The Greenwood Encyclopedia of Multiethnic American Literature

The Greenwood Encyclopedia of

MULTIETHNIC AMERICAN LITERATURE

Volume IV

N – S

Edited by Emmanuel S. Nelson

GREENWOOD PRESS
Westport, Connecticut • London

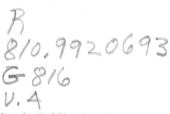

Library of Congress Cataloging-in-Publication Data

The Greenwood encyclopedia of multiethnic American literature / edited by Emmanuel
S. Nelson.
　　p. cm.
　　Includes bibliographical references and index.
　　ISBN 0–313–33059–X (set : alk. paper) — ISBN 0–313–33060–3 (v. 1 : alk. paper) —
ISBN 0–313–33061–1 (v. 2 : alk. paper) — ISBN 0–313–33062–X (v. 3 : alk. paper) —
ISBN 0–313–33063–8 (v. 4 : alk. paper) — ISBN 0–313–33064–6 (v. 5 : alk. paper)
　　1. American literature—Minority authors—Encyclopedias. 2. Minorities—United
States—Intellectual life—Encyclopedias. 3. Pluralism (Social sciences) in
literature—Encyclopedias. 4. United States—Literatures—Encyclopedias. 5. Ethnic
groups in literature—Encyclopedias. 6. Minorities in literature—Encyclopedias.
7. Ethnicity in literature—Encyclopedias. I. Nelson, Emmanuel S. (Emmanuel Sampath),
1954–
　　PS153.M56G74 2005
　　810.9'920693—dc22　　　　2005018960

British Library Cataloguing in Publication Data is available.

This book is included in the *African American Experience* database from Greenwood
Electronic Media. For more information, visit www.africanamericanexperience.com.

Library of Congress Catalog Card Number: 2005018960
ISBN: 0–313–33059–X (set)
　　　0–313–33060–3 (vol. I)
　　　0–313–33061–1 (vol. II)
　　　0–313–33062–X (vol. III)
　　　0–313–33063–8 (vol. IV)
　　　0–313–33064–6 (vol. V)

First published in 2005

Greenwood Press, 88 Post Road West, Westport, CT 06881
An imprint of Greenwood Publishing Group, Inc.
www.greenwood.com

Printed in the United States of America

The paper used in this book complies with the
Permanent Paper Standard issued by the National
Information Standards Organization (Z39.48–1984).

10 9 8 7 6 5 4 3 2 1

For Trevor again, with love

Set Contents

List of Entries

Guide to Related Topics

Okita, Dwight
Sone, Monica
Uchida, Yoshiko
Uyemoto, Holly
Yamada, Mitsuye
Yamamoto, Hisaye
Yamashita, Karen Tei
Yamauchi, Wakako

Jewish American Literature

Abish, Walter
Acker, Kathy
Agosín, Marjorie
Algren Nelson
Alkalay-Gut, Karen
Allen, Woody
Antin, Mary
Apple, Max
Asimov, Isaac
Auster, Paul
Behrman, S. N.
Bell, Marvin
Bellow, Saul
Bernstein, Charles
Berryman, John
Bessie, Alvah
Bloom, Harold Irving
Bodenheim, Maxwell
Broner, E(sther) M(asserman)
Brown, Rosellen
Budy, Andrea Hollander
Bukiet, Melvin Jules
Burnshaw, Stanley
Cahan, Abraham
Calisher, Hortense
Calof, Rachel Bella Kahn
Chabon, Michael
Chernin, Kim
Cohen, Sarah Blacher
Comden and Green
Dahlberg, Edward
Dame, Enid
Doctorow, E. L.
Elkin, Stanley
Elman, Richard M.

Endore, Guy
Englander, Nathan
Epstein, Joseph
Epstein, Leslie
Espinosa, María
Falk, Marcia
Fast, Howard
Faust, Irvin
Fearing, Kenneth
Federman, Raymond
Feinberg, David B.
Feldman, Irving
Ferber, Edna
Fiedler, Leslie
Field, Edward
Fierstein, Harvey Forbes
Finkelstein, Norman
Frank, Waldo
Freeman, Joseph
Fried, Emanuel
Friedman, Bruce Jay
Friedman, Stanford
Fries, Kenny
Fuchs, Daniel
Funaroff, Sol
Gelbart, Larry
Gerber, Merrill Joan
Ginsberg, Allen
Glickman, Gary
Glück, Louise
Glück, Robert
Gold, Herbert
Gold, Michael
Goldreich, Gloria
Goldstein, Rebecca
Goodman, Allegra
Graham, Jorie
Green, Gerald
Greenberg, Joanne [Goldenberg]
Grossman, Allen
Halper, Albert
Hart, Moss
Helprin, Mark
Hecht, Anthony
Hecht, Ben

Piercy, Marge
Pillin, William
Potok, Chaim
Prose, Francine
Rahv, Philip
Rakosi, Carl
Randall, Margaret
Raphael, Lev
Reich, Tova Rachel
Reznikoff, Charles
Rice, Elmer
Rich, Adrienne Cecile
Robbins, Doren Gurstein
Roiphe, Ann Richardson
Rolfe, Edwin
Rosen, Norma
Rosenfeld, Isaac
Rosten, Leo
Roth, Henry
Roth, Philip
Rothenberg, Jerome
Rudman, Mark
Rukeyser, Muriel
Salinger, J. D.
Sanford, John
Schaeffer, Susan Fromberg
Schulberg, Budd
Schwartz, Delmore
Schwerner, Armand
Segal, Lore [Groszmann]
Sephardic Literature
Shapiro, Alan
Shapiro, David
Shapiro, Karl
Shaw, Irwin
Sherman, Martin
Shulman, Alix Kates
Simon, Kate
Simon, Neil
Simpson, Louis
Sinclair, Jo (Ruth Seid)
Singer, Isaac Bashevis
Sklarew, Myra
Slesinger, Tess
Sontag, Susan

Spewack, Bella Cohen
Speigelman, Art
Stein, Gertrude
Stern, Elizabeth Gertrude
    Levin
Stern, Gerald
Strand, Mark
Swados, Elizabeth
Syrkin, Marie
Tarn, Nathaniel
Trilling, Lionel
Uhry, Alfred
Uris, Leon Marcus
Wallant, Edward Lewis
Wasserstein, Wendy
Weidman, Jerome
West, Nathanael
Whitman, Ruth
Wolf, Emma
Wolfert, Ira
Wouk, Herman
Yankowitz, Susan
Yezierska, Anzia
Yglesias, Helen
Yiddish Literature
Yurick, Sol
Zukofsky, Louis

Korean American Literature
Cha, Theresa Hak Kyung
Choi, Sook Nyul
Choi, Susan
Hahn, Gloria
Kang, Younghill
Kim, Myung Mi
Kim, Richard E.
Kim, Yong Ik
Korean American Literature
Lee, Chang-rae

Lithuanian American Literature
Lithuanian American Literature
Mackus, Algimantas
Šilbajoris, Rimvydas
Zolynas, Al

Mexican American Literature
Acosta, Oscar Zeta
Alarcón, Francisco X.
Alfaro, Luis
Anaya, Rudolfo
Anzaldúa, Gloria E.
Arte Público Press
Baca, Jimmy Santiago
Bless Me, Ultima
Border Narratives
Born in East L.A.
Bruce-Novoa, Juan
Burk, Ronnie
Candelaria, Cordelia Chávez
Cano, Daniel
Cantú, Norma Elia
Castedo, Elena
Castillo, Ana
Castillo, Rafael C.
Catacalos, Rosemary
Cervantes, Lorna Dee
Chavez, Denise
Cisneros, Sandra
Culture Clash
Cumpian, Carlos
Curiel, Barbara Brinson
De Casas, Celso A.
Del Castillo, Ramón
Fernández, Roberta
Flores-Williams, Jason
Fontes, Montserrat
Galarza, Ernesto
Garcia, Richard
Garcia-Camarillo, Cecillio
Gómez-Peña, Guillermo
Gonzáles, Jovita
Gonzales-Berry, Erlinda
Hinojosa-Smith, Rolando
House on Mango Street, The
Hunger of Memory
Islas, Arturo, Jr.
Jimenez, Francisco
Limón, Graciela
López, Josefina
Martínez, Demetria

Mena, María Cristina
Mexican American Autobiography
Mexican American Children's
　Literature
Mexican American Drama
Mexican American Gay Literature
Mexican American Lesbian
　Literature
Mexican American Poetry
Mexican American Stereotypes
Montalvo, José
Mora, Pat
Moraga, Cherríe
Nava, Michael
Navarro, Joe
Niggli, Josephina Maria
Niño, Raúl
Ortiz Taylor, Sheila
Paredes, Américo
De la Peña, Terri
Pineda, Cecile
Ponce, Mary Helen
Preciado Martin, Patricia
Quiñonez, Naomi Helena
Ramos, Luis Arturo
Ramos, Manuel
Rechy, John
Rivera, Tomás
Rodrígues, Joe D.
Rodriguez, Richard
Rodríguez-Matos, Carlos A.
Ruiz, Ronald
Ruiz de Burton, Maria Amparo
Sáenz, Benjamin Alire
Salinas, Luis Omar
Santiago, Danny [Daniel James]
Seguín, Juan N.
Soto, Gary
Suárez, Mario
Tafolla, Carmen
Tenorio, Arthur
Urrea, Luis Amberto
Valdés, Gina
Valdez, Luis
Vallejo, Mariano Guadalupe

Vásquez, Richard
Véa, Alfredo, Jr.
Villarreal, José Antonio
Villaseñor, Victor
Viramontes, Helena María
Zamora, Bernice

Native American Literature
Alexie, Sherman Joseph, Jr.
Allen, Paula Gunn
American Indian Movement
Apess, William
Black Elk [Hehaka Sapa]
Blaeser, Kimberley M.
Boudinot, Elias
Bruchac, Joseph
Ceremony
Chief Seattle
Conley, Robert J.
Cook-Lynn, Elizabeth
Dorris, Michael
Eastman, Charles Ohiyesa
Erdrich, Louise
Glancy, Diane
Hale, Janet Campbell
Harjo, Joy
Henry, Gordon, Jr.
Highway, Tomson
Hogan, Linda
House Made of Dawn
Johnson, E. Pauline
    [Tekahionwake]
Kenny, Maurice
King, Thomas
Love Medicine
Luther Standing Bear
Mathews, John Joseph
McNickle, William D'Arcy
Momaday, Navarre Scott
Mourning Dove (Hum-Ishu-Ma;
    Christine Quintasket)
Native American
    Autobiography
Native American Creation
    Myths

Native American Drama
Native American Mythology
Native American Novel
Native American Oral Texts
Native American Oratory
Native American Poetry
Native American Reservation
Native American Stereotypes
Occom, Samson
Ortiz, Simon J.
Owens, Louis
Peter Blue Cloud
Pocahontas [Matoaka]
Ray A. Youngbear
Revard, Carter
Ridge, John Rollin [Yellow Bird]
Riggs, Lynn
Rogers, Will
Rose, Wendy
Schoolcraft, Jane Johnston
Silko, Leslie Marmon
Tapahonso, Luci
Tracks
Trickster, Native American
Vizenor, Gerald
Walters, Anna Lee
Way to Rainy Mountain, The
Welch, James
Winnemucca, Sarah
Womack, Craig S.
Wounded Knee
Zitkala-Ša

Norwegian American Literature
Ager, Waldemar
Boyesen, Hjalmar Hjorth
Buslett, Ole Amundsen
Dahl, Dorthea
Janson, Drude Krog
Janson, Kristofer
Johnson, Simon
Norstog, Jon
Norwegian American Literature
Rølvaag, Ole Edvart
Wist, Johannes B.

Hashmi, Alamgir
Hejmadi, Padma [Padma
    Perera]
Iyer, Pico
Jasmine
Kitchner, Bharti
Kumar, Amitava
Lahiri, Jhumpa
Lakshmi, Vijay
Mehta, Ved Parkash
Mukherjee, Bharati
Nair, Meera
Narayan, Kirin
Nigam, Sanjay
Rama Rau, Santha
Shamsie, Kamila
Shankar, S.
South Asian American Film
South Asian American Literature
Suleri Goodyear, Sara
Sundaresan, Indu
Suri, Manil
Tharoor, Shashi
Vazirani, Reetika
Verghese, Abraham

Swedish American Literature
Hill, Joe [Joel Emanuel Hägglund/
    Joseph Hillström]
Sandburg, Carl
Swedish American Literature

Turkish American Literature
Turkish American Literature

Vietnamese American Literature
Cao, Lan
Donohue, Maura Nguyen
Hayslip, Phung Le Ly
lê thi diem thúy
Vietnamese American Literature

General Topics
Anti-Semitism
Assimilation
Bilingualism
Canon
Colonialism and U.S. Ethnic
    Literatures
Diaspora
Ellis Island
Ethnicity
Eurocentrism
Feminism and U.S. Ethnic
    Literatures
*Heath Anthology of American
    Literature, The*
Identity
Immigration
Liminality
MELUS
Multiculturalism
Pedagogy and U.S. Ethnic
    Literatures
Postcolonialism and U.S. Ethnic
    Literatures
Race
Racism
Whiteness

N

NABOKOV, VLADIMIR (1899–1997)   Russian American fiction writer, poet, critic, and translator. Born into privilege during the final years of Tsarist rule, Nabokov fled the Bolshevik Revolution and spent the rest of his life—in Germany, France, the United States, and, finally, Switzerland—in exile from his native Russia. The short stories, poems, and novels—including *The Defense* (1930), *Despair* (1936), *Invitation to a Beheading* (1938), and *The Gift* (1937–38)—that he published in Europe made important contributions to Russian-language literature. But after moving to the United States in 1940, he became adroit enough in English to create, in *Lolita* (1955) and *Pale Fire* (1962), masterpieces of Anglophone American literature.

Geographic and linguistic dislocation are recurrent themes in the works of Nabokov, who grew up in a wealthy household in which Russian, English, and French were mingled freely. Early on, he was unusually attentive to the medium of words, to the pleasures and restraints of the particular language in which he happened to be expressing himself. In his allusive and elusive autobiography, *Speak, Memory* (1951), Nabokov recalls being forced to abandon his idyllic life in St. Petersburg while still in adolescence. Art's desperate effort to arrest the flow of time would be the central theme of Nabokov's exquisite art. His family settled in Berlin, where Nabokov witnessed the assassination of his father at a political meeting. He graduated, with a degree in French literature, from Trinity College of Cambridge University in 1922, and, with his Jewish wife, Vera, he moved to Paris when the Nazis came to power in Germany. They left France in advance of the German army's

Vladimir Nabokov. *Courtesy of the Library of Congress.*

arrival, settling in Massachusetts, where, in 1941, Nabokov, an expert lepidopterist, found a job with Harvard's Museum of Comparative Zoology. His passion for butterflies is evident in their frequent appearance in his fiction as emblems of life's fragile, fleeting beauty.

Beginning in 1948, Nabokov taught literature at Cornell University. In *Pnin* (1957), he captured the pathos and absurdity of an émigré professor much like himself forced to function in an alien culture. The unexpected commercial success of *Lolita*, which American editors at first refused to publish, freed Nabokov to devote himself to writing. A first-person account, by Humbert Humbert, a middle-aged European transplanted in America, of his hopeless obsession with a pubescent "nymphet," the scandalous novel made its author notorious and rich. From 1959 until his death in 1997, Nabokov, famous for contrarian pronouncements, many of which were collected in *Strong Opinions* (1973), took up residence in a hotel in Lausanne. After childhood, he never felt at home.

After his work became widely read and studied, Nabokov set about making accessible the books that he, often under the pseudonym V. Sirin, had published in Russian but that were banned in the Soviet Union and, largely out of print, remained unknown in the United States. Publication of *The Stories of Vladimir Nabokov* (1995) allowed Anglophones to appreciate the full range and power of his short fiction from the 1920s to the 1960s, in Russian, English, and, in one instance, French. One of Nabokov's earliest projects, in 1923, was a translation of Lewis Carroll's *Alice in Wonderland* into Russian, but throughout his life he translated—his own work and others'—back and forth between Russian and English. Translation is central to *Pale Fire,* the story of a deranged critic, Charles Kinbote, who presumes to interpret the poetry of John Shade though he confronts American literature and life through the distorting prism of his own native language, Zemblan. Intent on making Russia's greatest poet, Aleksandr Pushkin, available to those who cannot read him in the original, Nabokov spent several years preparing an elaborate, four-volume, English-language edition of *Eugene Onegin* (1964) that includes the translator's commentary and a vehement defense of his view that translations should be literal renditions and conspicuously not the original.

Nabokov was born in Russia and did much of his most significant writing in the United States, but he could scarcely be considered part of a Russian American community. Though fascinated by its popular culture, he never fully assimilated into American society. And he scorned both the Tsarist sentimentalists and Soviet thugs who seemed to be all that remained of his vanished Russia. Nabokov was a brilliant, original writer who made enduring art out of art's rueful inability to bridge the gaps of time and place. (*See also* Russian American Literature)

Further Reading

Boyd, Brian. *Vladimir Nabokov: The American Years.* Princeton, NJ: Princeton UP, 1991.

———. *Vladimir Nabokov: The Russian Years.* Princeton, NJ: Princeton UP, 1990.

Wood, Michael. *The Magician's Doubts: Nabokov and the Risks of Fiction.* Princeton, NJ: Princeton UP, 1995.

Steven G. Kellman

NAHAI, GINA BARKHODAR (1961–)   Iranian-born American novelist. Nahai left Iran at the age of thirteen and was educated in Switzerland and the United States, where she has since spent the last thirty years. She received a master's degree in international relations from University of California at Los Angeles where her studies made her aware of the absence of historical material on Iran's long-standing Jewish community. She coauthored a study on Iran for the U.S. Department of Defense that involved interviewing many Iranian Jews fleeing Iran after the 1979 Revolution and the establishment of the Islamic Republic. She later earned a master of fine arts degree in writing from the University of Southern California, where she currently serves as an adjunct professor in the creative writing program. Her first novel, *Cry of the Peacock* (1991), spans two hundred years of Iranian history and deals in part with the many Shahs and dynasties of Iran, and specifically with Iran's nearly three-thousand-year-old Jewish population. Because Iranian Jews have been little understood or written about, Nahai's novel met with critical success both in the United States and abroad.

Nahai's second novel, *Moonlight on the Avenue of Faith* (1999), also deals with Iran's Jewish population and ghettos but this time includes the final destination for much of Iran's post-1979 Jewish migration: Los Angeles. Set in Tehran's Jewish ghetto and in the Iranian Jewish community in Los Angeles, *Moonlight* weaves a magical story of several generations of Iranian Jewish women. Nahai's depiction of Iranian Jewish culture and tradition is richly conveyed through both realism and fantasy. Some critics have equated her writing style with the magical realist tradition of Latin America.

Nahai draws on her own Iranian family for some of the colorful characters that people her novels. Her own paternal grandfather had two wives:

one Jewish and the other French Catholic. The two women lived in the same house and faithfully practiced their own brands of religious devotion and faith in the context of a predominantly Muslim society.

Unlike the two previous novels, *Sunday's Silence* (2003) has nothing to do with Iran and Jews but takes the remote and equally exotic locale of American Appalachia and the culture of snake handlers as its focus. After reporting on the world's war zones, the main character, Adam, returns home to the wild Appalachian mountains of Kentucky to investigate the death of his father, Little Sam Jenkins. Little Sam, an evangelist and a snake handler, was bitten by a snake his faith couldn't defeat, handed to him by one of his followers—a beautiful young Kurdish woman called Blue who was taken from her family in Central Asia as a child and brought to the United States. Like her earlier novels, *Sunday's Silence* explores some of the tensions of religious and cultural devotion to the past and the way that faith and fundamentalism are often linked together. (*See also* Iranian American Literature)

Further Reading

Goldin, Farideh. *Wedding Song: Memoirs of an Iranian Jewish Woman.* Lebanon, NH: UP of New England, 2003.

Karim, Persis, and Mohammad Mehdi Khorrami. *A World Between: Poems, Short Stories, and Essays by Iranian-Americans.* New York: George Braziller, Inc., 1999.

Kelley, Ron, and Jonathan Friedlander, eds. *Irangeles: Iranians in Los Angeles.* Berkeley: U of California P, 1993.

Persis Karim

NAIR, MEERA (1963–)   Indian American writer. She moved to the United States from India in 1997 and received a MA from Temple University as well as an MFA from New York University, where she was a *New York Times* Fellow. Meera Nair's first collection of short stories, *Video* (2002), was chosen as one of the best books of 2002 by the *Washington Post* and was a Kiriyama Prize Notable Book. It was also selected for the 2003 Asian American Literary Award. The title story, "Video," was the winner of the 2000 PEN/Amazon.com Short Story Award but was disqualified later as it ran afoul of one of the contest's technical rules: Fiction published with a circulation over five thousand was excluded, and another of her stories, "The Lodger in 726," had previously appeared in *The Threepenny Review*.

Video deals with universal topics such as adolescence, the constraints in marriage, and the ever-present pain of abuse in different cultural settings with details that go from the magical to the mundane. The ten stories in this collection are skillfully narrated by different personas. They cover both village life in India and the immigrant experience in the United States. And as many other diaspora narratives, the characters in Nair's stories are confronted with Western culture's influence on Indian traditions. The characters are not stereotyped though; neither are the surroundings specifically exotic. Nair shows a plurality of characters from different communities in India, social strata, and religious backgrounds. She has a command of authentic details, providing vivid portraits of life in India and in the United States.

The title story, "Video," is about a man torn between his desire and caring for his wife. It tells the crisis in the lives of a married Muslim couple of fifteen years, between Nasser and Rasheeda, from a man's point of view. The husband glimpses a pornographic film and asks his wife to expand their sexual repertoire, but she feels insulted and stops speaking to him. In "My Grandfather Dreams of Fences," Nair shows with compassion all sides of the story, which deals with a fifteen-year-old boy who witnesses his elderly grandfather being dispossessed of his land by trade union workers.

"Summer" deals with the theme of child molestation within an extended family; a girl is molested while rehearsing for a play. "The Lodger in Room 726" is about a boarding-house servant who takes excessive interest in a guest. "The Curry Leaf Tree" is about the conflicts in an arranged marriage between Dilip and Vanita. The man has a gift of smell for food, and his wife is the opposite of the traditional Indian dutiful women. Dilip's new wife has adapted quickly to the new environment in the United States, but he feels isolated. "The Sculptor of Sands" deals with magical realism, in the way of a fable, about jealous men in a town who ban a young man's gifts of sand sculptures to the public, which captivate the women of the town.

"A Warm Welcome to the President, Insh'Allah" is written with irony and humor about former President Clinton's visit to South Asia in 2000. The story is told from the perspective of a group of villagers in Bangladesh where they excitedly treat this event as the biggest happening and go to the extreme of building a bathroom exclusively for him. In another story Nair has captured the sad event during the destruction of the Babri Masjid in Ayodhya in 2001, which provoked Hindu-Muslim riots and caused deaths across India. "Sixteen Days in December" is a story of how the narrator, a female journalist, copes with her father's death after a stroke and her family's experience during the riots. (*See also* South Asian American Literature)

Antonia Navarro-Tejero

NAJARIAN, PETER (1940–)   Armenian American writer and artist. His works, *Voyages* (1971), *Wash Me on Home, Mama* (1978), *Daughters of Memory* (1986), *The Great American Loneliness* (1999), explore his protagonists' tensions in mediating between the rigid values and conventions of Old World Armenia with an ever-changing America whose promise of new possibilities seem narrowed as well.

Born in New Jersey, Peter Najarian, the son of an **Armenian Genocide** survivor, attended Rutgers University for a few years. His parents moved to London where he lived before returning to the United States, where he often lived in poverty while working on his writing. Najarian received a creative writing fellowship from Stanford in 1967. In the preface to *The Great American Loneliness,* he explains that the loneliness driving his search for selfhood was ultimately his love for art mirrored in friendships that defined America. William Blake's notion that contraries (e.g., *The Marriage of Heaven and Hell*) are necessary for progression is a key idea in understanding Najarian's writing, because failure was part of an ongoing writing process of self-discovery. A series of autobiographical narratives, *The Great American Loneliness* explores the fluid relationship between the past and present and how personal and ethnic Armenian **identity** is shaped by the creative energy this fluidity fosters.

In *Daughters of Memory*, perhaps Najarian's most provocative book, Zeke, the narrator, searches for his identity by coming to terms with his Armenian past and discovering his grandmother. Art and sexuality connect him to the creative process that allows this discovery of identity. The nude drawings of women in the book represent forms of the universal woman, their sexuality suggesting the intimate and creative experience, which is also the case in *The Great American Loneliness*. Najarian's use of explicit sexual language breaks with traditional Armenian American writing, revealing that the discovery of identity requires breaking with tradition and convention.

The problem of bridging past and present is addressed by a circle of Armenian women, including Zekes's mother, whose conversations evoke a traumatic past. Although his mother can only remember death, her stories help Zeke discover his grandmother through access to historical and personal meanings of his past. When Zeke visits Turkey, the friendly, innocent-looking Turkish boys on the bus present a stark contrast to the ugly, brutal perpetrators of the Armenian genocide. He observes, however, that the young passengers were not the perpetrators of the genocide, absent from their own history books. Healing and forgiveness become possible by recontextualizing the past in the present and looking toward the future. The Armenian woman he meets in Turkey whose family in America has disowned her for marrying a Turk reinforces the possibility that Armenians—not the past—define themselves. Zeke's sexual encounter with a Turkish prostitute signals his ability to rediscover his identity by moving beyond traditional Armenian/Turkish dichotomies. Through the fluid medium of art, Zeke continues his exploration of selfhood. (*See also* Armenian American Literature)

Further Reading

Der Mugrdechian, Barlow. "The Formation of an Armenian-American Identity: A Reading of Peter Najarian's *Daughters of Memory*." *Journal of the Society for Armenian Studies* 7 (1994): 101–13.

Robert Sirabian

NARAYAN, KIRIN (1959–) Indian American novelist and scholar. A noted anthropologist, Kirin Narayan has published two books on Indian folklore in which she destroys the boundaries between imaginative storytelling and academic discourse and analysis. Incorporating the art of storytelling, Narayan's only novel to date, *Love, Stars, and All That* (1995), is a gentle satire of university academic life and on some of the major academic modes of discourses—critical theory, postmodernism, and cultural and racial identities. The novel's major themes deal with the complex issues of the South Asian **diaspora, immigration, assimilation,** and the negotiation of **identity** in a multicultural world. Narayan follows in the tradition of Indian American women writers, such as **Bharati Mukherjee, Meena Alexander,** and **Chitra Divakaruni,** whose works also include the same themes that affect the South Asian diaspora.

Love, Stars, and All That brings together two worlds and identities that Gita, an Indian graduate student at the University of California at Berkeley, must negotiate, which is between the Western style of dating and the Indian system of arranged marriages and belief of cosmic destiny based on astrology. The autobiographical elements in the novel incorporate how Narayan was influenced by strong, liberated women in her life, her maternal grandmother and her mother, both white Americans. Growing up, Gita was influenced by her aunt, who had been a political revolutionary and possibly her father's lover. The novel is actually Gita's sexual awakening from her convent school experiences in India, to a brief Indian engagement, to a brief marriage with her professor, Norvin Weinstein, when she becomes involved with him as he is going through a painful divorce, and finally her first love affair.

Narayan's Gita is a complex woman, an "impossible collage": Americanized, Westernized, but also Indian, and searching for an independent and unique selfhood within the complex racial, national, and cultural identities that are a consequence of the diasporic dislocation. This is a coming-of-age novel but not a love story where the protagonist ends up marrying the hero. For example, the novel explores the importance of women's friendships with men, and there are two men who play an important part in her life: Timothy, a poet, and Firoze, a Parsi Indian and also a graduate student. At the end Gita and Firoze become lovers, but he is also her foil. For him, India is his homeland, the land of his parents, and of his culture and religion, but Gita sees two incomplete Indias from her newfound perspective in the United States, which she must attempt to make whole in her quest to create a complete identity within herself. (*See also* South Asian American Literature)

Further Reading
Kendall, Elaine. "One Girl's Invention of an American Self." *Los Angeles Times* (March 4, 1994): E4.

Ymitri Jayasundera

NATIVE AMERICAN AUTOBIOGRAPHY   Defining and discussing the Native American autobiography can be a worthy but complicated task. In Anglo American culture, the very definition of "autobiography," the story of a person's life written by herself or himself, would seem to eliminate many Native American autobiographies. Examination of the rich history of the Native American autobiography requires an expanded definition of "autobiography" as well as a basic understanding of the Native American culture.

Arnold Krupat, a foremost scholar on Native American literature, explains issues that complicate the study of Native American autobiographies in his works *For Those Who Come After* (1985) and *Native American Autobiography: An Anthology* (1994). First, although Native Americans were telling their stories thousands of years before any ethnographers arrived to do it for them, the stories were related orally. He writes, "Tribal people were oral people who represented personal experience performatively and dramatically to an audience." (Krupat, *Native American Autobiography* 3). For the Native American autobiography to exist in written form, someone else had to write it down in many instances. This leads to issues with authorship and accuracy. Is it an autobiography if it was not written by the person whom the story is about? Many Native American autobiographies were written down by ethnographers, so most scholars agree that an expanded definition of autobiography is necessary to the study of Native American autobiography. But Krupat has created two categories of Native American autobiographies to address this issue: "autobiographies by Indians" (written by the subjects themselves) and "Indian autobiographies" (written down by someone other than the subject).

Second, the principles that guide mainstream ideas about themes that should be present in an autobiography, such as emphasis on the individual's achievements, cannot usually be applied to Native American autobiography because the individual is "always subordinated to communal and collective requirements" (Krupat, *For Those Who Come After* 29). But Krupat and other scholars have, in recent years, worked to provide audiences with a greater understanding of Native American autobiography by examining its history and providing much-needed critical scholarship.

Probably the first Native American autobiography was written by the Reverend **Samson Occom** in 1768. Occom was a Mohegan who became a well-known Christian minister. His work is reflective of a period of time between the arrival of the white settlers and the Indian Removal in 1830. His words reflect the common sentiment of the white settlers of this period when he writes, "I was Born a Heathen and Brought up In Heathenism" (Krupat 106). During this time, Native Americans throughout the country were being converted to Christianity, and some who were converted were taught to write in English. Although there is little evidence of autobiographical writings of the Southwestern Native Americans who were also Christianized during this time, there were several Northeastern Native Americans who left behind autobiographical records.

The autobiographies of the nineteenth century would be quite different. The nineteenth century was the age of Indian war and Indian removal. Native Americans were considered obstacles to western expansion and were treated as such. Native Americans were removed to reservations, and those who resisted were often massacred. Though the United States government was ultimately successful in removing Native Americans to reservations, many Native Americans successfully resisted for periods of time. Many non-Indians wanted to help some of the most famous Native American resistors tell their stories. So the Native American autobiographies of this period were mostly collaborations between Native American storytellers and Euro-American recorders.

Perhaps one of the most famous of these collaborations is the collaboration between Black Hawk and Antoine Le Clair. Black Hawk was a traditional war chief of the Sac and Fox tribes who faced a period of imprisonment after resisting removal from his tribal lands. He was defeated in the Black Hawk War in 1832 and was imprisoned in several places before ultimately being allowed to return present-day Illinois. At this time, he expressed interest in narrating the story of his life to Le Clair who was a government interpreter for the Sac and Fox. Le Clair then recruited John B. Patterson to write the autobiography from Le Clair's notes. *The Life of Black Hawk* (1833) was quite popular and went through several editions. In 1882, Patterson revised the work, now titled *The Autobiography of Ma-Ka-tai-me-she-kia-kiak*, but because Black Hawk died in 1838, he had no say in this revision. Although this work is critical in the study of Native American autobiography and scholars are quick to point out that, without Le Clair and Patterson, Black Hawk's story would have been lost, there are clearly issues with accuracy in such a situation. And, unfortunately, no notes or transcripts exist from Le Clair's original interviews with Black Hawk.

Another famous Indian resistor was Geronimo. In 1886, a year before the Dawes Act, Geronimo and his band of about thirty Apache warriors were forced to surrender to an army of 2500. He, along with the other Apaches from the southwest, was sent to Florida. Like other tribes who were sent far from their homelands, the Apache became very sick, and many died. Later, Geronimo and other survivors were shipped to Fort Sill, Oklahoma. Geronimo would never see his homeland again.

While in Oklahoma, Geronimo met Stephen Melvil Barrett, a superintendent of the schools in Lawton, Oklahoma. Barrett persuaded Geronimo to tell his life story, but officers at Fort Sill objected. Barrett later got the project underway after he wrote to President Theodore Roosevelt, but Barrett was forced to write footnotes disclaiming any government responsibility whenever Geronimo made negative remarks about the army or any government official. Geronimo narrated his story in Apache, which was then translated to Barrett by a third party, Asa Daklugie, a son of an Apache chief. Again, there are no manuscripts of this collaboration. It is important to note that, although Geronimo seems to speak quite impersonally as he relates his story in terms of his entire culture, this is his way of relating the story of himself. *Geronimo's Story of His Life* was published by Barrett in 1906. Geronimo died considering himself a prisoner of war.

Perhaps the most famous Native American autobiography also comes from this period. *Black Elk Speaks* (1932) is a result of the collaboration between **Black Elk** and John Neihardt. Black Elk was a Sioux medicine man and was present at the infamous Custer fight of 1876 and later joined Buffalo Bill's Wild West Show. *Black Elk Speaks* includes details about Black Elk's great visions, his memories of the Custer fight, and his years with Buffalo Bill, but interestingly he makes no mention of the years he spent as a Catholic catechist.

After the **Wounded Knee** Massacre of 1890 where over 150 Native American men, women, and children were killed, there was little resistance from any Native American survivors. "The prevailing social Darwinism of the period suggested that the Indian must either step up to the next rung of the evolutionary ladder and become 'civilized' or, quite simply, go the way of the dinosaur and die" (Krupat 237). Now, in order to survive, it was thought that the Native Americans not only needed instruction in Christianity, but they also needed instruction in capitalism. Because the reservations were for the tribes (the group) as opposed to individuals, the U.S. government decided that it was now necessary to destroy the reservations. This was the purpose of the 1887 Dawes Act. It was also during this time that Indian schools began, most of which were abusive. Run by the Bureau of Indian Affairs or various churches, most of the Indian schools (though not all) were notoriously difficult for Native Americans. Native American children were forbidden to speak in their native languages and were beaten if they did so. But there were schools whose teachers at least attempted to provide a positive experience to their students, such as The Santee Indian School; the teachers at this school taught in Lakota as well as English. One positive to come out of this very difficult time is that the Native American autobiographies during this period were written by the subjects themselves. These autobiographies paint a complicated and realistic picture of the lives of many Native Americans. Autobiographies from this period include Gertrude Bonnin's (**Zitkala-Ša's**) autobiographical essay series published in the *Atlantic Monthly* in 1900. A Dakota Sioux, Bonnin experienced great success with her writing, overcoming both racial and gender oppression to be successful in a white man's world.

It is also at the beginning of the twentieth century that professional anthropologists began to interview "ordinary" Native American men and women who were representative of their culture. Influenced by Franz Boas, father of modern anthropology, these anthropologists spent several decades recording life histories of Native Americans. A result of this movement away from recording the lives of famous chiefs and warriors is that more women's autobiographies were recorded. Although there are numerous published examples of the collaborations between anthropologists and Native Americans, "Narrative of an Arapaho Woman" provides strong evidence of the anthropologists' quest during this time to write the stories of "average" Native Americans. In "Narrative of an Arapaho Woman," the anonymous subject relates the story of her life and, interestingly, makes no mention of whites, even though she would have certainly had encounters with them. "Narrative of an Arapaho Woman" was first published in *American Anthropologist* in 1933 by Truman Michelson.

In 1968, the U.S. Congress passed the Indian Civil Rights Act. Also, during this year, **N. Scott Momaday**'s novel *House Made of Dawn* was published, winning the Pulitzer the following year in 1969. These events mark the beginning of what many scholars refer to as the "Native American Renaissance." Momaday's autobiographical *The Way to Rainy Mountain* (1969) is similar to other modern Native American autobiographies in that the text relates his personal story in relation to his quest to understand his ancestors' culture. Momaday, a Kiowa, uses a sparse, lyrical style, clearly influenced by Native American orality, to tell the stories of himself and his family.

Leslie Marmon Silko, another modern Native American author, published her multiform autobiography, *Storyteller*, in 1977. According to Hertha Dawn Wong, Silko, like "other contemporary Native American writers . . . emphasizes how one's land and community, processed by memory and imagination and shaped into language, create one's personal identity" (187). Like Momaday, Silko is also known for her lyrical method of bringing the Native American oral tradition through in her writing.

Scholars agree that the Native American autobiography is an untapped resource for literary critique. The rich, complicated, and sometimes tragic history of the Native American peoples has provided the opportunity for important autobiographies to emerge. And as authors of Native American descent continue to merge cultural traditions, the Native American autobiography will continue to develop down an interesting path into the twenty-first century.

Further Reading

Krupat, Arnold. *For Those Who Come After: A Study of Native American Autobiography.* Berkeley: U of California P, 1985.

———. *Native American Autobiography: An Anthology.* Madison: U of Wisconsin P, 1994.

Wong, Hertha Dawn. *Sending My Heart Back Across the Years: Tradition and Innovation in Native American Autobiography.* New York: Oxford UP, 1992.

Crystal McCage

NATIVE AMERICAN CREATION MYTHS   Creation myths are not single-authored texts but a complex mesh of orally transmitted theories and traditions about how the world might have been created. Some of these tales of origin were for centuries taken very seriously, providing explanations for how the world is; others have a lighter touch and have a humorous or moral tone. Today they tend to be understood metaphorically, providing symbolic and sacred meanings for the purpose and creation of the world. Like Native American folklore in general, creation myths were told for sacred purposes and traditional education as well as entertainment.

Many Native American tribes possess the tradition of a Creator, who creates animals and plants and also humankind. He is known by the Chelan as the "Great Chief," by the Seminole and Comanche as "Great Spirit," and by the Chinook as Talapas, that is, "Creator." In the Iroquois tradition, the Creator is one of several Sky Spirits, who found the earth, saw it was beautiful, and created people. Often the Creator gives instructions as to how to care for the earth and be peaceful. The Lakota myth tells of him giving the first humans his sacred pipe and asking them to live by it. It is interesting that many Native American tales, although describing the formation of people, animals, and plants, are often silent about the creation of the earth, often implying that it may have preexisted the birth of the Creator. Some describe the Creator waking up, or journeying, and discovering the earth, rather than creating it. This reflects the importance of ecology in Native American traditional thought, in which the earth is the source of all that is good, and to respect the earth is to respect life itself.

Coyote is a creator figure found in many creation myths. He is sometimes represented as a **trickster** and sometimes as a wise, good old man. In the Chelan tradition Coyote is initially asked by the Creator to take care of the animals and make human beings, but then the job is taken away from him after he begins to believe himself as important as the Creator. Coyote tales often include a moral, surprise, or twist. In the Navajo creation myth, the people's careful deliberations as to how to place the stars are disrupted by Coyote's impatient throwing of a blanket containing the stars into the sky. The stars were scattered in a random pattern, where they remain today.

The role of women in Native American creation myth is significant. In an extended Navajo myth of creation, the Holy People who were the world's first inhabitants come under threat from monsters who try to kill them. They are rescued by Ever Changing Woman (Asdzaa Nadleehe), who marries the Sun. Their children, the Hero Twins, are given lightning bolts to fight the monsters. Many place-names in New Mexico commemorate these battles and the piles of stones that remained. Ever Changing Woman then plays a key role in creation, by creating four new clans from her own skin.

Several Native American creation myths tell the story of a great flood, in a theme that is echoed in mythologies around the world. The Lakota myth of creation tells how there was a world before this one in which people did not behave in a manner pleasing to the Creator. The Creator therefore sang songs to bring rain, which eventually split the earth apart and caused a terrible flood. Everyone died, except Kangi the crow, who pleaded with the Creator to make a new world and somewhere to rest. In the Chippewa tradition, the flood story is linked with the story of the Great Serpent, who is mentioned across North America as an agent of evil. The Chippewas tell how their hero Nanabozho's cousin was killed by the Great Serpent, who lived at the bottom of a lake. Nanbozho came to take revenge, lured the Serpent out of the water, and fired an arrow into his heart. In his anger he flooded the whole land, covering the highest mountain, and Nanbozho and his people were forced to survive on rafts.

Creation myths often describe advice-giving situations, such as the Chelan story. One story describes Youngest and Oldest Wolf Brothers creating human beings out of a dead Beaver. When the first human beings wake, they are given advice on survival and taught how to eat roots and huckleberries and how to fish for salmon. They are then directed to study preexisting rock paintings, which the animals tell them were drawn by the Creator. These give them the knowledge to produce bows and arrows and salmon traps. Such stories reveal Native American attitudes to the traditional knowledge and cultural artifacts passed on by their ancient ancestors.

They also reveal much about traditional Native American theologies. Creation myths often describe three worlds: an upper world, made of light; the earthly world; and a lower realm, made of darkness. The Najavo creation myth describes three preexisting underworlds and human beings arriving in this, the fourth, known as "Glittering World," through a magic reed. They then help to arrange and create the world around them. Animals with human features often play an important part in such stories, whether as creators, messengers, or protectors. This reflects the immense importance of the natural world and the animal kingdom in traditional Native American theology, which ascribes great significance to the role played by spiritual guides and animal guardians in a community's daily life. Unlike the Judeo-Christian tradition, in which Adam is given dominion over all the creatures of the earth, Native American stories show animals playing a key role in the formation of the human **race**. For the Haida, Raven literally created the human race, calling them out of a clamshell on the beach. In the Eskimo tradition, the Raven Father is the original Creator, who fed and taught the first humans to make canoes and clothing. In the Miwok creation myth, all the animals meet with Coyote in a powwow circle to discuss how man should be made. This reverses the common European view that humankind is superior to animals.

Because of the manner in which, like the Hebrew creation myth in the Judeo-Christian text, Genesis, creation myths of the American Native tradition were for centuries held as truth, and because many were for generations retold to white Americans as simple children's stories, it is easy for outsiders to mistake their continued symbolic significance in Native American culture as naïve. In fact, careful distinctions have always been made. In the Ojibwe language, for example, a creation myth is defined as an *Aadizookaan* or traditional story, as opposed to a *Dibaajimowinan*—a contemporary fact in a narrative. It is also important to distinguish the sacred retelling of a creation myth from a rejection of various current scientific theories of evolution. A belief in Native American cultural heritage needs to be distinguished from, for example, the literalist belief in biblical creationism found among some Christians.

It is also important to emphasize that creation myths are not merely stories. They can be viewed as indigenous literatures: moral and originating frameworks for Native American religious or spiritual outlooks; works of cultural property belonging to particular tellers, tribes, or regional and national groupings; and works of symbolic importance carrying significance and meaning for the whole world. In Native American tradition, the story itself is sacred, and retelling it is an act with symbolic effect. Like Native American literature in general, its history is that of being passed down orally and told in groups (often family, or ceremonial); this means that the texts in which it is written today are in some sense artificial, with the experience of the solitary reader (often in English translation) no substitute from hearing the tale told in its own context by an original teller.

Some Native Americans argue that the story is meaningless, divorced from its cultural context; others suggest that, read sensitively, the Native American traditions can give value and meaning to a materialist and urbanized society and that the transmission of traditional Native American creation myths to non-Native Americans may have something to teach. Nontraditional cultural traditions of reception for Native American stories include the collection of folktales into children's collections; the anthropological survey and categorization of narrative as part of a generalized survey of Native American cultural life; a romanticisation of Native American tradition as part of a generalized myth of the frontier; and, more recently, the incorporation of Native American stories into the generation of a New Age alternative religious movement. Recent Native American writers have protested their unattributed appearance on New Age Web sites, arguing that this represents cultural appropriation by a foreign group. Cultural property rights and religious issues of sensitivity have been invoked. Creation myths, however, remain a vital part of Native American cultural life. (*See also* Native American Mythology, Native American Oral Texts)

Further Reading

Einhorn, Lois J. *The Native American Oral Tradition: Voices of the Spirit and Soul.* Westport, CT: Praeger, 2000.

Ekkehart Malotki, and Michael Lomatuway'ma. *Hopi Coyote Tales: Istututwutsi.* Lincoln: U of Nebraska P, 1984.

Fletcher, Alice C. *Indian Story and Song from North America.* Lincoln: U of Nebraska P, 1995.

Shuldiner, David P. *Folklore, Culture and Aging: A Research Guide.* Westport, CT: Greenwood Press, 1997.

Kerry Kidd

NATIVE AMERICAN DRAMA   Oral performance is, of course, a standard feature of Native American oral tradition, but the earliest drama written by Native Americans can be traced to the Cherokee writer Lynn Riggs and his play, *The Cherokee Night* (1936). The full flowering of this genre by Native writers, both Canadian and American, waits until the larger movement called the "Native American Renaissance" of the late twentieth century. This movement, starting roughly with **N. Scott Momaday**'s Pulitzer Prize–winning novel, *House Made of Dawn* (1969), saw the emergence of many Native American writers in all genres. Although the number of Native playwrights is relatively small, these playwrights have nevertheless emerged as a potent force in Native literature.

Native American drama is a pan-tribal genre, with playwrights coming from many different tribal traditions and from different areas of North America. Thus, the style of Native drama ranges from Native traditionalism to historical pageant, from realism to existentialist drama in the mode of Bertolt Brecht. Thematically, Native drama addresses themes such as tribal loyalty versus individual identity, the effects of cultural stereotyping and cultural encroachment, and the ways in which older traditions can give strength to Native people.

Native American drama, unfortunately, has frequently been treated by critics and scholars less as drama than as ethnography. This is perhaps unsurprising because much Native American drama often consciously uses elements of ritual and performance specific to the author's tribal heritage. This view of drama as ethnography may also arise because of the relative richness of dramatic forms in Native religious rituals. For instance, the Navajo Chantways are intricately "staged" ritual dramas. Because of this, critics may sometimes emphasize the "primitive" nature of Native drama, even to the point of considering contemporary Native American playwrights as shamans or as primitive artists, even as backwater relics, rather than as self-conscious artists who are working in a contemporary medium.

In fact, Native American drama is the product of such a self-conscious, contemporary movement, albeit one with certain religious, social, even political overtones. In that sense, it is not quite drama that exists for its own sake, as entertainment, but instead is a body of work by diverse playwrights informed by an insistence that its audience take seriously Native North American realities.

Rollie Lynn Riggs (Cherokee) was born in the Oklahoma Territory and knew firsthand the reality of Native North American experience. As a playwright, Riggs's only noteworthy success was *Green Grow the Lilacs* (1930), a non-Native play that was changed by Rodgers and Hammerstein into the popular musical *Oklahoma!* Riggs's *The Cherokee Night* failed to make Broadway, instead being produced first in Rose Valley, Pennsylvania, near Philadelphia, and later at the University of Iowa, directed by Riggs himself. Riggs's themes in *The Cherokee Night* radiate from the slow realization that Cherokees' weakness comes not from being Cherokee but from being insufficiently Cherokee. Their tribal degeneration stems not from their tribal heritage but from forgetting their heritage.

The next significant moment in the history of Native American drama was the creation of a training program for Native American playwrights at the Institute of American Indian Arts in Santa Fe. Begun by Roland Meinholtz, the program recruited young people from all over the United States and enrolled them in a course of study intended to instruct them in dramatic technique and theatrical presentation. Though this program lasted only a few years, it nevertheless created a vanguard group of artists who had been encouraged not just to learn all they could about the theater but who had also written, acted in, directed, and produced experimental theater with Native American actors and tribal themes.

The first professional company to achieve national recognition from this vanguard was the American Indian Theater Ensemble (AITE), a group formed in 1972 as an adjunct of La Mama Experimental Theater Club. As a company-in-residence as La Mama, the AITE group produced experimental plays, one-acts, and enactments of tribal myths. Among their productions was *Body Indian,* by Hanay Geiogamah. Geiogamah also has had a number of other plays produced, among them *49* and *Foghorn.* The group also had a European tour.

By 1974 the group had changed its name to the Native American Theater Ensemble (NATE) and had moved to Oklahoma City. Their purpose in doing this was twofold. They wished to take their work into the heart of Indian country, to perform it for the people for whom it was intended. They also wished to draw from the strength of community.

AITE/NATE spawned a number of other theater groups: the Navajo-Land Outdoor Theater (1973), Spiderwoman Theater (1975), and Red Earth Performing Arts Company (1974). In addition, the Institute of American Indian Arts continued to be a launching pad for experimental artists. Spiderwoman Theater, in particular, has been a productive force for three decades, its best-known productions including *Winnetou's Snake Oil Show from Wigwam City* and *Power Pipes.*

As these groups provided support and, in some cases, facilities and feedback for Native playwrights, a number of playwrights rose to prominence in the genre. Among these playwrights are Bruce King (*Evening at the Warbonnet*), Annette Arkeketa (*Ghost Dance* and *Hokti,* among others), and William S. Yellow Robe (*The Independence of Eddie Rose* and *Starquilter,* among others).

In Canada, other groups arose. The most prominent of these groups was Native Earth Performing Arts (NEPA). Native Earth was based in the Native Canadian Centre in order to remain in the Native social context. The first works were collective creations, written and performed by the actors. The first show, *Double Take/A Second Look,* was created in collaboration with Spiderwoman Theatre, an outgrowth of Native American Theater Ensemble, and with Tukak Theatret, a Danish theater comprised primarily of Greenland Inuit, with musical direction by Tomson Highway. It consisted of a set of short scenes examining stereotypes about Native people around the world.

In 1986 Native Earth secured government funding and hired its first full-time staff, including Tomson Highway as Artistic Director. Also in 1986,

NEPA presented its first scripted work, Highway's *The Rez Sisters*. It was a breakaway hit, attracting large audiences across Canada and at the Edinburgh Theatre Festival. Prominent Native Canadian playwrights first produced at Native Earth include Drew Hayden Taylor (*Only Drunks and Children Tell the Truth* and *Toronto at Dreamer's Rock,* among others), Daniel David Moses (*Coyote City,* among others), Billy Merasty, Marie Humber Clements (*now look what you made me do* and *Urban Tattoo,* among others), and Monique Mojica (*Princess Pochahontas and the Blue Spots*).

Further Reading

Brask, Per, and William Morgan, eds. *Aboriginal Voices: Amerindian, Inuit, and Sami Theater.* Baltimore: The Johns Hopkins UP, 1992.

Darby, Jaye T., and Stephanie Fitzgerald, eds. *Keepers of the Morning Star: An Anthology of Native Women's Theater.* Los Angeles: UCLA American Indian Studies Center, 2003.

Geiogamah, Hanay, and Jaye T. Darby, eds. *American Indian Theater In Performance: A Reader.* Los Angeles: UCLA American Indian Studies Center, 2000.

———. *Stories of Our Way: An Anthology of American Indian Plays.* Los Angeles: UCLA American Indian Studies Center, 1999.

T. J. Arant

NATIVE AMERICAN MYTHOLOGY   Mythology is a cultural representation of symbolic realities that may hold multiple social significances or roles. The place of mythology in Native American culture is a significant one; although mythological representations, and figures from Native American myth, have found their way both into Native American literary works and into the mainstream of colonial American culture, it is important to bear in mind the exclusively oral nature of the Native American mythological traditions and the way in which they functioned as symbolic and truth-telling topos in a pre-literature society prior to the arrival of the first Europeans. Native American mythology is inseparable from Native American spirituality, and just as it is impossible—because more than a thousand tribes coexisted on the North American continent prior to the arrival of the Europeans, each with their own culture, oral tradition, and ritualistic tradition—to speak of a single Native American "spirituality" or religion, so it is also impossible to speak of a single Native American mythology. Nor should Native American mythology simply be viewed as "stories" but rather as the integration of a consciousness and worldview that is deeply concerned with the connection between individual, tribal identity, human and animal beings, and the entirety of creation. Native American mythology should also not be envisaged as belonging solely to the "stories" themselves. Rather, the interweaving of mythological, symbolic, and physical reality is for many Native Americans inescapable in the world around us, including the visible realities of nature.

For reasons of space, this article makes some generalizations about Native American myths and treats groups of different myths together. Many groups

Flying Eagle Man, war god of Zuni Pueblo, New Mexico. Hand-colored woodcut. *Copyright North Wind Picture Archives/North Wind Picture Archives. All rights reserved.*

of tribal myths share common features, such as a belief in animal spirits or a story relating to the Great Flood. This should not, however, be read as inferring that all different Native American cultures or myths are the same. It is also important to bear in mind the significant interrelation between myth and ritual: where in Western Judeo-Christian culture the religious ritual is generally thought to be the servant of theology, in Native American culture the myth and the ritual have a far closer relationship, and often the ritual has a greater clarity and precision for observers than the precise details of the particular myth invoked. Storytelling is seen as an art of knowledge in Native American culture: The distinction between "fact" and fiction is not always of use, as sources of cultural wisdom and historical understandings can conflict with "scientific" or literate historical ways of understanding the world. Traditionally, some stories are only shared at certain times of the year, or on special occasions: A distinction is often made between stories that are told only to entertain and those that also have an informational or teaching purpose. Myths such as "The Orphan and the Origin of Corn" (Creek) or "How the Buffalo Were Released On Earth" (Comanche) are clearly didactic, but "The White-Faced Bear" (Aleuts) is a cautionary story, rather than a myth of origins. Many myths provide explanations for the shape and diversity of animals, such as "How the Rabbit Stole the Otter's Coat" (Cherokee). Metis-Cree peoples of Canada forbid the telling of stories relating to the supernatural being Wisakecahk during the summer months (before the first falling of snow), because as well as being long these are culturally regarded as entertainment and have no place in a time of the year where all must work as hard as possible. This is attached to other beliefs about the proper seasonal telling of stories; the Cree peoples in general believe that the telling of fictional stories in the summer will lead to people being attacked by lizards, who come to suck their blood. During the summer, too, spirits are about and may take revenge if they are displeased by certain stories; and there is the risk of animals overhearing and being offended by the stories being told when they are wandering in the summer. Stories may be told through movement and dance as well as speech and seek to inform about the origins of sacred culture, as well as the physical world and cultural heritage.

In many Native American cultures, the role of storyteller is set apart and careful training is given to ensure an accurate record of traditional mythology from one generation to the next. Professional storytellers receive great honor in their tribe.

Many gods exist in Native American mythology. Some have animal identities and an enduring cultural life. For the Alonquins, Michabo is the god who, in chasing wolves into a lake, caused the great flood. Manabozho is another Alonquin deity, also known as the Great Hare. His **identity** (perhaps similar to that of Loki in European Norse mythology) is that of a **trickster**, a shape-changer and a creator. His identity was adopted into slave culture (and from there into mainstream American culture) as **Brer Rabbit**.

Native American mythologies are non-teleological. This contrasts with Western ideas of "progress," where scientific and technological innovations lead society to "improve" in departing from its past. Rather, Native American mythologies tend to stress continuity of spirit and place and provide a site of connection between present-day living storytellers and hearers and ancestral Native American values. Past and present intersect, as stories of explanation from the past are invoked to provide explanations and guides to behavior in the present. With other stories, the time and place is left unspecified, and myths are simply related in the sense of something that happened a long time ago. An example of this is the Cherokee legend that describes the origin of the Pheasant dance: it occurred as the result of a strange winter famine among the birds and animals. No nuts were to be found in the woods, and then the Pheasant discovered a holly tree, covered with nutritious berries and led his fellow creatures to it. The resultant dance of joy created the tradition of the Pheasant dance.

Such a story has a clear relation to seasonal tradition but not to any teleological or eschatological sequence of "truth." There is no linear "order," as in stories placed in sequence in a written book for example. Rather, myths are told at appropriate times of the year, or as and when they are felt to be appropriate to a specific course of behavior or occasion. Nor, historically, are they seen as abstract, fictional, or remote; rather, the details of the different mythological traditions are closely integrated with the questions and preoccupations of daily tribal life. As opposed to the Judeo-Christian and Islamic traditions, for example, they contain no concept of a savior, of a world that needs to be redeemed or transformed or of a fallen and intrinsically sinful humanity. Rather, they suggest a continued cycle of dependency between the earth, its peoples and animals, and the various deities who made (and are making) creation. A Cherokee myth about the origin of medicine describes how the animals grew angry with humans for taking too much of the earth's resources and invented disease. Then, when the humans begged for mercy, the plant kingdom took pity on them and provided remedies, one for each of the illnesses given to humankind. The vast majority of Native American myths preach interdependency with rather than domination over nature in this way and present humanity as having a cyclical relationship with creation. Because of this, the concept of the circular and the cyclical are central to the myths that are told. Even the location of sites of storytelling can be mythologically significant.

The language, as well as the content, of these mythologies has significant cultural resonance. Because of the context and method of transmission (oral narrative), the mythologies of Native Americans tend to be transmitted and retold in very simple language, suitable for an entire community to hear and understand. This is a consequence of the oral tradition of such societies and should not be misunderstood as signifying that these stories are themselves child-like or simple. Such stories can appear falsely simplistic or one-dimensional, if detached from their cultural environment. Cultural scholars may avoid this by rejecting attempts at a literary analysis of such specifically nonliterary texts. Additionally, respect must be paid by scholars to the linguistic heritage embedded in such texts: the languages, often near obsolete, in which these stories were originally told. Many stories today are told and retold in nonindigenous languages (mainly English). Some storytellers argue that the mythologies are meaningless, when so translated; others suggest that doing so can provide a means for young Native Americans to engage with their cultural background.

The history of scholarly appropriation and study of Native American mythologies is also highly contentious. Many were collected in the nineteenth and early twentieth centuries by white scholars. However, recent scholarly investigation has suggested that care needs to be taken to distinguish between the indigenous mythological heritage of Native Americans and the ways in which their mythologies have been recorded, absorbed, and incorporated into other cultures. In his study of the Sioux, Julian Rice argues that a significant historical process of cultural appropriation took place, in which Sioux and other spiritualities and mythologies were co-opted or distorted by the cultural perspectives of their collectors. Today a reappropriation of cultural heritage is taking place, as Native American collectors and storytellers themselves seek to reinscribe their heritage in the retelling and transmitting of stories. This is leading to changes in the way mythologies are transmitted, as well as stored. As well as the numerous paper and tape-recorded projects already in existence, there are a growing number of Indian-owned online libraries. (*See also* Native American Creation Myths, Native American Oral Texts)

Further Reading

Elk, Black, and John Gneisenau Neihardt. *Black Elk Speaks: Being the Life Story of a Holy Man of the Oglala Sioux.* Lincoln: U of Nebraska P, 2000.

Mohawk, John. "A Native View of Nature." *Resurgence* 178 (September/October 1996): 11.

Pritzker, Barry. *A Native American Encyclopedia: History, Culture and Peoples.* New York: Oxford UP, 2000.

Rice, Julian. *Before the Great Spirit: The Many Faces of Sioux Spirituality.* Albuquerque: U of New Mexico P, 1998.

Kerry Kidd

NATIVE AMERICAN NOVEL   The novel form is not indigenous to Native American art or culture; thus, Indian contributions to this genre did not appear until the mid-nineteenth century. As complex containers of often contradictory cultural, ethnic, and national experiences, Native American novels offer rich perspectives on what it means to live Indian in America and to write about that experience in an essentially non-Native form and language.

Although the novel as a genre has evolved over the centuries, in general it describes an extended fictional narrative composed of linked episodes. The Native American novel arose late, virtually disappeared for several decades, and reemerged more abundantly in contemporary times. In general, Indian novels have reflected both their artistic and cultural trends within Indian and American communities during the ebbs and flows of their production. Thus, the Native American novel over time represents a fusion of intercultural traditions and offers commentary on Indians' connections to and distance from mainstream Euro-American society and art. Although earlier novels tended to mimic their white counterparts, later publications show Natives adapting and revising mainstream models to contain their own cultural concerns and traditions. Today, the Native American novel is considered an integral part of the multicultural American literary **canon**, with distinctive indigenous features that set it apart as "Indian."

Early Novels (Nineteenth to Early Twentieth Century)

The first known Native American novel exemplifies both imitation and fusion. Published in 1854, **John Rollin Ridge**'s *Life and Adventures of Joaquin Murieta, the Celebrated California Bandit* is a conflation of European form and Indian content. Ridge's story is a fictional biography of a Mexican American outlaw named Joaquin Murieta, who soon became a lasting cult hero in the American West. The reader's sympathy is evoked for Murieta, also part Indian, as he seeks revenge on the whites who tortured him, his family, and his betrothed, and robbed him of his land. The story clearly evokes Native dispossession, as Ridge himself was a Cherokee Indian, but deals with this matter only indirectly; the book is otherwise wholly Western and has been compared usefully to Byronic and European romances. As a work of American literature, *Murieta* seems to have paved the way for subsequent dime novels and Westerns that became popular in the latter half of the century. Ridge's contribution to national letters, though largely unacknowledged, is an important example of the way Indian writers adopted not just the generic forms but the subject matter of the dominant culture. Serious meditations on Indian mistreatment and dispossession are sacrificed here in the service of an entertaining, colorful, popular tale.

Ridge's work responds to the concerns of his historical moment, which was still occupied with westward exploration and Indian removal. As expansion continued into the latter part of the century, and along with it, Native restriction to reservations, literary activity among individual tribes was limited. Many Indians remained illiterate, and the publications that did appear tended to be memoirs of the experience of migration, **assimilation** into white culture, or of children being shipped off to white boarding schools. Indians incensed by their unfair treatment at the hands of the federal government began composing treatises, scathing recollections, or defiant collections of tribal history. Sarah Winnemucca Hopkins (Pauite), Charles Eastman (Sioux), and Gertrude Bonnin (Sioux) all gained recognition for their important autobiographies and compilations of folk tales around the turn of the century. Although autobiography was by far the most popular mode of Native writing during this period, several Native American poets such as Alexander Posey (Creek) were publishing their works as well. Only one other novel was written by an American Indian in the nineteenth century: Sophia Alice Callahan's *Wynema* (1891). Callahan's work more self-consciously narrates the gap between Indian and white experience, with its mixed-blood female protagonist and a range of literary and cultural allusions both indigenous and European.

Several decades separated the novels by Ridge and Callahan; another lengthy span of years was to pass before novel writing picked up with fervor. During these transitional periods, Indians were becoming more and more engaged with narrating the terms of their own histories, their tribal memories, and their own identities within the dominant culture. In keeping with increased feelings of Native alienation, loss, and displacement, the novels of the twentieth century are more overtly concerned with issues of **race**, culture, land, and memory. The novel form reappeared in Native American letters in the 1920s with *Co-ge-we-a, the Half-Blood* (1927), which represents the first novel written by an Indian woman, an Okanogan named **Mourning Dove**. Much of the story signals a throwback to the dime-store Westerns of the previous century; so, too, does the 1928 novel *Long Lance: The Autobiography of a Blackfoot Indian Chief* by a Blackfeet Indian named Sylvester Long, which is in fact a fictional adventure story. Long's novel is, however, rich in ethnographical detail that would have been edifying to American readers. Mourning Dove's work, too, represents progress beyond the formulaic, as her concerns are particularly modern: a half-blooded Indian woman struggles to embrace the heritage embodied by both her grandmother and a similarly mixed-blood love interest, whom she ultimately rejects. It seems no coincidence that such Native novels made their return during the decade in which American Indians were finally granted the right to vote with the Indian Citizenship Act of 1924. The long era of political memoir writing, inspired in some way by this surge for recognition as individuals with sovereignty, could now give way to Indians' full participation in the artistic climate of the rest of the country.

This does not mean that these writers were satisfied with citizenship and assimilation, though; on the contrary, Native American struggles for tribal sovereignty, separate from that of the United States, would intensify over the course of the twentieth century, and such battles continue today in the political and legislative arenas. The Native American novel thus reflects a population in profound conflict with itself, its own roots, its relationship to American life and culture, and to the Western world at large. It is no coincidence that a substantial number of Native American authors are of mixed blood; this division and ambivalence forms the central theme of much of their literature. This conflict is apparent in the thematic preoccupations during the 1920s and 1930s, as represented in novels of the period by John Milton Oskison, **D'Arcy McNickle**, and **John Joseph Mathews**. Mathews's protagonist in *Sundown* (1934) is mixed not only in blood but in his affiliation, as he is unable to find refuge in either his Osage family and tradition or white culture, where he receives education and military training. McNickle, an extensively educated Flathead/Salish Indian, features a part-Spanish Indian whose attempt to reconcile his antagonistic heritages spurs a string of violent episodes. Oskison was the most well-known of these writers, and he was also the least Indian: only one-eighth Cherokee. His novels, which include *Wild Harvest* (1925) and *Brothers Three* (1935), reflect Natives' growing ambivalence about associating with the white world, even by individuals with more white blood than Indian.

The "mixed-breed" character will continue to haunt the novels written later in the century. Unfortunately, Native American literature experienced another hiatus in the 1940s and 1950s while the nation's tribes were undergoing traumatic reorganization and termination measures imposed by the Hoover administration in 1949. Attempts to assimilate Indians more comprehensively into American life met with resistance and resentment; consequently, the next generation of writers, resurfacing in the 1960s, struggled even more with issues of hybridity, nationality, and place. Fortunately, their redoubled challenges are answered by an increasing number of Native writers seeking voice and empowerment in literary activism.

Contemporary Novels (1969–present)

Despite the broad range of prolific Indian authors publishing during the first half of the century, the Native American novel did not receive widespread attention and acclaim until much later. The **Civil Rights Movement** of the 1960s encouraged Indian activism and struggles for sovereignty that continue into the present day, and it created a climate that particularly helped draw interest to marginalized groups generally. White readers and critics, still the major population, became more receptive to such struggles and worked to integrate more diverse voices in the literary canon. The two first and most influential contemporary Indian novelists were **N. Scott Momaday** and **Leslie Marmon Silko**. The Kiowa Momaday appeared on the literary scene first with his Pulitzer Prize–winning *House Made of Dawn* (1969). Silko's *Ceremony* (1977) was published eight years later, making her famous as the first contemporary female Indian novelist (some call her *the* first, though this is historically inaccurate). Both Momaday's and Silko's revolutionary novels feature a young male protagonist returning home after war, traumatized by battle but equally distressed about reintegrating into their communities. Thus, their stories become parables for the fractured, violent nature of everyday American Indian existence, the ruptures of assimilation and dislocation, and for Tayo, Silko's protagonist, the negotiation of mixed-race **identity**. Both novels invoke storytelling and tradition as means for healing, on both the individual and communal levels, but neither story ends entirely optimistically. Silko reaches for more universal, good-versus-evil themes that implicate all races and cultures; her art is also integrative, blending both traditional and Western elements into a whole and weave together story, poetry, pictures, and ceremony.

The challenging, unconventional styles of these two works also influenced a great number of writers who came after. Both Momaday and Silko chose complex narrative modes and chronologies, mixing not only genres but temporalities and realities. These qualities are considered uniquely "Indian" in their embracing of nonlinear historical and temporal elements and in their prioritizing of myth as a seamless component of reality; but they are also, in some ways, features typical of modern and postmodern writing generally, which tends to be disjunctive, complex, and experimental. Indeed, Indian authors often use these postmodern qualities to their advantage, reshaping them with Native American features. Ojibwa author **Gerald Vizenor**, for instance, reimagines the "crossblood" individual as a site of multiple cultural and historical experiences, a combination that is distinctly playful and liberating. His characters, embodying urban landscapes but charged with the importance of the past and tradition, have been described as **trickster** figures much like those indigenous to both Native and African American cultures. Vizenor's huge body of work includes well-known novels such as *The Trickster of Liberty* (1988) and *Heirs of Columbus* (1991).

Although many contemporary Native novelists engage in postmodern textual play, others remain focused on the past, the land, and the families that have lived and struggled there, meditating on their increased importance to contemporary cultural survival. **Louise Erdrich**, for example, a member of the Turtle Mountain Band of Ojibwa, has won unprecedented critical and popular acclaim for her interrelated novels tracing several generations of tribal families, beginning with *Love Medicine* (1984) and followed by *Beet Queen* (1986), *Tracks* (1988), and *The Bingo Palace* (1994). Critics have routinely praised Erdrich for her success in intimately creating a world populated by the peoples, places, and Native experiences she knows so well and, subsequently, bringing them to widespread attention in the American mainstream. **Linda Hogan**, a mixed-blood Chickasaw from Oklahoma, has extended her own purview still further, writing about several different tribes and their diverse communities and experiences and, in fact, creating fictional tribes as well. The cross-cultural message is similar, though, as Hogan writes extensively about the unifying plight of losing land, tradition, memory, and, along with it, a sense of affiliation and self. Her critical gaze turns on the greed of whites who rape the land and its people for resources and profit, particularly oil, as in her 1990 novel *Mean Spirit*. Her latest novel, *Power* (1998), describes a fictional tribe of Florida Indians and their negotiations between the American judicial system and the ancient laws of tribal governance and ecological balance.

Indeed, although many Native American authors decry the loss and contamination of their way of life to inimical American attitudes and institutions, many still struggle with their own very real connections to the white world. The mixed-blood figure thus remains a significant presence in novels by contemporary writers, as do the themes of assimilation, fragmentation, loss, and despair. Although his later works are less optimistic, **James Welch**'s *Winter in the Blood* (1974) exemplifies the importance of attaining peace and integration, as a Blackfoot Indian in Montana reaches back across memories and generations to come to terms with his own present dislocation and alcoholism. **Sherman Alexie**'s debut novel, *Reservation Blues* (1995), gestures across racial borders and brings the African American **blues** artist Robert Johnson onto the Spokane Indian reservation in a fictional merging of Native and black American musical forms and cultural experiences. LeAnn Howe's 2001 novel, *Shell Shaker*, fuses multiple temporalities that skillfully interweave the present moment with historical texture and myth, essentially creating a revisionist version of actual events—in this case, the murder of a Choctaw chief by his own people. **Louis Owens**, another Choctaw, also engages in rewriting history, mixing genres, the real and the surreal, the past and the present, in order to sketch a more accurate picture of complex contemporary Indianism. Perhaps his best-known novel to date, *Bone Game* (1994), is haunted simultaneously by a nineteenth-century murder and a string of contemporary serial killings; the book's half-Indian narrator, a displaced English professor, must figuratively return to his people and his tradition in order to realize ultimately that the murders are connected. So many Native novels reiterate this nonlinear temporality, reminding readers that the tragedies and triumphs of the past must be recalled and addressed consistently and overtly in order to make sense of—and ultimately to make peace with—the present.

Critical Approaches to the Native American Novel

It is undeniable that American Indian novels, like the Indians themselves, have pervaded and influenced American literature and culture on a number of levels. In its significant departure from the oral tradition that characterized the Indian narrative for countless generations, the novel form itself—not to mention the mainstream English language it adopts—represents a crucial compromise. In many ways, however, Indian authors have made the form their own, tampering with and enriching European tradition in turn. That is, the Native American novel is perceived to have distinctive qualities that derive from these oral and communal traditions: the fluid blending of storytelling and myth into the texture of real life, the focus on multiple generations of individuals within specific tribes, and the non-linear narrative forms hospitable to such themes.

Along with the increased production of Native American literature came increased efforts on the part of critics to understand and appreciate it. Previously, oral traditions and poetry had been examined mainly on the basis of what they could teach anthropologists and ethnologists about the curious ways of these indigenous peoples. The possibility that these works could represent serious and lasting pieces of literature simply did not occur to most reviewers until the twentieth century. Even then, the cultural allure of "primitivism" tended to contaminate even well-meaning attempts to gain knowledge and appreciation of Indian texts, much like the curious whites who flooded Harlem nightclubs in the 1930s seeking an authentic, "primitive" experience. In the 1920s, a critic named Mary Austin became a champion for indigenous American literature, lamenting the fact that mainstream students were likely to learn far more about European history and authors than about the Native inhabitants and artists of their own country. Austin was successful in bringing more sustained critical attention to Indian literatures, but her focus was largely on poetry.

Critical turns to the American Indian novel did not happen seriously until the auspicious coincidence of the Civil Rights Movement and the 1969 publication of Momaday's *House Made of Dawn*. Since then, annual sessions of the Modern Language Association and other major literary conferences and journals have been devoted to the exploration of Native American literature. Moreover, full-length dissertations and books have been written on the subject. Many of these investigations seek to understand the complex relationship between orally transmitted cultures and the bounded, Euro-American literary text. Marxist approaches have been used to analyze the Indian's vexed relationship to the material culture of the United States, which it is both dependent upon and detached from. Freudian models have been invoked to describe the alienation, fragmentation, and general psychological trauma incurred by a people so thoroughly oppressed and disrupted. Others, such as Arnold Krupat, have argued that such Western modes of criticism may be largely inappropriate for examining indigenous texts. One thing is certain: With the current popularity of airing multiethnic experiences and literatures, such discussions and debates about the Native American novel are sure to continue, deepen, and enrich the current **canon**—much as the novels themselves have done. (*See also* Native American Autobiography)

Further Reading

Alexie, Sherman. *Reservation Blues*. New York: Warner Books, 1996.

Allen, Paula Gunn, ed. *Studies in American Indian Literature: Critical Essays and Course Designs*. New York: Modern Language Association, 1983.

Krupat, Arnold. *The Voice in the Margin: Native American Literature and Canon*. Berkeley: U of California P, 1989.

Larson, Charles R. *American Indian Fiction*. Albuquerque, U of New Mexico P, 1978.

Oaks, Priscilla. "The First Generation of Native American Novelists." *MELUS* 5 (1978): 57–65.

Owens, Louis. *Other Destinies: Understanding the American Indian Novel*. Norman: U of Oklahoma P, 1994.

Wight, Andrew, ed. *Critical Essays on Native American Literature*. Boston: G. K. Hall, 1985.

Melanie R. Benson

NATIVE AMERICAN ORAL TEXTS   It would seem incongruous that nonliterate societies could produce literature. Yet although most Native American tribes had no written languages other than those that were the products of transliteration by ethnologists (notwithstanding the Maya of Mesoamerica, who employed hieroglyphics long before contact with Europeans; many other tribes, including the Kiowa and the Lenape, who used pictographs; and the Cherokee, who after 1819 employed a syllabary invented by mixed-blood Cherokee Sequoyah to write in their language) they all possessed vast bodies of oral literatures, commonly referred to as "folklore," repetitively spinning myths, epics, orations, and ritual dramas into the cultural fabric of their tribes. Unfortunately, serious study of Native American oral literature has too often been precluded by poor translations and the ethnocentrism of scholars who have historically evaluated these works based on the structural and aesthetic criteria established by Euro-American masterworks, as well as their own cultural biases.

Mythology, although undoubtedly an important component of Native American oral literature, is perhaps the least understood and most contentious. Historically, to the ethnologist in whom the tenets of cultural Darwinism were inculcated, a myth was little more than superstition, a tale unraveled by a storyteller to an audience in a technologically or scientifically barren culture to explain natural phenomena. Thousands of these myths were recorded by ethnologists in scores of monographs, related to them by tribal members, with the altruistic desire of the dominant culture to preserve them before the Native culture vanished (that is before it assimilated). This mentality has unfortunately perpetuated the notion that the only true Native cultures are those that are pre-contact, not recognizing that cultures are fluid and adaptable and that change does not negate political or literary viability. Myths therefore were dismissed as quaint artifacts relegated to the past, belonging to a dead people.

To Native peoples, however, a myth is a culturally owned truth, and its retelling and reenactment are vital to the continuation of not only the tribe, but also of the cosmology, and "is ongoing and relevant, not the [remnant] of a vanishing culture" (Womack 27). Contact does not eradicate the myth but rather informs and transforms it. The conflict between ethnographer and Native American is revealed in Vine Deloria Jr.'s *God Is Red*, in which Deloria challenges scientific notions of the arrival of Native Americans via a land bridge across the Bering Strait. Deloria counters the accepted scientific theory with traditional creation stories, such as the Navajo's emergence from an unpleasant underworld or the Creek's emergence from a fissure in the earth. Deloria's point is that these stories should be given credence by non-Native scientists, alleging that the stories are supported by suppressed archaeological evidence that threatens the mainstream theory. Deloria posits that non-Natives cannot consider **Native American creation myths** as truth because to do so elevates Native peoples to the status of original owners of the land, not as recent newcomers from Asia who can be displaced by other immigrants; blatant disregard for creation myths of Native peoples more importantly disputes their status as sovereign nations by denying that the oral literature comes from living, flourishing cultures and consigning it to ethnography.

Myths might elucidate not only the long distant past and the Creation but also the not-so-distant past in the tribe's history, as does an oral historical epic narrative, not unlike Homer's *Iliad* or the Anglo Saxon *Beowulf*, epic poems that originated as oral literature. One version of the Muskogean migration legend, for example, tells of the tribe's journey across the Mississippi River to the southeastern United States, led by two brothers, Chahta and Chikasha. A magical red and white striped pole, planted upright at the end of each day, determined the following morning their journey by pointing the direction of that day's route. Upon reaching the southeast, the brothers quarreled and separated, with one brother founding the Choctaw tribe and the other the Chickasaw.

Undoubtedly, the most controversial of the oral historical epic narratives is the Wallamolum, an alleged account of the Lenape people from the time of Creation to the seventeenth century, which also has the distinction of being recorded in pictograph form. Documented in the Wallamolum is the Lenape's migration across the ice-covered Bering Strait, their subsequent journey along the Rocky Mountains, and their settlement of eastern North America. The Wallamolum details the Lenape's battles with the Tallegwi tribe (recognized by some scholars as the Cherokee) and the Tallegwi's defeat at the hands of the Lenape and the Iroquois. University of Transylvania (in Lexington, Kentucky) professor Constantine Rafinesque received the Wallamolum in 1820 from an enigmatic Dr. Ward, and the pictograph account was preserved with red ink on long-since-vanished sticks, accompanied by verses in the Lenape language describing the drawings. Three translations of the Wallamolum are extant. In the latter part of the last century the authenticity of the Wallamolum came under fire, and some scholars believe that Rafinesque perpetrated a hoax, writing the verses first in

English, then translating them into Lenape. Also, Rafinesque may have been skeptical of the recent alleged discovery and translation of golden plates by Joseph Smith and the subsequent formation of the Church of Jesus Christ of Latter Day Saints; Rafinesque may have therefore created the Wallamolum in an attempt to dispel the commonly propounded assertion (one supported by Smith in the Book of Mormon) that the Native Americans were descendants of the Lost Tribes of Israel or to suggest the ease of duping the nineteenth-century scientific community. If it is an authentic document, however, the Wallamolum is perhaps the most important artifact relating to North American Indian culture.

An almost universal symbol in much of the oral literature of Native America is the **trickster**, usually characterized by the anthropomorphized Raven, Mink, or Blue Jay in the Pacific Northwest, Rabbit in the Southeast (known as Nanabozho in the Eastern Woodlands), or Coyote in California and the Southwest. The trickster figure has come to epitomize Native storytelling for Anglo audiences. At once a cultural hero and a cultural threat, the trickster—often depicted as a highly sexed male—serves to reinforce the boundaries of appropriate behavior by demonstrating undeniably inappropriate (and humorous) behavior. The trickster figure is found not only in Native American storytelling but also in oral literatures worldwide. For example, **Brer Rabbit** stories, which evolved from African trickster hare stories, came to the southern United States with slavery and often share similarities with Cherokee and Creek trickster rabbit stories. These similarities perhaps suggest that the oral literatures of African slaves and Native Americans may have intersected in the American Southeast.

Oratory is also a genre of Native American oral literature, and its prominence is indicative of the social status enjoyed by one who could effectively and eloquently communicate. An oration was often political, a means by which sovereignty was demonstrated diplomatically by challenging the rule of the dominant culture. No Indian-language versions of the most famous eighteenth- and nineteenth-century orations exist, and most orations first appeared in print years after their initial delivery and only in translation. For example, Rudolf Kaiser retraced the history of the well-known oration of **Chief Seattle** of the Suquamish and Duwamish Indians of Puget Sound, noting that the speech was made in 1853 and first published in a newspaper account in 1887. This 1887 version accepts the U.S. doctrine of Manifest Destiny and also details things that Seattle did not know about in 1853, such as the transcontinental railroad, while the version that gained prominence in the 1970s warns of "impeding white-caused ecological doom." The lack of a primary source in the original language often allows for editions that publicize current ideologies as well as perpetuate Pan-Indian or dominant-culture perceptions of Native Americans, such as the noble savage stereotype. Contemporary orations, however, delivered and recorded in Indian languages, and subsequently translated, offer perhaps more truthful Native perspectives of white-Indian relations.

The oral literature of Native America remains the vital expression of thriving cultures. Native American oral literature has also found its way into Native American written literature, in the works of **Louise Erdrich, N. Scott Momaday, Leslie Marmon Silko, Sherman Alexie**, Hanay Geiogamah, **Diane Glancy**, and **Maurice Kenny**, among others. As **Craig S. Womack** writes regarding Creek oral literature, although applicable to all Native American oral literatures: "The oral tradition is a living literary tradition, the standard by which Creek stories, oral and written, are judged. Like any other literary tradition, it consists of a complex body of genres [and structural components], as well as a relationship to larger Creek ceremony, society, politics, and government, that need to be explored in terms of formulating and analyzing approaches to Creek literary texts" (Womack 66). (*See also* Native American Oratory, Native American Stereotype)

Further Reading

Bierhorst, John. *Four Masterworks of American Indian Literature.* New York: Farrar, Straus & Giroux, 1974.

Bright, William. *A Coyote Reader.* Berkeley: U of California P, 1992.

Deloria, Jr., Vine. *God Is Red: A Native View of Religion.* Golden, CO: Fulcrum Publishing, 1994.

Hymes, Dell. *"In Vain I Tried to Tell You": Essays in Native American Ethnopoetics.* Philadelphia: U of Pennsylvania P, 1981.

Kroeber, Karl, ed. *Traditional American Indian Literatures: Texts and Interpretations.* Lincoln: U of Nebraska P, 1981.

Krupat, Arnold. *The Voice in the Margin: Native American Literature and the Canon.* Berkeley: U of California P, 1989.

Swann, Brian, ed. *Smoothing the Ground: Essays on Native American Oral Literature.* Berkeley: U of California P, 1987.

Vizenor, Gerald, ed. *Narrative Chance: Postmodern Discourse on Native American Literatures.* Albuquerque: U of New Mexico P, 1989.

———. *The Trickster of Liberty: Tribal Heirs to Wild Baronage.* Minneapolis: U of Minnesota P, 1988.

Wiget, Andrew, ed. *Handbook of Native American Literature.* New York: Garland Publishing, Inc., 1996.

Womack, Craig S. *Red on Red: Native American Literary Separatism.* Minneapolis: U of Minnesota P, 1999.

W. Douglas Powers

NATIVE AMERICAN ORATORY Throughout American history, Native American orators have spoken eloquently on topics ranging from the breaking of treaties by Euro-Americans to the preservation of Native lands and religious freedoms. During the earliest period of colonization, Native Americans, as peoples from primarily oral cultures, had little recourse but to turn to oratory to voice their grievances to both the colonial governments and the Euro-American citizenry occupying Native lands. Today, Native American activists such as Russell Means (Oglala Sioux) and Winona LaDuke (Ojibwe) still use oratory as a means of seeking redress for grievances. Some of the better-known orators also include Powhatan (Pocahontas's father), Pontiac (Ottawa), Tecumseh (Shawnee), William Apess (Pequot), Geronimo (Apache), and Crazy Horse (Oglala Sioux).

Many of the early speeches presented by Native leaders were given in their own languages and later translated into English for publication in newspapers and journals. The act of translation, in some cases, opened these speeches to alterations in style and structure. For example, Thomas Jefferson's inclusion of a translation of the Iroquois orator Tahgahjute's "lament" in the *Virginia Gazette* makes the speech more appealing to white audiences than it might have originally been. Likewise, because white listeners who often brought their own agendas to the table often transcribed the earliest Native American oral texts, they were also open to deliberate mistranslation to suit the translator's political goals. One example of a questionable oral text is **Chief Seattle**'s (Duwamish) speech: "Yonder sky that has wept tears of compassion" (1854). Not only are there multiple versions of the speech, but its language and structure (in it Seattle suggests that white people alone are smiled upon by God and paints Native American youth as malicious) suggest that it was written as propaganda. However, this is not to suggest that all Native American oratory was mistranslated (either deliberately or accidentally). Indeed, the majority of it comes to us from reliable translators who, if not representing each word spoken, are true to the goals and content of the speeches under consideration.

During the colonial period, Native American oratory often sought redress for injustices and the breaking of treaties. Tecumseh, a revolutionary Shawnee leader, spoke often to various Native American nations in an attempt to band them together to resist the encroachment of whites onto their lands. Speaking to the Choctaws and Chicasaws in 1811, he exhorts them to violently resist what he identifies as the tyranny of American rule and despairs the possible vanishing of his people. Comparable to standard political, prewar speeches of the contemporary era, Tecumseh clearly spells out the problems that have been and will be brought about by his enemies and relies heavily on the patriotism, fear, and brotherhood of his audience. Identifying the whites as the eventual cause of the "annihilation of our **race**" (Blaisdell 51), he points out that white America's actions are unjust and that they seek nothing more than all the lands and goods the Natives possess.

On the other hand, Native American oratory occasionally worked to support white America's causes (or at least to prevent further war with the whites). In a response to Tecumseh, Pushmatah (Choctaw) urges the same audience to choose a more prudent path than war. In this speech, Pushmatah concedes that America has indeed been unjust in its treatment of the Native Americans in the past yet is, at the moment of his speaking, "friendly dispossessed towards" the Native Americans (Blaisdell 54). War with them, he points out, would not only be unjust but also, due to lack of numbers, be futile and lead to further Native American deaths and losses. For Pushmatah, the logical route is to seek legal redress through Congress rather than war.

In the twentieth century, **American Indian Movement** (AIM) cofounder Russell Means, like Tecumseh, used oratory to argue for the sovereignty and rights of his people. In 1973, during the AIM occupation of **Wounded Knee**, Means argues that Native Americans are still at war with the United States. For him, the injustices suffered at the hands of white America are ongoing, and it is only recently that, "as a people we are beginning to see" them (Blaisdell 213). In 1977, Means also addressed the United Nations, identifying the United States as a "monster" and petitioning the United Nations for a Native American presence on the global level (Blaisdell 214). Pointing out that the United States is still perpetuating genocide on Native American peoples, he argues that the "international community" must step in and support Native Americans' "international rights" (214).

More recently, Winona LaDuke, environmental activist and Ralph Nader's Green Party running mate in 1996 and 2000, has spoken on a wide array of subjects from the environment to language to women's issues. Speaking at the Non-Governmental Organization (NGO) Forum in Hua-irou, China, LaDuke draws a connection between the earth and indigenous women and the ravaging of both by the colonial machine. To her, the destruction of Native lands and resources leads directly to the destruction of Native peoples through the loss of homes and the increase in pollution of both lands and bodies by "dioxins, organochlorides, and PCBs" (LaDuke 215). To LaDuke, this pollution occurs because of the denial of Native sovereignty and rights. Echoing the majority of Native American orators who preceded her, LaDuke argues for the recognition of Native self-determination and an end to the usurpation and destruction of Native lands and resources.

Even in this contemporary era of the printed (and even digitized) word, Native American oratory still plays a vital role in expressing concerns and arguing for political rights. No less eloquent than their ancestors, contemporary Native American orators speak passionately about crucial issues all Americans should hear and respect.

Further Reading

Armstrong, Virginia Irving. *I Have Spoken: American History Through the Voices of the Indians.* Athens, OH: Swallow Press, 1984.

Blaisdell, Bob, ed. *Great Speeches by Native Americans.* Mineola, NY: Dover Thrift Edition, 2000.

LaDuke, Winona. *The Winona LaDuke Reader: A Collection of Essential Writings.* Stillwater, MN: Voyageur Press, 2002.

Vanderwerth, W. C., ed. *Indian Oratory: Famous Speeches by Noted Indian Chieftains.* New York: Ballantine, 1971.

Carrie Sheffield

NATIVE AMERICAN POETRY   Although it has its roots and inspiration in the oral traditions of American Indian tribes, American Indian poetry, in the very strictest sense, is primarily a twentieth-century phenomenon;

prior to this time, the written and published works of Native American authors generally consisted of autobiographical stories and journalistic accounts of tribal life. The American Indian writers who did publish poetry in the late 1800s were better known both then and now for their works in other genres. Cherokee John Rollin Ridge primarily wrote fiction and auto-biography, but a volume of his poetry, *Poems,* (1868) was published posthu-mously by his wife. Likewise, Mohawk **Emily Pauline Johnson** published two volumes of poetry, *The White Wampum* (1895) and *Canadian Born* (1903), but is remembered for her short stories. And **Lynn Riggs** (Cherokee) pub-lished *The Iron Dish* in 1930 but is best known for his play *Green Grow the Lilacs* from which the musical *Oklahoma!* was derived.

Although these poets helped to prepare the way for the mainstream pub-lication of American Indian poets, the true Renaissance of writing by Native authors occurred in the middle twentieth century, propelled by two major events. The first was the publication of **N. Scott Momaday**'s novel *House Made of Dawn* (1969), which was awarded the Pulitzer Prize. The second was the rise of the **America Indian Movement** (AIM) and a resur-gence of political activism by young Native Americans, resulting in the occupation of Alcatraz, the Trail of Broken Treaties and the occupation of **Wounded Knee**, South Dakota. These events not only marked an increased interest on the part of non-Indians in listening to the voices and messages of American Indians but also a new determination by Indians to write in their own words about themes that are primarily Indian.

Though American Indian poets write in a form that is primarily Western (generally free and blank verse), they imbue that form with a sense of "Indianness" that makes it unique. What is particularly important for Indian poets is the connection between their writing and oral past of their people. Poets such as **Leslie Marmon Silko** (Laguna Pueblo) and **Simon Ortiz** (Acoma Pueblo) insist that their writing is but part of a cultural con-tinuum that stretches back to the oral tales, ceremonies, and songs of their tribes. Ortiz speaks on this in his poem "Survival This Way," suggesting that "the way" of surviving for a Native person is to participate in the cul-tural traditions of one's tribe, traditions that are passed from one genera-tion to the next. Likewise, **Wendy Rose** (Hopi/Miwok) suggests that poets participate in the preservation of tribal history by finding new words with which to express the old traditions, thereby grounding their work in those traditions.

A related theme explored by American Indian poets in their writing is **identity**, the struggle to define one's self as an American Indian set against the alienating effects of the modern world and its separateness from tradi-tional lifestyles and beliefs. Many American Indian poets explore what it means to be a part of a people whose ancestry goes back thousands of years and how tribal traditions and events can have meaning in a mechanized society. Because of their focus on cultural traditions, American Indian poets also emphasize the importance of history, both tribal and national; for these writers, making connections between past and the present are key to this dilemma of living as an Indian in the modern world.

Joseph Bruchac, an Abenaki poet and critic, notes that in addition to the awareness of and respect for tribal culture, American Indian poetry generally embodies a deep respect for the earth and the natural world and an understanding of the power of written words. For most American Indian writers, English is different than it is for white Americans because it is either their second language or at least second in significance to the language spoken by their tribe. Because of this, for Native poets, language is never simply ornamental or aesthetic but always powerful and purposeful.

The topic of the importance of words and the necessity of finding the right voice with which to speak is addressed frequently in American Indian poetry, sometimes through the use of voice. Wendy Rose often writes in voices that are not her own, speaking instead for those whose story has not been told or if told, has been misrepresented; in the poem "Truganiny," for instance, Rose speaks with the voice of an aboriginal woman whose stuffed body was put on display as the "last" of her people. When Rose does speak in her own voice, she describes herself not as singing or telling stories but only as making noise, an indication of her own search for the right words to express her meaning.

Language and words are imbued with power and meaning in the poetry of N. Scott Momaday (Kiowa). Though best known for his Pulitzer Prize–winning novel, he also published several volumes of poetry, the most notable being *The Gourd Dancer* (1976). In many of his poems, Momaday uses language as the connecting thread between the traditional past and the present, focusing especially on naming as a source of power even in the modern world. In the title poem, "Gourd Dancer," Momaday emphasizes the significance of a man's name being called in the context of a Giveaway Ceremony. For Momaday, words have power and the ability to recall an image or moment to mind as vividly as if the writer—or the reader—were experiencing the moment first hand. His reverence for language is evident in the lyrical imagery of his poems, which also celebrate the natural world and its importance. Many of Momaday's poems deal directly with images of nature, as in "The Bear," a description of an ancient and scarred bear, or in "Trees and Evening Sky," a pure imagist poem that vividly depicts a sunset. Place is also of key importance to Native writers; in "To A Child Running with Outstretched Arms in Canyon de Chelley," Momaday depicts the child embracing the "spirit" of the natural landscape in this sacred place. For Momaday, his Kiowa past, the natural world, and specific places and histories are all tied together by his use of and reverence for language, because words have the power to make things real.

Language also has power and significance for Simon Ortiz (Acoma Pueblo), but its power goes beyond the single word. For Ortiz, language is tied to the process of speaking and listening; the true meaning of an utterance comes not just from the meaning of a single word but rather in the understanding of the message as a whole. Ortiz uses language to articulate what it means to be Acoma, a people with a two thousand-year-old sense of identity, in the modern world. Part of the answer involves understanding one's past and connecting it to the present. In his collection *From Sand Creek* (1981), Ortiz connects the massacre of Cheyenne and Arapaho referenced in the title to other recent events in American history and in so doing, situates his own Native experience in this country within the continuum of American history in general. For Ortiz, violence in this country's history is a direct consequence of whites having lost this connection to their traditional past. In addition, Ortiz postulates a reverence for the natural world as a means of coping with the disconnect between traditional Indian life and the modern world; connecting one's self to nature is a means of connecting to a world that is broader in significance than merely the individual objects and inhabitants it contains. In "The Serenity in Stones," Ortiz expresses this clearly as he envisions a piece of turquoise as part of the sky and all that it represents. "A San Diego Poem" explores what happens when an American Indian loses that connection to the natural world: the narrator experiences isolation and fear while airborne because he has lost physical contact with the earth. Even upon landing, the narrator remains lost in the labyrinthine tunnels under the airport, which he describes as distinctly American, metaphorically buried in the concrete maze. Thus for Ortiz, physical and spiritual connection to the natural world is key to Indian identity in a world that contradicts or devalues the traditional way of life; the alternative is either violence or alienation and death.

In contrast to Ortiz, **James Welch** (Blackfeet-Gros Ventre) often expresses bitterness and anger over the events of recent history and their effects upon Native identity, which Welch sees as devastating. Skeptical of the possibility of retrieving traditions and history because of these dramatic changes, Welch's writing presents reservation life as a series of pointless attempts to defend a way of life that cannot be recovered. His poem "Harlem, Montana, Just Off the Reservation" is a bleak portrayal of life in a reservation border town, where Indians frequent the taverns and the whites are bigoted and ignorant. The setting of Welch's writing is often the bar rather than the natural world, and his characters, isolated by their poverty, are unable to connect with their spiritual past amid the bleak surroundings of the modern environment they inhabit. Even the natural world in Welch's writing is harsh and uncompromising, as can be seen in "Christmas Comes to Moccasin Flats," where the snow is not a cause for celebration but sends people huddling in their cabins and waiting for the next shipment of commodities to help them survive a hostile winter. For Welch, nature remains uncompromising and hostile, rather than a source of renewal and rebirth; there is little hope of repairing the broken connection between past and present.

One writer who does see the natural world as a means of renewal is Joseph Bruchac (Abenaki). For Bruchac, place is key; many of his poems' titles reference specific places, such as "Hawks Above the Hudson In March," an imagist style poem that centers on a lyrical description of hawks circling a frozen river. Bruchac writes with respect for the natural world; in "Bobcat, 1953," he emphasizes the connection between not only the narrator's past, as he remembers a story his grandfather told him, but also between the narrator and the animal, for he is one of the few able to sneak up on the wary bobcat. Bruchac's collection *This Earth Is a Drum* (1973) centers on the concept that planting and working a garden brings a person into close communication with the natural world. Bruchac also uses natural settings to make the connection between the modern-day and the larger cultural tradition of his people by retelling, in his poems, traditional tales of the Abenaki, inspired by a specific location. In "The Spreaders," Bruchac relates an Abenaki folktale about little men who accost unwary travelers in the heavily forested areas of upstate New York. Awareness of these connections, of how place maintains the connection between a traditional past and the chaotic present, is for Bruchac a way of maintaining Indianness and balance. In "Onondaga Lake," a sharp contrast is presented between the lake's pristine past as a watering hole for buffalo and its polluted and gray present. But still, Bruchac notes, the Indian people, despite their poverty and sorrow as represented by the polluted lake, are first to notice the changing of the seasons and the blooming of the flowers, because of their connection to traditional places, which Bruchac sees as key to maintaining an Indian identity.

Identity for Leslie Marmon Silko (Laguna Pueblo) can be found in the songs and stories of the American Indian's past. This is vividly explored in the poetry that intertwines within the pages of *Ceremony* (1977), poems that retell traditional stories of the Laguna and emphasize that the solution to the disconnect brought on by living in the modern world can be found by seeing one's self as part of a continuum of stories that reaches back to the time of creation. In "Toe'Ash: A Laguna Coyote Story," Silko makes this evident by updating the traditional coyote tales, applying the label of "coyote" to present-day politicians and businessmen who, although they attempt to be clever by promising the people food if they vote, end up being tricked themselves. This poem explicitly makes the connection between a traditional past and the modern present; Coyote's presence in the twentieth century implies not only a continuum but also the relevance of the old tales, which, Silko suggests, infuse modern life with meaning and promise.

Ray A. Young Bear (Mesquakie) also writes of the importance of maintaining connections between the physical world of his spiritual past, where spirits and animals have as viable a role as humans do, and the contemporary landscape, where the voices of the spirits and the memories of past events are distorted by the hustle and bustle of everyday life. Like Welch, Young Bear speaks of how the lives of traditional storytellers and wise men have changed in the contemporary world, as they appeal to modern technology, such as headphones and radio newscasts, in an attempt to hear the voices of the old gods. This juxtaposition of the traditional and the modern gives Young Bear's poetry a surreal quality that is often seen in the works of America Indian writers.

A similar surreal quality is present in the writings of **Louise Erdrich** (Chippewa). But here, the source of the surreal is located inside the individual, rather than in the natural world. Erdrich explores issues of gender roles and women's needs in her poems, which feature characters such as a woman who makes a "to do" list of things required for her to appease a god who is representative of the disapproving father or husband. Most of the characters in Erdrich's poems are women who seek justification from the male figures in their lives. But Erdrich generally ends her poems by affirming the importance of family and by suggesting that the darker emotions of anger, rage, and hatred can find a more constructive outlet in the energy needed to raise a family. Thus, for Erdrich, families help maintain one's identity.

Paula Gunn Allen (Laguna) also speaks of a struggle for identity, writing as a woman poet in an urban setting, separated from the traditional homeland and her people's history. In "Recuerdo," Allen recalls a moment when, climbing a mountain with her family, she believed she heard the voices of the old gods, voices that, as an adult living away from the sacred lands of the Laguna Pueblo, she now struggles to hear amid the clock ticking and other mechanized sounds of the urban environment. However, Allen insists that urban Indians can maintain contact with their ancestral past, suggesting that doubt, rather than technology, is their true enemy.

Linda Hogan (Chickasaw) also speaks of this doubt as she addresses the problems of living a divided life as, like Allen, an urban Indian who works and lives away from a reservation setting. Hogan most often associates moments of hearing those ancestral voices with images of sunlight and the dawn, so that light becomes equated with truth and belief. But in her more overtly political poems, Hogan inverts this dichotomy, envisioning darkness as the only place where the truth can be told, because in the light, one has to be polite and civil. Ironically, the poet must enter into darkness, where the truth about repression of Native peoples can be told, in order to bring this truth into the light. For Hogan, using language and words to make these stories real is a way of doing just that.

For **Joy Harjo** (Creek), a search for a confident voice manifests itself in the form of multiple voices speaking within a single poem. Many of the speakers in Harjo's poetry are inarticulate or mute; for them, the language they have available is insufficient to express their message. Even the poet in Harjo's work is often overcome by her inability to express the truth in words of a language that is not her own; in "Anchorage," the speaker is powerfully reminded of the history of Native peoples in North America by her encounter with a silent Athabascan woman, but she cannot find the words to express what she knows. Harjo suggests that there is always the potential for the poet to speak these transformative and clarifying words, and she speculates about the possibility of discovering a new and precise language that would enable her to express her thoughts in a way that English cannot.

Humor can be a way of using language to express the truth, and for **Sherman Alexie** (Spokane) it becomes a vehicle both for making connections to the past and for coping with the poverty and living conditions on the reservation. Humor enables Alexie to critique both Indians and white people, as he does in "The Native American Broadcasting System," where he suggests that if only one white man remained alive, he would reinvent himself as a Cherokee and create a modern-day Trail of Tears. This poem also expresses the effects of modernization on the traditional way of life by juxtaposing images of technology with icons from the Spokane traditional past.

American Indian writers use poetry, a borrowed form, as a means of addressing the key questions faced by Native peoples in the modern world. Their poems, even in the twenty-first century, continue to contemplate Indian identity and the importance of traditions, of maintaining connections to the past. For Native peoples attempting to live a balanced life amid the technology of today, this is an important issue that cannot easily be resolved.

Further Reading

Allen, Paula Gunn. *Studies in American Indian Literature: Critical Essays and Course Designs.* New York: MLA, 1983.

Bruchac, Joseph. "Many Tongues: Native American Poetry Today." *North Dakota Quarterly* 55 (Fall 1987): 239–44.

Castro, Michael. *Interpreting the Indian: Twentieth Century Poets and the Native American.* Albuquerque: U of New Mexico P, 1983.

Parini, Jay. "Native American Poetry." *The Columbia History of American Poetry.* Ed. Jay Parini. New York: Columbia UP, 1993. 728–49.

Patti J. Kurtz

NATIVE AMERICAN RESERVATION   Once the sole inhabitants of the entire landmass now known as the United States of America, Native Americans became gradually confined to smaller and smaller tracts of territory known as "reservations." The reservation system developed slowly and unsystematically during the course of American settlement and westward expansion: Europeans staked their claim to this new territory and removed the Indians each time they wanted to settle a region. Many treaties were drafted between the Natives and the settlers, most of which granted Native Americans parcels of land to the west of the new European settlements. But as post-Revolutionary "Americans" moved further and further west in the eighteenth century, these treaties were repeatedly nullified and renegotiated. Soon, Indians were relegated to small pieces of bounded territory scattered all across the country, surrounded and virtually imprisoned by the dominant settler culture.

These reservations were subject to the control and administration of the federal government. In 1824, the Bureau of Indian Affairs was created to provide management of the 55.7 million acres held for Native Americans at that time. Of the forty-five Commissioners of Indian Affairs since the Bureau's inception, only six have actually been Indian. Generally speaking, the Bureau would send white Indian agents, often uneducated about tribal life or otherwise corrupt, to oversee reservation life and activity. Beyond this surveillance, reservations were largely cut off from the laws, operations, markets, and culture of the United States at large; they functioned instead as isolated, often impoverished territories completely dependent upon the government's support. Indians leaving the reservation were often subject to arrest for trespassing. Thus, these previously nomadic tribes of hunters and explorers were forced to remain within constricted bounds, confined not just to new territory markers

Cheyenne people going to their reservation, 1870s. Hand-colored woodcut. *Copyright North Wind Picture Archives/ North Wind Picture Archives. All rights reserved.*

but to new lifestyles. Missionaries entered the reservations in hopes of bringing the light of Christianity to these "uncivilized" peoples, often setting up schools as well. Although many Indians were converted to European traditions, most remained attached to their own cultural beliefs and practices. This stubbornness led Americans to view the Indian as primitive and backward, and it prevented the reservation-bound tribes from gaining acceptance and respect from the dominant culture.

In February of 1887, the government initiated new legislation intended to help these alienated groups become "civilized" Americans. The Dawes Severalty Act proposed to accomplish this by changing fundamentally the structure of reservation life: in place of communally owned land, the government divided reservations into individual parcels and "allotted" them to Indians and their families. The expectation was that each person or family would farm their piece of land in the "American" way, but most Indians were unaccustomed to and unprepared for a rooted, agricultural lifestyle. Largely unable to support themselves, many Indians succumbed to poverty or sought escape in alcohol. Without providing sufficient preparation and support for the Indian's **assimilation**, the Dawes Act was a disaster. Within half a century, well over 50 percent of Native reservation land had fallen into white hands through fraud, trickery, or deals made with Native Americans too hungry or confused to demand a fair price.

Reservations still exist in America today, though many Native Americans have abandoned these communities and integrated into surrounding towns and cities. In 1953, a federal "termination" policy threatened to repeal reservation trusts in order to simultaneously deny tribal recognition and support; this policy was officially disbanded in 1970 by the Nixon administration, which promoted Indian "self-determination" instead. Indians who remain on reservations are still engaged in vigorous assertions of their rights as sovereign nations or in protesting the abuses of their lands as dumping sites for uranium waste or the depletion of natural resources. The **Civil Rights Movement** of the 1960s helped spur pan-tribal Indian activism as well. Even today, not all tribes are federally recognized; therefore, many have had to petition the government for tribal recognition and sovereignty, which gives them status as "domestic, dependent nations" with increased political autonomy and federal financial support. Many Native American authors, for example, **Sherman Alexie** and **Leslie Marmon Silko**, have compellingly documented the Indian's protracted struggle to negotiate the strange, shifting borders of their own Native land.

Further Reading

Alexie, Sherman. *Reservation Blues.* New York: Warner Books, 1996.

Lyman, Abbott. "Our Indian Problem." *North American Review* 167 (1898): 719–28.

Trennert, Jr., Robert A. *Alternative to Extinction: Federal Indian Policy and the Beginnings of the Reservation System.* Philadelphia: Temple UP, 1975.

Wildenthal, Bryan H. *Native American Sovereignty on Trial: A Handbook with Cases, Laws, and Documents.* Santa Barbara, CA: ABC-CLIO, 2003.

Melanie R. Benson

NATIVE AMERICAN STEREOTYPES The arrow-wielding savage and the sexualized Indian princess have been immortalized by Hollywood films, advertising, and sports team mascots. Despite a few exceptions, depictions of Native Americans bear little resemblance to the reality of most Native Americans today. Old stereotypes continue to be perpetuated, yet at the same time Native American film directors and writers today are deconstructing these images. These invented images are not only inauthentic to specific tribes, but they perpetuate the idea that all Indians are alike and that they are still living in the nineteenth century.

Hollywood Indians

Hollywood films have had a powerful impact on how most Americans view Native Americans: There have been thousands of films that portray

Native Americans since the beginning of the motion picture industry. Yet, although individual Europeans are usually identified as Irish, Polish, or Swedish in films, the over five hundred Indian tribes have, until recently, been lumped together. Films before the mid-twentieth century usually depicted Indians who were identified as one tribe, say Apache, but their rituals were from the Lakota Sioux and their clothes from the Navajo. If we were to come to conclusions about Indians based on *most* Hollywood films, we would think that there were no Indians before 1820 or after 1910. We would think that the "red man" was a Noble Savage, a Faithful Tonto, an exotic, virile barbarian, a Woodsy Christ figure, a druggy hippy, or pure evil, and that all Indian women were princesses and that Indians only speak in monosyllabic words ("How" or "Kemo Sabe").

It was not until the 1960s that Indians began to be portrayed as more fully human, with individual tribal cultures. In 1968, the **American Indian Movement** (AIM) was established and a series of incidents (the occupation of Alcatraz in 1968 and **Wounded Knee** Incident in 1973) led to more sympathetic films; however, most movies stayed with historical rather than contemporary settings, and white characters remained the main protagonists (e.g. *Little Big Man, Tell Them Willie Boy Is Here*, and *Thunderheart*). Richard Harris, the star of *A Man Called Horse* (1970), plays an Englishman who takes part in the Sun Dance ceremony and ironically shows the Sioux how to use a bow and arrow. *Dances With Wolves* (1990) was both praised for Kevin Costner's realistic touches (using the Lakota language with subtitles in English) and criticized for regressing to the vanishing Indian theme and the white-man-as-protagonist structure. In the film, the Sioux are treated as individuals; however, the Pawnee are purely evil Hollywood Indians. At the end, the white protagonists leave their Lakota friends to be slaughtered and oppressed by the U.S. government. Other films such as Disney's *Pocahontas* (1995) update the Indian princess stereotype and revise the historical events, much to the horror of many critics.

Yet the biggest impact of Hollywood's focus on mostly nineteenth-century Indians is the perpetuation of the myth that Indians are extinct, or that those both on reservations and off will soon be either assimilated or will self-destruct. Few Hollywood films have depicted the contemporary Native American. When the film *Pow Wow Highway* (1989), based on the book by David Seals, came out it was immediately a cult classic, especially with Native American viewers, because it was the story of contemporary Indians struggling with both cultural and political issues. Despite casting Indians in most of the roles, the lead role is played by Al Martinez, a non-Indian. But this is one of the first films to show Indians without feathers and loincloths, so despite its flaws it was a start to showing contemporary Indians in Hollywood film. The film also confronts the power of Hollywood movies and stereotypes about the spirituality of Indians when the main character mimics a jail break he watched on television and when an aunt makes fun of her nephew after he asks her to tell him the meaning of life—she just wants to be left alone to watch television.

Sherman Alexie's film *Smoke Signals* (1998), directed by Chris Eyre and based on Alexie's short story "This is what it means to say Phoenix, Arizona," also depicts young Indians on a reservation in a way that both alludes to and twists Hollywood stereotypes about Indians. Thomas is a storyteller, but his stories don't turn into new age, shamanistic trite sayings, and though Victor is a warrior, he is not a silent one. *Smoke Signals* is a road film, like *Pow Wow Highway,* but updated: it is the first feature film to have been written, directed, and coproduced by Native Americans, with Native Americans in all the lead roles. Alexie has said that the film's theme is loving someone despite his or her faults, a theme that transcends the focus on Indian characters.

Advertising and Sports Mascots

Stereotypes of Indians have been used to sell products so successfully that most consumers recognize the Indian maiden in nineteenth-century dress on packages of Land O' Lakes butter and the Indian chief on cans of Calumet baking power. And debate over the use of Indian figures as mascots or names of sports teams (the Braves, Indians, Chiefs, and Redskins, to name a few) continues today, with alumni of some universities threatening to stop giving funding if a team's name is changed for "political correctness."

Stereotypes in Literature

Hollywood, advertisers, and the sports world are not alone in creating and maintaining stereotypes about Native Americans. Written stories of Indian savagery were very popular in the sixteenth and seventeenth centuries. These "captivity" narratives were often adventure tales, filled with danger and violence. There is usually an exceptional "noble" Indian who establishes a connection with the captive, but for the most part, the Indians are portrayed as savages. In 1682 the best-selling book was *The Narrative of the Captivity of Mrs. Mary Rowlandson,* which pitted a Christian white woman against savage Indians. This theme continued in magazines, paintings, and dime novels well into the twentieth century.

In 1826, James Fenimore Cooper's novel *The Last of the Mohicans* established future stereotypical extremes of the Indian: the noble savage and the bloodthirsty savage. Five film versions exist of this novel. Native character Chingachgook is portrayed as a regal character, but he is also one of the last of this breed, beginning the myth of the vanishing Indian. Natty Bumpo, the white frontiersman, is one of the first in a line of Hollywood white frontiersman who is a better Indian than the Indians.

The late twentieth century gave rise to what is now called the Native American Literary Renaissance. These writers often explicitly address stereotypes. **Louise Erdrich** addresses the stereotypical Hollywood Indians embedded in American attitudes toward Indians in her 1984 poem "Dear John Wayne" from her collection *Jacklight* (1984). The poem confirms the power of Hollywood even one hundred years later as it depicts contemporary Indians growing increasingly uncomfortable while watching a John Wayne movie at a drive-in as the audience cheers when Wayne arrives to avenge the deaths of the white settlers. Other writers who depict the ambiguities of being both American and Native American today include **James Welch**, Sherman Alexie, Elizabeth Woody, **Leslie Marmon Silko**, and **Thomas King**, among many others.

Conclusion

Although film and literature may continue to maintain the stereotypes—both sympathetic and hostile—of Native Americans, with the ongoing presence of writers such as Sherman Alexie, who is attempting to challenge stereotypes in both the literary and film worlds, perhaps the stereotypical images of the nineteenth-century Indian will pass and Americans can begin to learn about the twenty-first-century realities of the various Indian cultures that have been influenced by and have influenced American culture.

Further Reading

Hirschfelder, Arlene, et al. *American Indian Stereotypes in the World of Children.* 2nd ed. London: Scarecrow Press, 1999.

Kilpatrick, Jacquelyn. *Celluloid Indians: Native Americans and Film.* Lincoln: U of Nebraska P, 1999.

Purdy, John. "Tricksters of the Trade: 'Reimagining' the Filmic Image of Native Americans." *Native American Representations.* Ed. Gretchen Bataille. Lincoln: U of Nebraska P, 2001. 100–18.

Reid, T. V. "Old Cowboys, New Indians: Hollywood Frames the American Indian." *Wicazo Sa Review* (Summer 2001): 75–96.

Rollins, Peter C., and John E. O'Connor, eds. *Hollywood's Indian: The Portrayal of the Native American in Film.* Lexington: UP of Kentucky, 1998.

Stacey Lee Donohue

NATIVE SON Published in 1940, **Richard Wright**'s novel was the first by an African American to become a Book-of-the-Month Club selection, albeit in significantly revised and expurgated form. Hailed as a touchstone of black literary naturalism and protest literature more generally, *Native Son* generated widespread controversy over its attribution of violent physical and sexual agency to its black male protagonist, Bigger Thomas.

The narrative is divided into three "books": "Fear," "Flight," and "Fate." The first introduces the reader to Bigger, a brutish, imposing figure who lives with his mother, brother, and sister in a run-down, rat-infested apartment on Chicago's South Side. Mr. Dalton, the landlord, employs Bigger as his family's chauffeur, and the first assignment is to drive Mary Dalton, the attractive and liberal-minded daughter, to the university. When she insists instead on having drinks with her communist boyfriend, Jan Erlone, Bigger has no choice but to go along for the ride. At the end of the evening, Mary is so intoxicated that Bigger is forced to carry her up to her bedroom. When the blind Mrs. Dalton appears in the doorway, a frenzied Bigger suffocates Mary out of fear of being caught in a space he knows is defended by a specifically racialized sexual taboo. Bigger gets rid of the evidence by decapitating the body and throwing it into the furnace.

"Flight" details Bigger's attempts to shake the authorities off his trail in the case of Mary's disappearance. He forges a ransom letter signed by "Red," briefly implicating Jan in the crime. Bigger confesses to the murder to his alcoholic girlfriend, Bessie Mears, but because he fears she will betray him, he rapes and then bludgeons her to death with a brick. A zealous manhunt, fueled by the hysteria surrounding the alleged defilement of white womanhood, ensues when Mary's remains are found and Bigger is identified as the prime suspect. He is soon tracked down and imprisoned amid calls for his lynching.

The third book unravels Bigger's fate at his inquest and subsequent trial. He is represented by Boris Max, a communist lawyer who argues that Bigger is less an individuated agent of violence and more a product of the blighted conditions into which he was born; the wretched state of Mr. Dalton's tenements has contributed to Bigger's depravity. When Bigger stands trial for murder, suspicion of his sexual violation of Mary characterizes the proceedings even though he will not and cannot admit to that facet of the crime. Despite Max's impassioned pleas, Bigger is sentenced to the electric chair as much for breaching racialized sexual codes as he is for murder.

A number of critics, most notably **James Baldwin**, have criticized Wright for subscribing to a deterministic literary practice that restricts the ways in which one is allowed to imagine black subjectivity. Bigger's narrative, in this regard, propagates the dominant white image, borne out of prejudice and fear, of the black male rapist. But that narrative can also be read as self-consciously defying another, equally damaging, racial mythos: the docile, accommodating "Uncle Tom." African American male authors writing in the hard-boiled (**Chester Himes**) and nationalist (**Amiri Baraka**) traditions have variously appropriated Wright's depiction of embodied black rage to further the work of resistant cultural and representational politics. (*See also* African American Novel)

Further Reading

Hakutani, Yoshinobu, ed. *Critical Essays on Richard Wright.* Boston: G. K. Hall, 1982.

Joyce, Joyce Ann. *Richard Wright's Art of Tragedy.* Iowa City: U of Iowa P, 1986.

Kinnamon, Keneth, ed. *New Essays on "Native Son."* Cambridge: Cambridge UP, 1990.

Rowley, Hazel. "The Shadow of the White Woman: Richard Wright and the Book-of-the-Month Club." *Partisan Review* 66.4 (1999): 625–34.

Kinohi Nishikawa

NAVA, MICHAEL (1954–)   Mexican American mystery novelist. Michael Nava is not only a novelist but also a lawyer and gay rights proponent. Nava's most popular works, the Henry Rios mystery novels, offer a less commonplace genre in Mexican American literature, the homosexual detective fiction, and also present commentaries on gay rights issues. Nava has also authored one nonfiction collection, *Created Equal: Why Gay Rights Matter to America* (1994), with Robert Dawidoff. Nava has also published some poetry, but, following his last published poems in *LA Poetry* in 1983, he has concentrated on prose. Nava has also edited a collection of short stories by gay and lesbian authors titled *Finale: Short Stories of Mystery and Suspense* (1997). His work has been anthologized in collections including *Friends and Lovers: Gay Men Write About the Families They Create* (1996), edited by John Preston and Michael Lowenthal; *Wrestling with the Angel: Faith and Religion in the Lives of Gay Men* (1996), edited by Brian Bouldrey; and *Las Christmas: Favorite Latino Authors Share Their Holiday Memories* (1999), edited by Joie Davidow and Esmeralda Santiago.

Born in Stockton, California, and raised in nearby Sacramento, Nava, a third-generation Mexican American, has a BA in history from Colorado College (1976) and a law degree from Stanford University (1981). Nava practiced law in the Los Angeles area following his graduation, but since 1995 he has lived in San Francisco, working in a private law practice.

Numbering among other authors writing in the gay mystery genre, such as J. M. Redmann and John Morgan Wilson, Nava is best known for his Henry Rios mystery novels. The seven Henry Rios novels, beginning with *The Little Death* (1986) and ending with the most recent, *Rag and Bone* (2001), all center on the protagonist, gay Mexican American lawyer Henry Rios in contemporary California. The city of Los Angeles provides a rich backdrop for Rios, Nava says, citing the city's diversity, the allure of the film industry, and the extremes of wealth and poverty (Forrest 9). Nava further states that "[T]o write about Los Angeles is to write about life itself" (Forrest 9). Rios is an engaging protagonist; however, he is not a "Utopian model of perfect self-acceptance" (Ortiz 123). He is an altogether human character who wrestles with his troubled upbringing in Los Robles, California, and appeals to a wide audience, as do the novels themselves.

The popular following the novels have garnered derives from Nava's insertion of social commentary into his work, balancing the art of fiction with moral insights. These issues include homosexuality, broken families, health concerns such as clinical depression and AIDS, and poverty. Amid all these topics Nava succeeds in drawing the reader both into the mystery and the underlying themes, carefully avoiding alienating the reader who may not identify with those topics such as homosexuality. As Ricardo L. Ortiz comments, "Rios' openness about his sexual and cultural identity allows Nava to demonstrate the ease with which these differences can acquire the status of significant but not incapacitating circumstances in the larger cultural and political environment in which Rios lives, and this without indulging in a too-stylized detective-fiction treatment, which would strain our ability as readers to suspend our disbelief" (122). Pivotal among these novels is Rios witnessing the death of his lover from AIDS in *The Death of Friends* (1996), the "apogee" of the series (Forrest 8).

Beginning in the first novel, *The Little Death,* Rios evidences characteristics that will mark his forays working with and challenging the legal system in efforts to publicize the need and secure justice for homosexual victims. Nava develops the same theme in the second novel in the series, *Goldenboy* (1988), winning the first annual Lambda Literary Award for Gay Men's Mystery/Science Fiction (1988). His subsequent novel, *How Town* (1990), earned Nava his second Lambda Literary Award for Gay Men's Mystery (1990); in *How Town* Henry defends a pedophile who is accused of murder. The other Henry Rios novels include *The Hidden Law* (1992), *The Death of Friends* (1996), *The Burning Plain* (1998), and the last novel, *Rag and Bone.* Nava has announced that *Rag and Bone* marks the conclusion of the Henry Rios novels, claiming that the frenetic pace of publishing and practicing law has fatigued him (Forrest 10). He also states, somewhat enigmatically, that "[T]he only thing that matters to me is the writing. Everything else is just noise" (Forrest 10).

In many ways *Rag and Bone* provides a capstone to the Rios novels. At the beginning of the novel, Rios has a heart attack, which prompts his reunion with his older sister Elena, who is a lesbian and a former nun and whose personal problems, which include an abusive husband, are introduced into the novel. Despite regaining his health, Rios suffers from a depression that stems in part from his lover's death from AIDS (*The Death of Friends*); this is ameliorated by the entrance of a new man into Rios's life, John, who is bisexual.

In an interview with Forrest, in response to the question "Why is *Rag and Bone* the last Henry Rios novel?" Nava replies that he is not interested in writing mysteries any more and that "the machinery of the murder and clues, all that, increasingly gets in the way of the stories I really want to tell" (9). Nava continues,

> When I started writing fiction, mysteries seemed to me to be an especially appropriate vehicle to explore the experience of being gay in this culture because, at least in the American tradition of crime writing, the protagonist is an outsider looking in, which describes the experience of most homosexual men and women. I suppose another reason I'm giving up the series is that I have said all I have to say about that experience, for now at least. Writing about being gay doesn't interest me much more at the moment than constructing a whodunit (9).

Collectively, the Henry Rios novels earned Nava the Bill Whitehead Award for Lifetime Achievement (2001).

Nava's nonfiction work, *Created Equal,* focuses on legal issues pertaining to gay rights. Nava and Dawidoff argue that gay men and lesbians deserve rights shared by all Americans and that they do not, contrary to popular belief, seek special treatment. *Created Equal* also engages with religious issues, arguing for much-needed tolerance. Furthermore, the authors support the cessation of discriminatory measures against gay men and lesbians, such as stereotyping, certain legislation, the military, gay marriage, and job discrimination; they also address issues of violence against gay men and lesbians. Moreover, *Created Equal* persuades the reader that the 1986 Supreme Court ruling (*Bowers v. Hardwick*) is a stumbling block against gay rights with regard to issues of privacy. The scholarly approach the authors take does not include moral arguments; the focus is purely on law and legislation. Overall, Nava and Dawidoff present a case that gay men and lesbians are denied certain rights, that this is constitutionally unacceptable, and that heterosexual Americans need to take an active interest in the issue of gay rights because it is a compelling contemporary American issue. At times written in a densely scholarly language, *Created Equal* nonetheless offers a cogent argument discussing gay rights. The text is not without its critics; Victoria A. Brownworth finds that there are certain flaws in the book, including a presumption of "racial and gender equity" and the exclusion of lesbian issues in the text (21).

Nava has been vocal in his defense of gay rights in other forms outside of the Henry Rios novels and *Created Equal;* along with Dawidoff, Nava authored an opinion piece in the *Los Angeles Times* titled "Why **Martin Luther King Jr.** Is a Gay Rights Hero" (January 16, 1994).

Nava can be situated within a coterie of Latino/a writers who actively engage with themes of homosexuality in their fiction and nonfiction. This focus earns Nava a place not only as a Mexican American author but also as a social critic. One can only wonder what is next in store for Nava following the conclusion of the Henry Rios novels. (*See also* Mexican American Gay Literature)

Further Reading

Brownworth, Victoria A. "Neo-lib glib: *Created Equal: Why Gay Rights Matter to America* by Michael Nava and Robert Dawidoff / A *More Perfect Union: Why Straight America Must Stand Up for Gay Rights* by Richard D. Mohr." *Lambda Book Report* 4.4 (May 1994): 21.

Forrest, Katherine V. "Adios, Rios." *Lambda Book Report* 9.8 (March 2001): 8–10.

Ortiz, Ricardo L. "Sexuality Degree Zero: Pleasure and Power in the Novels of John Rechy, Arturo Islas and Michael Nava." *Critical Essays: Gay and Lesbian Writers of Color.* Ed. Emmanuel S. Nelson. Binghamton, NY: Haworth Press, 1993. 111–26.

Lisa Nevárez

NAVARRO, JOE (1953–) Chicano poet and activist. Navarro's work as a poet (six chapbooks and a collection of children's poetry) is a direct outgrowth of his concerns as a teacher, parent, and political activist. His work as an activist began when he was still in high school and was expelled for wearing the brown beret as a symbol of Chicano pride. He then committed himself full-time to Chicano activism, helping to gain acquittal for seven young Latinos falsely accused of murdering a police officer. Later, he found work in a foundry and served as president of the union for six years.

In 1982, Navarro and his family moved to Colorado where Navarro finished high school and earned a college degree in Spanish, English, and teaching. Currently, he is an elementary school teacher in Hollum, California. There he is active in various civic organizations and was awarded the San Benito Community Spirit Award for organizing a parent and teacher alliance to ensure educational opportunities for children of minority or economically disadvantaged backgrounds. He also works with Apoyo Tarahumara: Tarahumara Support Committee, which delivers food to the Tarahumara Indians, a poor, indigenous community in the state of Chihuahua, Mexico.

Navarro's political concerns are most thoroughly explored in his first collection of poetry, *Reflections of an Aztlaneco* (1987), which is divided into six sections beginning with the personal and immediate "Experiences in the Barrio," "La Migra," and "Familia" and moving to the local and global "Education and Media," "Central America," and "South Africa." The theme of justice runs throughout this collection, whether it is for his daughter in "My Chicana Daughter" as she faces the **racism** of her educational system or for all people in "One Hundred Million Dollars to the Contras," which decries the illegal funding of war in Central America to the neglect of the poor in the United States.

Navarro's second major publication, a single poem titled *Awakening: Tribute to Malcolm X* (1992), describes a political awakening after which the speaker cannot return to a life focused solely on survival. The strength of this poem is its powerful lyricism. Here more than anywhere Navarro seems to enjoy the music of multisyllabic diction; this is a poem that asks to be read aloud. Navarro continues to explore the issues of **identity**, education, and politics in his continuing work, which includes *For the Sisters,* (1991), a collection exclusively about women navigating both Chicano culture and the culture of the United States; *Somos la Misma Raza: We Are the Same People* (1992); and *Ambidextrious: In Two Languages* (1999).

Although Navarro's work is not widely circulated, he gives frequent public readings and is a significant, contemporary voice in Chicano poetry. (*See also* Mexican American Poetry)

Further Reading

Del Castillo, Ramon. Introduction to *Reflections of an Aztlaneco: A Collection of Poetry by Joe Navarro.* Oakland, CA: Unity Publications, 1987.

Angela M. Williamson

NAYLOR, GLORIA (1950–)   African American novelist and anthologist. Alongside such figures as **Toni Morrison**, **Alice Walker**, and **Toni**

Cade Bambara, Gloria Naylor is a key voice in the rich outpouring of literature by African American women in the 1980s and 1990s. Her novels dramatize issues of community, connection, and **identity**, often through their focus on powerful but careworn women who tend to be the culture bearers for their communities. Orphans and those isolated from family, those seeking identity and community, also frequently people her fictions. Place plays an equally important role, as she tends to create very specific geographies that reflect her narrative structures. Connections interest her, as witnessed by her habit of placing at least one reference in each novel to a character or place or event from one of the others.

Naylor was born January 25, 1950, in New York City to parents who had just moved there from rural Mississippi, where they had been sharecroppers. She grew up in the Bronx and other areas of the city, including Harlem and Queens. A love of New York and of the foibles of its people and its neighborhoods is apparent in her fiction. Equally, however, Naylor displays an intuition for and understanding of the rural South, thanks to her parents' background and the family's frequent visits to family and friends there.

Naylor inherited a love of reading from her mother, who had worked extra hours in the fields in order to afford a library subscription. Naylor's mother also influenced her by joining the Jehovah's Witness during her daughter's adolescence. Upon high school graduation in 1968, Naylor was baptized in that faith, becoming in the process a minister. She began work as a switchboard operator in order to support her ministry. She continued as a missionary in New York, then in Dunn, North Carolina, and finally Jacksonville, Florida, through 1975.

At the age of twenty-five, Naylor broke with the Jehovah's Witnesses and entered college, first pursuing a nursing degree from Medgar Evers College. Deciding her strongest interests dwelt elsewhere, she changed both school and major, receiving a bachelor's degree in English from Brooklyn College, CUNY in 1981. Naylor married in 1980 but divorced the next year.

Essential to her development as a writer was the experience in 1977 of reading Toni Morrison's *The Bluest Eye*. She has described discovering for the first time that books were being published about her experiences, her life, her community. She has said *The Bluest Eye* gave her the authority to develop her own voice and to write the stories she knew. It also motivated her to pursue a master's degree from Yale in Afro-American studies, which she completed in 1983.

Naylor's first publication was a short story, "A Life in Beekman Place," published in *Essence* magazine in March 1980; its editor, Marcia Gillespie, strongly encouraged her to keep writing. It was also at this time in her life that Naylor began traveling outside the United States, visiting Spain and Tangiers in 1983.

Naylor's first novel, *The Women of Brewster Place* (1982), is told through seven interconnected stories, each featuring a different woman who has ended up living on a cul-de-sac that, once home to Irish immigrants, then Italian, is now populated primarily by African Americans. It has come to be a dead-end street, both literally and figuratively. The stories begin with that of Mattie Michael, who comes to Brewster Place as an older woman, having lost her house when she put it up as bond for her son, Basil, who fled rather than face a murder charge. As with each of the stories that follows, Mattie tells us about her years before Brewster Place: growing up with a doting but strict father, being beaten and thrown out by that father when she became pregnant, and taking up residence with Miss Eva, an older woman who eventually bequeaths her a house. Like Mattie's story, each woman's story seems close to an end once we see her arrive at Brewster Place, for the sense of a downward spiral that led them to this place and the poverty it holds mark it as a place of despair, not one of new beginnings.

Through the rest of the stories, Mattie remains as a figure who passes on the lessons she learned from Miss Eva, healing what she can of the pain around her—the fraught relationship of a young black nationalist to her disapproving mother, the rape of one member of a lesbian couple, and, in one of the most notable scenes, a young mother after the death of her child. Mattie thus takes her place as the older African American figure of wisdom who will reappear in Naylor's fictions, just as those figures do in much contemporary writing by African American women. Although there is no sense of an easy or happy ending for the women of Brewster Place, the novel does offer hope through community, as dawn breaks on the day of a block party. *The Women of Brewster Place* was awarded the American Book Award for best first novel in 1983. Oprah Winfrey spearheaded the transformation of the novel into a made-for-television film, broadcast in 1989, with Winfrey in the role of Mattie Michael.

Naylor's Yale master's thesis became her second novel, *Linden Hills* (1985). It also focuses on the dynamics within an African American community but does so in the context of a middle- and upper-class neighborhood. Modeled after Dante's *Inferno*, with a neighborhood arranged in concentric circles leading down to its center and the home of its founding family, and with its Virgil and Dante in the guise of two young men looking for handyman work for Christmas money, *Linden Hills* delivers a stinging critique of materialism and status seeking.

Mama Day, considered by many to be Naylor's most successful effort, appeared in 1988. A love story between George, a "stone city boy" from New York, and Cocoa (also known as Ophelia), from an island off the coast of the Georgia/South Carolina border, it is told in three narrative voices: George, Cocoa, and the communal voice of the island, Willow Springs. George is an orphan raised to believe in an extreme form of self-reliance while Cocoa has behind her generations of the Days, direct descendants of the slave woman, Sapphira Wade, who had wrested possession of Willow Springs from her master. Cocoa was raised by her grandmother and her great-aunt, Miranda "Mama" Day, one of the wise old culture-bearer women with deep knowledge of both the natural and the supernatural worlds. Miranda's given name is one of the many elements of *Mama Day* that put it in dialogue with Shakespeare's *The Tempest*, along with the island setting and the presence of conjurors. Naylor has stated that she found the structure to *Mama Day* while reading William Faulkner's *As I Lay Dying*.

Also in 1988 Naylor received a Guggenheim fellowship, followed by the Lillian Smith Award in 1989. In 1990 she founded One Way Productions, a film company to help bring *Mama Day* to the screen, although that has not yet been accomplished. One Way Productions has brought to the stage various works designed for children.

Naylor continued the magic realism and the multiple narrative voices she established in *Mama Day* with *Bailey's Cafe* (1992). Once again it is a novel comprised of the stories of seven people, but this time the structuring principle is music, particularly **jazz** and **blues**. Orchestrated by "Maestro," the proprietor of Bailey's Café whose name we never know, each woman (and one man dressed in women's clothes) takes center stage to tell her or his story at this way station of a café, an in-between place that inhabits nowhere and everywhere. Their stories resonate collectively through a shared element of each person having been defined by her sexuality; in interviews, Naylor has described the novel as a disquisition on the label "whore," demonstrating the various ways the term is used, and that finally no such thing exists. Naylor has also written *Bailey's Café* as a play; it had a successful run at the Hartford Stage in Connecticut in April 1994.

For the next few years, Naylor devoted much of her effort to compiling an anthology of African American writing, published in 1995 as *Children of the Night: The Best Short Stories by Black Writers, 1967 to the Present*. She conceived it as a follow-up to **Langston Hughes**'s 1967 *The Best Short Stories by Black Writers: 1899–1967*. Given that the thirty-seven stories "are recent; we are still within them," she chose to arrange them into topical categories, rather than chronologically, in order to avoid the sense of developmental progression. Her primary goal she describes as the selection of "the best to demonstrate, either thematically or structurally, mechanisms for surviving constant assaults against one's mind and spirit."

In 1998 Naylor returned to the setting of her first novel with *The Men of Brewster Place*, this time, as the title suggests, telling the story of the men who had such an impact on the lives of the women in her first novel (only one of the central characters did not appear in *The Women of Brewster Place*). The question each faces is, "What does it mean to be a man?"; each story shows an aspect of the complicated nature of that question in a society that has tried to deny maturity on the basis of skin color. The male gathering place is the barbershop, although it does not seem to hold out the same sense of power through community as the earlier work. Indeed, the final scene depicts just one man, "one tired warrior . . . one man standing is all that's needed." (*See also* African American Novel)

Further Reading

Awkward, Michael. *Inspiring Influences: Tradition, Revision, and Afro-American Women's Novels.* New York: Columbia UP, 1991.

Christian, Barbara. "Gloria Naylor's Geography: Community, Class, and Patriarchy in *The Women of Brewster Place* and *Linden Hills*." *Reading Black, Reading Feminist: A Critical Anthology.* Ed. Henry Louis Gates Jr. New York: Penguin, 1990: 348–73.

Felton, Sharon, and Michelle C. Loris, eds. *The Critical Response to Gloria Naylor.* Westport, CT: Greenwood Press, 1997.

Fowler, Virginia C. *Gloria Naylor: In Search of Sanctuary.* New York: Twayne, 1996.

Gates, Henry Louis, Jr., and K. A. Appiah, eds. *Gloria Naylor: Critical Perspectives Past and Present.* New York: Amistad, 1993.

Harris, Trudier. *The Power of the Porch: The Storyteller's Craft in Zora Neale Hurston, Gloria Naylor, and Randall Kenan.* Athens: U of Georgia P, 1996.

Kelley, Margot Anne, ed. *Gloria Naylor's Early Novels.* Gainesville: U of Florida P, 1999.

Montgomery, Maxine Lavon. "Authority, Multivocality, and the New World Order in Gloria Naylor's *Bailey's Café*." *African American Review* 29 (Spring 1995): 27–33.

———. *Conversations with Gloria Naylor.* Jackson: UP of Mississippi, 2004.

Naylor, Gloria, and Toni Morrison. "A Conversation." *Southern Review* 21 (July 1985): 567–93.

Stave, Shirley A. *Gloria Naylor: Strategy and Technique, Magic and Myth.* Wilmington: U of Delaware P, 2001.

Storhoff, Gary. "'The Only Voice Is Your Own': Gloria Naylor's Revision of *The Tempest*." *African American Review* 29 (Spring 1995): 35–45.

Ward, Catherine C. "Gloria Naylor's *Linden Hills*: A Modern Inferno." *Contemporary Literature* 28 (1987): 67–81.

Whitt, Margaret Early. *Understanding Gloria Naylor.* Columbia: U of South Carolina P, 1999.

Wilson, Charles E. *Gloria Naylor: A Critical Companion.* New York: Greenwood Press, 2001.

Kathryn West

NEAL, LARRY [LAWRENCE PAUL] (1937–1981)   African American poet, literary and music critic, playwright, journal editor, educator, and activist in the radical politics of the 1960s. He was born in Atlanta, Georgia, but he grew up in Philadelphia. He received his bachelor's degree in history and English from Lincoln University and his master's in politics and folklore from the University of Pennsylvania. He moved to New York City in 1964. Larry Neal's enduring legacy comes from his work within the **Black Arts Movement** (BAM) of the 1960s and 1970s to which he provided the founding ideology, concepts, and history. His most important contribution to the definition of the period is reflected notably in his essay "The Black Arts Movement" and an anthology he coedited with **Amiri Baraka** in 1968, *Black Fire: An Anthology of Afro-American Writing*, a collection of poetry, prose, and theoretical essays written by various adherents of the BAM. He also helped to found and edit several journals and magazines, including *Liberator, The Cricket, Black Theatre, The Journal of Black Poetry, Negro Digest, Essence,* and *Black World.* In general, these publications promoted the tenets of the BAM, including the idea that black art should be at the service of the black community. Neal also wrote two plays, *The Glorious Monster in the Bell of Horn* (1976) and *In an Upstate Motel: A Morality Play* (1981). Larry Neal's poetry appeared in *Black Fire* (1968), *Visions of a Liberated Future* (1989), and especially in two collections of poetry, *Black Boogaloo: Notes on Black Liberation* (1969) and *Hoodoo Hollerin' Bebop Ghosts* (1974). In using African culture, history, mythology, and orality, Neal was deliberate in promoting racial consciousness and social protest.

The BAM writers were committed to the belief that ethics and aesthetics cannot be separated; neither can black art and the black community. The black artist should address the aspirations of the black community and thus participate in the liberation of the black people. They also viewed art as performance, with emphasis on theater, because, for Neal, "theatre is potentially the most social of all the arts" (68) in that it relates directly to the aspirations of its audience. Neal and the BAM writers also committed to what Harold Cruse called, in *The Crisis of the Negro Intellectual* (1967), the "Triple Front" of cultural, economic, and political commitment. They also rejected restrictive conventions and instead opted for the fluidity of orality and unconventional forms.

In "The Black Arts Movement," Larry Neal argued that the BAM was "the aesthetic and spiritual leader of the Black Power concept" (62) and as such it should "speak directly to the needs and aspirations of Black America" (62). It rejected white cultural and political domination and called for black consciousness, pride, and self-determination. (*See also* Black Nationalism)

Further Reading

Callaloo 23 (Winter, 1985) [Larry Neal: A Special Issue].

Neal, Larry. "The Black Arts Movement." *Drama Review* 12.4 (1968).

Schwartz, Michael, ed. *Visions of a Liberated Future: Black Arts Movement Writings.* New York: Thunder's Mouth Press, 1989. 62–78.

Aimable Twagilimana

NEGRITUDE In its narrowest sense, Negritude is a movement of West Indian and African poetry in French that was centered in Paris and thrived from the late 1930s through the 1950s. Its most famous and influential figures are Aimé Césaire from Martinique, Léopold Senghor of Senegal, and Léon Damas from French Guiana. More broadly, Negritude refers to a French version of black self-awareness and **Pan-Africanism**. The word was apparently coined by Aimé Césaire and was first used in print in his seminal 1939 poem "Cahiers d'un retour au pays natal" ("Journal of a Return to the Native Land"). Césaire himself has defined Negritude as "a taking charge of one's destiny as a black man" (Kesteloot 105); Léopold Senghor defined it variously as "the spirit of Negro African civilization" (Kesteloot 102) and "the ensemble of black cultural values" (Kesteloot 103). Jean-Paul Sartre described Negritude as the antithesis of the European assertion of black inferiority.

Negritude took inspiration and ideas from a variety of sources: a questioning of Western rationality from French surrealism; anticapitalist and antiracist ideologies from the French Communist Party; and, from the **Harlem Renaissance**, a quest for an original black personality and a bold assertion of the dignity and equality of black people. Lilyan Kesteloot traces the origins of Negritude to the publication in 1932 of *Légitime Défense*, an artistic and political manifesto by Martiniquan students in Paris. Though suppressed by the French authorities after one issue, *Légitime Défense* had a profound effect on black students in Paris at the time and inspired a group led by Césaire, Senghor, and Léon Damas to found the newspaper *L'Etudiant Noir* (The Black Student) in 1934.

Over the following decade those three poets would write some of the seminal works of Negritude, but it was not until after World War II that Negritude as a cultural movement began to cohere and attract international attention. In 1947, the first issue of *Présence Africaine* was published simultaneously in Paris and Dakar, expressly to "define African originality and to hasten her acceptance into the modern world" (Jack, 58). Throughout the 1950s, *Présence Africaine* published a protracted exchange among key figures of Negritude and Pan-Africanism that came to be called the "Debate on the conditions of a national poetry for black people." Also in 1947, Damas published the first anthology of poetry from the French Empire; a year later, Senghor published his hugely influential *Anthology of the New Negro and Malagasy Poetry in French*, prefaced by Sartre's essay "Black Orpheus." With this anthology, Senghor helped established a sort of Negritude "**canon**," characterized by an emphasis on rhythm, image, and symbol and by its attempts to formulate a black aesthetic rooted in a common African past and a common experience of **colonialism**.

Further Reading

Jack, Belinda Elizabeth. *Negritude and Literary Criticism: The History and Theory of "Negro-African" Literature in French.* Westport, CT: Greenwood Press, 1996.

Kesteloot, Lilyan. *Black Writers in French: A Literary History of Negritude.* Trans. Ellen Conroy Kennedy. Philadelphia: Temple UP, 1974 [orig. pub. 1963].

Shane Graham

NEMEROV, HOWARD (1920–1991) Jewish American poet, novelist, short story writer, literary critic, and teacher. Howard Nemerov began his career echoing the works of the modernist poets T. S. Eliot, W. H. Auden, William Butler Yeats, and Wallace Stevens, but at the time of his death at age seventy-one, and after more than forty years and twenty-five books, he emerged as a leading American poet of great technical skill, wit, and versatility. A major poet writing in traditional verse forms, Nemerov uses irony, paradox, and often irreverent humor to comment on the balance between man's sense of himself and his place in the physical world.

Born into a Jewish family in New York City, Nemerov received his bachelor's degree from Harvard University in 1941. He served with the Royal Canadian Air Force and the U.S. Army during World War II, and following the war he taught in a number of universities, including Hamilton, Bennington, the University of Minnesota, and Brandeis. Beginning in 1969 and until his death, he taught at Washington University in St. Louis. Nemerov received most of poetry's major awards, including the Pulitzer Prize and the National Book Award for *Collected Poems* (1977), and he was both Consultant in Poetry to the Library of Congress (1963–64) and the third poet laureate of the United States (1988–99). His 1944 marriage to Margaret Russell produced three children.

He was a wry commentator whose casual, colloquial ease was displayed in tightly structured forms. The technical excellence of his poetry and his ability to write in diverse modes made Nemerov a leading voice in American poetry, though he refused to be identified with any particular school of poetry.

In such collections as *The Salt Garden* (1955), *Mirrors and Windows* (1958), and *The Western Approaches* (1975), Nemerov developed a growing concern with opposites and man's duality of vision. Nemerov's poetry displays a broad range of emotions and subject matter. Though his early poetry was thought to be derivative, academic, or dull, he developed a confident control in the way he used deceptively simple syntax to link the temporal and spiritual worlds. Although his poetry was not notably Jewish, it was filled with reflections on doubt and the human spirit. From his *Collected Poems* to *Trying Conclusions: New Selected Poems, 1961–1991* (1991), Nemerov alternated between skepticism and social satire, views also expressed in his prose works, including several books of criticism and five novels.

Howard Nemerov will be remembered as a leading American poet whose craftsmanship, sensibility, and discerning mind used the traditional verse form as a sounding board to discuss man's place in the modern world and his profound need to find a balance between innocence and existence.

Further Reading

Bartholomay, Julia A. *The Shield of Perseus: The Vision and Imagination of Howard Nemerov*. Gainesville: U of Florida P, 1972.

Labrie, Ross. *Howard Nemerov*. Boston: Twayne Publishers, 1980.

Meinke, Peter. *Howard Nemerov*. Minneapolis: U of Minnesota P, 1965.

Mills, William. *The Stillness in Many Things: The World of Howard Nemerov*. Memphis: Memphis State UP, 1975.

Gary Kerley

NEO-SLAVE NARRATIVE   In the wake of the Civil Rights, Women's Rights, and Black Power movements of the sixties and seventies, there has emerged a whole crop of imaginative **slave narrative**s that are the products of their authors' ancestral memories and reimagining of **slavery**. Adopting the voice of the fugitive slave and the structure of a slave narrative, these fictional works present an account of life in slavery, where the actual and the possible blend. They differ significantly from the traditional slave narratives best exemplified in **Frederick Douglass**'s *Narrative of the Life of Frederick Douglass, an American Slave, Written by Himself* (1845) and even in his fictionalized account of Madison Washington in the novella *The Heroic Slave* (1853) as well as Harriet A. Jacobs's *Incidents in the Life of a Slave Girl* (1861), published with only the name of **abolition**ist Lydia Maria Child as the editor on the title page. Jacobs's *Incidents* tells the story of a woman who enters into a sexual alliance with a white neighbor to escape the sexual advances of her master. Jacobs argues, "It seems less degrading to give one's self, than to submit to compulsion." The essence of a traditional slave narrative is well-captured in Douglass's oft-quoted sentence, "You have seen how a man was made a slave; you shall see how a slave was made a man." Douglass provides many scenes of the whipping of women, without any one of them offering any resistance. Whereas Douglass's narrative gives mainly the male point of view and values, according women a passive role, the new slave narratives authored by women offer the female slave as the protagonist and show female protagonists' resistance to servitude. Whereas the classic slave narrative purports to argue for the abolition of slavery and prove the slave's humanity, the neo-slave narrative focuses on the slave protagonist's individual experiences. Whereas the protagonist of a traditional slave narrative moves from slavery to literacy, identity, and freedom, the protagonist of a neo-slave narrative moves from slavery to family, community, identity, and freedom. Based on the premise that all slaves' experiences were not identical and that a number of slave stories were either destroyed or never told, the neo-slave narratives furnish imaginative accounts of slavery in which history and fiction intermingle. They provide fascinating variations on slave-master relationships and slaves' resistance to slavery, often with a humor usually absent from the traditional slave narratives.

A large majority of the neo-slave narratives have been the work of women. **Margaret Walker**'s *Jubilee* (1966) is perhaps the first neo-slave narrative. It tells the story of the author's maternal great-grandmother under the fictional name of Vyry and the black experience in slavery, the Civil War, and Reconstruction to 1870. Five years elapsed before the next neo-slave narrative appeared in **Ernest Gaines**'s *The Autobiography of Miss Jane Pittman* (1971). In the guise of taped interviews, Ernest Gaines presents in her own words the life story of its black female protagonist, who was born into slavery in the 1850s and is still alive in 1962. **Gayl Jones**'s *Corregidora* appeared in 1975. It tells about the sexual exploitation of the protagonist Ursa's great-grandmother and grandmother by their Portuguese master, Corregidora, as well as the impact of their legacy of slavery on Ursa, their freeborn twentieth-century child. **Ishmael Reed**'s *Flight to Canada* appeared one year later in 1976. Published in the bicentennial year of American independence, it tells the story of slaves living on the Virginia plantation of Massa Arthur Swille III, especially Raven Quickskill and Uncle Robin. Next appeared **Octavia Butler**'s *Kindred* (1979). In this neo-slave narrative the protagonist Dana Franklin, a modern day woman, travels back in time and space into the South of slavery times and learns from her own experience the devastating effects of slavery on the slaves' physical and mental health.

   Charles R. Johnson's *Oxherding Tale* (1982), **Sherley Anne Williams**'s *Dessa Rose* (1986), **Toni Morrison**'s *Beloved* (1987), and **J. California Cooper**'s *Family* (1991) are the outstanding neo-slave narratives of the 1980s and 1990s. In *Oxherding Tale,* the protagonist Andrew Hawkins, a young slave of mixed blood and well-versed in Eastern and Western philosophy, seeks freedom from slavery to marry the slave girl Minty whom he loves. He eventually passes for white and marries the daughter of his doctor who treats him for his opium withdrawal. Concerned with the deeper questions of self and being, it is a book in which "fiction and philosophy meet." In *Dessa Rose,* Williams interweaves documented stories of two historical characters, a pregnant slave woman who led a revolt on a coffle in Kentucky in 1829 and a white woman living in North Carolina who gave refuge to fugitive slaves in North Carolina in 1830 to create a most interesting neo-slave narrative. It also tells the story of a growing friendship between the two mothers—one, a black slave named Dessa Rose, and the other a white plantation mistress named Ruth Sutton (nicknamed Rufel). *Beloved* is also based on the true story of a slave woman, Margaret Garner, who tried to kill her four children rather than have the slave catchers take them back to slavery. This story is included in *The Blue Book,* which Morrison edited. Cooper's *Family* brings out the hard and miserable lot of the slaves as told by the disembodied voice of Clora, as she watches over her children's lives in slavery and out of slavery. It tells the success story of the light-skinned Sun, who is secretly taught to read by his slave master's daughter and is provided by her the ticket to his freedom. Literacy opens the door to prosperity as he becomes his employer's partner and later his son-in-law, but he does not do anything for his family, thus **signifying** Douglass's narrative.

   A comparison of the aforementioned works, with respect to the crucial aspects of slavery, reveals a wide variety of situations with one common thread that all slave owners look upon their slaves as property. As already noted, the narrative strategies range from taped interviews to travelling backwards through time and use of a disembodied voice of a dead slave that watches. Of all the slave masters, there is only Paul Garner in *Beloved* who does not physically abuse his slaves. Most slave masters treat slaves as less than human. Garner takes credit for turning "niggers into men." Of all the slave masters, only three encourage their slaves learning to read and write; they are Paul Garner, Massa Swille in *Flight to Canada,* and Masa

Polkinghorne in *Oxherding Tale,* who engages a private tutor to teach Andrew Hawkins to increase his value. In *Kindred,* Marse Tom Weylin whips the protagonist Dana Franklin when he catches her teaching the slave Nigel how to read; in *Family,* the new slave who can read and starts reading lessons to other slaves, is beaten to death. That slaves do not like this prohibition is well-expressed by the protagonist Dessa Rose in the novel of the same title: "May come a time when I forgive . . . the beatings, the selling, the killings, but I don't think I ever forgive the ignorance they [slave owners] kept us in." In addition to beatings, selling, and killings, slaves' punishments include branding with the letter "R" on the face in *Jubilee;* imprisonment in a sweat box and saltwater treatment in *Dessa Rose;* the use of an iron bit under the tongue in *Beloved;* and hanging of a pregnant woman and ripping the baby from the womb in *Kindred.* In *The Autobiography of Miss Jane Pittman,* Jane's beatings damage her womb, resulting in her inability to conceive. In *Flight to Canada,* however, Mammy Barracuda, at the behest of Massa Swille, bosses over Mrs. Swille and gives her Valium injections to keep her quiet.

Sexual oppression of enslaved women is rampant in these innovative narratives. Master Corregidora in Gayle Jones's novel of that title and the unnamed slave master of Fammy in *Family* are two outstanding examples of masters who sexually abuse their female slaves. Corregidora, the Portuguese slave master, sexually exploits both Ursa's great-grandmother and grandmother and further uses them for prostitution. His oppression stops only when Ursa's grandmother bites on his penis and flees to the United States to escape his wrath. In *Family,* the slave master fathered ten children of the slave Fammy, but nine of them are sold by the time they reach the age of three. Clora in that novel says that she has heard white ladies talking among themselves that "them nigger womens is sex fiends," putting all the blame on slave women, as if they force white men to have sex with them.

There are some plantation mistresses such as Flo Hatfield in *Oxherding Tale* who use slaves as their sexual servants and get them killed when they get tired of them. The protagonist Andrew Hawkins is sent to work for Flo Hatfield of Leviathan Plantation, when he tells Masa Jonathan Polkinghorne that he is in love with Minty and requests him to sign his manumission papers so that he could earn money to pay for his and Minty's freedom. Flo Hatfield uses Andrew for her sexual gratification but refuses to talk about his wages. When he loses temper with her, she sends him to the mines to get him killed. Andrew is, however, clever enough to escape alive, pretending to be an employee of Flo Hatfield's. Miz Lorraine in *Dessa Rose* uses Nathan for the same purpose and later sells him to trader Wilson.

Slave women deeply care about their families. Vyry in *Jubilee* and Always in *Family* are excellent examples. Even though she loves her husband, Randall Ware, she would not run away with him to freedom, leaving her children behind in slavery. Always, who is deeply interested in the advancement of her family, substitutes her son, named Soon, with her mistress's son so that her son gets all the advantages due to him being the sole heir of his father's estate.

Slave women in the neo-slave works are not the passive victims as they are shown in traditional slave narratives such as Douglass's. One method available to them to challenge the slave master's authority is to take their lives with their own hands. And quite a few of them resort to this method of resisting oppression. Alice in *Kindred* and Clora in *Family* commit suicide. Dana in *Kindred* kills Rufus when he assaults her sexually, and Fammy in *Family* kills the slave master and then stabs herself to death. Dessa in *Dessa Rose* kills her master and a number of white men, and the slave trader Wilson loses an arm to her. She says that she kills white men "cause I can." Dessa and other slaves in that novel conceive a scam of selling themselves to slavery again and again in different counties of Alabama in cahoots with Rufel. Dessa Rose expresses the slaves' viewpoint: "Oh, I tell you, honey, slavery was ugly and we felt right to soak the masters for all we could get."

Humor is also one of the important elements of the neo-slave narratives. When asked by Rufel what he did during slavery, Nathan in *Dessa Rose* responds that he worked for a slave trader who grew negroes by planting their toes in the ground and made them drink ink at night to give them color. This joke puts her and everybody else in good mood. Again in the same novel, there is a comic episode when the would-be-rapist Oscar is badly beaten by Dessa and Rufel when he tries to force himself on Rufel. In *Beloved*, Garner points out that Baby Suggs is a fine cook and a good cobbler. To prove his point, he shows his belly and the sample on his feet.

These meditations on slavery with their graphic description of horrifying physical and mental torture of their slave subjects and their signifying differences from the classic slave narrative manifest the many faces of the monster of slavery. These new versions of accounts of slavery help us in understanding the psychology of the oppressed and the truth about slavery. To sum up in the words of the protagonist Dessa Rose in the novel of that title, the study of these works of "rememory" helps in knowing about the reality of slavery and in "seeing ourselfs as we had been and seeing the thing that had made us."

Further Reading

Beaulieu, Elizabeth Anne. *Black Women Writers and the American Neo-Slave Narrative: Femininity Unfettered*. Westport, CT: Greenwood Press, 1999.

McDowell, Deborah E., and Arnold Rampersad, eds. *Slavery and the Literary Imagination*. Baltimore: The Johns Hopkins UP, 1989.

Rushdy, Ashraf H. A. *Neo-Slave Narratives: A Study in the Logic of a Literary Form*. New York: Oxford UP, 1999.

Harish Chander

NEUGEBOREN, JAY (1938–) Jewish American novelist and memoirist. In his autobiographical and fictional work, Jay Neugeboren has unflinchingly explored the aftermath of trauma, seeing in it a lens for exploring the contemporary American Jew as well as for grappling with his complicated relationship with his schizophrenic brother, Robert. The author of seven novels, three memoirs, and numerous short stories and essays, he has enjoyed consistent critical praise and has shown a persistent interest in depicting strong working-class Jews and in exploring the broader ethnic landscape of the American city of the 1950s and 1960s.

Neugeboren's writing is often haunted by an impression of belatedness, by a sense that the important events have taken place before the start of the narrative. In *Listen Ruben Fontanez* (1968), Harry Meyers is an aging high school teacher who has remained in a once-Jewish neighborhood. Twelve years earlier he captured, almost accidentally, the African American killer of a young Italian American child. The bulk of the novel deals with the distant aftermath of that instant, and it shows Harry waiting impotently for the killer's vengeance and struggling to reach his Latino students. In Neugeboren's first novel, *Big Man* (1966), former African American basketball star Mack Davis confronts his remaining opportunities a few years after he was caught in a point-shaving scandal. The action concerns a reluctant comeback that amounts to little, again showing a story that takes place after the climax of the protagonist's life.

In a similar vein, two of Neugeboren's finest novels, *The Stolen Jew* (1981) and *Sam's Legacy* (1973), deal with books that characters in the story have already written, and each quotes at length from the "earlier" work. In *The Stolen Jew,* the frame narrative tells the story of Nathan Malkin, the author decades earlier of a novel called *The Stolen Jew* about a young man spared conscription in Tsarist Russia when his father arranges for another Jew to be drafted in his place. Nathan, troubled by his good fortune and the difficulties that have led his brother to commit suicide, embarks on a doomed and daring scheme to sell invented alternate drafts of the novel in order to raise funds for Soviet Jews. Nathan's novel and his own story explore the vagaries of good fortune, asking how one character can enjoy comfort and health while another, without understandable cause, endures privation or mental illness.

In *Sam's Legacy,* erstwhile poker hustler Sam Berman is a young Jew struggling in the same sort of New York neighborhood as Harry Meyers. Most of his peers have left for the suburbs and, after his father departs for a retirement home in California, he inherits a memoir by a forgotten star of the Negro Baseball League. Among other claims, the memoir records a homosexual relationship with Babe Ruth, who freely admits that he is himself an African American merely passing as white. How much of that story is supposed to be true and how much the imagined history of a troubled man is never clear, but the undeniable power of the story almost dwarfs his own current difficulties.

Although many of his novels present characters who are nearly overwhelmed, his narrators typically offer muscular prose styles and challenge the idea of the Jew as merely a victim. The underrated *Before My Life Began*

(1985) recounts the story of David Voloshin, a young basketball star drawn into working with the last group of Jewish gangsters in Brooklyn. Although David has to flee and reinvent himself as Aaron Levin, he proves a strong and dynamic figure even in his new life.

Neugeboren has focused increasingly on memoirs since the early 1990s. *Imagining Robert* (1997) tells the painful story of his brother's mental illness, a topic he had touched on earlier through fiction in *Corky's Brother* (1989) and *The Stolen Jew*. In *Open Heart* (2003), he recounts how he discovered and then overcame his own heart disease through the help of several old friends. Such works show him turning the same critical eye to his own past that he uses on his narrators' pasts in his fiction. He remains a writer haunted by experience, unable to let go of the difficulties that have shaped him individually and as a Jew and bravely measuring his own strength and his own obligations to the people he loves.

Further Reading

Candelaria, Cordelia. "A Decade of Fiction by Jay Neugeboren." *MELUS* 5.4 (Winter 1978): 71–82.

Solomon, Eric. "Counter-Ethnicity and the Jewish-Black Baseball Novel: The Cases of Jerome Charyn and Jay Neugeboren." *Modern Fiction Studies* 33.1 (Spring 1987): 49–63.

Joe Kraus

NEW NEGRO   The term "New Negro" represents the emergence of evolving notions of a positive racial **identity** and of growing self-respect and confidence among African Americans. Historians and sociologists attribute several events to this concept. One was the return of military personnel following the end of World War I. African American soldiers returned to the United States only to find that America still was not a country where democracy was always practiced. Another event was the Great Migration where hundreds of thousands of African Americans moved from the rural South to urban Northern and midwestern cities seeking employment, a new start, and full citizenship. In addition, the formation of such organizations as the National Association for the Advancement of Colored People (NAACP), the National Urban League, and the Association for the Study of Negro Life and History helped solidify the idea that the "old Negro" no longer existed and that the "New Negro" had emerged. African Americans were casting off old ways of thinking, shedding feelings of inferiority and self-pity, seeking rights, and developing hopes and aspirations.

The term New Negro was in use as early as the latter part of the nineteenth century, appearing in newspaper editorials and books. However, the term came into prominence during the **Harlem Renaissance** following the publication of the anthology titled *The New Negro* (1925), edited by **Alain Locke**. Locke's opening essay is titled "The New Negro" and is considered the definitive explanation of this concept. This anthology is a special edition on

Harlem produced by the magazine *Survey Graphic*. The Harlem Renaissance defined a new age in African American cultural history with its artistic emergence and the outpouring of literature, art, and music. Along with novelists, poets, essayists, dramatists, artists, and musicians, the period also saw increased activity among political leaders and business leaders. Harlem, providing excitement and opportunity, was the center of activity and attracted African Americans from all areas of the United States; it was considered the cultural capital of black America.

The dates of the Harlem Renaissance are debatable. Some scholars set the beginning in 1910 and some set it in 1923. Some see it ending with the publication of **Zora Neale Hurston**'s *Their Eyes Were Watching God* (1937) or with the publication of **Richard Wright**'s *Native Son* (1940). Some regard the peak years as the decade of the 1920s or the period from 1923 to 1929.

The New Negro represented a positive racial identity; the African past was to be recognized and acknowledged. The New Negro possessed and exhibited a mood of confidence, energy, vitality, spontaneity, joy, energy, racial pride, and a new outlook.

Further Reading

Barksdale, Richard, and Keneth Kinnamon. *Black Writers of America: A Comprehensive Anthology.* New York: Macmillan, 1972. 467–79.

Gwendolyn S. Jones

NEWMAN, LESLÉA (1955–)   Jewish American writer of prose fiction, humor, children's books, and poetry. A prolific writer in many genres, Lesléa Newman is best known for her groundbreaking children's book *Heather Has Two Mommies* (1990), her novel *In Every Laugh a Tear* (1992), her poetic memorial to the victims of AIDS titled *Still Life With Buddy* (1997), and her numerous short story collections, including the recent *Best Short Stories of Lesléa Newman* (2004). Her work over the past two decades chronicles the tensions and the continuities between queer and Jewish cultural history.

In *Heather Has Two Mommies*, Newman presents one of her major themes—that nurturing love rather than legal status or blood relations defines a family. In her afterword to the tenth anniversary edition of *Heather*, Newman writes that her understanding that children being raised by gay and lesbian parents need to see their families positively depicted was partially a product of her own childhood memories: she did not see her Jewish family and traditions represented and thus felt the subtle but pernicious effects of cultural invisibility.

Rendering Jewish and queer lives visible in all their diversity is a significant aspect of Newman's literary project. Shayna Steinblatt, the protagonist of *In Every Laugh a Tear*, is a femme lesbian devoted to her aging grandmother, Tzeydl—and beginning a serious relationship with Luz, a butch Puerto Rican. Shayna has a tense relationship with her mother, Sylvia, who strives to deny her daughter's love life; this relationship becomes even more strained when Sylvia forces Tzeydl into a nursing home. As Shayna becomes her grandmother's advocate, she must acknowledge her grandmother's frailty and the imminence of her death. However, until the end, the relationship between grandmother and granddaughter is richly and lovingly depicted. When Shayna comes out to her grandmother, Tzeydl initially resists acknowledging Luz as Shayna's life partner. However, her unconditional love for Shayna and her recognition of Luz's good heart enable her to embrace Luz as a member of the family, and she even encourages Luz and Shayna to adopt a child. Ultimately, Shayna's feminist, woman-identified life is seen as continuous with, rather than a refutation of Tzeydl's.

"A Letter to Harvey Milk," one of Newman's most frequently anthologized works, is also a narrative of shared wisdom across generations. Barbara, a Jewish lesbian whose parents have rejected her, tries to reintegrate herself into the Jewish community by collecting life narratives from immigrants. Harry Weinberg, one of her writing students, provides her with memories of Harvey Milk, the first openly gay official in U.S. history and then relates a story that begins in the camps and ends in his own marriage bed; here, an old Jewish man becomes an ally by expressing fatherly pride in Barbara and by seamlessly interweaving gay and Jewish history.

Newman identifies her native language as Yinglish, a form of English that makes generous use of Yiddish phrases and syntax, and most of her works contain a Hebrew-Yiddish glossary for the benefit of non-Yinglish speakers. Indeed, Newman credits **Grace Paley** for teaching her that Yinglish might have literary qualities of its own rather than merely being a bastardization of the Queen's English. Yiddish is known as the *mamaloshen*, the mother tongue, and it seems no coincidence that the Anglicized remnants of this feminine language become a vehicle for constructing Jewish lesbian **identity** in the pages of Newman's work.

Newman received a grant from the National Endowment for the Arts for *Still Life With Buddy: A Novel Told in Fifty Poems*. In that work as well as in "Whatever Happened to Baby Fane," Newman chronicles the life and death of a man in the last stages of AIDS. Throughout her substantial body of work, Newman focuses her writerly eye on the ravages of an epidemic that was neglected until it was too late for too many, the genocidal legacy of the **Holocaust**, and the **anti-Semitism** of supposedly progressive lesbian-feminist communities. However, alongside such depictions of death, despair, and oppression, Newman inscribes narratives of resistance and of joyous lesbian love. Indeed, her capacious and generous vision of the world is one of her distinctive writerly attributes. (*See also* Bilingualism)

Further Reading

Meyers, Helene. "The Lesbian and the Mishpachah: Newman's *In Every Laugh a Tear.*" *Studies in American Jewish Literature* 22 (2003): 46–51.

Helene Meyers

NG, FAE MYENNE (1956–)   Chinese American novelist and short fiction writer. Born in San Francisco, of Chinese parents, Fae Myenne Ng holds an important place in Asian American literature because of the complex narrative structure and the characters' resistance to a stabilized ethnic **identity** in her novel *Bone* (1993). Ng's intriguing book tells the stories of a Chinese American family of first-generation parents and American-born daughters. Her short stories have been published in magazines and have been anthologized.

A national best seller, *Bone* reveals the hidden aspects and family secrets in the lives of Chinese immigrants in San Francisco's Chinatown through the first-person narrative of the eldest daughter, Leila. The book's title, *Bone*, refers to the tradition of Chinese Americans, who send the bones of the deceased relatives back to China so that their spirits can return to their homeland. *Bone* illuminates the complexities of Leila's relations with her mother, Mah, stepfather, Leon, her half-sisters, Ona and Nina, and her husband, Mason Louie. All Ng's main characters are memorably individualized and undergo a process of development throughout the narrative. *Bone* questions American society's tendency to assume a consistent heritage and history for its ethnic members through revealing the multitudinous identity negotiations within Chinese Americans.

The rupture incurred by shifting frames of place and time in Ng's novel precludes an easy reading or simple interpretation. Rather, Ng presents several complex issues without providing clear answers: the reasons for Ona's suicide, the breakup of Mah and Leon, as well as Nina's anxiety covered up by her seemingly indifference and distancing from the family. Such unresolved questions are designed as challenges for the readers. The complications of the family life are illustrated through Leila's current life and her memory to connect the past with the present and in the process to challenge the common assumptions about the immigrant experience and their ethnic identity.

Ng has a skillful way of giving voice to larger societal issues through her characters' concerns that at times become controversial. Entering America as a "paper son," Leon never recovers from his obsession with physical documents. Nevertheless, his suitcase full of papers cannot fulfill the request for proof of his legitimate identity. Through making the absent become present and the silent gain a voice, Ng's literary construction recapitulates and claims her male ancestors' position in American history. Through the genre of fiction, Ng witnesses, through Leila's eyes, the tragic impact of exclusionary laws and economic exploitation on the lives of Chinese American men and women. By addressing immigrant men's lives, *Bone* thus expands and deepens the discourse on gender identity and suggests hybridity within "Chinese America." (*See also* Chinese American Novel)

Further Reading

Kafka, Phillipa. "Fae Myenne Ng, *Bone*: 'Nina, Ona, and I, We're the Lucky Generation'." *(Un)doing the Missionary Position: Gender Asymmetry in Contemporary Asian American Women's Writing.* Westport, CT: Greenwood Press, 1997. 51–78.

Kim, Thomas W. "'For a Paper Son, Paper Is Blood': Subjectivation and
   Authenticity in Fae Myenne Ng's *Bone*." *MELUS* 24.4 (Winter 1999): 41–56.

Lan Dong

NG, MEI (1966–)   Chinese American novelist. Mei Ng's novel *Eating
Chinese Food Naked* (1998) has won her recognition as one of the younger
generation of Chinese American writers. Using food and sexuality as metaphors, Ng's book centers on protagonist Ruby Lee's pursuit for her ethnic
and gendered identity that is entangled with her relation to her family and
her partners. It is reminiscent of **Maxine Hong Kingston** and **Amy Tan**'s
works in its narrative focus on the mother-daughter relationship from an
immigrant family. Ng's fiction also shares **Gish Jen**'s witty style and sense
of humor. Yet, it distinguishes itself from previous generations of Chinese
American writers by the complexity of its female protagonist and the poignant portrayal of the bittersweet relations among the Lees.

The novel starts with the summer after twenty-two-year-old Ruby gradu-
ates from Columbia University and returns home at the Lee's Hand Laundry
in Queens, New York, to live temporarily with her first-generation immigrant parents. Through the interlaced narratives of Ruby's adulthood in the
present and her memory of childhood, readers are exposed to the secret cor-
ners of the Lee's family life. Ruby's parents, Franklin and Bell, are stuck
within the indifference and misunderstanding that have accumulated
between them over the years. The tension has never been released between
Ruby's father and her elder brother Van, who has been a long-time rock-and-
roll fan and is now a husband and a father of three. Ruby's elder sister Lily,
who lives in the apartment above the laundry, has distanced herself from the
rest of the family through locking up things in her drawer and within her
mind. Ruby reevaluates the relations among her family members from
whom she has tried hard to escape before college. As the youngest daughter,
Ruby finds it difficult to negotiate between her bossy father and her
estranged mother. Working as a temp now and then over the summer, she
has plenty of time to reconsider the process of her growing-up that has been
filled with love for her parents and uncertainty about her ethnic **identity**.

Ruby's struggle over her ethnic and gender identity is intertwined with,
and at times reflected by, her confusion and obsession with her sexuality.
As the vital metaphor, sexuality is Ruby's means to react to racist assumptions and to seek for her female subjectivity as an ethnic American woman.
Similarly, food also functions as a symbol of identity and power. Living
with her patriarchal husband for decades, Bell constantly takes control in
her reserved territory: the kitchen. Following her mother around the stoves
and cupboards as a child, Ruby holds the faith that food—the ways of
cooking, serving, and eating—integrates cultural meaning and a person's
identity. Ng ends her novel with Ruby moving into an apartment with
more understanding of her family and herself. (*See also* Chinese American
Novel)

Further Reading

Barnhart, Sarah Catlin. "Mei Ng." *Asian American Novelists: A Bio-Bibliographical Critical Sourcebook*. Ed. Emmanuel S. Nelson. Westport, CT: Greenwood Press, 2000. 267–70.

Lan Dong

NIGAM, SANJAY (1959–)   Indian American novelist and medical doctor. Sanjay Nigam's position in literature is directly related to his ability to chronicle the contemporary search for meaning, identity, and truth through colorful characters and stories. Originally born in India, his family came to America while he was an infant. Nigam began writing fiction during his medical residency and his short stories were featured in *Grand Street*, *The Kenyon Review,* and *Story*. His collection of shorter work, *The Non-Resident Indian and Other Stories,* was published in 1996. Also a physician, Nigam was named by *Utne Reader* as one of ten writers who represent the changing face of fiction.

His first novel, *The Snake Charmer* (1998), centers on Sonalal, a Delhi man who is "the best charmer in all India." Early in the novel he and his beloved cobra, Raju, reach a pinnacle in their performance, a moment of improvised perfection in an ancient art. When he hits a wrong note, Raju bites him; enraged, Sonalal bites the snake in two. Though he destroys his livelihood, the charmer receives temporary fame and wealth as a result. Sonalal then begins a circular journey to reconcile the truth that he cannot put his snake back together with his own efforts to do so. The image of a "snake biting its own tail" becomes a central metaphor as Sonalal seeks redemption in reclaiming the things he seemingly destroyed—sublime art, love, and even the meaning of life. The journey gives the reader a satirical glance of modern Delhi as a place of clashing cultures and changing caste identity.

Nigam's latest novel is *Transplanted Man* (2002). The protagonist, troubled insomniac Dr. Sunit "Sonny" Seth, rescues a patient from the brink of death after a kidney transplant only to learn the man later dies from heart failure. This serves as the catalyst for another journey of discovery as the book examines the connections between comically flawed characters, and ultimately, the juxtaposition of East and West, expatriation and repatriation, meaning and existence.

As a physician, researcher, and professor, Sanjay Nigam has also published widely in medical journals. He currently practices and teaches at the University of California—San Diego Cancer Center. (*See also* South Asian American Literature)

Further Reading

Chadwell, Faye A. Review of *Transplanted Man*. *Library Journal* 127 (August 1, 2002): 215.

Dwyer, Janet Igraham. Review of *The Snake Charmer*. *Library Journal* 123 (April 15, 1998): 114.

Lowenthal, Michael. Review of *The Snake Charmer. New York Times Book Review* 103 (August 9, 1998): 19.

Zaleski, Jeff. Review of *Transplanted Man. Publishers Weekly* 249 (July 8, 2002): 29.

David R. Deborde

NIGGLI, JOSEPHINA MARIA (1910–1983) Mexican American playwright, fiction writer, and poet. Although born of Scandinavian American parents, Niggli spent her formative years in northern Mexico, which heavily influenced her work that focused on the tropes of bicultural and bilingual existence.

In 1910, Niggli was born in Monterrey, Nuevo Leon, Mexico, while her father was managing a cement plant. These formative years, although short, influenced Niggli's life and writing career. In 1913, Niggli was sent to live in Texas in order to escape the violence of the Mexican Revolution. In 1925, Niggli entered Incarnate Word College, where her English teacher encouraged her to write. She won prizes in the *Ladies Home Journal* and in the National Catholic Poetry Contest. Her father helped to further her writing career by paying for the printing of her first collection of poetry, *Mexican Silhouettes* (1928).

In 1931, Niggli completed her degree in philosophy and history. Niggli remained in San Antonio where she began working with San Antonio Little Theatre (SALT) in order to refine her writing skills. Niggli decided to make this endeavor more formal and moved to North Carolina in the summer of 1935 to enroll in a playwright graduate program called the Carolina Playmakers. Niggli honed her playwriting skills, writing *The Fair God, The Cry of Dolores, Azteca,* and *Soldadera,* all of which are considered historical plays about Mexico. She completed her MA in 1936 with the play *Singing Valley.*

In 1945, Niggli wrote the novel for which she is best known, *Mexican Village.* Made up of ten intertwined short stories, the pieces focus on the people living in one small village in Mexico. Although some critics have charged Niggli with using stereotypes for some of the characters, other critics credit her for the diversity found within them. Although some of the men could be categorized as macho and womanizers, others are more introspective and respectful of women. Most importantly, Niggli's collection forecasts one of the major themes found in more contemporary Chicana/o literature, the importance of living biculturally. One of the main characters in *Mexican Village,* Robert Warren, must grapple with a mixed Anglo and Mexican heritage to ultimately decide to identify as a Mexican by changing his name to Roberto Ortega. In addition, her innovative use of language (use of direct translation from Spanish to English) continues to be seen today in the work of **Sandra Cisneros,** Estela Portillo Trambley, and others.

Niggli continued writing, publishing a play, *The Ring of General Macías,* and two novels, *Step Down, Elder Brother* (1947) and *A Miracle of Mexico* (1964). The majority of Niggli's work incorporated Mexican folklore and traditions to help forward her stories and show the humanity of her characters. She died in 1983 and is buried in San Antonio, Texas.

Further Reading

Herrera-Sobek, María. "Josephina Niggli: A Border Writer and Precursor of Chicano/a Literature." *Mexican Village.* Josephina Niggli. Albuquerque: U of New Mexico P, 1994. xvii–xxxi.

Paredes, Raymund. "The Evolution of Chicano Literature." *MELUS* 5.2 (Summer 1978): 71–110.

Nancy K. Cardona

NIÑO, RAÚL (1961–)   Mexican American writer and poet. Niño's major accomplishment, *Breathing Light* (1991), is a compendium of poems imbued with love remembrances, a changing **identity,** and the vicissitudes of an immigrant. Born in Monterrey, Mexico, Niño immigrated to America with his mother at the age of ten. The family lived in Texas and later settled in Chicago. While at Loyola University, Niño became a member of the self-appointed *Generacion Mojada* (Wetback Generation), a group of Latino intellectuals that included, among others, **Sandra Cisneros** and **Luis Rodriguez**. Niño's poetry celebrates the memory of his past left behind in Mexico, the language he forgot and the new culture in which in he grew up. His lyrics reflect a personal search, a quest to find an identity. His poetry is more cultural than political; he misses in the north what he left behind in the south.

"Monterrey Sketches," for example, is a metaphysical journey back to his place of origin. He has ambivalent feelings toward a strange yet familiar place. There is rage and happiness; there is regret and hope; there is drifting apart and belonging. There are allusions to a father's rejection, a mother's shame and a young, growing rage. In "February on Eighteenth Street," the setting of his angst is poles apart. His lyrics long for a warm, familiar place like Monterrey; this yearning is set, ironically, in the middle of a cold street in a Chicago winter. The poem is infused with memories, but also with regrets. The map of Mexico in the store window of a Slavic neighborhood reflects the deep ambivalence of a mystified self. In "Hijo de la Malinche," he asserts his identity as an American, not just as an American of Hispanic origin. The poetic voice stresses the epistemology of America as a land of immigrants and points to the unacknowledged Hispanic contribution to America's grandeur.

Not everything in Niño's poetry is ambivalent about identity and **immigration**. His lyrics deal with lost loves and celebration of life. "Phantom Fraulein," for instance, is a erotic recollection of happiness, excitement and abandonment to pleasure. He writes of those risky, never-ending nights with a phantom woman, which result in complete exhaustion. The poem is an homage to past experiences that persist in the infinite quarters of memory. In "Sleep Hermosa," the confessionalist nature of Niño's poetry and the celebration of pleasure appear again. This pleasure, however, is waning. The lyrics point to resting bodies pinned down by lasting climaxes. Love, passion, and excitement, as any human sentiment, are withering away.

Further Reading

Cumpian, Carlos. *Emergency Tacos: Siete Poetas en Picante.* Chicago: March/Abrazo Press, 1989.

Jorge J. Barrueto

NISHIKAWA, LANE (1956–) Japanese American playwright, producer, director, actor, and theater educator. Lane Nishikawa was born Sansei (third generation Japanese American) in Wahaiwa, Hawai'i, raised in San Diego, and attended San Francisco State University. He is known for his one-man shows, and he received a Solo Performance Fellowship from the National Endowment for Arts and a National Japanese American Citizens League Ruby Yoshino Schaar Playwright award. He has taught at San Francisco State University, the University of California at Santa Barbara, California State University at Monterey Bay, Stanford University, and the Asian American Theater Company (AATC, founded in 1973), where he served as a director from 1986 to 1994.

Nishikawa's career as a theater artist started when he met a university counselor, who introduced Nishikawa to her sons, Marc and Eric Hayashi, and to the Asian American theater movement in San Francisco. Marc and Eric were active in the Asian American Theater Workshop (later became AATC) lead by Chinese American playwright Frank Chin, who trained Asian American performers and created plays in which Asian American performers could play substantial and dignified roles. Nishikawa formed a lifelong friendship with Marc (actor-director) and Eric Hayashi (lighting designer), and the trio collaborated on many plays. Nishikawa's first notable role as an actor was in Amy Sanbo and Lonny Kaneko's *Lady Is Dying* (1977) directed by Frank Chin. Since then, he has performed in Steve Okazaki's *Tokyo Time* (1987), Wayne Wang's *Eat a Bowl of Tea* (1989), Okazaki's *American Sons* (1998), and other plays.

Not being able to find a meaningful role in a play early in his career as an actor, Nishikawa started to write his own one-man play about an audition-interview, *Life in the Fast Lane* (1980). In 1981 he directed and performed *Life in the Fast Lane* as part of AATC's New Playwrights Series. He wrote a sequel to this play, another one-man show, titled *I'm on a Mission From Buddha* (1989). Along with *Mifune and Me* (1994), *Life in the Fast Lane* and *I'm on a Mission From Buddha* make Nishikawa's trilogy of solo shows. In these plays, Nishikawa problematizes Asian stereotypes, celebrates Asian American **identity**, and sets straight the historical records, particularly of Japanese internment camps during World War II.

The best-known work by Lane Nishikawa is perhaps *The Gates of Heaven* (1994), a play he coauthored with Victor Talmadge. Nishikawa met Talmadge in 1993 when both were performing in the American Conservatory

Theatre's *The Duchess of Malfi. The Gates of Heaven* was inspired by experiences of the authors' fathers and deals with a soldier in the all-Nisei (second generation Japanese American) 442nd Regimental Combat Team and a Jewish prisoner in World War II. Unlike his other plays, which were staged but not published, this play is anthologized in *Asian American Drama: 9 Plays from the Multiethnic Landscape* (1991).

Further Reading

Janes-Brown, Paul. "A Mirror for Maui: Don't We Ever Learn From History?" *American Theatre* 19.9 (November 2002): 9.

Kaplan, Randy Barbara. "Lane Nishikawa (1956–)." *Asian American Playwrights: A Bio-Bibliographical Critical Sourcebook.* Ed. Miles Xian Liu. Westport, CT: Greenwood Press, 2002. 251–62.

Kyoko Amano

NISSENSON, HUGH (1933–) Jewish American novelist, short story writer, and journalist. In his economical and beautifully wrought stories, novels, and reportage, Nissenson grapples with problems of belief in God after the **Holocaust**, the spiritual and ethical complexities and tension inherent in the fact of modern Israel, and the possibility for redemption in a violent, fractured world.

Nissenson's first collection of short stories, *A Pile of Stones* (1965), announced him as a Jewish American writer of unusual breadth. Unlike most Jewish American writers, who had concentrated their fiction almost exclusively on Jewish life in America, Nissenson's book ranges across a wide spectrum of modern Jewish existence. Divided into three sections—"Then: Poland," "Now: Israel," and "Then and Now: America"—the stories revolve around the central Jewish concepts of free will and belief in an inscrutable God. The first story, "The Groom on Zlota Street," set in Warsaw during the first decade of the twentieth century, is exemplary. In spare, evocative prose Nissenson tells the story of Yecheil, an Orthodox Polish Jew who sells whips. In the story's climactic scene Yecheil reveals that the titular groom has offered to purchase one whip each time Yechiel allows the groom to pull his beard—a common form of anti-Semitic abuse. Yechiel's pointed refusal—and subsequent beating at the hands of the groom—illustrates that it is possible, even and especially in the face of adversity—to choose dignity over abasement and puts one's faith in a providing God.

The role of God in a world filled with apparently meaningless suffering saturates the entirety of Nissenson's oeuvre, including his next two books: *Notes from the Frontier* (1968)—extended reportage on Israel—and *In the Reign of Peace* (1972), a second collection of short stories. Based on two years spent living in Israel, *Notes from the Frontier* is an unblinking portrait of the new Jewish state struggling to define its moral ground. In his unsentimental prose Nissenson offers first hand accounts of gory, corpse-strewn battlefields in the aftermath of the Six Day War and of regular Israelis coping with the demands of warfare and nation building. The abundance of bloated corpses, war-ravaged landscapes, and socialist, secular sermons preached by kibbutz members raises a question central to Nissenson's writing: Is humane civilization possible without God?

The answer, both in *Notes from the Frontier* and *In the Reign of Peace*, appears to be an unqualified "no." The title story from Nissenson's second short story collection is arguably the most telling example. Set on a kibbutz, the story involves a discussion between the narrator, a secular kibbutz member, and Chaim, a religious Jew who works on the kibbutz as a hired hand. Chaim is perplexed by fact kibbutz members' abandonment of Judaism for socialist ideology. To demonstrate the inadequacy of such misplaced faith, Chaim points out a mouse trapped in a hole in the ground being eaten alive by ants. To the narrator's protest that such suffering is, however unfortunate, simply unavoidable, Chaim responds, "But not in the reign of peace. . . . When the Messiah comes."

The reader is, of course, free to be swayed or not by Chaim's argument, but Nissenson seems to have concluded that a world without God is a world bound to suffer in seemingly inexplicable and unavoidable ways. Yet according to Jewish tradition, the Messiah may be hastened either by a world unified in belief of by a world become completely debased and immoral. It is this second, more frightening scenario that forms the basis of Nissenson's first novel, *My Own Ground* (1976). Set in New York during the years of Jewish **immigration** and revolving around the sexual enslavement of a rabbi's daughter by an evil Jewish pimp, the novel is mired in debased behavior including whoredom, suicide, and murder. By far the darkest of Nissenson's work, the novel leaves little hope for redemption of any kind. As critic Alvin Rosenfeld notes, "*My Own Ground* is meant to disabuse us once and for all of both the normative secular and religious options for a better future" (56).

Although Nissenson published another novel, *The Tree of Life* (1985), *My Own Ground* marks his last work to date on Jewish themes. Although Nissenson has received relatively little critical attention, his steadfast engagement not only with Jewish themes but with the central concepts of Jewish belief secures his place as a Jewish American writer of central importance.

Further Reading

Berkove, Lawrence, "American *Midrashim:* Hugh Nissenson's Stories." *Critique* 20 (1978): 75–82.

Rosenfeld, Alvin. "Israel and the Idea of Redemption in the Fiction of Hugh Nissenson." *Midstream* 26 (April 1980): 54–56.

Jeremy Shere

NO-NO BOY   **John Okada**'s first and only novel, *No-No Boy* (1957), is a book about the plight of Japanese Americans in the immediate aftermath of World War II. The title of this book derives from the history of the **internment** of Japanese Americans during World War II. On February 19, 1942, President Franklin D. Roosevelt issued Executive Order 9066 under which about 12,000 Japanese and Japanese Americans were "relocated" throughout the Pacific Coast region to desolate internment camps. In 1943, the War Department decided to recruit internees and they were administered a Selective Service questionnaire. As a security-clearance measure, internees were asked about their willingness to serve in the American forces and were compelled to forswear allegiance to Japan. The protagonist, Ichiro Yamata is among those who answered "no" to both questions and, like other "no-no boys," was jailed for disloyalty.

The novel begins with the protagonist, Ichiro being released and returning to his now disinterred family in their home in Seattle. As a "no-no" boy, Ichiro feels the weight of his uneasy position as a Japanese American in postwar America. His veteran peers treat him with great disdain and he feels both guilty and hostile toward his parents. Over the course of the novel, each character Ichiro meets provides different ideas of how Japanese Americans can fit in America. His mother, a native of Japan, is proud of his son's refusal to be drafted and will not accept Japan's loss. She is blind to the fact that her son, having grown up in America, is necessarily American. Ichiro's younger brother Taro, thinking that his "no-no" boy brother has tarnished the reputation of his family and community, is so desperate to prove his American **identity** that he completely rejects his Japanese heritage and joins the U.S. military. Emi, a mother figure and lover to Ichiro suggests to him that he learn to forgive America. Kenji, who is an amputee veteran, dreams of a world in which every American citizen can become simply "American" irrespective of his or her race. *No-No Boy* ends with Ichiro still struggling with the question of what it really means to be American to come to terms with his identity as a Japanese American.

In the vignette of devastating effects of the internment, Okada depicts an era when the ideal of American abstract citizenship is called into question. Ichiro's predicament provides a number of pertinent topics for recent studies on **immigration**, citizenship, and parallels between domestic policies against Asian immigrants and the U.S. foreign policies beyond its national borders. (*See also* Japanese American Novel)

Further Reading

Chu, Patricia P. *Assimilating Asians: Gendered Strategies of Authorship in Asian America.* Durham, NC: Duke UP, 2000.

Kim, Elaine H. *Asian American Literature: An Introduction to the Writings and Their Social Context.* Philadelphia: Temple UP, 1982.

MacDonald, Dorothy Ritsuko. "After Imprisonment: Ichiro's Search for Redemption in *No-No Boy.*" *MELUS* 6.3 (Autumn 1979): 19–26.

Yogi, Stan. "You Had to Be One or the Other: Oppositions and Reconciliation in John Okada's *No-No Boy.*" *MELUS* 21.2 (Summer 1996): 63–77.

Seongho Yoon

NORSTOG, JON (1877–1942) Norwegian American writer. Norstog immigrated to the United States in 1902, when he was twenty-five and had published (with little success) a volume of poetry in Norway. After a brief period in Iowa and Minneapolis, he moved to North Dakota, where he homesteaded. He had little interest in farming, however, and spent his time writing books that he printed on a small press and bound himself—all in a primitive cabin on his land—and then tried to sell. He may have been the most ambitious of Norwegian American writers—and had the fewest readers. Most of his work may be divided into three categories: voluminous verse dramas about biblical characters, novels on immigrant and religious themes, and lyric and narrative verse. The first category includes the 324-page *Kain* (Cain, 1912), *Moses* (1914), *Josva* (1916), and many more. Cain is a guilt-ridden hero of epic proportions, who loves the God who has cursed him. He becomes a powerful prophet yet, when he has a vision of the crucifixion of Christ just before he dies, he also realizes that God's design of redemption does not include him and that he is forever damned.

Norstog's early novels, such as *Ørnerud* (1907), express an idealistic view of **immigration** as a potential renewal of Norwegian values. He is far more pessimistic in his complex, even chaotic, late trilogy, *Exodus* (1928, 1930, 1931), which gives a bleak picture of the consequences of acculturation and the predicament of the immigrant artist through its protagonist, the sculptor Sigbjørn, who shares many character traits with the author himself. The narrative moves between a cabin in Wisconsin and a settlement in North Dakota, an unlikely place for the studio of a sculptor of large-scale allegorical images. At the thematic center of the first two volumes is the nature and process of Americanization and the question of how the Norwegian and the American traditions may be united, a union symbolically expressed in the troubled marriage between the sculptor and his Anglo American wife, Ruth, and the death of their young daughter. In the third volume, Sigbjørn is consumed both by guilt and hatred for his wife, who he believes is plotting to weaken him as an artist. After the completion of his major work, a sculpture showing the Temptation of Christ, he seeks death, praying for the salvation of mankind and for judgment rather than forgiveness for himself. His last work of fiction, *Når elvane møtest* (When the rivers meet) in 1934, is different from his other work in that none of the characters is an immigrant. The hero, the Reverend Samuel Huntington, combines a social conscience with religious fervor in a campaign that begins locally, in an American city, and grows to an international movement for peace and social justice. Norstog's only work to achieve some popularity is a narrative sequence of lyrics, *Tone* (1913). (*See also* Norwegian American Literature)

Further Reading

Øverland, Orm. *The Western Home: A Literary History of Norwegian America.*
   Northfield, MN: The Norwegian-American Historical Association, and
   Champaign: U of Illinois P, 1996. 293–309.

Orm Øverland

NORWEGIAN AMERICAN LITERATURE   An American literature in the Norwegian language began in the 1850s with the first Norwegian immigrant newspapers and printing presses. By 1930, with a decline in immigration, the economic depression, and the rapid assimilation of the second and third generations, the publication of books dwindled. Novels, short stories, and poems nevertheless continued to appear in a declining number of newspapers and journals for a few decades after World War II.

The potential audience for literature in the Norwegian language was modest. Compared to the German-speaking immigrants in the nineteenth century and Spanish-speaking immigrants in the twentieth, Norwegian immigrants and their descendants are a small population group. The census for 1850 has 12,678 Norwegian-born individuals; for 1880 the number is 181,729. The 1890 census reflects a significant growth in **immigration**: 322,665 Norwegian-born Americans, a number that remained stable in the following three decades. The children of immigrants were also part of the immigrant community, and in 1890 the combined number of the first and second generation was 606,316. They numbered more than a million by 1920. Their geographical concentration, however, may explain how so small a population could support a substantial literature: Although the Norwegian-born were only 3.49 percent of the total population in 1890, they were 7 percent of the population of the midwestern states. Norwegian American literature was primarily produced in the upper Midwest.

By the time Norwegians began to arrive in the 1830s and 1840s virtually all were literate, and writing was the only means of communication between those who left and those who stayed at home. The many immigrant letters give a collective narrative of the experience of settlement in a new land and are the earliest instances of American writing in the Norwegian language. They established central themes in Norwegian American literature: breaking up from the old home, the journey, the difficulties of settlement, the cultural and religious conflicts created by migration, the organization of new family lives and immigrant societies, acculturation, and the troubled relations between generations created by migration.

The first immigrant publications were newspapers that had two important functions: to maintain ties with the old country and to introduce immigrants to their new country. A metaphor used for both functions was the bridge, in one instance a bridge of memory to the Old World, in the other a bridge into a new and strange society. The newspapers included popular fiction, some pirated from Norwegian sources, some translated from English, and soon subscribers, mainly immigrants with limited formal education, began to submit their own prose and verse for publication. The newspapers had printing presses, and the publishers of newspapers soon also became publishers of journals and books by immigrants with literary ambitions. Thus there was a close correspondence between newspapers and literary publishing in this as in other immigrant communities.

Religious literature and practical handbooks were dominant early genres, but there was an increasing amount of fiction and poetry. By the 1880s Norwegian American literary institutions were established in the Midwest: Books of all kinds were published, distributed, and reviewed; journals and newspapers brought poetry, fiction, essays, and reviews into a large number of immigrant homes; and reading societies, libraries, and a variety of local and regional associations with some degree of cultural ambition had important educational functions. By the second and third decades of the twentieth century, the literary production in Norwegian was not only large and diverse but a number of authors of considerable quality and ambition were publishing regularly.

Most Norwegian immigrants were Lutheran, and religion was an important motivating factor for writing and publishing. Theologians were of course active in this field, but also many lay people wrote books of devotion. Religious autobiographies were a popular genre, as was religious verse.

Drama, on the other hand, was an underrepresented literary genre, even though theater was a popular entertainment in most immigrant groups at the turn of the nineteenth century. The reason why relatively few plays were published may be that they were written for amateur productions and not thought of as literary texts for reading. In Chicago in the 1860s a remarkable immigrant, Marcus Thrane (1817–90), wrote plays for his own theater company. He had been the organizer of the first labor organization in Norway in the 1840s, and in the wake of the general reaction in Europe after the revolutions of 1848 he had been sentenced to prison. Thrane had a wide experience and was schooled in political thought as well as in literature and music, but his plays were intended for the entertainment of an uneducated audience.

By the 1890s Norwegian American literature was sufficiently varied and diverse to be a good business for several thriving publishing houses—in Chicago and Minneapolis as well as in smaller towns all over the Midwest. Many books, however, were published privately. Popular writers ranged from the pious Ulrikka Bruun (1854–1940) to the scandalous Lars A. Stenholt (1850–1911), the first with amateurish verse and didactic novels, the latter with a large number of popular novels, many based on newspaper accounts of contemporary events such as ghastly murders and violent strikes. Two who deserve special mention are Knut M. O. Teigen (1854–1914) and Peer O. Strømme (1856–1921). Teigen, who had a degree in medicine, satirized the foibles of his immigrant culture in short fiction and verse while Strømme, who had a degree in theology and for a while was a Lutheran pastor, achieved popularity with his novel *Hvorledes Halvor blev Prest* (1893; translated as *How Halvor Became a Minister*, 1960), his humorous journalism, and his heartwarming verse. Both were born in the early Norwegian settlement of Koshkonong in Wisconsin, demonstrating that Norwegian could be the preferred language of native-born Americans.

Most writers had an idealistic motivation such as religious dedication, radical politics, a sentimental and idealized notion of what it meant to be Norwegian, a vision of the value of language and culture maintenance, or a sense of the need for a spiritual or cultural awakening of their ethnic group. Indeed, one feature shared by writers, journalists, and other leaders of European immigrant groups was their insistence that not only should immigrants maintain their language and their culture, but that their national traditions made them the best Americans. One writer who was inspired by such ethnic idealism was the prolific **Simon Johnson** (1874–1970), whose fiction is marred by sentimental idealism and a belief in the excellence of all things Norwegian.

Most immigrants came from the uneducated classes in Europe. A remarkable exception is **Kristofer Janson** (1841–1917), who was a highly regarded author and educator before emigration. In Minneapolis in the 1880s and 1890s he was a Unitarian minister and contributed to local newspapers, published books with local publishers, and edited his own journal. The women's movement in the United States had a radicalizing impact on both Kristofer Janson and his wife, **Drude Janson** (1846–1934), and her first novel, *En saloonkeepers datter* (1889; translated as *A Saloonkeeper's Daughter,* 2002), is a remarkable contribution to late nineteenth-century women's literature.

The self-taught Hans A. Foss's (1851–1929) first novel, *Husmands-gutten* (1885; translated as *The Cotter's Son,* 1963), tells the oft-told story of the poor cotter's son, born on the same day and baptized in the same water as the wealthy farmer's daughter. They grow up loving each other but are kept apart by class barriers. Although he is diligent and honest the hero is doomed to remain poor and despised in Norway. But, happily, he is cheated and fooled by the cruel and wealthy farmer and emigrates to the United States, where, with perseverance and hard work, he is able to prove himself. As might be expected in popular fiction, he returns as a wealthy man on the day the bankrupt farmer's property is auctioned. He buys the farm and marries his beloved, who has faithfully waited. No wonder the novel was immensely popular. Foss's later novels show his increasing concern with American society and politics. *Hvide slaver* (1892; White Slaves) promotes the views of radical Populism and is influenced by the utopian fiction of the late nineteenth century such as Ignatius Donnelly's *Cæsar's Column* (1891) and Edward Bellamy's *Looking Backward* (1888). **Ole A. Buslett** (1855–1924) was a more ambitious writer. A romantic idealism characterizes his early efforts, but he, too, became increasingly concerned with contemporary social and political issues. Among his most interesting books are the utopian fantasy novel, *Glans-om-Sol* (1912; Splendor-of-Sun), his autobiographical novel, *Fra min ungdoms nabolag* (1918; From the neighborhood of my youth), and an allegorical vision of a multicultural America, *Veien til Golden Gate* (1915; translated as *The Road to the Golden Gate,* 2000).

The wide range of Norwegian American literature may be suggested through brief mention of two poets: Julius Baumann (1870–1923) and

Agnes Wergeland (1857–1914). Baumann wrote poems and stories as he worked on farms, lumber camps, and sawmills on coming to the Midwest and was encouraged by the reception of his first contributions to newspapers and journals. His main poetic themes are love and family, the immigrant experience, and memories of the country he had left, and he expressed them in well-crafted, conventional poems that became very popular with his immigrant audience. Wergeland was not a representative immigrant. She immigrated in 1890, after achieving a doctorate in history at the University of Zurich, to pursue an academic career that was impossible in Norway, where women were still barred from the university. After a fellowship at Bryn Mawr and temporary appointments at the University of Chicago, where she was denied tenure in spite of her substantial articles in prominent journals, she accepted an appointment as professor of history and French at the new University of Wyoming. Here she began to write articles and verse for immigrant publications in the Midwest and was encouraged to publish more poetry even though her critics found it difficult and puzzling.

The writers who may best represent the achievement of this immigrant literature are **Dorthea Dahl** (1881–1958), **Jon Norstog** (1877–1942), **Johannes B. Wist** (1864–1923), **Waldemar Ager** (1869–1941), and **Ole Edvart Rølvaag** (1876–1931). Dahl had no education in Norwegian and published in both English and Norwegian, mainly in church publications. She is at her best in her many short stories, in particular "Kopper-kjelen" (1930; translated as "The Copper Kettle," 2000). Norstog's two major themes are religion, for instance in his many biblical verse dramas, and the importance of the old-world heritage. Both come together in his ambitious trilogy, *Exodus* (1928–1931). Wist was editor of the Norwegian American newspaper with the longest life, *Decorah-Posten* (1874–1972), and his fiction was serialized here. His most successful work is an entertaining trilogy about the remarkable career of an immigrant who comes to Minneapolis in the 1880s and later becomes proprietor and political boss of a town in northwestern Minnesota (1920–22). Ager began his career as a writer of didactic temperance fiction but developed to become one of the most professional of Norwegian American writers. With his late novel, *I Sit Alone* (1931), he achieved acceptance by a major publisher in New York, a recognition denied other Norwegian American writers with the exception of Rølvaag. Rølvaag is undisputedly the greatest American novelist to write in Norwegian. Most of his work is available in translation, and his best novel, *Giants in the Earth* (1927), the first volume of a trilogy about two generations of a midwestern immigrant family, has achieved the status of a minor classic.

As Norwegian American literature gradually grew in quality and quantity, it also began to show signs of its inevitable decline. An immigrant culture is a transitional culture, a stage in a collective as well as individual **assimilation** process. Neighborhoods, institutions, and organizations gradually take on more and more of the characteristics of the dominant culture until differences eventually become largely symbolic. Immigrant culture is, however, also transitional in the sense that individuals are constantly moving through it: they may be part of it on arrival but choose to leave it for a place in the dominant culture when they feel fully assimilated. It is, moreover, transitional in the sense that although it may be a comfortable home for the first generation, it is often resisted by the second and may seem irrelevant to the third. The gradual loss of the language, which is essential to the distinctness as well as the vitality of a culture, was an essential factor in the decline of Norwegian American literature.

There were also external developments that hastened the decline of most European immigrant literatures in languages other than English. The rapid growth in immigration from the 1880s gave rise to antiimmigrant attitudes and xenophobia. With the outbreak of World War I, nativism was strengthened by a fear of the perceived disloyalty of the foreign-born. These developments resulted in an intense Americanization campaign that demanded that immigrants forget their past, including their language, cease to be "hyphenated," and become "100% Americans." The growing antiimmigration sentiment resulted in the so-called Quota Act of 1924 that, along with other economic and demographic factors, led to the end of mass immigration in the course of the 1920s. This spelled the end of most immigrant literatures in languages other than English. Because immigrant languages rarely survived beyond the second generation and immigrant cultures depended on a constant renewal of their unstable populations by new immigrants, a diminishing population who had Norwegian as their preferred language was no longer able to provide the necessary support for a Norwegian American literature.

From its early newspapers in the 1850s through its period of flowering in the 1920s this literature had the important function of giving expression to the experiences and aspirations of an immigrant group. In a 1920 promotional pamphlet for Augsburg Publishing House, the writer Nils N. Rønning expressed his perception of the complementary relationship between a majority and a minority literature: "As Americans, we feel that the literature of this country is our literature, expressing and interpreting our common American life; but as Americans of Norwegian descent, having our own peculiar characteristics, history, traditions, institutions, and problems, we need also a literature of our own." Some decades later, however, most native-born Norwegian Americans felt stronger ties to their "common American life" than to the "peculiar characteristics" of the immigrant generation. There was no longer a need for a Norwegian American literature.

Further Reading

Gulliksen, Øyvind T. *Twofold Identities: Norwegian-American Contributions to Midwestern Culture.* New York: Peter Lang Publishing, 2004.

Haugen, Einar. *The Norwegian Language in America: A Study in Bilingual Behavior.* 2 vols. Philadelphia: U of Pennsylvania P, 1953.

Øverland, Orm. "From Melting Pots to Copper Kettles: Assimilation and Norwegian-American Literature." Ed. Werner Sollors. *Multilingual America: Transnationalism, Ethnicity, and the Languages of American Literature.* New York: New York UP, 1998. 50–63.

———. *The Western Home: A Literary History of Norwegian America.* Northfield, MN: Norwegian-American Historical Association, and Champaign: U of Illinois P, 1996.

Thorson, Gerald Howard. "Pressed Flowers and Still-Running Brooks: Norwegian-American Literature." Ed. Wlodomyr T. Zyla and Wendell M. Aycock. *Ethnic Literature Since 1776: The Many Voices of America.* Lubbock: Texas Tech P, 1978. 375–94.

Orm Øverland

NOTES OF A NATIVE SON   Published in 1955 and reprinted with an added preface in 1984, *Notes of a Native Son* made **James Baldwin** one of the most revered essayists of his generation, and it continues to be celebrated as a moving testament of a black male artist's search for **identity** at a number of crossroads in his life.

The collection consists of ten essays divided into three parts. The first part examines the problem of racial representation in American popular culture. "Everybody's Protest Novel" has Baldwin revisiting his childhood fascination with Harriet Beecher Stowe's *Uncle Tom's Cabin* (1852) to condemn it on the grounds of its sentimentality and patronizing stance toward the enslaved African Americans in whose name it promotes the abolitionist cause. "Many Thousands Gone" provides an interesting corollary to this critique in its suggestion that **Richard Wright**'s *Native Son* (1940) and particularly its protagonist, **Bigger Thomas**, corroborate dehumanizing, one-dimensional images of black subjectivity borne out of white prejudice and fear. Supplemented by an occasional piece on Otto Preminger's film *Carmen Jones* (1954), these essays point out the violent limitation of aesthetic possibilities, of black self-expression as such, that results from an artist's commitment to rigid ideological positions and so-called "protest" literature.

Part 2 outlines African American political disillusionment within the context of urban blight in "The Harlem Ghetto" and "Journey to Atlanta." In the former Baldwin offers a perceptive analysis of the strained sociopolitical relations between blacks and Jews, conditioned as they are by religious and class prejudices that circumvent genuine "interracial understanding." The title essay, the only one written expressly for this volume, appears at the end of the section and presents Baldwin's meditation on the death of his father, whose bitterness about **race** relations in United States he inherits yet nevertheless wishes to overcome.

The last part combines discussion of race, color, and national identity in four essays that came out of Baldwin's travels through Western Europe. After brief observations on French colonial subjects and the American student colony in

Paris, Baldwin turns to a more explicitly autobiographical mode in "Equal in Paris" and "Stranger in a Village." The former recounts his eight-day incarceration over a stolen bed sheet from a hotel; the latter remembers a trip to a remote Swiss village where Baldwin was the first "real" black person its inhabitants had encountered. Despite the diaspora orientation of these essays, they constitute some of Baldwin's most astute diagnoses of the race "problem" in the United States. Indeed, the sense of alienation he feels and embodies in Europe dedicates him more fully to the cause of racial justice in America.

Black nationalist artists have criticized Baldwin's work for not being militant enough in its advocacy of black cultural and political self-expression. Yet the thrust of these essays is profoundly political in its promotion of the different, possibly more complex, aesthetic modes and ways of seeing that are available to African American artists in the field of cultural production. (*See also* African American Autobiography)

Further Reading

Balfour, Lawrie. *The Evidence of Things Not Said: James Baldwin and the Promise of American Democracy.* Ithaca, NY: Cornell UP, 2001.

Ford, Nick Aaron. "The Evolution of James Baldwin as Essayist." *James Baldwin: A Critical Evaluation.* Ed. Therman B. O'Daniel. Washington, DC: Howard UP, 1977. 85–104.

McBride, Dwight A., ed. *James Baldwin Now.* New York: New York UP, 1999.

Standley, Fred L., and Nancy V. Burt, eds. *Critical Essays on James Baldwin.* Boston: G. K. Hall, 1988.

Kinohi Nishikawa

NOVAK, MICHAEL (1933–)   Slovak American novelist and prolific writer on philosophical, religious, and socioeconomic topics. His activity in ethnic affairs and studies has concerned not only Slovaks but other nationalities and involved him in government and diplomatic activities at the national and international level. Since 1978 Novak has been at the American Enterprise Institute where he is currently the George Frederick Jewett Scholar in Religion, Philosophy, and Public Policy and also Director of Social and Political Studies.

Novak has published two novels. *The Tiber Was Silver* (1961) presents what it would be like for an American to study for the priesthood in Rome from winter 1956 through spring 1957. Richard McKay is an Irish American from Gary, Indiana, who is pursuing theological studies as a member of an international religious congregation. During the months of the novel, Richard grapples to understand his relationships with fellow seminarians, be true to himself with his spiritual advisor, assess his interactions with senior members of his religious congregation, and evaluate his feelings for a young Irish American woman, attracted to being a painter like Richard himself. Although McKay explores who he is in the ambience of pre-Vatican II (1962–65) Catholic society and culture, by the end of the novel he is ordained a priest. In sharp contrast is *Naked I Leave* (1970). Slovak American

Jon/Jonathan Svoboda has left a Catholic seminary and during the many months of the novel completes his doctorate in English at Columbia University, supporting himself as a journalist especially during the early months of the Catholic Church ecumenical council, Vatican II. Against the background of interactions with family, various friends, and acquaintances experiencing their own turmoil and crises unfold Jon's sexual liaisons with four women. Jon even becomes involved in some Eastern European political intrigue. Like St. Jerome, whose "nakedness" at birth and death exemplifies his strong desire to be "naked"—his essential self—before God, Jon is by the end utterly himself before God and the reader but no closer to the genuine feminine love he so craves. The novel's concluding marker—"end of the beginning"—is a dubious endpoint in Jon Svoboda's life.

The Guns of Lattimer (1978) is a mostly nonfiction narrative on the massacre of unarmed miners—mostly Slovak, Polish, Lithuanian—near Hazelton, Pennsylvania, on September 10, 1897, and the subsequent trial through March 9, 1898. In this peaceful march to Lattimer Mines with a call for a strike, nineteen miners are killed and at least thirty-nine wounded. The fifty-two verses of "Ballad of the Deputies" from the Hazelton *Daily Standard* of Sept. 17, 1897, introduce and set the tone for this catastrophe fostered by a lack of cultural understanding and poor communication between the opposing sides that anger and fear helped ignite into an historical tragedy. Novak's passionate Slovak ethnic interest and talent have effected an engaging account of a terrible happening through which the ethnic American miners finally have their voice heard. (*See also* Slovak American Literature)

Gerald J. Sabo

NUGENT, RICHARD BRUCE (1906–1987)   African American writer and artist. Nugent was the only member of the **Harlem Renaissance** who was openly gay in both his life and his artistic endeavors. Nugent was born in 1906 into a prominent Washington family, and he decided early in life that he wanted to lead a bohemian life, refusing to seek regular employment and devoting himself to artistic pursuits instead. In 1925 Nugent met **Langston Hughes** at the renowned salon given by Washington poet Georgia Douglas Johnson, and the two struck up a close friendship. When Hughes invited "Ricardo" to join him on a trip to New York, where Langston was to receive two literary prizes sponsored by *Opportunity* magazine, Nugent accepted the invitation, unaware that this trip would irrevocably alter his life.

Nugent was fascinated by the vibrant artistic atmosphere of Harlem and Greenwich Village and soon became a member of the "Niggerati," a group of young and rebellious writers, which included Hughes, **Zora Neale Hurston**, **Countee Cullen**, Aaron Douglas, and **Wallace Thurman**. Nugent eventually shared a rooming house at 267 West 136th Street, dubbed "Niggerati Manor," with Hughes and Thurman, who would publish *Infants of the Spring* (1932), a thinly veiled portrait of the Niggerati. Nugent is depicted in the satirical novel as Paul Arbian, a bohemian and painter of erotic subjects, who admires Oscar Wilde, Joris-Karl Huysmans, and Charles Baudelaire. Like his fictional alter ego, Nugent seemed more interested in attending parties than in pursuing a literary career, and his first publication took place by happenstance: when Langston Hughes found Nugent's poem "Shadows" discarded in a trash can, he forwarded it to *Opportunity*, a magazine sponsored by the National Urban League, which published it in October 1925. Countee Cullen included the poem together with Nugent's "Cavalier" in the anthology *Caroling Dusk* (1927). "Sadhji," Nugent's first published short story, appeared in **Alain Locke**'s groundbreaking anthology *The New Negro* (1925). The morality tale is set in Africa and features Mrabo, a young warrior who is in love with the chieftain's son, Mrabo. Alain Locke encouraged Nugent to transform the short story into a one-act play, which was published in Locke's *Plays of Negro Life* (1927) along with an original musical score by William Grant Still. The premiere of the play took place in 1932 at the Eastman School of Music in Rochester, New York.

Nugent's most important and controversial literary work, "Smoke, Lilies, and Jade" (1926), appeared in the first and only issue of *Fire!!*, a quarterly "devoted to younger Negro artists" and intended to question the prevailing tendency in literature to show blacks exclusively in a positive light. The story, which is considered the first work by an African American to deal explicitly with homosexuality, combines elements of fin-de-siècle literature with stream-of-consciousness techniques. Subtitled "A Novel, part I," it is clearly autobiographical and opens with Alex, a young artist, lying on his bed, smoking a cigarette, too languid to write or draw. Being an artist, he does not feel the need to earn a living. Eventually, Alex rouses himself and steps outside, cruising the dark streets. He meets a stunning, Spanish-speaking stranger whom he calls "Beauty" and who, according to Thomas W. Wirth, is modeled after Juan Jose Viana, Nugent's Panamanian lover. The two men spend the night together, and Alex realizes that he is able to love two people at the same time—his girlfriend Melva and Beauty. Alex's seeming bisexuality, however, becomes questionable at the end of the story when Alex's final thoughts concentrate on his male lover and his previous statement "one *can* love two at the same time" is reduced to "one *can* love."

Nugent was aware of the controversial nature of this work, and he published it as well as his earlier poems and "Sahdji" under the pseudonym Richard Bruce in order to spare his family any embarrassment. Partly because of the scandalous "Smoke, Lilies, and Smoke" and partly because of Nugent's reluctance to actively pursue a literary career, his subsequent published output dwindled considerably. He turned to painting and the theater and toured the United States and Europe as a nonspeaking member of Dubose Hayward's play *Porgy*. Having been interested in dance for a long time—his younger brother Pete performed on Broadway and established his own company—Nugent appeared as a dancer in *Run, Lit-*

tle Chillun on Broadway in 1933. In the 1930s he became involved with the Federal Arts Project and the Federal Theatre and was a founding member of the Harlem Artists Guild, an organization dedicated to supporting black artists.

In 1952 Nugent married Grace Marr, a nursing supervisor, who was aware of her husband's sexual orientation. Their marriage lasted for seventeen years until she committed suicide in 1969. In the 1960s Nugent helped to establish the Harlem Cultural Council, serving on its board of directors. As the last surviving member at the center of the Harlem Renaissance, Nugent proved an invaluable resource for researchers. Nugent died on May 27, 1987, of congestive heart failure. Although most early chroniclers of the Harlem Renaissance neglected Nugent, his importance as the movement's "gay rebel" has now been firmly established thanks to numerous critical studies and Thomas H. Wirth's long overdue 2002 collection of the writer's published and unpublished works. Richard Bruce Nugent also plays a pivotal role in *Brother to Brother* (2004), writer-director Anthony Mackie's cinematic exploration of the gay side of the Harlem Renaissance. (*See also* African American Gay Literature)

Further Reading

Nugent, Richard Bruce. *Gay Rebel of the Harlem Renaissance: Selections from the Work of Richard Bruce Nugent.* Ed. Thomas W. Wirth. Durham, NC: Duke UP, 2002.

Karl L. Stenger

NUYORICAN   A term used as a proper noun to describe persons of Hispanic (particularly but not exclusively Puerto Rican) descent living in New York City, especially on the Lower East Side. As an adjective it may apply equally to the particular Spanglish dialect spoken by New York City's Hispanic population or to anything created or manufactured by a Nuyorican.

The term is a fusion of the words "New York" and "Puerto Rican." Other Hispanic immigrant groups have come to accept the label as pertaining to them as well, although many reject any and all association with this term. Often seen as politically charged, there are many different perspectives on the word: some see the word as a source of pride in their cultural ancestry, while others see it as evidence that either the Hispanic population is spreading its influence too far or, conversely, that North American culture is eroding the essence of being Latino.

The largest movement of Puerto Ricans from the island to the mainland in the twentieth century occurred after World War II. By that point, every Puerto Rican had officially been declared a U.S. Citizen by the Jones Act of 1917, the Great Depression had passed, and industry was doing well in the U.S. mainland. The ease with which Puerto Ricans could travel into and out of the country coupled with the opportunity for wages higher than those offered in Puerto Rico brought many Puerto Ricans to New York. This Puerto Rican workforce could come to New York to earn more money than was possible on the island and could return to their homeland at any point. As many immigrant groups have done historically, the Puerto Ricans coming to New York settled here close to one another; in this case it was the Lower East Side of Manhattan, or "Loisaida," as many call it affectionately.

Linguistically, "Nuyorican Spanish" is a variant of other Spanglish dialects. "Spanglish" is any combination of the English and Spanish lexicons or grammars, although it is mostly associated with the interjection of English words into Spanish syntax, as in, "Voy a chequear el correo." The English verb "to check" is inserted into the Spanish and treated as a regular verb. Nuyorican Spanish includes Spanish of mostly Puerto Rican character but also demonstrates other Carribean and Central American Spanish influences.

Nuyorican influence in the arts has been most prominent in spoken word poetry, although some Nuyorican influence may be noted in the plastic arts as well. Miguel Algarín, retired English professor at Rutgers University, founded the Nuyorican Poets' Café circa 1973 as a forum for young poets to be heard, especially those whose voices would not otherwise be heard. The Nuyorican Poets' Café has grown to be one of the most critically acclaimed and popular venues for young artists coming from traditionally underrepresented groups. The Café hosts nationally famous poetry slams as well as concerts, theatrical performances, and is host to art exhibits and comedy performances as well. The Nuyorican Poets' Café is also involved in many community outreach programs. (*See also* Bilingualism)

Further Reading

Algarín, Miguel, and Bob Holman, eds. *Aloud: Voices from the Nuyorican Poets' Café*. New York: Henry Holt and Company, 1994.

Algarín, Miguel, and Miguel Piñero, eds. *Nuyorican Poetry : An Anthology of Puerto Rican Words and Feelings*. New York: Morrow, 1975.

Morales, Ed. *Living in Spanglish: The Search for Latino Identity in America*. New York: St. Martin's Press, 2002.

Santiago, Esmeralda. *When I Was Puerto Rican*. New York: Vintage, 1994.

Santiago, Roberto. *Boricua: Influential Puerto Rican Writings*. New York: Ballantine, 1995.

Stevens, Ilan. *Spanglish: The Making of a New American Language*. New York: Rayo, 2003.

Teck, Bill. *The Official Spanglish Dictionary*. New York: Fireside, 1998.

Alexander Waid

NYBURG, SIDNEY LAUER (1880–1957)   Jewish American novelist, lawyer, and community activist. Nyburg is best known for his 1917 novel, *The Chosen People*, which was praised in its day as one of the most important novels from the Jewish American experience. Nyburg wrote four other works of fiction, all of which express concern for social causes as well as a deep connection to the city of Baltimore.

Nyburg was the descendant of Dutch Jewish immigrants and grew up in relative comfort in Baltimore, graduating with a law degree from the University of Maryland in 1901. His first collection of stories, *Final Verdict: Six Stories of Men and Women*, appeared in 1914, when Nyburg was already established as a community leader and public figure. Three novels followed, including the melodrama *The Conquest* (1916), *The Chosen People* (1917), and a psychological romance, *The Gate of Ivory* (1921). Nyburg also compiled a collection of "Legends of Old Baltimore" titled *The Buried Rose* (1931). For ten years he was the director of the Associated Jewish Charities in Baltimore and served on a number of other committees and organizations, including the Legal Aid Department, which provided free legal advice to new immigrants and the poor.

There was a substantial split during this period between the Jews of Western European descent (predominantly German, but also Austro-Hungarian, Dutch, and French), who largely came to the United States between the 1830s and 1860s, and the "new immigrants" from Eastern Europe (especially Russia, Lithuania, and Poland). The German Jews had, to a great extent, already found success in the United States and had assimilated alongside their non-Jewish countrymen in cities such as Baltimore, Cincinnati, St. Louis, and New York. When the new immigrants arrived, they seemed culturally backward, politically radical, and religiously orthodox to the Americanized German Jews. What was worse, the possibility that non-Jews would lump the German Jews together with these "Easterners" threatened to undermine all of the societal gains that this earlier generation had accumulated. Nyburg's community involvement helped to bridge this gap, and *The Chosen People* deals compellingly with this tension and other issues faced by Jewish Americans at the beginning of the twentieth century.

The novel's protagonist is Philip Graetz, a young Reform rabbi who has recently become the spiritual leader of the major German Jewish synagogue in Baltimore. His congregants are, for the most part, wealthy lawyers and businessmen. His attempts to bring religious ethics come to a head when a strike breaks out among Eastern European Jewish workers at a factory that is owned by the president of Graetz's congregation, Clarence Kaufman. Graetz tries to mediate between the two parties but is rebuffed by both: To the workers the rabbi is seen as too assimilated, corrupted by the easy life of American wealth and to Kaufman and his colleagues the rabbi is hopelessly naïf.

Graetz's counterpart is the Russian-born lawyer David Gordon, who is much more savvy in his efforts to conflate, and then dispel, the conflict. Gordon becomes the novel's hero as someone who is able to balance political activism with street savvy, ethnic **identity**, and worldly idealism.

The Chosen People also tackles the subject of intermarriage, when Rabbi Graetz meets and falls in love with a non-Jewish nurse. Nyburg's portrayal in the novel contrasts from most other works of the period by being neither vociferously supportive of these relationships as the symbol of Jewish integration into American society nor vehemently against them as indicative of the breakdown of Jewish morality and cultural character.

In all, *The Chosen People* is one of the most nuanced novels about the Jewish American experience, and Nyburg's status as a writer and community leader is exemplary of the achievement of Jewish Americans at the beginning of the twentieth century.

Further Reading

Fine, David M. "Attitudes Toward Acculturation in the English Fiction of the Jewish Immigrant, 1900–1917." *American Jewish Historical Quarterly* 63 (1973): 45–56.

Sol, Adam. "Searching for Middle Ground in Abraham Cahan's *The Rise of David Levinsky* and Sidney Nyburg's *The Chosen People*." *Studies in American Jewish Literature* 16 (1997): 6–21.

Adam Sol

NYE, NAOMI SHIHAB (1952–) Arab American poet, writer of children's and young adult's literature, and folksinger. Nye's poetry has been widely published, achieving considerable literary prominence and winning numerous awards, thus situating Nye as one of the most prominent Arab American poets currently living in the United States. Born to an American mother and a Palestinian father, Naomi Shihab Nye grew up in various places in the United States and the Middle East, including St. Louis, Missouri; Jerusalem; and San Antonio, Texas.

Nye's work has received great critical acclaim for its insightful and discerning descriptions of everyday experiences, with her poetry acting as a transformative lens through which the ordinary is made novel and even extraordinary. A strong sense of place is embedded in Nye's poetry, which is informed by her Palestinian American background and her encounter with the cultures of the Middle East, the United States, and South America, among others. The vivid cultural portrayals in Nye's poetry overlap and intermingle, producing a rich array of cross-cultural images that overcome geographical boundaries, thus acting as bridges between different ethnicities, **race**s, and cultures.

Nye's poetry collections include *Different Ways to Pray* (1980) and *Hugging the Juke Box* (1982), both of which won the Voertman Poetry Prize, as well as *Yellow Glove* (1986), *Invisible* (1987), *Mint* (1991), *The Red Suitcase* (1994), and *Fuel* (1998). Her collection of selected poems, *Words Under the Words*, was published in 1995, followed by *19 Varieties of Gazelle: Poems of the Middle East* (2002), nominated for the National Book Award. She has been the recipient of several awards and fellowships including a Guggenheim fellowship, the Witter Bynner Fellowship from the Library of Congress, the I. B. Lavan Award from the Academy of American Poets, and four Pushcart prizes.

In addition to her poetry, Nye is also widely known for her literature targeting children and young adults and for featuring fiction, essays, and translated poetry. *Sitti's Secret* (1994), a picture narrative, focuses on the relationship that an Arab American girl living in the United States has with her grandmother living in a Palestinian village, poignantly detailing ways by which they overcome the linguistic and geographical borders separating them. Nye's first novel for young adults, *Habibi* (1997), also involves a journey to the Middle East, one undertaken by an Arab American female protagonist visiting her father's native Jerusalem during the 1970s. This autobiographical narrative portrays the tensions inherent in the Palestinian-Israeli conflict, adding a complex level to an adolescent's perspective. Other children's texts by Nye include the illustrated books *Benito's Dream Bottle* (1995) and *Lullaby Raft* (1997).

Naomi Shihab Nye. *By permission of Steve Davis, photographer, and Naomi Shihab Nye, 2005*

Nye has also edited several poetry anthologies, including *This Same Sky: A Collection of Poems from around the World* (1992), which contains the work of 129 poets from 68 different countries, as well as *The Tree Is Older Than You Are* (1995); *I Feel a Little Jumpy Around You* (1996); *The Space Between Our Footsteps: Paintings and Poems from the Middle East* (1998), which was republished as *The Flag of Childhood: Poems from the Middle East* (2002); and *Salting the Ocean: 100 Poems by Young Poets* (2000).

After reading with three other poets from Texas at the University of North Texas Poets in Concert Series, Nye's work was published as part of *Texas Poets in Concert: A Quartet* (1990). In her book of essays titled *Never in a Hurry: Essays on People and Places* (1996), Nye ruminates on a wide-ranging collection of experiences extending over a period of thirteen years. This mix of personal essays, with topics varying between the Arabic language, the people she has known (including her neighbor Pablo Tamayo), and the places she has lived in (such as San Antonio where she still currently resides), widen the scope of this writer's literary endeavors, while at the same time attesting to Nye's unchanging poetic and humanistic perceptions. (*See also* Arab American Novel, Arab American Poetry)

Further Reading

Hilal, Deema. "Bordering on the Borderless: The Poetry of Naomi Shihab Nye." *Al-Jadid: A Review & Record of Arab Culture and Arts* 8.39 (2002): 7, 17.

Majaj, Lisa Suhair. "Arab American Literature and the Politics of Memory." *Memory and Cultural Politics: New Approaches to American Ethnic Literatures*. Ed. Amritjit Singh, Joseph Skerrett, and Robert E. Hogan. Boston: Northeastern UP, 1996. 266–90.

———. "Two Worlds: Arab-American Writing." *Forkroads: A Journal of Ethnic-American Literature* 1.3 (1996): 64–80.

Milligan, Bryce. "Writing To Save Our Lives: An Interview with Naomi Shihab Nye." *Paintbrush: A Journal of Contemporary Multicultural Literature* 18.35 (1991): 31–52.

Orfalea, Gregory. "Doomed by Our Blood To Care: The Poetry of Naomi Shihab Nye." *Paintbrush: A Journal of Contemporary Multicultural Literature* 18.35 (1991): 56–66.

Spaar, Lisa Russ. Introduction to *Texas Poets in Concert: A Quartet.* Ed. Gwynn, R. S., et al. Denton: U of North Texas P, 1990. 2.

Carol Fadda-Conrey

O

OCCOM, SAMSON (1723–1792) Native American author, missionary, and activist. The earliest known published Native American author, Presbyterian minister and Mohegan tribal leader, Samson Occom occupies an important place in American Indian literary history. Occom's *Sermon on the Execution of Moses Paul* (1772) was widely disseminated during his lifetime. Paul, a fellow Mohegan who had been sentenced to death for murder, had requested that Occom preach at his execution, and the sermon was so well received by the large crowd of spectators that it was published almost immediately. Occom's short autobiographical sketch, *A Short Narrative of My Life,* was written in 1768, but was not published until 1982. The *Narrative* not only provides a valuable record of Native American life in the eighteenth century, but also documents Occom's growing sense that Indians could not rely on the promises of whites to adequately fulfill the spiritual and material needs of Christian converts.

Occom grew up in Connecticut, in the homeland of the Mohegans, and studied under the minister Eleazar Wheelock. In addition to being a Mohegan councilor, Occom served as a missionary to the Oneidas and taught school in Montauk, where he married a Montauk woman. As his *Short Narrative* makes clear, the money granted him by the mission society was insufficient, and in order to support his growing family Occom took on a variety of odd jobs in addition to his teaching and preaching. Nevertheless, financial worries were constant.

In 1765, Wheelock asked Occom to travel to England to raise funds for an Indian mission school (later Dartmouth College). He promised that he would care for Occom's family in his absence, but upon his return Occom found that Wheelock had not kept his promise. Occom's disappointment at finding himself so exploited by a man he had considered a mentor resulted in his gradually distancing himself from white Christians, recognizing that the only people who had the Indians' best interests at heart were Indians themselves. As a result, Occom began to focus his energies on creating a new community of Christian Indians that would not be dependent upon white benefactors. This vision came to fruition in the 1773 founding of Brotherton, New York, an intertribal community of Christian Indians drawn largely from New England tribes, which was supported by the local tribes of the Iroquois Confederacy and for whom Occom served as minister.

In addition to sermons and his autobiographical narrative, Occom also composed hymns and, in 1774, published a popular hymnal that included both his own hymns and hymns by other New England writers.

Over the course of his life, Occom had a growing belief in the importance of Indian self-determination and sovereignty. In addition to his work as a Christian missionary among Indians, Occom also preached the right of Indians to determine their own destinies. (*See also* Native American Autobiography)

Further Reading

Brooks, Joanna. *American Lazarus: Religion and the Rise of African-American and Native American Literatures.* New York: Oxford UP, 2003.

Peyer, Bernd. *The Tutor'd Mind: Indian Missionary Writers in Antebellum America.* Amherst: U of Massachusetts P, 1997.

Miriam H. Schacht

O'CONNOR, EDWIN (1918–1968)   Irish American novelist. Edwin O'Connor deals with the importance in life of family and the Catholic Church, and is interested in the differences among the generations, the gravity of politics, and the passing of traditions. His works include *The Oracle* (1951), *The Last Hurrah* (1956), *The Edge of Sadness* (1961), for which he won the Pulitzer Prize for Fiction in 1962, *All in the Family* (1966), and *The Best and the Last of Edwin O'Connor* (1970), published posthumously by Little, Brown and Company and edited by Arthur Schlesinger Jr.

O'Connor's 1956 novel *The Last Hurrah* is often rumored to be about Democratic career politician James Michael Curley, a former Boston mayor and former Massachusetts governor. Like Curley, the protagonist Frank Skeffington has also been governor of his state, and like Curley, who lost his mayoral reelection campaign in 1948, Skeffington loses his. Regardless of this possible connection, *The Last Hurrah* is the tale of the seventy-two-year-old Irish American Skeffington who decides to once again run for reelection as mayor of "the city," and whose loss brings on a stroke and death. The novel follows Skeffington from the night he announces he will run, through the campaign, the night of the election, and into his death and funeral. Along the way, we learn Skeffington is a narcissist. He loves himself, but says he loves the people, and is running for reelection for the people. O'Connor skillfully reveals his character's traits through dialogue. Often, what is said in public is quite the opposite of what is said in private, Skeffington often having something witty to say regardless. O'Connor's own narrative language mirrors that wit, making for a solid tone.

O'Connor has the aging Skeffington lose the election, consistent with the author's interest in the changing of the times. Skeffington is an old-time politician. The youth want change. They do not want a big boss politician. In the world of the novel, it used to be that what got one into office was being a Democrat, Irish, and Catholic. But in these changing times, a weak, politically inexperienced candidate is desired by those who wish to manipulate politics from behind the curtain. O'Connor shows the power of the media, with its biased newspaper. In the end, it is Kevin McCluskey who wins the election, a candidate empowered by many special interest groups. With Skeffington losing, he dies. The world in which Skeffington could live is gone, and so he must be gone, too.

Skeffington's nephew, Adam Caulfield, is another major character in the book. His name comes from the biblical story, and he is a young, innocent newspaper cartoonist, functioning as an observer, and confident of Skeffington. Through Skeffington, Adam is brought into this politically corrupt environment. As Adam becomes more aware of this political world, his innocence is stolen from him. Following Adam, the reader's innocence is stolen, too.

In part because of its success, *The Last Hurrah* was made into a film in 1958, starring Spencer Tracy (*Guess Who's Coming to Dinner?*) and directed by John Ford (*The Grapes of Wrath*).

O'Connor's *The Edge of Sadness* won him the Pulitzer Prize for Fiction. The narrator of *The Edge of Sadness*, the alcoholic, middle-aged priest Father Hugh Kennedy, opens the novel saying the story is not about him, but of course it is. He is a native returning to the church of his youth as the new pastor. The times have changed, and the once strong parish has become run down. Back home, Father Hugh reunites with old friends: John Carmody, who has become a priest turned nihilist, and John's sister Helen, a love interest from Father Hugh's youth. The novel meditates on what a priest is and what the vows mean. The priest gets up to do God's work and must love the people. The irony and tragedy of the priest is that he must be humanly alone. In the end, the novel puts forth a hopeful message. A better tomorrow can be built on the present. Remembering the good times of the past will only make one miserable. Working to build a better future from the lackluster present will make one happy. (*See also* Irish American Novel)

Further Reading

Duffy, Charles F. *A Family of His Own: A Life of Edwin O'Connor.* Washington, DC: Catholic U of America P, 2003.

Rank, Hugh. *Edwin O'Connor.* New York: Twayne, 1974.

Rogers, James Silas. "Blessed Words: Duality of Language in Edwin O'Connor's *The Edge of Sadness.*" *Providence: Studies in Western Civilization* 6.2 (2001): 29–41.

Stephen Oravec

O'CONNOR, MARY FLANNERY (1925–1964) Irish American author of short stories and novels. Flannery O'Connor is best known as a Southern writer whose "Christ-haunted" characters achieve redemption through an epiphany brought on by an act of violence. She resisted the label of "Southern writer" and in fact produced a body of work that, though set in the South and populated with unmistakably Southern characters, transcends the region. Her fiction is often described as Southern gothic or grotesque.

O'Connor, the only child of Edward Francis O'Connor and Regina Cline O'Connor, was born in Savannah, Georgia, a cosmopolitan city where Catholic families like the O'Connors were less rare than they were in other parts of the South. Her religion served more to mark O'Connor as an outsider than did her Irish American heritage. In 1938 O'Connor's father became ill, and the family moved to Andalusia, the Cline family home near Milledgeville, where, except for a few years, O'Connor would remain for the rest of her life.

After graduating from high school, O'Connor earned a degree in sociology from Georgia State College for Women (now Georgia College and State University) at age twenty. She attended the writer's workshop at the State University of Iowa on scholarship, earning an MFA in 1947. O'Connor remained at Iowa an additional year to work on her novel, then was accepted at Yaddo, the writer's colony in Saratoga Springs, New York. In the spring of 1949 she left Yaddo, and by September she had settled in with friends Sally and Robert Fitzgerald in Connecticut to work on her novel.

In December 1950, when O'Connor was finishing *Wise Blood*, she suffered her first attack of lupus, the autoimmune disease that killed her father when she was fifteen. Although lupus patients today have a good prognosis with proper treatment, in O'Connor's day they did not. In early 1951 O'Connor moved back to the family home in Milledgeville, where, with her mother's help, she learned to live within the limitations of the disease. When she felt well, O'Connor wrote for three hours in the morning, received visitors, read, and carried on an active correspondence. After the publication of *Wise Blood* in 1952, she accepted speaking engagements, attended conferences, and visited friends. Although O'Connor was on crutches beginning in September 1955, she continued to be active. By the time of her death in 1964 she had published two novels and numerous short stories.

Wise Blood (1952) is the story of Hazel Motes, who denies the religion of his grandfather, an evangelical preacher. Hazel is haunted not only by the image of his grandfather, but also by the feeling that Jesus is haunting him. Hazel establishes the Church Without Christ to prove that Jesus is a liar and that sin does not exist. After murdering a man who parodies Hazel and his church, Hazel returns to his rooming house and spends several months scourging himself, wrapping his chest in barbed wire and putting stones in his shoes. Finally, he blinds himself with lime. Later, Hazel is found dead in a ditch, and Hazel's land-lady is asked to identify his body. She looks at his ruined eyes and sees a sign that Hazel has followed the star of Bethlehem, suggesting that the Christ who haunted Hazel has found him.

The Violent Bear It Away (1960) dif-fers from *Wise Blood* in that it shows the internal conflict, rather than the outward appearance, of a character struggling with religion. As the book opens, Old Mason Tarwater dies at the breakfast table, having instructed his grand-nephew, four-teen-year-old Francis Marion Tar-water, to give him a Christian burial and baptize the boy's retarded

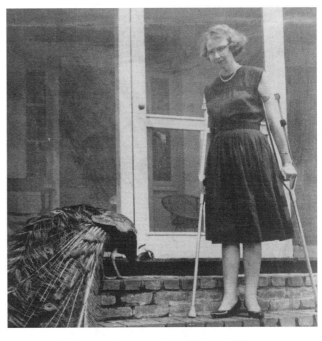

Flannery O'Connor. *Courtesy of the Library of Congress.*

cousin, Bishop Rayber. The boy begins digging the grave but does not com-plete the task. He burns the house, believing Old Tarwater is inside, and runs off to the home of his uncle, George F. Rayber, a high school teacher and reli-gious opposite of Old Tarwater. He intends to laugh in the face of his great-uncle's beliefs; he will resist baptizing Bishop. At the crux of the novel, young Tarwater, perhaps accidentally, drowns Bishop, at the same time involuntarily delivering the words of baptism, setting him on the course prophesied by Old Tarwater. O'Connor is best known for her short stories, which continue to be widely anthologized and taught in high schools and colleges. They are char-acterized, as are her two novels, by violence and grotesque characters. In "A Good Man Is Hard to Find," a grandmother and her family are shot to death by escaped prisoners. "Greenleaf," replete with images of classical mythology and Christianity, shows Mrs. May stabbed in the heart by a scrub bull and dying with a beatific smile on her face. In "Good Country People," an atheist tries to seduce a Bible salesman and is shocked when he steals her prosthetic leg. In "Revelation," Mrs. Turpin believes she has received a message from God when a college girl hits her in the face with a book and calls her a wart hog from hell. One collection of stories, *A Good Man Is Hard to Find* (1955), was published during O'Connor's lifetime. Two others, *Everything That Rises Must Converge* (1965) and *The Complete Stories* (1971), were published posthumously.

In addition to the Kenyon Fellowship, which she was awarded in 1953 and 1954, O'Connor won a Ford Foundation grant in 1959 and a posthumous National Book Award in 1971 for *The Complete Stories of Flannery O'Connor.*

She won first prize O. Henry awards for "Greenleaf" in 1957, for "Everything That Rises Must Converge" in 1963, and for "Revelation" in 1964; and second prize O. Henry awards for "The Life You Save May Be Your Own" in 1954 and for "A Circle in the Fire" in 1955. (*See also* Irish American Novel)

Further Reading

Giannone, Richard. *Flannery O'Connor: Hermit Novelist.* Urbana: U of Illinois P, 2000.

Orville, Miles. *Flannery O'Connor: An Introduction.* Jackson: UP of Mississippi, 1991.

Paulson, Suzanne Morrow. *Flannery O'Connor: A Study of the Short Fiction.* Boston: Twayne, 1988.

Whitt, Margaret Earley. *Understanding Flannery O'Connor.* Columbia: U of South Carolina P, 1995.

Claudia Milstead

ODETS, CLIFFORD (1906–1963) Jewish American playwright. Clifford Odets was considered to be the most promising playwright of the 1930s, and the plays he wrote during that decade brought him great success. But many critics now consider them dated, focusing as they do on Depression Era issues. And, while his later works declined in quality and popularity, all but one of his plays were produced on Broadway. Furthermore, his socialist dramas of the thirties render him important in theater history, as does his influence on such postwar playwrights as **Arthur Miller** and Tennessee Williams.

Odets initially pursued an acting career, with limited success; however, his endeavors led to his involvement with the Theatre Guild and subsequently its offshoot, the socialist-oriented Group Theatre, for which he would become the foremost dramatist.

Waiting for Lefty (1935), which calls for unionization and a strike among taxi drivers, launched Odets's fame and won Yale's George Pierce Baker Drama Cup. Considered by many to be his masterpiece, this one-act play also raised the status of agit-prop (agitation propaganda), a popular genre during the Depression, while exposing the effects of the country's dismal economic situation, the evils of capitalism, and anti-Semitic views. *Awake and Sing!* (1935), the title of which comes from the Bible's Book of Isaiah, manifests similar views. Set in a Bronx apartment, it depicts the struggles of the Berger family to, as Odets put it, live "life amidst petty conditions." This play also argues for change, primarily through the Bergers' young son Ralph, who by the end of the play vows to help bring about a new society. *Paradise Lost* (1935), like *Awake and Sing!*, centers on a family beset by tragedy and reiterates the theme of hope and renewal. Many critics, in fact, note the importance of Odets's concentration on Jewish families in America, particularly the rich language he creates.

Till the Day I Die (1935), one of the first anti-Nazi plays to be produced on Broadway, is based on a letter that appeared in the socialist publication

New Masses and is one of the earliest theatrical assaults on fascism. The play depicts the efforts of the underground resistance, as well as themes of betrayal and homosexuality in a political environment.

In *Golden Boy* (1937), generally considered Odets's most popular work, the playwright breaches the strictures of agit-prop in an intriguing blend of leftist and Faustian themes. It centers on a brazen young Italian American, Joe Bonaparte, a gifted violinist who turns to boxing to earn fame and fortune. As he does so, however, he becomes increasingly arrogant and egotistical. On the night of a major fight, beleaguered by his father's disappointment in him and angered at his girlfriend's abandonment, Joe fights with powerful emotion, only to learn later that his opponent died from his blows. Feeling like a murderer and finally recognizing the loss of his music career, Joe speeds off into the night and is killed in a car crash, presumably a suicide.

Rocket to the Moon (1938), Odets's last play of the 1930s, moves from a focus on socialist themes to an examination of human relationships. The title, like that of *Awake and Sing!,* suggests the possibility of renewal and happiness, depicting various tangled love affairs of an idealistic young woman, Cleo. Through her experiences, she grows and matures, ultimately rejecting all of her paramours to seek new roads and the kind of love for which she longs.

Odets's subsequent plays include *Night Music* (1940), *Clash by Night* (1941), and *The Big Knife* (1949). *The Country Girl* (1950), which was made into a successful film in 1954, is the only play in which Odets doesn't address socialism, while *The Flowering Peach* (1954) is a Jewish American rendition of the Biblical tale about Noah and the Ark.

Besides his stage work, Odets was active as a screenwriter, though many of his scripts remain unpublished. Among his more well-known screenplays are *The General Died at Dawn* (1936), *None But the Lonely Heart* (1944), *The Greatest Gift*—later released as *It's a Wonderful Life* (1944)—*Sweet Smell of Success* (1957), and *Wild in the Country* (1961), which earned a Drama Award from the American Academy of Arts and Letters.

Odets's socialist views and dramas caused him to be labeled a Communist by the House Un-American Activities Committee (HUAC) in 1947. Although he was a member for only a few months, he remained sympathetic to the cause and was summoned to testify before the HUAC in 1951. (*See also* Jewish American Theater)

Further Reading

Cooperman, Robert. *Clifford Odets: An Annotated Bibliography, 1935–1989.* Westport, CT: Meckler, 1990.

Demastes, William W. *Clifford Odets: A Research and Production Sourcebook.* Westport, CT: Greenwood Press, 1991.

Flexner, Eleanor. "The New Realism." *American Playwrights: 1918–1938.* New York: Simon and Schuster, 1936. 290–302.

Gould, Jean. "Clifford Odets." *Modern American Playwrights.* New York: Dodd, Mead, 1966. 186–201.

Mendelsohn, Michael J. *Clifford Odets: Humane Dramatist*. DeLand, FL: Everett/ Edwards, 1969.

Miller, Gabriel, ed. *Critical Essays on Clifford Odets*. Boston: G. K. Hall, 1991.

Murray, Edward. *Clifford Odets: The Thirties and After*. New York, Ungar, 1968.

Shuman, R. Baird. *Clifford Odets*. New York: Twayne, 1962.

Weales, Gerald. *Odets: The Playwright*. New York: Methuen, 1985.

Karen C. Blansfield

O'HARA, FRANK (1926–1966)   Irish American poet and art critic. Since his death Frank O'Hara has been recognized as one of the most important American poets of the mid-twentieth century. O'Hara wrote poems lush with Irish Catholic sentimentality, honest accounts of homosexual life, tributes to New York City, and praise of high and popular art for its own sake. Witty, prolific, and generous, he anchored an influential multiethnic salon of avant-garde writers and artists.

O'Hara had a happy childhood in Grafton, Massachusetts, but, as he came to terms with his homosexuality, he grew increasingly restless there. A devotee of classical music, he planned to attend the New England Conservatory and pursue a career as a concert pianist, but, instead, he enlisted in the wartime Navy. He served from 1944 to 1946 in the Pacific and then attended Harvard from 1946 to 1950.

O'Hara's first literary mentor was the poet and professor John Ciardi; his first roommate was the artist Edward Gorey; and his first close poetic ally was fellow student John Ashbery. Poets visiting Harvard during his time there included Wallace Stevens, W. C. Williams, T. S. Eliot, Stephen Spender, Dylan Thomas, Marianne Moore, and Robert Frost. All influenced O'Hara, as did the French and Russian surrealists. At Harvard he encountered anti-Catholic, anti-Irish prejudice for the first time. Although these biases and anti-homosexual sentiment had little effect on O'Hara's own success, he vehemently opposed all forms of **race**-, ethnicity-, gender-, and sexuality-based discrimination throughout his life.

After graduating from Harvard, he attended the master's degree program in creative writing at the University of Michigan, where he won the 1951 Hopwood Prize for poetry. In the fall of that year, O'Hara moved to New York. Over the next fifteen years, his coterie of writers and visual artists would include Ashbery, Kenneth Koch, James Schuyler, LeRoi Jones/ **Amiri Baraka**, **Allen Ginsberg**, **Jack Kerouac**, **Diane di Prima**, **Gregory Corso**, Jackson Pollock, Willem De Kooning, Larry Rivers, Jane Freilicher, Mark Rothko, Helen Frankenthaler, Michael Goldberg, Franz Kline, and Grace Hartigan. During this period O'Hara produced hundreds of poems, many of them inspired by friends and lovers, most written spontaneously, often in bars and cafés, at his desk at the Museum of Modern Art (the museum of which he eventually became an Associate Curator), or aboard trains traveling between New York and the Hamptons (the place where he spent most of his summers). O'Hara put little effort into publishing his work, but in his lifetime six books of his poems saw print: *A City Winter, and Other Poems* (1951), a collaboration with Rivers; *Meditations in an Emergency* (1957); *Odes* (1960), a collaboration with Goldberg; *Second Avenue* (1960); *Lunch Poems* (1964); and *Love Poems* (1965).

Although varied, O'Hara's poems typically foreground speakers' engagement with a world in motion. Among his best early poems are "Second Avenue" (1952), a surrealist city epic; "To the Harbormaster" (1953), an often anthologized extended metaphor; and "To the Film Industry in Crisis" (1955), a medley of popular culture allusions and existential meditations. Among his best later poems are "A Step Away from Them" (1956), the first of what O'Hara called his "I do this, I do that" pieces; "Homosexuality" (c. 1956), a candid portrait of homosexual life; "In Memory of My Feelings" (1958), a vivid autobiographical poem; "A True Account of Talking to the Sun on Fire Island" (1958), a reflection on the poet's vocation; "The Day Lady Died" (1959), a speaker's encounter with Billie Holiday's death; and "Biotherm" (1962), a multivoiced dramatic love poem.

As he grew older, O'Hara spent ever more time curating museum exhibits, writing art criticism (notably a monograph, *Jackson Pollock* [1959] and the "Art Chronicles" columns in *Kulchur* magazine [1961]), and attending cocktail parties. His last years were marked by alcoholism, erratic behavior, and flagging poetic productivity. He wrote only seventeen poems over the last three years of his life, which ended on Fire Island in the summer of 1966 when O'Hara was struck and killed by a beach taxi.

While O'Hara lived his poetry gained little attention, and most of that for contributions to the anthology *New American Poetry* (1960). After he died, however, most of his poems, including manuscripts that friends had rescued from his apartment, were published in *The Collected Poems of Frank O'Hara* (1971), which won a National Book Award. Several other collections followed: *Selected Poems* (1973); *Art Chronicles* (1975), a collection of criticism; *Standing Still and Walking in New York* (1975), a collection of essays and notes; *Poems Retrieved* (1977); and *Early Writing* (1977).

Further Reading

Elledge, Jim, ed. *Frank O'Hara: To Be True to a City (Under Discussion)*. Series ed. Donald Hall. Ann Arbor: U of Michigan P, 1990.

Ferguson, Russell. *In Memory of My Feelings: Frank O'Hara and American Art*. Berkeley: U of California P, 1999.

Gooch, Brad. *City Poet: The Life and Times of Frank O'Hara*. New York: Alfred A. Knopf, 1993.

Perloff, Marjorie. *Frank O'Hara: Poet Among Painters*. New York: Brazilier, 1977.

George Guida

OKADA, JOHN (1923–1971) Japanese American novelist. Okada's only published work of fiction, *No-No Boy* (1957), has been recognized at home and abroad as a classic of Asian American literature and widely examined in anthologies, literary histories, Asian American studies, and scholarly journals.

Before the novel was rediscovered by **Frank Chin** and other Asian American writers in the mid-1970s, John Okada's *No-No Boy* had been ignored for almost two decades. When first published in 1957, the novel was not only neglected by the American dominant public, but also unwelcome in the Japanese American community. Its first edition of 1500 copies had not sold out when John Okada died in obscurity in 1971. The negative response to the novel surprised its publisher, Charles E. Tuttle, who assumed that the Japanese American community "would be enthusiastic about it." On the contrary, they "were not only disinterested but actually rejected the book" (*Aiiieeeee!* xxxix). In the afterword of the second edition in 1976, Frank Chin, in addition, said that he "got the impression his family was ashamed of the book" (256). After Okada's death, his widow wanted to offer all of his manuscripts to the Japanese American Research Project at the University of California at Los Angeles, but the manuscripts were rejected, and the widow was even encouraged to destroy the papers.

Set just after the end of World War II, *No-No Boy* begins with Ichiro Yamada's return to the Japanese American community in Seattle from a two-year prison term. A twenty-five-year-old Nisei, Ichiro is imprisoned for refusing the draft and answering "No-No" to the two questions on the loyalty oath issued by the War Department in 1943. The first question asks "Are you willing to serve in the armed forces of the United States on combat duty whenever ordered?" The other reads "Will you swear unqualified allegiance to the United States of America and faithfully defend the United States from any or all attack by foreign or domestic forces, and foreswear any form of allegiance or obedience to the Japanese emperor, to any foreign government, power, or organization?" Ichiro's double negative to both inquiries regarding his loyalty and combat duty makes him an outcast in the Japanese American community and a traitor to the country. Moreover, he is labeled a "no-no boy." *No-No Boy* depicts Ichiro's reunion with his family and a rapid sequence of encounters with friends, neighbors, and strangers. The succession of events illustrates Ichiro's step from the trauma of being a no-no boy and his journey to reestablish an **identity** out of fragments.

In the pursuit of a "whole" identity, Ichiro first tries to understand why he said, "No-no." After two years in jail, he is still uncertain about his actions. His probing begins with his reunion with the family. Through examining his relationships with them and tracing his development from childhood into adulthood, Ichiro gradually understands the formation of himself as a no-no boy. Fractured and disjointed by the war, the family includes atypical Japanese: a patriotic and maniac mother, an ineffectual and alcoholic father, and a rebellious and malicious brother. Clinging to her fanatical loyalty to Japan, the mother cannot admit the Japanese defeat in the war. Unable to accept the outcome of the war, the mother isolates herself socially and psychologically. No longer able to live in a fantasy filled with Japan's glorious victory and her eventual return to Japan, the mother finally drowns herself in a tub full of water. Although regarding the mother as a crazy woman, Ichiro wonders: Who is crazy? The mother? Or those who were so delirious as to fight for a country that denied them? In contrast to the mother as a "rock" who usurps the head of the family, Ichiro's father is a "round and fat and cheerful-looking" man. He is called by Ichiro "a baby," "a fool," and even "a goddammed, fat, grinning, spineless nobody." Of his father, says Ichiro, "He should have been a woman. He should have been Ma." In addition to the eccentric parents, Ichiro's younger brother, Taro, feels shame for his parents' "Japaneseness" and Ichiro's "no-no" status. On his eighteenth birthday, Taro waits no longer to join the "American" army to prove his loyalty. In order to show his disassociation from Ichiro's treason and gain acceptance of his peers, Taro betrays his brother, leading Ichiro to be beaten by his friends. Unwilling to be a "Japanese" brother or a "Japanese" son, Taro desires an identity—an American one—separate from his parents' and his brother's.

In the novel not only Japanese Americans but also other ethnic groups suffer from being excluded from the mainstream of America. Blacks, Japanese, Chinese, Mexicans, Filipinos, and Jews all strive for recognition as complete persons, namely Americans. But being American in the novel is characterized by a practice of inclusion and exclusion. As the members of these ethnic groups cannot assume the primary attribute of the dominant culture (i.e., white skin), they can never cross "the unseen walls" to become American. In agonies of unfulfillment, they turn against one another and impose racial discrimination on other groups. In the novel the blacks ask the "Japs" to go back to Tokyo; in turn, the Japanese despise the blacks and feel superior to the "Chins," who may see themselves better Asians since China was America's ally during the war. **Racism** gnaws at the heart of each ethnic American, disfigures the spirit of every community, and finally damages the nation as a whole.

Beginning with Ichiro's return home—the onset of a quest for an identity—*No-No Boy* ends with his still-ongoing search for the meaning of his existence. Constantly examining his "half of self," either Japanese or American, Ichiro is obsessed with recurrent guilt as a no-no boy, worthy of nothing: He turns down two jobs, a chance to go back to the university, and love from Emi. Although concluding on a note of "hope," the novel emphatically depicts Ichiro as a solitary seeker, one still compulsively journeying to an indefinite destination. (*See also* Internment, Japanese American Novel)

Further Reading

Chin, Frank, et al. *Aiiieeeee: An Anthology of Asian American Writers.* Garden City, NY: Doubleday, 1974.

Ling, Jinqi. "Race, Power, and Cultural Politics in John Okada's *No-No Boy.*" *American Literature* 67.2 (1995): 358–81.

Yogi, Stan. "'You Had to Be One or the Other': Oppositions and Reconciliation in John Okada's *No-No Boy.*" *MELUS* 21.2 (Summer 1996): 63–77.

Fu-jen Chen

OKITA, DWIGHT (1958–)   Japanese American poet and playwright. Dwight Okita identifies himself as Japanese American, gay, and Buddhist, and he uses those elements in his work. As a third-generation Japanese American (Sansei), Okita is a voice for his parents' generation, the Nisei, many of whom were interned in relocation camps during World War II. He is best known for two widely anthologized poems, "In Response to Executive Order 9066: All Americans of Japanese Descent Must Report to Relocation Centers" and "Notes for a Poem on Being Asian American."

Dwight Okita was born in Chicago. Both of his parents were held in relocation camps during World War II, his father only briefly before joining the 442nd Battalion and his mother for four years, beginning at age fourteen. After the war, both resettled in Chicago. They met at a church picnic, eventually married, and had two sons.

Okita began writing poems in elementary school and first had a poem published in high school. In 1983 Okita earned a bachelor's degree in creative writing from the University of Illinois at Chicago. After college, Okita held several jobs and wrote poems on weekends, at night, and during his train commute. When a number of his poems had been published in Chicago-area periodicals, Tia Chucha Press published his collection, *Crossing with the Light* (1992).

When he realized that the "canvas of poetry" had become too small, Okita began to write plays. "Richard Speck," a comic monologue about the mass murderer who killed eight student nurses a block from the Okita house in the summer of 1966, was produced by the American Blues Theatre in 1991 as part of a larger work, *Monsters.* It was published in *Yellow Light: The Flowering of Asian American Arts* (1999). *The Rainy Season,* about a romance between a Japanese American man and a Brazilian man, was produced in February 1993 and published in *Asian American Drama: Nine Plays from the Multiethnic Landscape* (1997). *The Salad Bowl Dance,* commissioned by the Chicago Historical Society and produced in 1993, depicts the lives of Japanese Americans who settled in Chicago after World War II. In 1995 Okita won the Joseph Jefferson Citation for outstanding new work in Chicago theater for his collaboration on *The Radiance of a Thousand Suns: The Hiroshima Project* (1998).

Despite the potentially political nature of his subject matter, Okita has no desire to promote any particular points of view. He says he writes to help the reader discover a new way to see the world.

As a follower of the Sokka Gakkai sect of Buddhism, Okita chants daily, not only to create good karma, but also to prepare himself to be in the right place at the right time. He is now writing his first novel, *The Prospect of My Arrival.*

Further Reading

Chiu, Christina. "Dwight Okita." *Lives of Notable Asian Americans: Literature and Education.* New York: Chelsea House, 1996. 106–13.

Milstead, Claudia. "Dwight Okita: A Net of Images." *Voces de America.* Ed. Laura
　　Alonso Gallo. Cadiz, Spain: Editorial Aduana Vieja, 2004.

Claudia Milstead

OLSEN, TILLIE (1912 or 1913–)　　Jewish American writer, political
activist, feminist, and teacher. Born to working class, socialist Jewish immigrants, Tillie Olsen came of age during the Great Depression, taking up her
parents' legacy of political activism. These life circumstances did much to
shape her writing. As Olsen has said, "I believe that the heritage of those
socialist communist Jews, that heritage that is less than a hundred years old,
is in a way our most living heritage. . . . That is part of what I feel is my Yiddishkeit, *my* Jewish heritage, that need to change the world and eradicate
those breeding grounds for hatreds and ignorances" (Frye 79). Although the
quantity of Olsen's published work remains small, it has received considerable acclaim. She is best known for the four short stories collected in *Tell Me a
Riddle* (1962). Two of these stories, "I Stand Here Ironing" and "Tell Me A
Riddle," have been widely anthologized and are frequently taught in college
classrooms; the latter story won the O. Henry Award for best American short
story in 1961. Her other published fiction includes the short story "Requa"
(1970) and the unfinished novel *Yonnondio: From the Thirties* (1974). Her nonfiction includes *Silences* (1978), a description of the social and economic circumstances that prevent writers from writing; *Mother to Daughter, Daughter to
Mother: Mothers on Mothering: A Daybook and Reader* (1984), which Olsen
shaped and selected; and *Mothers and Daughters: That Special Quality, an
Exploration in Photography* (1987), edited with her daughter, Julie Olsen
Edwards, and Estell Jussim. Olsen is also important for the role she has
played in expanding the literary **canon** by helping to republish the work of
neglected working-class and women writers (notably Rebecca Harding
Davis's *Life in the Iron Mills*).

　　Born Tillie Lerner, the second of six children to Samuel and Ida Lerner in
Omaha, Nebraska, Olsen's birth date was not recorded. Her parents had fled
Czarist Russia following their participation in the abortive 1905 revolution.
Samuel Lerner would become the state secretary of the Nebraska Socialist
Party, and Olsen remembers meeting Eugene Debs as a young child. Olsen
grew up in a multiethnic, multiracial working-class community and benefited from the rich cultural life of the left. Her family was poor but valued literacy, and she developed a passion for reading and writing from a young
age. Most of her peers left school after the eighth grade, but Olsen "crossed
the tracks" and attended the prestigious Omaha Central High through the
eleventh grade where she became acutely aware of the power of economic
differences to shape people's lives. From an early age Olsen felt driven to
write, keeping journals and composing poetry. She has described her "colleges" as literature, motherhood, and activism. In 1931 she joined the Young
Communist League (YCL), moved to Kansas City, worked in a tie factory,
and was jailed for passing out leaflets to packinghouse workers. Olsen's first

child was born when she was nineteen, the same year she began writing *Yonnondio*, as she was recovering from incipient tuberculosis that she had developed in jail. She moved to California to continue organizing for the YCL and was jailed again for supporting the San Francisco Maritime strike in 1934. In 1936 Tillie Lerner began living with her future husband, Jack Olsen, with whom she bore and raised three more daughters.

Begun in 1931 and ultimately published as an unfinished novel in 1974, *Yonnondio: From the Thirties*, takes its title from a Walt Whitman poem, "Yonnondio! Yonnondio! . . . unlimn'd they disappear." Yonnondio, a Native American word meaning a lament for the lost, is an appropriate title for a book that was lost for almost forty years and for Olsen's passion to bring the untold stories of working-class lives to literature. In the novel, the father struggles to support his growing family, first as a coal miner, then as a tenant farmer, and finally as a meat packer. His wife, already overwhelmed with several small children, has a miscarriage and almost dies. Yet, there is hope for the future, especially in the eldest child who, like her mother, is sensitive to beauty and has the ability to dream. "The Iron Throat," the first chapter of what would become *Yonnondio*, was published in the *New Republic* in 1934. Robert Cantwell praised it as a "work of early genius," and Olsen was sought out by editors and publishers but couldn't be reached because she was in jail, a situation that led to protests on her behalf. Olsen's life as an activist, worker, and mother would leave her little time to write fiction, and the novel was put aside, "lost." In a note to the reader Olsen describes coming across parts of the old manuscript and the process of reconstructing it.

Tillie Olsen's dilemma was to combine her gift for literary expression with her commitment to working-class people, to women's experience, and to progressive social struggles, "to rise but not get separated," as she put it (Frye 162). The four stories of *Tell Me a Riddle* (1961) are a profoundly beautiful expression of this dilemma. Olsen has referred to these stories as "pieces," because her original intent was to write a longer work. "Pieces" is also descriptive of her prose style, which is characterized by fragments, nonlinear plots, multivocal points of view, and shifting time frames. The result is a highly condensed mode of story telling that demands active reader involvement, creates a deep empathy between her readers and her characters, and affirms a worldview not often associated with the techniques of literary modernism that she employs. Yet, there is an organic relationship between Olsen's style and subject matter. Her condensed prose suggests the pressures under which she wrote, which, in itself, is an important subject of her stories: the pattern of discontinuity and silences imposed upon women and the working class. The stories in *Tell Me a Riddle* are loosely connected, with some of the same characters reappearing in three of them. Written during the virulent anticommunism of the 1950s, they reflect a sense of loss and the betrayal of idealism by the larger culture. Each of the stories explores the ways that personal and social experience are intertwined by focusing on family relationships, especially, although not exclusively, mother and daughter relationships, as they are shaped by the larger environment. Finally, each story insists on the resilience of the human spirit to reclaim what has been lost and damaged.

"I Stand Here Ironing," the most well known of the stories, is told in the first person voice of a mother reflecting back on the difficult circumstances of her oldest daughter's life. An unknown caller (probably a school counselor or a teacher) has asked the mother to come in, because her daughter, Emily, needs help. Throughout the story the mother is ironing and remembering years marked by poverty, illness, war, the mother's own inexperience and lack of resources, and the less-than-positive "help" of intervening institutions. As the mother moves the iron back and forth she weighs the effect of these circumstances and her own responsibility. Despite the mother's anguish, however, it becomes clear that Emily, a talented comedic performer, has a strong spirit and is more than a product of the negative circumstances that her mother has cataloged in her imaginary conversation with the caller. The story ends with the mother's plea to let her daughter know that she is "more than this dress on the ironing board, helpless before the iron."

Technically more complex, the three stories that follow explore the hunger for human community. "Hey Sailor, What Ship?" is about an aging, alcoholic merchant marine who has lost his community due to "the death of the brotherhood." "O Yes," drawing on Olsen's experiences attending black churches, explores an interracial friendship between two mothers and their daughters. "Tell Me a Riddle," the longest and the finest of the stories, takes its title from a Randall Jarrell poem. The epigraph, "These Things Shall Be," comes from an old socialist hymn. Dedicated to her parents and two others of their generation, Olsen memorializes the power of their revolutionary beliefs and the struggle of their everyday lives. The story involves three generations of a family, but focuses on the grandparents, Eva and David, beginning with the "gnarled roots of [their] quarrel." Married for forty-seven years they cannot agree on where to live in their old age, and, as it turns out, Eva is dying of cancer. The elderly couple travel to the homes of their children, where Eva remembers the past, her experience of motherhood as "a torrent [that] drowned and immolated all else." Now she seeks "coherence, transport, meaning" in an older self. Reliving events from her revolutionary youth in Russia, Eva moves from silence to speech. As Eva recovers the power of her belief in the struggle for a better world, the rift with her husband is healed, and a profound connection is created with her granddaughter, Jeannie.

The feminist movement that emerged in the early 1970s embraced Olsen's work and the values her life represents. Invited to teach and lecture at several colleges and universities, Olsen made important contributions to the recognition and understanding of women and working-class writers not previously studied. She has been the recipient of numerous awards and honorary degrees, and has generously discussed her life and work in a number of published interviews with writers and scholars. Residing most of her life in San Francisco, she currently lives next to her daughter in Berkeley.

Further Reading

Frye, Joanne S. *Tillie Olsen: A Study of the Short Fiction.* New York: Twayne Publishers, 1995.

Nelson, Kay Hoyle, and Nancy Huse eds. *The Critical Response to Tillie Olsen.* Westport, CT: Greenwood Press, 1994.

Pearlman, Mickey, and Abby H. P. Werlock. *Tillie Olsen.* Boston: Twayne Publishers, 1991.

Lynn Orilla Scott

OLSON, CHARLES (1910–1970)   Part-Irish, part-Swedish American poet, literary critic and theorist, teacher. Known for his experimental verse, communal vision for society, and interest in native cultures, Charles Olson's life and work reflect his belief that Western culture's many contributions to the development of the rational mind have also resulted in alienation from the natural world.

Born in Worcester, Massachusetts, Olson's mother was of Irish descent. His father, a Swedish immigrant who became a postman, made attempts to unionize and establish fair labor practices, which likely contributed to Olson's later interest, from 1941 to 1944, in working for the American Civil Liberties Union as well as a division of the Office of War Information established to protect U.S. minorities as ethnic wartime tensions in America increased. When the war concluded, Olson abandoned his interest in politics in favor of devoting himself to the literary training he had received as a student at Wesleyan and Harvard Universities.

As a teen, Olson had met the Irish poet William Butler Yeats during a trip to Europe that he had won in a national speaking contest, but it was primarily during the years that Olson began lecturing at Black Mountain College, an experimental farming and arts center in North Carolina, that his friendships with other prominent artists and thinkers widened and began to influence his writing. Among these figures were the poets Ezra Pound, Robert Duncan, and Robert Creeley; the geographer Carl Sauer; the painters Franz Kline, Josef Albers, and Robert Rauschenberg; and the musician John Cage. During this period, Olson separated from his first wife, Constance Wilcock, and began his second common-law relationship with Elizabeth Kaiser, one of the college's music students. Olson lectured and eventually became rector at the school from 1951 until it closed in 1956. Having passed many summers as a youth in nearby Gloucester, Massachusetts, Olson chose to return to this familiar setting while giving poetry readings and lectures at other colleges. From 1963 to 1965 he taught at the State University of New York at Buffalo, but his second wife, with whom he had one child, was killed in a car accident in 1964. Cancer prevented him from teaching for more than a few weeks at the University of Connecticut teaching assignment he accepted in 1969.

Olson's work, which takes the form not only of poetry but essays, letters, reviews, scholarly books, plays, and a memoir, demonstrates his interest in artistic experimentation and his belief that language should be a continual process of finding a voice that is vibrant and new. For that reason, his writing is sometimes associated with earlier experimental poets such as Walt Whitman, T. S. Eliot, and Ezra Pound, but also with the poets William Carlos Williams, Wallace Stevens, and **Denise Levertov**. Interested in words as forms, sounds, and performances, Olson explored the creative uses of language as a means of perceiving the world immediately, directly, and intuitively. Despite the diversity of his concerns, this interest in establishing a more natural relationship with the world and its cycles informs his most famous scholarship, literary theories, and poetry.

Olson was first recognized for his 1947 study of Herman Melville, *Call Me Ishmael*, which saw *Moby-Dick* as an allegory of Western culture's long history of wandering the earth and Ahab as the epitome of human self-interest and alienation. He saw Ishmael, on the other hand, as the passive observer whose selflessness allows him to live in unity with his surroundings, a theme that can be detected throughout Olson's later work. In 1949 he published his best-known poem, "The Kingfishers," which anticipates the postmodern rejection of European imperialism and **colonialism** by celebrating the indigenous cultures of the New World. *Projective Verse* appeared the following year, an essay written to clarify the poetic process Olson used to write the poem. He devoted his later years, however, to his most elaborate work, *The Maximus Poems*, an epic series begun in the early fifties and published in three volumes in 1960, 1968, and posthumously in 1975. As with *Call Me Ishmael* and "The Kingfishers," *The Maximus Poems* explore the extent to which European values are responsible for the materialism, greed, and egocentrism in contemporary American culture. A writer whose interests spanned native New England to Aztec culture, the scope of Charles Olson's poetry and other work was as innovative as it was ambitious.

Further Reading

Christensen, Paul. *Charles Olson: Call Him Ishmael*. Austin: U of Texas P, 1978.

Clark, Tom. *Charles Olson: The Allegory of a Poet's Life*. Berkeley, CA: North Atlantic Books, 2000.

Robert W. Rudnicki

O'NEILL, EUGENE GLADSTONE (1888–1953)

Irish American playwright. Eugene O'Neill has long been regarded as America's foremost playwright. He has been the only American dramatist to be awarded a Nobel Prize for drama (1936). His dramatic work also received four Pulitzer Prizes. O'Neill's tragic vision of American life—marked by an emerging harsh realism and probing expressionism—began a new era of serious drama on the

Eugene O'Neill. *Courtesy of the Library of Congress.*

American stage. Rejecting the commercial forms of melodrama and farce, O'Neill was the first American playwright to treat the stage as a serious literary medium. His plays explored characters trapped by poverty, alcoholism, **race**, and prostitution. Alienation and marginalization marked a frequent existential theme. O'Neill's realism was more brutal and graphic than that of the Norwegian Henrik Ibsen and the Swedish August Strindberg, two pioneers in realism in the theater, and more American and contemporary than the Celtic Irish tradition that inspired him. O'Neill's playwriting spanned the first half of the twentieth century and included forty-nine plays. His repertory includes such masterpieces as *Beyond the Horizon* (1920, Pulitzer), *The Emperor Jones* (1920), *Anna Christie* (1922, Pulitzer), *Strange Interlude* (1928, Pulitzer), *The Iceman Cometh* (1946), and *Long Day's Journey into Night,* (1956, Pulitzer posthumously).

O'Neill was born November 27, 1888, into an Irish Catholic theatrical family in a New York boarding hotel. His father, James O'Neill, was an accomplished nineteenth-century Shakespearean actor, often playing opposite the legendary actor Edwin Booth. But the elder O'Neill traded in his Shakespearean roles for the financial rewards of melodrama in commercial theater, a choice that both James and his son Eugene would always regret. O'Neill's father made a small fortune through repeated performances in the lead role of *The Count of Monte Cristo*, a stage adaptation of Alexandre Dumas père's novel. Ella Quinlan, his mother, was a genteel woman of deep Catholic faith. As a young girl she envisioned her life devoted to chamber music and the simple purity of a nun's life. But after meeting James O'Neill, a matinee idol of the time, she suddenly abandoned her dreams in order to marry the older romantic actor. She would often regret the loss of her spiritual dreams.

This storybook romance was short-lived. The birth of three sons and the hard-road life of a touring theater company produced discord in the family. As the youngest son, Eugene O'Neill spent much of his early years in hotel rooms, on trains, and backstage as the family crisscrossed the country from one theater to the next. O'Neill's autobiographical masterpiece, *A Long Day's Journey into Night*, painfully reveals the stormy family life in which the playwright grew up. His father, miserly and insensitive, blames himself and his family for the loss of his artistic possibilities. O'Neill's mother, addicted to morphine because of Eugene O'Neill's difficult birth in a hotel room, longs for the serene life behind church walls that she had long-before abandoned.

A sense of rootlessness was to plague Eugene O'Neill throughout his life. He was dispatched to various boarding schools, never staying at any school long enough to form close friendships. At the age of eighteen he entered Princeton University, but was expelled his freshman year for playing a prank on the university's president. This brought an end to O'Neill's formal education.

In 1909 he secretly married Kathleen Jenkins, his first of three wives. Days after the marriage, O'Neill shipped out on a tramp steamer to go gold prospecting in Honduras. After the mining venture failed, he led the life of a wanderer and derelict, frequenting bars and prostitutes along rough waterfronts in Buenos Aires, Liverpool, and New York City. O'Neill's encounters with the outcasts working aboard ships and along wharves later supplied many of the realistic details for such plays as *The Hairy Ape* (1922) and *The Iceman Cometh*. But his vagabond life proved deleterious. The effects of heavy drinking led to an attempted suicide. O'Neill finally returned to his father's home (dubbed the Cristo cottage because it was purchased with box office receipts from the Dumas play) in New London, Connecticut, for a long recuperation.

Upon his return, O'Neill and Kathleen were divorced. A son, Eugene O'Neill Jr., had been born in O'Neill's absence. In 1918 O'Neill married Agnes Boulton, the writer with whom he had two children: a son, Shane, and a daughter, Oona. He divorced Agnes in 1928 and married actress Carlotta Monterey with whom he lived until his death.

In 1911 O'Neill was still convalescing from the aftermath of his dissolute odyssey as a seafarer and nervous about his future. He was twenty-three years old and desperate to find his role in life. When the young Irish American found himself in the audience of the Irish Players performing in New York, he had an epiphany. The company was touring America from the famed Abbey Theatre in Dublin. His Irish ancestry resonated with the authentic realism and social commentary in the drama of George Bernard Shaw, John Millington Synge, William Butler Yeats, Lady Gregory, and other distinguished Irish dramatists of the time. O'Neill decided that night to become a playwright.

But O'Neill's health took a turn for the worse. The following year he was confined to the Gaylord Farm Sanitarium in Connecticut for tuberculosis, the fate of the younger son, Edmund, in *Long Day's Journey into Night*. It was during his lengthy recuperation in 1912 that O'Neill read voraciously, took stock of his life, and began seriously to write plays. He filled his old seaman's chest with play scripts. He then enrolled in George Pierce Baker's famous playwriting course at Harvard from 1914 to 1915. Although O'Neill did not finish the course, he gained much needed technical experience from Baker's formal instruction in dramatic composition. The unproven playwright also gained confidence.

O'Neill's dramatic style would not follow the traditional plots or themes staged by The Irish Players. O'Neill's vision for drama was to find an American voice and eschew what he saw as the provincial ideas belonging to Ireland. O'Neill's drama would more clearly echo the Swedish dramatist August Strindberg in his evocation of quintessential modern themes probing alienation and fragmentation from the social body. Instead of the conventional concerns of Irish **identity**, freedom, and economics, Strindberg's tragic themes in the realism of *Miss Julie* and the expressionism in *The Ghost Sonata* became O'Neill's model. O'Neill was also greatly influenced by the German Gerhart Hauptmann.

O'Neill began his apprenticeship as a playwright at a highly auspicious time in American theater. The tide of realism sweeping across the stages of Europe signaled a current of change for theaters on the Yankee shores. Over the next four decades, O'Neill would revolutionize American theater by putting onstage raw aspects of life that were both personal and universal. His artistic career can be viewed in three stages.

O'Neill's early plays drew upon his rag-tag sea adventures and his wastrel years. This apprentice period represents O'Neill's contributions to the short, or one-act, play genre. His recognized sea plays include *Bound East for Cardiff* (1916), *In the Zone* (1917), *The Long Voyage Home* (1917), and *The Moon of the Caribbees* (1918). These four plays were written between 1913 and 1917 and produced in 1924 under the collective title *S.S. Glencairn*. This group of plays staged serious subjects that were then marginalized in the American theater: anarchists, prostitutes, derelicts, disenfranchised workers, and the poor. Prior to O'Neill's redefinition of the domain of the theater, these lower-class denizens primarily filled comedy roles onstage. O'Neill's serious treatment elevated these characters into genuinely tragic figures. The playwright also plumbed metaphysical dimensions such as God's injustice to humankind.

While writing the sea plays, O'Neill took part in what is now regarded as a revolutionary movement that has forever changed American theater. Seeking a stage for his unproduced scripts, O'Neill, in 1916, joined the experimental Provincetown Players. This impromptu and impoverished theater group—bringing together such literary names as Jack Reed, Louise Bryant, Robert Edmund Jones, and Susan Glaspell—produced new plays in its small, dilapidated playhouse on a wharf in Providence, Massachusetts. It was here that O'Neill's apprentice plays, *Bound East for Cardiff* and *The Long Voyage Home*, were first produced. The young playwright quickly made a name for himself. These chronicles of a seafarer's travails staged by the Provincetown Players led to his success on New York and other stages.

O'Neill's middle creative period is remarkable for its prodigious number of plays. Between 1920 and about 1943 he finished twenty long plays and a number of shorter works. His first full-length play, *Beyond the Horizon,* was staged on Broadway at the Morosco Theatre (February 2, 1920). Steeped in tragic realism, *Beyond the Horizon* centers on two brothers—one a realist and the other an idealist—who follow opposite paths in life. The practical brother returns home after making his fortune to find his younger brother defeated and dying on his failed farm. O'Neill's poignant final scene depicts the tragic brother gazing out beyond the distant horizon. The young playwright returned to the theme of lost dreams, a motif indelibly etched in his mind by the litany of lamentations of his father, mother, and brother. The carefully crafted realism in *Beyond the Horizon* impressed critics enough to award O'Neill his first Pulitzer for drama. This success launched O'Neill's reputation in America and abroad.

Some of O'Neill's most distinguished short plays include *The Emperor Jones* and *The Hairy Ape.* These expressionistic pieces reveal the playwright's exploration of grand themes through metaphysical realms and symbolism.

The Emperor Jones is O'Neill's inquiry into the problem of race in America in the early part of the twentieth century. Haunting in its dark jungle setting and drum sounds, this terrifying play, a reverse **diaspora**, centers on Brutus Jones, an African American Pullman porter and con artist who establishes himself as the king on a tropical island. When Jones attempts to flee with the royal treasure, the natives pursue him through the shadowy jungle. As Jones blindly runs in a circle, the drumbeats intensify. O'Neill's ingenuity becomes evident as audiences recognize that Jones' desperate flight, both Darwinian and Jungian, brings him back to his beginning. The setting, lighting, and off-stage sound effects create a disturbing and alien universe, one in which Jones finds that he does not belong.

The Hairy Ape is O'Neill's experiment in weaving together the threads of realism and expressionism—genres successfully woven in the novel and painting—into a dramatic fabric. The achievement is anti-realism, a grounded surrealism. Exploring what O'Neill described as his "big ideas," *The Hairy Ape* questions the advent of futurism, the runaway optimism America had placed in mechanization and industrialization—at the sacrifice of human identity—in the early decades of the twentieth century. The tragedy focuses on the story of Yank, a coarse but self-confident coal stokeman who works in the fiery depths of a luxury liner. His image of himself is incongruent with how the world perceives him. His shipmates below decks find him overly boastful and self-assured, while the privileged society on the liner's upper decks reject his unrefined language and ape-like body. Yank discovers that he does not fit in the world. He leaves the ship, wanders through New York, and finally stumbles into a zoo where he comes face to face with a caged ape, and Yank recognizes his commonality with the ape. After Yank befriends the ape by releasing him, the animal kills his alter ego and benefactor and tosses Yank's body in the cage. Yank can find no place or home in the world. O'Neill's juxtaposition of the two creatures dramatizes the feeling of human alienation and displacement in the post–World War I world. After writing the play, O'Neill remarked that Yank's struggle is primeval—"man and his struggle with his own fate."

During this middle period of playwriting, O'Neill worked with a number of themes. *Anna Christie* is the story of an immigrant prostitute with a heart of gold; *Desire Under the Elms* (1924) situates the Greek tragic themes of incest, retribution, and fate in a New England home; *Ah, Wilderness* (1933) represents O'Neill's only comedy. *Ah, Wilderness* was written as a reply to critics who charged that the dramatist could not write a comedy.

O'Neill's middle period of writing climaxes with the play *Mourning Becomes Electra* (1931). This is the playwright's great American epic drama that is grounded in the Greek Oresteia trilogy by Aeschylus and the Electra tragedies of Sophocles and Euripides. The play brings to fruition O'Neill's long desire to link a momentous period of the American past with Hellenic tradition. *Mourning Becomes Electra*, set in New England following the Civil War, relates the story of the Mannon family. Christine is the wife of returning Civil War general Ezra Mannon. Conspiring with her lover, Adam, Christine plots the murder of her husband on the eve of his return. The daughter Lavinia takes revenge on her treacherous mother by convincing her brother Orin to kill their mother's lover and accomplice. Suffering from the loss of her lover, Christine commits suicide. Orin, guilt-ridden over his mother's death, kills himself, leaving Lavinia alone in the family mansion. *Mourning Becomes Electra*, a stark look at human tragedy fixed by fate, remains a haunting realization of the impact that the foundation of Greek tragedy continues to have in theater.

By the middle of the 1930s, the world had taken serious note of O'Neill's dramatic craft. He was awarded the Nobel Prize in 1936, but did not attend the award ceremony in Stockholm, Sweden because of illness.

Several of O'Neill's most significant plays were written during his mature period, nearly a decade after he had received the Nobel Prize. This era of extraordinary creative accomplishment was preceded by almost a decade during which the dramatist had no new plays produced. The Nobel Prize had gained him worldwide notoriety and he seemed to relish in the acclaim.

The Iceman Cometh is arguably one of O'Neill's masterpieces. The play is a further exploration of O'Neill's past. It is set in Harry Hope's grim saloon on the Lower West Side of New York, a setting reminiscent of seedy bars like Jimmy-the-Priest's and the Hell Hole that O'Neill had frequented decades earlier during his sea adventures. The time is 1912, the same year that O'Neill had attempted suicide. *The Iceman Cometh* explores the sordid existence of a group of drunken derelicts and prostitutes who idle away their lives. The characters hang on to pipe dreams that they boast about fulfilling someday. Their dreary existence changes suddenly with the appearance of Hickey, a voluble and electrifying salesman who charges the derelicts to act on their dreams. Rebirth seems imminent from the Christian symbolism, and audiences, through Hickey's prodding, come to believe that rehabilitation is possible for this rathskeller humanity. Ironically, the bar dwellers' dreams are dashed as the hero Hickey is unmasked as a madman who murdered his wife to give her peace from his brutality.

The first American Broadway premiere of *The Iceman Cometh* occurred at the Martin Beck Theatre (October 9, 1946). *The Iceman Cometh* was the last play to be produced on Broadway during O'Neill's lifetime. The playwright was always present for rehearsals, as was his habit at all of his productions. But on opening night, O'Neill was too ill to attend. The drama opened to a divided reception, mainly attributable to the length of the play that O'Neill would not allow to be cut. This lukewarm response greatly disappointed O'Neill. It was not until ten years later—three years after O'Neill's death—that a revival of *The Iceman Cometh* was risked. Under the direction of José Quintero and with Jason Robards Jr. in the role of Hickey, *The Iceman Cometh* opened to acclaim in the Off Broadway Circle in the Square Theatre. This successful revival led to a resurgence of interest in O'Neill's unique repertory.

A year after the failure of *The Iceman Cometh* in 1946, O'Neill's *A Moon for the Misbegotten* (written 1943) was hurried into production to shore up sagging doubts about the playwright's future. The play continues the character of James Tyrone Jr., O'Neill's theatrical avatar, who is a drunken and scheming landowner. O'Neill would later once again revive the Tyrone family in his last play *A Long Day's Journey into Night*. *A Moon for the Misbegotten* pits a poor and crude Irish American father and daughter, who are tenant farmers, against Tyrone, their landlord. This work, unlike O'Neill's other plays, includes themes of affection and forgiveness. The play opened in Columbus, Ohio (February 20, 1947), and then toured other midwestern cities such as Pittsburg, Detroit, and St. Louis. The try-out run met numerous obstacles including censors who objected to the script's graphic language. Despite O'Neill's hopes, the fate of *A Moon for the Misbegotten* proved to be another failure. The play wasn't staged on Broadway until after the artist's death.

Several significant plays were posthumously produced on Broadway after O'Neill's death in 1953. These include *A Touch of the Poet* (written 1939–41, performed and published, 1957), and the long celebrated *Long Day's Journey into Night* (written 1939–41, performed and published 1956).

Long Day's Journey into Night is considered O'Neill's single greatest contribution to American classics. The play is highly experimental in the use of stark realism and exploratory expressionism. It also exhibits the playwright's daring techniques and innovative concepts. *Long Day's Journey into Night* is O'Neill's most poignant autobiographical work, a haunting recreation of the bitterness and acrimony he witnessed living in his father's home. The play substitutes the four members of the Tyrone family—James, the father; Mary, the mother; Jamie, the older brother; and Edmund, the younger brother—for the O'Neill family: James, Ella, Jamie, and Eugene. In

Long Day's Journey into Night, the father is an aging and disappointed actor; the mother is addicted to drugs; the older son is a resentful alcoholic; and the younger son embodies the disillusioned youth of America. Edmund, like O'Neill, suffers from tuberculosis. Defeat for the characters hangs in the air as palatable as the setting's heavy ocean fog. For *Long Day's Journey into Night* and other plays, O'Neill remains recognized as America's greatest contribution to world theater.

The story behind the play's posthumous publication is as gripping as the play itself. O'Neill finished writing the play in 1941, but it was not published until 1956, three years after his death. In his will O'Neill had directed that the play should not be published until twenty-five years after his death. O'Neill made this last request because the play nakedly portrays the strife, alcoholism, and drug addiction within the O'Neill family home at the Cristo cottage. This caveat was to shield living family members from the embarrassment that the play would foster. Many of O'Neill's plays include autobiographical material, but none so transparently reveals the hidden shortcomings of his father, mother, and brother, as does *Long Day's Journey into Night.* Despite the author's wishes, his widow, Carlotta, made the play available for publication in the third year following O'Neill's demise. Random House, O'Neill's long-time publisher and to whom the author had entrusted the manuscript for sake keeping, respected O'Neill's last judgment and refused Carlotta's request to publish the script. Yale University Press, however, agreed to publish the play. *Long Day's Journey into Night* was an immediate best seller, and its successful stage performance assured O'Neill's place in American and world theater.

During his final months, after a long illness, O'Neill suffered physically and emotionally. His last days seemed as though he had written a part for himself in one of his tragedies, as he had in his autobiographical play *Long Day's Journey into Night.* The Parkinson's-like affliction that had slowly paralyzed him and brought a halt to his writing years earlier was now rapidly consuming his body. His public image had plummeted with the recent failures of *The Iceman Cometh* and *A Moon for the Misbegotten.* Depressed, he sought isolation by moving alone into a secluded hotel room. He cut himself off from all friends and visitors except his wife and his doctor. He could no longer write to absolve himself of his demons. The past continued to haunt him. His father and mother were long deceased, but memories of their tragic flaws lived on in O'Neill. He also felt acutely culpable for the disintegration of his relations with his own children. His older son, Eugene O'Neill Jr., had committed suicide at the age of forty. His younger son, Shane, had drifted into a life of alcoholism. And his daughter, Oona, was estranged from him. She had angered her father when, at the age of eighteen, she had married the comic actor Charlie Chaplin, who was O'Neill's age. Eugene O'Neill died at the age of sixty-five, on November 27, 1953, in a Boston hotel room.

O'Neill's life and rich **canon** of expressive plays remain a central part of American theater culture. The playwright's principal manuscripts and letters are housed at the Yale Collection of American Literature. O'Neill's legacy continues to be studied through such groups as the Eugene O'Neill Foundation and the Eugene O'Neill Society. (*See also* Irish American Drama)

Further Reading

Alexander, Doris. *Eugene O'Neill's Creative Struggle: The Decisive Decade, 1924–1933*. University Park: Pennsylvania State UP, 1992.

Engel, Edwin A. *The Haunted Heroes of Eugene O'Neill*. Cambridge, MA: Harvard UP, 1953.

Miller, Jordan Y. *Playwright's Progress: O'Neill and the Critics*. Chicago: Scott, Foresman, 1965.

Shaughnessy, Edward L. *Down the Night and Down the Day: Eugene O'Neill's Catholic Sensibility*. Notre Dame, IN: U of Notre Dame P, 1996.

Sheaffer, Louis. *O'Neill, Son and Playwright*. Boston: Little Brown, 1968.

Winther, Sophus Keith. *Eugene O'Neill: A Critical Study*. New York: Russell and Russell, 1961.

Michael D. Sollars

ONG, HAN (1968–)   Filipino American playwright and novelist of Chinese ancestry. Han Ong was born and raised in Manila, later emigrating with his family to Los Angeles in 1984. Ong moved to New York in the mid-1990s, where he has since remained. Ong's dramatic work earned him early recognition as a prolific and inventive playwright with telling and often acerbic descriptions of Asian experiences in contemporary America. Frequent focuses of his work include themes of dislocation, loneliness, and alienation, and the lives of marginalized individuals and disreputable groups.

His play *Bachelor Rat* (1992) comprises a series of vignettes from the life of Dada, a young promiscuous gay man; *The Middle Finger* (adapted from Frank Wedekind's *Spring Awakening*) explores the developing identities of several Catholic schoolboys growing up under social pressure from parents and teachers in the Philippines. Ong's more than thirty plays include *Reasons to Live* (1992), *The L.A. Plays* (1993), *The Chang Fragments* (1996), *Watcher* (1998), *Mysteries* (2001), *Swoony Planet*, and, most recently, *Savage Acts* (2004), cowritten with Kia Corthron, Jorge Cortinas, Sung Rno, and Alice Tuan. His performance pieces include the solo works *Symposium in Manila* (1992) and *Corner Store Geography* (1993), and the collaborative work with **Jessica Hagedorn**, *Airport Music* (1994). He has worked extensively with New York's Ma-Yi theater company, which focuses on developing and performing work by writers of Asian descent.

In Ong's first novel, *Fixer Chao* (2001), William Narciso Paulinha, a gay Filipino hustler, is enlisted by Shem C., a washed-out writer, to scam trendy New Yorkers. Under Shem's guidance, William becomes Fixer Chao, a Feng Shui master who dispenses expert and expensive consultations on interior decoration to a cast of spoiled and self-indulgent marks. Ong's second novel, *The Disinherited* (2004), follows the return of a writing professor,

Roger Caracera, from New York to the Philippines for his father's funeral. Surprised by a half-million-dollar inheritance, Caracera attempts to make up for his father's business practices by giving it back to former employees and the local community. In Caracera, Ong paints an ambivalent portrait of an expatriate Filipino coming to terms with his geographical displacement and the legacy of his family's industrial success.

Ong's awards include the Joseph Kesselring Prize in 1993, and the Macarthur Fellowship in 1997, making him among its youngest recipients. (*See also* Filipino American Novel)

Further Reading

Eng, Alvin. Interview with Han Ong, et al. *Tokens: The NYC Asian American Experience on Stage.* Philadelphia: Temple UP, 2000: 408–44.

Maslin, Janet, "Fixer Chao: Oh, That Cashmere Throw, It's So-o-o New York, No?" *New York Times* (April 5, 2001).

Tompkins, J. H. "Han's World." *San Francisco Bay Guardian* (April 15, 1992).

Ty, Eleanor, "Abjection, Masculinity, and Violence in Brian Roley's *American Son* and Han Ong's *Fixer Chao.*" *MELUS* 29.1 (Spring 2004): 119–36.

Alex Feerst

OPPEN, GEORGE (1908–1984) Jewish American poet. Oppen was born in New Rochelle, New York, to a wealthy, assimilated family, and grew up there and in San Francisco, where the family moved in 1918; his father changed the family name from Oppenheimer to Oppen in 1927. Oppen came to reject the commercial values of his family, becoming a poet and later a leftist. He gave up poetry for twenty-four years in favor of political activism, because he didn't believe that poetry could be turned into politics or that poetry could be made to be politically useful.

Feeling America to be a hostile environment in which to be an artist, Oppen and his wife, Mary, moved to France in 1929 with a small inheritance he had received on turning twenty-one; they lived in France until 1934. Oppen's first book, *Discrete Series* (1934), was published by the Objectivist Press, a cooperative publisher Oppen formed with **Charles Reznikoff**, William Carlos Williams, and **Louis Zukofsky**. The book's elliptical, somewhat fragmentary poems attempt to construct meaning through empirical fact rather than through the poet's sensibilities or emotions.

In 1935 the Oppens joined the Communist Party. Having given up poetry, Oppen was a labor organizer and factory worker during the next several years; both Oppens were arrested several times and investigated by the Federal Bureau of Investigation (FBI). Drafted, Oppen served in Europe in World War II (being denied promotion because of his political beliefs) and was seriously wounded in 1945, receiving a Purple Heart and several other decorations at his honorable discharge. After further FBI harassment, the Oppens moved to Mexico; they returned to the USA in 1960, their names having been removed from the FBI Security Index in 1957. However, the FBI continued visiting them until 1966.

Oppen began writing poetry again in 1958; his second book, *The Materials*, approaching words and things as the poem's materials, but also admitting more emotional associations with and personal response to the objects it notates (including the poet's biography) than his earlier work had allowed, was published in 1962. Oppen's fourth book, *Of Being Numerous* (1968), an examination of the city as humanity's greatest accomplishment and expression, but also of the alienation and oppression that distort that accomplishment, won the Pulitzer Prize in 1969, exposing him to a larger poetic audience. His *Collected Poems* (1975) was nominated for a National Book Award. The Oppens moved to San Francisco in 1967; in the late seventies, as his work continued to gain wider recognition, Oppen began to suffer symptoms of Alzheimer's disease, which grew acute before his death in 1984. Oppen's *New Collected Poems,* including previously unpublished and uncollected poems, was published posthumously in 2002.

Along with **Carl Rakosi**, Charles Reznikoff, and Louis Zukofsky (all also Jewish writers), Oppen was a leading member of the poetic group known as the Objectivists. Following in the footsteps of Ezra Pound and William Carlos Williams (who was affiliated with the group) and developing from Imagism, with its emphasis on hard, clear imagery and clean, uncluttered language, Objectivism sought both to treat the concrete objects of the world directly and for their own sakes (rather than as symbols or metaphors) and to treat the poem itself as an object in the world.

Oppen's work does not just describe the material world, though that is one of the things it does elegantly and precisely. His spare, almost lapidary poems enact, as well as convey, perceptions, exploring both the world of nature and the urban world, especially that of New York City. They also expose the social facts of that world, challenging its injustices, inequalities, and exploitation. The long title poem from *Of Being Numerous,* originally called "Another Language of New York," kaleidoscopically explores both the physical structure of the city and the structures of class oppression of which the city is built as much as it is built of bricks and glass and girders.

Oppen's last two books, *Seascape: Needle's Eye* (1973) and *Primitive* (1978), are more elliptical, compressed, and syntactically fractured than much of his earlier work, while, if anything, even more intensely lyrical.

The economy, density, concentration, and rhythmic assurance of Oppen's work have been widely celebrated and much emulated. For many younger poets, his poetry has been an important link with the Modernist tradition. He has come to be regarded as a major figure in twentieth-century American poetry. (*See also* Jewish American Poetry)

Further Reading

Freeman, John ed. *Not Comforts//But Vision: Essays on the Poetry of George Oppen.* Devon, UK: Interim Press, 1985.

Hatlen, Burton, ed. *George Oppen, Man and Poet.* Orono, ME: National Poetry Foundation, 1981.

Heller, Michael. *Conviction's Net of Branches: Essays on the Objectivist Poets and Poetry.* Carbondale: Southern Illinois UP, 1985.

Oppen, Mary. *Meaning a Life: An Autobiography.* Santa Barbara, CA: Black Sparrow Press, 1978.

Reginald Shepherd

OPPENHEIMER, JOEL LESTER (1930–1988)   Jewish American poet and scholar. Joel Oppenheimer's place among American poets rests on his unique use of language, themes, and symbols to portray things familiar in the human experience. With a career spanning nearly forty years, Oppenheimer stands out as a unique voice in poetry; his life and work represent an important period of social change in American history.

Joel Oppenheimer was born on February 18, 1930, on a cold morning in Yonkers, New York. He would later tell people that he often felt cold throughout his life, and he believed this was because it was such a cold day when he was born. Indeed, Oppenheimer was a sensitive child, perhaps a character trait that would lead him into his chosen work. Oppenheimer did well in school, but would not do well at Cornell University or the University of Chicago, a reality that would lead him to a college experience that would forever change him. Oppenheimer attended North Carolina's Black Mountain College from 1950 to 1953. Black Mountain College was recognized as a radically liberal institution where forward thinkers could be supported. The college was owned and operated by faculty who developed curriculum focused on music, theater, and literature. Oppenheimer flourished in this environment, and his education as a poet began; he would later be remembered as one of the most famous poets to come out of the group at Black Mountain, a group full of famous American names. Oppenheimer, however, would never receive his degree, as he left school early to support his wife and her child.

In spite of this setback with his education and the miserable jobs that would follow, Oppenheimer would continue to work on his poetry after he left Black Mountain College. His first book of poetry, *The Dutiful Son* (1956), is a collection of poetry focused on the mixed feelings of marriage, fatherhood, and domesticity, grouped by tone rather than date of composition. The collection received little critical attention, but did get a positive review in the *New York Times.* It was small, but it was the beginning. His second book of poetry, *The Love Bit and Other Poems* (1962), published after Oppenheimer's separation from his first wife and children, addressed sadness and bitterness over lost relationships and received more attention. Oppenheimer's first play to see production, *The Great American Desert*, would open in 1962 to much acclaim and success. Then, in 1964, he met the woman who would later become his second wife, but, just as his career and personal life improved, Oppenheimer became increasingly neurotic. He was fearful of buses, the subway, and airplanes. And, according to biographer Lyman Gilmore, Oppenheimer's inability to travel would have an impact on his career, as he was not able to travel to give his poetry more national exposure.

In 1966 Oppenheimer was appointed to direct St. Mark's Poetry Project, and his reputation grew as his poetry continued to get positive reviews in major New York publications. He also became involved in the anti-Vietnam protest movement during this time. In 1967 Oppenheimer published *Sirventes on a Sad Occurrence*, which is considered one of his masterpieces, and gained even more recognition when it was published in his third major book of poetry, *In Time: Poems 1962–1968* (1969). In 1969 Oppenheimer was appointed writer-in-residence and became a professor at City College of New York. Oppenheimer would continue to teach for the rest of his life and would be a well-respected professor despite the fact that he had never completed his bachelor's degree. In 1982 Oppenheimer became a professor of communication at New England College.

Oppenheimer would also continue to write until his death from lung cancer in 1988. He would publish other books of poetry (of which Oppenheimer said all contained a central theme), short stories, and two works of nonfiction: a book about the New York Mets, *The Wrong Season* (1973), and a biography of Marilyn Monroe, *Marilyn Lives!* (1981).

Oppenheimer's work is known for its thematic depth and stylistic simplicity. Important images in his work are nature, sexuality, and painful isolation. His work was autobiographical and was often painful for him to write, but Oppenheimer's ability to tap into the concerns of man and to assert his worldview that reality has meaning only when it is perceived make him an important American poet and an important contributor to Jewish American and New York culture.

Further Reading

Gilmore, Lynn. *Don't Touch the Poet: The Life and Times of Joel Oppenheimer.* Jersey City: Talisman House, 1998.

Thibodaux, David. *Joel Oppenheimer: An Introduction.* Columbia, SC: Camden House, 1986.

Crystal McCage

ORNITZ, SAMUEL (1890–1957) Jewish American novelist and screenwriter. Born in New York City to a merchant family, Samuel Ornitz grew up to be a champion of social activism. Becoming a social worker after a few years of college, Ornitz went on to serve as assistant superintendent of the Society for the Prevention of Cruelty to Children in Brooklyn, investigate labor conditions in coal mines, work for freeing the Scottsboro Boys, and help found the Hollywood Anti-Nazi League. He is most famous for the role he played in the "Hollywood Ten," the group of witnesses who, in 1947, refused to answer questions by the House Un-American Activities Committee about their roles in the Communist Party. As a result, Ornitz was sentenced to a year in prison in 1950. He never renounced his membership in the Communist Party. Ornitz first moved to Hollywood in 1928, and there he wrote and coauthored many

Samuel Ornitz testifying before the House Un-American Activities Committee. *Courtesy of the Library of Congress.*

screenplays, including *Follow Your Heart* (1936), his first movie project, cowritten by **Nathanael West** and Lester Cole. However, it is *Haunch Paunch and Jowl* (1923), Ornitz's sole novel, which has received the most critical acclaim. Written in three "feverish" months, *Haunch* first appeared anonymously as an autobiography of a judge who had died five years earlier, but, in reality, it is a fictional piece of literature. The book's protagonist is Meyer Hirsch—selfish, conniving, and unlikable—the complete opposite of Samuel Ornitz.

Haunch Paunch and Jowl is a poetic, philosophical, and political novel that documents the life of Meyer Hirsch from the time of his boyhood to his rise as a Superior Criminal Court Justice of New York. Instead of chapters, Ornitz divides the narrative into seven "periods," each containing several scenes. This unique, play-like style foreshadows the screenwriting that Ornitz would begin five years later. The prose style in *Haunch* is semi–stream of consciousness, full of ellipses, sentence fragments, repetition, and run-ons. Ornitz alternates between dialogue, including long speeches by various characters, straight narration, and poetic musings.

Considered to be a foundational work in Jewish American literature, *Haunch* contains an array of viewpoints on the economic position of Jews, generational issues with Judaism, and the pros and cons of intermarriage between Jews and gentiles. As a child member of the Ludlow Streeters, a Lower East Side gang, Hirsch rejects the Orthodox Judaism his mother embraces, and then goes on to "pass" as a practicing Jew, only to gain wealth and power as a lawyer and then a judge. Hirsch, a man shockingly void of morality, cares more about profit than his ethnicity and religion. Lionel Crane, a Jewish psychologist who passes as gentile, functions as the antithesis of Hirsh's character. Crane criticizes "Professional Jews" like Hirsch, who exploit hard-working Jews in the name of lucrative gain and vanity. If Crane is the opposite of Hirsch, two characters, Esther and Davie, similarly function as his foils. Both physically beautiful and idealistic, unlike Hirsch who is an overweight realist, Davie and Esther each marry a non-Jew, creating public scandal. Poetic Davie marries Billie, a former prostitute, for love. After his sudden, tragic death his non-Orthodox marriage complicates his funeral, as the majority of the congregation refuse to defile their burial ground with his sinful body. When Esther, Hirsch's unattainable fantasy, marries Barney Finn, an Irish philanthropist, after he inherits millions, the newspaper headlines read, "Poor Jewish Girl Marries Millionaire Sociologist." In reality, Esther and Barney have been close companions for several years, but the anti-Semitic paper portrays the Jewish woman as money-grubbing.

It is arguable that *Haunch Paunch and Jowl* is primarily a denouncement of capitalism. Much of Hirsch's money-making ideology is learned from his uncle, Philip, an antiunion, vicious capitalist who travels the road to wealth, not concerned that it is paved with the backs of workers. In fact, it is Philip who pushes Hirsch in the direction of practicing law. It is understandable that Hirsch and Philip, who at the start of the book are so poor they only have two dishes for a household of four, want to rise out of poverty, but the novel is full of characters who find charitable means of creating secure financial situations. Ornitz uses the ruthless nature of Hirsch and his uncle to symbolize the greedy capitalist agenda of the United States.

Haunch Paunch and Jowl was rereleased by Markus Wiener in 1986 as *Allrightniks Row*, Hirsch's final destination, a part of Riverside Drive that housed wealthy "Professional Jews." A crucial early work about Jewish Americans and capitalism, Ornitz's novel is an enduring political work of art.

Further Reading
Japtok, Martin. "Socialism and Ethnic Solidarity: Samuel Ornitz's *Haunch Paunch and Jowl.*" *MELUS* 28.3 (Fall 1999): 21–37.

Rubin, Rachel. *Jewish Gangsters of Modern Literature.* Urbana and Chicago: U of Illinois P, 2000.

Danielle Angie

ORTIZ, SIMON J. (1941–)   Acoma Pueblo poet, fiction writer, essayist, and storyteller. One of the preeminent figures in contemporary Native American literature, Simon J. Ortiz's vast body of work offers consistent testimony to the continuing presence of indigenous Americans in their ongoing struggles against centuries of colonial oppression. While Ortiz became recognized in the 1970s with the publication of his poetry collection titled *Going for the Rain* (1976), no single text marks Ortiz's influence in Native American literature. Rather, it is Ortiz's enduring commitment to writing as an act of decolonization and resistance over decades that has built his reputation as not only a powerful writer and speaker, but as an artist of integrity and heart.

Although Ortiz views himself as a storyteller in all of his literary productions, he is best known as a poet. Ortiz grew up in the small village of *Deetseyamah* (McCarty's) in Acoma Pueblo, New Mexico, and his poetry is firmly rooted in *nuu yuh Aacquemeh hano ka-dzeh-nih* ("the Acoma people's

Simon J. Ortiz. *AP/Wide World Photos.*

language"). While his poems address themes from Coyote (or **trickster**) mischief to working in New Mexican uranium mines, their syntax, structure, format, and repetitions emphasize *Aacquemeh* orality, often achieving the breath-paced quality of language chanted or sung. Like most Native writers, Ortiz struggles with the inherent contradiction of attempting to transmit his indigenous oral tradition in written form, a condition that distances language from the intimacy of its spoken and performed context. Especially in more recent works, such as *Out There Somewhere* (2002), Ortiz includes words, phrases, and entire poems in his *Aacquemeh* language. In doing so, Ortiz simultaneously foregrounds the continuing presence of this precolonial language and demonstrates the Acoma people's abiding resistance to colonial attempts to eradicate the language that forms the very basis of their culture and worldview. In *Aacquemeh* language, Ortiz finds a palpable quality arising from the contours and textures of his homeland and community, in contrast to the abstractions of European languages such as English or Spanish, which easily migrate because they are not rooted in specific sacred geographies. Still, Ortiz believes that all languages possess spiritual energy and life force, a world-making power that demands of writers and speakers great responsibility because words carry with them tangible social and political consequences.

Of Ortiz's many collections of poetry, his own favorite volume is *from Sand Creek* (1981), which won a Pushcart Prize. Both autobiographical and historical, *from Sand Creek* is Ortiz's poetic manifesto bearing witness to the brutality of United States imperialist policies that frame war as righteous at the expense of innocent people slaughtered and also the veterans who return damaged and disenfranchised after fighting for their country. The Veteran's Administration (VA) Hospital in Fort Lyons, Colorado, is the setting of *from Sand Creek*. Fort Lyons was also the military headquarters for the U.S. troops who, along with seven hundred Colorado Volunteers under the command of reverend Colonel John W. Chivington, massacred and mutilated one-hundred five Cheyenne and Arapaho women and children and twenty-eight men (in an encampment of about six hundred people) on November 29, 1864. The Cheyenne leader Black Kettle had been promised peaceful habitation for his people at this site by the U.S. government, and was flying a flag of peace presented by President Lincoln when the massacre took place. In this forty-five-poem cycle—with one or two brief declarative sentences preceding each untitled poem on the facing page—the VA Hospital becomes the zone in which Ortiz reveals the intimate histories of wounded veterans. These histories include his own, as Ortiz was a patient in the Fort Lyons VA Hospital between 1974 and 1975, where he was treated for alcoholism. In *from Sand Creek,* Ortiz considers his position as a Native, an American, and a veteran within complex cycles of American imperialism against Native peoples, whether on domestic or foreign soil. He explores the layers of innocence, ignorance, and complicity that allow such assaults against human life and dignity to continue, and frames a vision for the future in which love, compassion, historical consciousness, and cross-cultural understanding replace exploitation, hatred, and destruction.

Just as Ortiz's *Aacquemeh* oral tradition finds expression through poetic form, so does the process of oral narrative lend itself to Ortiz's short fiction. *Men on the Moon* (1999) collects the nineteen short stories originally published as *Fightin'* (1983), plus seven additional stories (most published first in the anthology *The Man to Send Rain Clouds* [1974], edited by Kenneth Rosen, and in Ortiz's 1978 collection, *Howbah Indians*). Ortiz has made minor revisions to a few of the stories in *Men on the Moon,* just as a traditional Native storyteller incorporates slight changes in the telling of her or his stories over time. The landscapes of Ortiz's stories include the familiar terrain of his southwest *Aacquemeh* homeland, a lonely migrant work camp in rural Idaho ("Woman Singing"), and the urban strangeness of the streets of San Francisco, where earnest white hippies play at being "real Indians" ("The San Francisco Indians"). Ortiz's direct language and quiet tone amplify the themes of his more political stories involving the abuse of power by colonial authority against Native peoples, such as an incident with a racist policeman ("The Killing of a State Cop") or a young Pueblo man's flight from federal Indian boarding school ("Pennstuwehniyaahtse: Quuti's Story"). Other stories register powerfully in more intimate contexts, as when a Laguna Pueblo couple helps their white Oklahoma neighbors mourn the death of a younger brother, who stepped on an American mine in Vietnam, by giving the Okie couple an ear of white corn and a ceremonial corn husk bundle in traditional Laguna fashion ("To Change Life in a Good Way"). These stories illustrate the small details of life within its epic sweep through human relationships and attempts at understanding, some of which succeed, some of which fail, and many of which remain unresolved and under negotiation. Ortiz has stated that from earliest memory he has always existed inside language, and that language has always existed in the form of stories. In a different manner than his poems, Ortiz's short fiction cultivates a similar narrative intimacy between reader and author that both reveals the values that shape Ortiz's **identity**, and allows readers to be moved.

In addition to his many collections of poetry and short stories, Ortiz has written three children's books and has edited a number of important Native American literary anthologies, including *Earth Power Coming* (1983) and *Speaking for the Generations* (1998). The influence of Ortiz's literary production in subverting mainstream stereotypes of Indians and promoting literature as an act of Native self-determination, resistance against colonialism, and an assertion of cultural and political sovereignty has inspired his own and future generations of Native writers, as well as a wide non-Native literary public. When Ortiz began to write, he knew of few Native American writers, so his curiosity and love of words led him to read everything from Emily Dickinson to the Beat poets. Yet, it is the role of language in oral narrative, song, prayer, and other speech acts within his *Aacquemeh* culture that has laid the enduring foundation for Ortiz's writing. (*See also* Colonialism and U.S. Ethnic Literatures, Native American Poetry)

Further Reading

Wiget, Andrew. *Simon Ortiz*. Boise, ID: Boise State UP. 1986.

Wilson, Norma. "Language as a Way of Life: The Poetry of Simon J. Ortiz." *The Nature of Native American Poetry*. Albuquerque: U of New Mexico P, 2001. 45–64.

Jane Haladay

ORTIZ COFER, JUDITH (1952–)   Puerto Rican–born poet and novelist, raised in the United States. Ortiz Cofer is one of the most versatile writers in the United States and has established herself as a very popular and innovative author. Her work often uses code-switching, alternating between Spanish and English and mixing the two, as a way of reinforcing her Puerto Rican and American heritage and adding artistic value to her writing.

Of all the novels and poetry collections Ortiz Cofer has written, her autobiographical work, *Silent Dancing: A Partial Remembrance of My Puerto Rican Childhood* (1990), best showcases her talents. Written as a series of creative nonfiction essays followed by poems that add commentary at the end of each chapter, *Silent Dancing* presents the story of a young Ortiz Cofer and her family's migration from Puerto Rico to the U.S., namely to Paterson, New Jersey. Her father, who enlisted in the Navy, brought his family to the mainland and struggled against all odds to achieve a better life. Once here, he was immediately made aware of the prejudice he would face, especially among landlords who preferred not to rent to Puerto Rican families and who were used to having Jewish tenants. Still, he strongly believed that the United States was the best place for his family, so he did as much as possible to keep them from being dragged down by the daily grind of living in tenement housing. During the times that her father had to be away for extended periods of time, Ortiz Cofer and her family would return to Puerto Rico, and this, in turn, kept her ties to the island strong. At the same time, this pattern of shifting between two cultures made it more challenging for her to grow up without much cultural conflict. In this way, *Silent Dancing* provides a collage of stories and poems that focus on the many facets of immigrant life that so many Puerto Ricans experience. For example, it details the bicultural, bilingual worlds of Puerto Ricans who, at times, are made to feel like they have no home.

A common theme in Ortiz Cofer's writing is the role of women in Latino/ Puerto Rican worlds. Although Ortiz Cofer has claimed that her own grandmother, who had progressively nontraditional views, would have laughed at the idea that she was a feminist, there is no doubt that Ortiz Cofer's work demonstrates a deep awareness and understanding of the challenges that Latinas face in predominantly patriarchal societies. In fact, she has dedicated a significant number of works to this issue; *Woman in Front of the Sun: On Becoming a Writer* (2000), *Sleeping with One Eye Open: Women Writers and the Art of Survival* (1999), *The Line of the Sun* (1989), and *The Year of Our Revolution: New and Selected Stories and Poems* (1998) all concern themselves with women's roles in such spheres as the family, the workplace, relationships, politics, and even literature.

As someone who takes very seriously the importance of story-telling traditions, Ortiz Cofer demonstrates through her writing that women have played a pivotal role in Puerto Rican culture, in keeping that tradition alive. Her works detail how stories about mythical figures, told to young girls, have the effect of serving as warnings to them about how to behave ladylike. Her female characters are strong, often in control of relationships even when the male head of the household earns the wages. One of her most widely acclaimed novels, *The Line of the Sun* (1991), which was nominated for the Pulitzer Prize, looks closely at women who find that their fight for equality can succeed only if it is to be supported by a network of women. Just as she does in other works, Ortiz Cofer draws on the spiritual traditions of the Caribbean with characters who perform Santeria. No doubt inspired by her own upbringing, the novel depicts a young woman who grows up living in Paterson and Puerto Rico. Ortiz Cofer grew up surrounded by relatives and family friends who believed in the supernatural—her grandfather claimed to communicate with spirits. Quite often in her stories, however, females are the ones who are most affected by spiritual and religious practices.

Ortiz Cofer's poetry switches between English and Spanish, in part because so much of her poems center on life in a bicultural, bilingual world. A frequently anthologized poet, Ortiz Cofer weaves Spanish words, expressions, and names in her poems as a way to capture artistic truth. It is not uncommon for her poems to be written almost entirely in English, with the exception of one or two words that stand out and provide important meaning and significance. The poem, "Fulana," for instance, contains only one word in Spanish—the title's namesake. A word that means a female "so and so," *fulana* loses its true connotation in English. Hence, in such a case, and in similar other occasions, Ortiz Cofer's use of Spanish is not only warranted but crucial toward developing a poem that captures the emotions in an experience that takes place in more than simply a monolithic world, but in a world full of bicultural encounters. Such use of Spanish distinguishes her from other Latino poets, many of whom use Spanish as a reflection of dialects and speech patterns that are found in many Latino households. These poets' use of Spanish is much more prevalent, and, to a certain degree, can be said to address bilingual readers. As a result, Ortiz Cofer's writing has been praised by many mainstream critics.

Ortiz Cofer has earned many accolades and awards for her work. She has been the recipient of fellowships from the National Endowment for the Arts and the Witter Bynner Foundation, and has received such awards as Best Book of the Year from the American Library Association, for *An Island Like You: Stories from the Barrio* (1998), a Paterson Book Prize, the O. Henry Prize for Short Story, the Pushcart Prize, and the first Pura Belpre Medal. Her work has appeared in such prominent publications as *Best American Essays 1991, The Norton Book of Women's Lives,* and the *O. Henry Prize Stories.* She has been a featured speaker in conferences, literary festivals, and symposia throughout the United States and is currently a professor of English and creative writing at the University of Georgia. (*See also* Puerto Rican American Poetry, Bilingualism)

Further Reading

Acosta-Belen, Edna. "A *MELUS* Interview: Judith Ortiz Cofer." *MELUS* 18.3 (Fall 1993): 83–97.

Davis, Rocio G. "Metanarrative in Ethnic Autobiography for Children: Laurence Yep's *The Lost Garden* and Judith Ortiz Cofer's *Silent Dancing." MELUS* 27.2 (Summer 2002): 139–58.

Faymonville, Carmer. "New Transnational Identities in Judith Ortiz Cofer's Autobiographical Fiction." *MELUS* 26.2 (Summer 2001): 129–57.

Ocasio, Rafael. "Puerto Rican Literature in Georgia?: An Interview with Judith Ortiz Cofer." *Kenyon Review* 14.4 (Fall 1992): 43–51.

Rangil, Viviana. "Pro-Claiming a Space: The Poetry of Sandra Cisneros and Judith Ortiz Cofer." *Multicultural Review* 9.3 (September 2000): 48–51, 54–55.

Jose B. Gonzalez

ORTIZ TAYLOR, SHEILA (1939–) Chicana novelist, poet, teacher, and scholar. Born in Los Angeles, Sheila Ortiz Taylor completed her doctoral studies at the University of California at Los Angeles in 1972 and later relocated to Florida, where she currently works as a professor of English at Florida State University. She is the author of the novels *Faultline* (1982), *Spring Forward/Fall Back* (1985), *Southbound* (1990), and *Coachella* (1998); a poetry collection, *Slow Dancing at Miss Polly's* (1989); and a volume of autobiography with illustrations by her sister Sandra, *Imaginary Parents* (1996).

Ortiz Taylor's novels confirm that she is one of the finest comic writers in Chicana/o literature, a field whose boundaries she has also constantly challenged. Indeed, beginning with *Faultline,* which has the distinction of being the first "lesbian" novel by a Chicana, Ortiz Taylor has played a pivotal role in the establishment and development of queer Chicana writing. Her novels form a body of work that accepts as axiomatic the slippery, unpredictable and mutually transformative nature of identificatory processes and social relations. By exploring the complex lives of lesbians who shift between distinct identity options with ease and without compunction, Ortiz Taylor is able to provide subtle, complex, and often hilarious critiques of conventional understandings of motherhood, marriage, family structures, race relations, and purportedly secure sexualities, genders, and ethnicities. *Faultline*, and its sequel *Southbound*, for example, focuses on the chaotic travails faced by Arden Benbow as she attempts to win a costly custody battle, dodge snooping social workers, relocate from Los Angeles to Florida, foil her father-in-law's smuggling operation, and construct an alternative "queer" family comprising her six children, her lover Alice, a black drag-queen nanny, and three hundred voracious pet rabbits.

Despite the uniqueness of her writerly voice, Ortiz Taylor has had a troubled reputation in the field of Chicana/o literature. This status may reflect her literary emphasis on lesbian relations, her challenge to rigidly structured and conceived identity categories, and the elusive or absent Chicana presence in her fiction. As the few critical treatments of her work argue, her early novels, in particular, have been regarded in Chicana/o studies as unconcerned with Chicana/o identificatory terrains and, thus, as falling somehow outside the Chicana/o literary **canon**. While such readings have been contradicted by the novel *Coachella*, and the memoir *Imaginary Parents*, both of which explicitly foreground Chicanoness, the critical neglect of Ortiz Taylor suggests that her writing continues to present classificatory challenges to the ethnic parameters of Chicana/o fiction. (*See also* Mexican American Lesbian Literature)

Further Reading

Bruce-Novoa, Juan. "Homosexuality and the Chicano Novel." *Confluencia* 2.1 (Fall 1986): 69–77.

———. "Sheila Ortiz Taylor's *Faultline*: A Third-Woman Utopia." *Confluencia* 6.2 (Spring 1991): 75–87.

Christian, Karen. "Sheila Ortiz Taylor." *Latin American Writers on Gay and Lesbian Themes: A Bio-Critical Sourcebook.* Ed. David William Foster. Westport, CT: Greenwood Press, 1994. 300–304.

———. *Show and Tell: Identity as Performance in U.S. Latina/o Fiction.* Albuquerque: U of New Mexico P, 1997.

———. "Will the 'Real Chicano' Please Stand Up? The Challenge of John Rechy and Sheila Ortiz Taylor to Chicano Essentialism." *Americas Review* 20.2 (1992): 89–104.

Paul Allatson

OSBEY, BRENDA MARIE (1957–)   African American poet. Brenda Marie Osbey is a New Orleans native. Her poetry reflects the tension between her city's competing European and Afro-Caribbean cultures. Unlike previous generations of New Orleans writers, Osbey illustrates cultural contact and hyphenated **identity** through formal innovations that privilege afro-francophone aesthetics. Critics see Osbey's poetry as an occasion to discuss the presence of the past in contemporary black art, especially that presence which highlights the legacies of **slavery**, non-Western forms of divination, and hybridity. They cast Osbey as a weaver of psyche and setting, a poet through whom New Orleans becomes maternal and strong, but (like a coastal city below sea level) in a perpetual state of danger.

Her poems are usually localized to the Faubourg Tremé, a neighborhood that includes the historic site of Congo Square—an antebellum lodestone of African cultural survival and renewal. Her long poetic sequences, specifically the book-length poem *Desperate Circumstance, Dangerous Woman* (1991), assume a narrative form that combines multiple voices with call-and-response structures, nursery rhymes, ring games, and references to voodoo ceremonies. *Desperate Circumstance* reminds one critic of poet Robert Hayden's long poem "The Middle Passage" (1962) in its ensemble of voices and cultural traditions. New Orleans folk legends become, in Osbey's poetry, living symptoms of larger acts of cultural violence. Osbey traces these acts not only through official contact zones (like the **Middle Passage** or Congo Square), but also through family relationships. For instance, the title poem of Osbey's first book, *Ceremony for Minneconjoux* (1983), tells the story of an adolescent girl who was conceived in a reluctant moment of sexual contact between people of different marginalized groups. Through the alternating voices of grandmother, mother, and daughter (the title character), Minneconjoux becomes an assemblage of memories about her own conception blended with "life lessons" handed down from women for whom sex has been a plague. The poem is punctuated by points of contact between "creole" and "indian" blood that likewise conflate sexual and familial narratives. Her most recent book, *All Saints: New and Selected Poems* (1997), which received the American Book Award, demonstrates Osbey's position as an "insider" of clandestine religious and cultural communities. Yet she never translates her "exotic" cultural knowledge strictly into an entertainment enterprise.

Unlike her nineteenth-century "local color" predecessors, Osbey does not write in Creole patois, since such a technique represents an ethnically deformed version of official language and culture. However, on the strength of a recent Camargo Fellowship (2004), Osbey is writing an Afro-francophone volume of poems (the first to be written by a New Orleanian since 1845). Tentatively titled *Canne à Sucre*, this volume will be a collection of original poems in French, Creole, and English translation. Not only a work of poetry, the volume will be the fruition of Osbey's nearly two decades of research on the history of free blacks in New Orleans.

Further Reading

Bryan, Violet Harrington. *The Myth of New Orleans in Literature: Dialogues of Race and Gender.* Knoxville: U of Tennessee P, 1993.

Lowe, John. "An Interview with Brenda Marie Osbey." *Southern Review* 30.4 (1994): 812–23.

Jason Arthur

OSTRIKER, ALICIA (1937–)   Jewish American poet, literary critic, and editor. Swimming against the tide of traditional academic concerns, much of Ostriker's writing focuses on women's complimentary and conflicting roles in the personal and professional spheres: the nursery and the boardroom. It was exceptional to write about motherhood when Ostriker began her career, although it is commonplace now. With eight books of poetry and several major critical studies, including the controversial 1986 book *Stealing the Language: The Emergence of Women's Poetry in America*, to her credit, Ostriker is ranked as one of the leading poet-critics in America today. Ostriker is also a full-time academic, a professor at Rutgers University in New Jersey, where she has taught since 1965.

Ostriker's concern with motherhood as an act of love is central to her verse. In an interview in *Belles Lettres*, Ostriker said, "My guess is that the experience of maternity saturates every single thing I do. Maternity augments one's vision, one's sense of reality, one's sense of self. I believe that I'm maternally motivated toward the world and not just toward my children. Certainly I'm maternally motivated toward my students, who are a big part of my life. But in addition, my views of art, history, politics, all sorts of issues are in part determined by that double experience that motherhood brings of idealism and practicality. Children represent at once infinite hope and stony intractability—and the world is like that, too" (Rosenberg 27). The poems in *Once More Out of the Darkness, and Other Poems* (1971) and *A Dream of Springtime* (1979) give a universality to the events that Ostriker was experiencing: pregnancy, childbirth, family relationships, and professional development. The nontraditional poems in *The Mother/Child Papers* (1980) again give a universality to personal events: in this instance, the joy of giving birth juxtaposed to a mother's horror of the violence of war. Indeed, Ostriker's lack of separation between herself and the world is one of her greatest strengths as a poet, awakening the reader's own shock of recognition.

By 1982, when *A Woman Under the Surface: Poems and Prose Poems* debuted, Ostriker included overtly feminist themes, alluded to poems by other female writers, and reworked myths about women. Four years later, in *The Imaginary Lover*, Ostriker again focused on feminist concerns, calling forth comparisons to her contemporary **Adrienne Rich** and their forerunner H. D. [Hilda Doolittle]. In "Surviving," for instance, Ostriker focuses on her mother, a symbol for all female artists who were unable to reach their potential. *The Crack in Everything* (1996) once more merges the poet's own experience with universal female concerns, as some of the poems movingly describe Ostriker's fight against breast cancer. In "Mastectomy," Ostriker triumphs over despair with her characteristic sly wit.

Ostriker is equally well regarded for her feminist literary criticism. *Writing Like a Woman* (1983) traces the unfolding of feminist writing though the works of the "Confessional" poets Anne Sexton and Sylvia Plath and the feminist poet Adrienne Rich. In *Stealing the Language: The Emergence of Women's Poetry in America* (1986), Ostriker compares and contrasts the poetic styles of male and female writers to prove her thesis: poetic styles emerge from experience particular to each gender. This work sparked fiery controversy, with some critics taking Ostriker to task for not including less traditional poets, while others praised her insights and achievement in breaking new ground.

Ostriker is also deeply concerned with her heritage as a Jew. This is especially evident in the poems in *Green Age,* in which Ostriker rails against the restrictions imposed on Jewish women in Judaism due to its patriarchal emphasis. For instance, in "A Meditation in Seven Days," she enters where only men are welcome. In "The Book of Life" from the same collection, Ostriker reflects on the strength she draws from her religious roots, notably the support of female creators.

Ostriker's two landmark revisionist critical studies on the Bible, *Feminist Revision and the Bible* (1992) and *The Nakedness of the Fathers: Biblical Visions and Revisions* (1994) are especially well regarded.

In addition to her frank feminist themes and deep concern with her religious heritage, Ostriker's poetry is visionary in the tradition of the eighteenth-century British poet William Blake. Like Blake, Ostriker showed early talent in both poetry and art. Ostriker first intended to become an artist, but she decided instead to concentrate on literature and earned her BA in English from Brandeis University in 1959. Ostriker used Blake as the subject of her PhD dissertation at the University of Wisconsin in 1964. That study, *Vision and Verse in William Blake,* became her first published work the following year. Ostriker's interest in Blake has continued: In 1977, she edited a volume of his complete poetry. "One reason I worked on Blake," she noted in an interview, "is that his writing is so revolutionary. He was a proto-feminist; he explores the meaning of maternity and paternity in our culture more deeply than any previous poet; and he writes about the experience and the significance of sexuality more interestingly and more powerfully than any poet before D. H. Lawrence." (Rosenberg 26). As with Blake, Ostriker's vision of how the world might be is rooted in the reality of how the world really is. Her verse seeks to cure the world's wrongs through the power of our imagination, mercy, and love.

The narrator in "The Class" from *The Crack in Everything* says that her role is to give her students authorization to express their feelings in their writing. This is certainly true of her own writing as well. For her mastery of styles, voices, and forms in poetry, trenchant feminist literary criticism, deep humanity, and accessibility, Alicia Ostriker is rightly classified as one of the preeminent Jewish American poets, scholars, and literary critics of our age. (*See also* Feminism, Jewish American Poetry)

Further Reading

George, Diana Hume. "Repairing the World." *Women's Review of Books* XVI.3 (1998): 10–11.

Rosenberg, Judith Pierce. "Interview with Alicia Ostriker." *Belles Lettres* 3 (1993): 26–9.

Laurie Rozakis

OWENS, LOUIS (1948–2003)   Native American novelist, critic, and educator. Born of mixed Choctaw, Cherokee, and Irish heritage, Owens's work centers on the issues and possibilities within mixed-blood **identity**. A prolific writer, Owens published five novels, two critical studies of John Steinbeck, short stories, and multiple essays before his death in 2003. His acclaimed *Other Destinies: Understanding the American Indian Novel* (1992) is viewed as one of the foremost critical studies of Native American literature.

In *Other Destinies*, Owens investigates the projects of the Native American novel and its writers to redefine the identity of Natives in the twenty-first century. He posits that Native writers navigate between false conceptions of "Indians" in order to form for themselves and their readers an identity. This process also relies heavily upon community (re)formation as well as rejection of mainstream America's continual mission of forced **assimilation**.

Similarly, in his novels and especially in his essay collection *Mixedblood Messages: Literature, Film, Family, Place* (1998), Owens deals extensively with the issues of identity that arise from mixed heritage. Also in *Mixedblood*, Owens investigates stereotypical representations of Native Americans through popular cinema. The remaining essays deal with Native environmental concerns as related to traditional native beliefs, as well as several autobiographical essays that touch upon the real in his fiction.

Owens's first novel, *Wolfsong* (1991), follows Tom Joseph's evolution from a college student to a defender of the environment, following in his uncle's footsteps. Throughout the novel, the author sets figures largely as a protagonist, highlighting the inextricable nature of place and identity. Owens's project of correcting "Indian" myths remains present also in this book.

Both *The Sharpest Sight* (1992) and *Bone Games* (1994) follow Cole McCurtain and his family. *The Sharpest Sight* falls into the genre of murder mystery, which serves to underscore Cole's quest for self. Through the course of the novel, Cole returns to his Choctaw roots, which allows him both to locate his identity and solve the mystery. *Bone Games* follows Cole to Santa Cruz as a professor of Native American literature. Santa Cruz surrounds Cole with violence, both spiritual and physical. To fend off the evil, Cole must enjoin the help of his family and friends, who constitute community and redefine Cole's identity.

In the above novels, as well as his last two, *Nightland* (1996) and *Dark River* (1999), Owens explores again and again the question of identity for Native Americans. Through layered plots and attention to event time and sequence, Owens reveals the dependence of present on past, accentuating the importance of discovering and embracing the true past, no matter how painful. Throughout his prose, Owens demands that Natives be allowed to author their own identities, pasts, and futures. (*See also* Native American Novel)

Further Reading

LaLonde, Chris. *Grave Concerns, Trickster Turns: The Novels of Louis Owens.* Norman: U of Oklahoma P, 2002.

———, guest ed. *Studies in American Indian Literature.* 10.2 (1998) [Special Issue on Louis Owens].

Anastasia D. Wright

OZICK, CYNTHIA (1928–)   Jewish American essayist and fiction writer. Cynthia Ozick has written substantially on the relationship of humanity and the art it creates. Her other major themes are the dichotomous nature of a person bound by Jewish tradition in a profoundly Greco-Roman society, such as modern America; and the ambivalence in an identity that is both intellectual and female. She discusses these themes in both her essays and fiction. Her essays also comment on other writers' conflicts between humanity and art, as well as the expectations of women in literature, the reclamation of both Jewish and women writers, and the need for English writers to further accept Jewish language and philosophy in their writings.

Ozick's first major publication is the novel *Trust.* Written over the course of six years and finally published in 1966, the novel presents many of Ozick's lifelong themes. In an attempt to pay homage to the early twentieth-century writers she read while working in her parents' drugstore, such as Henry James and T. S. Eliot, she echoes their writing styles. In *Trust,* Ozick's anonymous protagonist attempts to discover her personal and psychological **identity**. The novel is accepted for publication the same year Ozick's first child is born, and Ozick nurtures both the novel and the infant at the same time. This complex novel receives very little acclaim, thus Ozick dedicates herself to her short fictions, novellas, and essays. Many of these pieces are first published by *The New Yorker.* However, her essays are in published collections throughout the last quarter of the twentieth century.

The Pagan Rabbi and Other Stories (1971) contains three of her most important pieces. "The Pagan Rabbi" records the tragedy of a rabbi lulled from the study of the holy books in Jewish culture by his fascination with nature's sexual energy as he is seduced by nymphs. The rabbi's wife destroys the journal that catalogues her husband's descent from being the interpreter of the *Torah* to a pagan nature lover in order to protect her family from the inevitable scandal, and her people from the taint of animism. "Envy; or, Yiddish in America" chronicles a Jewish scholar looking for a

Yiddish translator. He finds one, a young woman who is too modern and American to want to resurrect yet another suffering Jewish poet from pre-Nazi Europe. "Virility" discusses the nature of sexism in literary criticism when a man steals his aunt's poetry to publish. The critics hail the works as great masculine poetry. Once the deception is revealed, critics who review the poetry describe it as girlish in its tone and quality.

In 1976, her second collection of novellas, *Bloodshed and Other Stories*, was published. The major story of this collection, "Usurpation (Other People's Stories)," deals with the conflicts of a writer whose religious background warns against creating idols and the idolatry of creating fictional gods in one's storytelling.

In *Levitation: Five Fictions* (1982), Ozick's most memorable character, Ruth Puttermesser, first appears. Despite the magical overtones in Puttermesser's life, Ozick's life is closely mirrored in this character. Puttermesser is the character Ozick returns to approximately every ten years for which to write a new story. Both Ozick and Puttermesser have uncles whose existence encouraged their intellectual pursuits. Ozick's uncle Abraham Regelson is a Hebrew poet, and Ozick composed poetry in his honor. Puttermesser's uncle Zindel teaches his niece Hebrew language and law, as well as telling her that being named after a butter knife is really a name of honor. A butter knife only cuts butter to feed people and never kills. Later in "Puttermesser: Her Work History, Her Ancestry and Her Afterlife," the text reveals that a reader cannot trust the author in this case; Uncle Zindel died years before Puttermesser was born. Uncle Zindel's inclusion reminds readers that Jewish Americans must have a link to their past, even if the link is imaginary.

The second Puttermesser story in this anthology is "Puttermesser and Xanthippe." Puttermesser is now a New York City bureaucrat, who is trapped in the political chaos of nepotism and corruption. After she is fired from her job, she unconsciously creates a golem. In European Jewish folklore the golem is a synthetic human created from clay. When the Jewish community has been in danger, the learned members of the community create the golem. Once Puttermesser brings the creature to life, she names it Leah. However, the creature wants to be called Xanthippe, after Socrates's wife. The golem pronounces that she will be a critic to all philosophers. Together Puttermesser and Xanthippe overturn the political machine and create a paradisiacal version of New York. Puttermesser has created a plan to destroy the city politics and crime, and Xanthippe gathers the grassroots support among the various ethnic populations to elect a nonpartisan mayor, Puttermesser herself. The paradise is destroyed by Xanthippe's sexual appetites, and buried by Puttermesser's willingness to use nepotism and murder as political tools against her construct and daughter. Puttermesser will return in other stories over the years. The two Puttermesser stories in *Levitation and Other Stories* eventually will be collected in *The Puttermesser Papers* (1997). The other stories in *The Puttermesser Papers* are

"Puttermesser Paired," in which the protagonist marries a man who resembles George Eliot's lover, George Lewes; "Puttermesser and the Muscovite Cousin," deconstructs the image of the hapless and heroic Soviet Jew as Puttermesser meets her stylish Russian cousin who is business savvy. She has traveled to America in order to sell Lenin medals. The final story is "Puttermesser in Paradise," and the protagonist discovers that without life's challenges, knowledge and accomplishment are meaningless. These particular stories emphasize the ambivalence between a Jewish American's Jewish and Greco-Roman heritages, the need for art in human existence, and the fragility of human endeavors.

Ozick published two books in 1983. Besides *The Cannibal Galaxy* novel, her first collection of essays, *Art and Ardor,* was published by Knopf. *The Cannibal Galaxy* studies schoolmaster Joseph Brill's life as he loses his family to the Nazi deportation of French Jews to concentration camps, and copes by obsessing over an obscure writer. As he becomes the schoolmaster of a school designed to fuse Aristotle's teachings with Jewish tradition, he meets a mother of one of his students who attempts to teach him both the pedagogical theory that he lacks to create a fused curriculum, and that the Jewish tradition already has the logic he seeks, if only he can reclaim it for himself. The title is derived from the idea that the universe eats its extraordinary members, such as the Jewish legends of Jonah, who is swallowed by a whale, and Joseph, who is imprisoned by the Pharaoh.

Art and Ardor is Ozick's earliest essay collection, yet still is the most important in terms of her thoughts as a scholar, reader, and philosopher of English and American fiction. In this collection, she discusses Edith Wharton, Thomas Hardy, and Virginia Wolf, as well as argues against the biological determinism for women, and takes part in the feminist project of reclaiming lost texts by women when she discusses German-Jewish writer Gertrud Kolmar. However, her essays on fellow Jewish writers and their American subjects discuss the paradoxes of Jewish writers who use varieties of subjects to discuss the damaging boundaries created by the use of ethnic backgrounds. These writers include Truman Capote, **Isaac Bashevis Singer**, **Bernard Malamud**, Maurice Samuel, and **Harold Bloom**. The most important and often reprinted essay in this collection, "Toward a New Yiddish," demands a recreation of a Jewish language that transcends geographic and cultural boundaries. The original essay is written in 1970. However, as her 1983 preface points out, she believes that the international language is no longer needed. With some more introductions of Jewish concepts into English, that international language would serve as the literary tongue of the Jewish diaspora. One other intriguing essay is the review of the English translation of Bruno Schulz's work. Schulz was a Polish Jewish author who was assassinated in 1942. Her interest in Schulz's work, combined with a rumor that Schulz's missing manuscript of *Messiah* was discovered in Stockholm, inspires her to write her 1987 novel, *The Messiah of Stockholm.*

The *Messiah of Stockholm* addresses the themes of a person of Jewish descent needing Jewish heritage and the travails of a people who need to authenticate themselves through fakery and surrender of their ideals. The protagonist, Lars Andemening, is Bruno Schulz's child, and is not even born when his father dies. His review work at a Stockholm newspaper is underappreciated because he tends to review pieces that are philosophical. These concerns are guided by his understanding of his father's passions. Once he surrenders to the editor's demands of reviewing popular culture, he is accepted by the staff and the readership. After this **assimilation** of literary concerns, he is offered the chance to buy the missing *Messiah* manuscript from a forger and his daughter, who falsify the authentication of the manuscript and hope to use Lars to legitimize their scam. Lars, who has been passive throughout the book, becomes an agent in his own life and destroys their pretence. Then he starts talking to his coworkers and buys the essential tools of society, the telephone and the word processor, so that he can enter into the modern discussions.

In 1989 another collection of her essays, *Metaphor and Memory,* was published. Ozick continues her literary discussions about authors such as Henry James, **Saul Bellow** and Shalom Aleichem, and Shmuel Yosef Agnon, the winner of the 1966 Nobel Prize for Literature. In "Bialik's Hint," she returns to the idea of English as the "new Yiddish" and how the Jewish parables, or *midrashim,* could be an asset to English writings. She also criticizes the nature of creating literary ghettos for ethnic writers, since American society and the discussions of the eighteenth-century Enlightenment condone a dissemination of ideas across cultural boundaries.

Besides Puttermesser, "The Shawl" and "Rosa" from 1989 are Ozick's most anthologized fiction. "The Shawl" is the story about Rosa and her infant daughter in a World War II concentration camp. The infant survives starvation and discovery by sucking on the fringes of the shawl and remaining silent. When the infant is discovered and killed by the concentration camp guards, Rosa can only watch, or she will be killed as well. In "Rosa," the shawl still keeps the infant alive in her mother's life. Rosa, now retired to Florida in her sixties, sees her daughter as a grown woman, and uses her as an excuse not to enter into society. Once she meets a fellow Polish refugee at a Laundromat, her prejudices about the real refugee Jews are deconstructed. She realizes she must reenter society as it is, and recognizes that the shawl as a colorless rag that smells of saliva is only a reminder of her lost daughter. Ozick adapts "The Shawl" into a play called "Blue Light" in 1994, which is renamed "The Shawl" in its 1996 New York City debut.

Ozick continues to write essays, poems, and edit numerous collections, including *The Complete Works of Isaac Babel,* published in 2001. Her works appear in *The New Yorker, Partisan Review,* and other magazines. There is little doubt she will continue to be an important critical and fictional voice in the twenty-first century. (*See also* Jewish American Novel)

Further Reading

Bloom, Harold, ed. *Cynthia Ozick.* Modern Critical Views series. New York: Chelsea House Press, 1986.

Cohen, Sarah Blacher. *Cynthia Ozick's Comic Art: From Levity to Liturgy.* Bloomington: Indiana UP, 1994.

Friedman, Lawrence S. *Understanding Cynthia Ozick.* Understanding Contemporary American Literature series. Columbia: U of South Carolina P, 1991.

Kauvar, Elaine M. *Cynthia Ozick's Fiction: Tradition and Invention* Bloomington: Indiana UP, 1993.

Lowin, Joseph. *Cynthia Ozick.* Twayne's United States Author's series. Boston: G. K. Hall and Co., 1988.

Statlander, Jane. *Cultural Dialectic: Ludwing Lewisohn and Cynthia Ozick.* New York: Peter Lang, 2002.

Strandberg, Victor. *Greek Mind/Jewish Soul: The Conflicted Art of Cynthia Ozick.* Madison: U of Wisconsin P, 1994.

Amy Becker-Chambless

P

PAKISTANI AMERICAN LITERATURE.   *See* South Asian American Literature

PALEY, GRACE (1922–)   Jewish American short story writer, poet, activist. Grace Paley was born in the Bronx, New York, the third child of Manya and Isaac Gutseit (subsequently Americanized to Goodside). Her parents were Russian Jews who emigrated together from the Ukraine to the United States in 1906 at the age of twenty-one, having been previously exiled for radical activities by Czar Nicholas II (Isaak to Siberia, Manya to Germany), then released by the amnesty following the birth of the czar's son. Isaac's New World trajectory is echoed by one of Paley's fictional characters who, under "the protection" of the American flag "and working like a horse . . . [had] read Dickens, gone to medical school, and shot like a surface-to-air missile right into the middle class." Grace Goodside grew up in an extended family that included her grandmother and aunt, where Yiddish, Russian, and English were all spoken, providing a rich linguistic background that is often mentioned in discussions of her sensitivity to language and its varied inflections. She attended Hunter College and New York University (where she studied poetry with W. H. Auden) without taking a degree from either. In 1942 she married Jess Paley, with whom she had a daughter and a son. They separated in the late 1960s and divorced in 1972, the year that Grace Paley married Robert Nichols. Grace Paley taught for many years at Sarah Lawrence College and has also taught at Columbia and Syracuse University, City College of New York, and Dartmouth College.

Grace Paley's literary reputation is based primarily on her three volumes of short stories, *The Little Disturbances of Man* (1959), *Enormous Changes at the Last Minute* (1974), and *Later the Same Day* (1985), all subsequently published together as *Collected Stories* (1994). She has, however, written in a variety of literary forms, including poetry and personal and political essays. Indeed, she wrote poetry from childhood on, whereas she did not write her first short story until she was over thirty. Paley has sometimes characterized this shift by saying that in her poems, "it was really me speaking to the world," but in "writing stories, it was really me getting the world to speak to me." In moving away from her earlier poetry, where she was "stuck in [her] own voice" (Bach 76), to short stories in which she was able to hear and use other people's voices, Paley developed a narrative voice that is like no other. The "orality" of her language, her remarkable ear and ability to capture the cadences of actual speech (what she calls the language of home and street), has been repeatedly praised. At the same time, her language is marked by a poetic distillation and inventiveness that testifies to Paley's literary apprenticeship as a poet. Although rooted in familiar experiences of everyday life, her stories are characterized by abrupt leaps and unexpected foreshortenings and interpolations, sometimes incorporating metafictional and surrealistic elements as well. Moreover, her blend of humor, irony, and pathos is distinctively her own, even when the narration and dialogue are placed in the mouths of a range of different characters. Most of her stories concern the adult children of middle and Eastern European Jewish immigrants, but she also uses a variety of other urban American voices—Irish American, Italian American, Hispanic American, and African American. Taken together the stories create a vibrant, complex community—its neighborhood streets, parks, schools, and kitchens; the same characters often reappear from story to story, thereby thickening the texture of their imagined experience. Paley, who does not like the word *ethnic,* describes herself as "a regional writer . . . an urban writer with a New York focus" (Bach 11).

The title of Paley's first collection of stories, *The Little Disturbances of Man: Stories of Women and Men at Love,* indicates her modest claim for these short stories about private lives (hers was the World War II generation whose male writers wrote big war novels), while the subtitle subverts its apparent acceptance of the generic "Man" to encompass both genders; it was tellingly (if unintentionally) altered to *Stories of Men and Women in Love* by the publisher who reprinted the collection, thus inverting the order of the genders and erasing the original subtitle's playful suggestion of the combative nature of amorous relations between the sexes. (The subtitle is dropped entirely in the *Collected Stories.*) Although some stories in all three collections have male narrators or are told from a male point of view, Paley's interest in the experiences of women has always predominated. Indeed, in her second and third collections, relations between women and children and friendships among women displace her earlier focus on relations between women and men. Over time Paley has become more assertive about the importance of private life, repeating in interviews that although she didn't realize it when she began to write about the everyday lives of women and men, she has since come to recognize that this was actually a very political task. And while her stories continue to foreground private relations, they are set with increasing specificity within a wider political context, in which characters have political as well as personal lives. With Paley's development, too, the balance between humor and pathos has shifted. Tragedy has never been absent from Paley's world, but in her earlier stories the dominant key was upbeat, whereas in the later stories the canvas has darkened; as Paley's characters have aged, their children have met with assorted disasters and the world has grown increasingly scary. Still, though qualified by her characters' sadder experiences, Paley's later stories retain her characteristic buoyancy, humor, and irony, along with her humanity and commitment to personal possibility.

Paley has also continued to write poetry. Indeed, since shifting her center of gravity from New York City to Vermont in the 1980s, it has become her favored form. Giving a reading in a local church in August 2003, she suggested that her move to Vermont was responsible for this return to poetry, since, living away from New York, she felt she "no longer had the lingo" necessary for story writing. Yet if her prose is conditioned by long years of writing poetry, the published poetry of her later years (*Leaning Forward* [1985], *New and Collected Poems* [1992], and *Begin Again: Collected Poems* [2000]), with its apparently "natural" rather than "literary" language, suggests, in turn, its indebtedness to linguistic skills developed through writing stories about daily life. Paley herself has repeatedly said that writing short stories is much closer to writing poetry than it is to writing novels.

In addition her literary output, Paley has been a tireless activist on behalf of both community and global issues, identifying herself as "a combative pacifist and cooperative anarchist." During the Vietnam War she was a founder of the Greenwich Village Peace Center and was active in the War Resisters League, being jailed briefly several times. She visited North Vietnam in 1969 as a member of a peace mission that brought back three American prisoners of war and in 1973 was a delegate to the World Peace Congress in Moscow, representing the War Resisters League. She has opposed U.S. support for repressive regimes in Latin America and been involved in a variety of actions on behalf of the feminist and antinuclear movements. She has also traveled to China, Nicaragua, and San Salvador. Paley's extensive political engagement is reflected in her collections of political essays and poems, the 1989 *Peace Calendar: 365 Reasons Not to Have Another War* and *Long Walks and Intimate Talks* (1991), and in her political, literary, and autobiographical essays and poems collected in the volume *Just as I Thought* (1998).

Although Paley is sometimes referred to as a "writer's writer," she is also much in demand for her public readings and ability to connect with her audience. Her literary achievement has been acknowledged by numerous awards: a Guggenheim Fellowship in 1961, a grant from the National Endowment for the Arts in 1966, and an award from the National Institute of Arts and Letters for short story writing in 1970. In 1980 she was elected to the National Academy of Arts and Letters, and in 1985 awarded a PEN/Faulkner Prize for fiction. In 1987 she was awarded the Senior Fellowship of the Literature Program of the National Endowment for the Arts, designed to honor those who have "expanded the boundaries of this nation's literary heritage." Befitting her **identity** as both a native New Yorker and an adoptive Vermonter, Paley received the first New York State Edith Wharton Citation of Merit in 1986 (becoming the first State Author of New York) and in 2003 she was named to a four-year term as Vermont's State Poet.

Further Reading

Aarons, Victoria. "Margins of Hope: Grace Paley's Language of Memory." *A Measure of Memory: Storytelling and Identity in American Jewish Fiction.* Athens: U of Georgia P, 1996. 123–70.

Arcana, Judith. *Grace Paley's Life Stories: A Literary Biography.* Urbana: U of Illinois P, 1993.

Bach, Gerhard, and Blaine Hall, eds. *Conversations with Grace Paley.* Jackson: UP of Mississippi, 1997.

Heller, Deborah. "The Work of Faith in the Stories of Grace Paley." *Literary Sisterhoods: Imagining Women Artists.* Montreal: McGill-Queens UP, 2005. 89–147.

Isaacs, Neil D. *Grace Paley: A Study of the Short Fiction.* Boston: G. K. Hall & Co., 1990.

Taylor, Jacqueline. *Grace Paley: Illuminating the Dark Lives.* Austin: U of Texas P, 1990.

Deborah Heller

PAN-AFRICANISM   An umbrella term for a variety of movements and ideas, Pan-Africanism advocates political and cultural unity of Africans and people of African descent throughout the **diaspora**. Since at least the early nineteenth century, various thinkers have articulated a shared set of Pan-African ideas and assumptions: Africa as homeland or mother figure with a glorious past; independence and self-governance for and solidarity between peoples of African descent; the existence of a distinct African personality and culture in which Africans and their descendents should take pride; and hope for a future united Africa. Politically, Pan-African ideas were profoundly influential on anticolonial and postcolonial nationalists like Kwame Nkrumah of Ghana, Julius Nyerere of Tanzania, Léopold Senghor of Senegal, and Jomo Kenyatta of Kenya. Such ideas also provided the ideological foundation for political entities such as the Organization of African Unity and the African Union, for black nationalist groups from the Black Panther Party to the Nation of Islam, and for ill-fated efforts to establish a federation of West Indian states. Culturally and aesthetically, Pan-

Africanism's influence was felt in virtually every black cultural and literary movement of the twentieth century, from the **Harlem Renaissance** to **Negritude** poetry to Rastafarianism to the **Black Arts Movement**.

Arguably the earliest articulations of Pan-African ideas arose in the context of the "Back to Africa" movement that proposed **immigration** of free black Americans to West Africa in the nineteenth century. One of the earliest such projects was sponsored by the American Colonization Society (ACS), founded in 1816 by an unlikely alliance of slaveholders and **abolition**ists to settle free American blacks in Liberia. Despite the ACS's explicitly racist rhetoric and despite the failure of the initial experiments in emigration due to disease and poor planning, the ACS colonization project marked the beginning of a number of waves of immigration to West Africa. By the late nineteenth and early twentieth centuries, the arguments for the African American colonization of West Africa—including those offered by Bishop Turner, Alfred Charles "Chief" Sam, Martin Delany, and Henry McNeal Turner—had cohered into a cogent assertion of blacks' capacity for and rights to self-governance.

The pro-emigrationists found ideological allies in a number of other black intellectuals in the United States, the West Indies, South America, and Africa. Journalists, historians, clergymen, educators, and businessmen—including J. A. B. Horton, Benito Sylvain, James Johnson, George Washington Williams, J. E. Casely-Hayford, Carter G. Woodson, John Edward Bruce, and Arthur Schomburg—contributed various components to Pan-African thinking, from notions of a glorious African past and triumphant future, to anticolonial and black nationalist sentiments, to the legitimization of the study of African history and culture. Arguably, though, the most important early exponents of Pan-African ideas were Alexander Crummell, an Episcopalian minister from New York, and Edward Wilmot Blyden, a West Indian journalist and Presbyterian minister who took up residence in Liberia after its independence in 1847. These two men helped synthesize the various strands of black emigration movements, nationalism, and anticolonial sentiment into a relatively coherent set of ideas that later came to be called Pan-Africanism. The term itself first came into widespread use with the Pan-African Conference in London in 1900. **W. E. B. Du Bois** played a pivotal role at that conference, as he did at many similar gatherings through the first half of the twentieth century, earning him the nickname the "Father of Pan-Africanism."

The other central figure in twentieth century Pan-Africanism was **Marcus Garvey**, who embraced and gave new life to the old slogans "Back to Africa" and "Africa for the Africans." Garvey not only advocated independent black republics in Africa that could serve as a homeland for black people, but also promoted pride and self-reliance in black populations throughout the diaspora. Garvey did more than any other figure of his time to popularize Pan-Africanism and embed its assumptions in the thinking of the black masses throughout the world.

The assumptions of Pan-Africanism have recently come under question, however. Most notably, Kwame Anthony Appiah has argued that Pan-Africanism is historically rooted in the very notions of racial essentialism that underlay **slavery** and white domination. Nevertheless, even Appiah acknowledges that, were Pan-Africanism to be grounded in some basis other than biological or religious racialism, it could help forge invaluable political, cultural, and economic alliances among some of the world's poorest and most disenfranchised populations.

Further Reading

Appiah, Kwame Anthony. *In My Father's House: Africa in the Philosophy of Culture.* New York: Oxford UP, 1992.

Esedebe, P. Olisanwuche. *Pan-Africanism: The Idea and Movement, 1776–1991.* Washington, DC: Howard UP, 1994.

Walters, Ronald W. *Pan-Africanism in the African Diaspora: An Analysis of Modern Afrocentric Political Movements.* Detroit: Wayne State UP, 1993.

Shane Graham

PARADISE　The seventh novel by Nobel Prize–winning African American author **Toni Morrison**, *Paradise* (1997) interweaves the story of Ruby, an all-black town in Oklahoma, with the story of five displaced and damaged women living in a large old house (the "convent") ten miles down the road. *Paradise* is sometimes considered to be the third of Toni Morrison's planned trilogy on love that leads to murder: sexual love (*Jazz*), mother love (**Beloved**), and the love of God.

The novel begins with nine male leaders from Ruby massacring the castaway women in a modern-day witch hunt and execution. Ruby has changed for the worse, and only women who don't live under the protection and control of men (and thus of God) could be responsible. Through nine chapters named after the women in the book, the history of each woman at the convent and of the town of Ruby is revealed.

The main themes in the novel include memory versus truth; history as a construct that can be not only inaccurate but harmful; patriarchal religious empowerment of men to control, belittle, abuse, and murder women; racial discrimination; and "color" discrimination among African Americans. The novel also provides a model for rewriting the history of Christianity itself if necessary. The style is modernist, with sharp shifts in time, place, and point of view, making the reader work to put the pieces of the puzzle together. The modernist style also has a postmodernist goal: The reader learns through the experience of reading the novel that anyone can be misled by words. Even the best critics, for example, write that the motto on an oven in Ruby is "Beware the Furrow of his Brow," because that phrase is repeated over and over, while the actual phrase on the oven is mentioned only once, by the outsider Richard Misner, in the chapter called "Seneca."

The argument over the motto on the oven—the Word—is ironic, as are the inaccuracies, inconsistencies, and omissions in the history of Ruby that no one notices or admits to. Morrison's epigraph to the novel comes from the Gnostic gospels, which show what accounts of Jesus were rejected from the **canon**ical New Testament. Ruby represents this canonical religion, while Consolata represents a healing alternative; the last scene of the novel finds Consolata figured as the dead Jesus in a posture similar to Michelangelo's "Pieta." Meanwhile, the people of Ruby tell confused and contradictory accounts of the massacre, because its meaning in the history of Ruby has yet to be established. History is created out of the present moment, and not the moment out of history.

Further Reading

Peach, Linden. *Toni Morrison.* 2nd ed. New York: St. Martin's, 2000.

Tally, Justine. *Toni Morrison's (Hi)stories and Truths.* Piscataway, NJ: Transactions Publishers, 1999.

Barbara Z. Thaden

PAREDES, AMÉRICO (1915–)   Chicano scholar, poet, and fiction writer. In an academic career spanning several decades, Paredes's analyses of cultural life along the Texas-Mexico border influenced a wide range of scholars, writers, and musicians, paving the way for a school of cultural criticism that would come to be known in the late twentieth century as "border studies." It was only recently, however, that Paredes also became renowned for his creative work, and his novels, short stories, and poetry (written over many decades as well, but only published in the 1990s) have attracted the attention of scholars and the wider reading public.

Paredes was born and raised in Brownsville, Texas, a small town at the state's southernmost tip, along the Texas-Mexico border. In 1915, the year of his birth, the border region witnessed violent *tejano* uprisings and brutal reprisals at the hands of the Texas Rangers, events that would ultimately find their way into Paredes's scholarship and creative work. After graduating from high school, Paredes attended Brownsville Junior College and worked as a proofreader and staff writer for the *Brownsville Herald* newspaper before entering the U.S. Army. While in uniform he was a reporter and political editor for the Army newspaper, *Stars and Stripes.* Paredes was discharged after covering the Tokyo war crimes tribunals. Following a brief stint with the Red Cross, he studied at the University of Texas at Austin, where he received undergraduate and graduate degrees in English, with a special focus on folklore studies. His masters thesis, "Ballads of the Lower Border" (1953), a comparative analysis of *tejano* and European folk songs, paved the way for his dissertation, "El Corrido de Gregorio Cortez, a Ballad of Border Conflict" (1956). The latter was published in only slightly edited form by the University of Texas Press as *"With His Pistol in His Hand": A Border Ballad and Its Hero* (1958).

"With His Pistol in His Hand" has proven one of the most influential works of folklore scholarship ever written. Scholars such as Renato Rosaldo and María Herrera-Sobek, writers such as **Gloria Anzaldúa** and

Oscar Casares, and musicians such as Tish Hinajosa have credited the book as inspiration for their work. The book offers a biographical and historical study of "El Corrido de Gregorio Cortez" [The Ballad of Gregorio Cortez], as well as a consideration of the social and cultural conditions necessary for border balladry. A tight-knit agricultural community that paid little attention to the international boundary, Border (with a capital B) culture gave rise to the expressive genre, Paredes argues, and encroaching modernization and Anglo cultural hegemony during the early twentieth century gave rise to heroic acts of resistance exemplified by Cortez. (The book inspired a feature film, *The Ballad of Gregorio Cortez* [1982], directed by Robert M. Young and starring Edward James Olmos.) An impressive academic career followed for Paredes: he was a lifelong professor of English at the University of Texas at Austin, he edited the *Journal of American Folklore* from 1968 to 1973, he was president of the American Folklore Society, he received the prestigious Charles Frankel Prize from the National Endowment for the Humanities, and he was inducted into the *Órden del Augila Azteca* [Order of the Aztec Eagle], the highest honor bestowed by the Mexican government upon noncitizens. During the 1960s, Paredes helped found the Center for Mexican American Studies at the University of Texas, serving as its first director; today the Center for Cultural Studies at the University of Texas bears his name, as do public schools in Austin and Brownsville.

Paredes wrote several more books—most notably, *A Texas-Mexican Cancionero: Folksongs of the Lower Border* (1976) and *Folklore and Culture on the Texas-Mexican Border* (1993)—and several dozen articles that paved the way for subsequent analyses of transnational cultural formations (the school of cultural criticism known today as "border studies"). Late in his career, **Arte Público Press** published *George Washington Gómez: A Mexicotexan Novel* (1990), a book Paredes wrote in the 1930s. The novel follows the title character from his birth, amid the so-called border troubles of 1915, through a vexed elementary and high school education, and into a career as a Washington lawyer and Army intelligence officer on the eve of World War II. The novel thus follows the traditional bildungsroman plot, but set against the backdrop of Anglo-*tejano* cultural tensions in the town of Jonesville-on-the-Grande (a thinly veiled version of Brownsville).

The following year, Arte Público published a collection of poetry written primarily in the 1930s and 1940s (*Between Two Worlds* [1991]). The poems offer compelling evidence of a voice caught, not just between the United States and Mexico or between English and Spanish, but also between the United States and Japan, and between an urban modernity and a recrudescent agrarianism. Paredes then brought out *The Hammon and the Beans and Other Stories* (1994). The short story collection, written during the 1940s and 1950s, provides fictional accounts of life along the Texas-Mexico border and in occupied Japan. *The Shadow* (1998) was Paredes's second novel and last major work. The historical novella, set in postrevolutionary Mexico, explores a complex and conflicted milieu, in which ethnic, class, political, and regional loyalties compete for prominence.

Paredes's work, Ramón Saldívar observes, serves as a "crucial" model for subsequent Chicano prose fiction "in historical, aesthetic, and theoretical terms" (27). Without it, Chicano literature and Chicano studies would arguably look vastly different today. (*See also* Border Narratives)

Further Reading

Garza-Falcón, Leticia. *Gente Decente: A Borderlands Response to the Rhetoric of Dominance.* Austin: U of Texas P, 1998.

Saldívar, José David. *Border Matters: Remapping American Cultural Studies.* Berkeley: U of California P, 1997.

Saldívar, Ramón. *Chicano Narrative: The Dialectics of Difference.* Madison: U of Wisconsin P, 1990.

Michael Soto

PARINI, JAY (1948–)   Novelist, poet, biographer, editor, and literary critic. One of the foremost Italian American men of letters, Parini has a body of work that, indeed, resists simple categorization. Born and raised in a Pennsylvania coal-mining community and earning his BA at nearby Lafayette College, Parini has represented his immigrant, working-class background in his writing, particularly in the poetry collection *Anthracite Country* (1982) and his second novel, *The Patch Boys* (1986). Yet this author also lived for years in Scotland, earning his PhD at the University of St. Andrews in 1975, and his oeuvre evinces a wide-ranging sensibility, embracing as it does a highly regarded biography of John Steinbeck (*John Steinbeck*, 1995), a popular research compendium (*The Columbia History of American Poetry*, 1993, coedited with Brett C. Miller), and novels that dramatize the life of Jewish intellectual Walter Benjamin (*Benjamin's Crossing*, 1997) and Russian novelist Leo Tolstoy (*The Last Station*, 1990). Parini's dozens of essays (many collected in *Some Necessary Angels*, 1998) similarly address subjects as various as the TV series **The Sopranos**, the poets John Donne and Gerard Manley Hopkins, and the pleasures of life along the southern Italian coast.

Parini's first book was poetry, *Singing in Time* (1972), published while still a graduate student in Scotland. Not long after, he began contributing essays and reviews to journals such as *Scottish International*, *Antaeus*, and *Chicago Review*. He returned to the United States to take a position at Dartmouth in 1975 and there, in 1976, helped found the *New England Review*. Three years later he brought out his first booklength work of criticism, **Theodore Roethke**: *An American Romantic*, then the following year his first novel, *The Love Run* (1980). He moved to Middlebury in 1982 and with the appearance of *Anthracite Country* that year and *Patch Boys* not long after, Parini began to achieve national recognition.

The poems in *Anthracite Country* are characterized by disarming honesty and emotional intensity, while *The Patch Boys*, a coming-of-age tale set in

Parini's hardscrabble home territory, is marked by gritty realism. Both works met with a highly favorable critical reception. The poems that followed (*Town Life*, 1988) were less place-specific, though also critically well received, and the next novel, his Tolstoy book, *Last Station* (1990), was a greater departure. Set in 1910 and told from six different points of view, among them the aged Tolstoy and the young Russian writer Mikhail Bulgakov, the novel makes considerable demands on the reader but nonetheless stands as Parini's greatest success to date, a book featured on the cover of the *New York Times Book Review* and praised by many critics as one of the finest American novels.

None of the author's books since have won so much attention and admiration—not even the superficially similar *Benjamin's Crossing*, which details a refugee existence leading up the philosopher's suicide in 1940. But Parini, to be sure, has continued undeterred, both with his editing (for example, the popular textbook, *An Invitation to Poetry*, first published in 1987) and his shorter work. He currently contributes to an impressive array of journals, among them *The Atlantic* and *The New Yorker*, and has won major awards like the Guggenheim Fellowship (1992–93) and, at Middlebury, the Axinn Professorship.

With his prolific output, Parini came round eventually to addressing his own ethnic heritage. His 1992 novel, the relatively lighthearted *Bay of Arrows*, features a contemporary Italian American academic whose peregrinations were aligned with those of Christopher Columbus, five centuries earlier. Then in 1997, Parini effected his most direct address thus far of his immigrant legacy, in the form of a substantive anthology edited with A. Kenneth Ciongoli (president of the National Italian American Foundation), titled *Beyond the Godfather: Italian American Writers on the Real Italian American Experience*. Pulling together the reflections and insights of some twenty-three authors, the anthology is a milestone in the development of Italian American writing.

Parini and Ciongoli appeared together again in 2002, as coeditors on the slim and glossy overview *Passage to Liberty: The Story of Italian Immigration and the Rebirth of America*. That same year also saw a more moving and deeply probing exploration of the same issues in the novel *The Apprentice Lover*. The story is set mostly on Capri, but its narrator and protagonist is the novice writer Alex Massolini, of hardscrabble Pennsylvania stock, the grandson of an immigrant and the son of a GI who fought in the Italian campaign during World War II.

Yet this summary of the author's career to date, while thick with titles and encomiums, nevertheless leaves out a number of accomplishments. Chief among these is the biography *Robert Frost: A Life*, published in 2000, which won the Chicago Tribune-Heartland Award for the best work of nonfiction that year. Parini published a 1998 collection of poetry, *House of Days*, he has edited a well-regarded selection from American autobiographies (as well as other texts), and he has contributed introductions to recent editions of **F. Scott Fitzgerald**, Edgar Allan Poe, and others. The sheer volume of work can seem to call into question its intelligence and power, but Parini himself may have justified his literary fecundity when he declared, in an interview for *Contemporary Authors*, "In a sense, I use writing to pay attention to the world, to explain it to myself." Certainly a number of his works have helped explain Italian Americans to themselves and to others, and his career as a whole offers a happy contrast to the unfortunate thug stereotype, still all too prevalent, of Italian Americans. (*See also* Italian American Novel, Italian American Poetry, Italian American Stereotypes)

Further Reading

Bayley, John. "A Household on Its Head." Review of *The Last Station*. *Times Literary Supplement* 28 (December–January 1990–91): 1408–9.

Ciongoli, A. Kenneth, and Parini, Jay, eds. *Beyond the Godfather: Italian American Writers on the Real Italian American Experience*. Dartmouth C: UP of New England, 1997.

Condren, Edward. "Tolstoy's Final Days." Review of *The Last Station*. *Los Angeles Times Book Review* (October 9, 1990): 4.

Grudin, Robert. "Everywhere an Exile." Review of *Benjamin's Crossing*. *New York Times Book Review* (June 29, 1997): 12.

Jarman, Mark. "Shifting Sands: *The Columbia History of American Poetry*." *Hudson Review* 47.4 (1995): 641–47.

Schiff, Stacy. "Coming of Literary Age." Review of *The Apprentice Lover*. *New York Times Book Review* (March 31, 2002): 22.

Seymour, Miranda. "Tolstoy in Torment." Review of *The Last Station*. *New York Times Book Review* (July 22, 1990): 1+.

Spiegelman, Willard. "History by Many Hands." Review of *The Columbia History of American Poetry*. *Kenyon Review* 17.3–4 (1995): 219–29.

John Domini

PARKER, DOROTHY (ROTHSCHILD) (1893–1967) Jewish American poet, playwright, novelist, humorist, short story writer, and critic. Parker was born in New York City to a Jewish father and a Scottish mother, J. Henry and Eliza Rothschild. Her mother died when Parker was an infant, and her stepmother, also Scottish Presbyterian, sent her to Catholic school to erase her "Jewish upbringing." After her expulsion from the convent school for describing the Immaculate Conception as "spontaneous combustion" she was then sent to Miss Dana's, an exclusive New Jersey girls' school, where she received a classical education. Parker grew up both confused by and ashamed of her religious background as reflected in her anti-Semitic poem "Dark Girl's Rhyme" (1926) and contemporaries of Parker noted that she often announced, unasked, that she was half Jewish.

After graduating from Miss Dana's, Parker worked as a copywriter for *Vogue*, but she soon became famous as *The New Yorker's* pseudonymous literary critic, "Constant Reader," where she praised Ernest Hemingway and criticized A. A. Milne's *The House at Pooh Corner* (1928) with the comment: "Tonstant weader fwowed up." In keeping with her near obsession over her Jewishness, her first book review for *The New Yorker* was on a novel about

Dorothy Parker. *Courtesy of the Library of Congress.*

anti-Semitism. During the 1920s and 1930s, Parker was a celebrity within New York's literary and theatrical world. As a member of the Algonquin Round Table, a group of mostly Jewish writers who met regularly at the Algonquin Hotel to share gossip and wit, Parker's remarks were reported (and often misquoted) in newspaper columns, including the famous "Men seldom make passes/ At girls who wear glasses." Her poetry and fiction, most often from a woman's perspective, depicts such themes as unhappy love affairs and marriages, and middle-class morality; Parker was a social satirist as much as a humorist, attacking all forms of hypocrisy, including sexual and racial oppression.

After leaving review writing, Parker focused her attention on writing verse, short fiction, screenplays, and dramas, and at the same time, living a life of heavy drinking, numerous love affairs, and depression. Her first collection of poetry, *Enough Rope* (1926), which alternatively sympathizes with the woman whose heart is broken and criticizes the myth of romantic love, was a national best seller, and her second volume, *Sunset Gun* (1928), which continued to address themes of lost love, was also critically acclaimed. With her 1931 collection, *Death and Taxes,* her poetry became more pessimistic. "Laments for the Living" (1930), her first short story collection, was praised by critics for its use of dialogue and its ongoing commentary on human behavior, particularly the often senseless and restrictive upper-class woman's life. "Big Blonde," from the 1930 collection and her most anthologized work today, is a sympathetic portrait of one Hazel Morse, a woman who is tragically dependant upon men for emotional and economic needs, a woman who struggles to fulfill society's expectations. Although she spent over thirty years writing fiction, Parker produced fewer than fifty stories and most of Parker's fame rests on works published before 1938. In 1944, Viking came out with *The Viking Portable Dorothy Parker,* which was reissued in 1973 under the title *The Portable Dorothy Parker.*

Parker's personal life was not so successful. Her first marriage in 1917 to Edwin Pond Parker II, a Wall Street broker, was brief and lonely (he was away for two years' military service). By the end of the 1920s, Parker had attempted suicide three times and increasingly turned to alcohol. She married her second husband, actor Alan Campbell, in 1933, divorced in 1947, and remarried in 1950, yet she and Alan still collaborated on sixteen screenplays, including the 1937 *A Star Is Born*, which was later nominated for an Academy Award. Campbell was eleven years her junior and, like Parker, half Jewish. Like many writers of her day, she was directly involved in politically liberal causes. Parker was fined five dollars for being in a Boston demonstration protesting the execution of Sacco and Vanzetti. During World War II, Parker gave fund-raising speeches including one for the Emergency Conference to Save the Jews of Europe. Her association with the American Screen Writers Guild and the Anti-Nazi League, two left-wing organizations, led the House Un-American Activities Committee (HUAC) to investigate her as a possible Communist sympathizer during the 1950s. She refused to cooperate and charges against her were ultimately dropped. She continued to write, mostly reviews, in the 1960s, but ill health and continued depression made it increasingly difficult. Parker died in 1967.

Parker's suggestions for her own epitaphs have become famous: "Excuse my dust" and "If you can read this, you've come too close." Contemporary readers continue to find her portraits of woman's lives humorous, painful, and relevant. In keeping with the sympathy she felt for social causes and the oppressed, and perhaps due to her own identification as a dispossessed Jew, Parker left her estate, plus copyrights and royalties, to **Martin Luther King Jr.** and the NAACP.

Further Reading

Bloom, Harold, ed. *Jewish Women Fiction Writers.* Philadelphia: Chelsea House, 1998. 104–19.

Calhoun, Randall. *Dorothy Parker: A Bio-Bibliography.* Westport, CT: Greenwood Press, 1993.

Meade, Marion. *Dorothy Parker: What Fresh Hell Is This?* New York: Villard, 1988.

Stacey Lee Donohue

PARKER, GWENDOLYN M. (1950–)   African American novelist and autobiographer. Gwendolyn Parker's two published works center on middle-class African Americans who confront racism prior to the Civil Rights Movement of the 1950s and 1960s and during the last quarter of the twentieth century. In Parker's debut novel, *These Same Long Bones* (1994), the residents of the African American enclave of Hay-ti in Durham, North Carolina, look to Sirus McDougald, bank president, insurance executive, and builder, when white investors in McDougald's development project in the late 1940s sabotage the project by building substandard and unsafe houses. McDougald, who is still grieving over the mysterious death of his young daughter, is challenged to look beyond his personal pain and act on his community's behalf. Prior to the aforementioned incidents, McDougald realizes his childhood dream of becoming a "race man," an African American male whose successes benefit other members of his community. In Parker's auto-biography, *Trespassing: My Sojourn in the Halls of Privilege* (1997), she describes inheriting the roles of race child and race woman from her prominent Durham, North Carolina family, a family that includes her great-grandfather, Dr. Aaron McDuffie Moore, who was a cofounder of North Carolina Mutual Life Insurance and an influential figure in the development of a number of Durham institutions. Several weeks before Parker's ninth birthday in 1959, her family moved from their middle-class African American community to Mount Vernon, New York. Parker's life then evolves into patterns of the first African American, one of the first African Americans, and/or one of the first African American females to attend Kent School, an exclusive boarding school in Connecticut; attend Radcliffe College; become an attorney with the Wall Street firm of Cadwalader, Wickersham, and Taft after receiving JD and LLM degrees from New York University; and become a director at American Express. *Trespassing*, while chronicling Parker's academic and professional achievements, also documents her disenchantment with corporate America because of its racism, sexism, and class discrimination. Although Parker pos-sesses impeccable academic as well as professional credentials, her col-leagues consistently view her as an intruder; for example, she wears a pinstripe suit, dons a name tag, and has a briefcase, just like her white male counterparts at a luncheon for lawyers, yet Parker's appearance does not convince the man next to her that she is a lawyer. In this autobiography that was published four years before September 11, 2001, Parker writes that she wants to respond she is a terrorist after he questions her; instead she nods an affirmative response. After ten years of feeling like a permanent outsider in predominantly white male environments, Parker, at the age of thirty-six, walks away from the corporate world and embraces her writing talent. *These Same Long Bones* and *Trespassing* herald an auspicious beginning for Gwen-dolyn Parker's career as a writer. (*See also* African American Autobiography)

Further Reading

Woodard, Loretta G. "Gwendolyn M. Parker." *African American Autobiographers: A Sourcebook.* Ed. Emmanuel S. Nelson. Westport, CT: Greenwood Press, 2002. 295–98.

Linda M. Carter

PARKS, GORDON (1912–)   African American photographer, writer, filmmaker, musician, and composer. A remarkably prolific artist in numer-ous forms, Parks is one of the most versatile American artists of the twenti-eth century. Just as his work has spanned a remarkable number of overlapping forms, the range of his subject matter reflects the diversity of his life experiences. As a photographer alone, he has been equally at home treating fashion models and the poor of Brazil, his friend the heiress Gloria Vanderbilt and members of the Black Panthers.

Parks had already gained recognition for his photographs when he trained under the Farm Security Administration during the Depression. After serving as a correspondent during World War II, he found work for *Vogue* and then *Life*. Early in his long career with *Life*, Parks displayed his unusual ability to gain the trust of his subjects, scoring a journalistic scoop with his portrait of a young gang leader in Harlem. Assigned to *Life*'s Paris bureau in 1950, Parks experienced the same relief at the relative freedom from American **racism** as many African American writers and artists and met one of his artistic heroes, **Richard Wright**. Upon returning to the United States, he covered the burgeoning **Civil Rights Movement** and formed relationships with **Malcolm X** as well as other figures from the Nation of Islam and the Black Panthers, all of whom have figured in his photographs and writings. Numerous books came from his work for *Life*, notably *Flavio* (1978), which tells the story of the impoverished Brazilian boy he had photographed for the

Gordon Parks, on set. *Winger/The Kobal Collection.*

magazine. Parks's photography represents an important contribution to the photojournalistic tradition he inherited from socially conscious artists of the Depression. His most distinctive photographs are deeply humanistic portraits of individuals, often in black and white, which translate his ability to gain his subject's trust into a connection the viewer can share.

Parks's numerous books record his remarkable life story. His best-selling novel *The Learning Tree* (1963) fictionalized his experiences growing up in poverty in Kansas. The autobiography *A Choice of Weapons* (1966) continues the story, recounting the struggles that followed the death of his mother. *To Smile in Autumn* (1979) tells the equally remarkable story of his working life, while *Voices in the Mirror* (1990) provides an overview of all these periods. All are affecting literary works and important documents of twentieth-century and African American history.

In 1968 Parks wrote, directed, and produced a film adaptation of *The Learning Tree*. He went on to direct films including *Shaft* (1971) and *Leadbelly* (1976) and to influence numerous younger African American filmmakers. He has combined his prodigious talents by writing scores for films as well as concert music and publishing several volumes that interweave his poetry and photography. The multi-genre retrospective, *Half Past Autumn*, which toured from 1998 to 2004, allows us to appreciate the full range of his extensive achievement and influence. (*See also* African American Film)

Further Reading

Berry, S. L. *Gordon Parks*. New York: Chelsea House, 1991.

Donloe, Darlene. *Gordon Parks: Photographer, Writer, Composer, Film Maker*. Los Angeles: Melrose Square, 1993.

Laura Tanenbaum

PARKS, ROSA (1913–) African American activist called the mother of the **Civil Rights Movement**. Born in Tuskegee, Alabama, on February 4, 1913, Parks grew up in an era when blacks had very few rights and schools and other public facilities were segregated. From the very beginning, Parks recognized these injustices and vehemently fought against them. In her book, *Rosa Parks: My Story* (1992) written with Jim Haskins, she gives details about her youth, her family, and her contribution to the Civil Rights Movement. For years, Parks's story was minimized, transforming a defiant act—her refusal to give up her seat to a white man on a segregated bus in Montgomery on December 1, 1955—to the story of a timid woman who was just simply too tired to get up. *Rosa Parks: My Story* challenges this misconception.

Prior to providing the impetus for what became the Montgomery bus boycott, Parks was already committed to securing civil rights for people of color. Her husband, Raymond Parks, was an active member of the NAACP and was deeply involved in voter registration rights for blacks. In 1943 Parks too became active in the NAACP, and served as secretary of the Montgomery branch during a time when few women were active members. That same year she tried to register to vote, but was denied the right. It would be two years before Parks would be granted a certificate for voting. In 1943, while on the way to make her second attempt to register to vote, Parks challenged bus segregation for the first time. Parks was asked to get off a bus because she entered it from the front. When she refused, the driver grabbed her coat sleeve and demanded that she get off the bus. After this incident, she avoided this driver, consciously choosing not to ride the bus if he was driving it.

In the 1950s the NAACP began to develop a plan for filing a suit against Montgomery. Parks knew bus segregation would soon be challenged in an important way. The NAACP began to think about the type of person they must choose to challenge bus segregation. When Claudette Colvin was arrested, it seemed they had a plaintiff who could help them develop a strong case against the city. A detailed petition was developed and presented to the bus company and to officials in the city with hopes of improving public transportation for blacks. The requests in the petition were denied, however. Then it was discovered that Claudette would soon be a single mother, and so the NAACP would need to continue searching for a female willing to challenge segregation.

While the NAACP continued to look for determined candidates who might help strengthen a case against Montgomery, Parks boarded a bus driven by the driver who had forced her off the bus in 1943. On this particular day, Parks sat in the first row of the black section along with three other passengers. The driver asked them to get up, but none of the passengers moved. Eventually the other three passengers stood up, but Parks did not. Parks was taken into custody, bail was set, and a court date was scheduled. E. D. Nixon, president of the Montgomery branch of the NAACP, asked Parks if she would serve as plaintiff with the support of the NAACP. That same night Jo Ann Robinson and others began to put plans for the boycott in place. Parks will forever be remembered as the woman who dared to challenge segregation and, with the help of others, won.

Further Reading

Garrow, David J., ed. *Martin Luther King, Jr. and the Civil Rights Movement*. New York: Carlson Publishing Inc., 1989.

KaaVonia Hinton-Johnson

PARKS, SUZAN-LORI (1964–) African American playwright. Suzan-Lori Parks is one of the most prominent, challenging, and daring contemporary playwrights. Her works are remarkably original and stylized, combining boisterous humor with an underlying darkness. Parks uses theater as a way to explore, deconstruct, and recreate history, primarily that of African Americans, much of which has been lost or overlooked. Her fundamental interest is in time: how people pass through it and how it interacts with history. Thus, her plays often center on specific segments of American history, such as Abraham Lincoln's assassination.

Additionally, Parks's plays are characterized by playful, kinetic language that combines the vernacular and the mystical; long monologues; rhythmic, poetic, and jazzy dialect (she has said she often dances or listens to **jazz** while writing); repetition and revision that replicates African American oral traditions, and a nonlinear, nonrealistic style. As highly theatrical spectacles, her plays depend heavily on sound through such devices as lack of punctuation, linguistic compression ("Whaduhya think?" or "Whatdoyou say"), and phonetic spelling ("ugho instead of "ago"). This formal verbal complexity further contributes to the refreshing uniqueness of her work and affirms her assertion that her plays must be spoken, not just read—yet it also makes her plays quite difficult to summarize.

Parks initially gained public recognition with *Imperceptible Mutabilities in the Third Kingdom* (1989), which won her the 1990 Obie Award for Best New American Play and acclaim from critics as a vital new voice in American theater. Organized into four "Parts" (and a Reprise), each presenting a distinct set of characters, the play explores African Americans as a curious species placed under a microscope—a kind of scientific racial classification—

Suzan-Lori Parks. *AP/Wide World Photos.*

as well as the 1865 Emancipation, the **Middle Passage**, the longing for home, and the oppressed (or "imperceptible") possibilities for social change and advancement.

The Death of the Last Black Man in the Whole Entire World (1990), Parks's second major play, is divided into five "Panels," framed by an "Overture" and a "Final Chorus." Incorporating biblical, literary, historical, and folkloric imagery, the play explores the disparity between African and American, depicting characters eternally trapped between these two identities. Again, history is presented, not sequentially, but through repetition, both in language and events. The *Last Black Man* continually seems to die but never does, while a number of births offset the notion of death.

Another major success came with *The America Play* (1993) set in what Parks calls The Great Hole of History (in the middle of nowhere) that serves as a kind of theme park. The central character—the Foundling Father, a gravedigger—bears an uncanny resemblance to Abraham Lincoln, and in Act One, he recounts how he left his family to head West, to this Great Hole. There he devised a vaudeville act in which he impersonated Lincoln at Ford's Theatre, with tourists paying to imitate John Wilkes Booth, assassinate the President, and then leap from the balcony. In Act Two, the Foundling Father's wife and son are digging in the Great Hole for clues to his life, discovering in the process historical artifacts such as a bust of Lincoln, his bones, and his boots. Periodically, the Foundling Father reappears to enact scenes from *Our American Cousin* (the play Lincoln saw the night he was killed). Again, Parks is exploring history as the characters attempt to excavate their own personal and collective racial pasts.

Topdog/Underdog (2001), which Parks wrote in three days and which earned her a Pulitzer Prize, continues this bizarre Lincolnian saga. Much more conventional in structure than her other works, *Topdog/Underdog* focuses on two brothers, jokingly named Lincoln and Booth by their late father. Lincoln—or Linc, as he is called, suggesting some relationship to the "missing link"—is a master of three-card monte. However, since he also looks remarkably like Abraham Lincoln, he abandons this illegal street game to play the same role as his (presumed) ancestor at an amusement arcade, where he is repeatedly assassinated, day after day. Linc is proud to have a decent and legal job, even though it means performing in whiteface. In contrast, Booth continually attempts to attain his brother's con game techniques, fueling a jealousy that leads to a bizarre and fatal conclusion.

Other major plays by Parks include *In the Blood* (1999), which takes a satiric stab at Nathaniel Hawthorne through a central character named Hester, a homeless mother of five children from different fathers, who lives under a bridge, survives on welfare, and is exploited by nearly everyone she encounters, including some of the children's fathers. The play examines attitudes towards poverty and social responsibility, as well as gender, class, racial, and generational divides. *Fucking A* (2000), for which Parks wrote the music and lyrics, continues this Hawthorne association with another character named Hester, this one a backroom abortionist who is struggling to earn enough money to free her son, Monster, from prison, after twenty years of incarceration. A kind of revenge tragedy, the play culminates in a bloody finale and incorporates themes similar to *In the Blood*, including brutality and the evil of injustice.

Parks's only historically based play, *Venus* (1996), earned her another Obie for Best New American Play. *Venus* explores the real-life character of Venus Hottentot, a deformed, disfigured black woman who was brought to England in the nineteenth century for display as a theatrical sideshow freak. Other plays by Parks include *Betting on the Dust Commander* (1987), *Pickling* (1988), *Greeks* (1990), and *Devotees in the Garden of Love* (1992). In 1990, Parks produced the film *Anemone Me*, and in 1996, she wrote the screenplay for *Girl 6*, produced and directed by Spike Lee. In 2003, she published her first novel, *Getting Mother's Body*, and she is currently adapting **Toni Morrison**'s novel *Paradise* for Oprah Winfrey's film company as well as working on a stage musical about the Harlem Globetrotters, titled *Hoopz*.

Parks's many honors include a Guggenheim Fellowship; Leila-Wallace Reader's Digest Award; W. Alton Jones Grant from the Kennedy Center Fund for New American Plays; *New York Times* Most Promising New Playwright Award; Whiting Writers' Award; NEA Playwriting Fellowships; grants from the Rockefeller Foundation, Ford Foundation, and NEA; California Institute of the Arts Alpert Award in Drama; the PEN-Laura Pels Award for Excellence in Playwriting; and a MacArthur "Genius" Award. (*See also* African American Drama)

Further Reading

Bernard, Louise. "The Musicality of Language: Redefining History in Suzan-Lori Parks's 'The Death of the Last Black Man in the Whole Entire World'." *African American Review* 31.4 (1997): 687–99.

Bigsby, C. W. E. *Modern American Drama: 1945–2000.* Cambridge, UK: Cambridge UP, 2000.

Brubaker, Sharon M. "Suzan-Lori Parks." *African American Dramatists: An A-to-Z Guide.* Ed. Emmanuel S. Nelson. Westport, CT: Greenwood Press, 2004. 336–46.

Dixon, Kimberly D. "An I am Sheba me am (She be doo wah waaaah doo wah, O(au)rality, Textuality and Performativity: African American Literature's Vernacular Theory and the Work of Suzan-Lori Parks." *Journal of American Drama and Theatre* 11.1 (1999): 49–66.

Drukman, Steven. "Suzan-Lori Parks and Liz Diamond: Doo-a-diddly-dit-dit." *Drama Review* 39.3 (1995): 56–75.

Elam, Harry, and Alice Rayner. "Echoes from the Black (W)hole: An Examination of *The America Play* by Suzan-Lori Parks." *Performing America: Cultural Nationalism in American Theater.* Ed. Jeffrey D. Mason and J. Ellen Gainor. Ann Arbor: U of Michigan P, 1999. 178–92.

Frieze, James. "Imperceptible Mutabilities in the Third Kingdom: Suzan-Lori Parks and the Shared Struggle to Perceive." *Modern Drama* 41 (Winter 1998): 523.

Garrett, Shawn-Marie. "The Possession of Suzan-Lori Parks." *American Theatre* (October 2000): 22–26+.

Jiggetts, Shelby. "Interviews with Suzan-Lori Parks." *Callaloo* 19.2 (1996): 309–17.

Miller, Greg. "The Bottom of Desire in Susan-Lori Parks's *Venus*." *Modern Drama* 45.1 (2002): 125–39.

Rayner, Alice, and Harry Elam Jr. "Unfinished Business: Reconfiguring History in Suzan-Lori Parks's 'The Death of the Last Black Man in the Whole Entire World'." *Theatre Journal.* 46.4 (1994): 447–62.

Ryan, Katy. "'No Less Human': Making History in Suzan-Lori Parks's *The America Play*." *Journal of Dramatic Theory and Criticism* 8.2 (1999): 81–94.

Solomon, Alisa. "Signifying on the Signifyin': The Plays of Suzan-Lori Parks." *Theatre* (Summer–Fall 1990): 73–80.

Wilmer, S. E. "Restaging the Nation: The Works of Suzan-Lori Parks." *Modern Drama* 43.3 (2000): 442–52.

Karen C. Blansfield

PASSING   **Nella Larsen**'s *Passing* (1929) remains one of the most intriguing novels of the **Harlem Renaissance**. The novel's plot pivots on the relationship between two main characters, Irene Redfield and Clare Kendry, who are light-skinned enough to pass for white. Irene, who is married to a Harlem-based physician, passes for white whenever she can use her pseudo-whiteness to gain social privileges that she would otherwise be denied. Clare, however, is married to a pathologically racist white businessman who believes that his wife is white. So Clare conceals her cultural **identity** and passes for white on a full-time basis.

The novel begins with an accidental meeting of Irene and Clare in a sleek Chicago restaurant after having lost touch with each other for over a dozen years. They reestablish their friendship. Irene feels vaguely tantalized by Clare and her beauty, her toughness and daring, and her casual disdain for upper-class conventions. Yet she also feels faintly uneasy with the emotional intensity that begins to characterize their friendship. In the second section of the novel, Clare visits Irene in New York; the visit, ostensibly, is prompted by her desire to reconnect with her roots but her motives remain ambiguous. And Irene becomes increasingly puzzled by her own fascination with Clare. Irene's feelings become more complicated when she begins to suspect that her husband and Clare might be having an affair. In the final segment of the novel, Larsen stages a dramatic confrontation: Clare's racist husband, in search of Clare, wanders into a glamorous party in Harlem and finds her there. Moments later Clare falls out of a window and dies. Whether her fatal fall is an accident, suicide, or murder is left to the reader's speculation.

A novel of manners, *Passing* offers an articulate critique of the values and foibles of the black upper class of the 1920s. More importantly, Larsen's use of the phenomenon of passing deconstructs the very concept of **"race"** by subverting the presumed rigidity and impenetrability of racial categories. But perhaps the most daring aspect of the novel is its subtle exploration of transgressive sexuality: on the surface it appears to be a conventional novel about two married women, but subtextually it hints at lesbian desire.

Since the mid-1980s *Passing* has generated substantial critical attention. This renewed academic interest is at least partly due to the novel's curiously postmodern sensibility: *Passing* points to the instability, even the performative and fictional nature, of all identities.

Further Reading

Davis, Thadious. *Nella Larsen: Novelist of the Harlem Renaissance.* Baton Rouge: Louisiana State UP, 1994.

Grayson, Deborah R. "Fooling White Folks, or, How I Stole the Show: The Body Politics in Nella Larson's *Passing.*" *Bucknell Review* 39.1 (1995): 27–37.

Wald, Gayle. *Crossing the Line: Racial Passing in Twentieth-Century U.S. Literature and Culture.* Durham, NC: Duke UP, 2000.

Youman, Mary Mabel. "Nella Larsen's *Passing*: A Study in Irony." *CLA Journal* 18 (December 1974): 235–44.

Emmanuel S. Nelson

PEDAGOGY AND U.S. ETHNIC LITERATURES   The impact of U.S. ethnic literatures on American literary pedagogy has been profound. Curricula and syllabi are more diverse and inclusive and minority writers and texts receive significant scholarly and popular attention. **Canon**ical texts are often approached in new, fruitful ways, focusing on the politics of injustice and the ways ideology shapes discourse. Yet the challenges for instructors and students of U.S. ethnic literature remain. Fortunately, scholar-teachers of U.S. ethnic literatures continue to engage in serious, ongoing reflection about principles, objectives, and practices.

Pedagogy of U.S. ethnic literatures is deeply embedded in multiculturalism, an identifiable ideology, political movement, and educational movement. Built on the recognition that democratic ideals of egalitarianism and justice often go unrealized, **multiculturalism** seeks to redress such injustices and inequities through increased inclusion of racial, ethnic, and other marginalized social groups in cultural, social, educational, and political arenas. But the debate between multicultural and "traditional" educators is ongoing. In general terms, traditionalists charge multiculturalists with politicizing curricula and classrooms through the infusion of multiculturalism, while progressivists argue that curricula and classrooms are and always have been political, biased toward Western, white male experience and knowledge. Progressivists, therefore, seek to include voices and perspectives of previously marginalized groups in curricula. Some who are critical of current multicultural approaches to education countercharge that emphasizing exclusions based on race, class, gender, and sexual orientation does not serve diversity because it divides students. Rather, they see multiculturalism as purely political, defined in terms of what some have called "oppression studies."

In literary studies, culture wars take the form of "canon wars," a term coined by Gerald Graff and William Cain, which indicates controversies over the texts that should be studied, taught, and even appreciated or revered. Traditionalists appeal to the past, to God, to natural laws, or to foundationalist claims to Truth. Revisionists, however, view cultural diversity as America's foundation; curricular diversity, then, not the "Great Books" of Western civilization, form the basis for understanding American society's multicultural composition. Moreover, revisionists tend to subscribe to postmodernist, antifoundational claims to truth, knowledge, and morality; the "Great Books," therefore, provide only one version of truth rather than Truth with a capital "T." By including texts, voices, worldviews, philosophies, and belief systems of previously excluded groups, revisionists claim, the curricula encourages students to develop multiplicity in their approach to knowledge.

Yet many versions of multiculturalism exist, ranging from the "liberal" to the "radical," each representing particular philosophical and political beliefs. Liberal multiculturalisms go by many names: "corporate," "liberal," "boutique," and "institutionalized." They tend to focus on the study of all different cultures and nationalities and the "appreciation" of everything another culture has to offer, at least on the surface. Multiculturalism, according to these versions, is the celebration of different customs, foods, dress, and religious holidays. In the study of U.S. ethnic literature, liberal multiculturalism is manifested in efforts to make curricula and syllabi representative and inclusive; as such, students experience a smorgasbord of ethnic writers as they move their way from one culture to another, often by using one of several available anthologies.

But this approach to U.S. ethnic literature has been criticized on several grounds. First, it may reinforce **assimilation**ist and universalist values through thematic focuses such as "family," "home," and "love." Students are encouraged through a liberal multicultural approach to U.S. ethnic literature to think that except for surface differences, such as where we live or what we celebrate, "underneath we're all alike." Students tend to read unfamiliar texts from their own perspectives, thereby appropriating and erasing difference. **Leslie Marmon Silko**'s short story, "Yellow Woman," for example, is often interpreted as a feminist tale of a woman's break from the mundane domestic sphere, which stifles her imagination and passion. However, when read through the context of traditional Cochiti and Pueblo Yellow Woman tales, Silko's story resists a white feminist perspective.

Similarly, adding or replacing old texts with new ones may lead to diversification but does not transform literary studies. The add-on approach, as many scholar-teachers have called it, forces ethnic texts into white, male ways of reading and teaching. It likewise focuses on diversity at the expense of issues of inequity and injustice; real-world political gains do not inevitably accrue from diversification of the literary canon. Thus many scholar-teachers of U.S. ethnic literatures call for new kinds of teaching approaches that neither eliminate cultural difference nor ignore systemic injustices. For example, it is not enough to add African American writer **Ernest Gaines**'s *A Lesson Before Dying* into a course on American literary modernism, even though this text shares some modernist features. Rather, pedagogical approaches to *A Lesson Before Dying* should account for the particulars of **race**, class, and gender as these categories of difference modify or challenge modernist characteristics. Jefferson's efforts to regain his humanity after having been called a "'dumb animal'" by his defense attorney are deeply embedded in what Grant Wiggins, another character, calls the "black man's burden," dating to **slavery.**

In response to what are seen by many as liberal multiculturalism's shortcomings, critical multiculturalists address the politics of race and other social categories of difference. Critical multiculturalists advocate a critique of the power relations that work to undermine efforts at equality and attempt to focus on and thus remedy the uneven distribution of goods, power, and access to knowledge. Critical multiculturalisms attend to power, structural inequalities, injustice, discrimination, and hate.

In critical multicultural literature classrooms, students study power dynamics in U.S. ethnic literatures. For example, critical multicultural pedagogies interrogate individualist ideologies that blindly promote notions of equal opportunity and merit-based achievements. Students examine countless topics, including education, advertising, television, family, and literature. Students may, for example, analyze Chicana writer **Sandra Cisneros**'s *The House on Mango Street* and Chicano writer **Tomás Rivera**'s *. . . y no se lo trago la tierra/And the Earth Did Not Devour Him* against the backdrop of individualist ideology as generally articulated in canonical literature, television, and film. Furthermore, critical pedagogists have moved away from a focus on literary interpretation to what has been called a "politics of interpretation." That is, critical multiculturalists ask students to consider the ways their reading practices are shaped by cultural forces, such as race, class, and gender, and how they might try on unfamiliar ways of reading.

Objectives

The conflicts between liberal and critical multiculturalisms impact pedagogical objectives of U.S. ethnic literatures. Why do we teach texts by U.S. ethnic writers? Do we teach these texts to foster understanding of cultural difference, to promote aesthetic appreciation, to sharpen awareness of language use, or to hone socially just attitudes? Do we teach ethnic literature so that our minority students can see themselves in American literary history and thus develop or reaffirm self-worth? These important questions remain largely unresolved, except that many scholar-teachers assume all are important, even if difficult to include together in any one course.

In particular, for many instructors, multiethnic literary studies should engage issues of justice and equity and prepare students for active democratic participation. Many instructors have thus made their literature classes sites of antiracist, antisexist, anticlassist social change, spaces for cultural critique. For some of these instructors, U.S. ethnic texts are powerful vehicles for conveying how oppression and discrimination harm individuals and cultural groups. While acknowledging that transformations in politics and ethics do not usually occur through one or two semesters of literature study, these instructors nonetheless view reading literature by ethnic writers as an important first step toward social engagement and change.

Other teacher-scholars, however, question such motives and objectives, usually along two lines. First, is it fair or appropriate, they ask, to impose an instructor's moral and political agenda on students? Are teachers of U.S. ethnic literatures hypocritical in their refusal to accept students' conservative viewpoints when multiculturalists advocate respect for and acceptance of difference? Additionally, some instructors worry about how to grade fairly students whose politics are disagreeable to themselves and their disciplinary claims. Moreover, when an instructor's viewpoint dominates classroom dialogue, how will students participate in knowledge making?

Some opponents of what has been called "politicized teaching" argue that students may merely mimic the teacher to please her.

For others, the emphasis on politics belies aesthetic appreciation. Efforts to broaden the canon to include diverse, previously marginalized voices were conducted with recognition of the socially constructed nature of literary excellence. As a result, criteria for constituting literary "greatness" became increasingly nebulous. Some scholar-teachers believe that a further consequence has been the privileging of "political" U.S. ethnic literatures–those texts that advance social justice agendas–at the expense of considerations of a text's aesthetic dimensions. Recently, however, multiculturalists have begun to acknowledge that aesthetics and politics are often inseparable, and efforts to more clearly identify and invent ethnic aesthetics are underway, particularly in African American, Chicano/a, Asian American, and Native American literary critical communities.

Teaching Multiculturally

Among the most crucial pedagogical questions for U.S. ethnic literatures is *how* these texts should be read and, subsequently, taught. Should these texts simply be added to an instructor's standard or familiar course syllabus, fit in as the instructor deems appropriate? What about the cultural, ethnic, and racial contexts of multicultural texts? Do we ignore these and teach texts according to familiar paradigms, forms, genres, and other formal qualities of literature, or should other kinds of critical approaches be brought to these texts? Many instructors of multiethnic literature agree that new critical categories and paradigms are necessary.

Chicano writer **Rudolfo Anaya**'s *Bless Me, Ultima* will serve as one example. This text is readily taught within the traditional framework of a coming-of-age novel, the bildungsroman, in which a young protagonist (typically white, male, and middle class) develops into a more mature individual through a standard pattern of making choices, breaking away from societal institutions, overcoming obstacles, undergoing a spiritual crisis, and finally, recognizing one's self-**identity** and place in the world. In *Bless Me, Ultima* the protagonist, Antonio (who narrates the story retrospectively), adheres to many of these traditional patterns. He moves away from the security of his mother's home to experience life and discover himself, and he encounters numerous tests along the way, including the violent killings of the sheriff and Lupito as well as knowledge of sin. Antonio must choose between the confinement represented by the farms of his maternal family, the Lunas, or the freedoms represented by his paternal family, the Márezes, and their history as *vaqueroes* (cowboys). The novel follows a fairly linear pattern that readers, especially students, find accessible and familiar.

But scholars of Chicano/a literature have identified many distinctive cultural elements in the text, such as references to Mexican Catholicism, code-switching, Aztec myth and symbol, New Mexican and Southwest folklore, and the importance of modernization's threat to agricultural and ranching ways of life in the small towns of New Mexico in the early 1940s. La Llorona, the wailing woman of the river in Mexican myth and folklore, permeates Antonio's self-discovery. La Llorona is associated with the women in the novel, most pointedly Antonio's mother, Maria, who offers warmth and security that Antonio must deny if he is to become a man. By understanding the significance of La Llorona, readers understand Antonio's story, not only in universal terms of growing up, but through the lens of Mexican folklore which was very much a part of Antonio's (and Anaya's) childhood.

Feminist perspectives are also crucial to effective multiethnic pedagogy, but some ethnic feminists find mainstream feminist critical frameworks limiting. Observing that feminist criticism was initiated by and based upon white, middle-class women, critics and teachers of texts by women of color charge that mainstream feminist interpretive frameworks often omit the racialized ethnic contexts embedded in this body of work. Accordingly, they argue that women of color are multiply marginalized by gender, race, **ethnicity**, class, and other categories of difference. As a result of this perspective, scholarship in multicultural literary studies argues for providing students with relevant cultural information as they read and interpret texts within feminist frameworks.

One common mainstream approach to texts by women writers of color is to consider the text within larger categories of women's traditions, such as narrative strategies, voice, and themes. For example, feminist critics tend to view women's connections to one another as a need for reassurance that they are not alone as writers and creators, even though patriarchal culture has long viewed the woman writer as deviant or as "monsters." One only need look at Charlotte Perkins Gilman's white, middle-class protagonist (in her widely read short story, "The Yellow Wallpaper,") who is completely isolated, with the exception of the woman she imagines in the wallpaper; while her creative energy at the story's end can be read as subversive, she ends up institutionalized for her alleged madness. This traditional reading of women's relationships can be productively applied to a text like African American writer **Alice Walker**'s *The Color Purple*, illuminating the female relationships that sustain Celie and ward off descent into madness, which would seem utterly understandable given the abuse she suffered as a young girl and an adult. Celie's developing relationships with the women around her—Shug, Sofia, Squeak, and even her sister Nettie, who she is able to communicate with through letter writing—parallel her healing of mind, body, and soul.

However, because many identified women's traditions were ascertained with or by white, middle-class women writers and may not apply to women of color or poor women, mainstream feminist notions of women's connections do not account for the decidedly African American nature of women's networks of support that derive from African cultural systems and black slaves' experiences during American **slavery**. Thus Celie's mutually supportive relationships with Shug, Sophia, Squeak, and Nettie become crucial to her development as a fully realized human being. Through such support, Celie can resist the patriarchal rhetoric that seeks to destroy her: Alphonso's admonitions that she tell no one about the rape, his vicious words about her ugliness, and Albert's hurtful contention that she is worthless. Additionally, Celie's writing reveals the creativity passed through generations of African American women. Walker honors black women's conscious and unconscious struggles to be creative despite the oppressive conditions in which they have historically lived. Celie's sewing activities aid her acquisition of black women's agency as they directly connect Celie with a community of women, past and present.

Teaching Methods

Infusing the curricula with multicultural perspectives refers to teaching practices as well as content and critical approach. It is the recognition that teaching practices are always politically constituted. In a multicultural classroom, subjects are approached in multiple ways and through multiple perspectives rather than top-down and single (teacher) voiced. All students' voices must be heard to make the classroom a genuinely democratic setting where everyone contributes to meaning-making. Such pedagogy recognizes that all students bring valuable experiences and knowledge to their readings of texts, and that students must feel free to express their views in a mutually informing conversation of ideas. Teaching from critical multicultural perspectives means helping students, especially women and students of color, to feel safe in classrooms and to realize that their ideas are valued.

The Instructor

The instructor of U.S. ethnic literatures faces enormous challenges. The notion of identity politics in literary studies continues to provoke passionate debate about whether one's ethnic background should determine what texts one can appropriately teach. That is, must Native American literature be taught by Native Americans? Must Asian American literature be taught by Asian Americans? Although some ethnic literature specialists continue to believe that white instructors should not teach ethnic literature, most acknowledge the pragmatic implications of such limitations; discouraging white instructors from teaching U.S. ethnic literatures would severely undermine advances in curricular diversification. Many also look beyond pragmatics to assert that any instructor, regardless of race or ethnicity, can commit to teaching any literature well through sustained study of the literature and relevant culture and history.

Finally, instructors of U.S. ethnic literatures understand that bringing issues of race into the classroom is risky, unpredictable, discomforting, and potentially explosive. Instructors of multiethnic literature face numerous challenges including marginalization by the institution; negative student responses to multicultural content, including defensiveness, resistance, apathy, anger, resentment, or guilt; and lower course ratings. Yet despite (or because of) these challenges, there is an urgency and excitement about multiethnic pedagogy among teachers, scholars, and students. When instructors teach about and with race, ethnicity, class, gender, and other social categories of difference, they raise the stakes for students and themselves. They push students to think and feel beyond what they are accustomed to, and instructors must do the same for themselves. Teachers who choose to teach U.S ethnic literatures can expect the unexpected, but the unexpected often brings the most meaningful moments inside or outside the classroom.

In many ways, effective teaching of U.S. ethnic literatures requires collaboration and sharing of ideas. An enormous amount of theoretical and pedagogical scholarship exists and all instructors and students should take advantage of these resources. In addition to the books listed below, which only begin to tap available resources, the following journals are recommend: *MELUS, College English, College Literature,* and *Pedagogy: Critical Approaches to Teaching Literature, Language, and Culture. (See also* Feminism, Womanism, Pedagogy and U.S. Ethnic Literatures)

Further Reading

Alberti, John, ed. *The Canon in the Classroom: The Pedagogical Implications of Canon Revision in American Literature.* New York: Garland, 1995.

Brannon, Lil, and Brenda M. Greene, eds. *Rethinking American Literature.* Urbana: NCTE, 1997.

Goebel, Bruce A., and James C. Hall, eds. *Teaching a "New Canon"? Students, Teachers, and Texts in the College Literature Classroom.* Urbana: NCTE, 1995.

Grobman, Laurie. *Teaching at the Crossroads: Cultures and Critical Perspectives in Literature by Women of Color.* San Francisco: Aunt Lute, 2001.

Jay, Gregory S. *American Literature and the Culture Wars.* Ithaca, NY: Cornell UP, 1997.

Maitino, John, and David R. Peck, eds. *Teaching American Ethnic Literatures.* Albuquerque: U of New Mexico P, 1996.

TuSmith, Bonnie. *All My Relatives: Community in Contemporary Ethnic American Literatures.* Ann Arbor: U of Michigan P, 1993.

Laurie Grobman

PELLOWSKI, ANNE (1933–)   Polish American author of children's literature, storyteller, essayist, and children's advocate. Anne Pellowski is likely America's best internationally known and most highly acclaimed professional storyteller and author of children's literature. She has lectured, performed, and consulted in approximately one hundred and fifteen countries and has developed a worldwide audience. In 1966 Pellowski established the Information Center on Children's Culture, an agency of the United Nations, and directed the Center until 1982. Pellowski has established a repertoire of stories and indexed literature from around the world.

In recognition of her achievements—scholarly, administrative, and artistic—on behalf of children, Pellowski has received numerous awards and honors. Among these are the Grolier Award of the American Library Association (1979) and the Constance Lindsay Skinner Award of the Women's National Book Association (1980) for "extraordinary contributions to the world of books and, through books, to society." Her citation for the latter award nicely summarizes Pellowski's work and career:

Author, teacher, librarian, storyteller, and world traveler, she fosters understanding through folktale and fable, fact and fiction. Using the magic of words and pictures, she educates adults and enchants children everywhere. With vitality, commitment, and vision, Anne Pellowski transforms every year into the Year of the Book, every hour into the Children's Hour.

It was not, however, until 1981 and 1982, with the publication of her Wisconsin farm tetralogy (*Stairstep Farm: Anna Rose's Story* [1981], *Willow Wind Farm: Betsy's Story* [1981], *First Farm in the Valley: Anna's Story* [1982], and *Winding Valley Farm: Annie's Story* [1982]) that Pellowski established herself as not only a dominant figure in the realm of children's literature but a model for the handling of ethnicity in that field and a major voice in Polish American literature.

Pellowski's tetralogy is a remarkable achievement. The four books trace the life of a single Polish American family from a time just after its arrival in the Latsch Valley of Wisconsin until the closing decades of the twentieth century: *First Farm* is set in 1876, *Winding Valley Farm* in the early 1900s, *Stairstep Farm* in the late 1930s, and *Willow Wind Farm* in the 1980s. In each book the protagonist and character whose point of view dominates the volume is a young daughter in the family, approximately six years old. In books two and three the young protagonists are the daughters of the main character of the previous volume; in the last book she is the niece of the previous protagonist. The tetralogy, then, is linked by its cast of characters, setting, ethnic cohesion, and themes, although the themes vary somewhat from generation to generation; it is also linked in the accuracy of its picture of rural life, by skillful storytelling, and as a remarkable record of **immigration**, family life, traditions, **ethnicity**, **assimilation**, and childhood.

Exceptionally well written, the volumes excel in several elements of fiction. Perhaps most remarkably, Pellowski achieves the delicate and difficult task of maintaining an informative and coherent narrative while reporting the story convincingly from the perspective of a six-year-old child.

The tetralogy is also remarkable as a contribution to a new kind of children's literature that presents life unflinchingly to its adolescent audience. The stories are not bowdlerized in a way that distorts reality and confuses children; they treat "sadness as well as joy, fear as well as courage, death and aging as well as life and birth—but always in the context of a loving family environment" (Napierkowski 95). Here are stories that enable children to grow intellectually and to deal honestly with a range of emotions.

It is, however, as a model of the treatment of neglected ethnicity in which the tetralogy breaks new ground. Not until recently has ethnicity received in the realm of children's literature the recognition it plays in the lives of millions of Americans; this is, of course, particularly true for frequently neglected groups such as Polish Americans. Anne Pellowski has argued that "one of the first rights of children is the right to an identity—personal and national"; she has worked assiduously to guarantee that right for all children. Her tetralogy presents a marvelous record of Polish American life and provides a model, without apology or chauvinism, of the presentation of ethnicity to children. (*See also* Polish American Novel)

Further Reading

Koloski, Bernard. "Children's Books: Lois Lenski, Maia Wojciechowska, Anne Pellowski." *Something of My Very Own to Say: American Women Writers of Polish Descent.* Ed. Thomas S. Gladsky and Rita Gladsky. Boulder, CO: East European Monographs, 1997. 144–69.

Napierkowski, Thomas J. "Anne Pellowski: A Voice for Polonia." *Polish American Studies* VLII.2 (1985): 89–97.

Thomas J. Napierkowski

PERDOMO, WILLIE (1967–) **Nuyorican**/African American poet and spoken word artist. Willie Perdomo's place in U.S. poetry falls somewhere between American **Langston Hughes** and Chilean Pablo Neruda. Born and raised in Spanish Harlem, Perdomo's poetry reflects the politics, social struggles, and urban scenery involved in being a black male Puerto Rican in Spanish Harlem. His poems, many of them spoken word, maintain the natural rhythms and flavors of Harlem street parlance and are informed by a keen poetic eye, his studies, and much artistic honing. Perdomo refined much of his poetic voice in the regular spoken-word competitions at the Nuyorican Poets' Café (founded by Miguel Algarín circa 1973), where he earned the title of Grand Slam Champ. He has been called by some the poet laureate of Puerto Rican New Yorkers. Perdomo is the author of several collections of poetry, including *Where a nickel costs a dime* (1996); *Smoking lovely* (2003); a children's book, *Visiting Langston* (2002); and a bilingual edition of poetry, *Postcards of el Barrio* (2002). His poems have appeared in numerous anthologies including *Aloud: Voices from the Nuyorican Poets' Café* (1995), *Bum Rush the Page: A Def Poetry Jam* (2002), *Step into the World* (2001), *Listen up!: A Spoken Word Anthology* (2000), and *Poems of New York* (2002). His work has also appeared in several magazines including the *New York Times Magazine, Bomb,* and *Urban Latino.* Perdomo has appeared in a number of PBS documentaries as well as HBO's Def Poetry Jam. He was the 2001 recipient of the New York Foundation for the Arts (NYFA) Poetry Fellowship, and in 1996 he received the NYFA Fiction Fellowship. He lives in New York.

His first collection of poems, *Where a nickel costs a dime* (1995), depicts a New York rife with drugs, AIDS, crime, violence, and also with hope and beauty. Its rhythms are informed by a wide range of influences from salsa to hip-hop beats to everyday life on the streets of East Harlem. *Postcards of el Barrio* (2002), Perdomo's second book, is a bilingual collection of poetry, published by Isla Negra Editores. His latest collection, *Smoking Lovely* (2003), follows in the footsteps of *Where a nickel costs a dime*, and is sold with an audio CD of the poet reading his works. As in his first collection, the reader is thrown into a New York full of social class struggles, **race** and race **identity**, violence, linguistic freedoms and problems, and love and tenderness. Perdomo continues with his street-smart lyrics and rhythms and maintains the intense eye of the poet he established in *Where a nickel costs a dime.*

Perdomo has also written *Visiting Langston* (2002), a children's picture book in verse illustrated by Bryan Collier. The book tells the tale of a young girl visiting the home where **Langston Hughes**, the influential African American writer, had once lived. (*See also* Bilingualism, Puerto Rican American Poetry)

Further Reading

Algarín, Miguel, and Bob Holman, eds. *Aloud: Voices from the Nuyorican Poets' Café.* New York: Henry Holt, 1994.

Stavans, Ilan. *Wachale!* Chicago: Cricket Books, 2001.

Alexander Waid

PERELMAN, S. J. (1904–79) Jewish American essayist, satirical journalist, surrealist, humorist, screenwriter, and playwright. He was born in Brooklyn, New York, to Russian immigrants, but grew up in Providence, Rhode Island. He began working as a cartoonist, but his commentaries on the cartoons grew more and more extensive so he became a writer. He said he was a crank who bruises easily, and when bruised writes. He worked for the *New Yorker* magazine, won an Oscar for screenwriting *Around the World in Eighty Days*, and collected his essays in over twenty books. His wit and biting social commentary were popular for almost fifty years.

Some of Perelman's last, and perhaps best, pieces were based on a seven-month global tour. *Eastward Hal*, a masterpiece of satiric railing, is an episodic travelogue recording his perilous and riotous journeys around the world, all in an attempt to ridicule the false values of various societies.

In France he observes that when taking a shower, one must remember that soap is not supplied, fats being conserved exclusively for soups. While shaving, the tin medicine cabinet covered in cheap plastic collapses into the sink, cutting him badly. But his rendition makes us laugh. His encounters with various vicious mechanical devices, and their success in completely mauling him, are the memories he has of Paris.

His trip to Iran coincides with the worst heat wave and the greatest pollution in forty years. He cannot get a hotel and is harassed by everyone he meets. Brooding on the thought that this treatment is not quite the rosewater and iced sherbet promised in Omar Khayyam, he trudges on. Finally, having bribed his way into a hotel (a funny tale in itself), he changes and goes for a walk in Tehran. It is a terrifying experience mainly due to the "world's most demented thoroughfares." He stops at a cafe for lunch. There he describes the antics and pratfalls of the Iranian waiters, comparing them to the Three Stooges. For instance, when a diner sees a roach on the curtain above his head and informs the staff, the waiter takes a folded newspaper, strikes at the insect and misses, but precipitates a thick shower of dust, all falling on the table and the food. Unconcerned, the waiter moves on.

Of Israel, he says, it takes great magic, ingenuity, and manpower to recreate Grossinger's, the Miami Fontainebleu, and the Concord Hotel on a barren strand in the Near East. The Soviet Union contains sanitariums that ignite more hypochondria in the onlooker than Thomas Mann's *Magic Mountain.*

Clearly, Perelman's great wit can at times seem dated and his references occasionally obscure. But the majority of his writings retains their high humor and can be appreciated for their insightful display of human characteristics and foibles. His writing highlights the flawed social mores and vulnerabilities of the twentieth century. And even if we don't laugh quite as loudly as we did in 1950, we surely can understand the human condition he reveals and satirizes so well.

Further Reading

Gale, Steven. *S .J. Perelman: A Critical Study.* New York: Greenwood Press, 1987.
Herrmann, Dorothy. *S. J Perelman: A Life.* New York: A Fireside Book, 1986.

Robert J. Toole

PÉREZ FIRMAT, GUSTAVO (1949–) Cuban American writer best known for his poetry, life writing, and literary scholarship. Pérez Firmat's work exemplifies the experience of the "one-and-a-half" generation: "Born in Cuba, Made in the U.S.A.," he explains in the title of the prologue to his memoirs, *Next Year in Cuba: A Cubano's Coming-of-Age in America* (1995). The inclusion of Pérez Firmat in the lists of the three leading publishers of Spanish-language or bilingual literature by Latino writers in the United States—Bilingual Press/Editorial Bilingüe (Tempe), **Arte Público Press** (Houston), and Ediciones Universal (Miami)—both affirms his broad appeal and secures his place in this literary canon. Pérez Firmat was elected to the American Academy of Arts and Sciences in 2004.

As a "one-and-a-halfer," Pérez Firmat has written more in English than in Spanish, and the underlying voice that unifies his literary oeuvre and even some of his criticism—whether English, Spanish, or bilingual—invariably explores Cuban exile and the attendant paradoxes of language, place, and identity. Pérez Firmat's play with the copulative verb *ser,* "to be," for example, acquires a special sadness vis-à-vis a search for identity (his own and his children's) realized through a prism that necessarily brings together icons of Cubanness with the American experience. Pérez

Firmat's collected poetry to date appears in *Carolina Cuban* (1987), *Equivoca-ciones* (1989), and *Bilingual Blues* (1995). A master of the short poem, Pérez Firmat is at his most compelling as he weaves bilingual word play and a keen sense of humor to make sense of the fragmented self of exile. "Vo(I)ces," the title of the Spanish-language preface to the bilingual poetry of *Carolina Cuban,* encapsulates both this aesthetic of brevity and the collab-oration between Pérez Firmat's Spanish and English voices. Pérez Firmat's autobiographical writing—*Next Year in Cuba*, its Spanish variant *El año que viene estamos en Cuba* (1997), and *Cincuenta lecciones de exilio y desexilio* (2000)—is no less poetic than his poetry is autobiographical. In the "les-sons," he takes the opportunity of his fiftieth birthday to return to the chal-lenges and pleasures of writing exclusively in his mother tongue. The three works form a poignant contribution to the growing body of memoirs of Latin American immigration and exile in the United States. Pérez Firmat's novel *Anything But Love* (2000), the erotic story of a Cuban exile professor, is a fictional showcase for his preferred topics.

Pérez Firmat's research includes pioneering studies in fields as disparate as Hispanic avant-garde fiction and literature of the Americas, along with a distinguished body of criticism on Cuban and Cuban American literature and culture, which he enriches with the privileged perspective of memoir. In *Tongue Ties: Logo-Eroticism in Anglo-Hispanic Literature* (2003), he extends his scholarly reach well beyond the Cuban context to study Anglophone writing by native or heritage speakers of Spanish from Spain and the Americas, culminating in the confessional epilogue "I'm Cuban—What's Your Excuse?" (*See also* Cuban American Autobiography, Cuban American Poetry, Bilingualism)

Further Reading

Pérez Firmat, Gustavo. Interview with Bruce Allen Dick. *Michigan Quarterly Review* 40.4 (2001): 682–92.

Catharine E. Wall

PETER BLUE CLOUD (1933–)   Native American poet. Also known by his Mohawk name, Aroniawenrate, Blue Cloud was born to the Turtle Clan of the Mohawk tribe in Kahnawake, Quebec, Canada. Native Ameri-can literary critic Joseph Bruhac regards him as an elder of the current gen-eration of Native American poets, whose work reflects a deep commitment to poetry and the Native American struggles for sovereignty. Blue Cloud received the American Book Award from the Before Columbus Foundation in 1981. He has worked as an ironworker, logger, carpenter, and woodcut-ter, but his literary career began with his work as poetry editor for *Akwanse Notes.* He has published extensively (more than sixteen books) and two of his books have been translated into German. However, many of these works are out of print. Fortunately, much of his work has been collected and republished recently in *Clans of Many Nations: Selected Poems 1969–1994* (1997). His poetry also appears in a wide variety of anthologies, including

Songs from This Earth on Turtles Back (1983), *A Coyote Reader* (1993), and *Nothing But the Truth: An Anthology of Native American Literature* (2000).

Blue Cloud is known for combining contemporary and political concerns with poetic ones. His first published volume, *Alcatraz Is Not an Island* (1972), is an anthology that reflects the history and occupation of the area, in the context of the **American Indian Movement**'s pan-tribal activism. His first book of poems, *Turtle, Bear and Wolf* (1976), connects contemporary activist issues with mythic histories—these animals feature significantly because of their relationship and embodiment of these Mohawk clans. In *White Corn Sister* (1979), Blue Cloud recreates the history of the arrival of Europeans, the first treaties and how they were broken, and Sullivan's march. He takes what may be abstract in history books and breathes emotion into it; histories of genocide and violence have had deep and ongoing effects in contemporary Native American life and we feel them deeply in his work.

Blue Cloud's poetry invests continuity and tradition with imagination. He is perhaps most famous for his poems and stories about Coyote, a **trickster** figure that appears across North American indigenous cultures, as in *Elderberry Flute Song* (1982) and *The Other Side of Nowhere* (1990). His work, however, refuses an anthropological attempt at replication or recording of tradition; it is rather a reinvention and continuation of it. Continuity, in Blue Cloud's work, depends on the individual voice, which then connects to a larger tradition. These traditions are both culturally specific, reflecting his Mohawk and Iroquois background, and deeply connected to a pan-Indian sensibility. This interconnection shapes even Blue Cloud's name, which in a rare published interview with **Joseph Bruchac**, he explains is a gift from the Paiute—Blue Cloud is a translation of his Mohawk name, Aroniawenrate. This sense of interconnection and interdependency between Native American cultures, between the old and the new, and between people and their surroundings (the landscape, the animals) animates Blue Cloud's poetic sensibilities and drives his work into the future. (*See also* Native American Poetry)

Further Reading

Bruchac, Joseph. *Survival This Way: Interviews with American Indian Poets.* Tucson: U of Arizona P, 1987.

Eliza Rodriguez y Gibson

PETERSON, LOUIS STAMFORD (1922–1998)   African American playwright, actor, television and movie scriptwriter, and professor. Louis Peterson grew up in Hartford, Connecticut, graduated from Morehouse College in Atlanta, studied at the Yale University School of Drama, and received an MA in acting and theater studies from New York University. He has written four plays, *Take a Giant Step* (1954), *Entertain a Ghost* (1962), *Crazy Horse* (1979), and *Another Show* (1983), and dozens of scripts for many popular television programs and Hollywood movies. Beginning in 1972 he taught for more than twenty years in the Department of Theatre Arts at the State University of New York at Stony Brook. Peterson died of cancer on April 27, 1998.

Peterson's first play, *Take a Giant Step*, is also his most successful and best-known work. A coming-of-age drama, *Take a Giant Step* focuses on a black male teenager who grows up in a predominantly white neighborhood and attends a mostly white school. It reveals his sense of alienation, sexual anxiety, conflicts with white peers and adults, and his struggle to forge his own sense of self. The play premiered on Broadway and elicited very favorable responses from critics as well as theatergoers.

Peterson's other three plays, however, were considerably less successful, both critically and commercially. *Entertain a Ghost,* partly autobiographical, examines the tensions between an interracial couple and the incremental collapse of their marriage. *Crazy Horse,* too, deals with the difficulties of sustaining an interracial relationship in the face of social disapproval and internalized hostilities. *Another Show,* Peterson's last play, explores the impact of a young man's suicide on his loved ones.

Disappointed by the lackluster reception accorded to his later plays, Peterson turned to television and movie screenwriting. He was enormously successful. He wrote individual episodes for many popular television series such as *Dr. Kildare* and *Wagon Train*. He wrote the screenplay for **William Saroyan**'s *The Confessions of Nat Turner* and authored the film script for his own play, *Take a Giant Step*, which became a successful commercial movie.

Further Reading

Abramson, Doris E. *Negro Playwrights in the American Theatre*, 1925–1959. New York: Columbia UP, 1969.

Delatiner, Barbara. "Playwright Eyes a New Giant Step." *New York Times* (February 20, 1983): E19.

Hill, James L. "Louis Stamford Peterson." *African American Dramatists: An A-to-Z Guide.* Ed. Emmanuel S. Nelson. Westport, CT: Greenwood Press, 2004. 347–351.

Trevor A. Sydney

PETRY, ANN (1908–1997)   African American novelist, short story writer, essayist, and poet. Ann Petry is the author of two milestones in African American literature: *The Street*, which is the first novel by an African American woman to sell more than a million copies; and *Miss Muriel and Other Stories*, which is the first short story collection by an African American woman writer. Ann Petry, the daughter of Peter Clark Lane Jr. and Bertha (nee James) Lane, was born above her father's drugstore in Old Saybrook, Connecticut, on October 12, 1908. Although Petry has been compared with other novelists such as **Richard Wright** and **Chester Himes**, and has been hailed as a literary foremother of such writers as **Toni Morrison** and **Gloria Naylor**, it appeared that Petry, who was also the granddaughter of a chemist, would follow in her family's footsteps and become a pharmacist. After graduating from Old Saybrook High School (1925) and receiving the PhG degree (1931) from the School of Pharmacy at the University of Connecticut, Petry worked at her family's drugstores in Old Saybrook and Old Lyme, Connecticut from 1931 to 1938, the year she married George Petry and moved to Harlem where she began her writing career. Petry, a fourth-generation Connecticut native, returned to Old Saybrook in 1947 when she and her husband purchased a two-hundred-year-old house and lived there until her death a half-century later. She never resumed her career as a pharmacist.

When Petry arrived in Harlem years after the **Harlem Renaissance** had ended, she worked as an advertising representative and journalist for New York's *Amsterdam News* (1938–41) as well as a reporter and editor of the woman's page for Adam Clayton Powell Jr.'s newspaper, the *People's Voice* (1941–44). During Petry's tenure at the *People's Voice*, she wrote about Harlem events in "The Lighter Side," a weekly column. Petry, who had been writing short stories as early as her college years, published her first story, "Marie of the Cabin Club" (1939), under the pseudonym of Arnold Petri in the *Baltimore Afro-American*. Prior to Petry's first novel, the *Crisis* published three of her stories: "On Saturday the Siren Sounds at Noon" (1943), "Olaf and His Girl Friend" (1945), and Like a Winding Sheet" (1945), which was also published in *Best American Short Stories* (1946), edited by Martha Foley. A Houghton Mifflin editor, after reading "On Saturday the Siren Sounds at Noon, encouraged Petry to apply for the publishing company's literary fellowship which offered $2400 and publication of her work. She submitted the opening chapters of her first novel, *The Street*, and won the fellowship in 1945. One year later, Houghton Mifflin published *The Street*, which was followed by her second novel, *Country Place* (1947). In 1949, the year that her daughter Elizabeth was born, Petry wrote her first children's book, *The Drugstore Cat*. Among the works that followed were essays such as "Harlem" (1949) and "The Novel as Social Criticism" (1950); Petry's third novel, *The Narrows* (1953); three children's nonfiction works, *Harriet Tubman: Conductor of the Underground Railroad* (1955), *ituba of Salem Village* (1964), and *Legends of the Saints* (1970); the previously mentioned *Miss Muriel and Other Short Stories* (1971); and three poems published in 1976, "Noo York City 1," "Noo York City 2," and "Noo York City 3," as well as two poems published in 1981, "A Purely Black Stone" and "A Real Boss Black Cat."

The Street, Petry's most popular novel, is also her most critically acclaimed. Unlike *Country Place*, which narrates a white veteran's return to his small New England town after World War II, and *The Narrows*, which reveals the tragic consequences of an interracial affair in a New England community, *The Street* presents the devastating effects of an urban environment on a mother and son in the 1940s. Petry's young, African American protagonist, Lutie Johnson, quits her job as a live-in maid for a family in Old Saybrook, leaves her adulterous husband, works as a hand presser in a steam laundry by day, takes stenography courses at night, passes civil service exams at least four times, and finally lands a job as a file clerk. When she arrives in Harlem and rents a three room apartment on 116th Street, she naively believes that the dismal tenement conditions she and her eight-year-old son, Bub, endure are merely temporary and that her hard work will guarantee them an improved lifestyle. Lutie anticipates climbing the ladder of success; instead she and Bub fall from the ladder into misery's pit. Petry, when creating Lutie, was undoubtedly influenced by her trailblazing, successful female relatives who refused to let their race and gender hinder their existence as they became chiropodists, pharmacists, teachers, and businesswomen. Petry imbues her female protagonist with the content of her mother, aunts, and sister's characters: their ambition, determination, and tenacity. Consequently, although Lutie does not succeed, her quest to eradicate limitations placed upon her transform Lutie into the prototype for subsequent African American female characters of the twentieth and twenty-first centuries, and *The Street* remains an American masterpiece. (*See also* African American Novel)

Further Reading

Clark, Keith. "A Distaff Dream Deferred? Ann Petry and the Art of Subversion." *African American Review* 26.3 (1992): 495–505.

Ervin, Hazel Arnett. *Ann Petry: A Bio-Bibliography.* New York: Hall, 1993.

Ervin, Hazel Arnett, and Hilary Holladay, eds. *Ann Petry's Short Fiction: Critical Essays.* Westport, CT: Praeger, 2004.

Holladay, Hilary. *Ann Petry.* New York: Twayne, 1996.

McKay, Nellie Y. "Ann Petry's *The Street* and *The Narrows:* A Study of the Influence of Class, Race, and Gender on Afro-American Women's Lives." *Women and War: The Changing Status of American Women from the 1930s to the 1950s.* Ed. Maria Diedrich and Dorothea Fischer-Hornug. New York: Berg, 1990. 127–40.

Linda M. Carter

PICANO, FELICE (1944–)   Italian American writer. In his review of *Looking Glass Lives* for the *Lambda Book Report*, Latino author Jaime Manrique compares Felice Picano to Joyce Carol Oates, emphasizing their prolific output and their willingness to write within a broad range of genres. He might have added that, like Oates, Picano has exhibited a continuing fascination with several paradoxes: the ways in which the mainstream and the margins of American life represent both congruent and discrete parts of the national experience; the ways in which sexuality both defines and is extraneous to personal **identity**; and the ways in which paranormal forces exert an extraordinary influence on events and yet seem to be a relatively commonplace phenomenon within ordinary experience.

Picano was born in New York City, and after completing his baccalaureate degree in 1964 at Queens College of the City University of New York, he became a social worker for several years. Then, for the next decade, he was employed alternately as a periodical editor or as a buyer for bookstores. In 1977, he founded Sea Horse Press, and in 1980 he cofounded the Gay Presses of New York. He continued his work with both presses until 1994. Since 1974 he has earned most of his income from his writing, though he has supplemented the income from his books by writing for a wide variety of newspapers, general periodicals, and special-interest journals. In addition, his work has been very frequently anthologized.

In the 1970s Picano established himself as an author of very commercial mainstream fiction, producing such novels as *Smart as the Devil* (1975), *Eyes* (1976), and *The Mesmerist* (1977). In all of these novels, he effectively combined suspenseful plots with an intense psychological interest in his characters. So, when he decided to "come out" as an author and to focus on openly gay characters and themes, it seemed to some that he was sacrificing his commercial success when, in actuality, he was able to insure the continuing success of his books by maintaining the basic approach to storytelling that had made his mainstream fictions popular. His "gay" novels include *An Asian Minor: The True Story of Ganymede* (1981), *Late in the Season* (1981), *House of Cards* (1984), the highly acclaimed *Like People in History* (1995), and *Looking Glass Lives* (1998).

Indeed, in the 1980s, Picano joined with a half-dozen other gay writers, including Andrew Holleran and Edmund White, to form the Violet Quill Club, which informally did much to promote a marketplace for gay authors and gay readers. One of Picano's most highly regarded novels, *The Book of Lies* (2000) is, in part, a *roman a clef* based on the Violet Quill Club. On the other hand, in his autobiographical writings, Picano has often couched his disclosures by placing them within a fictional frame. For instance, his second autobiographical volume is titled *Men Who Loved Me: A Memoir in the Form of a Novel* (1989). And his other autobiographical books—*Ambidextrous: The Secret Lives of Children* (1985) and *A House on the Ocean, A House on the Bay: A Memoir* (1997)—can be classified as creative nonfiction because of the variety of fictional techniques that Picano employs to great effect within the narratives.

Picano has also produced several collections of poems (including *The Deformity Lover and Other Poems* [1978] and *Window Elegies* [1986]) and several collections of short fiction (*Slashed to Ribbons in Defense of Love and Other Stories* [1983], *The New York Years: Stories* [2000], and *Counting Backwards* [2001], which collects both stories and essays). Several of his plays have been produced Off Off Broadway, most notably, *Immortal* (1986) and *One O'Clock* (1986). (*See also* Italian American Novel, Italian American Gay Literature)

Further Reading

Findle, Bob. "Still with the Quill: An Interview with Felice Picano." *Harrington Gay Men's Fiction Quarterly* 3.1(2001): 27–32.

Freis, Kevin S. "Prelude to Process: Sources of Felice Picano's Life Writing: An Interview Based on Oral and Written Communication." *A/B: Auto/Biography Studies* 15 (Summer 2000): 37–61.

Herren, Greg. "Felice Picano: Sex, Lies, and Manuscripts." *Lambda Book Report: A Review of Contemporary Gay and Lesbian Literature* 8 (November 1999): 6–8.

Hewitt, Chris. "A Portrait of Felice Picano." *Art & Understanding* (August 1994): 38–45.

McQuain, Kelly. "Lies and Lives: Interview with Felice Picano." *Art & Understanding* (November 1999): 49–52.

Meyerhofer, Will. "Felice Picano (1944–)." *Contemporary Gay American Novelists: A Bio-Bibliographical Critical Sourcebook.* Ed. Emmanuel S. Nelson. Westport, CT: Greenwood Press, 1993. 298–308.

Pela, Robert L. "A Writer's Journey: Felice Picano Talks about His Latest Novel, a Tale of Love and Travel through Time." *The Advocate* (September 15, 1998): 64.

Martin Kich

PIERCY, MARGE (1936–)   Jewish American novelist, poet, playwright, and activist. Marge Piercy is a highly prolific writer whose work has succeeded in reaching a large audience while making innovative use of multiple genres to treat the central political and social issues of the day. Particularly concerned with recording women's experiences, Piercy holds an important place in the emerging canon of contemporary feminist writers. Jewish **identity** has also been a recurring concern and she has contributed to the development of Jewish **feminism** and to the exploration of Jewish women's concerns in literature.

Piercy's novels and poetry share a direct style that emphasizes the details of everyday life, character, and events rather than intricate games of language, an approach that allows her to explore complex social and political issues while remaining accessible to a wide audience of readers. Many of her novels have been intentionally published as mass-market trade paperbacks because of her wish that readers, especially women, who do not often go to bookstores might come across her work in the supermarket or at the airport. Her realist approach has been praised by many critics for its direct yet innovative treatment of such issues as feminism, **racism**, and class. Some critics have faulted her for using her novels to schematically advance political ideas. For Piercy, however, the feminist idea that "the personal is political" means that politics are reflected in everyday experiences and vice versa. Thus in her novels discussions of war and peace are juxtaposed to household conflicts; similarly, her poetry collections might weave together accounts of women's struggles with harassment and domestic violence with odes to life in the country or to one of her cats. Her poetry uses wit and a colloquial style to gain the reader's attention and to delight even as she draws attention to difficult issues. The natural world has become an increasingly important concern in her poetry, and her recent work displays the influence of the landscape of Cape Cod where she currently lives with her husband, the writer Ira Wood.

Women on the Edge of Time (1976) and *He, She and It* (1991) have received particular attention for their use of the genre of future-based speculative

Marge Piercy. *Photo by Ira Wood, Leapfrog Press.*

fiction to explore feminist issues. These novels draw on and contribute to a means of exploration found in the work of writers including Margaret Atwood, Johanna Russ, and Charlotte Perkins Gilman. *Women on the Edge of Time*, which Piercy has identified as her personal favorite, juxtaposes a hopeful future in which men and women live in harmony with nature and take part equally in the birth and raising of children to live in a dystopic city in which technology rules everyday life and a rigid hierarchy structures all social interactions. The historical novels *Gone to Soldiers* (1987) and *City of Dark, City of Light* (1996) also display the scope of Piercy's vision, imagining the role of women in World War II and in the French Revolution, respectively, using extensive research to immerse the reader in the daily experience of her characters. Piercy has also reworked the genre of the romance in novels like *Small Changes* (1973) and *Braided Lives* (1988) in order to critique traditional male/female relationships and reveal the danger of the unquestioned belief in romance and marriage as the be-all and end-all of a woman's experience. The first section of *Small Changes* is ironically titled "The Happiest Day of a Woman's Life"; readers learn quickly that the wedding portrayed is anything but.

Piercy's work frequently explores the experiences of women marginalized for multiple reasons. Class issues and the experiences of working-class women, concerns underrepresented in contemporary American fiction, have had an important place in her work, especially in the novels *The High Cost of Living* (1978) and *The Longings of Women* (1994). Many of her works depict women who are lesbian or bisexual, and, unlike some white writers, she has not shied away from depicting characters of diverse ethnic and racial backgrounds or from depicting racial conflicts, as in the conflict over gentrification central to *Going Down Fast* (1969). Piercy's Jewish heritage has long been central to her work; Jewish ritual is particularly important to the stories told in *Summer People* (1989), *Gone to Soldiers*, and *He, She and It*, and in her poems reworking Jewish traditions collected in *The Art of Blessing the Day* (1999). She has written about how Jewish feminists can reinvent ritual and criticized the tendency of some feminists to see Judaism as a particularly sexist tradition. Her work can be understood as part of a growing

canon of feminist Jewish writers including **Grace Paley,** Robin Morgan, and **Adrienne Rich**.

While her work has sought to bear witness to the diversity of contemporary women's experiences, she presents a coherent vision of the feminist values she believes can guide us to a more just world. Central to this vision is the value of connection and mutuality and the dangers of hierarchies, isolation, and separation. This is reflected in the fact that many of her novels center, not on a single character, but on a web of relationships, deploying innovative stylistic devices in order to balance multiple points of view. Her vision of political writing is suggested in the title of her poetry collection *To Be of Use* (1973). She has written poems for specific occasions including demonstrations devoted to a range of causes as well as a sequence of poems, "The Chuppah," for her own wedding to Ira Wood. Her ethical vision of writing includes supporting the work of other women writers. She edited the collection *Early Ripening: American Women's Poetry Now* (1987) and frequently contributes reviews of women writers whose work she considers important.

Piercy's memoir *Sleeping With Cats* (2002) speaks candidly of the experiences that have fueled her writing and politics, interweaving photographs and her own poetry to tell this interconnected story. Raised in a working-class Jewish family in Detroit, she attended the University of Michigan where she found herself marked as an outsider. The atmosphere of political and artistic repression of the fifties and the damage done to women who were forced to turn to illegal abortions shapes her important novel *Braided Lives* (1982). After leaving graduate school to pursue writing, Piercy became highly involved in the Civil Rights and antiwar movements of the 1960s. Like many women activists, she became disenchanted with the sexism of these movements and turned her attention to the growing feminist movement in the 1970s. She has explored the political experiences of this period throughout her work, particularly in the novels *Dance the Eagle to Sleep* (1970) and *Vida* (1979). The moving poems of *My Mother's Body* (1985) suggest how her relationship with her mother helped to spark her desire to the tell stories of women who cannot tell their own in both her writing and in her activism. Piercy's work has always insisted on the complexity of the relationships between men and women, and while she does not hesitate to depict the pain caused by sexism, we can also see in her work the hope for more equal partnerships. Much of her recent poetry pays tribute to this hope by drawing on the experience of her marriage to Ira Wood, with whom she cowrote the play "The Last White Class" (1980) and the novel *Storm Tide* (1998).

Further Reading

Shands, Kerstin W. *The Repair of the World: The Novels of Marge Piercy.* Westport, CT: Greenwood Press, 1994.

Walker, Sue, and Hammer, Eugenie, eds. *Ways of Knowing: Essays on Marge Piercy.* Mobile, AL: Negative Capability Press, 1991.

Laura Tanenbaum

PIETRI, PEDRO (1943–2004)   Puerto Rican poet and playwright. Pedro Pietri was born in Ponce, Puerto Rico, and immigrated to the United States in 1945. He is a prolific writer, who has produced twenty-three plays, two books of poetry, and a narrative. Like some of his contemporaries, including Miguel Algarin and Sandra Maria Esteves, Pietri often mixes both Spanish and English in his work. This combination, which he calls Spanglish, embodies the sense of duality that Pietri's speakers and characters often feel about their identity.

Pietri's plays have been presented in New York and in San Juan, including *The Living Room* (1975), *What Goes Up Must Come Down* (1976), *Dead Heroes Have No Feelings* (1978), *Jesus Is Leaving* (1978), and *Mondo Mambo/A Mambo Rap Sodi* (1990). In addition, two of his plays have been published, *Illusions of a Revolving Door* (1992) and what is perhaps his best-known drama, *The Masses are Asses* (1984). The testament to this play's popularity is the fact that it has been performed by such great actors as Raul Juliá and has been translated into Spanish as *"Las Masas son Crasas."*

Along with Algarin and Esteves, Pedro Pietri is considered one of the founders of the Nuyorican poets. Adopting the name *Nuyorican* as a reference both to the city and to their Puerto Rican origins, these poets were part of the Beat Generation that produced such figures as **Allen Ginsberg** and **Jack Kerouac**. Pietri's poetry is oral, meant to be read out loud, and resonating with the sounds of the streets. Pietri's appearance, of a tough motorcycle club member, belies his personality. Although he is exuberant and loud-flashy, his words often convey a thoughtful, carefully measured message. His poetry reflects this contrast. *Traffic Violations* (1983), is a collection of poems that perfectly illustrates this notion, as it seems to be a haphazard amalgam of disconnected thoughts by speakers recalling their nights of drunken debauchery. When read more carefully, however, the poetry reveals speakers who are in tune with their surroundings as well as their inner voice. "I Hate Trees," for example, at first glance seems to be a sixteen-page rant with little connection to the poem's title. In fact, the poem is an elegy to Pietri's brother, and its poignant recollection of their friendship is one of Pietri's most powerful pieces of verse.

Puerto Rican Obituary (1971), however, is by far Pietri's most popular work. It is an appeal to ethnic pride as a defense against the broken promises of the American dream. The woes of discrimination and prejudice are countered by a call for defiance and nonconformity. The poem begins by referring to five recent immigrants who are the symbolic representation of all Puerto Ricans in New York. Using repetition, Pietri emphasizes how, despite the fact that these immigrants worked hard, all that they ever gained was death. Thus, the American dream was always beyond their reach even though they had learned to follow this new society's rules. These five immigrants, Juan, Miguel, Milagros, Olga, and Manuel, in fact all pursue the American dream in their own way. Juan waited for his lottery ticket to win, Miguel waited for the welfare check to help, Milagros waited for her children to take care of her, Olga waited for a raise, and Manuel waited for a promotion. Their waiting, however, was in vain, as they all died before these things became reality.

Although the poem casts blame on American society for inculcating these false dreams on Puerto Rican immigrants, Pietri also makes it clear that Puerto Ricans can choose not to embrace this illusion. The Puerto Ricans who have not yet died will die soon, the poem claims, because they continue to forget their roots by attempting to impress their bosses and trying to learn "correct" English. Most significantly, those left behind also choose to discriminate against each other based on socioeconomic status. This is a conscious choice, it seems, since, if they had remembered that they were not just American but also Puerto Rican, their souls would be in a place where black skin is the color of love.

Pedro Pietri's place in Puerto Rican literature cannot be overstated. The popularity of his plays continues, and to date they have been directed by such renowned figures as José Ferrer. His poetry is equally influential. Now translated into thirteen languages, *Puerto Rican Obituary* is a living testament to the far-reaching scope of Pietri's bilingual, biracial, bicultural, Nuyorican message. This message, shaped by Pietri's Vietnam experiences and his life in the New York streets of the 1960s, continues to influence a new generation of writers. (*See also* Bilingualism, Puerto Rican American Poetry)

Further Reading

Hernandez, Carmen Dolores. *Puerto Rican Voices in English: Interviews with Writers.* Westport, CT: Praeger, 1997.

Luis, William. *Dance Between Two Cultures: Latino Caribbean Literature Written in the United States.* Nashville: Vanderbilt UP, 1997.

Mohr, Eugene. *The Nuyorican Experience: Literature of the Puerto Rican Minority.* Westport, CT: Greenwood Press, 1982.

Stavans, Ilan. *The Hispanic Condition: Reflections on Culture and Identity in America.* New York: HarperCollins, 1995.

Eduardo R. del Rio

PIETRZYK, LESLIE (1961–)   Polish American novelist and short story writer. Leslie Pietrzyk is the author of approximately fifty short stories published in journals such as *Iowa Review, Gettysburg Review,* and *New England Review* and in various anthologies. In the course of her career, she has won numerous awards including *Shenandoah*'s Jean Charpiot Goodheart Prize for Fiction (1996), *Descant*'s Frank O'Connor Memorial Award (1996), and the Whetstone Prize (1996). It was not, however, until the publication of her first novel, *Pears on a Willow Tree* (1998), that Pietrzyk was recognized as a major new figure on the American literary scene and emerged as one of the leading authors in the current renaissance of Polish American literature. She has recently published her second novel, *Year and a Day* (2004).

Pears on a Willow Tree was greeted with more acclaim in prestigious venues, both in the United States and abroad, than the first novel of any other Polish American. The *Washington Post*, for example, reported that it "marks the debut of a genuine and fully developed talent with a most promising future." The *New York Times Review of Books* hailed Pietrzyk's "untapped gifts of eye and ear" and "her skill at characterization." The novel is the story of four generations of Polish American women "bound together by recipes, reminiscences, and tangled relationships" made even more complicated by their various responses to the family's story of **immigration** and ethnic **identity**. In the course of the century covered in the novel, the women of the first two generations, mother and daughter, hold tight to the family's traditions and identity while the granddaughter flees both, and the great-granddaughter struggles to recover and understand what her mother has rejected. A synopsis of the novel gives no indication of its literary strengths, thematic sophistication, and ethnic impact.

Characterization is particularly impressive in the novel. Ginger, for example, the daughter of the third generation who flees family and identity, is a chilling portrait of an alcoholic mother. The nuances of similarities and contrasts between the four generations and the complexities of their relationships are delivered through Pietrzyk's deft handling of characterization. Essential to Pietrzyk's achievement with characterization is her exceptional handling of point of view; each representative of the four generations of Marchewka women tells her part of the story in a limited first person point of view. Pietrzyk establishes the different identity and perspective of each woman with subtlety and maintains them with the skill of a mature artist. Contributing to the characterization and point of view is a remarkable attention to language. Pietrzyk is not only sensitive to the nuances of language in the Polish American home—an early dominance of Polish, a macaronic stage, and the triumph of English with a continuing presence of Polish, if only in words and phrases—she is exceptionally skilled in reflecting them in dialogue and points of view.

The themes of *Pears on a Willow Tree* are not new; the complex relationships between mothers and daughters, the "reverberations" of immigration, and the struggle with the question of what it means to be a woman have been addressed by countless authors. The success of Pietrzyk's handling of these themes resides in the "affection and clarity" with which she treats them and in her insistence that, for all of their universality, there is uniqueness to the struggle of each individual, each family, and each ethnic group to come to terms with such fundamental issues of life. Furthermore, Pietrzyk focuses the themes on the motif of storytelling and the women's attitudes toward the family's stories. Rose, the great-grandmother, assures her mother in Poland she will tell the stories to her American daughter and that her daughter will remember them. Helen, the American daughter, finds the Polish stories difficult to understand in the new country but passes them on. Ginger, Helen's daughter, wants new stories and leaves the family to find them. Finally, Amy,

Ginger's daughter, recovers the stories (new and old, Polish and American), tells them to her infant daughter, and is confident that the daughter will put them into books and win awards for them.

Two elements are significant about this motif. The fact that women are the storytellers reinforces both Polish **feminism** and the feminist strain of Polish American literature. It also reminds readers that without their stories, no ethnic group can survive. Pietrzyk's work has contributed mightily to the preservation of the Polish American story and readers of all backgrounds have expressed their appreciation. (*See also* Polish American Novel)

Further Reading

Harleman, Ann. "The Matriarchs." *New York Times Book Review* 148 (October 4, 1998): 21.

Merullo, Roland. *"Pears on a Willow Tree:* An Immigrants' Tale That Bears Plentiful Fruit." *Washington Post* (October 19, 1998): D09.

Thomas J. Napierkowski

PILLIN, WILLIAM (1910–1985) Jewish Russian American poet and ceramic craftsman. Pillin published nine volumes of poetry: *Poetry* (1939), *Theory of Silence* (1949), *Dance Without Shoes* (1956), *Passage After Midnight* (1958), *Pavanne for a Fading Memory* (1963), *Everything Falling* (1971), *The Abandoned Music Room* (1975), *To the End of Time: Poems New and Selected (1939–79)*, and *Another Dawn* (1984). His poems have been published in over one hundred journals including *New Republic, Saturday Review, Southwest Review,* and *Epos. Poetry* magazine awarded him the Jeanette Sewell Davis Prize (1937). He and his wife Polia have designed and exhibited hundreds of pieces of ceramic pottery.

Although Pillin shunned the idea of being a cult figure, he is identified with California's Papa Bach bohemians, writing of "socialism of the heart" and "anarchic space" ("That which is good is simply done"). He considered his influences more European than American or English.

As a poet, he writes of the suffering of Jews, yet sometimes in a dispassionate tone. In "The Requirement," he is thankful for having survived the **Holocaust** while his "burning cousins" did not; he mentions "strange German ovens" and speaks of Jews cremated in "Thor's ovens," yet he thanks God for fire. He is also unorthodox in advocating for victims, preferring "loudmouth, unhappy, conniving jews," the "scum" of the ghettos, whom no one mourns. He defends rude neighbors, rotting walls, and pavement cracks as reminders that we all could fall so low. His view of life, described as "delicate dissonances" and as a "nectarine with a violent core," reiterates the fickleness of fate and man's penchant for violence.

In spite of his apparent pessimism, his verses reveal optimism and reverence. Although not subscribing to the rituals of Judaism, he tries his "ignorant best" to extend love. In "Two Jewish Poems," he sees God as forgiving and extols the virtue of labor rather than asking "favors" of God. Through imagery, alliteration, and metaphor, his lyrical verses depict the beauty of the everyday world where even small things matter and his poetry is a softly fading "lamp of metaphor." Mundane life is made up of quiet door-ways and soft lamplights but he prefers life as a sonata, sleep as a "winding sheet," kiln's clay as "tomorrow's meal," awareness as an "eager trout" ("Passage After Midnight"). He delights in mythology, allusion, and mysti-cism, likening a jaunt to Ocean Park to adventure with Merlin, Shahrazad, and Sinbad; having Pan accompany him to a poetry reading; alluding to Niobe and Rachael in talks with his grandfather and Lazarus with his doc-tor; and lamenting his vulnerability without his grandmother's magic.

Pillin died of a heart attack in 1985, after a life rich with poetry, music, friendship, and art.

Further Reading

Dickey, James. "Five Poets." *Poetry* 94 (1959): 121–22.

Novak, Estelle Gershgoren, ed. *Poets of the Non-Existent City: Los Angeles in the McCarthy Era.* Albuquerque: U of New Mexico P, 2002.

Rolfe, Lionel. "Hidden Links." *In Search of Los Angeles.* L.A.: California Classics, 2002.

Donna Kilgore-Kimble

PINEDA, CECILE (1932–)   Mexican and Swiss American novelist, autobiographer, and theater director. Cecile Pineda, born and raised in New York, moved to San Francisco in 1961 and has lived in the Bay Area ever since. She has published five novels: *Face* (1985), *Frieze* (1986), *The Love Queen of the Amazon* (1992), *Bardo 99* (2000), and *Redoubt* (2000). She has also published a fictional memoir, *Fishlight: A Dream of Childhood* (2001). *Face* won the Sue Kaufman Prize awarded by the American Academy and Insti-tute of Art and Letters, the Gold Medal from the Commonwealth Club of California, and was nominated for The American Book Award for First Work. Prior to her career as a novelist, Pineda founded an ensemble com-pany in San Francisco called Theatre of Man, which she directed from 1969 to 1981, staging a dozen dramatic productions, including original adapta-tions of T. S. Eliot's *Murder in the Cathedral* in 1969 and Franz Kafka's *The Trial* in 1975.

Face takes place in the 1970s and is set in the Whale Back, a "slum dis-trict" in Rio de Janeiro, Brazil. The novel tells the story of Helio Cara, a bar-ber, who suffers a devastating accident. He falls down a flight of stairs, disfiguring his face beyond recognition. (The word "cara" in Spanish and Portuguese translates to "face" in English.) Too poor to afford reconstructive surgery, and rejected by his lover, coworkers, and neighbors, Helio leaves the capital and returns to his home village in the "Hinterland," where he teaches himself basic surgical techniques and thus begins the arduous task of recon-structing his face and his identity.

Pineda's second novel, *Frieze*, traces the life of Gopal, who lives in India in the ninth century. As a sculptor of friezes, he is an artisan, a high-skilled worker better off than the slaves but still exploited by the ruling classes. He is forced to migrate to Java, leaving his family behind, to carve 120 friezes in the temple of Borobudur. The friezes narrate the life of Siddhartha Gautama, the Buddha, also known as "The Enlightened One." The builders of the temple promise to pay him ten pieces of gold when he completes the project, which takes twenty years to finish; instead, having seen the beauty and truth of Gautama's narrative, they send their henchmen to blind him by putting hot iron to his eyes. *Face* and *Frieze* are modernist narratives: In addition to telling interesting stories thematically, they also offer self-reflexive commentaries on the act of novel writing.

Pineda further demonstrates her concern with modernist self-reflection in her third novel, *The Love Queen of the Amazon*. The novel's Peruvian protagonist, Ana Magdalena Figueroa, is married to a man who is writing a novel titled *The Love Queen of the Amazon* and Ana's lover owns a boat he names "The Amazon Queen." Thus the novel is about Ana, but it is also metafiction—fiction about itself. Whereas *Face* explores the consequences of losing the façade of one's identity, *The Love Queen* examines the specificity of gendered identity from a woman's point of view in a fictional world dominated by men. Pineda's magical realist *Love Queen* has been compared to the works of Jorge Luis Borges, Gabriel García Márquez, and Mario Vargas Llosa. *The Love Queen* can be read as both a tribute to these writers and a critique of the male-oriented discourses that inform much of Latin American fiction.

In her two "mononovels," Pineda delves even deeper into philosophical questions concerning the limits and possibilities of history. In *Redoubt*, Pineda asks an impossible question: What would the twentieth century say and how would it feel if it were to take the form of an individual consciousness? More importantly, how would this consciousness be different if it took the form of Woman rather than Man? In *Bardo 99*, Pineda constructs a narrative that mediates between the poles of various abstract binaries: chance and necessity, accident and causality, birth and death, modern and postmodern, and peace and war. Imagine waking up one day alone, not knowing where you are, how you got there, or where you are headed. This is the Kafkaesque predicament in which Joseph Viek, the protagonist of *Bardo 99*, finds himself, not unlike the predicament of humankind itself in the modern period. Pineda's autobiographical novel, *Fishlight*, is narrated from the perspective of a five year old. Terribly funny and gut-wrenchingly heartbreaking, *Fishlight* traces the influences of an eccentric Mexican father and an overbearing Swiss mother on the thinking and feelings of a young girl as she comes to consciousness of the world.

Given the particular kinds of conflicts represented in Pineda's fiction, one may conclude that her novels are largely philosophical in nature. Pineda also writes, however, about issues that have been important to Chicana/o writers since the 1960s: examining the formation and problems of **identity**, imagining subjects capable of effecting historical change, criticizing patriarchy and **racism**, exposing the devastation caused by forced migration, depicting social class contradictions, and arguing for a conception of art and literature as political.

Further Reading

Christian, Karen. *Show and Tell: Identity as Performance.* Albuquerque: U of New Mexico P, 1997.

Magill, Frank N. "Book Review of *Face.*" *Masterpieces of Latino Literature.* New York: HarperCollins, 1994. 157–60.

Rodriguez, Barbara. "Making Face, Making Race: Prosopopoeia, Autobiography, and Identity Construction in Cecile Pineda's *Face.*" *Autobiographical Inscriptions.* Oxford: Oxford UP, 1999. 177–204.

Marcial Gonzalez

PIÑERO, MIGUEL (1946–1988)   Poet, playwright, screenwriter, and actor. Miguel Piñero is best known for his award winning play *Short Eyes*, which became both a Broadway show and a commercial film during the 1970s. He also wrote and acted in television crime dramas such as *Kojak*, *Barretta*, and *Miami Vice*. Some critics report that contemporary Hollywood images of Latinos, specifically criminals, are based on Piñero's depictions created for the previously mentioned television programs. A prolific and eloquent writer, Piñero is also credited, along with Miguel Algarín, as being one of the founders of the **Nuyorican** Poets' Café. His life was depicted in the 2000 film *Piñero*, directed by Leon Ichaso.

Considered by many scholars and critics to be a real life "outlaw," his writing, as well as his life, was a testament to his refusal to conform to the mainstream's status quo and its ideals for success. His writing can be described as a counter-discourse (connecting him to such exiled writers as the Cuban **Reinaldo Arenas**, and the Puerto Rican Manuel Ramos Otero) to the belief that an individual must conform to a homogenous mentality and a uniform way of life in order to achieve success as prescribed by mainstream society. Rather, his writing reflects life as he lived it and experienced it. In essence, his writing and life experiences were nonapologetic; his writing depicted life on the streets, the underworld, characters such as drug dealers and prostitutes—individuals who lived their lives in complete opposition to conventional social expectations. Unlike many contemporary media depictions of modern-day outlaws, gangsters, and drug lords, the characters and descriptions created by Piñero were based on his own experiences in the streets with the people he encountered and associated with.

His plays in particular showcase his belief in living life as an individual, avoiding conformity and presenting a reality that has often been ignored. As a matter of choice and style, his plays often attacked "the comfortable aesthetics of the middle-class theater goers" (Kanellos 1997, 245). His work also criticized **racism**, "exploitation of the poor, **colonialism** (in Puerto Rico), greed, and materialism" (Kanellos 245–46).

Another aspect of his writing touches on how Puerto Ricans on the island view those individuals who call themselves "Nuyoricans" as Americanized versions of what a Puerto Rican is—and at the same time a threat to Puerto Rican island culture. This attitude is best represented in the film *Piñero* where the poet is attacked by some of his Puerto Rican audience members during a presentation of his poetry. Piñero's response was that his Nuyorican **identity** reflected his condition—a Puerto Rican who was "transplanted" to New York and who had to adapt to his environment in order to survive.

Further Reading

Acosta-Belén, Edna. "Beyond Island Boundaries: Ethnicity, Gender, and Cultural Revitalization in Nuyorican Literature." *Callaloo* 15.4 (Autumn 1992): 979–98.

Kanellos, Nicolás, ed. *The Hispanic Literary Companion.* New York: Visible Ink, 1997.

Luis, William. "From New York to the World: An Interview with Tato Laviera." *Callaloo* 15.4 (Autumn 1992): 1022–33.

Enrique Morales-Diaz

PLUMPP, STERLING (1940–) African American poet. Sterling Plumpp, raised in an extended family sharecropper household in Clinton, Mississippi, is a professor emeritus at the University of Illinois at Chicago, where, since 1971, he has taught in the African American Studies and English departments. Plumpp is known for his deeply reflective poetry, rich in self-examination and reflection upon the maturation process as viewed through African American history in vivid sweeping portrayals. Such poems constitute the bulk of his early volumes of verse, such as *Portable Soul* (1969) and *Steps to Break the Circle* (1974). He later wrote a more autobiographical work of poetry, *Clinton* (1976), which received an Illinois Arts Council Literary award. The success of his two longer works, *Clinton* and *Steps to Break the Circle*, brought him considerable acclaim.

In both works, he continues his exploration—which he began in his first work of prose, *Black Rituals* (1972)—into the psychological and historical development of African Americans as it relates to oppression. Plumpp, who refers to his early life in Mississippi as a peasant existence, struggles to come to terms with anger and a sense of rejection. He attempts to break all associations with cultural affinities related to this subsistence existence. Yet, he finds in the **blues** of his southern migrant past an anchor and source of spirituality. This theme of uprooting and rerooting is central to *Clinton* and *Steps To Break the Circle*.

In *Black Rituals*, Plumpp names **James Baldwin** as a major influence along with **Haki R. Madhubuti**. Poems in Plumpp's *The Mojo Hands Call, I Must Go* (1982), awarded an Illinois Arts Council award, resemble some of Baldwin's works: The facts of his life become the foundation for imaginative meditations on society and history. In the early seventies, Plumpp joined the Organization of Black American Culture and worked closely with fellow member Haki R. Madhubuti on several editing projects. The work of Plumpp, however, reflects a departure from the black aesthetic movement that Madhubuti was aligned with and revisits an earlier time, as evidenced by the employment of biographical material, black vernacular, and southern black folk life. He looks to writers such as **W. E. B. Du Bois**, **Sterling A. Brown**, and **Richard Wright** as sources of inspiration.

In more recent times, Plumpp has received attention for his use of **jazz**, **blues**, and **spirituals**; in 2003 Plumpp received the Keeping Blues Alive in Literature award. As shown in *Martin Scorsese Presents the Blues: A Musical Journey* (2003), **John Edgar Wideman**'s essay, "A Riff on Reading Sterling Plumpp's Poetry," draws parallels between the blues tradition and Plumpp's writing style as seen in Plumpp's compression of language, remarkably varied and broad expanse of form, and employment of blues-oriented ambiance, scenes, topics, and tone. *Blues Narratives* (1999), for example, uses the voices of a male and several female narrators who tell the stories of their lives. *Velvet BeBop* (2003) celebrates the blues tradition, speaks in a language of riffs and blues formations, and dialogues with many of the great innovators in the African American musical tradition. Much of Plumpp's work is about self-examination, preservation of southern black folklife, and collective liberation of black people.

Further Reading

Cunningham, James. "Baldwinian Aesthetics in Sterling Plumpp's Mojo Poems." *Black American Literature Forum* 23.3: 505–18.

Roland Barksdale-Hall

POCAHONTAS [MATOAKA] (c. 1595–1617) Daughter of Wahunsonacook, headman of the Algonquian-speaking Powhatan Confederacy of Tidewater Virginia; mythologized in American literature as an Indian princess and epitomized in Vachel Lindsay's poem *Our Mother Pocahontas* as "the mother of us all." The centerpiece of her narrative—her alleged rescue of Captain John Smith from the hands of bloodthirsty tribesmen, as described by Smith in his *Generall Historie of Virginia, New England, and the Summer Isles* (1624)—falsely suggests her desire to abandon Powhatan culture and asserts English triumph over the indigenous peoples of the Virginia colonies. In Smith's narrative, she retains her "Indianness" as an exotic, colluding Other who invites colonization through seduction. Scholars have conjectured that Smith invented the rescue, or misinterpreted a ritual adoption ceremony.

Pocahontas's true story delineates her subjugation, however, far more than Smith's yarn. More of a captive than a friend to the English colonists at Jamestown, she was held as ransom for food and the release of English prisoners. During her captivity, she may have been coerced into conversion and marriage to the widower John Thomas Rolfe. Rolfe had much to gain as the founder of the tobacco industry (the result of his hybridization of two tobacco species), and his letter to Governor Dale asking for permission to marry Pocahontas suggests that the motive was not romantic but political ("but for the good of this plantation, for the honour of our countrie, for the glory of God, for my owne salvation, and for the converting to the true knowledge of God and Jesus Christ, an unbelieving creature, namely Pokahuntas"). Obliterating her Indian **identity**—and, importantly, her identity as an Indian woman—was her conversion, in which she abandoned her traditional belief system and assumed a Christian name; her marriage, in which she became under English law the property of her husband; and her subsequent childbirth, in which she passed Native ownership of Virginia to her English son. The register of her death at Gravesend, England, recorded March 21, 1616/1617, reads: "Rebecca Wroth wyffe of Thomas Wroth/gent[leman] a Virginia Lady borne was buried/in the Chauncell."

The nineteenth-century theater established the myth of Pocahontas and the Indian princess. In 1808, James Nelson Barker's melodrama The Indian Princess, ou la Belle Sauvage premiered in Philadelphia. The first play by an American-born playwright about an American Indian subject (and the first of almost twenty Pocahontas plays that dominated the century), The Indian Princess reinforces Smith's version of Pocahontas's recognition of the technological and religious superiority of the messianic white men who have come to save the Indians from their savagery, and she is prepared to die to defend the English.

Further Reading

Allen, Paula Gunn. *Pocahontas: Medicine Woman, Spy, Entrepreneur, and Diplomat.* San Francisco: Harper San Francisco, 2003.

Price, David. *Love and Hate in Jamestown: John Smith, Pocahontas, and the Heart of a New Nation.* New York: Knopf Publishing, 2003

Tilton, Robert S. *Pocahontas: The Evolution of an American Narrative.* Cambridge: Cambridge UP, 1994.

W. Douglas Powers

POLISH AMERICAN LITERATURE IN POLISH   In 1938 immigrant historian Artur Waldo dedicated his sketch of Polish American literature to the "Forgotten Writers of American Polonia." If their names were already forgotten in 1938, while many of them were still alive and some were still publishing, how much more obscure they are today, nearly seventy years later. However, the literature they produced was an important element in the genesis of Polish America. And that literature was written in Polish.

Among the best-kept secrets of ethnic American literature is the existence of immigrant literary traditions outside the English language. Operating beneath the American cultural radar and often drawn from community life, works written by immigrants in their native tongues can offer a rare, unaccommodated view of immigrant social, political, and cultural worlds.

Although Polish Americans did not enter the American literary mainstream until much later, by the 1880s they had already begun developing a literature of their own in the Polish language. Producing and distributing novels, short fiction, poetry, and plays through their own publishing networks, Polish immigrant writers supplied readers with works which reflected their own experiences and interests. Poles are not unique in this—other immigrant groups have done the same, with much overlap in subject matter and publication patterns. However, the historical circumstances of Poland's political dismemberment by Prussia, Russia, and Austria-Hungary from the final years of the eighteenth century until the end of World War I resulted in strategies of national survival which shaped the work of Polonia's earliest immigrant writers and gave it a distinctive, clearly articulated purpose. That purpose was the formation of a Polish national consciousness among the mostly peasant immigrant readership in the United States.

That literature was enlisted in the national cause is consistent with trends among Polish writers in Europe during the same time period, after the crushing failure of armed insurrections against Russian rule in 1830 and 1863 had forced a rethinking of strategies of resistance to foreign rule. In order to sustain Polish national consciousness, patriots turned to "organic work"—that is, the building of social, economic, and cultural foundations through grassroots education and local development. Peasants, who traditionally had not been considered part of the body politic, were increasingly encouraged to revise their traditional identification with the local community or parish—the *okolica*—and embrace a larger, national collectivity as Poles. The content of and criteria for that Polishness was hotly debated, as Polish writers used their work to promote various models of nationhood. Immigrant writers, influenced by the same trends and with a reading public drawn from different regions, cultural backgrounds, and social strata, recognized a unique opportunity to transform their readers from *tutejsi*—locals—into Poles. Literature was only one component in this project, which was shared by American Polonia's leadership overall. But it was a vital component.

Even a quick acquaintance with the literary culture created by Poles of the Great Wave **immigration**, from roughly the 1870s through the 1930s, undermines the popular image of Polish Americans (and Slavic Americans in general) as silent and passive. Newspapers and magazines proliferated, lending libraries became a part of even the smallest communities, local theater flourished, and book publishers released thousands of titles. In the process, individual lives were transformed and a culture was created. As one immigrant remembered, "Those books and newspapers opened my eyes, so that from then on I felt what I was and what Poland was, what a series of battles she went through for her national unity, about the heroes and traitors" (Dziembowska I:489).

Publishers sprang up wherever Poles were settled, particularly in Chicago; Buffalo; Detroit; New York City; Stevens Point, Wisconsin; and Toledo, Ohio, where Antoni Paryski operated Polonia's most prolific newspaper and book publishing company from 1889 until his death in 1935. Like Paryski, many publishers were affiliated with newspapers, which greatly facilitated production and distribution of the inexpensive books that immigrants could afford. Most books were priced at five to twenty-five cents, and many were given away as premiums for newspaper subscriptions. Paryski even employed "education agents" who sold his goods in taverns and other immigrant gathering places. Among the thousands of fiction and nonfiction titles offered by Paryski and other immigrant publishers were hundreds of novels, novellas, short stories, sketches, collections of poetry, and plays written by immigrants themselves, "based on Polish-American conditions," as so many were subtitled. Many other works were self-published by their authors, or appeared only in newspaper or magazine serialization.

As early as 1870, the poems of Teofila Samolińska were being printed in the Polish immigrant press. With the 1873 staging of her play *Emancypacja kobiet* (The Emancipation of Women), Samolińska also established herself as one of Polonia's earliest dramatists. In 1881, the first Polish immigrant novel was published. These pioneering efforts were quickly followed by other writers, who recognized the importance of offering readers a literature based on their own experiences and concerns. Helena Staś, one of the most prolific of Polonia's authors, argued that immigrants "don't understand Mickiewicz or Słowacki. . . . But they would understand a literature created for them, based on their lives. That's the only way the national spirit will survive in a foreign land" (*Na ludzkim targu* 180).

Staś and her contemporaries created a diverse literature. It included works of social protest like her 1910 novel, *Na ludzkim targu* (In the Human Market) and immigration sagas like Czeslaw Łukaszkiewicz's *Anioł stróż i djabeł stróż* (Guardian Angel and Guardian Devil, 1931). There were detective stories and potboilers like Henryk Nagiel's often-reprinted *Kara Bożaidzie przez oceany* (God's Punishment Crosses the Ocean, 1896). Political intrigue was a popular theme, as in Stanisław Osada's *W dniach nędzy i zbrodni* (In Days of Misery and Crime, 1908), which dealt with President McKinley's assassination by Polish American Leon Czołgosz. Polish immigrant writers also produced songs, vaudeville-style stage reviews, collections of poetry (including the bilingual *Antologia poezji polsko-amerykańskiej* [Anthology of Polish-American Poetry], 1937, edited by Tadeusz Mitana), radio soap operas, romance novels, patriotic plays, social satires, religious conversion tales, and anti-clerical exposés.

By the 1920s, Polish immigrant literature was well established and prominent authors had emerged. But the reality of a reborn Polish state after World War I was also testing Polonia's allegiances and identity. It was during this time, in fact, that several of the most important writers returned permanently to Poland. At the same time the second generation, with facility in English and its own developing culture—Polish American rather than Polish—was coming of age. Writers continued to produce works in Polish, but increasingly they dealt with the concerns of the second generation as it struggled to balance its widening experience outside the ethnic community with its continuing loyalty to Polishness and to Poland. Notable among works of this era are Melania Nesterowicz's novels of manner, including the popular *Sprzedawaczka z Broadwayu* (The Salesgirl from Broadway, 1937), which was also produced for the stage and for radio. Although works like these became increasingly sophisticated in the 1920s and 1930s, the momentum of the early years was fading. With the exception of a handful of poets like **Victoria Janda** who wrote in both Polish and English, a second generation of authors writing in Polish failed to emerge.

However, World War II and its aftermath brought a new wave of Polish immigrants to this country. Along with new problems and possibilities for Polonia, this meant a revitalization of Polish-language writing in America. The old publishing networks had deteriorated and were judged inadequate or irrelevant by the new immigrant cohort, many of whom, unlike the Great Wave immigrants, were well educated and city bred. Feeling the same need for a literature that reflected their experiences—so different from those of the earlier immigrants and their American-born children—they created their own publishing enterprises. Some, like the Roy (Rój) company, were transplanted from Poland. But they also turned to publishers in London and France, which became the venues for a worldwide community of émigré intellectuals. Émigré writers in the United States like Stanisław Barańczak and Czesław Miłosz became international figures, rarely writing about American Polonia (and, in the case of Miłosz, sparking controversy when he did by disparaging Polish American ethnic culture). But other writers like **Danuta Mostwin**—a sociologist by profession—focused, like the author-activists of half a century before, on immigrant problems and experiences (see Danuta Mostwin, *Testaments: Two Novellas of Emigration and Exile.* trans. Marta Erdman, 2005). Poetry, along with memoirs of the war years, were popular literary forms, but with fewer immigrant publishers in operation, many writers self-published their work. Polish-language theater survived, but performing companies preferred the works of European Polish writers to homegrown ones like Antoni Jax and Szczęsny Zahajkiewicz of the previous generation. The creation and consolidation of a Polish identity was no longer an issue—after all, these writers and readers had come from an established Polish state. But writers continued to engage issues of cultural survival in America, adding to them their political concerns about a Communist Poland to which they could not return.

The crackdown on the Solidarity labor union and the imposition of martial law in Poland in 1981 brought yet another wave of immigrants to the United States. They were joined by an even larger group, the *wakacjusze* or "vacationers," Poles who entered this country on tourist visas with the intention of working under the table, often staying for years at a time and establishing lives and families here. While new immigrant publishers emerged, usually small enterprises based in Polonian centers like Chicago and New York, writers also benefited by international contacts in a world made smaller by technology. Janusz Głowacki, a playwright living in New York since 1981, is the most prominent of the Solidarity-era émigré writers. His 1987 play *Hunting Cockroaches*, originally published in Polish as *Połowanie za karaluchy*, is a semi-absurdist look at a Polish actress and her husband struggling to find meaning in their new lives in New York. Other writers, most notably Zofia Mierzyńska and Edward Redliński, deal unflinchingly with the experiences of Polish illegals. Mierzyńska's novels about women workers, most notably *Wakacjuszka* (The Vacationer, 1985), bear much in common, in theme and subject, with turn-of-the-century works, particularly in their focus on village Poles transplanted to urban America; Redliński's artistically sophisticated novels like *Dolorado* (1984) include bitter depictions of the situation of illegal workers. In 1997 his *Szczuropolacy* (Rat-Poles), published in Poland in 1994, was made into the tragi-comic film *Szczęśliwego Nowego Yorku* (Merry Christmas and Happy New York). Like many of Polonia's most prominent writers of the turn-of-the-century immigration, both Mierzyńska and Redliński eventually returned to Poland. And, also like turn-of-the-century writers, both have been criticized for airing the immigrant community's dirty laundry. But until Polish immigrant works are made available in English translation, these issues, like the literature itself, will continue to exist in the shadows of American literary discourse. (*See also* Polish American Novel).

Further Reading

Dziembowska, Janina, ed. *Pamiętniki emigrantów: Stany Zjednoczone* [Emigrant memoirs: United States]. Warsaw: Książka i Wiedza, 1977.

Gladsky, Thomas S., and Rita Holmes Gladsky, eds. *Something of My Very Own to Say: American Women Writers of Polish Descent.* Boulder CO: East European Monographs, 1997.

Jacobson, Matthew Frye. *Special Sorrows: The Diasporic Imagination among Irish, Jewish, and Polish Immigrants in the United States.* Cambridge, MA: Harvard UP, 1995.

Kruszka, Wacław X. *A History of the Poles in America to 1908.* Part I. Trans. Krystyna Jankowski. Ed. James S. Pula. Washington, DC: Catholic U of America P, 1993.

Majewski, Karen. *Traitors and True Poles: Narrating a Polish-American Identity, 1880–1939.* Athens: Ohio UP, 2003.

Waldo, Artur. "Polish-American Theatre." *Ethnic Theatre in the United States.* Ed. Maxine Seller. Westport, CT: Greenwood, 1983. 387–417.

Zaborowska, Magdalena J. *How We Found America: Reading Gender through East European Immigrant Narratives.* Chapel Hill: U of North Carolina P, 1995.

Karen Majewski

POLISH AMERICAN NOVEL   Novels in English by writers of Polish descent have had a relatively recent history, beginning with stories published in the 1920s. Polonia's fiction writers have predominantly explored themes linked to an historical evolution of concerns about ethnicity in the context of America's melting-pot culture: anxieties about **assimilation**, revitalizing memories of immigrants, the erosion of ethnic communities, the alienation of descent generations from their Polish roots, and the reconnection to a Polish cultural heritage by contemporary descent generations.

Reconstituting the Immigrant Past

Monica Krawczyk is distinguished as Polonia's first professional fiction writer in English. Throughout the 1920s and 1930s she wrote stories that focused on the rural life of Polish Americans in her native Minnesota. Her work first appeared in magazines such as *Good Housekeeping* and *Country Home,* and it was later published as a collection, *If the Branch Blossoms,* in 1951. Krawczyk's portrayals of domestic country life underscore the upheavals that Polish American families experienced before the mid-twentieth century as they shifted from an Old-World patriarchal structure to a New World orientation that gave women a more central position in the household. Her female protagonists are conduits for two sets of lessons juxtaposed in her stories. They maintain customs brought from the Old World that bring joy, solace, and stability to the family—a role in which they fulfill the ethnic expectations assigned to their gender. But Krawczyk's heroines in fiction also demonstrate another set of lessons from the New World. In her prize-winning story "No Man Alone" it is the mother who advocates the acquisition and use of modern inventions such as the telephone; she also persuades her old-fashioned husband to break out of his rural isolation and attend meetings of an American community organization known as the Grange Club where he will learn about new scientific farming techniques. With her insightful portrayals of strong Polish American immigrant women who help their families maintain their own ethnic traditions and also adapt to American society, Krawczyk was a pioneer in showing Polonia a positive vision for the accommodation of transformed roles both in gender and in **ethnicity**.

Set in Wisconsin, **Wanda Kubiak**'s novel, *Polonaise Nevermore* (1962), provides a complex portrayal of an immigrant settlement by agrarian Polish Americans. Her depiction underscores the divisions within this group, especially those that emanate from the opposing pulls of assimilation and nationalism. These are epitomized in the conflict of two families concerning the future role of the Catholic Church recently built by the settlement. Through her detailed descriptions of the varied folk Polish customs that are practiced by different groups in the settlement, Kubiak emphasizes the fact that the immigrants come from a country comprising areas that differ greatly. Although she underscores divisions within the ethnic community, Kubiak also portrays American and Polish characters who discover a strong kinship between their two cultures, such as the democratic and patriotic ideals they have historically shared. The author proposes that a pluralistic vision of the New World, rather than cultural isolation acerbated by Old World divisiveness, is the most helpful response of the Polish immigrants to the demands of their new environment.

In contrast to Kubiak's depiction of a divided ethnic community, **Anne Pellowski**'s series of novels for young people offers an image of Polish American life that is secured by its strong historical basis on the values of family, culture, community, and religion. The author acts as a guide through four generations of her family's history; the novels are set in the Latsch Valley of Wisconsin and written as a tetralogy: *Willow Wind Farm* (1981), *Stairstep Farm* (1981), *Winding Valley Farm* (1982), and *First Farm in the Valley* (1982). Each book portrays a Polish American childhood that is structured on a series of vignettes. The first volume focuses on the present generation who maintain few of the visible signs of ethnicity, especially the Polish language. However the author emphasizes the coherence of the Polish American life that is based on a sense of community and the natural incorporation of folk traditions and celebrations into daily routine. The author stresses the centrality and abiding significance of the Catholic Church for each generation of Polonia, so that even if contemporary generations forego Polish terms for their ethnic traditions, the symbolic and spiritual significance of each ritual endures. Pellowski employs a very effective narrative structure in her series of novels by retracing the family's saga backwards in time so that the last volume focuses on her immigrant roots. Thus, because the context of connection to historical realities is so firmly established at the end of her saga, the reader is left with a heightened impression about the significance and value of Polish traditions.

A succession of descent novelists, notably Phillip Bonosky and Matt Babinski, have turned their attention to what might be designated the second major stage in the saga of Polonia—the struggles of immigrant families to realize their aspirations by making a great leap from an agrarian culture and mentality to the brutal stresses and demands of a working-class environment. In the course of this difficult transition, and for several decades to come, Polish-Americans became known as especially active in the struggle for workers' rights. The value of Bonosky's and Babinski's novels is that they provide a three-dimensional depiction of the socioeconomic and political evolution of Polonia's working-class culture.

Phillip Bonosky's novel, *Burning Valley* (1953), offers a sociopolitical retrospective of labor unrest and union struggles during the 1920s and 1930s in the ethnic industrial communities of western Pennsylvania and West Virginia. He depicts a Polish American worker, Benedict, who challenges a hierarchy of church, state, and corporate leadership that thwarts the attempts of workers to better their lot in life. The author presents Benedict as a working-class hero with an emerging political consciousness who can rally fellow workers against the forces of the economic status quo. Bonosky's historical portrayal is valuable as a realistic depiction of a protagonist who realizes that he must defend political ideals that directly oppose the conservative values espoused by the religious and business traditionalists within his Polish American community.

In *By Raz 1937* (1978), Matt Babinski structures his story of working-class struggle around his boyhood past, focusing on the Polish American mill workers' environment in Worcester, Massachusetts, during the Great Depression. The author depicts the perceptions of the protagonist, Raz, who must make assessments about two contrasting faces of his community in order to determine the future course of his life. On one side he sees ruined lives and socioeconomic decay of the collapsed mill industry produced by the collapsed chimera of the American dream. Opposite this blight, within his own ethnic community, he finds hope, moral strength, and emotional support through his Uncle Eevon, who helps Raz explore his Polish **identity**. As part of Babinski's probing analysis of the Polish working-class community, he depicts Raz's discovery that, along with the stability of traditional culture and religion, this environment harbors the danger of stagnation and isolation from the vitality of the world outside. The author also shows his protagonist's ability to evolve beyond the myopic perspectives of his community when Raz decides to go to college and chooses a career in art. This choice eventually also proves to be a way for Raz to disseminate his Polish cultural heritage to the broader society, and thus to come to terms with his ethnicity.

Loss of Ethnicity

For several decades after World War II, there was a mass exodus of second and third generation Polonia from traditional ethnic communities; many Polish Americans loosened ties to their cultural heritage by anglicizing their names and by dropping the use and teaching of Polish at home. A number of descent writers, like Richard Bankowsky and Darryl Poniscan, published works during the 1960s and 1970s that explored the alienation and the disaffection of Polish America's contemporary generation.

Richard Bankowsky's tetralogy—*A Glass Rose* (1958), *After Pentecost* (1961), *On a Dark Night* (1964), and *The Pale Criminals* (1967)—explores the theme of the eroding Polish American community through a focus on the fate of one Polish American family and its descendants. The Macheks immigrate to America in the early 1900s to settle in a New Jersey factory town that remains the emotional and spiritual center for succeeding generations of the family. This saga about the fate of the Polish peasant in America is the antithesis of the histories of successful **assimilation** prevalent in many previous Polish American novels. Bankowsky employs a wide array of narrative techniques and thematic approaches to convey this complex history of clan disintegration. The Macheks and their descendants submit to vice and despair in their fall from the New World paradise that their immigrant ancestors tried to create. At the end of the history there is some hope of a return to grace for the family when the last remaining member retires to a Catholic sanctuary and lives out his days with respect and wisdom. Bankowsky's gloomy depiction of an ethnic family's disintegration in America surely gave Polonia's community food for thought regarding the disaffection and alienation of its younger generation during the turbulent 1960s in America.

Darryl Poniscan's fiction about contemporary working-class Polish Americans expands the theme of the ethnic as cultural outsider. Three of his novels, *The Last Detail* (1970), *Goldengrove* (1971), and *The Accomplice* (1975), explore the lives of descendants from the Buddusky family who originate from the decaying Polish coal-mining community in northeastern Pennsylvania called Andoshen, the focus of a fourth novel, *Andoshen, Pa* (1973). Poniscan's protagonists are young men who strive unsuccessfully to escape the limitations of their traditional, downtrodden ethnic communities. Whether they choose the route of the rebel, the upwardly mobile professional, or the criminal drifter, they are depicted as trapped by an ethnicity that confines them to the lowest socioeconomic ranks. Poniscan's view of this generation is that it is truly alienated—through cultural and emotional distance from their ethnic communities and through condemnation by the larger world as despised losers.

Recuperating Ethnicity

The 1980s ushered in a cultural renaissance for Polonia. Political upheaval in Poland during the period of the Solidarity trade union movement and its aftermath brought many Polish refugees to America, including writers and intellectuals who helped to renew interest in Polish American ethnicity and a cultural reconnection with Polish "roots." The election of a Polish Pope boosted Polish America's view of itself. A new generation of descent fiction writers, **Stuart Dybek**, **Gary Gildner**, **Anthony Bukoski,** and **Suzanne Strempek Shea**, began to reexamine the possibilities of recuperating and redefining Polish American ethnicity.

In some ways Stuart Dybek's stories about his Chicago-based Polish American communities seem to focus primarily on the erosion of ethnicity, particularly in the context of the decay of inner-city neighborhoods. Stories in his collections *Childhood and Other Neighborhoods* (1980) and *The Coast of Chicago* (1991) feature protagonists who are young second- or third-generation descendants and who appear unconscious of their own "Polishness" or else associate it with the disintegration of their urban environment. Only fragments of Polish tradition and language remain, and these are associated with the traces of the older immigrant generation of relatives and neighbors who are dying off. Almost as a form of defense against this neighborhood decay, Dybek's protagonists use their imaginative capabilities to transform the bleak and gritty emptiness of their environment into a realm of mystery and romance. Certain old immigrant customs and traditions appear strange to Dybek's young protagonists and are invested with a fascinating grotesquerie. In "Blood Soup," from *Childhood and Other Neighborhoods*, two brothers search outside their own neighborhood to obtain the main ingredient for the *czarnina* (a Polish soup made with duck's blood) that their ailing grandmother wants to make as a cure for her illness. However, they discover that the blood cannot be legally purchased. Thus, their quest turns into an exotic adventure leading them into an underworld of threatening places where they confront bizarre eccentrics like the insane elderly Polish recluse Pan Gowumpe who maintains an illegal aviary. Dybek's later collection of stories, *The Coast of Chicago* (1991), is marked by a shift in narrative tone. He conveys sense of lyrical fondness for the old ethnic working-class neighborhoods and many aspects of Polish cultural heritage, if still unfamiliar, are here depicted as both exotic and restorative. In "Chopin in Winter" the story's young protagonist lives among a group of Polish American families who are traumatized by misfortune and strife. When a neighbor begins to incessantly play piano music that the boy doesn't recognize as Chopin's music, his gruff old Polish grandfather forces his grandson to learn about the composer and his significance for Poles. The boy is thus left with a legacy of pride in his Polish cultural heritage and a valuable appreciation for the uplifting and consoling powers of art in one's life. In other stories in the same collection, Dybuk stresses aspects of Chicago ethnic neighborhoods that show how they adapt in response to the changes within the American social fabric: through interethnic marriages, tolerance of "otherness," and an elevated social and moral awareness. His fiction emphasizes that although they are no longer traditional Polish American communities, these environments have redefined themselves as mosaics of ethnicities, in opposition to the homogenization inherent in the melting-pot ideal of becoming "All-American."

Gildner, who is a poet and novelist, is a good example of a descent author who began to explore his ethnic identity most fully in the latter part of his career. His early works tend to incorporate elements from his Polish American background in a peripheral manner. His first novel, *The Second Bridge* (1987), features Bill Rau, who is half Polish and suffers a mental breakdown after the collapse of his marriage and his child's death. Although Gildner does not dwell on ethnicity as a crucial element of characterization, his protagonist harks to his upbringing in an ethnic home. The security and stability he experienced with his Polish American family acts as a poignant counterpoint to the current chaotic life he now leads. Gildner was able to explore his cultural roots thoroughly some years later when he visited Poland as a Fulbright lecturer at Warsaw University. Shortly after his return, *The Warsaw Sparks* (1990), a record of his Polish experience, was published, exemplifying the extent to which his artistic imagination has become more fully engaged with aspects of his Polish heritage.

Anthony Bukoski's fiction focuses on the specific concerns of the ethnic communities in the Superior Great Lakes region of the United States, and his narrative themes are similar to those that preoccupy other descent writ-

ers of current generations. Throughout several collections of his stories—
Children of Strangers (1993), *Polonaise* (1999), and *Time Between Trains*
(2003)—he expresses for many Polish Americans their sense of distance
from Poland's past and its cultural heritage. He portrays this estrangement
as a form of alienation between older and younger generations. It is
through his unique narrative style that Bukoski has revitalized the fictional
treatment of this topic. He focuses on the emotional states of his characters
whose innermost thoughts and feelings are expressed though stream-of-
consciousness or dreamlike revelations. Thus, he effectively conveys the
feeling of urgency that accompanies his protagonists' need to reconnect
with their Polish roots through older relatives and neighbors. In the story
"Old Customs," he depicts the last hours of communication between a
young girl and her dying immigrant great-aunt. With poignancy and
despair the girl narrates how she strives to understand her aunt's memories of her Polish childhood, told in broken English. She sees her cultural
heritage disappearing with her aunt's death and her own loss of fluency in
Polish. Throughout his writing, Bukoski perceives the importance of language as a key connection with ancestry. Thus, as an important contribution to the Polish American literature, his fiction plays an important part in
strengthening to Polish cultural roots. Suzanne Strempek Shea is a contemporary Polish American woman writer whose realistic narratives portray
young women who link an exploration of their ethnicity with a quest for
self-definition that often conflicts with the restrictive gender roles prescribed by their tradition-bound families. Her novels are set in the working-
class neighborhoods of Massachusetts; the culture and traditions of Polish
American life play an especially prominent part in two works. The heroine
of *Selling the Lite of Heaven* (1994) is forced to rethink the course of her life
when her hopes for a traditional marriage are shattered. After she challenges her immigrant mother, who demands that she pursue the role of the
acquiescent Polish American daughter, the young woman finds the inner
fortitude to pursue life goals that are more compatible with her evolving
self-definition. In *Hoopi ShoopiDonna* (1996), the element of Polish American
popular culture plays a central role. By following her own life's dream of
forming an all-girl polka band, the heroine flouts traditional ethnic expectations for women. Polka music is an important motif in the novel, since it
bonds the family together and also provides a channel for the heroine's
self-definition. Ultimately, Strempek Shea's heroines show that the Polish
American family can survive the challenges of the modern world through
creative adaptability

Many fresh voices have emerged from the community of Polonia's fiction
writers: Denise Dee, Melissa Kwasny, and **Leslie Pietrzyk**, to name a few.
Some explore topics reflecting contemporary issues that challenge traditional ideas about ethnicity. The themes that absorb these authors lead back
to the central concern and question that has engaged authors of Polish
American fiction from its very inception: "What does it mean to be Polish

American?" (*See also* Polish American Literature in Polish, Polish Émigré Writers in the United States, Polish American [Literary] Stereotypes)

Further Reading

Bukowczyk, John J. *And My Children Did Not Know Me: A History of the Polish-Americans.* Bloomington: Indiana UP, 1987.

Gasyna, George Z. "Inscribing Others: Polish-American Writers After the Great Divide." *Living in Translation: Polish Writers in America.* Ed. Halina Stephan. Amsterdam: Rodopi, 2003. 331–77.

Gladsky, Thomas S. *Princes, Peasants and Other Polish Selves: Ethnicity in American Literature.* Amherst: U of Massachusetts P, 1992.

Gladsky, Thomas S., and Rita Holmes Gladsky, eds. *Something of My Very Own to Say: American Women Writers of Polish Descent.* East European Monographs Series. New York: Columbia UP, 1997.

Diana Arlene Chlebek

POLISH AMERICAN (LITERARY) STEREOTYPES For the great majority of Polish immigrants, America represented an opportunity to recreate Polish culture in the New World, a place where religious, cultural, and even political traditions could be maintained and discussed through the Polish language. Subsequently, in the late nineteenth and early twentieth centuries, Polish immigrants and many of their descendents wrote in their own language, directing their efforts exclusively toward the ethnic community. For these and other reasons, the literary portrayal of Polish culture and ethnicity in the larger culture was constructed, not by the Poles themselves, but by host culture writers. The literary representation of Polish ethnicity by American writers of Polish descent appears generations later and necessarily takes different forms.

To speak, therefore, of the characterization of Poles in American literature is to acknowledge that two radically different forms of representation are at work—often simultaneously. More to the point, host culture writers have described Poles and Polish Americans through the prism of American sociopolitical topics and as reflections of America's own cultural fears and frustrations, aspirations and ideals. The result is that, throughout the nineteenth century and well into the twentieth, Polish characters and their cultural heritage are, for the most part, American cultural constructs. One might go so far as to describe Polish characters in American literary works as cultural stereotypes created to respond to the sociopolitical and ideological climate and issues of the times.

The 1830s are a case in point when, for the first time, Poles and Poland appear in American letters. In 1831 the Poles rose unsuccessfully against their Russian oppressors and attracted the world's attention. The exiles in Paris, including Frederick Chopin, excited revolutionary sympathies and James Fenimore Cooper, in his "Letter to My Countrymen" (published in American newspapers) and in his participation in a Paris-based Committee to Aid Poland, stirred American hearts as did the arrival in New York harbor of two boats of Polish officers sentenced to exile by the Tsar. Immediately, in poems, novels, and plays, America rushed to sympathize with the Polish cause. This response was, in part, a historical reflex, dating back to the Revolution when two young Polish officers, Casmir Pulaski and Thaddeus Kosciusko, served America's interests without reservation, creating an indelible impression in the American temper. In addition, Poland's historically democratic instincts served to justify and complement America's own developing ideological self-portrait. That is to say, Americans, enamored with New World egalitarianism and Old World culture, viewed the Poles as an idealized us—a blend of democrat and aristocrat whose character and breeding resembled the portrait of the natural aristocrat discussed by Jefferson and the American gentleman described at length by James Fenimore Cooper.

Rather than pointing out cultural differences, writers sought to show that Poles are indeed just like us. So eager were 1830's writers, such as Samuel Knapp (*The Polish Chiefs*), Robin Carver (*Stories of Poland*), Silas Steele (*The Brazen Drum or Yankee in Poland*), and Susan Rigby Morgan (*Polish Orphan*), to link American and Polish history, that the destiny of the characters in their works parallels America's own: to point the way to freedom and to sacrifice all for the cause. Poles in these works are defenders of Christianity and freedom, bearers of enlightenment and culture, and foes to tyranny and oppression. In response to the 1831 Uprising, poems appeared in scores of American periodicals and newspapers in which poets referred to "glorious liberty," "righteous cause," "freedom's temple," "tyrant's shackles," and other patriotic flourishes reminiscent of the poetry the American Revolution. In short, Poles are admirable combinations of culture, patriotic tenacity, and democratic instincts—perfect representations of the national idealized self in Jacksonian America.

The image of the Pole as a bearer of culture, natural aristocrat, and sympathetic victim of oppression persisted throughout the nineteenth century. Louisa May Alcott, for example, modeled the main male character of *Little Women* (1868) after a Pole she had met in Switzerland, where he had come after participating in yet another attempt by Poles to rise against their oppressors. In the novel, Laddie (Wladislaw) is the embodiment of Victorian manliness. In addition, Alcott wrote "My Polish Boy" (1864) and "The Baron's Gloves" (1869) which also feature refined, patriotic, God-fearing Polish aristocrats. Although Polish characters appear infrequently in American letters in the nineteenth century, whenever they do appear, they unmistakably bear resemblance to the portraits offered in the 1830s. In Mary Ives Todd's *Violina: A Romance* (1904) and Rupert Hughes's *Zal: An International Romance* (1905), the Polish protagonists are rooted in Polish history and described as kinsman of Kosciusko and Pulaski and the officers of 1831 celebrated in America's periodical press. Once again, Poles are represented as patriotic and poetic; in *Zal*, for example, Ladislaw, the protagonist, writes an opera about the 1830 uprising. Highly educated and cultured, they speak French, know music, and possess fine manners and breeding. Todd explains that there are "no braver, more liberty loving people on earth."

In the latter part of the nineteenth century, the ongoing debate about America's racial, religious, and ethnic makeup was rekindled with the arrival of millions of eastern and southern European immigrants who, in many ways, did not resemble their predecessors. Perhaps as many as 2,000,000 Polish peasants, for example, responded to the demand for labor in American industry. These Poles were neither natural aristocrats, nor military officers, nor musicians. They were peasants fresh from the village with little awareness of high culture or learning. They had little sense of either national **identity** or of their own **ethnicity**. Almost immediately what had been a consistent literary image of the Pole as a European beau ideal was transformed in the periodical press into that of a cultural deviant who reflected America's conscious and unconscious fears of Catholicism, Slavic physiognomy, peasant coarseness, and sexual virility. Furthermore, writers and politicians ignored the nuances of cultural difference and lumped immigrants together into a composite representation of the "Other."

The periodical press charged that the immigrants brought with them a dangerous political philosophy—a combination of socialism, anarchy, and distrust for democracy. Catherine Metcalf Roof's *Strangers at the Hearth* is illustrative. She describes the new immigrants as the raw waste of Europe, hoodlums who endanger the ideals of the founding fathers. The Slav, according to Roof, is used to a life as simple as a dog's in a kennel. In novels such as Richard Henry Savage's *The Anarchist* (1894), Edward S. Van Zile's *Kings in Adversity* (1897), and Thomas Dixon Jr.'s *Comrades* (1901), Poles enter the mainstream of political literature in reactionary novels designed to stir up fear about the new proletariat and about radical anarchist politics. At the same time, writers with a different political ideology began to write about the plight of the immigrant working-class poor. A number featured Polish characters, including I. K. Friedman, Jack Fletcher Cobb, and James Oppenheim. Cobb drew upon a stereotype quickly fashioned from the American imagination: Joe is brutish, slow-witted, violent, "a damned animal," in the eyes of the foundry foreman. A realization of cultural fears for many Americans, the image of the Pole as anarchist and as proletariat was quickly countered, however, by fuller, more rounded representations of the new immigrants as transformational agents and nation builders.

Karl Harriman was such a writer. In *The Homebuilders* (1902), his characters are neither radicalized workers, nor downtrodden immigrants and dangerous anarchists. He presents the Poles in their own milieu as newly arrived urban workers. He makes it clear that dual ancestry does not come easily, a point dramatized in "The Day of the Game" (1909) where we discover that John Adams, the hero of the Michigan victory over Cornell, is actually Jan Adamovsky who has hidden his Polish identity to assimilate more easily only to discover that he has lost his cultural heritage in the process. Harriman's sensitive portrayal of Adamovsky makes it clear that some Americans recognized the trials of transplant in more than two-dimensional terms. For example, Frances Allen introduced the Polish farmer into American literature. In *The Invaders* (1913), she captures America's ambivalence toward the Polish peasant. On the one hand, her Poles are uneducated and socially backward. On the other, they are industrious and family centered. America prefers, Allen seems to say, the Poles of an earlier period. Thus she praises Stefan Posadowski, whose manners and breeding are a stark contrast to the peasant farmers in her novel. When he performs Chopin, he instructs the townspeople about the "real Poland," one quite different from the villages from which Allen's Polish farmers originated. Allen's willingness to see cultural difference in the new immigrants while still preferring an idealized literary model perfectly illustrates the sociopolitical climate of the period.

In the post–World War I period, America confronted an agricultural crisis, particularly in New England where farms suffered from neglect and the movement West that left agricultural regions deserted and undermanned. The crisis was further exacerbated by the great immigration and an influx of Poles into the Connecticut River valley which some regarded as a threat to New England's heritage. Many began to see immigrants as threats to the established American way of life. Rather quickly, writers turned to the Pole as a way to discuss a new and vital sociopolitical issue. Beginning with Edith Miniter (*Our Natupski Neighbors*, 1916), writers produced approximately a dozen novels about the immigrant on the land—despite the fact that relatively few Poles turned to farming in the United States. In these works, **Edna Ferber**, Gladys Hasty Carroll, Annette Esty, Cornelia Cannon, and others suggested that Polish peasants were perhaps a solution and not a problem. In their novels they presented Polish characters as transforming agents in a region where the best blood has gone west; the land is worn out; and the American garden is in ruins. Into this typological wasteland enter the Poles, the new chosen people whose mission is to reclaim a lost America. In contrast to the withered and withdrawn Yankees, they are robust, vigorous, and prolific. Polish women are life-giving; Polish men are industrious and thrifty, efficient and self-reliant. Infusing the land with a blend of passion, industry, faith, and a willingness to learn new methods and a new American way of life, they rejuvenate the region and the people and the garden blossoms once more. In novels published between the wars, writers employed this typological approach and Polish characters to address America's concerns about the declining status of agriculture, about the particular decline of farming in New England, and, more importantly, about the nation's lingering doubts about the new immigrants.

With the appearance of the Polish farmer in American literature, another version of the Polish self appeared almost simultaneously in the proletarian literature of the 1930s and 1940s. When writers responded to the Great Depression and to the unresolved problems of capitalism and industrialism by pointing out that the American worker suffered the burden of an unresponsive system, Poles and Polish Americans assumed yet another literary identity—this time as proletariat and protester. Between 1935 and 1955, approximately twenty-five works of political fiction featured Polish characters. For the first time, important writers wrote about Poles, not to introduce aliens to American audiences, but rather to examine the presence of a large ethnic group in the context of a major political movement. The immediate result was the association and identification of Polish Americans with the oppressed urban worker whose future, if he had any at all, rested in the collectivized movement of the working class. Transformation is, in fact, implicit throughout this fiction except that class struggle replaces the greening of New England and Polish ethnic comes to mean economic victim. Such victimized figures appear in the protest narratives of William Carlos Williams, Jerome Bahr, **James T. Farrell**, and Adam Wolak.

But Poles in protest fiction are usually passive voices—victims of social neglect, economic injustice, and a political system for which they are unprepared. Lester Cohen's Poles, for example, are models of the ethnic citizen who has given more to his country than his country has given to him. Mrs. Witkowski scrubs floors and her husband opens a "crummy little grocery" that fails. Daughter Stella is beaten and raped by an official who was elected to protect her rights. The ethnic Poles understand that they are helpless against such odds and they take it. Cohen offers little consolation in a world which is "always going to be this way" unless America changes politically. In proletarian literature, ethnic and worker come to mean almost the same thing. Consequently, Poles were enlisted to serve yet another cause—a vision of a new American ideology consisting of populist solidarity, proletarian vigor, and national diversity. This representation of the Polish self as an expression of American cultural tensions continues through World War II and into the postwar period with the characterization of the Poles as tragic victims of war, refugees, and the economic by-product of America's failure to live up to its promises to serve the needs of all its citizens. One need only read such works as Helen MacInnes's *While Still We Live* (1944), Ida Wylie's *Strangers Are Coming* (1941), and Millard Lampell's *The Hero* (1949), to see examples of such characterizations. To be sure, these cultural/ethnic portraits are largely the product of lesser-known writers with limited readership and influence. So too were the literary representations offered earlier.

In the second half of the twentieth century, however, all this changed as major American writers produced best-selling and highly regarded works that featured Poles and Polish American characters. In the works of **Nelson Algren**, Tennessee Williams, **William Styron**, Jerzy Kosinski, James Michener, **Isaac Bashevis Singer**, **Saul Bellow**, **Phillip Roth**, and **Leon Uris** among others, the Polish self was reintroduced to new and larger audiences. Surprisingly, with the exception of Jewish American writers, these writers turned to cultural representations already ingrained in the American temper and in the American literary imagination.

In the 1940s, Nelson Algren recalled the great debate that had earlier questioned the prospects of immigrant success. Algren's portrait of the Pole as proletarian and social deviant recalls similar representations in the works of Cobb and Vogel, except that Algren's Chicago Poles have become proletarian misfits. Unlike their immigrant parents, Algren's Polish Americans think that deceit, petty crime, violence, and asocial behavior are perfectly natural. The protagonist of one story boasts about his jail record and a childhood spent preying upon the unsuspecting. Lefty Bicek, the young protagonist of *Never Come Morning* (1942), rapidly declines into mayhem and murder. And Frankie Majcinek in *The Man with the Golden Arm* (1949) is a drug addict. As their names indicate they belong to a hybrid culture, marked by alienation from the past and the present. Tennessee Williams' Stanley Kowalski in *A Streetcar Named Desire* (1947) poses a similar threat to Anglo America in that he too represents America's lingering suspicions about this new ethnic group. For Blanche, he is "an animal . . . survivor of the stone age . . . swelling and gnawing and hulking." This emanates from her view of him as "a healthy Polack." Stanley knows, as does his creator, Tennessee Williams, that "the Kowalskis and the Dubois have different notions." But the Kowalskis are on the rise and Belle Reve ends up in ethnic hands. By the end of the play, the Kowalskis and the Dubois have switched power positions, a shift that greatly troubled Williams who insisted that the message of his play was "if we don't watch out, the apes will take over." Thus Algren and Williams, despite their literary achievements, fail to advance the literary representation of the Polish self, turning instead to familiar methods to describe America's doubts about the agenda of the ethnic proletariat.

With the worsening of the cold war, Jerzy Kosinski and James Michener, in radically different ways, invested their Polish characters with the requisite qualities that American readers had come to expect. Kosinski, in the style of writers and journalists at the turn of the century, blurs ethnic distinctions so that to most readers his characters appear to be generic Slavs. Given, however, his own Polish origins and telltale cultural signs in his fiction, there is little doubt that many of his protagonists are Polish refugees and exiles. Unlike their literary ancestors in the 1830s, however, they are not culture-bearing aristocrats, pure in spirit and noble in behavior. Instead, we find deracinated selves whose neuroses exemplify the political neuroses of the cold war and whose paranoid behavior directly flows from cold war experiences, real and imagined. Kosinski's most successful novel, *Steps* (1969), features a young Polish intellectual who escapes from mental collectivization, a mindless bureaucracy, and political torture. In fleeing Poland for America, he presents himself as an immigrant self waiting to be reborn as an American self. In this sense Kosinski offers his American readers a self-assuring rejection of East European socialism and a Polish character that reinforces American cultural and political "superiority."

By and large James Michener does the same in his best-selling novel *Poland* (1983). Seizing upon world interest in the Solidarity movement of

1980–81 and the subsequent political crackdown, Michener rushed into print with a novel that offers a sweeping and heroic view of Polish history. For one thing, Michener offers Reaganite America assurance of the rightness of the American way. For another, he presents a fictional vision of a country whose "history" mirrors America's own ideological imprint. Self-described as an "inspirational saga of a people who not only survived catastrophe but who were capable of building on that very destruction," the novel draws upon the images, icons, and traits of national character most appealing to and "felt" by Americans, including the historical antecedents of Polish and American historical kinship. By tracing the roots of two distantly related families, the Buks and the Bukowskis, Michener juxtaposes princes and peasants who together represent the character of the nation. In so doing, he captures the ambivalence that characterizes America's historical fondness for the genteel tradition tempered by an egalitarian predisposition. Moreover, Michener binds Poles and Americans through a symbolic marriage that reinforces the notion of the two nations as an extended family. The novel ends with Janko Buk visiting America where he is delighted to discover that Poland thrives in Detroit, Chicago, and other American localities. Buk's warm reception is that of a distant but like-minded relative, and he, correspondingly, is amazed to meet "so many men who know my country so intimately."

Not surprisingly, some members of the Polish American community have not appreciated the representations of Poles and Polish Americans in the work of Algren, Williams, Kosinski, and Michener. Their dissatisfaction was especially directed toward William Styron's *Sophie's Choice* (1979) and the subsequent film version starring Meryl Streep. In Sophie, Styron offers a sophisticated, educated, and cultured Pole who, having suffered through the war in Warsaw and in Auschwitz, finds herself as a refugee in Brooklyn. The characterization of Sophie is rooted, of course, in the works of nineteenth-century writers who characterized the Pole as a European beau ideal. By and large, Sophie, whose father is a university professor, fits that conception. Unfortunately, Sophie's father is also an anti-Semite and Sophie herself must conform to the wishes of her Nazi captors and thus Poles become enmeshed in the **Holocaust** in Styron's novel even as they were in history.

The public tendency to associate the Holocaust exclusively with European Jews and to confuse Polish victims with Nazi perpetrators because many of the death camps were located in Poland, produced yet another version of the Polish literary self—the Pole as anti-Semite. This caricature appears rather abruptly and almost synonymously with postwar revelations of Nazi atrocities. For example, in *Coming Home* (1945), Lester Cohen unexplainably indicts the Polish family in his novel. Although Mr. Witkowski never says or does anything to justify the accusation, Cohen writes that "when Hitler was killing Jews, Witkowski looked upon it with some amusement." Cohen's reflex action, a product in part of short term memory regarding 500 years of relative peace and good will between Poles and Jews in Poland, was almost immediately taken up by other Jewish American writers, including Saul Bellow, **Bernard Malamud**, and Phillip Roth. Leon Uris had a particular argument with history. In some of his novels he offers an image of Poland as a "nation of thirty million with only two million newspaper readers. A nation of feudal lords and serfs in this twentieth century. A nation which worships a black madonna as African Zulus prayed to sun gods." Uris further belittles Polish character and culture when he introduces the commander of the Polish Home Army who "has the perpetual arrogance of a Polish nobleman and a medieval mentality. His class has misused the wealth of Poland, legalized serfdom for private gain, and has carried the inbred hate of centuries toward Jews." Isaac Bashevis Singer, who looked upon Poland with sentiment in his fiction, did not resist employing stereotypes already in practice in **Yiddish American literature**. In contrast to the tradition introduced in the nineteenth century, his aristocrats are barbarians, not beau ideals, and his peasants are rogues, not redemptive agents. The Polish peasant is slow-witted, superstitious, and animalistic. The gentry are fornicating, drunken brutes. Both are anti-Semites. With Singer's help, in postwar Jewish American literature, yet another cultural stereotype of Poles and their American descendents emerged—the scapegoat—the embodiment, not of European enlightenment, but of European and American transgressions against Judaism.

With the flowering of ethnic, minority, and women's literature in the last quarter of the twentieth century, American writers of Polish descent, discussed elsewhere in this volume, with trepidation, found something of their very own to say. By the 1990s, **Stuart Dybek**, **Anthony Bukoski**, **Gary Gildner**, **Suzanne Strempek Shea**, **Leslie Pietrzyk** and others had created an ethnic voice and perspective that needed no "mainstream" cultural interpretation, guidance, or representation. This is not to say that they have completely avoided two-dimensional or predictable characterizations. What is more important is that they have forever altered the representation of Poles and Polish Americans in American literature through their sensitive and insightful studies of the human condition within the perspective of the ethnic community.

Further Reading

Gladsky, Thomas S. *Princes, Peasants, and Other Polish Selves: Ethnicity in American Literature.* Amherst: U of Massachusetts P, 1992.

Gladsky, Thomas S., and Rita K. Gladsky, eds. *Something of My Very Own to Say: American Women Writers of Polish Descent.* Boulder, CO: Eastern European Monographs, 1997.

Thomas S. Gladsky

POLISH ÉMIGRÉ WRITERS IN THE UNITED STATES The history of Polish authors writing in their native language in the United States parallels the trends in Polish **immigration** to America. The initial wave of immigrants, generally of peasant background, arrived at the end of the nineteenth and the beginning of the twentieth century. They came from a Poland that did not exist as a unified country, but was partitioned between Russia, Prussia, and Austria. After Poland obtained its independence in 1918, the immigrants continued to arrive, although in lesser numbers. A second, very different group of immigrants, mainly from the middle-class, war-displaced intelligentsia, came with the outbreak of World War II in 1939 and the subsequent establishment of People's Poland under Soviet domination. The third wave began after 1956, when the political atmosphere in Poland allowed for foreign travel. Those arrivals often felt alienated, even persecuted, in Poland and sought refuge abroad. That wave of immigration continued intermittently until the Solidarity movement managed to wrestle power from the Communist government in 1989.

The Polish-language literature written in the United States is closely linked to the native literary tradition, although it adjusted to and accommodated the American experience. Correspondingly, writers who arrived within one of the three currents of immigration had a specific notion of their relation to the home country and a different understanding of the purpose of literature. The initial group of authors, writing for an audience of recent immigrants, addressed the acculturation problems of the new arrivals and did so in the form of popular literature that was widely published in immigrant newspapers and journals. The immigrant authors came from the intelligentsia and professional classes. Some had writing experience in Poland, although none of them gained a permanent place in the history of Polish literature. In the United States those writers produced detective novels, family sagas, adventure stories, and romances which addressed an ethnic identity in flux and modeled the correct Polish values against the progressive Americanization of Polish immigrants. The first known immigrant novel in Polish appeared in 1881. Since that time an extensive tradition of popular literature in the native language guided recent Polish immigrants through the process of acculturation. With Poland's independence acquired after World War I, the national element decreased in popular literature, but novels and short stories continued to help recent immigrants to find a new identity while cultivating a sense of collective cultural heritage.

An altogether different literature emerged between the years 1939 and 1956. It was the outbreak of World War II that was instrumental in introducing a new model of immigrant literature, one generated from the most fertile current of the Polish cultural tradition—its Romantic past. The formation of postwar Poland under Soviet control added further impetus for the development of the immigrant writer's role as the preserver of an authentic Polish culture that could no longer be cultivated in the home country. Rather than defining themselves as Polish émigré writers, these authors considered themselves exiles and so stressed their opposition to the status quo in Poland. Following the outbreak of the World War II, many prominent writers, who were well established on the Polish literary scene, sought refuge in the United States. This group was shaped by its experience in independent Poland, and faced both the German and, later, the Soviet occupation of the country. Among this group, the dominating current was poetry, oriented in its appeal to a highbrow audience, which shared the ethos of the Polish intelligentsia of the period between the wars.

The Polish literary tradition strictly distinguishes between Polish American literature created for Polish immigrants in the United States and Polish exile literature beginning in 1939 and ending in 1989. The institution of exile literature was not a new one in Polish culture. Its tradition goes back to the first half of the nineteenth century when the leading Romantic poets found themselves immigrating to France following the failure of a Polish uprising against the partitioning powers. The response of the Romantic poets to the foreign setting provided a model situation for the role of a Polish writer in exile. According to the Romantic ethos, the poet/writer was cast in the role of a moral leader and preserver of the authentic Polish culture that could not be cultivated at home for political reasons. The impact of the Romantic tradition on Polish culture and in particular on the mission of the writer can hardly be overestimated. The role of the writer-in-exile has, ever since, been surrounded by a Romantic aura and designated as a political-cultural mission that goes beyond the normally understood function of literature.

World War II created a similar political situation. Soon after the outbreak of the war, several writers and poets found their way to the United States. Already in 1941, three important Polish authors, Jan Lechoń (1899–1956), Kazimierz Wierzyński (1894–1969), and Józef Wittlin (1896–1976), arrived in New York. In the early postwar period, New York appeared as one of the majors center of Polish literary exile, although it was somewhat overshadowed by London and Paris, which sheltered literary communities with a lively publishing scene dominated by the journal *Kultura* (Paris) and the weekly *Wiadomości* (London). The new arrivals largely followed the Romantic topos of preserving the memory of Polish culture in relative isolation both from Poland and from the American setting. Jan Lechoń perhaps best personified that generation of writers in exile. He was a poet and critic, who also worked for Radio Free Europe and was very preoccupied with the Romantic mission of the writer. In addition to numerous volumes of poetry, he wrote sketches on American culture, *American Transformations* (1959), and a three-volume *Diary* (1967) addressing the situation of a writer in exile. Kazimierz Wierzyński was probably the most outstanding poet of the war emigration. His poetry volumes, *Crosses and Swords* (1946), *The Earth's Substance* (1960), and *Black Polonaise* (1968), were widely acclaimed among the Polish audience. He also wrote a biography, *The Life and Death of Chopin* (1949). Józef Wittlin authored a major essay "The Splendor and the Squalor of Exile" (1957), published a collection of essays *Orpheus in the Inferno of the Twentieth Century* (1963), and was mainly known as a translator of Homer and author of an important antiwar novel, *Salt of the Earth*, which in 1943 was awarded prizes by the American Academy of Arts and Letters and the National Institute of Arts and Letters.

Following a relative liberalization of the Polish political system in 1956, many writers active in postwar communist Poland began arriving in the United States. They usually came after a sojourn in Western Europe. Some were attracted by job offers, others received grants, and still others came looking for professional opportunities. The majority entered the United States on a temporary basis and eventually settled into more or less permanent residency. Directly or indirectly, politics constrained their lives to such an extent that an interval abroad, which they had expected to be momentary, turned into exile as a result of a withdrawn passport, the "anti-Zionist" campaign of 1968, the collapse of the Prague Spring (1968), or the social destabilization that followed the state of martial law imposed in Poland in 1981.

Writers, who left Poland after the Thaw of 1956 and established a politically neutral expatriate existence in America, were generally conscious of the advantages which emigration offered to them and yet felt clearly constrained by the topos of the exile in their home culture. The exilic narrative traditionally celebrated the uniqueness of the national tradition and promoted in exile the concept of nationality and Polish statehood. While the postwar diaspora zealously cultivated the image of the exiled writer, obedience to the Romantic canon was no longer an option for writers who emigrated from Soviet-controlled Poland. In turn, American media welcomed those writers as Eastern European dissidents, even though only a few of them actually played that role in the home society. Assumed or real dissidence and the cold war image of Eastern Europe provided a useful bridge through which an emigrant author could enter the discourse of the new country.

Just like in the Romantic period, poetry was best represented among the émigré writers and it enjoyed the highest prestige. Czesław Miłosz (1911–2004), the winner of the 1980 Noble Prize for Literature, had come to the United States in 1960 from France, where he briefly worked in the Polish diplomatic service. His book, *The Captive Mind* (1953), dealt with the intellectuals' adjustments to communism and brought him recognition as a political writer. Miłosz was critical both of the Romantic tradition and of the avant-garde. He wrote numerous volumes of poetry, among which *A Treatise on Poetry* (2001) explains his own understanding of the poetic art. He wrote about the shape of history and the destiny of modern man. Although he located himself within the European poetic tradition, he extensively interacted with the American scene and translated American poetry. Miłosz, who taught Polish literature at the University of California at Berkeley, also published important prose works like *The Issa Valley* (1955), *The Native Realm: A Search for Self-Definition* (1968), and *The Emperor of the Earth: Modes of Eccentric Vision* (1977). His views of America are presented in a volume titled *Visions from San Franscisco Bay* (1982). Another poet, Stanisław Barańczak (1946–), was a political dissenter in Poland who came in 1980 to teach Polish literature at Harvard University. He authored a book of essays, *Breathing under Water and Other East European Essays* (1990), and several collections of poetry. The fusion of poetry and politics permeates his writings. His poetry destroys the automatic perception of language and obliviates the boundary between art and life. Volumes of his poetry in English include *Under My Own Roof: Verses for a New Apartment* (1980) and *Selected Poems: The Weight of the Body* (1989). Another kind of poetry is practiced by Tymoteusz Karpowicz (1921–), who came to the United States in 1973 as a participant in the Iowa International Writing Program. He taught Polish literature at the University of Illinois in Chicago. His poetry functions as a mode of thinking and hypothecizing about the world and represents a strategy of condensed philosophizing. Difficult to translate, his long poems consisting of hundreds of pages, appear only in Polish.

Among the best prose writers is Henryk Grynberg (1936–), who focuses on the experience of the Polish Jews during the **Holocaust**. His texts are frequently based on individual personal accounts as he seeks to cultivate the memory of the life and death of the Jewish community in Poland. Among his semi-documentary narratives are *Children of Zion* (1997), *The Jewish War and the Victory* (2001), and *Drohobycz, Drohobycz and Other Stories* (2002). Jerzy Kosinski (1933–91), another prose writer, has been assigned both to American and Polish American literature. Although he was an immigrant from Poland, Kosinski wrote in English and his novels reached great popularity in the United States. Among his novels, the best known are *The Painted Bird* (1965); *Steps* (1968), for which he received the National Book Award; *Being There* (1971), which was made into a movie; and *The Hermit of 69th Street* (1988). A part of the American celebrity scene, Kosinski committed suicide in 1991 in New York. A Polish journalist, novelist, and music critic, Leopold Tyrmand (1920–85) came to the United States with the idea of contributing to American culture his distinctly Polish experience and knowledge. He wrote for various American periodicals and published *Notebooks of a Dilletante* (1967), *The Rosa Luxemburg Contraceptives Cooperative: A Primer on Communist Civilization* (1972), and *Tu w Ameryce, czyli dobre rady dla Polaków* (Here in America, or Good Advice for Poles, 1975). **Eva Hoffman** (1945–) came from Poland as a teenager and later worked as a book review editor for the *New York Times*. Her first book, *Lost in Translation: A Life in a New Language* (1989), addressed the complexities of adjusting to the new culture and the new language environment. She has also written about the postsocialist transformations in Eastern Europe in *Exit into History: A Journey Through the New Eastern Europe* (1993) and about the history of the Polish Jews in *Shtetl: The Life and Death of a Small Town and the World of Polish Jews* (1997).

Poles have also made contributions to American theater. Jan Kott (1914–2003), theater critic, essayist, and performance theorist of international reputation, is best known for his commentaries on Shakespeare's plays. More than half of his work was produced in emigration including *The Eating of the Gods* (1970), *Theater Notebook 1947–1967* (1968), *The Bottom Translation* (1987), *Memory of the Body: Essays on Theater and Death* (1992), and his own reminiscences, *Still Alive* (1994). Like Kott, Janusz Gowacki (1938–) had considerable success in American theater. A journalist by training and a prose writer in Poland, he came to the United States in 1981. His two plays, *Hunting Cockroaches* (1985) and *Antigone in New York* (1997), received numerous American awards. His dramatic works were published in English as *Hunting Cockroaches and Other Plays* (1990).

Since 1989, the United States no longer needs to function as a haven for the dissident and exiled Polish writers. With the collapse of the Soviet bloc, many authors keep residences both in Poland and in the United States. The concept of émigré literature has largely lost its validity in the current literary scene in Poland with writers publishing and living on both sides of the ocean.

Further Reading

Danilewicz-Zielinska, Maria. *Szkice o literaturze emigracyjnej* [Sketches about the Emigrant Literature]. Paris: Instytut Kultury, 1978.

Gladsky, Thomas. *Princes, Peasants, and Other Polish Selves: Ethnicity in American Literature.* Amherst: U of Massachusetts P, 1992.

Hoffman, Eva. *Lost in Translation: A Life in a New Language.* New York: Penguin Books, 1989.

Klimaszewski, Bolesław. *Pod znakiem potu, łez, i dolara: Polonia amerykańska w zwierciadle literatury polskiej* [Under the Sign of Sweat, Tears and the Dollar: American Polonia as Reflected in Polish Literature]. Krakow: Uniwersytet Jagielloński, 1990.

———, ed. *Słownik pisarzy polskich na obczyźnie 1939–1980* [Dictionary of the Polish Writers Abroad 1939–1980]. Warsaw: Interpress, 1993.

Leonard, Nathan, and Arthur Quinn. *The Poet's Work: Introduction to Czesław Miłosz.* Cambridge, MA: Harvard UP, 1991.

Majewski, Karen. *Traitors and True Poles: Narrating a Polish-American Identity 1980– 1939.* Athens, OH: Ohio UP, 2003.

Miłosz, Czesław. *The History of Polish Literature.* 2nd edition. Berkeley: U of California P, 1983.

Stephan, Halina, ed. *Living in Translation: Polish Writers in America.* Amsterdam: Rodopi, 2003.

Zaborowska, Magdalena. *How We Found America: Reading Gender through East European Immigrant Narratives.* Chapel Hill: U of North Carolina P, 1995.

Halina Stephan

POLITE, CARLENE HATCHER (1932–) African American novelist. Carlene Hatcher Polite was a talented dancer and active member of the **Civil Rights Movement** before she moved to Paris at the age of thirty-two to write. Polite was elected to the Michigan State Central Committee of the Democratic Party in 1962, served on the Detroit Council for Human Rights, participated in the 1963 Freedom Now Rally, organized the Northern

Negro Leadership Conference, and was active in the NAACP. Polite was a student at the Martha Graham School of Contemporary Dance and performed with the Concert Dance Theater of New York City between 1955 and 1959 and with the Detroit Equity Theater and Vanguard Playhouse between 1960 and 1962. During these years, she was also a guest instructor of dance at Wayne State University. Polite has said that she did not move to Paris in search of a "racial equality unrealized by the American Black community," but simply to write without distraction. Her two novels, *The Flagellants* (1967) and *Sister X and the Victims of Foul Play* (1975), both exhibit a strong Parisian influence. Polite currently resides in Buffalo, where she has taught creative writing and African American literature at the State University of New York.

The Flagellants tells the story of the tempestuous relationship between Ideal and Jimson, two African Americans living in Greenwich Village and struggling with the roles assigned to them by a racially oppressive culture. The lovers are the flagellants; they constantly abuse each other verbally and physically as a result of feelings of alienation, hostility, absurdity, and hopelessness in what they see as a miserable society. There are elements of existentialism throughout the book, and Ideal can be categorized as an idealist who conveys an occasional hope that the relationship is promising and meaningful. But this perfect union with Jimson is not practical or possible, and the sour disintegration of the relationship is bitterly yet skillfully depicted. Ideal finally tells Jimson to leave at the end of the novel, and her final words imply that she is at last executing her free will. However, the existentialist sense of an uncertain future is apparent because the two have separated temporarily before, and it is up to the reader to decide if Jimson will really leave for good this time.

In *Sister X and the Victims of Foul Play*, Black Will and Abyssinia recall episodes of the life and death of their close friend Sister X Arista Prolo. Black Will is a traveling ex-convict and romantic who aspires to an ideal African community. Abyssinia, a seamstress, refuses the enticements of rich male caretakers while struggling with the "Dead World" idea that living is a luxury and one is obligated to suffer in order to survive. Sister X was an exotic dancer who sacrificed her dreams for a paycheck and died in an attempt at resistance. She represents the constant battle between life and money, inherent human right and governing ideology. The novel is not only an emotional portrayal of pure friendship, but also a scornful commentary on our contemporary value system, which Polite perceives as an economic game. This book also ends on a note of uncertainty; it is unclear if Sister X dies from an accidental fall or is intentionally pushed, in which case the motives for murder might be fiscal greed or racial hate or both. There are elements of flagellation between the main characters in this novel as well, but it does not contain the absolute despair of *The Flagellants*. Black Will's final statements guarantee that he and Abyssinia have the power to exercise their own free will and consequently escape the tragedies of life.

The language and style of Polite's novels are controlled and poetic. The emotional complexities of life are artistically expressed through the experiences of the African American, and the author's background in dance is effectively exhibited in the lessons, disciplines, and unsettling personal performances in both works. The French connection, Black folklorist tradition, **race** relations, and the potential of free will to correct social injustice are all themes shared between these unique, fascinating, and influential novels. (*See also* African American Novel)

Further Reading

Busch, Frederick. Review of *Sister X and the Victims of Foul Play. New York Times Book Review* (November 23, 1975): 24.

Lottman, Herbert. Review of *The Flagellants. New York Times Book Review* (April 21, 1968): 7.

Newson, Adele. "The Poet's Distance Achieved Through a Parisian Sojourn: Carlene Hatcher Polite's *The Flagellants.*" *Middle Atlantic Writers Review* 7 (June 1992): 22–26.

Kim Kather

PONCE, MARY HELEN (1938–)   Mexican American short story writer, novelist, and teacher of Chicano Studies. Mary Helen Ponce is one of the early Chicana writers of the 1980s who depicts in her stories the Los Angeles Mexican community of the 1940s and 1950s. Many of her short stories, in English and Spanish, have been published in periodicals in the United States and Mexico and in a collection titled *Taking Control* (1987). Her two other monographs are *The Wedding* (1989), a novel that received mixed reviews due to its naturalistic portrayal of the Pachuco subculture of the 1950s, and *Hoyt Street: An Autobiography* (1993) a unique, almost ethnographic, narrative of Ponce's life growing up on Hoyt Street in Pacoima, California.

Even though many of her works were published during the same period as other Chicana writers like **Sandra Cisneros** and **Ana Castillo**, Mary Helen Ponce is actually of a different generation. Her literary style is closer to that of Mario Suarez than to 1980s Chicana novelists. Much of her writing material originates from her cultural experiences as a little girl during World War II and as a teenager during the 1950s. Ponce's narratives recreate the lives of immigrant workers, of women coping with the exigencies of day-to-day living, and of the social affairs of working-class Mexican Americans.

As the title suggests *Taking Control* is a collection of narratives that frequently portray characters that survive unusual circumstances and learn to take control of the future direction of their lives. Stories, such as "La Josie" and "The Painkillers," present women having to cope with personal and intimate feelings about their relationships and their bodies, topics that are not typically addressed in Chicana literature. For instance, in "The Painkillers" Ponce creates the narrative of a woman who has undergone surgery for a hysterectomy. In another story, "The New Affirmative Action Officer," Ponce describes how sexism affects the main character, putting her in the embarrassing position of having to explain that her frequent job absences are due to intimate female problems.

The Wedding is a curious novel that can be interpreted in several ways. Some reviewers consider it an insulting parody or a satire of Chicano culture while others view it as a realistic portrayal of the subculture of the Pachucos and their gangs. It is the story of the wedding of Blanca and Cricket that takes place in the San Fernando Valley of Southern California sometime in the 1950s. Blanca works at a poultry factory plucking feathers from turkeys, saving all her money for her wedding dress, while Cricket is primarily involved with his homies from the Tacanos gang and their rivals the Planchados. The actual wedding day turns out disastrously, with every imaginable dreaded mishap occurring, including the sickness of Blanca and the wedding party. Spanish is used intermittently throughout the novel, as well as *caló*, the slang of the Pachucos. According to Ponce, the novel is meant to be honest, but to Chicanos who are familiar with San Fernando Valley culture the story may read as a humorous satire.

Mary Helen Ponce was born in Ventura and raised in Pacoima, California, the tenth of eleven siblings, eight daughters and three sons. While she was enjoying her childhood, her brothers and sisters were going to dances and working in homes as housekeepers and in the aircraft plants. These are the stories from *Hoyt Street: An Autobiography*, a vivid narrative of life in a Mexican American enclave with solid traditions, rituals, and memorable characters. Ponce had a happy childhood growing up in her large loving family that she clearly describes in fine detail. There is the scent from the kitchen stove, the textures from the cloth on the sewing machine, the laughter in the house and on Hoyt Street, and they're all skillfully preserved in this memoir. This well-crafted work can be read as a history, an ethnography, and as a life story.

Further Reading

Ikas, Karin. "Mary Helen Ponce: Author and University Instructor." *Chicana Ways: Conversations with Ten Chicana Writers*. Reno: U of Nevada P, 2002. 175–203.

McCracken, Ellen. "Subculture, Parody, and the Carnivalesque: A Bakhtinian Reading of Mary Helen Ponce's 'The Wedding'." *MELUS* 23.1 (Spring 1998): 117–31.

Rafaela G. Castro

PORTUGUESE AMERICAN LITERATURE   Portuguese American literature cannot compare in bulk with other emergent contemporary American literatures. Portugal is a small country and for the last five centuries–since the Age of the Discoveries in the sixteenth century—a few million individuals immigrated to its former colonies in Africa and Brazil. During the twentieth century, others settled in a few Western European countries as well. But the Portuguese population in North America—the United States and Canada—has never reached the million mark. In the United States, the Portuguese have traditionally settled in southeastern New England, metropolitan New York, and New Jersey, as well as in central California. During the last third of the nineteenth century, many Portuguese settled in Hawai'i. It is during this period that the mass movement of the Portuguese into the United States took place, even though a smaller influx had made its way there from the early sixteenth to the mid-nineteenth century. This exodus was first triggered by the whaling industry in New England and later by the job opportunities in the local textile industry. In New England and in the Mid-Atlantic states, most of these ethnics were mill and construction workers, but in California they prospered in the dairy industry and in intensive farming. Those who went to Hawai'i worked in the sugar and pineapple plantations.

Most Portuguese came from the Azores and Madeira islands; others arrived from the Cape Verde islands, a Portuguese colony in Western Africa that became an independent nation after the democratic revolution in Portugal on April 25, 1974. The Continentals hailing from mainland Portugal followed them and arrived in greater numbers about a half-century later. The earlier Portuguese immigrants who arrived before World War I were predominantly illiterate and generally of peasant background. After the restrictive **immigration** acts of the early 1920s, Portuguese immigration to the United States waned. Since the late 1950s, the influx of Portuguese immigrants has increased, especially into southeastern New England and the Mid-Atlantic states. These were generally literate and not exclusively from a rural background as in the past.

Several scholars have noted that these conditions and patterns of immigration influenced the literary output of Portuguese American writers. Compared to other ethnic literatures in the United States, Portuguese American literature can still be defined as a relatively young literature. Most of the writings pertaining to the first group of immigrants are usually written in a simple, unadorned style. These writings appeared in the mid 1930s and often reflect the educational level of these writers. They tend to focus on the immigrant experience. Whereas some focus on how much they miss the Azores and its simple ways of life, others prefer to ponder their new American experience. Francis Rogers has distinguished between ethnic literature and immigrant literature. "True ethnic literature," he claims, "is a literature of maturity." Ethnic literature "normally has to be written by immigrants resident here for many years and by descendants born here. The ethnic literature of Americans of Portuguese descent and birth forms part of American literature, not of Portuguese literature. It treats American problems, not Portuguese problems." In his view, immigrant literature, instead, would include "the volumes of poems and journalistic essays written in their native language by recent immigrants, writers who are, for the moment at least, transplanted Portuguese." This group often includes ex-university or ex-seminary students who "remain in close intellectual and even publishing contact with their fatherland. A portion of them tend to be highly critical of democratic America, which they have barely come to know. They are not really ethnics, and they are not really writing ethnic literature" (425). On this issue, Nancy T. Baden notes "in the first period, the term 'immigrant' is appropriate, but with the more sophisticated recent writers we find people able to enter the established ethnic community, observe, participate, and even criticize the life of the Luso-American enclave and yet, simultaneously maintain their connections with the homeland" (23–24). Such is the case with the writings of Onésimo T. Almeida, which appeal both to a Portuguese American audience and to audiences in Portugal and the Azores.

The first group would include, for example, an immigrant versifier as Guilherme Silveira da Glória. He was born on the island of Pico in the Azores in 1863. Formerly a priest, he settled in Sacramento, California, and founded a Portuguese-language newspaper, *A Liberdade.* He published *Poesias* (1935) and *Harpejos* (1940). Some of the poems in the former collection reflect an excessive admiration for Salazar's nationalism and right-wing dictatorship (1926–74). Arthur Vieira Ávila was born in 1888 on the island of Pico and also migrated to California. He was active in Portuguese-language journalism on the West Coast and ran a radio program. Both volumes of poetry, *Desafio Radiofónico* and *Rimas de Um Imigrante,* which he collected in 1961, a year before his death, reflect his broadcasting activity, his sentimentality, and his Portuguese patriotism. Father José Reinaldo Matos, born in the North of continental Portugal in 1925, immigrated to the United States in 1967 and settled in Cambridge, Massachusetts. His poems, which are more sophisticated than most by the two previous writers, reflect not only his religious fervor to the point of resembling prayers, but his nostalgia and longing for his native land. José Joaquim Baptista Brites was born in 1945 in a village in the center of continental Portugal. He immigrated to the United States in 1970 after having worked as a jet mechanic for the Portuguese airline, and settled in Bethlehem, Pennsylvania. The poems in *Poemas sem Poesia* are hardly ethnic and usually verge on universal themes and are more Portuguese than ethnic. This volume includes pieces dealing with the immigrant's experience, but do not paint a dreamland Portugal as we often encounter in several poems written by the previous poets. While some of them depict reality, namely the colonial war in Guiné-Bissau, Angola and Mozambique, they also touch upon the defects in the New World. This volume was followed up by *Imigramar* (1984).

The number of prose writers is even smaller. Alfred Lewis (Alfredo Luiz) of Los Baños, California, was born on the island of Flores in 1902. Following in the footsteps of his father, at age nineteen he migrated to California. His first novel, *Home Is an Island* (1951) is a highly autobiographical piece. His poems are collected in *Aguarelas Florentinas* (1986). His novel does not contribute much to Portuguese American literature, but it contains a repository of information on life in the Azores during the early twentieth century. It recreates his childhood in Flores while focusing on food, the living conditions in the Azores, clothes, superstitions, and Catholicism. It is a good source for those wishing to understand the mentality and way of life of Azorean immigrants arriving in the United States. The novel traces the early childhood of José de Castro, a young man who grows up dreaming about America and eventually leaving his homeland in search of a better life. According to Rogers, Elvira Osorio Roll's novel *Hawaii's Kohala Breezes* (1964) is "the single most important piece of United States-Portuguese ethnic literature" (417). Roll was born in Honolulu in 1888 and became a schoolteacher. She also wrote *Background: A Novel of Hawaii,* which only incidentally touches upon the Portuguese in Hawai'i. For Rogers, the former is the very first work focusing on American issues, and not Portuguese as those by her predecessors. The primary importance of this novel lies in the Damus family's insistence that the Portuguese are white, that is, Caucasian, while focusing on a girl of Portuguese descent who has fallen in love with a *haole,* a white Anglo, and who must overcome interethnic tensions.

Immigrant autobiographies written in English are Laurinda C. Andrade's *The Open Door* (1968) and Lawrence Oliver's *Never Backward* (1972). Andrade was born on the island of Terceira in 1899. A self-reliant, independent woman, she arrived in America in 1917, one month after the United States entered World War I. She settled in New Bedford, Massachusetts and for a while worked in the textile industry. While combating tuberculosis and using her determination and strong religious faith, she became a schoolteacher. She entered New Bedford High School in 1924 and in 1931 earned her baccalaureate from Brown University's Pembroke College. She followed it by a Master's from Columbia University. In 1942, she introduced bilingual education in the New Bedford public schools. The other one, *Never Backward,* focuses on the story of a poor, unschooled immigrant boy born on the island of Pico in 1887 who immigrated to the United States in 1903. Oliver's autobiography focuses on how he acquired an education and became a successful businessman and a leader in the Portuguese community in San Diego, California. From his house on Point Loma he had a full view of the bay first revealed to Europe in the sixteenth century by Cabrillo [João Rodrigues Cabrilho], a Portuguese navigator sailing for the Spanish crown.

Born in 1901 in Lisbon, José Rodrigues Miguéis is a good example of the established writer who emigrated to the United States mostly because of his opposition to Salazar's regime. Upon completing his degree in Law from the University of Lisbon in 1924, he moved to Brussels to study education. After his graduation in 1933, he returned to Portugal and was simultaneously an attorney, a public prosecutor, and a high-school teacher. He emigrated to the United States in 1935 and became an American citizen in 1942. He settled in New York City and worked as a translator, a freelance writer, and an editor for the *Reader's Digest.* Baden has noted that his collection of short stories *Gente da Terceira Classe* (Third-Class Passengers) includes the "most sustained treatment" of "immigrant experience in the United States" and that some of these are only thinly fictionalized. This story focuses on a group of passengers in third-class steerage on a ship sailing to the United States via Southampton. In "O Viajante Clandestino" (The Stowaway) we witness a stowaway being caught jumping ship and his fear of deportation. "Natal Branco" (White Christmas) focuses on a hard-working Portuguese immigrant family who has succeeded in New York. An educated immigrant from the second wave of immigration to the United States, Miguéis is an important figure in twentieth-century Portuguese literary history mainly because of his contributions to the novel and short story genres. Miguéis's writings have been widely acclaimed because he capitalized on his self-imposed exile and successfully explored the problems and feelings of the immigrant. Miguéis's acute perception in those stories of immigrants torn between their native land and country of birth— especially in the United States—continues to draw the attention of emerging Portuguese American writers and scholars interested in Portuguese American literature.

Unlike Miguéis, Jorge de Sena (1919–78) was not only a writer, but also a literary critic and a scholar who taught, at first, at the University of Wisconsin at Madison, and, afterwards, at the University of California at Santa Barbara. What both writers have in common is that they express their impressions of America in Portuguese. In the case of Sena, these have been collected in *Sequências*, in the section titled "América, América, I Love You." The poems in this sequence are superficial and reflect an author who resists a full immersion in American society. In some of these poems he satirizes the stereotypes surrounding American attitudes towards sexuality and how the country's puritanical heritage has shaped the discourse on sexuality. In others, he shows the liberal side of America, namely sexual promiscuity and homosexuality in such pieces as "O Culto da Virgindade" (The Cult of Virginity) and "As Peúgas" (The Pair of Socks). Other poems range from satirizing the sacrosanct belief in private property ("O Direito Sagrado" [The Sacred Right]) and conspicuous consumption, to the nonadmittance of patients in hospitals without financial guarantee or insurance coverage ("Doença Urgente" [Sudden Illness]). Most of these pieces evolved from stereotypes and generalizations about American ways and life. "América, América, I Love You" leads us on a trip to the eccentricities and excesses in American life, and it also conveys to us how Sena's professed love for America was ironical and caustic.

The contribution of John Dos Passos (1896–1970) is at the opposite side of the spectrum from Miguéis and Sena. His paternal grandfather emigrated from the island of Madeira and settled in Philadelphia as a shoemaker about 1830. Although he is one-fourth Portuguese, George Monteiro has noted that Dos Passos was ashamed of his ethnic background and even viewed it as an encumbrance, especially in his social and professional lives. While making a significant impact on American literature with *USA* and other works, it was only later in his career that he published *The Portugal Story: Three Centuries of Exploration and Discovery*. His interest in Brazil also dates from this period. Dos Passos was an American of a predominantly Anglo-Saxon background, and his Portuguese side played a minor role in his writings.

Onésimo T. Almeida also belongs to the second wave of immigrants. He was born in the island of São Miguel and educated in the Azores, Lisbon, and Brown University, where he is currently a faculty member. An advocate for Portuguese American writings, he also contributed to the foundation of the Gávea-Brown press. He published *Da Vida Quotidiana na Lusalândia* (1975) in Portugal. Originally a collection of essays Almeida had published in the *Portuguese Times* of New Bedford from January 1973 to April 1975, on occasion, this work reflects the author's unpopular opinions on such issues as: what is a Portuguese American, the conservative political views of Portuguese immigrants, and the mixture of language and customs typical of the American experience. Some of these pieces encourage self-examination so that most Portuguese Americans do away with their provincial ways. In *Ah! Mónim dum Corisco* (1978) lampoons Portuguese Americans so that they may reflect on themselves. His more recent work includes titles such as *(Sapa)teia Americana* (1983), *L(USA)lândia–A Décima Ilha* (1987), *Que Nome É Esse, Ó Nézimo?* (1994), and *Rio Atlântico* (1997), where he pursues some of these issues.

With **Thomas Braga**, **Katherine Vaz**, and **Frank Gaspar,** Portuguese American literature has come of age. Their writings belong to American ethnic literature since they completely fulfill Almeida's and Rogers's criteria for what constitutes ethnic literature in America. In Braga's *Portingales* (1981); Katherine Vaz's *Saudade* (1994), *Mariana* (1997), and *Fado & Other Stories* (1997); and Frank Gaspar's novel *Leaving Pico* (1999) and some poems in *The Holyoke* (1988), *Mass for the Grace of a Happy Death* (1994), and *A Field Guide to the Heavens* (1999), these third-generation American-born voices attempt to retrieve their ancestor's roots so as to learn more about where they came from. Although some of their writings reflect an interest in Portuguese culture and often cast an eye on the dynamics of life in Portuguese American communities, these authors are fully accommodated to the mainstream, and their writings are an integral part of contemporary American literature.

Further Reading

Almeida, Onésimo Teotónio. "Duas Décadas de Literatura Luso-Americana: Um Balanço (1978–1998)." *Veredas* 1 (1998): 327–47.

Baden, Nancy T. "Portuguese-American Literature: Does It Exist?" *MELUS* 6 (Fall 1979): 15–31.

Duarte, Maria Angelina et al. "A Literatura Luso-Americana: Que Futuro?—Uma Mesa Redonda." *Gávea-Brown* 2 (1981): 14–32.

Monteiro, George. "'The Poor, Shiftless, Lazy Azoreans': American Literary Attitudes Toward the Portuguese." *Proceedings of the Fourth National Portuguese*

Conference: The International Year of the Child. Providence, RI: The Multilingual/Multicultural Resource and Training Center, 1979. 166–97.

Pap, Leo. "Portuguese-American Literature." *Ethnic Perspectives in American Literature: Selected Essays on the European Contribution.* Ed. Robert J. Di Pietro and Edward Ifkovic. New York: MLA, 1983. 183–96.

Rogers, Francis M. "The Contribution by Americans of Portuguese Descent to the U.S. Literary Scene." *Ethnic Literature Since 1776: The Many Voices of America.* Ed. Wolodymyr T. Zyla and Wendell M. Aycock. Lubbock, Texas: Texas Tech P, 1978. 409–32.

Silva, Reinaldo Francisco. "Representations of the Portuguese in American Literature." *Dissertation Abstracts International.* October 1998, 59.4. New York University, 1998. DA 9831767.

Suárez, José I. "Four Luso-American Autobiographies: A Comparative View." *MELUS* 17.3 (Summer 1992): 17–32.

Reinaldo Francisco Silva

POSTCOLONIALISM AND U.S. ETHNIC LITERATURES   A postcolonial perspective interrogates the effects of **colonialism** on all aspects of culture and **identity**, past and present. More broadly, it refers to the necessity of understanding imperial power and domination in the making of culture, both literary and nonliterary. After **Edward Said**'s *Orientalism* (1978), the making of an empire, or the apparatus by which European powers controlled the lands and economies and subordinated the languages and cultures of the colonies, was seen to be as much discursive as coercive. Discursive power is reflected in the knowledge generated about the colonized—their "character" and their culture (civilizational history, literature, religion)—on the basis of a difference that renders them other, different and inferior to the colonizer. Emancipation for the postcolonial nation or individual would, ideally, require a decolonization of colonial epistemology, a resistance to Eurocentric ways of knowing and seeing. This is in every way a complex and continuing process that involves the transformation of knowledge, history, and identity.

Settler Colony and Internal Colonizer

It should be noted right away that the case of settler colonies, like Australia, Canada, and the United States, is very different from those of the colonies in Asia, Africa, and the Middle-East that were occupied by European powers. American literature as a whole may not be considered postcolonial, although some critics referring to the United States as a colony of Britain include the United States in the category of the postcolonial. Although the United States liberated itself from the status of being a colony of Britain in the War of Independence, it conquered territories and enslaved others, in a process of internal colonialism. More accurately, in the context of U.S. ethnic literature, the *postcolonial* serves as a critical lens with which to read the asymmetrical experience of those ethnic groups negatively marked by **race** and the histories of imperial annexation and internal colonialism. The post-colonial lens brings to view the picture that is erased by the dominant his-toriography and the nation-building of the settlers.

Myth of Immigrant Literature and the Erasure of Empire

In popular mythic imagination, America is a nation of immigrants, whose shores received all with grace. Such an understanding obscures many impor-tant differences. First, it ignores the prior claim to the land of Native tribal peoples, colonized by European Americans. The civilizing mission of the col-onizers was carried out in Indian missionary and off-reservation boarding schools where English and Anglo-American culture replaced native lan-guages, names, and customs. The African slaves were not immigrants: the Middle Passage and the transatlantic slave trade, part of European empire-building, were integral to the prosperity of the Americas. The Mexican Americans did not consider themselves immigrants, since they had lived on the land prior to Anglos, but had found themselves displaced when the United States forcefully annexed Mexico in 1848, taking over the Southwest-ern states. Puerto Rico and Hawai'i were annexed in 1898; in both states, belonging to the United States is an ambivalent matter. Asian immigrants—mostly subjects of the British and French empires from eighteenth to the mid-twentieth century—were categorized as yellow and brown peoples and sub-ject to the color line. Among all the *immigrants,* Asians alone were the targets of various discriminatory laws that prevented them over the first four decades of the twentieth century from owning property, acquiring citizen-ship, and intermarrying with whites. Eventually they were barred from entering the United States, a prohibition that was annulled in 1965.

Post–Civil Rights Era and "Decolonization"

The 1964 Civil Rights Act, achieved after decades of struggle, may be said to be the U.S. counterpart to formal decolonization in the third world. In the U.S. academy after 1965, some important changes took place that decisively challenged the dominant understanding of culture and national identity. Inspired by the black struggle for equality, emancipatory move-ments of various subordinated populations, those of women, American Indians, Chicanos, and Asian Americans, heightened consciousness of the politics of race, class, and gender. This revolution facilitated the creation of various ethnic studies departments, such as black studies or African Amer-ican studies, Native American studies, Asian American studies, Chicano studies, and women's studies; these disciplines fostered scholarship that de-centered the dominant paradigms. The terms "people of color" and "women of color" came to be used in the 1980s to promote solidarity in the face of racist discrimination.

Alongside "minority" voices claiming their rights and asserting their agency with the politics of difference, diasporic postcolonial intellectuals brought to bear their own understanding of colonial dominance. In the 1980s the English departments were in a crisis as the traditional **canon** of literature came to be resisted by critics of color. The dominant ideal of **assimilation** into the Anglo-Saxon "mainstream" was challenged. Feminists of color questioned the hegemony of white liberal feminism. Jewish feminist writer **Adrienne Rich**'s essay "Resisting Amnesia: History and Personal Life" in her collection of essays *Blood, Bread, and Poetry* (1986) reflects a postcolonial consciousness as it sketches the reconstruction of the past a democratic feminist history must accomplish. Resisting the ideology of assimilation, she interrogates the hegemonic narrative of American identity. Thus the exclusive focus on gender gave way to an emphasis on gender, race, and class, and **whiteness** became a subject of inquiry in cultural studies programs.

It must be noted that the radical critique of race was blunted by the official discourse of **multiculturalism** in the 1980s, which emphasized an apolitical diversity, as if a genuine pluralism was simply about being inclusive. The discourse of "celebrating" multiplicity or difference was a muffling of the counter-discourse of inequality, which stressed how difference was historically constructed and maintained. The latter also recognized that even though race was a colonial fabrication that could be deconstructed, the pervasive effects of race were lasting and continuing and needed to be redressed. Intersecting with the emergent discourse of racialized ethnicity, postcolonial scholarship amplified in the 1990s the critique of empire in the Americas from 1492 to the present.

Further, diasporic postcolonial intellectuals in the United States complicate the relationship of **ethnicity** to nationality. Their transnational context refers U.S. ethnicity to a global politics. With the United States already shaping a world globalized by capitalism, the postcolonial perspectives enable a transnational literacy that is basic for democratic futures. To an extent, this local-global linkage was what earlier intellectuals of the black **diaspora**—such as **Marcus Garvey**, Aime Cesaire, Franz Fanon, Edward Brathwaite, C. L. R. James, to name but a few of the black Caribbean intellectuals—offered the black liberation movement in the United States in the 1920s through the 1960s and 1970s.

Literature

The relationship between postcolonialism and U.S. ethnic literature may be grasped by examining some texts that thematize issues pertaining to colonial relations and their aftermath. One of the main themes of this literature concerns the reclamation of historical and cultural group memory. If one of the aims of colonial subjection was to suppress this memory, then an activity vital to postcolonial agency is remembering and reconstructing the past. The entire literary oeuvre of Native American writer **Leslie Silko** and African American writer **Toni Morrison** has been shaped by postcolonial imperatives to challenge, restore, and heal from a colonial past whose baneful effects continue to mould present identities. The same may be said for Asian American novelist **Maxine Hong Kingston** and Chicana writer **Gloria Anzaldúa**.

Leslie Silko's *Almanac of the Dead*, an epic narrative of the five-hundred-year history of the Americas told from the vantage of the indigenous, documents the violence of that history, and concludes with the vision of the vanquished regaining their land. *Beloved*, Toni Morrison's complex narrative of "rememory," maps across three generations the psychic violence unleashed by **slavery**. This historiographic novel is guided by the imperative to reclaim the stigmatized past and represent it in ways that restores the subjectivity and agency of those erased in dominant historiography and literature. Other black novels that recover history include **Charles Johnson**'s *Middle Passage* (1990), a novel set in 1830 about the slave trade, and **Ishmael Reed**'s *Flight to Canada* (1976), which blurs fact and fiction, using anachronisms such as an American Civil War-era slave escaping via bus and airplane, to make a darker point about present freedoms.

The ethnic writer serves as griot and shaman diagnosing the ills of their community. Toni Morrison's *The Bluest Eye* (1970) delineates the causes of the self-internalized hatred in the black community. **Alice Walker**'s *Color Purple* (1982) depicts black women suffering from and resisting the racial and sexual violence imposed by white and black patriarchy. In African American writer **Toni Cade Bambara**'s novel *The Salt Eaters* (1980), racial and sexual oppression makes Velma Henry, a committed civil rights activist, suicidal; it takes old healer Minnie Ransom to restore her.

Several novels reflect the numbing alienation felt by protagonists cut off from the traditional ways of their culture. **N. Scott Momaday**'s *House Made of Dawn* (1968) and Leslie Silko's *Ceremony* (1977) both portray young American Indian men, World War II veterans, who return to find themselves displaced in their communities and alienated from themselves. Abel and Tayo, the respective protagonists, are healed by the intervention of traditional healers; the narratives draw upon Navajo ritual ceremony and Pueblo myth so that the novels incorporate the healing modality of the oral tradition. Toni Morrison's *Song of Solomon* (1977) reconnects Milkman Dead, a lost young black man from the north, with the southern ancestral history and folklore he was disconnected from. All three novels attest to the saving power and necessity of storytelling, of narrative's ceremonious capacity to renew cultural memory and rewrite subjection into something enabling and sustaining. African American novelist **Paule Marshall**'s *Praisesong for the Widow* (1983) is a narrative about a black couple's estrangement from their culture in their struggle to achieve the American dream; after her husband's death, the widow Avey mourns and heals in a saving reconnection with her African Caribbean roots. Chicano novelist **Rudolfo Anaya**'s *Bless Me, Ultima* (1972) is about the wisdom of the traditional healer Ultima, whose alternative cosmology makes a lasting impression on Antonio, a young New Mexican boy.

Valuing cultural traditions and artists deemed insignificant by the dominant society has been a significant part of the work of marginalized ethnic literatures. Alice Walker's *In Search of Our Mothers' Gardens: Womanist Prose* (1983) refers to the neglect of literary foremothers, from the slave poet Phyllis Wheatley to the novelist Zora Neale Hurston whose grave lacked a marker. Chinese American novelist Maxine Hong Kingston wrote *China Men* to commemorate the forgotten ancestors and their stories in the new world. **Paula Gunn Allen**'s collection of essays *The Sacred Hoop: Recovering the Feminine in American Indian Traditions* (1986) is one among many Native American works that reflect the need to name and safeguard silenced traditions and stories.

Language as the vehicle of cultural memory and identity acquires a critical significance in several texts dealing with bilingual consciousness. Examples are Chicano author **Richard Rodriguez**'s *Hunger of Memory: The Education of Richard Rodriguez* (1983), Chinese American novelist Maxine Hong Kingston's *Woman Warrior: Memoirs of a Girlhood Among Ghosts* (1976), **Sandra Cisneros**'s *The House on Mango Street* (1984), and the Puerto Rican writer **Victor Hernandez Cruz**'s mixed-genre work, *Panoramas* (1997). The anthology *Tongue-Tied: The Lives of Multilingual Children in Public Education* (2004) includes first-person accounts by Chinese Americans Amy Tan and Maxine Hong Kingston, Native American (Spokane) **Sherman Alexie**, African American writer **bell hooks**, and Chicano Richard Rodriguez. The bilingual and mestizo/a character of the literature of the Southwest with Native and Chicano/a heritages is exemplified by Gloria Anzaldúa's *Borderlands* (1987) which takes up the U.S.-Mexican border as a policed zone and as a metaphor for an emergent postcolonial identity; the latter is conceived as hybrid, with the borderland cast as neither a place of losing one's identity through assimilation, nor recuperating a prior identity untouched by colonization.

Essays are an important genre in U.S. ethnic literature as they perform an important function of delineating the sociopolitical issues and themes of concern to the ethnic group. **Audre Lorde**'s *Sister Outsider: Essays and Speeches* (1984) includes the essay made famous by the feminist movement, "The Master's Tools Will Never Dismantle the Master's House." June Jordan, a poet known for her powerful poems of antiimperialism, racism, and sexism, as in *Naming Our Destiny: New and Selected Poems* (1989), is also author of *Technical Difficulties: African American Notes on the State of the Union*, a collection of fine political essays. Elizabeth Cook-Lynn, *Why I Can't Read Wallace Stegner and Other Essays* (1996) discusses the critical issue of tribal sovereignty, and the blind spots of writers such as Wallace Stegner, in whose writings she sees as erasure of indigenous presence and culture. Toni Morrison, *Playing in the Dark: Whiteness and the Literary Imagination* (1992) writes about white American literature's relationship to race and the black presence in the nation, a relationship most often ignored by critics. Leslie Silko, *Yellow Woman and a Beauty of the Spirit* (1996), writes about the

Native American heritage, from the importance of the land and of stories to the Pueblo people, to her outrage over the government's long-standing, racist treatment of Native Americans. **Ana Castillo**'s essays *Massacre of the Dreamers: Essays on Xicanisma* (1987) are, as the subtitle of a later edition indicates, "reflections on Mexican-Indian women in the United States 500 years after the conquest." Huanani-Kay Trask's collection of essays *From a Native Daughter: Colonialism and Sovereignty in Hawai'i* (1999) protests U.S. colonization of Polynesian land and culture.

Postcolonial Dislocations

Writers who are immigrants from the postcolonial nations invariably complicate the relationship of **ethnicity** and nationality. Autobiography is a genre that accommodates the multiple displacements and relates a collective ethnic memory to an individual one. Further, it is perhaps the only genre that allows a full articulation of the historical and cultural specificity that is so easily elided in the United States, and whose invisibility creates the sense of exile. Shaped by postcolonial India, writer **Meena Alexander**'s *Fault Lines* (1993) reflects an identity that exceeds the boundaries of India and the United States. The postcolonial immigrant body is simultaneously without a history in the United States, even as it somatically incarnates and registers a different history. This ambivalence is further negotiated in *The Shock of Arrival: Reflections on a Postcolonial Experience* (1996). Other American autobiographies that narrate the experience of British (post)colonialism as formative to their own identities in the United States are **Jamaica Kincaid** (Antiguan), **Michelle Cliff** (Jamaican), Leila Ahmed (Egyptian), and **Shirley Geok-lin Lim** (Malaysian). Afro-Caribbean novelist Jamaica Kincaid brings to bear the formative experience of British colonialism in Antigua in much of her work.

In her work of nonfiction, *A Small Place* (1988), Kincaid reflects on the failure of decolonization in Antigua and links this failure to the island being run by the neo-colonial tourist industry that caters to Europeans and Americans at the expense of the local people. In *Among the White Moon Faces: An Asian-American Memoir of Homelands* (1996) Chinese Malaysian writer Shirley Geok-lin Lim writes of her colonial English education and her experiences of multiple discriminations, from colonial British, ethnic Malays, and Americans, who grasped none of her historic specificity. Leila Ahmed's *Border Passage: From Cairo to America—A Women's Journey* (1999) speaks of her homeland Egypt, the complexities of Arab nationalism, her education in England, and her life as a Muslim woman in the American academy where Islam is stigmatized. Palestinian American writer and literary critic Edward Said's *Out of Place: A Memoir* (1999) describes his early years in Palestine, Egypt, and Lebanon and his subsequent education in the United States and charts the conflicting influences that created the outsider in him.

To conclude with Said's work is befitting since it is his writing that formally inaugurated the field of postcolonial studies. Much of the U.S ethnic literature that we consider from a postcolonial perspective is literature that attempts to connect the individual with the collectivity that gives it meaning. The act of representation becomes an act of bearing witness, of expressing commitment and hope toward a better social order. The work of postcolonial studies in the United States is ongoing as the conditions that generate the critiques continue well into the twenty-first century.

Further Reading

Arteaga, Alfred, ed. *An Other Tongue: Nation and Ethnicity in the Linguistic Borderlands.* Durham, NC: Duke UP, 1994.

JanMohamed, Abdul, and David Lloyd, eds. *The Nature and Context of Minority Discourse.* New York: Oxford UP, 1990.

Kaplan, Amy, and Donald Pease, eds. *Cultures of United States Imperialism.* Durham, NC: Duke UP, 1993.

Lowe, Lisa. *Immigrant Acts: On Asian American Cultural Politics.* Durham, NC: Duke UP, 1996.

Lubiano, Wahneema, ed. *The House That Race Built: Black Americans, U.S. Terrain.* New York: Pantheon. 1997.

Palumbo-Liu, David, ed. *The Ethnic Canon: Histories, Institutions, and Interventions.* Minneapolis: U Minnesota P, 1995.

Saldivar, José David. *Border Matters: Remapping American Cultural Studies.* Berkeley: U California P, 1997.

Schmidt, Peter, and Amritijit Singh, eds. *Postcolonial Theory and the U.S.: Race, Ethnicity, and Literature.* Jackson: U of Mississippi P, 2000.

Sharpe, Jenny. "Is the United States Postcolonial? Transnationalism, Immigration, and Race." *Diaspora* 4.2 (Fall 1995): 181–99.

Gurleen Grewal

POTOK, CHAIM (1929–) Jewish American novelist. Chaim Potok was born Herman Harold, (Hebrew names Chaim Tsvi) to Polish immigrant parents in 1929. He went to religious schools and, because of his keen interest in literature, his parents worried that it would distract him from his religious studies. He did pursue his theological studies, however: Ordained at age twenty-five as a Conservative rabbi, Potok became a chaplain in the United States Army and saw active service in Korea. He then taught at the University of Judaism, married, and became editor of *Conservative Judaism* and then the Jewish Publication Society. He also spent some time in Israel.

As a young teenager Potok was captivated by reading *Brideshead Revisited* by Evelyn Waugh. This novel describing Roman Catholic upper-class English culture on the verge of World War II taught him, he later claimed, the value of using literature to describe different worlds and first gave him the idea of trying to use his literary talent to depict Orthodox Jewish life. This was in contrast with Orthodox tradition, in which such literary endeavor was viewed with disapproval. In 1967 his first novel, *The Chosen*, was published. It depicted the world of two Jewish friends, one the son of a Hasidic rabbi and one a boy from a more secular Jewish family. Their relationship is torn apart by the tensions in the Hasidic community surrounding the foundation of Israel.

The Chosen achieved instant commercial success, and was followed by a sequel, *The Promise,* two years later. In this novel the Hasidic friend has begun to doubt the faith of his father, and refuses to become a *tzaddik* (Jewish leader) in his turn. Such tensions between the secular and the religious dominate Potok's work, with reflections on questions of Jewish **ethnicity** and Israeli-North American Jewish politics interweaving with questions about the value of literature and the worth of the intellectual life.

In *My Name Is Asher Lev,* Potok directly addressed some of the tensions he had himself found in balancing literary and artistic endeavor with his upbringing in an Orthodox Jewish community. *Asher Lev* becomes controversial not merely for depicting his mother in a Crucifixion (a taboo Orthodox Jewish subject) but for daring to use visual artistic form at all (this is prohibited by strict Orthodox tradition). *Davita's Harp* (1985) reverses the pattern of secularization of cultural **identity** present in many Potok novels by presenting a central character who has grown up with a secularized Jewish identity and finds himself increasingly drawn to the tradition of Kabbalic mysticism.

Potok was a Talmudic scholar and worked on the Jewish Publication Society of America's translation of the Hebrew Bible. As well as his many novels, he also wrote the acclaimed *Wanderings: Chaim Potok's History of the Jews* (1978), which sold over 100,000 copies; a work of literary criticism, *The Jew Confronts Himself in American Literature* (1975); a collection of short stories for teens, *The Zebra and Other Stories* (1998); a book of moral reflections, *Ethical Living for a Modern World* (1985); and many short articles and reviews. *In The Beginning,* an autobiographical piece of writing, was published in 1975. In 1981 *The Chosen* was made into a film, starring Robbie Benson. Potok also wrote for the theater. In 1988 he wrote a theatrical adaptation of *The Chosen.* This was followed by *Out of the Depths* and *Sins of the Fathers: The Carnival and the Gallery* (two one-act plays), and *The Play of Lights,* which were all premiered in Philadelphia in 1992. *Old Men at Midnight,* published in 2001, was his final work. It deals with experiences of cultural loss and transformation across three eras, as stories told by different men to a single woman. The subject matter ranges from Russia and Poland to contemporary America and wartime Japan.

Issues of ethnic identity were at the heart of Potok's writings. His books did not prescribe a particular view of Judaism, or American identity: rather they dealt with the difficulties and confusions in the tensions between traditionalist and contemporary (secularizing) idioms. He often contrasted the relative certainties of European Jewish tradition with the political dilemmas and controversies marking Jewish identity today. However, when asked how he felt about being described as an American Jewish writer, Potok famously remarked that he preferred to be seen as "an American writer writing about a small and particular American world." Nor was his work focused solely on the American community. Two of his later works, *I Am the Clay* (1992) and *The Book of Lights* (1981), focused upon the experience of both Koreans and outsiders in the damage wrought by war in Korea. However, Potok differs from other American Jewish writers of his generation such as **Philip Roth** and **Saul Bellow**, in that his characters do not take an **assimilation**ist approach to the issue of Jewishness in twentieth-century America. Their books tended to minimize or even scorn the world of religious Judaism. By contrast, Potok places the Jewish religious experience at the very heart of much of his creative work. As Potok expert Daniel Walden comments, Potok is unusual in that, like his childhood hero Evelyn Waugh, he wrote as a believer rather than an agnostic or a skeptic. This did not diminish his appeal, but rather broadened it. He received many fan letters from readers of other faiths. Potok himself commented that the appeal of his work was so broad because he had "stumbled quite inadvertently upon the central problem of any system of faith in the secular culture." Therefore, his work had meaning to non-Jewish readers too.

Within his faith commitment, Potok was constantly concerned to highlight the need for tolerance and the need to listen with respect to those from different faiths and perspectives. In a 1983 interview, he said, "I submit that the price you pay for listening is far less than the price you pay for not listening and disappearing. I'm not altogether certain that a fundamentalism of necessity has to argue that it is the only reading of the human experience in order to stay alive. There has got to be another way of articulating one's commitment to a body of ideas—a way other than saying, 'I'm right and everybody else is wrong.' And that's what we have to learn in the next half a century to a century, otherwise we are just not going to be around to talk to ourselves anymore."

His views on ethnic diversity and interaction revolved around a theme of "core" culture. At the heart of every culture, he once said, there were core ways of seeing the world. This contrasted with the "umbrella" way in which many cultures intersected in modern life. Culture fusion—the positive meeting of cultures—happened when "something is yielded by both sides. The ideal would be that out of the fusion something new would result. You hope when you give something up that you gain something back." This contrasted with culture confrontation, when stress was caused by the encounter with a different ideology, or perspective on the world. Rather than seeing culture and faith as one dimensional, Potok stressed the role of mystery and ambiguity in our approach to and understanding of the world. In *My Name is Asher Lev,* his central character tries to describe his work: "I call that ambiguity. Riddles, puzzles, double meanings, lost possibilities, the dark side to the light, the light side to darkness, different perspectives on the same things. Nothing in this whole world has only one side to it. Everything is like a kaleidoscope. That's what I'm trying to capture in my art. That's what I mean by ambiguity."

Potok's work is marked by a belief in the universal power of hearing and telling stories. In *Zebra and Other Stories*, a character notes, "I think losing your soul is when you can't tell a story about something that has happened to you."

Further Reading

Kremer, S. Lillian. *Witness Through the Imagination: Jewish American Holocaust Literature*. Detroit: Wayne State UP, 1989.

Walden, Daniel, ed. "The World of Chaim Potok." *Studies in American Jewish Literature* 4 (1985).

Kerry Kidd

POTTER, ELIZA (1820?–?)   African American autobiographer. Potter's 1859 socially conscious autobiography is the first behind-the-scenes book written by an African American woman. Although it is an autobiography, *A Hairdresser's Experience in High Life* does not provide a lot of personal information about Potter. Indeed the particular details of her life come from the Cincinnati, Ohio, censuses. We do know that she was a mulatta from Kentucky who worked as a maid, a wet nurse, a governess in Europe, and, lastly of course, a hairdresser. She was briefly married in Buffalo, New York, and gave birth to two children in Philadelphia, Pennsylvania, whom she supported with her work. She moved to Cincinnati in 1840.

Instead of focusing upon her personal life, Potter discusses the evils of **slavery**, how she learned her hairdressing craft, and the caprices of her white customers, of which she speaks with contempt. Being a mulatta, Potter existed on the fringes of the white and African American worlds of Cincinnati, but she still managed to create her own **identity**. However, Potter was not just an observer: She helped slaves escape and at one point was jailed for a few months because of her assistance. She also took care of and trained African American women to become hairdressers and placed their children in an orphanage that lists her as the "lady manager." Her candid and clear language, at times contemptuous of slave owners, **abolition**ists, slave mistresses, and patrons, is nonetheless articulate and straightforward. Obviously, Potter was a strong-willed, direct, and determined woman. She had to be to survive in her world.

Furthermore, what makes Potter admirable is that she independently supported herself through her hairdressing and raised her children by herself. She was financially well-off and owned her own house, which was a major feat for that time. Besides that, she found the time to help other African Americans who were less fortunate. Unfortunately, Potter eventually disappears from history. The 1861 Cincinnati census does not list her, so she must have left the city sometime before. Why she left is open to conjecture. Maybe it had something to do with the subject matter of her autobiography.

Although Potter does not give much information about her personal life from her autobiography, she lives up to the promise of its title. Her in-depth commentaries on the vagaries of fashion, the whims and secrets of her white customers, and social injustice toward herself and other African Americans demonstrated a woman keenly aware of the world around her. Perhaps that is why Potter did not talk much about herself; her autobiography was about the world that never fully accepted her. Still, Potter clearly provides us with an inner glimpse into a world that few people will ever have. (*See also* African American Autobiography)

Further Reading

Huot, Nikolas. "Eliza C. Potter." *African American Autobiographers: A Sourcebook.* Ed. Emmanuel S. Nelson. Westport, CT: Greenwood Press, 2002. 298–302.

Devona Mallory

POWERS, JAMES EARL (1917–1999) Irish American Catholic short story writer and novelist whose stories are focused almost exclusively in Illinois and Minnesota. He was born in Jacksonville, Illinois, and studied at Northwestern University in Chicago. He spent thirteen months in jail for being a conscientious objector and refusing to join the military in World War II. Most of Powers's stories are concerned with Catholic religious orders and the life within rectories, monasteries, and convents. Although not a religious writer (in the sense that there are no miracles, grand voices from above, or otherworldly occurrences), he does concern himself with the everyday lives of religious people.

As we all know too well (especially in the twenty-first century), Catholic priests and nuns have the same foibles, weaknesses, prejudices, and shortcomings that all human beings have. They fight life's nuisances and troubles everyday, often losing the battle. They are not all smug, pious, overly serious, lifeless creatures. They often bemoan their sometimes gloomy existences and long for an entirely new or free state. There is a similar struggle in all of us. Powers reflects these feelings and emotions in all his tales.

In several of his stories (e.g. "Lords Day") he bitingly portrays the feelings of neglect and belittlement that many of the sisters feel about their status in the Catholic hierarchy. They know that they are second-class in the world they have chosen. They do most of the menial, uninspiring, physical labor, and are under the priest's controls and whims. From sighs and sorrowful, annoyed glances, the reader senses their (if not despair at least) resigned acceptance. They are often shown with extremely work-hardened, reddened hands, sore backs and knees, haggard looks, and tired voices. Yet they are mainly lighted with smiles, albeit weak and unconvincing ones, trying to gain merit or grace from their patience and goodness. And they perform their tasks with game-like efficiency and even with fun. In some ways the nuns appear childlike and completely innocent. Nevertheless, as with the priests, they have their small rebellions and defiances. For example, when Sundays, supposed to be days of rest, are unexpectedly made workdays, for the nuns, the disapproval is displayed in various subtle but unmistakable acts and words, especially when the priests are going off to the theater or to play golf. Powers also clearly reveals the various personalities, for, of course, they are not all of one mold. He relates (in some respects) tragic incidents in humorous, often extremely hilarious ways. We never feel the heaviness or sadness that might easily arise from such stories (except in "Lions, Harts, Leaping Does"). Although the points are made lightly and humorously, they cannot be missed.

Some critics accuse Powers of superficiality because he is seemingly so easy and lighthearted. They say he has no depth or complexity. They are wrong. Not all of his tales are concerned with daily, prosaic, all-too-human problems. Some are about deep philosophical issues, such as life and death, salvation and damnation, and ultimate good and evil. In "Lions, Harts, Leaping Does" Powers exhibits his most penetrating, and arguably, the most important analysis ever of a priest's meaningful and severe spiritual problems. His complete and insightful study of Father Didymus, and his agony of the soul, is moving and tearful. We anguish over the poor, aged, gray man's struggle with, what is for him, his failing faith, his trivial life, and his impending disgraceful death. When even an apparently devoted, cloistered priest is unsure of his motivations, intents, and ultimate deliverance, how can we of the secular world ever hope for a chance at salvation? The priest evolves during the short story into a firm believer in spirituality as the highest value. He shifts from self-judgment, self-doubt, self-condemnation, guilt, and feelings of empty unworthiness to total resignation and acceptance, willing to be judged on his last day by compassionate spirits rather than by bitter critics. But does he achieve redemption? Powers leaves readers pondering Didymus's eternal fate (and their own). "Didymus" could be read as "did he miss." This marvelous character study is the best story of its kind in American literature. Powers won the National Book Award for his excellent novel *Morte D'Urban* (1963) and received a nomination for the fine *Wheat That Springeth Green* (1988), but his short stories are his highest achievements. A short story collection, *Look How the Fish Live* (1973), won a National Book Award.

Further Reading

Hagopian, J. V. *J. F. Powers*. New York: Twayne, 1968.

Lebowitz, Naomi. "The Stories of J. F. Powers: The Sign of Contradiction." *Kenyon Review* XX (Summer 1958): 494–99.

Sisk, John. "The Complex Moral Vision of J. F. Powers." *Critique* II (Fall 1958): 41–58.

Robert J. Toole

PRECIADO MARTIN, PATRICIA (c. 1940–) Mexican American public historian and short story writer. The majority of Preciado Martin's work focuses on oral history, and this concern is reflected in her short stories, which draw upon the theme of tradition. More specifically, Preciado Martin explores how people lived their lives in the past and how others deal with their heritage in the face of progress.

Patricia Preciado Martin is a native of Tucson, Arizona. She is an honors graduate of the University of Arizona. Her first publication, *Images and Conversation: Mexican Americans Recall a Southwestern Past* (1983), began her exploration of oral histories that is furthered in *Songs My Mother Sang to Me: An Oral History of Mexican American Women* (1992) and her most recent project, *Beloved Land: An Oral History of Mexican Americans in Southern Arizona* (2004), written in collaboration with Pulitzer Prize–winning photographer José Galvez. In 2000 she was given the Distinguished Public Scholar Award by the Arizona Humanities Council

Preciado Martin has written three collections of short stories, *Days of Plenty, Days of Want* (1988), *El Milagro and Other Stories* (1996), and *Amor Eterno* (2000), for which she has been awarded the Border Regional Library Association Award. Preciado Martin's work is populated with Mexican American characters who lead a way of life in Tucson and its environs that has withstood cultural change for multiple decades. Her attention to language further emphasizes this, with characters speaking Spanish, English, and a combination of the two.

In *El Milagro and Other Stories,* the reader is introduced to characters whose heritage shapes their very being. Some lament its inability to withstand the pressures of modern day life and others simply deal with the changes. In the second story, "Dichos, Proverbs," the main character is made to visit her grandmother, Mamnina, every Saturday, and although she claims to dread the weekly ritual, the reader learns that she looks forward to the visit when she indicates that the closer she comes to the house, the better she feels. During this visit, Mamanina counsels the ninth grader through a series of proverbs that make relevant the values of the past in the present. At the same time, Preciado Martin indicates that younger generations must also deal with these changes, with characters understanding that this heritage is a valuable asset that they must try to reclaim.

Preciado Martin has continued to explore this theme in *Amor Eterno*, with each short story based upon a type of love (e.g. mother's love, enchanted love, desperate love, etc.) that is framed by the lyrics of a love song, further emphasizing the story's specific theme. In "Amor Inolvidable: Unforgettable Love," a young woman learns why her ninety-year-old great aunt, Nina Jacinta, sets her table with a third place setting. At the same time the reader learns about women's handicrafts as they were practiced by Nina Jacinta and her mother. Altogether, the story shows how the past shapes the present as the narrator attempts to learn more about her great aunt's life.

Further Reading

Bellver, Pilar. "La Historia Oral Como Autobiografica Cultural: Dos Ejemplos Chicanos." *Aztlán: A Journal of Chicano Studies* 24.2 (1999): 49–72.

———. "'Songs That My Mother Sang to Me': y la construccion de la identidad Chicana." *Debate Feminista* 10.19 (1999): 231–53.

Nancy K. Cardona

PRIDA, DOLORES (1943–)   Cuban American dramatist, ranked among the most important playwrights of contemporary Latino theater in the United States. Prida's plays range in style from that found in realistic musical theater to that of the nonrealistic theater of the absurd. Her thematic material is informed by issues of ethnic, gender, and class identities, and tends to explore the options available to Latinos within a society that, while it values its traditional customs, is concurrently interested in exploring the possibilities offered by a new, emerging hybrid culture.

Prida, born in Cuba, was brought to the United States as a child by her parents, and since 1961 has resided in New York City. She attended Hunter College, majoring in Latin American literature. She has written for the stage and television and has taught workshops on play writing in New York and in other parts of the country. In the early 1980s, she was the director of the New York–based Association of Hispanic Artists and was the editor of its newsletter, *AHA*. In 1989 Mount Holyoke College awarded her an honorary Doctorate of Humane Letters for her contributions to the American theater. Since 1996, Prida has been a senior editor at the bilingual national monthly magazine *Latina Magazine*. At *Latina Magazine*, she is responsible for translating and editing all of the material that appears in Spanish and writes two sections for each issue, the "The Ñ Generation" and the advice pages titled "Dolores Dice: Old-Fashioned Consejos for a New Millennium." Keeping in mind the lifestyle of its readership—primarily young, professional, bilingual, bicultural, "cool" Latinas and their friends—*Latina Magazine* is an energetic promoter of the hybrid language, Spanglish, a language found in all of Prida's plays.

Dolores Prida has published a collection of five plays, *Beautiful Señoritas and Other Plays* (1991), in which she has mapped the urban landscape and covered most of the important topics of her generation. "Beautiful Señoritas" is a musical satire of women's roles and the images that Latino culture has of these roles. Prida's love of the strong Cuban Spanish tradition of the musical comedy as well as that of the American musical is expressed in a mannered theatricality, one of her defining characteristics. Judith Weiss, a critic of Latin American and Latino theater, attributes the satire and humor in "Beautiful Señoritas" to Prida's insider's knowledge of two musical traditions, which in turn helps her to turn her own lyrics against the dominant ideology.

Beautiful Señoritas and Other Plays also includes "Coser y Cantar," "Savings," "Pantallas," and "Botánica." Perhaps it is in the two-person one-act play, "Coser y Cantar," that Prida best makes use of Spanish and English, and of her knowledge of the two cultures represented by these two languages. The character *Ella* operates within a traditional Latin American mindset and speaks in Spanish, while *She* represents the Americanized Latina who speaks in English and displays a new way of thinking. But "Coser y Cantar," first produced in 1981 and in regular production since then, does not privilege one culture above the other. A radio play version taped for National Public Radio has been broadcast nationwide several times.

Another of Prida's most popular plays is "Botánica." Commissioned in 1991 by New York's Teatro Repertorio Español, "Botánica" was in resident production in Spanish for nine years. With its vivid dialogue and distinctive setting, "Botánica" brings to life the delicate balance that Millie, representing the youngest of three generations of women, must negotiate in her assimilation process. The play is set in Doña Geno's herbal shop in East Harlem, a self-contained world that can be found in every major metropolis in the United States. Although all of the characters are Puerto Rican, Doña Geno could just as easily be a Cuban *santera* or a Mexican *curandera* who serves her community with herbal remedies for maladies that are both physical and psychic. Doña Geno's granddaughter, Milagros, has just graduated from a New Hampshire college where she majored in business. In college she changed her name to Millie and has come home a changed person who desires to succeed in what she considers "a bigger life" in the world of banking in Manhattan. Prida avoids taking the easy way out in the plot and negotiates a possible solution for Millie, offering her a way to contribute in her own manner to her community with her newly acquired skills, a message that no doubt has wide audience appeal.

Two of Prida's more recent plays have also had successive staged presentations. "Casa Propia" ("A House of One's Own," 1998), based in part on the advice given by Virginia Woolf in "A Room of One's Own," is about a group of women in search of a space of their own. The play won the 1998 Fannie Mae Foundation "American Dream" play competition. Her latest play, "Four Guys Named José and Una Mujer Named María" (2000) is a comedy musical review of the most-loved Latin songs of all times; its soundtrack was issued in February 2001 as an audio CD. The musical is about four guys named José, all U.S.-born, whose parents came from different countries in Latin America; they befriend one another when they find themselves stranded in a Nebraska snowstorm. Longing for the songs of home, they put on a show at the VFW hall, celebrating well-known singers such as Desi Arnaz, Julio Iglesias, José Feliciano, Santana, and Selena, among others. A full Off Broadway production from September 2000 through March 2001 at the Angel Theatre in New York was followed by an equally successful run in Miami at the Actors Playhouse from October 2001 to February 2002. The musical then went on to the West Coast in 2004, playing at the Oregon Cabaret Theater in Ashland, the Teatro Visión in San José, California, and the International City Theater in Long Beach, California. With its family-oriented, dazzling dancing, "Four Guys Named José and Una Mujer Named María" will no doubt become a staple offering in season ticket series that feature the most beloved plays of the American musical theater.

Prida has three more works in Progress: "LIPS*—The Play (*Latinas in Power . . . Sort Of)," a comedy about a networking group of professional Latinas who meet on a regular basis in New York City; "The Electric Maraca," a play with music about a Cuban restaurant-owner and his fading business who still has personal dreams in the Big Apple; "The Saxophone Man," a full-length musical developed at INTAR's Playwrights-in-Residence Laboratory in New York, which is under the direction of another major Cuban American playwright, **Maria Irene Fornes**. (*See also* Bilingualism)

Further Reading

Weiss, Judith. "The Theaterworks of Dolores Prida." Introduction to *Beautiful Señoritas & Other Plays*. Judith Weiss, ed. Houston: Arte Público Press, 1990. 7–16.

Roberta Fernández

PRINCE, MARY (1788–?)   First black woman to publish a **slave narrative**. Mary Prince was born in Bermuda in 1788 and spent the first four decades of her life in **slavery**, enduring brutal circumstances under several different owners. After being separated from family members as a child, she worked as a household slave in Bermuda and Antigua and as a laborer on a salt plantation on Turk Island. Prince endured harsh working conditions, sexually exploitative owners, and brutal physical punishment that left her suffering from lifelong scars, as well as crippling rheumatism. In 1828, she escaped to freedom while accompanying her owners on a trip to London. At the time, British law forbade slavery on English soil, although slavery was still allowed in British colonies. Taking advantage of her newfound right to freedom, Prince sought the aid of the Moravian Church, which she had joined in the West Indies, and the British Anti-Slavery Society. Unable to return to Antigua and reunite with her husband without risking reenslavement, Prince told her story to Susannah Strickland, a poet and **abolition**ist, and, with Prince's permission, her tale was subsequently edited and published by Thomas Pringle, the secretary of the Anti-Slavery Society, who would also become Prince's employer in London.

The History of Mary Prince, A West Indian Slave, Related by Herself (1831) was the earliest firsthand published account of the brutality that women suffered under the system of slavery. Although only twenty-three pages long in its initial printing, Prince's narrative was both popular and controversial when it was published in London, running to a third edition the year it was published and stirring intense debate about the nature of the institution of slavery in the West Indies and the conditions endured by slaves. In simple but eloquent language, Prince strongly discounted the pro-slavery arguments which held that blacks were basically content to be slaves, revealing the emotional toll taken by the separation of families, as well as the physical suffering caused by harsh conditions and brutal punishments. When proponents of slavery, including her former master, challenged the authenticity of Prince's claims and impugned her character, Prince gave evidence in British courts to support her assertions. In telling her story and disputing the biased assertions of slavery's supporters, Prince set an example which would later be followed by numerous former slaves, both men and women.

Although she briefly became a celebrity in England, Prince was still unable to purchase her freedom and return to the West Indies. Instead, she remained in England, at least until after 1833, when she disappeared from the public record. Today Prince's narrative stands as an important early text for scholars of slave narratives, black women's life-writing, and Caribbean literature.

Further Reading

Morton, Nanette. "Mary Prince." *African American Authors, 1745–1945: A Bio-Bibliographical Sourcebook.* Ed. Emmanuel S. Nelson. Westport, CT: Greenwood Press, 2000. 357–65.

Sharpe, Jenny. *Ghosts of Slavery: A Literary Archaeology of Black Women's Lives.* Minneapolis: U of Minnesota P, 2003.

Todd Dapremont

PRINCE, NANCY GARDNER (1799–?) Free-born African American and Native American travel writer, lecturer, social reformer, **abolitionist**, and philanthropist. Best known for her autobiographical travel writing, her most famous text, *A Narrative of the Life and Travels of Mrs. Nancy Prince, Written by Herself* (1850), begins with a proud declaration of both her African and Native American heritage and tells the tale of her life from early childhood, through her conversion to Christianity in her teen years, followed by her many adventures in Salem, the West Indies, Russia, and the American South.

Prince was an unusual woman, and her text is an unusual amalgamation of travel writing, spiritual confession, autobiography, and cultural criticism. From the first pages of her text, she seeks to expand her nineteenth-century readers' understanding of what being an American means by providing the historical roots and antecedents of her family. She is a quintessential American for she is the granddaughter of a Native American woman and an African man who fought on the side of American independence in the American Revolution. A dedicated Protestant, she rescued her sister from a life of prostitution in Salem, and during the ten years she lived outside the United States with her husband, Nero, an employee of the Russian tsars, she worked for both religious and social reform in Russia. A successful business owner, hiring white Russian women to work for her in her St. Petersburg seamstress shop, Prince studied the customs of the Russian people and offered spiritual guidance to the women she employed.

Following a spate of bad health, Prince returned to the United States. In the wake of the death of her husband and the emancipation of the West Indies, Prince sailed to Jamaica to raise money for church schools there. Her text provides a significant eyewitness account of the decolonization and emancipation of the West Indies from the point of view of a middle-aged, free-born, nineteenth-century African American and Native American woman who, though a citizen of a nation that permitted **slavery**, had also lived abroad for ten years in a country where her color did not limit her social status or success. She is a harsh critic of hypocrisy and chicanery, whether perpetuated by West Indian blacks or Anglo-missionary whites, when members of either group attempted to attain personal advantage at the expense of others.

Although her book was published in America and went through three editions (1850, 1853, 1856) Prince's life in America after having lived abroad was financially unsatisfactory. She died in poverty and obscurity as America entered its own period of political and social unrest: the Civil War.

Further Reading

Fish, Cheryl. "Journeys and Warnings: Nancy Prince's Resistant Truth Telling in New England, Russia, and Jamaica." *Black and White Women's Travel Narratives.* (2004). 24–64.

Gunning, Sandra. "Nancy Prince and the Politics of Mobility, Home and Diasporic (Mis)Identification." *American Quarterly* 53.1 (March 2001). 32–69.

Moody, Jocelyn. "Rejecting Sentimentalism: Nancy Prince." *Sentimental Confessions: Spiritual Narratives of Nineteenth-Century African American Women.* (2001). 77–102.

Darcy A. Zabel

PROSE, FRANCINE (1947–) Jewish American novelist, short story writer, essayist, and scholar. Francine Prose is the author of highly acclaimed works of fiction, including *Household Saints* (1981), *Hungry Hearts* (1983), *Big Foot Dreams* (1986), *Primitive People* (1992), *Hunters and Gatherers* (1995), *Guided Tours of Hell* (1996), and *Blue Angel* (2000) (which was nominated for a 2000 National Book Award). Her work has been published in such periodicals as *The Paris Review, GQ, The Atlantic Monthly,* and *The New Yorker.* A contributing editor at *Harper's* and a Director's Fellow at the Center for Scholars and Writers at the New York Library, Prose also writes about art for the *Wall Street Journal.* Francine Prose is the recipient of numerous grants and awards, and she has taught at the distinguished Iowa Writers' Workshop, the Sewanee Writer's Conference, and the Johns Hopkins University. She currently resides in New York City.

Francine Prose is a postmodern satirist whose fiction explores how pop culture infiltrates the contemporary individual's consciousness, what happens when old frames of reference collide with the new, and the pretense associated with academia and social life. Although her fiction reflects contemporary concerns, Prose's oeuvre also demonstrates an interest in the Jewish folktale tradition. Questions of faith, morality, freedom, individuality, and community are propagated by Prose's portrayals of everyday life, and these queries are propelled by a keen eye for detail, a tuned ear for dialogue, and a passion for storytelling. Prose often delineates an understated heroism in the everyday struggles of her protagonists, which are frequently contrasted to the lofty aspirations and ideas perpetuated by the media and academic institutions. Enmeshed in the many themes that pervade Prose's work are interrogations of contemporary forms of contradiction and hypocrisy, the performative nature of social life, the delicate balance between artifice and reality, and the roles fabrication, myth-making, and nostalgia play in the present day. Some of her most recent work investigates the dangers of extreme political correctness and over-protectiveness in a culture inundated with violence, crime, and concomitant fear.

In *Blue Angel,* Prose lampoons academic ethics and the political correctness that has run away from common sense. At the center of the novel is Ted Swenson, a creative writing professor at a second-rate college who enjoyed a modicum of success with his first novel. Since writing his novel, Swenson has fallen into a funk of malaise and disillusionment with his writing and teaching career. It has been a long time since he has written anything of merit or since any of his students have shown any promise. Once a talented young writer named Angela Argo joins his writing seminar, however, Swenson begins to believe in the art of writing again and serves as enthusiastic mentor to the intriguing Argo. Unfortunately, Angela is more interested in the prospect of getting Swenson's editor to consider her novel-in-progress than she is in anything Swenson might have to offer her. Swenson's editor's refusal to view Argo's work leads to a series of specious accusations against the creative writing professor that are played out in a ludicrous but all-too-realistic academic hearing. Through her satirical look at the political, social, and theoretical landscapes of academia, Prose boldly aims her incisive perceptiveness at such contentious issues as the extreme nature of sexual harassment policies and gender politics. In doing so, Prose subverts and complicates old and new stereotypes, but not without engendering sympathy for her protagonist. Prose's *Hunters and Gatherers* is a cutting portrayal of the New Age movement. Martha, a fashion magazine fact checker whose emotional life is in disarray, joins a community of individuals who practice goddess worship. In typical iconoclastic fashion, Prose details Martha's revelation that even a well-intentioned matriarchy can succumb to jealousy and competition. The group's lack of genuine spiritual guidance and tradition, combined with their derivative ceremony rituals, causes the community's dynamic to break down. In this way, *Hunters and Gatherers* is a tale for the new age. Prose's *Primitive People* illustrates some of the more absurd elements of contemporary American culture through the eyes of an illegal Haitian immigrant who serves as a nanny to children of self-absorbed parents. Simone, a Haitian au pair, flees the turbulent brutality of Port-au-Prince only to find that she has escaped to a place that is no less chaotic and aberrant. Once again, it is Prose's sharp eye for irony and satire that unearths the dark truths underlying the opulent, resplendent lives of the wealthy denizens of the Hudson Valley in upstate New York.

In the two novellas that make up *Guided Tours of Hell,* Prose's American characters' perceptions of sex, history, politics, and reality are challenged while they attempt to mix business with pleasure in Europe. The title work's protagonist, Landau, a second-rate playwright from New York attending a conference on Kafka in Prague, becomes immersed in a disgraceful ego-charged struggle with a concentration camp survivor. Likewise, the main character of "Three Pigs in Five Days," Nina, confronts her own personal hell while in Paris writing an article on a whorehouse-turned-hotel. *Bigfoot Dreams* is a caustic examination of disreputable journalism, *Hungry Hearts* is the story of an actress who is possessed by a dybbuk, and *Household Saints* deals with issues of religion, morality, tradition, and superstition as they present themselves in New York's Little Italy in the 1950s. Prose brings Jewish legend and folktale to life in her children's books, *Dybbuk: A Story Made in Heaven* (1996) and *The Demon's Mistake: A Story from Chelm* (2000). *After* (2003), Francine Prose's first novel for teens, explores the stifling repression and over-guardedness that the students of Central High must endure following a massacre at a neighboring school.

Francine Prose continues to deal with issues of **feminism**, morality, contemporary culture, narrative, aesthetics, and myth in her nonfiction. In *The Lives of the Muses* (2002), Prose explores the complex, interdependent relationship between artist and muse. The nine women featured in Prose's exposé challenge the traditional notion of the female muse as passive object exploited by the artist. In fact, the women depicted in Prose's work demonstrate that there are many variations on the theme. Among other muse figures, Prose documents how Yoko Ono sought to compel John Lennon into the role of muse, portrays Gala Dali as a mastermind at marketing husband Salvador's art while concurrently catapulting her own notoriety, and details how Hester Thrale's adulterous relationship with Dr. Samuel Johnson kept his depression from completely inhibiting his writing. Originally a lecture as part of the New York Public Library's Seven Deadly Sins Series, Prose's *Gluttony* (2003) examines the many facets of our obsessions with food and diet, and reveals how these preoccupations evolved out of our demonization of self-indulgence. In addition to charting various images of gluttony in history and literature, Prose questions the morality of the institutions that have condemned it. In medieval times, Prose points out, gluttony was deemed a moral and spiritual aberration. Today, gluttony is considered an illness linked to such phenomena as self-destruction and the fear of intimacy. Prose argues that this evolution of gluttony from spiritual to psychological abnormality does not allow the individual to celebrate indulgence as an assertion of gratification and desire. As part of the ongoing National Geographic Directions Series, Prose combines personal narrative and travel writing with art, history, and cultural criticism in *Sicilian Odyssey* (2003). In her book, Prose examines the diverse mythical and cultural legacies associated with the beautiful Mediterranean island of Sicily, and explores what the island can disclose about maintaining beauty in the midst of violence. In addition to books on the muse-artist relationship, gluttony, and cultural criticism, Prose has contributed a chapter to the renowned *On Writing Short Stories* (2000) and has written a witty introduction to the provocatively titled *Master Breasts: Objectified, Aestheticized, Fantasized, Eroticized, Feminized by Photography's Most Titillating Masters* (1998).

Further Reading

Aarons, Victoria. "Responding to an Old Story: Susan Fromberg Schaeffer, Leslea Newman, and Francine Prose." *Daughters of Valor: Contemporary Jewish American Women Writers*. Ed. Jay L. Halio. Newark: U of Delaware P, 1997. 112–25.

Prose, Francine. "What Makes a Short Story?" *On Writing Short Stories*. Ed. Tom Bailey. New York: Oxford UP, 2000. 3–12.

Alex Ambrozic

PUERTO RICAN AMERICAN AUTOBIOGRAPHY   If what distinguishes memoirs from autobiography, as it has been suggested, is the emphasis on community rather than the individual, then the foundational Puerto Rican American first-person accounts fall unquestionably under the rubric of the former. Neither the *Memorias de Bernardo Vega* (1977), written in Spanish, nor **Jesus Colon**'s *A Puerto Rican in New York and Other Sketches* (1961), both recognized by critics as fundamental texts in the history of Puerto Rican literature in the United States, aims to represent the protagonist only, but an individual life submerged in the social and political history of the Puerto Rican community on the mainland. Readers looking for details about the intimate lives of these two individuals will not find them in these texts. The period covered by both books spans roughly a hundred years, beginning with the mid-nineteenth century. Although the personal, albeit public, eyewitness story Bernardo Vega (1885–1965) and Jesus Colon (1901–74) have to tell begins in the second decade of the twentieth century, when they both arrived in New York in search of a better life, Vega's book summarizes the state of the Puerto Rican settlement in the metropolis from about 1850 through a story told to him by a relative who had preceded him. This narrative strategy serves to trace the ongoing struggle of a colonized people in the continental United States and in crafting what is considered to be, by all accounts, a unique document for the study of the Puerto Rican community's forebears.

Written by Bernardo Vega, the manuscript of the *Memorias* was edited by César Andreu Iglesias, Vega's longtime friend, ten years after the author's death. Born in Cayey, Puerto Rico, the self-taught Vega worked as a cigar maker since an early age. Like others in the cigar industry, then at the vanguard of the labor movement, he embarked on a long fight for social justice that led to his involvement in myriad political, cultural, and labor organizations, some of which he helped create, and his collaboration in a number of progressive and socialist newspapers of the first half of the twentieth century. Vega paints a large fresco of Hispanic life in the boroughs of New York, with episodes relating to diverse topics, such as the fight of the working-class migrants for their rights and their daily interaction with other ethnic groups. Vega also records the intense activity displayed by the community in support of the independence of their native land from Spain, and later their participation in local politics. He also maps out the expansion of neighborhoods to accommodate the growth of the Hispanic community that, by 1927, may well have numbered over 100,000 inhabitants. These numbers would increase significantly in the 1940s and 1950s as a result of the push for industrialization in Puerto Rico and the concomitant displacement of peoples.

Whereas Vega offers a panoramic view of Puerto Ricans in the continental United States, Jesus Colon, another self-educated cigar maker with whom Vega would cross paths in the fight for justice, zooms in to offer thumbnail sketches of this history in *A Puerto Rican in New York and Other Sketches*. The book opens with a scene of reading in a cigar factory in Puerto Rico that lingers in the memory of the narrator. Colon recalls how the resonant voice of the *lector* (a person hired to read to the cigar makers while they worked) would reach his nearby room, filling it with the sounds of world literature and political philosophy. This opening vignette suggests a link between word and work that Colon would pursue later, when he went into journalism and labor organizing. Many of the sketches included in the book reflect his lifelong interest in reading and writing, often as a means to defend the rights of disenfranchised constituencies and to counteract the widespread misinformation on Puerto Ricans found in the mainstream media of his times. During more than fifty years, he collaborated in numerous progressive newspapers published in Spanish and English. The essays included in *A Puerto Rican in New York and Other Sketches* represent only a portion of the ones he wrote. In 1993, a selection of Colon's unpublished sketches appeared under the title *The Way It Was and Other Writings,* edited by Edna Acosta-Belén and Virginia Sánchez Korrol. Colon, a black Puerto Rican, has been credited with defining a Puerto Rican tradition in New York that served as a source of inspiration and resistance to subsequent waves of migrants from the island.

Whereas the characters that populate the above books are largely from the working class and racialized sectors of the Puerto Rican colony with a strong class-consciousness, Pedro Juan Labarthe provides a window into the mindset of a different type of character in *The Son of Two Nations: The Private Life of a Columbia Student* (1931). The only child of a dressmaker and an educated and wealthy man who soon dilapidates his fortune, Labarthe becomes a pro-American Puerto Rican who advocates the annexation of the island to the United States. Following many hardships after his arrival in New York in 1924 (only a few years after Vega and Colon), Labarthe succeeds in entering Columbia University on a scholarship, where he obtains a degree that allows him to ultimately dedicate himself to teaching. If the narratives by Vega and Colon are read like memoirs, Labarthe's book is clearly an autobiography that stresses his *petite histoire* and his own ability to rise above penury in pursuit of the American dream.

The topic of **race** addressed by Colon informs **Piri Thomas**'s autobiographical novel *Down These Mean Streets* (1967), a classic in Puerto Rican literature and the most accomplished work within a subgenre that brings ghetto life to the fore in the tradition of **Malcolm X**'s autobiography. The main character in *Down These Mean Streets*, a second generation, *mestizo* Puerto Rican, agonizes over the binary racial context predominant in the United States, which precludes his mixed racial heritage. Dehumanizing social conditions in the New York urban *barrio* drive the protagonist into confrontation with the law, and into jail. Thomas's other books, *Savior, Savior, Hold My Hand* (1972) and *Seven Long Times* (1974), describe respectively his rehabilitation, religious conversion, commitment to social work, and experiences in jail. All three fall under the genre of autobiographical novels.

Although the above narratives stressed a male point of view that left little room for women's perspectives, the last two decades of the twentieth century saw a blossoming of autobiographical accounts authored by female writers that placed women in center stage, always in relation to their surroundings. The first, **Nicholasa Mohr**, won acclaim with novellas and short stories of growing up in the Puerto Rican *barrio* of East Harlem, all with female characters that face up to adversity and come out strengthened by the experience. Instead of delving in the violent, drug-ridden culture found in sectors of inner cities, Mohr chooses to underscore the resilience of the average barrio family in the face of discrimination. Partly autobiographical, *Nilda* (1973) and *Felita* (1979) are two of Mohr's popular novellas that fit this description, displaying a female perspective that was lacking in the literature written by Puerto Ricans. Mohr's feminist concerns, which are evident in the collection of short stories *Rituals of Survival: A Woman's Portfolio* (1985) and other books, are also reflected in *Growing Up Inside the Sanctuary of My Imagination* (1994), an autobiography proper, where the narrator's creative skills are the tools employed to escape prescribed gender roles within Hispanic patriarchal society. Like Thomas's work, and the **Nuyorican** poetry of the 1970s, Mohr's narratives signal the coming-of-age of a Puerto Rican literature grounded in the streets of New York.

Survival, a recurrent theme in Puerto Rican literature, is thoughtfully approached in *Getting Home Alive* (1986), a hybrid book of prose and poetry, the outcome of a collaboration between a mother, **Rosario Morales**, and her daughter, **Aurora Levins Morales**, both creative writers. Their joint story crisscrosses not only generations, but also languages and religions. Rosario was born in New York shortly after her parents migrated from Puerto Rico in 1929, and years later, after marrying a Jewish man of Russian ancestry, made the return trip to the island, where she gave birth to Aurora. Afterward, the family moved to Chicago. Although at times the family struggled economically, both women consider themselves relatively privileged; therefore, the survival skills they hone are aimed at a larger world in which social inequality, police brutality, profit-driven multinationals, and abuse against women proliferate, making it difficult to get "home alive." Although they denounce the current state of affairs, they also celebrate their mixed racial and ethnic heritage and the multiple identities that result from that mix. One of the collection's most disseminated pieces is the "Ending Poem" in which the alternating, bilingual voices of both women reconstruct their genealogies and recognize their diasporic condition as well as their "wholeness." Ironically, only by acknowledging their multiple racial and ethnic make-up—and by remaining committed to the struggle for a better future—do they make it "home" alive.

The topic of **identity** is also crucial to **Judith Ortiz Cofer**, an award-winning poet, essayist, and fiction writer, the author of *Silent Dancing: A Partial Remembrance of a Puerto Rican Childhood* (1990). Highly skeptical of the act of remembering, the autobiographical prose and poetry of *Silent Dancing* capture discrete, defining moments in the narrator's journey toward self-discovery. Cofer was born in the town of Hormigueros, Puerto Rico, and moved to Paterson, New Jersey, in 1955. Her move was far from permanent, however, as every time her father, a U.S. Navy officer, was on duty, she, her mother, and her brother went back to the island to her grandmother's home, where several of the stories in *Silent Dancing* are set. There, while listening to the stories from the Puerto Rican oral tradition told by women relatives, the narrator begins to construct her gender and ethnic subjectivity. Accustomed to the back and forth movement of transnational migrants, neither of these identities comes across as one-dimensional. Rather, they are the outcome of a negotiation between the identity models provided by her ancestors and others learned through the English language. Cofer embraces a self-image that suits her bicultural reality; it includes a Puerto Rican **identity** that implicitly transgresses national borders and official languages. Currently Franklin Professor of English at the University of Georgia, Cofer is a prolific writer, with books such as the much-praised *The Line of the Sun* (1989) and *The Latin Deli* (1993) to her credit.

Also engaged in cultural negotiations, Esmeralda Santiago looks back down memory lane in *When I Was Puerto Rican* (1993) to offer a gendered narrative of growing up in a town near Bayamón, in the Puerto Rican countryside, and the city of Santurce. Santiago, who went on to migrate to the United States, graduating from the Performing Arts High School in New York and later Harvard University, endows her persona with an inquisitive character, one that with time leads her to question the double standard for men and women inherent in patriarchal society. The oldest daughter in a family of six children, the narrator suffers the tension and bickering between her parents due to her father's adulterous and complacent conduct. His unfaithfulness, along with his lack of ambition, prompts the mother to enter the labor market and, later, opt for migration. Only the last fifth of the book is set in Brooklyn, where the children attend public schools. The book was quickly translated into vernacular Spanish by the author herself and published in 1994. Although the use of the past tense in the title would seem to imply a conversion narrative, in the prologue to the Spanish edition Santiago portrays herself as a hybrid Puerto Rican writer who embraces both the *jíbaro* (hillbilly) tradition and American culture. In *Almost a Woman* (1998), a sequel, Santiago focuses on her sexual awakening as she grows into a young adult who establishes some distance from her indigenous culture as well as family values and traditions. The book highlights the tense relationship between mother and daughter as much as between native and adopted cultures.

Whether emphasizing the individual or the community, the autobiographical genre has served Puerto Ricans to negotiate between their two cultural worlds and expose the marginalized and "other" space from which they write due to nationality, **ethnicity**, **race**, class, or gender. Their self-referential narratives reveal commonalities across ethnic experiences as well as uniqueness, one largely derived from their neocolonial condition. (*See also* Bilingualism, Feminism)

Further Reading

Aparicio, Frances R. "From Ethnicity to Multiculturalism: An Historical Overview of Puerto Rican Literature in the United States." *Handbook of Hispanic Cultures in the United States: Literature and Art.* Ed. Francisco Lomelí. Houston: Arte Público Press, 1993. 19–39.

Flores, Juan. *Divided Borders: Essays on Puerto Rican Identity.* Houston: Arte Público Press, 1993.

Hernández, Carmen Dolores. *Puerto Rican Voices in English. Interviews with Writers.* Westport, CT: Praeger, 1997.

López, Iraida H. *La Autobiografía Hispana Contemporánea en los Estados Unidos. A Través del Caleidoscopio.* Lewiston, NY: Mellen Press, 2001.

Mohr, Eugene V. *The Nuyorican Experience. Literature of the Puerto Rican Minority.* Westport, CT: Greenwood Press, 1982.

Iraida H. López

PUERTO RICAN AMERICAN DRAMA   When the United States annexed Puerto Rico, today officially known as the Commonwealth of Puerto Rico, in 1898 after the Spanish-American War, it found its new charge to be a poverty-stricken island of coffee and sugarcane farmers. Today, Puerto Rico is primarily an urban society relying on industry and tourism as its major sources of means. Spanish, U.S., and Afro-Caribbean cultures have mixed together on the island to form a dynamic, specifically Puerto Rican culture. Spanish explorers established San Juan in the early sixteenth century and maintained control of the island until the end of the nineteenth century. Although Spanish is still the predominant language of Puerto Rico, English is spoken by many Puerto Ricans, and both languages have intermingled to form a uniquely Puerto Rican patois. Puerto Rico has several museums, libraries, and other cultural centers, including the Luis A. Ferré Fine Arts Center, a theater for drama and for musical events, in the capital city of San Juan. Puerto Rico has produced many playwrights, including the world famous and influential René Marqués, and many noted stage and film actors, including José Ferrer, Rita Moreno, Raul Julia, and Benicio Del Toro.

Since 1898, many Puerto Ricans have immigrated to the United States, though improved living conditions on the island had induced a small return to Puerto Rico by the end of the twentieth century. Many have remained in the United States, however, with the number of Puerto Ricans living in the United States rising from about 70,000 in 1940 to more than 3,000,000 at the end of the twentieth century, mostly in New York, though the population has recently shifted somewhat to other areas of the country.

During the great migration of Puerto Ricans to the United States, especially to New York City in the 1940s and 1950s, Puerto Rican drama began to flourish in New York's theater scene, eventually supplanting Spanish theater as the dominant form of Hispanic theater in the United States. Hispanic theater in its various forms represents several nationalities and continues to thrive in New York and in other major American cultural centers, with Puerto Rican artists continuing to make great contributions to American and world theater.

Puerto Rican American drama has often proved difficult to categorize. Puerto Ricans are American citizens whose culture is primarily Spanish in origin. However, Puerto Rican American drama is rarely anthologized in collections of American plays. Rather, Puerto Rican American plays are generally lumped with Mexican American, Caribbean American, Spanish American, and other ethnic groups of plays into a generic category called "Hispanic." Puerto Rican American drama reflects this confusion, dealing with themes of the Puerto Rican islander's longing for a "better life" in the States balanced against themes of the Puerto Rican immigrant in the States struggling to hold on to the family and Catholic values of home. At the same time, Puerto Rican American drama examines **racism**, sexism, and other forms of prejudice that Puerto Rican Americans experience in the United States.

Puerto Rican theater flourished on the island in the 1940s after the founding in 1938 of the Areyto Group by Emilio S. Belaval. The Areyto Group explored Puerto Rican history, delving into issues of slavery and encroaching modernization. The group also created plays centering around Puerto Rico's national folk hero, the jíbaro. A farmer of modest means, the jíbaro began appearing in Puerto Rican literature in the mid-nineteenth century and remained popular well into the twentieth century as a symbol of the land and the spirit of Puerto Rico, a spirit often difficult to maintain during the rapidly changing twentieth century.

Puerto Rican dramatist Rene Marqués was studying playwriting in New York on a Rockefeller grant in 1940 when he began to develop a keen awareness of the Puerto Rican experience in the United States. Upon returning to San Juan, he wrote *La Carreta* (1953), a play about a rural Puerto Rican family that moves to San Juan and then to New York City in search of better living conditions. The family's journey is filled with pain and loss as it is crushed beneath an unrealizable American dream that is not meant for them. Although Marqués wrote the play in Puerto Rico, its world premiere was a

Spanish-language production directed by Roberto Rodríguez Suárez in New York. It ran in an English-language production titled *The Oxcart* Off Broadway in 1966 starring Raul Julia and directed by Lloyd Richards, now known for his work with **August Wilson**. The original 1953 production is generally credited with birthing the Puerto Rican theater movement in New York. Suárez, himself a native Puerto Rican, moved to New York after matriculating at the University of Puerto Rico and established himself as an important catalyst in the growth of Puerto Rican American theater. His play *The Betrothal* (1958) captures the uncertainty of the transition of Puerto Rico from an agrarian colony to an industrial United States territory. Cultures and generations clash before a tapestry of religion, family, and the growing pains of modernization.

In 1954 Suárez and a group of colleagues founded the Nuevo Círculo Dramático, the first permanent Hispanic theater in New York. For five years the theater functioned as a theater school as well as a performance space. Soon other Hispanic theaters began to open and, in some cases, to flourish in New York City. Puerto Rican actress Miriam Colón, who had appeared in the 1966 production of *The Oxcart,* founded the Puerto Rican Traveling Theatre (PRTT) in 1967. Traveling the boroughs of New York City, PRTT performed in English and in Spanish. The group continues to operate, training new theater artists as it maintains its touring companies, and has had many popular successes, including Edward Gallardo's *Simpson Street* (1979), which spoke to a generation of Puerto Rican Americans who had been born in the States and thus had no memories of Puerto Rico but still felt bound together as a community because of their Puerto Rican heritage. *Simpson Street* explores the dynamics between this new generation of Puerto Rican American and their forebears as well as exploring the Puerto Rican American woman experiencing the effects of the U.S. women's liberation movement while combating the culturally instilled machismo of the Puerto Rican male.

Other Puerto Rican theaters to come along in the wake of the success of PRTT include the South Bronx's history-exploring Pregones Touring Puerto Rican Theatre Collection, the ensemble-oriented Shaman Theater Repertory Company, and Manhattan's radical **Nuyorican** Poets' Café. These theaters reach out to a traditionally disenfranchised audience that feels it has nothing in common with the mainstream face of contemporary Broadway and Off Broadway theater. All of these theaters have been profoundly informed by the experimental New York theater of the 1960s: the theater of La Mama, the Group Theatre, and other companies radical in approach to performing techniques and subject matter.

Miguel Algarín founded the Nuyorican Poets' Café in 1973 in order to provide a home in which creative artists, particularly of the underclass, could congregate and exchange creative energy and ideas. One of the café's earliest participants was **Miguel Piñero**, whose influential prison drama *Short Eyes* (1973) was then playing at Joseph Papp's Public Theater in New

York. *Short Eyes* was an enormous critical and popular success and, though not a Poets' Café production, brought attention to the café because of Piñero's involvement with the company. The Poets' Café's mission has always seemed to bolster the disenfranchised "Other" at odds with the hegemony, whether because of race or class. It has constantly endeavored to create a theater that reflects the truth of the gritty life of the streets, and Piñero and Algarín often roamed the streets of New York in the early days of the 1970s, recruiting prostitutes, junkies, and other street people as actors for the company. Originally setting out to attract a working class audience, the Nuyorican Poets' Café did not take long to begin attracting a diverse audience made up from many social classes as word of its unique setting and mission spread. Patrons could sit and order a few beers while watching a play or poetry reading. Not restricted to works by Puerto Rican American playwrights, the café has fostered works by playwrights as diverse as **Amiri Baraka** and **Ntozake Shange**. William Burroughs dropped in frequently during the 1970s to read new work aloud. As the Nuyorican Poets Café proceeds into the twenty-first century, it has become famous for its Poetry Slam competitions and forays into Hip Hop Theater.

Puerto Rican American playwrights born in the United States have dealt in recent decades with many of the same cultural **identity** conflicts that Puerto Rican-born playwrights dealt with in the 1950s and 1960s, though strategies and techniques have changed. Oscar A. Colón's *Siempre en Mi Corazón* (1986) explores issues of identity as its main character returns home to Puerto Rico after having left twenty years earlier to marry and live in the States. Carmen Rivera's *Julia* (1992) deals with issues of gender, education, and the transition from being an islander to a New Yorker. Edward Iván López, though born in Puerto Rico, was raised in New York. His *Spanish Eyes* (1982) explores issues of cultural identity through the framework of an intercultural marriage.

Perhaps the most successful Puerto Rican American playwright thus far is **José Rivera**, author of the popular *Marisol* (1992), *Cloud Tectonics* (1995), *References to Salvador Dalí Make Me Hot* (2000), and *Sueño* (1998), a freewheeling adaptation of Pedro Calderón de la Barca's Spanish Golden Age classic play *Life is a Dream* (1636). Rivera was born in Puerto Rico but raised on Long Island, where he saw his father work as many as three jobs at any one time to support his family. Rivera's work has been criticized by some for "not being Hispanic enough" and by others for being "too Hispanic." Full of excess and fantasy, Rivera's plays are often classified as "magic realism," and he does count Gabriel García Márquez as an influence. His plays negotiate the space between the real and the fantastic, as in *Marisol*'s exploration of a postapocalyptic New York. Ruptured violently, society must begin anew as the old order falls. Populated with angels and idiots, the play explores issues of gender and religion against a backdrop of dreams and nightmares. It has proven popular among regional theater groups since it premiered at the Actors Theatre of Louisville in 1992 and won the 1993 Obie Award for Outstanding Play.

Rivera claims to come from a family of storytellers, which he cites as an intrinsic part of being Puerto Rican. His family's stories, he says, blur the lines between fantasy and reality, and this trait is evident in his own play-writing. Rivera's plays have been produced all over the country at such prestigious theaters as the Public Theater/New York Shakespeare Festival, which sponsors the annual Festival Latino; Playwrights Horizons; and the Mark Taper Forum. He has received Fulbright, National Endowment for the Arts, Rockefeller, and Whiting Foundation grants. Rivera makes his home in Los Angeles.

Further Reading

Algarín, Miguel & Lois Griffith. *Action: The Nuyorican Poets Café Theater Festival.* New York: Touchstone, 1997.

Antush, John V., ed. *Nuestro New York: An Anthology of Puerto Rican Plays.* New York: Mentor, 1994.

———, ed. *Recent Puerto Rican Theater: Five Plays from New York.* Houston: Arte Público Press, 1991.

Gallardo, Edward. *Simpson Street and Other Plays.* Houston: Arte Público Press, 1990.

Rivera, José. *Marisol and Other Plays.* New York: Theatre Communications Group, 1997.

———. *References to Salvador Dalí Make Me Hot and Other Plays.* New York: Theatre Communications Group, 2003.

Jeffrey Godsey

PUERTO RICAN AMERICAN GAY LITERATURE   Puerto Rican literature has traditionally focused on themes that deal with various forms of **identity** (ethnic, cultural, national, or political). Contemporary literature not only continues to focus on the political status of the island, but also touches on family, tradition, culture, and gender relations. Diasporan writers also discuss topics of political importance and issues pertaining to their identity as either Puerto Ricans in the United States, as Nuyoricans or Neo-Ricans (Puerto Ricans in the United States who do not reside in New York).

However, the literature available from writers on and off the island rarely deals with sexuality as it pertains to same-sex relationships. Although there have been exceptions within the last decade, such as Angel Lozada's *La Patografía* (1998) and *Las Siete Palabras* (1999), and Mayra Santos-Febres's *Sirena Selena Vestida de Pena* (2000), not much is available in reference to gay Puerto Rican men. What literature there is on sexuality focuses on the male/female dichotomy that exist in Puerto Rican society, connected to *machismo* and *marianismo*—ideals that each man and woman must adhere to in order to be accepted by society. According to Puerto Rican anthropologist Rafael L. Ramírez, *machismo* is "invariably defined as a set of attitudes, behaviors, and practices that characterize men" (11). Puerto Ricans have often adopted a homogenous conformity, and as a result those who have left the island have brought into the diasporic communities values that continue to encourage individuals to conform to specific behavioral patterns based on their gender. Among U.S. Puerto Ricans most affected by these notions are Puerto Rican gay males, who are often perceived as anomalies to Puerto Rican masculinity and manhood.

The gender-stratified expectations of Puerto Rican society continue to inform the behavior of many, even second-generation Puerto Ricans living in the United States. As Ramírez states, "The masculine ideology, because it is a social construction that favors the masculine and belittles the feminine, places us men in a universe of categories and symbols of power that we reproduce daily. This ideology forms and guides us in our behavior as men" (15–16). However, what happens when gay Puerto Ricans do not conform to mainstream society's expectations? What happens when they refuse to accept that they must behave according to prescribed notions of proper male conduct?

Puerto Rican men find that they must reinforce the belief that the role of the "macho" or "real" man is to conquer, possess, and dominate. As a result, mainstream society on and off the island has marginalized the unique element that homosexuality adds to the diasporan experience. For the U.S. Puerto Rican gay man, the task of being able to identify himself is a challenging one as he is forced or expected to conform to both North American as well as Puerto Rican ideologies of masculinity devoid of a homosexual identity, and conform to a homogenous homosexual identity in the United States that ignores ethnic differences.

Added to these pressures is the fact that, according to David Román, both Catholicism and machismo have "combined to undervalue—if not foreclose—a 'Latino' gay identity." For this reason, some of the literature by U.S. Puerto Rican gay writers presents an internalized *machista* attitude as seen in the ways that gay men relate to each other. Some scholars such as Donald Hall would argue that this is so because there is an expectation that even homosexual relationships must reflect the ways individuals in mainstream society relate to each other: There must be a "man" and a "woman" in every relationship. This parallels Román's statement with regards to gay Latinos—machismo has played an integral role in the ways U.S. Puerto Rican gays label themselves and affects whether they identify themselves as gay or not.

However, some contemporary U.S. Puerto Rican gay writers have opted to confront the pressures imposed by the mainstream societies they are a part of in order to appropriate a sense of self that is devoid of any classification other than the one they choose. As Larry La Fountain-Stokes writes, there is a "critical mass of openly self-identified queer cultural producers" that defies any imposition pertaining to an ethno-sexual identity; the choice is up to the individual. Among these contemporary "producers" who seek to (re)present a reality often ignored by scholars who speak and write of the diasporan experience are writers, poets, and playwrights like Larry La Fountain-Stokes, Roberto Vázquez-Pacheco, Arturo Sandoval, Emanuel

Xavier, Angel Lozada, Moisés Agosto-Rosario, Rane Arroyo, Guillermo Román, Edgardo Alvarado-Vázquez, Elliot Torres, and Aldo Alvarez, whose work not only embraces their characters' and their own sexualities, but mutually acknowledges an ethnic identity that U.S. mainstream gay communities force them to deny in order to belong. Embracing their ethnic identity in the United States comes in many forms: Some writers protest mainstream society's images and biases about Puerto Ricans in general, while others explore relationships that ignore any form of categorization and focus on male/male sexual relationships as well as on the characters' relationships with their family members. They demystify stereotypes that exist with regards to the ways that U.S. Puerto Rican gays relate to their own culture and to mainstream society. Their work often focuses on "family . . . identity and its ramifications within two distinct cultures, the attempts to assimilate into U.S. gay culture . . . the efforts to cultivate a [Puerto Rican] gay culture in the United States" (Román). It presents experiences centered on an ethno-sexual identity. Their writing (re)presents an attempt at incorporating themselves within the fixed definition of what it means to be a Puerto Rican man, both in the United States and Puerto Rico, and share their own diasporic experiences. At the same time they attempt to break with the imposed masculine man/feminine woman dichotomy, rejecting conformity and defining for themselves their *puertorriqueñidad* (Puertoricanness), or what it means to be Puerto Rican.

These queer cultural producers differ in experiences and artistic style. However, an attribute that their writing shares in common is an autobiographical approach, a counter-attack against heteropatriarchal norms that force U.S. Puerto Rican gay men to conform to the ideals of the society they live in, and at the same time embrace the values imposed by the ethnic culture they are a part of. Thus, the process of constructing an identity within the diasporan communities can be considered a deconstruction of fixed characteristics that marginalize them because they do not conform to accepted notions of Puerto Rican masculinity.

For instance, Robert Vázquez-Pacheco's "Brujo Time" focuses not only on his character's sexuality, but on reconciling with his Puerto Rican heritage, which his family members denied him because they wanted him to succeed and attain the American dream. Like Vázquez-Pacheco's character, La Fountain-Stokes's autobiographical voice in "My Name, Multitudinous Mass" embraces not only his sexuality but even alludes to a more universal Latin American/Latino gay identity, specifically within the confines of a culture that believes homosexual behavior to be non-Puerto Rican/un-American.

Emanuel Xavier's "Banjee Hustler," an excerpt from his 1999 novel *Christ Like*, looks at gay Puerto Rican/Latino life in New York City, focusing on the realities that many Latino gay men face when they are not accepted by their families and must learn to survive by any means necessary. Xavier, primarily a poet, embraces his ethnic roots as seen in his poem such as "Americano" and "Burning Down the House."

Rane Arroyo in *The Singing Shark* (1996) and *Home Movies of Narcissus* (2002) also addresses ethnic and sexual identities. For example, in his poem "The Singing Shark Dream, or Toto, I Don't Think We're in Tegucigalpa Anymore," he makes references to being the son of "Tony and María," protagonists of *West Side Story*. Both a memorial and protest, this poem explores the images and biases mainstream society has about Puerto Ricans in the United States, and it also touches on the influence these images have on the way society in general view ethnic groups, and the behavioral expectations for Puerto Ricans in general.

Five Years of Solitary (2002) by Elliot Torres is a series of poems, like Xavier's *Americano* (2002), that explore the individual life of a Puerto Rican gay man and his perspective not only on his ethnicity and sexual identity, but also on his particular perspective of the world around him. *Undaunted: A Poetic Journey* (2004) picks up where his first volume leaves off in a continuing exploration of life as a gay Puerto Rican in the United States, affirming an identity that the individual is supposed to deny because it is considered "un-Puerto Rican."

The emerging Puerto Rican gay writing in the United States continues to explore the intersections of ethnicity and sexuality. Speaking from the ethnic and sexual margins of American society, the writers continue to make a radical a revolutionary attempt at interpolating themselves within the diasporan Puerto Rican community that has not embraced them because of who and what they are and the Anglo society that continues to perceive them as outsiders.

Further Reading

Acosta-Belén, Edna. "Beyond Island Boundaries: Ethnicity, Gender, and Cultural Revitalization in Nuyorican Literature." *Callaloo* 15.4 (Autumn 1992): 979–98.

Alvarez, Aldo. Blithe House Quarterly: A Site for Gay Short Fiction. www.blithe.com/bhq7.1/index.html [Winter 2003—The Puerto Rican Issue].

Cruz-Malavé, Arnaldo, and Martin F. Manalansan IV, eds. *Queer Globalizations: Citizenship and the Afterlife of Colonialism.* New York: New York UP, 2002.

Manrique, Jaime with Jesse Dorris, eds. *Bésame Mucho: New Gay Latino Fiction.* New York: Painted Leaf Press, 1999.

Román, David. "Latino Literature." *GLBTQ: An Encyclopedia of Gay, Lesbian, Bisexual, Transgender and Queer Culture,* www.glbtq.com/literature/latino_lit.html.

Ramírez, Rafael L. *What It Means to be a Man: Reflections on Puerto Rican Masculinity.* Trans. Rosa E. Casper. New Jersey: Rutgers UP, 1999.

Enrique Morales-Diaz

PUERTO RICAN AMERICAN LESBIAN LITERATURE   Like other Latina writers, Boricua (the indigenous term for Puerto Rican) lesbian writers confront the complexities of **race, ethnicity**, and class within a dual cultural **identity** defined between the homeland of Puerto Rico and the mainland of the United States. The duality of two cultures, exemplified in the nation's two names (the colonial one of "Puerto Rico"—meaning "rich port"—and its indigenous Taíno one of Borinquen) is an ever-present theme in Puerto Rican literary production in general. For many lesbian writers, the notion of exile becomes a metaphor for the double and triple **diaspora** that they experience as both migrants between two geographic spaces and as marginalized voices within two heterosexually dominant patriarchal worlds. They must work through both a sense of urgency to address sociopolitical issues such as independence and colonization yet also are compelled to speak to the double silence surrounding women's voices generally and lesbian voices in particular. Given these personal and political exigencies, contemporary Puerto Rican lesbian texts represent the self, family, friends, and the larger world through a lens of social critique and rebellion that often defies traditional literary genres and language boundaries. Both defined and not-defined by borders, Puerto Rican lesbian writing is fluid and multifaceted reflecting the many levels of self to be negotiated in the creative process.

As part of Latino/a cultural production, Boricua lesbian writing is necessarily bilingual: Texts may be exclusively in Spanish or in English, or may move between the two languages in a creative play of difference and invention. The bilingual nature of many of these texts not only structurally sets the reader up for accepting difference; it also provides an innovative avenue of resistance to cultural **assimilation**. As linguistic alienation and isolation give way to linguistic liberation, so too does lesbian existence gain a space for authentic expression through that language play. Contemporary self-identified Puerto Rican lesbian writers not only connect sexual and sociocultural identities through multiple languages, but also by blurring the lines around their literary production as essayists, short story writers, playwrights, spoken word artists, and poets, and their work as sociopolitical activists and intellectuals. Given their immediacy and accessibility, the cultural production of contemporary Puerto Rican lesbians is most prominent in these areas of artistic and social expression.

Juanita Díaz-Cotto's 1987 anthology *Compañeras: Latina Lesbians* (published under the pseudonym Juanita Ramos) is a vital contribution to lesbian writing and is illustrative of the diversity of creative identities among the *puertorriqueñas* represented there: Rota Silverstrini is a poet, editor, and writer; Brunilda Vega, poet and social worker; Cenen, an African Boricua short story writer and poet, to name only a few.

As with other rights movements that gained ground from the civil and social transformations of the late twentieth century, the 1970s and 1980s marked the moment when self-identified Boricua lesbians began to produce and publish works that reached a wider audience. Rather than give up multiple identities of color, *raza* (race), African roots, and the diasporic condition, these writers sought to articulate and explore those differences. Nemir Matos Cintrón's *Las Mujeres no Hablan Así* and *Proemas para Despabilar Cándidos* and **Luz María Umpierre**'s texts such as *The Margarita Poems* and *For Christine: Poems and One Letter* are late twentieth century poetic contributions that challenge the tradition of censure and prejudice that women loving women experience. Although Matos Cintrón utilizes a direct vocabulary that relies on metaphors of nature to create a highly eroticized poetry, Umpierre's work largely connects sexuality and issues of personal oppression to **racism** and **colonialism**. Both poets necessarily challenge and transgress phallocentric discourse by naming the unnamable. Umpierre in particular has been the subject of much critical inquiry, especially because her work's form and content was one of the first to militantly defy boundaries of language and ritual. Boricua poet and photographer Samantha Martínez, who primarily publishes in online venues, echoes this need to write for sanity and for her survival.

More recently, Aixa Ardín's sensual and political collection of poetry, *Batiborrillo* (meaning "Hotchpotch"), continues the themes expressed by her precursors in a poetry marked by rebellion and open expression of lesbian desire. Like many Puerto Rican writers, Ardín relies on references and vocabularies specific to island culture to bring her underground poetry to the surface. In the first poem of the collection, "Poesía para Mayra Montero," Ardín playfully calls herself a *plátano*—but one that cannot be used for traditional dishes. In "Pa-ul" the great island rainforest of El Yunque provides a metaphor of healing for one who dies of AIDS. As is the case with many Latina writers, Ardín plays on the gendered nature of Spanish grammar, anthropomorphizing words like "la imaginación" into a girlfriend, a best friend. Informed by lesbian sexuality and also by a rejection of colonization, these poems are out and proud, and are representative of both the rage and celebration found in writings by women-identified women.

Family is central to Latino culture and thus is an important theme in Puerto Rican lesbian writing. Radical lesbian feminist and Puerto Rican poet Teresita Bosch explains how familial estrangement is overcome by identifying and working through common spaces of oppression: in her work, coming out as a lesbian is paralleled to the repression of language that her mother experiences as the price to be paid for striving towards a middle class lifestyle within an Anglo culture that demands assimilation of difference.

Since the publication of Ramos's anthology, online journals and websites such as *Conmoción* (which published between 1995 and 1996) have begun to provide forums for Latina lesbian writing. Yet the most visible and current cultural production has been in terms of theater and spoken work, especially within the **Nuyorican** context. Among the most notable figures here are Bronx born Puerto Rican lesbian writer, actor, and producer Janis Astor del Valle who founded Sisters on Stage, and Brenda Cotto who, with Noelia Ortiz, wrote the wholly woman identified 1996 play *Motherlands*, which also explores the complexities of mother-lesbian daughter relationships.

In all its varied forms, Puerto Rican lesbian cultural production is intricately tied to the larger reclamation and insertion of the feminine within Boricua culture and heritage. (*See also* Bilingualism)

Further Reading

Blasius, Mark. *Sexual Identities, Queer Politics.* Princeton, NJ: Princeton U Press, 2001.

Chanady, Amaryll, ed. *Latin American Identity and the Construction of Difference.* Minneapolis: U of Minnesota P, 1994.

Chávez-Silverman, Susana, and Librada Hernández, eds. *Reading and Writing the Ambiente: Queer Sexualities in Latino, Latin American, and Spanish Culture.* Madison: U of Wisconsin P, 2000.

Cruz-Malavé, Arnaldo, and Martin F. Manalansan IV, eds. *Queer Globalizations: Citizenship and the Afterlife of Colonialism.* New York: New York UP, 2002.

Dolores Costa, Marìa. *Latina Lesbian Writers and Artists.* New York: Harrington Press, 2003.

Gómez, Alma, Cherríe Moraga, and Mariana Romo-Carmona, eds. *Cuentos: Stories by Latinas.* Brooklyn: Kitchen Table Press, 1983.

Martínez, Elena. *Lesbian Voices from Latin America: Breaking Ground.* New York: Garland Publishing, 1996.

Ramos, Juanita. *Compañeras: Latina Lesbians.* New Cork: Routledge, 1994.

Rivera, Carmen. *Kissing the Mango Tree: Puerto Rican Women Rewriting American Literature.* Houston: Arte Público Press, 2002.

Romo-Carmona, Mariana. *Conversaciones: Relatos por padres y madres de hijas lesbianas y hijos gay.* San Francisco: Cleros Press, 2001.

Sánchez González, Lisa. *Boricua Literature: A Literary History of the Puerto Rican Diaspora.* New York: New York UP, 2001.

Torres, Lourdes, Inmaculada Pertusa. *Tortilleras: Hispanic and U.S. Latina Lesbian Expression.* Philadelphia: Temple UP, 2001.

Colleen Kattau

PUERTO RICAN AMERICAN NOVEL   The first major wave of Puerto Ricans settled in New York in what would come to be known as Spanish Harlem, the Bronx (El Barrio), and the Lower East Side (Losaida) between the American Civil War and the World War I. Published novelists of this generation were few and they often wrote in Spanish. A few, however, including William Carlos Williams, published novels in English. Williams represents his generation's critique of the American dream and his advocacy of a progressive, even radical, politics of social and institutional reform. Like many of his contemporaries as well as his successors, Williams was an activist as well as a novelist, offering free care to low-income patients in his medical practice. However, another early Puerto Rican American novel, Pedro Juan Labarthe's *The Son of Two Nations* (1931), tells a largely **assimilation**ist story where Pedro, a Puerto Rican boy, embraces the American dream and through education and hard work becomes more American than Puerto Rican. *The Son of Two Nations* resembles classic immigrant novels of the early twentieth century more than it does later Puerto Rican American novels. In 1917 the Jones Act granted citizenship to Puerto Ricans just as the second generation of Puerto Rican Americans, and the first born in the United States, came into the world. This is the generation that launched Puerto Rican American literature as we know it. In addition to the novel, throughout its history much Puerto Rican American literature takes the form of the short story, picking up perhaps on the popularity of this genre in Latin American letters. Poetry has also been important in Puerto Rican American letters with such figures as Tato Laviera and more recently the **Nuyorican** Poets' Café. Many Puerto Rican American novelists also write short stories and poetry. The second generation of Puerto Rican American writers saw the Puerto Rican community in New York grow to over fifty thousand people. They were active in the Young Lords party and advanced their radical civil rights program; all were concerned with delineating a Puerto Rican American **identity** that belongs in America even as it resists either assimilation of second class citizenship. They often call themselves Nuyorican, emphasizing their ties to New York but also asserting that they are not simply a hyphenated community, rather an organized part of an America whose only language is not English.

Piri Thomas's *Down These Mean Streets* (1967) launches the contemporary Puerto Rican American novel and still serves as the exemplary Puerto Rican American text. In *Down These Mean Streets*, we find many characteristics that continue to define the Puerto Rican American novel: a form of the coming of age novel, a blending of Spanish and English, a focus on the place of El Barrio, and an exploration of Puerto Rican Americans as an American ethnic group negotiating a complex set of questions about **race**, culture, language, place, gender, sexuality, and class. Piri narrates *Down These Mean Streets*, recounting his early childhood in Spanish Harlem, his encounter with racism in other parts of Harlem, and the necessary turn to violence for survival. Even as he tries to understand his relationship to black American, Puerto Rican, and poor Anglo American communities, Piri becomes increasingly caught up in a life of drugs and crime and eventually ends up in prison. Seven years in Sing Sing prison and Comstock correctional facility force him to reconsider whether violence is the best way to assert his manhood and whether gangs and drugs are viable means of survival.

At the same time as *Down These Mean Streets*, a number of similar novels appear. They share not only the themes but also many formal elements of *Down These Mean Streets*. At the same time, each novel offers a distinct perspective on *barrio* life. Manuel Manrique's *Island in Harlem* (1966) actually precedes *Down These Mean Streets* by a year to tell the story of Antonio. Antonio's life is much like Piri's, but Manrique offers a more complex consideration of young women than does Thomas. In *Down These Mean Streets*, girls serve as the vehicles through boys to express their masculinity. *Island in Harlem* portrays Margarita, the stereotypical virgin from Puerto Rico who saves Antonio at the risk of her own perdition. But *Island in Harlem* also presents another girl, Lilliam, who is neither the typical virgin nor the typical whore: She is a smart, savvy young woman aware of the sexual power plays that go on in the barrio, and she is able to enter into them as a player, not just an object. It will take years and the appearance of women writers for more nuanced portrayals of girls to appear in a Puerto Rican American novel. Other novels in the tradition of *Down These Mean Streets* include: Lefty Barreto's *Nobody's Hero* (1976), Edwin Torres's *Carlito's Way* (1979), Abraham Rodríguez Jr's *Spidertown* (1993), and Ernesto Quiñonez's *Bodega Dreams* (2000). One notable variation on *Down These Mean Streets* are the novels of Nick Cruz Humberto Cintrón where the trajectory of poverty, violence, and drugs leads not to redemption and the return of the prodigal son, but to his final departure from the barrio and from the community.

In the 1980s, a number of Puerto Rican American women writers question the paradigms of the Puerto Rican American novel set up by Thomas. **Nicholasa Mohr, Judith Ortiz Cofer,** and more recently Esmeralda Santiago write coming-of-age novels and employ a vernacular mix of Spanish and English, but theirs is a domestic rather than a street vernacular, and their community starts with the family rather than the gang or the block. These women describe the domestic life of Puerto Rican Americans, what happens inside the buildings that the boys are always leaving or entering only to be fed, comforted, or chastised by mothers, sisters, and girlfriends. Mohr, Cofer, and Santiago reveal the complex experience of Puerto Rican American girls who serve as linguistic and cultural translators for their families in welfare offices and schools, as well as in the arena of gender relations, negotiating the differences between the roles of girls and women in Puerto Rican and in American contexts.

Mohr's *Nilda* (1976) was the first novel written by a Puerto Rican American woman. Like Piri, Nilda grows up in Spanish Harlem in the 1940s. One of her brothers follows a path similar to Piri's, but Nilda remains closely tied to her mother, responsible for maintaining the home either by cooking and cleaning or by communicating with the Home Relief Office. Nilda negotiates her identity as a Puerto Rican American in a variety of interior spaces: homes, buildings, and institutions. Nilda struggles to make school a place where she can learn skills that will help her to survive in New York and to make New York more hospitable to Puerto Rican Americans.

Santiago's work covers many themes similar to Mohr's, although she writes of the experiences of later waves of Puerto Rican immigrants, of those of Mohr's generation and the next who were born in Puerto Rico and came to the United States as children. Santiago's novels, starting with *When I Was Puerto Rican* (1993), include much less of a mix of Spanish than do many other Puerto Rican American novels and are written in a much more "standard" English, but she also translates all of her own work into Spanish, suggesting that this literature is of interest not only to Puerto Rican Americans and to Americans, but also to Puerto Ricans on the island. Santiago's second novel, *América's Dream* (1996), makes an important move in its questioning of the ideal of Puerto Rico that stands as a sort of "Paradise Lost" in the background of so many Puerto Rican American novels.

The twenty-first century has already seen not only a new novel by Cofer, *The Meaning of Consuelo* (2003), but also the emergence of a new generation of Puerto Rican American authors who write about the changing faces and the enduring identity of Puerto Rican Americans. Ed Vega's *No Matter How Much You Cook or Pay the Rent You Blew It Cause Bill Bailey Aint Never Coming Home Again* (2003) is a novel of epic proportions following its female protagonist, Vidamía Farrell, as she negotiates not only her own mixed heritage (she is half Puerto Rican and half Irish) but also the increasingly mixed neighborhoods of New York.

The barrios of New York remain the place of the Puerto Rican America novel, its language remains a mixed Spanish and English vernacular, and its themes continue to turn on the understanding of hybrid identity in the context of poverty and discrimination, but now the Puerto Rican American novel has a wide and nuanced cast of characters: Well-developed women and men who not only assert their identity but also explore its limits. (*See also* Bilingualism)

Further Reading

Flores, Juan. *From Bomba to Hip-Hop.* New York: Columbia UP, 2000.

Luis, William. *Dance Between Two Cultures.* Nashville: Vanderbilt UP, 1997.

Mohr, Eugene V. *The Nuyorican Experience.* Westport, CT: Greenwood Press, 1982.

Sánchez-González, Lisa. *Boricua Literature.* New York: New York U Press, 2001.

Keja Lys Valens

PUERTO RICAN AMERICAN POETRY Puerto Rican literature in all genres flourished in the United States throughout the twentieth century. The political status of Puerto Rico as an Estado Libre Asociado (Associated Free State) of the United States complicates the easy classification of this corpus as ethnic "American" literature. Designations such as "mainland" and "continental" literature can be cumbersome, and "Puerto Rican American" is inappropriate. The social, historical, and cultural impact of the 1960s **Civil Rights Movement** brought the terms "Neorican" and "**Nuyorican**" into currency despite the island origin of "Nuyorican" as a derogatory term for Puerto Rican New Yorkers. "Boricua," which Lisa Sánchez-González defines as a "term of self-affirmation in the stateside community" (1), is another culturally appropriate designation (and broader than "Nuyorican"). These terms describe the Puerto Rican literature produced, primarily in English, as part of multiethnic American literature beginning in the late 1960s. Several periodicals are indispensable sources of Puerto Rican, Nuyorican, and Boricua creative writing, interviews, scholarly criticism, and literary essays over the years: the literary magazines *Revista Chicano-Riqueña* (1973–85) and its continuation, *The Americas Review* (1986–99); the scholarly journal *The Bilingual Review/La Revista Bilingüe* (founded in 1974); and the two-issue Chicago **diaspora** magazine *The Rican* (1971–74). This body of literature also enjoys varying degrees of regional or national renown, significance, and distribution through the book publications of Bilingual Press/Editorial Bilingüe (established by the *Review* in 1976) and **Arte Público Press** (founded by Nicolás Kanellos in 1979), as well as the research and publishing activities of the Recovering the U.S. Hispanic Literary Heritage project (since 1992).

The Two Islands

In "La guagua aérea" (1983), a poetic essay about back-and-forth migration between Puerto Rico and New York, Luis Rafael Sánchez recounts an anecdote about a woman who identifies New York as her place of origin in Puerto Rico. This poignant and paradoxical truth underscores the role of place and **identity** in the Puerto Rican experience in the twentieth century, and the rich motif of the two islands is a recurring image in the Nuyorican aesthetic. Alfredo Matilla and Iván Silén wrote in similar terms about the shared experience of Puerto Rican poets: "The poets became brothers crossing a bridge of airplanes that span language" (xviii). Several anthologies have highlighted the continuities and differences between the literatures of the two islands by bringing together writers from Puerto Rico and the mainland. The editors necessarily must consider place of residence, national identity, language choice, and aesthetic and literary affiliations, and consequently the introductions, biobibliographies, and other critical apparatus of these compilations provide invaluable secondary source information. Matilla and Silén's *The Puerto Rican Poets/Los poetas puertorriqueños* (1972) was the first anthology of this type. The publication of this volume in a popular poetry series from Bantam Books alongside such significant (and now classic) anthologies as *The Black Poets* (1971; ed. Dudley Randall) and *The Voice That Is Great Within Us: American Poetry of the Twentieth Century* (1970; ed. Hayden Carruth) is evidence of the place of Puerto Rican poetry in the changing American literary canon of the early 1970s. María Teresa Babín and Stan Steiner's *Borinquen: An Anthology of Puerto Rican Literature* (1974), published by Knopf, also afforded the potential for mainstream attention during the crucial period of development of Puerto Rican literature in the United States. An important feature of *Borinquen* is its chronological and thematic breadth, which extends from the pre-Columbian oral tradition and early colonial historiography (Juan de Castellanos's sixteenth-century epic poem *Elegías de varones ilustres de Indias*) to psalms by a Lower East Side priest, David García, in the radical tradition of liberation theology. (Significantly, and an additional indication of the burgeoning Latino literary and cultural movements in the United States, Steiner also coedited, with the playwright **Luis Valdez**, a comparable early volume of Mexican and Chicano literature, *Aztlán: An Anthology of Mexican American Literature* [1972]). Julio Marzán's *Inventing a Word: An Anthology of Twentieth-Century Puerto Rican Poetry* (1980) gave much less room to Nuyorican poetry than did the previous anthologies, but nevertheless acknowledges the continuities between the two groups, particularly with respect to a shared tradition of social protest and colloquial expression, as exemplified by **Pedro Pietri** and **Victor Hernández Cruz**. Much more recently, Roberto

Santiago has taken the same composite approach to Puerto Rican literature in *Boricuas: Influential Puerto Rican Writers—An Anthology* (1995).

On the other hand, Miguel Algarín and Miguel Piñero's now-**canon**ical *Nuyorican Poetry: An Anthology of Puerto Rican Words and Feelings* (1975) and Faythe Turner's comprehensive *Puerto Rican Writers at Home in the USA: An Anthology* (1991) cover only Nuyorican and Boricua literature. Algarín explains in the afterword that Nuyorican poets need to "[define] the qualities of the space in which [they] live" and so "locate their position on earth, the ground, the neighborhood, the environment" (181). Turner indicates the same notion with the geographical specification of "at home" in the expressive title of her anthology. From the 1970s forward, this space, position, or home is not the island, but New York and other places in the diaspora. Regardless of the relative merits of the chronological, geographic, thematic, or aesthetic scope or limitations of each of these anthologies published over a twenty-year period (1972–91), however, all are indispensable to a comprehensive understanding of the field of Puerto Rican poetry in the United States.

Nuyorican Poetry

The Nuyorican movement was firmly in place by the mid-1970s. In 1979 Soledad Santiago published "Notes on the Nuyoricans" in the *Village Voice,* New York's alternative weekly. These notes constitute a sweeping essay on the arts, culture, and institutions of the Nuyorican experience during a decade of vast changes in all sectors of U.S. society. The Nuyorican Poets' Café emerged as a literary and cultural arts venue on the Lower East Side in 1975, founded by poet Miguel Algarín, who with dramatist **Miguel Piñero** also compiled the anthology, *Nuyorican Poetry,* that introduced the poetry and poetics of this experience. Numerous New York organizations, institutions, and venues also supported the dissemination and promotion of Puerto Rican and Nuyorican literature and intellectual culture at the time, including the Association of Hispanic Arts (AHA), El Museo del Barrio, the New Rican Village Cultural and Educational Center, Repertorio Español, and Taller Boricua. The location of venues of this kind in neighborhoods such as El Barrio (also known as East Harlem or Spanish Harlem) and the Lower East Side (Loisada), bolstered in turn by the broader-reaching activities and missions of AHA and the Repertorio, granted important visibility for Nuyorican activities both within and outside of the community.

The best-known single-author book of the Nuyorican movement is *Puerto Rican Obituary* (1973) by the late **Pedro Pietri** (1944–2004), published by the radical Monthly Review Press. The thirty-two poems treat a variety of issues relating to the Puerto Rican experience in New York as seen through the eyes of a vociferous social critic: work, poverty, life in the housing projects, drug abuse, unemployment and underemployment, and the disintegration of Puerto Rican identity in the face of a hostile dominant culture. In extreme antiestablishment spirit (inherited in part from both Beat poetics of the 1950s and the social activism of the 1960s) Pietri parodies, satirizes, and blasphemes everything from mindless consumerism and authority figures to such mainstream texts as the Lord's Prayer and the Pledge of Allegiance. *Puerto Rican Obituary* includes poetry of contrasts. Puerto Rico and New York, Puerto Ricans and non-Puerto Ricans, Spanish and English, dark skin and light skin, death and life, the self and the other, rich and poor—all these oppositions come together to explore the loss of cultural identity of a group marginalized by social and political circumstances. Pietri's sharp wit and keen sense of social justice combine with a streetwise approach to poetry as oral performance to shape these differences into a multifaceted and conflicted vision of Puerto Rican reality in New York.

Irony, satire, comedy, and tragedy are the dominant modes in this self-proclaimed verse obituary, and Pietri employs both traditional and unconventional poetic and rhetorical techniques to lay bare this problem and the attendant wrath, hostility, and frustration. The hallmarks of his compositional style include intricate patterns of rhyme and repetition, the intercalation of written and oral found material, and a reliance on orality and Nuyorican speech patterns. Language—whether English or Spanish, broken or not—is also a theme in *Puerto Rican Obituary*. For instance, Juan, Miguel, Milagros, Olga, and Manuel—the generic Puerto Rican New Yorkers of the title poem, "Puerto Rican Obituary"—implausibly take lessons in broken English. Pietri revisits this ironic motif in "The Broken English Dream," which nominally underscores the linguistic ramifications of how the so-called American dream has eluded Puerto Ricans in the United States. Alfredo Matilla and Iván Silén used this same clever turn of phrase in the context of both islands: "Puerto Rican poetry of the twentieth century, in Puerto Rico as well as New York . . . is a summons to awaken from this broken English dream and assume the Puerto Rican and Latin-American essence that belongs to us" (xviii). The aptness of this concept to a sociopolitical critique notwithstanding, Miguel Algarín embraces the literary practice of code-switching in Nuyorican expression, as he explains in "Nuyorican Language," the introduction to *Nuyorican Poetry*, the anthology he edited with Piñero: "We come to the city as citizens and can retain the use of Spanish and include English. . . . The interchange between both yields new verbal possibilities, new images to deal with the stresses of living on tar and cement" (15). Two recent books that variously document, analyze, and contextualize this hybrid language—Ed Morales's *Living in Spanglish: The Search for a Latino Identity in America* (2002) and Ilan Stavans's *Spanglish: The Making of a New American Language* (2003)—underscore the growing acceptance of Spanglish as a linguistic and cultural phenomenon and exemplify an increasingly broader approach to U.S. Latino literature.

The modes of communication and topics that Pietri practiced in *Puerto Rican Obituary* and Algarín theorized in "Nuyorican Language" provide common ground for many other poets of the same period, beginning with those anthologized in *Nuyorican Poetry*. Along with Pietri, the other principal poets in Algarín and Piñero's anthology are **Sandra María Esteves**, Lucky CienFuegos, and Algarín and Piñero themselves. They wrote primarily in free verse and in English with sporadic Spanish or **bilingualism**. Most of the *Nuyorican Poetry* writers did not go on to distinguish themselves beyond the anthology, though: Later compilations and studies neither include nor name more than a few of the poets from the 1975 book. Nor did every important Nuyorican poet appear in the Algarín and Piñero anthology. Victor Hernández Cruz is notably absent, even though he already had published three books of poetry and an anthology by that time, most prominently *Snaps* (1969) and *Mainland* (1973), both with Random House. By the same token, Cruz and some of the *Nuyorican Poetry* poets (Algarín, Esteves, Pietri, Piñero, and **José Angel Figueroa**) continued publishing into the 1980s and even beyond, thus bridging the gap between the Nuyorican and post-Nuyorican periods, and defying neat periodization based on a specific cut-off date. As a corpus, this work runs the gamut from the protest and praise poetry of the Caribbean Latina of color Esteves, to Figueroa's visually conscious verse in *Noo Jork* (1981), and Piñero's allegiance to the catchy orality and musical rhythms that inspire many Nuyorican poets (and that critics and music lovers recognize as an early configuration of rap lyrics and slam poetry).

During this post–*Nuyorican Poetry* transitional period, a new generation simultaneously began to emerge and introduce aesthetic changes, as Frances Aparicio has noted (28). Louis Reyes Rivera published his poetry and edited anthologies, established the small press Shamal Books, and wrote a spirited introduction for Esteves's first book, *Yerba Buena* (1980). In *La Carreta Made a U-Turn* (1979), Tato Laviera presented a realistic alternative to René Marqués's treatment of return migration in the play *La carreta* (1951; pub. 1963). **Martín Espada** explored the particulars of Puerto Rican identity, his experiences in the broader Latino community, and radical causes throughout the Americas. The anthology Espada edited for the progressive Curbstone Press, *Poetry Like Bread: Poets of the Political Imagination from Curbstone Press* (1994; rev. 2000), exemplifies the extent of his commitment to a political aesthetic in contemporary U.S. and Latin American poetry. The work of **Judith Ortiz Cofer** and the mother-daughter collaboration of **Rosario Morales** and **Aurora Levins Morales**, *Getting Home Alive* (1986), added the perspectives of women and Latinas. Jack Agüeros, the former director of El Museo del Barrio (1976–1986), challenged the established precepts of two time-honored forms, the sonnet and the psalm, in his first book, *Correspondence between the Stonehaulers* (1990). Two essential books provide comprehensive access to this breadth of Nuyorican poetry as it developed from its beginnings into the 1990s, Faythe Turner's *Puerto Rican Writers at Home in the USA: An Anthology* and Carmen Dolores Hernández's *Puerto Rican Voices in English: Interviews with Writers* (1997). In addition, Turner introduces a new poet, Magdalena Gómez, and two others not usually included in this group, **Luz María Umpierre** and Julio Marzán. Hernández similarly assembles voices from different generations; her comparative chronology of writers and events from 1922 to 1996 is a notable contribution to the study of Nuyorican and Latino cultural and publishing history.

Into the Twenty-first Century

At the turn of the twenty-first century, two works of popular art—a novel and a film—have immortalized the earlier decades of Nuyorican literature. The up-and-coming New York novelist Ernesto Quiñonez, raised in El Barrio by his Puerto Rican mother and Ecuadorian father, pays homage in *Bodega Dreams* (2000) to the heyday of his Nuyorican literary forebears. The protagonist visits the hallowed halls of El Museo and Taller Boricua, for example, and Agüeros, Algarín, CienFuegos, Espada, Esteves, Pietri, and Piñero appear at a climactic moment; the final section of the novel, "A New Language Being Born," pointedly marks the cultural relevance of Spanglish. León Ichaso's *Piñero* (2001) celebrates the work of the late Piñero (1946–88) and, by extension, the entire Nuyorican scene of the 1970s and 1980s. The release of the biopic gave room for the *New York Times* to address the current state of Nuyorican poetry and performance. Mireya Navarro shows in "The Poetry of the Nuyorican Experience" that the scene has changed. At the Nuyorican Poets' Café, a new generation reads, performs, and slams alongside non-Puerto Ricans, as Miguel Algarín and Bob Holman's anthology *Aloud: Voices from the Nuyorican Poets' Café* (1994) clearly illustrates. Pietri later groused about slams as well as about being excluded as coeditor of this Nuyorican anthology (Hernández 118–19), but his poetry appears there nonetheless. Nor was everyone pleased with the lionization of Piñero; Espada and Esteves openly questioned the choice (Navarro B3).

Such considerations bring to the fore the ongoing relevance of comprehensive access to Boricua poetry and its place in the broader contexts of Latino and American poetry. Several anthologies of the 1990s responded to the trend of documenting the Puerto Rican presence within a pan-Latino context: *After Aztlán: Latino Poets of the Nineties* (1992; ed. Ray González), *Paper Dance: 55 Latino Poets* (1995; ed. Victor Hernández Cruz, Leroy V. Quintana, and **Virgil Suárez**), *El Coro: A Chorus of Latino and Latina Poetry* (1997; ed. Martín Espada), and *¡Floricanto Sí! A Collection of Latina Poetry* (1998; ed. Bryce Milligan, Mary Guerrero Milligan, and Angela de Hoyos). The encyclopedic undertakings of the Recovering the U.S. Hispanic Literary Heritage project under the editorship of Nicolás Kanellos, *Herencia: The Anthology of Hispanic Literature of the United States* (2002), and *En otra voz: antología de la literatura hispana de los Estados Unidos* (2003), offer another model for showcasing Boricua and other Latino poetry within Hispanic literature. A current anthology might follow the example of *Aloud* and feature the new voices (such as Mariposa, Ed Morales, **Willie Perdomo**, Mayda del

Valle, and others) among not only those of earlier periods, but also as part of the corpus of American poetry, where they rightfully belong.

Further Reading

Algarín, Miguel. Introductions and afterword. *Nuyorican Poetry: An Anthology of Puerto Rican Words and Feelings.* Ed. Algarín and Miguel Piñero. New York: Morrow, 1975. 9–20, 23–27, 81–91, 129–31, 181–82.

Aparicio, Frances R. "From Ethnicity to Multiculturalism: An Historical Overview of Puerto Rican Literature in the United States." *Handbook of Hispanic Cultures in the United States: Literature and Art.* Ed. Francisco Lomelí. Houston: Arte Público Press; Madrid: Instituto de Cooperación Iberoamericana, 1993. 19–39.

Flores, Juan. *Divided Borders: Essays on Puerto Rican Identity.* Houston: Arte Público Press, 1993.

Hernández, Carmen Dolores. *Puerto Rican Voices in English: Interviews with Writers.* Westport, CT: Praeger, 1997.

Kanellos, Nicolás. "An Overview of Hispanic Literature in the United States." *Herencia: The Anthology of Hispanic Literature of the United States.* Ed. Nicolás Kanellos et al. New York: Oxford UP, 2002. 1–32.

———, ed. *Biographical Dictionary of Hispanic Literature in the United States: The Literature of Puerto Ricans, Cuban Americans, and Other Hispanic Writers.* Westport, CT: Greenwood Press, 1989.

Lindstrom, Naomi. "Cuban American and Continental Puerto Rican Literature." *Sourcebook of Hispanic Culture in the United States.* Ed. David William Foster. Chicago: American Library Association, 1982. 221–45.

Matilla, Alfredo, and Iván Silén. Prologue. *The Puerto Rican Poets/Los Poetas Puertorriqueños.* Ed. Matilla and Silén. Bantam Poetry. New York: Bantam, 1972. xiii–xviii.

Mohr, Eugene V. *The Nuyorican Experience: Literature of the Puerto Rican Minority* [Contributions in American Studies 62]. Westport, CT: Greenwood Press, 1982.

Morales, Ed. *Living in Spanglish: The Search for a Latino Identity in America.* New York: St. Martin's Griffin, 2003.

Navarro, Mireya. "The Poetry of the Nuyorican Experience." *New York Times* (January 2, 2002): B1+.

Sánchez-González, Lisa. *Boricua Literature: A Literary History of the Puerto Rican Diaspora.* New York: New York UP, 2001.

Santiago, Soledad. "Notes on the Nuyoricans." *Village Voice* (February 19, 1979): 1+.

Wall, Catharine E. "Latino Poetry." *Critical Survey of Poetry.* 8 vols. Ed. Philip K. Jason. 2nd rev. ed. Pasadena: Salem, 2003. 4825–32.

Catharine E. Wall

PUERTO RICAN STEREOTYPES   Similar to other minoritized groups in the United States, Puerto Ricans also deal with stereotyped notions of themselves held by the dominant (Anglo) culture. As Ilan Stavans discusses in his book *The Hispanic Condition* (2001), since the 1960s the U.S. government has repeatedly talked about "the Puerto Rican problem," usually referring to "criminality, the preponderance of drugs, the lack of education, poverty" and other malaises associated with working class barrios (47). In addition, Puerto Ricans are also seen as docile: "lacking self-esteem, domesticated, harmless, submissive, gentle to the point of naiveté, out of touch with themselves" (47).

Throughout the years, Puerto Rican literature in the United States has contested these stereotypes by providing a context upon which they are addressed, explained, and subverted. For instance, **Piri Thomas**'s *Down These Mean Streets* provides an insight into the life of a young Puerto Rican raised in the New York City's barrio who struggles to find a space in a world that seems to tell him he is insignificant (or dangerous) because he is a dark-skinned Puerto Rican. Because of the political relationship between Puerto Rico and the United States, Puerto Rican literature on the island has also dealt with and contested these notions. For instance, in his play *La Carreta* (The Oxcart) René Marquéz details the story of a family (a matriarch and her three children) looking for a way to improve their living conditions while attempting to stay together. Set in the 1940s, poverty in *La Carreta* is not the result of a cultural trait, nor is it the result of individual laziness or lack of self-esteem, but the result of an economic system in flux and disarray. In their search for a better life for themselves and their family, the main characters engage in a migratory cycle where they move from the countryside on the island to the city (San Juan), to New York, and back to the island. The topic of migration (especially migration in search of a better life) is present in much of the Puerto Rican literature and popular culture in general (e.g., music, art, press, etc.). Migration is also the central topic in Luis Rafael Sanchez's "short story turned motion picture" *La Guagua Aérea* (The Air Bus), which provides insight into the economic reasons for the constant migration of between the island and the United States, while tweaking the stereotype of submissiveness in the character of Don Faustino, the figure narrating the events. Also set in the 1940s (because of monumental changes in the economic system at the time, the 1940s marked the beginning of massive migration from the island of Puerto Rico to the U.S. mainland), Don Faustino seems like the stereotypical *jíbaro* from the countryside: the domesticated, harmless, submissive and "kind to the point of being naïve" Puerto Rican from the countryside. However, he is the one character who, in the middle of the flight, provides a heartfelt and compelling statement as to why he is flying for the first time to New York, while responding to the scolding inquiries of another Puerto Rican, one who has been portrayed throughout the story as an "Americanized" Puerto Rican. In the end, his stereotypical characteristics are the ones pushing him to fight for his land and, thus, his heritage.

The works of **Judith Ortiz Coffer**, *An Island like You* (1995) and *Silent Dancing* (1991), and **Esmeralda Santiago**, *When I Was Puerto Rican* (1993) and *Almost a Woman* (1998), are very important in this discussion, for they offer alternative representations of Puerto Rican **identity** via migration.

Ortiz Coffer, for instance, presents the reader with her own account of Puerto Ricanness, which she associates with her childhood, as she travels back and forth from the island to New Jersey. Santiago's account also involves detailed discussions of a Puerto Rican childhood, in this case a "one way trip" to the United States with her mother and her siblings. Santiago's family migrates to the barrio in New York, but different from the stereotypes associated with this environment, Santiago presents us with a poor but strong and caring family. It is clear through her account that their poverty is not the result of a cultural defect, but rather the result of imposing economic, political, and social structures. Thus, in the hands of Puerto Rican authors, Puerto Ricanness becomes a contesting and contested identity, in direct opposition to the traditional stereotypes associated with this **ethnicity**/nationality.

Further Reading

Stavans, Ilan. *The Hispanic Condition: The Power of a People.* New York: HarperCollins, 2001.

Carmen R. Lugo-Lugo

PUZO, MARIO (1920–1999)   Italian American novelist and screenwriter. Well-known for his all-time best seller, *The Godfather* (1969), Mario Puzo had written two earlier novels that received critical acclaim. His earlier novels were his attempts to fulfill a dream of becoming an artist and escaping the ghetto world in which he had been born. Puzo's early encounter with such writers as Dostoyevsky in his local library strengthened his belief in art and, enabled him to understand the New York world he grew up in. However, it would not be art but war that would enable Puzo to escape his environment and eventually return to it through writing. Out of his experiences in Europe during and after World War II he crafted his first novel, *The Dark Arena* (1955), and ten years later he returned to his life experiences growing up in a New York "Little Italy" to create *The Fortunate Pilgrim* (1965), which is a classic of Italian American literature.

In *The Dark Arena*, the protagonist, Walter Mosca returns home from serving in the American occupation army in Germany. Unable to take up where he left off before the war, Mosca returns to Germany as a civilian employee of the occupation government and resumes his life as a black marketer. With this novel he joined other veterans of World War II, including James Jones and **Norman Mailer**, in recounting experiences of war and postwar America. Although the novel received some good reviews, he was disappointed that it did not make much money. For his next work, *The Fortunate Pilgrim*, Puzo reached into his own childhood to tell the story of how an Italian immigrant woman keeps her family together in New York's "Hell's Kitchen" neighborhood through the deaths of two husbands and succeeds in moving them all safely to the dream home in Long Island. The novel focused on the mother/son relationship, so important to Italian culture and so ignored in American culture. Critics agree that this novel, by far, is the writer's masterpiece. Although he again received excellent reviews, it brought him even less financial reward. Deep in debt, he began looking for a way out and took an editor's advice to develop a novel around a small gangster figure in *The Fortunate Pilgrim.*

With the publication of *The Godfather* Puzo was instantly promoted to celebrity status. The timing of the novel's publication had much to do with its rapid climb to number one and its long stay (sixty-seven weeks) on the *New York Times* best seller list; it came off the press in the middle of the ethnic revival period of the 1960s. It also followed nationally televised congressional hearings on organized crime and the publication of Peter Maas's nonfiction bestseller, *The Valachi Papers,* through which

Mario Puzo. *AP/Wide World Photos.*

mobster-turned-informer Joe Valachi testified on his activities inside organized crime. Mafia had become a familiar term in American culture.

Most people read the novel as an allegory of a decadent America in the post–World War II period. But the novel is better read as the struggle to protect a family and preserve it, no matter the cost, in a hostile environment. If the Corleone family is to be preserved, it must avoid total assimilation into American culture. With this in mind, Puzo's novel reaches beyond the surface of popular culture to give great insight into Italian American ethnicity.

The Godfather has done more to create a national consciousness of the Italian American experience than any work of fiction or nonfiction prior to or since its publication. It was the first novel that Italian Americans, as a group, reacted to either positively or negatively. It appeared during a time when Italian Americans were just beginning to emerge as an identifiable cultural and political entity. Even though this book was much more a work of fiction than any of the earlier, more autobiographical novels written by Italian Americans, the novel created an identity crisis for Italian Americans throughout the nation. Antidefamation groups denounced Puzo for creating a bad image of Italians in America; young Italian American kids formed "Godfather" clubs; and real mafiosi claimed Puzo knew what he was writing about. For a while, Puzo wrote a number of essays on the subject of Italian America that appeared in major national magazines. Although often undermining the image of Italians that he created in *The*

Godfather, these essays are also quite critical of the Italian American's behavior in American society. After the publication of *The Godfather* and the release of the first two films based on the novel, *The Godfather* (1972) and *The Godfather Part II* (1974), Puzo dropped out of the public spotlight and wrote screenplays for *Superman* (1978) and *The Godfather Part III* (1990). He would go on to write six more novels, *Fools Die* (1978), the story of a gambler in Las Vegas; *The Sicilian* (1984), based on the historical brigand Salvatore Giuliano; The *Fourth K* (1990), an attempt to create an international thriller around a member of the Kennedy family who becomes president of the United States; *The Last Don* (1996) and *Omerta* (2000) in which he tries to return to the familiar material of *The Godfather;* and *The Family* (2001), a dramatization of the events surrounding the famous Borgia family, powerbrokers of the Italian Renaissance. This last novel, co-completed by his friend Carol Gino, was published posthumously. Although most of these later works were based on Italian Americans, many involved in organized crime, none of the works ever achieved the artistry of *The Fortunate Pilgrim* or the success of *The Godfather.* Though social scientists and literary scholars may forever debate the value of Puzo's work as social documents and art, it cannot be denied that Mario Puzo was one writer who has left a permanent imprint on the American cultural scene through his representation of *italianita* and his creation of a mythic filter through which Italian American culture would be read. (*See also* Italian American Film, Italian American Novel, Italian American Stereotypes)

Further Reading

Gardaphe, Fred. "Mario Puzo's Great Italian American Dream." *Italian Signs, American Streets: The Evolution of Italian American Narrative.* Durham, NC: Duke UP, 1996. 87–98.

Messenger, Christian. *The Godfather and American Culture: How the Corleones Became "Our Gang.* Albany: State U of New York P, 2002.

Puzo, Mario. *The Godfather Papers and Other Confessions.* New York: Fawcett, 1972.

Fred Gardaphe

Q

QUIN, MIKE (1906–1947) Pseudonym for Paul William Ryan, prolific Irish American journalist, poet, labor movement activist, radio newscaster, and detective fiction writer (under the pseudonym Robert Finnegan). Mike Quin was a gifted storyteller whose vivid accounts of the social injustices suffered by working-class Americans during the 1930s and 1940s chronicled a dark side of American cultural history; these stories of the dispossessed include *And We Are Millions: The League of Homeless Youth* (1933), *Dangerous Thoughts* (1940), *More Dangerous Thoughts* (1941), and the posthumously published *The Big Strike* (1949), an in-depth account of the Great Maritime Strike of 1934.

By the age of nineteen, Ryan, who had left school at fifteen to support himself in clerical positions and as a sailor, had committed himself to a career in professional writing; for the next twenty-two years, he wrote tirelessly, often at night, to produce novels, poems, fables, satires, lampoons, newspaper columns, and nonfiction accounts that illustrated the struggles and suffering of the under-classes whose labor powered capitalist institutions. Born and raised in an industrialized Irish American working-class neighborhood of San Francisco, he gained an insider perspective on the social problems created by poverty, unemployment, disease, and ethnic prejudice; his childhood experiences contributed to the highly developed social consciousness later reflected in all genres of his writing. His sensitivity to the plight of working-class men and women led Ryan to become politically active in trade union and communist organizations, such as the John Reed Club of Hollywood. He contributed regularly to leftist periodicals such as *Partisan Review* and *Western Worker*, which later became *People's World.*

In 1933 his sympathy for unemployed vagrant youth during the Depression resulted in his first major publication as Mike Quin: *And We Are Millions: The League of Homeless Youth.* This pamphlet collects the histories and testimonials of American youth prosecuted for vagrancy during the early years of the Depression. He then turned his attention to the plight of Mexican workers being deported amid the rampant unemployment of the early 1930s, highlighting the tragic irony that those being represented as "useless" to American society were the same workers whose labor had built roads and bridges all over California in the 1920s.

During the 1934 West Coast maritime strike, in which two strikers from a group of picketing dockworkers, seamen, and teamsters were killed by San Francisco police, Quin contributed poems, satires, sketches, and anecdotes to the International Longshoremen and Warehousemen's Union's *The Waterfront Worker.* His book-length account of the union struggle for improved working conditions, *The Big Strike,* creates a riveting narrative sympathetic to the strikers' perspective. Now heralded as a seminal work that provides historical insight into the origins of contemporary labor unions, it was never published in Quin's lifetime: No commercial book publisher was willing to take the manuscript when he wrote it in 1936. That same year Quin began a career as a radio newscaster for the Committee for Industrial Organization, the "CIO Reporter on the Air," to further circulate the labor perspective. In the 1940s he acted as the Public Relations Director for the CIO, renamed as the Congress of Industrial Organizations, in California.

In spite of the serious content, much of his writing reflects a dry, ironic sense of humor, as seen in the Socratic dialogues that shape his numerous sketches of "Mr. Murphy and Mr. O'Brien." His sketch of Bongo and Wowsy was incorporated into the musical *Meet the People,* and **Theodore Dreiser** encouraged him to write for the theater. Dreiser had been so impressed with Quin's 1940 collection *Dangerous Thoughts* that he wrote a letter comparing its author to Voltaire, Rabelais, and Paine. Dreiser and Quin went on to become friends, and Dreiser wrote the Introduction to *More Dangerous Thoughts* in 1941.

In order to "make crime pay," Ryan embarked on a promising career as in detective fiction in his late thirties. Under the pseudonym Robert Finnegan, he quickly produced a trilogy of novels—*The Lying Ladies* (1946), *The Bandaged Nude* (1946), and *Many a Monster* (1948)—all of which follow the socially conscious detective Dan Banion as he searches for truth and for himself amidst the unstable environment of postwar America. These well-written crime novels earned Ryan, as Finnegan, popular acclaim, but failing health prevented him from developing Banion's character in further novels. In 1944 Ryan had married Mary King O'Donnell. Their only child celebrated her first birthday the month before the exhausted Ryan succumbed to the pancreatic cancer that took his life in August 1947. (*See also* Irish American Novel)

Jacquelyn Scott Lynch

QUIÑONEZ, NAOMI HELENA (1951–) Chicana scholar, writer, and activist. As part of a generation of socially committed Chicana and Chicano intellectuals, Quiñonez has, over the course of her professional career, served in public administration, as an educational administrator, and most recently as an associate professor of Chicana and Chicano studies at California State University campus at Fullerton. She is also an editor of books and cultural/art journals, the author of two published volumes of poetry, and a tireless advocate for public educational and literary resources—working with library systems in the greater Los Angeles area, as well as social service agencies in California. She was cofounder and codirector of United Artists of Los Angeles, a community-based cultural production organization. Her poetry has been published in more than twenty anthologies and journals, including *After Aztlán* (1992), *Chicana Creativity and Criticism* (1997), and *From Totems to Hip Hop* (2003). Her scholarship in Chicana and Chicano studies is interdisciplinary, shaped by both literary and historical concerns; indeed her dissertation *Hijas de La Malinche* (1997) is a historiography of first-wave Chicana writers. She has received numerous awards and accolades, including grants from the National Endowment for the Arts, the California Arts Council, and most recently from the Rockefeller Foundation. She has also tirelessly worked to convene conferences and symposia that bring together creative, critical, and political concerns, and beginning in the 1980s has read at countless events throughout the Southwest, as well as in Mexico and Nicaragua.

This synthesis of the public and the private, the aesthetic and the activist is also reflected in Quiñonez's poetry. Critic Francisco Lomelí sees her as part of a group of writers whose writing and public reading is a form of activism—their work engages the reader/auditor in such a way that will inspire social change. This activist strand is clearly evident in her two published collections, *Sueños de Colibri* (1986) and *The Smoking Mirror* (1998), as well as in her anthologized work. The publication of her first collection places her squarely in an emerging tradition of experimental Chicana writers such as **Sandra Cisneros** and **Helena Maria Viramontes**, who explore questions of aesthetics and politics as they write of the everyday experiences of Chicanas—embedded as they are in larger social constructions of sexuality, race, class, and gender. Quiñonez often writes arresting descriptions of a multicultural Los Angeles, infusing the everyday with mythic significance. For example, the title of her most recent work is a reference to Nahua myth, and this direct engagement with the mythic, an ongoing motif in her poetry, reflects her deep concerns with spiritual questions, especially as they offer the potential for empowerment. Her meditations on memory are always inflected by the specifics of place and the experiences of women.

Indeed, Quiñonez's poetic voice is centered in the experiences, perspectives, and spiritualities of women. Her engagements with Chicana and Chicano history, myth, and culture are deeply feminist, multicultural, and egalitarian; her work expands our understanding of the power of language in shaping not only readers and writers but also the world. (*See also* Mexican American Poetry)

Further Reading

Apodaca, M. Linda. "Naomi Quiñonez: Images in Cultural Poetics and Gender." Proceedings of the 1st Annual International Conference on the Emerging Literature of the Southwest Culture. El Paso: U of Texas P, 1996. 9–13.

Lomeli, Francisco. "Ars Combinatoria in Naomi Quinonez: From Trobadora to Anti-Word Synthesizer." *Confrontations et Metissage.* Ed. Elyette Benjamin-Labarthe. Bordeux: Editions le Maisons Des Pays Iberiques, 1995. 261–70.

———. "Naomi Helena Quiñonez." *Dictionary of Literary Biography.* Vol. 209. Eds. Francisco A. Lomeli and Carl R. Shirley. Detroit: Gale, 1999. 226–31.

Eliza Rodriguez y Gibson

R

RACE   Most scholars today hold that the idea of *race* as an identification or category for classifying people is a social invention. Recent discoveries in the field of genetics have particularly discredited biological notions of race because more genetic variations exist within a socially defined racial group than between different races. To say that race is a social construct, however, is not to deny the reality of **racism**, or the effects of these social attitudes and beliefs about human difference upon various groups, both in the past and in the present. It does shift the focus of historical and literary investigations to the changing meaning of race in U.S. culture and the instrumental value that ideologies (or sets of beliefs) about race had in justifying inequalities such as in slavery or immigration restrictions, nation building, the management of class conflict, imperialism, westward expansion, cultural shifts in gender roles and norms, and political resistance movements. At the beginning of the twenty-first century, some people wished for or predicted the end of race as a significant marker of identity as the U.S. population becomes increasingly heterogeneous and individuals multiracial. Many peoples of color, on the other hand, continue to value race as an important source of belonging and an essential tool to rally political struggles for social justice and equality in the face of continuing institutional and cultural racism. Because art is a product of its historical context, critical race scholars have increasingly investigated the work that literature has played both in constituting U.S. society's ideas about racial **identity** and difference, but also in creating counter traditions resisting these dominant beliefs and authoring an alternative racial (or nonracial) identity.

Most scholars trace modern ideas about race to the categories of thought invented during the Enlightenment. Although eighteenth- and nineteenth-century historians located the origin of race thinking in Greek thought, the Greeks did not tie their system of classifying differences among people to a biology of race, and their practice of slavery was not reserved for people of specific skin colors or physical features. With the development in the seventeenth century of Enlightenment investigations into natural history and anthropology, philosophers began to turn from earlier metaphysical and theological explanations for the ordering in nature and society toward a more empirically based description and classification. Originally, to eighteenth-century theorists, these observable physical differences resulted from climate and social environment, which over time placed groups at various stages of civilization. In key works, however, such as the 1795 edition of Natural Variety of Mankind, Johann Friederich Blumenbach, the father of modern anthropology, started to tie natural or physiological distinctions such as pigment or anatomy to innate and mental distinctions. Blumenbach spoke of five divisions of mankind: the Caucasian, Mongolian, Ethiopian, American, and Malay. To explain the diversity of mankind from the original Biblically based unity, he argued that, in addition to climate-based differences, each racial group had a life force or soul that determined its place in the hierarchy of civilizations. Blumenbach's ideas would influence historians who saw in theories of genius and blood explanations for differences in national character. In his reinterpretation of Greek and Roman history, Barthold G. Niebuhr (1813) would imply that each nation had a hidden and noble natural past that could be legitimated by scientific investigation and that served as a driving, if not determining, force of history. Although the word race had entered the European lexicon sometime in the Middle Ages to designate lineage or purity of descent in class or kinship, it slowly shifted to a genealogy of natural inheritance that was linked to national and cultural characteristics.

In the first half of the nineteenth century, race continued to have malleable meanings, and U.S. writers used the term race loosely as a convenient rhetoric to denote a number of differences, from nation, class, region, and skin color. Yet over the course of the nineteenth century, race would acquire a new scientific authority and would be associated—for the first time—specifically with biological differences. The intellectual movement toward biological notions of race must be connected to their value for a number of historical and socioeconomic developments. Many historians link the rise of race thinking to the need to justify **slavery** and **colonialism**. Although certainly scientific racism was appropriated to legitimate slavery and imperialism, it is important to see how it served the larger purpose of reconciling the conflict within the United States between professed beliefs in equality and the persistence of—and desire for—inequality. A language of race helped to naturalize differences and to provide an immutable ground to imagined communities of nation, class, and region.

In the nineteenth century, race particularly worked, according to a number of labor historians, as a divide-and-conquer strategy that separated working-class European descendants from the slave and free people of color. Although initially Africans, like many European immigrants, were brought to America as indentured servants, colony leaders introduced the differentiating language of race to create a buffer class of "whites" to identify with the planters and, in turn, to defend the established interests of the status quo. Although European stereotypes of Africans and Asians have exited for centuries, these groups were enslaved, or indentured, in the case of the Chinese and South Asians, not simply because of racism. Rather, these stereotypes developed into full-blown theories of biologically based racial inferiority because of the political utility this race thinking had in providing a cheap labor force for a trans-Atlantic plantation economy and for developing an enfranchised class of free white citizens who would identify with the ruling elite.

The assigning of racial meaning in the nineteenth century, however, was also a variegated system, whereby a group could have more than one racial classification. Although various European immigrants such as the Irish and later the Eastern European Jews were "white" in contrast to the African American, they were considered "black" or a racial other compared to the Anglo-Saxon.

The designation of the Anglo-Saxon as a separate race, one descended from the original English settlers in New England and the South arose as an important racial ideology in the nineteenth century. New Englanders continually invoked the superiority of the Anglo-Saxon race to rationalize their national prominence, their class leadership (especially in contrast to more recent immigrants), and their right to a manifest destiny in the West and overseas. The so-called Anglo-Saxon race believed they had inborn traits of self-discipline, individualism, domestic life, and intellectualism that set them apart from other races who never had—and never would—reach such a stage of evolutionary development. Thus, the Anglo-Saxons had a manifest destiny to dispossess the Native Americans and Mexicans of their land and to seize the Pacific coast before the Chinese and other "Mongolians" could settle it. Likewise, because certain racialized groups, such as the Chinese, were considered incapable of these Anglo-Saxon traits, they were deemed fundamentally unassimilable—permanent aliens who would later be barred from **immigration** with the **Chinese Exclusion Act** of 1882 (and 1888 and 1892). Not surprisingly, these exclusions also coincided with the economic depression of the 1880s, when many "nativist" workers resented cheap "foreign" labor.

The spread of race thinking in the nineteenth century also occurred because of its value in strengthening nationalism. Earlier ideas of citizenship were based on civic ideals or actions in the public sphere, but nineteenth-century theorists turned to ideas of race to provide a social cohesion and order based on nature and not politics: national membership would derive from sharing a common racial character, language, culture, and color. In his "Essay on the Inequality of the Human Races" (1853), Arthur de Gobineau, who is often called the father of modern racial thought, reimagined historical progress in terms of racial struggle. The spirit of the dominant race was key to the survival of the nation and to the future evolution of civilization, and countries had a duty to preserve their best racial traits. Likewise, the Scottish anatomist John Knox would greatly influence many prominent New England thinkers by promoting a similar determinist racial history and organic idea of national characters. Such theories would shape later debates over immigration, naturalization, and the exclusion of designated racial groups well into the twentieth century.

In the last decades of the nineteenth century, race thinking is particularly evident in the national debates over social Darwinism and degeneration. Although Darwin himself argued against a causal link between physical (racial) features and behavior, that did not stop social theorists from appropriating his ides of evolution and the survival of the fittest to naturalize capitalist modernization, immigration restriction, and imperialism. Social positivists borrowed particularly three key principles from Darwinian influenced science: first, that history was purposive and progressed according to laws of nature, such that the triumph of the superior racial civilization was inevitable; second, that all human society was constrained by natural laws and, therefore, human beings and races were no different from animals in battling for the survival of the fittest; and, third, that mental abilities were related to physical characteristics. The pioneer criminologist Cesare Lombroso in *The Man of Genius* 1891 is particularly known for having argued that physical traits such as facial angle, ear shape, or cranial size provided a true indication of mental ability and criminal behavior. Mental deficiencies were carried as visible signs on an "abnormal" body, which was different from a Western Greco-Roman classical ideal. Such theories were adopted not only by conservatives elites who could feel reassured of their continued leadership because of the natural evolutionary progress of the superior race but also by liberals who believed that social change went hand-in-hand with racial improvement.

Complementary to this belief in the inevitability of racial conflict and progress, on the other hand, was an anxiety about degeneration, a fear that would lead to support for eugenics. Many theorists in the last decades of the nineteenth century and the first part of the twentieth century feared that immigration, miscegenation, and other social changes (dance halls and public parks) that permitted racial mixing would cause racial dilution and usher in the decline and fall of the Anglo-Saxon nation. Such fears at the turn of the century lent support to many regulations on female sexuality and reproduction, as well as exhortations for increased birth rates among Anglo-Saxon women to offset the reproductive excess of immigrant races, including Southern and Eastern Europeans as well as Africans and Asians. Some initial support for white women's suffrage also stemmed from a similar desire to create a white voting block and government majority. To some theorists, such as Max Nordau in *Degeneration* (1895), experimental art forms as well were a sign of a mind atrophied by modern excess and racial pollution, and antimodernist aesthetic views arose out of overt, as well as more subtle, racial anxieties. In his *Inquiries into Human Faculty* (1883), when speculating on nations' racial future, Francis Galton first introduced the term *eugenics*, believing that a nation's average intelligence, racial behavior, and culture could be improved through racial engineering and selection. After the increase in labor movement strikes and the great wave of immigration from Eastern and Southern Europe starting in the 1890s, degeneration moved from a subcurrent of U.S. social thought to the center as differences in blood and race loomed as the causal agent of many social tensions.

In the first half of the twentieth century, race theory would undergo another important alteration, as an understanding of race would shift from biology to culture. Frank Boas, a German Jew who immigrated to the United States in 1887, would be a key figure in the redefining of race. In his influential *The Mind of Primitive Man* (1911), he would vehemently oppose racial theories of identity by asserting that physiological and morphological features of race had no determination on inherited cultural traits. Race and culture had to be studied separately. Although Boas's idea would shape the thinking of key African American public intellectuals such as **W. E. B. Du Bois**, most theorists took up Boas's call for the primacy of culture to preserve dominant ideas of racial difference. Racial identities were now understood as discrete cultural genealogies that had created the soul or consciousness of the race, and, as a consequence, racial segregation and hierarchies would persist as cultural divides. Prior to World War II many U.S. writers saw themselves as fashioning the cultural identity of America, which was frequently spoken of as a racial one. In response, many writers of color saw themselves as forging a racial consciousness and identity figured as an opposing cultural nationalism. The twentieth-century debate within many communities of color over **assimilation** versus separatism cannot be understood apart from this shift toward linking nation, race, and culture. Building a strong minority identity through resisting assimilation depended on recovering or maintaining the culture (language, beliefs, manners) of one's ancestors and the home country against a U.S. race-based nationalism.

Post–World War II U.S. culture has been greatly enriched by the art movements within various communities of color based on models of cultural nationalism, whether the **Black Arts Movement**, the Chicana/Chicano Movement, or the collective of Asian American writers that produced the landmark *Aiiieeeee!* anthology in 1974. Tied to political movements based on an identity politics, these art movements gave individuals a sense of belonging and a shared consciousness, and mobilized collective political struggles that transformed the United States toward greater political and social justice.

Starting, however, in the 1970s there began a shift to think of these identities along models of **ethnicity** rather than race. Although Chicana and Chicano activists in the 1960s and 1970s spoke of La Raza (or "the race") to describe a pan-Latin identity, many view such collective identifications, whether of Hispanic or Latino, as a false term of unity and collectivity imposed by an Anglo-European media, entertainment industry, and government. Prior to coming to the United States, most people of Latin American and Caribbean descent would have identified themselves in national rather than racial terms and certainly would not have designated themselves within the United States binary racial system as simply either black or white. As a consequence, Latinas and Latinos have had two competing and shifting historical trajectories in response to race as an identity category: first, to acknowledge that U.S. Latinas and Latinos have become a racialized population and to use this portrayal as a "race" (if not a homogeneous one) to fight against discrimination and to seek the inclusion of people of Spanish-speaking descent in affirmative-action programs under the Equal Protection Clause; and, second, to resist Latinoness/Latinaness as a racial category, instead, recruiting ethnic paradigms to define *Latinidad* as a set of shared cultural practices, customs, and language. Among African Americans, the shift from the term "black" to "African American" also indicates a rethinking of racial identities in terms of ethnicity rather than biology. What unites the great diversity of black people is less a shared racial essence than a shared historical experience, collective memory, and expressive style that derives from their African diasporic cultural heritage.

The history of Asian American in the United States (a collective racial classification that can also trivialize cultural and historical differences) has been complicated by their shifting racialization within the bipolar system of U.S. race relations. In the past Asians were assigned a place in American society as both black and white. In the nineteenth century, for example, the Chinese's status within national censuses shifted, being considered white in 1860, Chinese in 1880, and lumped as black in 1900, if they were not born in China. After the 1952 Walter-McCarran Act reversed earlier Asian exclusion laws and allowed "non-white" citizens to be naturalized, Chinese, Korean, Japanese, and South Asian immigrants have often been seen as model minorities, who were nearer white, but they were often treated and designated as nearer black, being economically and socially discriminated against. As a result, many Asian diasporic immigrants felt pressured to adopt the racial prejudice against African Americans and to disassociate themselves from them as part of the assimilation process.

At the end of the twentieth century and the first part of the twenty-first century, a number of theorists have turned from cultural theories of racial difference to explore questions of hybridity and creolization, and some predict that this will in turn change how people think of their membership in socially defined groups. Despite the continuing appeal of race as a positive source of identity, it can also marginalize or exclude the diversity of people who identify with this category, particularly in recent years, many sexual minorities. Many theorists believe as well that cultural theories of racial identity perpetuate false myths of the purity of a white U.S. culture, which, from the beginning, has always been shaped by the unrecognized contributions of minorities. U.S. culture is embedded with African, Asian, and Latin diasporic influences, and thus the color line between U.S. culture and African, Asian, and Hispanic American culture is always an arbitrary or tenuous one. Finally, any stagnant notion of racial identities would belie a long history of racial border-crossing, in which European-descent people and individuals of color have interacted, intermarried, and initiated productive interchanges that have created a continuum of racial identities that are never stable, always hybrid, and, most accurately, multiple.

Further Reading

Delgado, Richard, and Jean Stefanic. *The Latino/a Condition: A Critical Reader.* New York: New York UP, 1998.

Gossett, Thomas F. *Race: The History of an Idea in America.* 2nd Edition. Oxford: Oxford UP, 1997.

Hannaford, Ivan. *Race: The History of an Idea in the West.* Washington, DC: Woodrow Wilson Center, 1996.

Jacobson, Matthew Frye. *Whiteness of a Different Color: European Immigrants and the Alchemy of Race.* Cambridge, MA: Harvard UP, 1998.

Lowe, Lisa. *Immigrant Acts: On Asian American Cultural Politics.* Durham, NC: Duke UP, 1996.

Niro, Brian. *Race.* New York: Palgrave MacMillan, 2003.

Oboler, Suzanne. *Ethnic Labels, Latino Lives: Identity and the Politics of (Re)Presentation in the United States.* Minneapolis: U of Minnesota P, 1995.

Omi, Michael, and Howard Winant. *Racial Formations in the United States: From the 1960s to the 1990s.* New York: Routledge, 1994.

Said, Edward. *Orientalism.* New York: Vintage, 1979.

Takaki, Ronald. *Iron Cages: Race and Culture in 19th-Century America.* New York: Oxford UP, 1990.

Stephen Knadler

RACHLIN, NAHID (1947–) Iranian American novelist and short story writer. In 1964 Rachlin left her home in Ahvaz in the southern oil-producing region of Iran to attend college in the United States; it was a time when many Iranians were being encouraged to study abroad to receive higher education, because few advanced educational opportunities existed in Iran. Rachlin attended college at Lindenwood College in St. Charles, Missouri, and, like so many other Iranians of her generation, she remained in the United States after completing her degree. She later moved to New York City and took graduate courses in creative writing. She met and married her American husband and eventually settled in the United States.

Rachlin is the author of *Veils: Short Stories* (1992), and several novels including *The Heart's Desire* (1995), *Married to a Stranger* (1993), and *Foreigner* (1979).

Nahid Rachlin. *Photo by Howard Rachlin. Courtesy of Nahid Rachlin.*

Because her work represented the first published voice of an Iranian woman written in English, Rachlin's writing is often considered pioneering among Iranian Americans. Her work also touches on her own biography as one of the earlier generations of Iranian women who were educated and settled in the United States and whose writerly voice and vision reflect her own struggles to come to terms with her **identity** as an Iranian woman living outside her country of birth.

Rachlin's writing represents a common sentiment among early Iranian immigrant writing. She grapples with the dizzying effects of **immigration**, of living between and in two cultures, and with the issues of cross-cultural marriage. Unlike some of the Iranian male writers, such as Taghi Modaressi and Manoucher Parvin, with whom she is a contemporary, Rachlin's writing is much less focused on overt social and political issues taking place in Iran. Her characters and perspective are informed by an internal, female sensibility that focuses more directly on issues of cross-cultural displacement, and the difficulties of locating an identity in the aftermath of immigration. As a woman in a writerly tradition that has largely excluded women, Rachlin articulates through her characters some of the anxieties and ambivalences of participating in two cultures, Iranian and American, that assign very different roles and limitations for women. As such, Rachlin is especially concerned with issues such as male-female relationships, expectations of marriage, and the desire to transgress some of the roles and limitations set by Iranian culture.

In her first novel, *Foreigner,* Rachlin draws on her own biography, creating in her protagonist a model for her own experience as an immigrant Iranian woman. Feri, an Iranian woman in her thirties, left Iran to study and work in the United States, where she married an American and eventually settled down. Fourteen years later, she decides to return to Iran to visit her family. She finds herself strangely pulled by the old Iranian culture, where she confronts as never before the question of where she belongs and how she wants to live. Her second novel, *Married to a Stranger,* deals with a young woman in the context of modern Iran. The protagonist, Minou, marries a man of her own choice and anticipates that her life will be different from the lives of other Iranian women, but she soon finds out that he is not what she expected. The novel focuses on her disappointment and her attempt to reorder her life.

In her latest novel, *The Heart's Desire,* Rachlin again explores cross-cultural marriage and the difficulties of articulating a solid identity when one has lived a life in two very different cultures. In this story, which parallels a number of true-to-life scenarios of American women paired with Iranian men who came to this country during the 1960s and 1970s, American artist Jennifer Sahary and her Iranian-born husband Karim, an academic, leave their comfortable home in Athens, Ohio, with their six-year-old son, Darius, to visit Karim's family shortly after the end of the Iran-Iraq war. Although Jennifer had been to Iran on an earlier visit, she finds the Iran of post-1979, steeped in an anti-Americanism that makes her uncomfortable. This parallels Karim's recollections of the increasing anti-Iranian feeling during the period when he was living in the United States. The trip to Iran arouses in him a desire to be more connected to his culture of origin and results in an increasing strain on the couple's twelve-year relationship. While in Iran, Karim finds out that some of his classes on his college campus in Ohio are given to other professors, and this begins a process of asking whether he shouldn't remain in Iran. This novel explores the ways that individuals are the products of historical trends and events that have an impact on the way they view themselves.

Rachlin's explorations of cross-cultural existence and, in many ways, the difficult choices that accompany this journey are central themes in all of her novels as well as in many of her short stories. Her work compassionately highlights the differences in two cultures that have a shared history but are perhaps the bedrock of why there are often common misperceptions about each of these cultures. Rachlin's narrative goal perhaps lies first and foremost in her desire to unhinge Iranians and Iranian culture from some of the stereotypes that are often promulgated in the U.S. media and to sensitively question each culture from inside the mind of her characters. Much of her work does contain an implicit, if understated, critique of Iranian patriarchy. Her characters, rather, benefit from their existence in two cultures, and as such they experience both positive and negative in both cultures. (*See also* Iranian American Literature)

Further Reading

Milani, Farzaheh. *Veils and Words: The Emerging Voices of Iranian Women Writers.* New York: Syracuse UP, 1992.

Naficy, Hamid. *The Making of Exile Cultures.* Minneapolis: U of Minnesota P, 1993.

Sullivan, Zohreh T. *Exiled Memories: Stories of Iranian Diaspora.* Philadelphia: Temple UP, 2001.

Persis Karim

RACISM   Racism refers to belief in a racial hierarchy based on unchangeable characteristics or assumed physiological traits as well as to practices that discriminate against a people because of their perceived or ascribed racial identities. Sometimes labeled *white supremacy* in the United States, racism still affects nearly every aspect of life and remains a central theme in a great body of American writing.

Racism cannot exist without a concept of **race**. Drawing from the biological sciences and social Darwinism, the notion of race categorizes the human species into different varieties or types on physiological grounds such as skin, hair color, physique, and facial features. Invidious distinctions based on differences in these traits among Negroes, Caucasian, Asiatic Mongols, Moors, and others have been used by Europeans to impose systems of imperialism, **colonialism**, and **slavery**. The distinctions of race are made meaningful in the contexts of culture, intellect, and morality to justify the racial superiority of the white men and women and to legitimize prejudice and hostility toward other peoples. The history of American racism dates back to Christopher Columbus's "discovery" of America in the late fifteenth century. For this so-called discovery, Native Americans paid a great price. As the first victims of American racism, American Indians, seen as subhumans, were virtually annihilated by acts of European violence and their spread of unfamiliar diseases. These wiped out more than 90 percent of American Indians of coastal New England. Their lands were stolen, their towns destroyed, their religious structures defiled, and their languages lost due to a long history of colonization and forced **assimilation**.

The next victims of American racism were Africans introduced to the New World as slaves. These peoples were shipped from Africa across the Atlantic Ocean—the notorious **Middle Passage**—primarily to Spanish and Portuguese colonies in the Caribbean, Mexico, and Central and South America in the early sixteenth century. From this trade, a system of American slavery developed and was fully established by about 1680. Slavery on American soil grew at such a fast rate that, by 1750, there were over 200,000 African slaves. Throughout most of the colonial period, opposition to slavery among white Americans was virtually nonexistent. Settlers in the seventeenth and early eighteenth centuries lacked a later generation's belief in natural human equality and saw little reason to question the enslavement of Africans. In molding a docile labor force, they resorted to harsh measures, including liberal use of whipping and branding, and inculcated in Africans a sense of black inferiority, helplessness, and dependence and a belief in the superior powers of their white masters. By 1860, near the start of the Civil War, the African American population had increased to 4.4 million, but the vast majority remained slaves. America condoned institutional slavery from 1619 up until the passage of the Thirteenth Amendment to the Constitution abolishing "slavery and involuntary servitude" on December 18, 1865. But constitutional abolition freed African Americans only halfway in their escape from racism. Questionable legal strategies, named for an antebellum mistral show character, called **Jim Crow** laws were enacted in the last third of the nineteenth century after Reconstruction by legislatures of the Southern states to legally impose racial segregation. Despite challenges for many decades, many of these persisted until the 1960s in many Southern states and systematically codified in law and state constitutional provisions the subordinate position of African Americans in society. Most such legal steps were aimed at separating the races in public spaces (restaurants, boardinghouses, theaters, parks, schools, hospitals, accommodations, and transportation) and denying black Americans their civil rights. Laws regulating segregation and disfranchisement were not only legitimized by the U.S. Supreme Court but also supported by brutal acts of ceremonial and ritualized mob violence such as the notorious lynching practiced by the Ku Klux Klan. Since the 1960s, the Supreme Court has struck down most such laws, but de facto segregation and disenfranchisement remain in many locales, as do other forms of racial discrimination against African Americans.

Like American Indians and African Americans, many immigrants have encountered racism to a great or certain degree, and even some European immigrants—Italians, Irish, Poles, and Jews—have not been immune to racist discrimination. But only Japanese Americans have ever been interned in the United States. In February 1942, two months after the Japanese bombing of Pearl Harbor, the federal government, under President Franklin D. Roosevelt, legalized the relocation of approximately 120,000 people of Japanese ancestry. Taken from their homes, mainly on the West Coast, they were forced into **internment** camps, also known as relocation camps, in Idaho, Arizona, Utah, California, Arkansas, Colorado, and Wyoming. Simply as *Japanese* Americans, they were seen as "enemy aliens" or, worse, "the enemy" in their own homeland. In the name of national security, this horrible act was perpetrated by the American government without regard for due process or legal remedy and most, even after repatriation, lost their most valued possessions. Like that of the Japanese, the history of Chinese **immigration** into the United States has been characterized by official policies of racist exclusion and violence. Chinese immigrants encountered harsh conditions, including what is called *institutionalized* racism. The **Chinese Exclusion Act** of 1882, the first and only immigration law in American history to target a specific nationality, banned the entry of "lunatics," "idiots," and all "Chinese laborers" into the United States. Designated as "aliens ineligible for citizenship," Chinese immigrants were unable to own land or work in California and other states. The Chinese Exclusion Act was renewed in 1892, again in 1902, and was not repealed until 1943 when China allied itself with the United States in World War II. In more recent American history, racist attitudes have been directed toward immigrants from south of the border. Rapidly becoming the largest minority in the United States, Mexican Americans and other Hispanic groups are playing a vital role in the borderlands of the American Southwest and beyond. Although Mexican Americans in the North American Southwest trace their history to pre–Anglo-American times, it was the 1848 Treaty of Guadalupe Hidalgo that brought a radical turning point for Mexican Americans. The treaty took the lands of thousands of Mexicans residents in former Mexican territories and thrust them into the United States within the region known as the American Southwest. There, as underclass American citizens, they have faced dual wage structures, job segregation, and racist treatments that force them to serve mostly as poorly paid laborers, ranch hands, farm workers, or domestic servants. In Texas during the 1930s, a sign that read "No dogs nor Mexicans allowed" was commonly written on restaurant facades.

Racism has been present blatantly or subtly throughout Anglo-American literature, and some writings have even been **canon**ized as American classics. From writers in the colonial period (particularly the Puritans) through writers of the frontier in the eighteenth century (such as James Fenimore Cooper) to nineteenth-century realist and naturalist writers (Samuel Langhorne Clemens, William Dean Howells, and Thomas Dixon, for instance)—virtually all either overtly or covertly express racist attitudes in their works. Also known as Mark Twain, Clemens is seen by many critics as a racist as well as a realist: his realist's aim to truly represent society has been called into question because his *critique* of a social problem paradoxically helps to perpetuate it. Twain's racism is evident not merely in his use of racial slurs (e.g., "nigger") but also in the racial stereotypes of Native Americans, blacks, and Chinese. In *The Adventures of Tom Sawyer* (1876), for example, the villain of the novel, Injun Joe, acts out of more than just an evil nature. He is evil *because* of his Indian blood, a claim that other characters in the novel reiterate repeatedly and also take as a cause of his sadistic nature and the vengeful fantasy Twain attributes to him. Racist expressions about Indians also appear in Twain's *Innocents Abroad* (1869) and *Roughing It* (1872). In the latter work, Twain labels "Goshoot" Indians as "gorilla," "kangaroo," and "Norway rat."

Beside Indians, Twain's racism also targets African Americans. In *The Adventures of Huckleberry Finn* (1884), Twain addresses the issue of slavery in antebellum America. His abundant use of racial slurs such as "nigger" has been excused by some readers as a necessity for its realistic historical context. Likewise, some excuse Twain because his protagonist, Huck, offers a powerful speech against racism. Even so, Twain's racism is embedded deeply in the relationship between Huck and Jim, a runaway slave who is Huck's companion. Extending beyond racism directed toward Native Americans and African Americans, Twain's play *Ah Sin* (1877), written with Bret Harte, is a reminder of the racist legacy of California's literary frontier. Ah Sin, a Chinese, is treated with contempt as a "slant eyed son of the yellow jaunders," a "jabbering idiot," and "a moral cancer," yet such a racist portrayal of Ah Sin in the eyes of Twain "reaches perfection."

Described by biographers as like a Huck Finn roaming the Michigan woods barefoot and wearing a straw hat, Ernest Hemingway once said that "all modern American literature comes from one book by Mark Twain called *Huck Finn*." Like Twain, Hemingway has been reread with racial issues in mind. A racist or an anti-Semite (along with other labels including misogynist, homophobe, cultural imperialist, and elitist), Hemingway uses the term *nigger* to refer to African Americans in his works and the word *kike* litters his personal letters. *The Sun Also Rises* (1926) well illustrates the ethnic hatreds of the upper classes in the 1920s. There, the portrayal of Robert Cohn reveals the author's **anti-Semitism**. In the eyes of Hemingway's narrator, Jake Barnes, Cohn is the one who possesses every negative personality trait and, most of all, a disfigured *Jewish* nose. Even as Barnes notes that Cohn's nose was flattened in a boxing match, he also avers that the blow "certainly improved" it.

Refuting presuppositions of American racism, ethnic American writers demonstrate their shared concern in their writing. The first body of ethnic writing to emerge, African American literature presents some of the most revealing investigations of racism. Early in the nineteenth century, slave narratives recount the dehumanizing effects of slavery. In probably the period's most famous African American text, *The Narrative of Frederick Douglass, an American Slave, Written by Himself* (1845), **Frederick Douglass**, born into slavery in Maryland, details his own experiences in slavery and articulates his dignity as a man. Refusing to submit himself to his master, he declares, "You have seen how a man was made a slave; you shall see how a slave was made a man." Although by a century later slavery is no longer present, racial discrimination still intrudes upon every aspect of the lives of African Americans and positions them as "invisible" men. **Ralph Ellison**'s *Invisible Man* (1952) depicts a quest for **identity** within the system of American racism. Ellison's unnamed black narrator's search for self-definition begins with an indictment of racial discrimination: "I am invisible, understand, simply because people refuse to see me." In her novels, Pulitzer and Nobel Prize winner **Toni Morrison** explores the history of racial hatred perpetrated upon black Americans. In her first novel, *The Bluest Eye* (1970), Morrison, also writing from a feminist perspective, describes how racism defines standards of beauty that militate against blacks, women especially, and leads to tragic consequences. That black is not beautiful has been determined by (northern) European standards of blond, blue-eyed beauty. In Morrison's novel, the child Pecola's obsession with Shirley Temple and a desire to have "the bluest eyes" cause her to descend into madness. In her tragic story, Morrison illustrates another form of the soul-killing impact of American racism on African Americans.

Exploring the unspeakable issue of the Japanese American internment, **John Okada**'s *No-No Boy* (1957) was neglected by the American dominant public and unwelcome in the Japanese American community for almost two decades after publication. The disfiguring effects of racism on the individual psyche, the family, the Japanese American community, and other ethnic Americans prevail throughout the novel. The novel also shows that blacks, Japanese, Chinese, Mexicans, Filipinos, and Jews all strive for recognition as complete beings, namely as Americans, but so far few are able to cross the "unseen walls" constructed by racism.

As old as Columbus, American racism is marked by epithets rooted in color ("The Yellow Peril," "the Red threat," "the Brown Menace") and heinous slogans ("A good Indian is a dead Indian"). Although legal statutes supporting racism have been struck down in America, racism's effects nonetheless continue to permeate American letters and society. Once dominant but now operating on the culture's fringes, white supremacy movements are still recurrent phenomena in the United States, as are racist organizations including the Ku Klux Klan, Christian Identity theology, skinheads, and neo-Nazi organizations.

Further Reading

Grice, Helena, et al. *Beginning Ethnic American Literatures.* Manchester, NH: Manchester UP, 2001.

Fu-jen Chen

RAHMAN, AISHAH (1936–)   African American playwright, professor of English at Brown University, and cofounder of Blackberry Production Company. Her birth name was Virginia Hughes, but she changed it after converting to Islam. She began writing plays in the sixth grade, but her professional career started in 1972 with the play *Lady Day: A Musical Tragedy.* In 1988 she received fellowships from the New York Foundation for the Arts and the Rockefeller Foundation. She also won the Doris Abramson Playwriting Award for *Mojo and the Sayso* (1989), which focuses on a family that has to learn to cope with trauma.

Rahman's dramatic language, which relies heavily on music and dance, keeps her apart from the realistic tradition. Although she does employ certain realistic conventions, she is regarded as an avant-garde playwright due to her experimentation with forms. In fact, as part of the Black Theater Movement of the 1960s, Rahman seems to create a new black aesthetic that reconstructs African American art. Most of her plays explore the experience of being black and female in a world that marginalizes and stereotypes both. Like many women of color, Rahman attempts to foreground female voices and recover black women's subjectivities.

The breaking of silence, which is a central concern in many African American women artists, is evident, for example, in her book *Unfinished Women Cry in No Man's Land, While a Bird Dies in a Gilded Cage* (1977), where the voices of several unwed and pregnant women are heard. The women's recollections of how they became pregnant underline their present plight and foreground the pain of the decision to give up their babies for adoption.

In terms of form, *Unfinished Women* is an example of Rahman's **jazz** aesthetic that makes music and dance an essential aspect of her work. More specifically, Charlie Parker's saxophone music that accompanies the play becomes a metaphor for the African American woman's experience, and in the end brings together the living, the unborn, and the dead. Speech, music, and movement participate simultaneously in the creation of meaning, or rather of multiple meanings and experiences.

The themes of pain and separation are also explored in *Chewed Water* (2001), Rahman's successful attempt at prose. Biographical in nature, the book recounts Virginia Hughes's experience of growing up, which culminates in her dramatic decision to give up her three-month-old son, Kevin, for adoption. The story is narrated in an impressionistic way, and the language, vivid and lyrical, records the pain of dispossession while simultaneously painting a romantic portrait of postwar Harlem. (*See also* African American Stereotypes)

Further Reading

Davis, Thadious M. "Aishah Rahman's *Writing in the Dark:* The presence of an Absence." *Obsidian III: Literature in the African Diaspora* 1.1 (1999): 56–72.

Massa, Suzanne Hotte. "Aishah Rahman." *African American Dramatists.* Ed. Emmanuel S. Nelson. Westport, CT: Greenwood Press, 2004. 352–457.

Chrysavgi Papagianni

RAHV, PHILIP (1908–1973)   Jewish American literary critic. Philip Rahv is best known as the cofounder of the main organ of the New York intellectuals circle, *Partisan Review* (1934–2003; Rahv left the magazine in 1970). Born Ivan Greenberg in Kupin, Ukraine (then part of the Russian Empire), he and his family settled in Palestine after the Russian Revolution and civil war. In 1922 Rahv left his parents and joined his older brother in America, where he took a name both westernized (Philip) and emphatically Jewish (Rahv, which means "rabbi"). His intellect and future career were shaped by poverty. Standing in bread lines and sleeping on park benches made him a Marxist; studying alone in the New York Public Library made him an intellectual and critic. Although his theories were rooted in Marxism, Rahv never felt compelled to take the official Communist Party line. Instead he described his guiding critical principle as the historical insight labeled by Friedrich Nietzsche as a "sixth sense."

Partisan Review, founded in 1934 by Rahv and William Phillips, began as an outgrowth of the John Reed Club, an artistic branch of the American Communist Party. The aims of *Partisan Review,* as described in the first edition, were to present revolutionary literary writings both creative and critical, to support the working class, and to defend the Soviet Union. Under Rahv's editorship, works by significant essayists, novelists, and poets filled the pages of the magazine; **Richard Wright, Lionel Trilling**, Edmund Wilson, **James T. Farrell**, John Dos Passos, **Theodore Dreiser**, James Agee, William Carlos Williams, Elizabeth Bishop, Wallace Stevens, and Pablo Picasso are only some of the authors to appear, although their works were not always explicitly political. A few of the major works published in *Partisan Review* include Saul Bellow's novella *Sieze the Day,* sections of T. S. Eliot's poems from *Four Quartets,* and the first translation of Erich Auerbach's critical work *Mimesis.*

In 1937 *Partisan Review* broke away from the Communist Party, remaining Marxist in philosophy while declaring independence from the party line. Rahv sometimes took unpopular positions, whether political, literary, or both. Most people who considered themselves intellectuals held an isolationist position in 1941, when he wrote an editorial in favor of U.S. involvement in World War II. In "Proletarian Literature: A Political Autopsy" (1939), he criticized the genre as the work of a political party disguised as that of the working class; in "**F. Scott Fitzgerald** on the Riviera" (1934) Rahv's Marxist opposition to the wealthy class lovingly portrayed by Fitzgerald did not interfere with what **Mary McCarthy** recalled as a tender and sympathetic review of the novel at hand.

Rahv was not only an editor but a critic of American and Russian literature whose works appeared in his own magazine and elsewhere. His most remembered essay, "Paleface and Redskin" (1939), mapped a division between two schools of American writing exemplified by Henry James and Walt Whitman, two writers of the late nineteenth century who held opposite views about the value of experience and the value of consciousness. Although he does not envision a reconciliation between thoughtful "palefaces" such as James and boisterous "redskins" such as Whitman in the essay, he returns to the question and finds a new resolution in "The Cult of Experience in American Writing" (1940). Here he says that James and Whitman have a common ground in an emphasis on experience in writing, although as "palefaces" and "redskins" they take different approaches. Although early Americans preferred the sacred to the secular world of experience, and Europeans focused more strongly on the intellect, the best feature of modern American writers was in their down-to-earth particulars. For Rahv, this phenomenon is an outgrowth of different historical currents in Europe and America, and he predicts a new strand of literature affected by America's growing engagement with the rest of the world in the twentieth century.

Although primarily a figure of the 1930s, Rahv continued working through his death in 1973, teaching literature at Brandeis University and founding *Modern Occasions* (1970–73), the last 1930s-style intellectual magazine. He lived to complain about the "pornographic" tastes of the 1960s and see the death of the apolitical New Criticism he objected to, although not to complete his own planned volume on the novels of Dostoyevsky.

Further Reading

Cooney, Terry A. *The Rise of the New York Intellectuals: Partisan Review and Its Circle.* Madison: U of Wisconsin P, 1986.

Gilbert, James Burkhart. *Writers and Partisans: A History of Literary Radicalism in America.* New York: Wiley, 1968.

Jaime Cleland

RAISIN IN THE SUN, A **Lorraine Hansberry**'s *A Raisin in the Sun* (1959), whose title comes from a **Langston Hughes** poem, is a groundbreaking play that endowed Hansberry with the distinction of being the first African

American female to have a play produced on Broadway. The play also established Hansberry as the first African American, the first woman, and the youngest American playwright to win the New York Drama Critics Circle Award for Best Play of the Year, and her play helped pave the way for African American as well as female playwrights.

A compassionate domestic drama structured as a well-made play, *A Raisin the Sun* tells the story of the Younger family living in a cramped Southside Chicago slum, yearning for a better life. Their hopes center around a $10,000 life insurance check that the family matriarch Lena (Mama) is due in the wake of her husband's death. Conflicts arise over how to use the money: Mama wants to buy a house for her family and set aside a portion to fund her daughter Beneatha's hope of becoming a doctor; however, her son, **Walter Lee Younger**, dreams of investing in a liquor store, envisioning himself a wealthy businessman. When Mama makes a down payment on a house in a white neighborhood, Walter Lee is furious. But she entrusts the remaining money with Walter Lee, instructing him to set up a fund for his sister's medical education and to put the rest in a bank account in Walter's name.

Meanwhile, a representative from the white community where the Youngers plan to move—Mr. Lindner—attempts to bribe the family into selling back the property at a profit, but his offer is rejected. However, after Walter Lee foolishly turns over the remaining money to a scam artist rather than following Mama's instructions, he is ready to capitulate. But when Lindner arrives to finalize the deal, Walter Lee, galvanized by the strength of his family, announces that he has changed his mind, and the end of the play depicts the Youngers leaving their slum for their new home.

A Raisin in the Sun features characters who, for better or worse, may be considered stereotypes: Mama is the stern matriarchal figure; Walter Lee is the angry young man straining to escape subservience to the white man; Beneatha is struggling to reconnect with her African roots, rejecting the affections of a wealthy but assimilated suitor in favor of a Nigerian lover who wants to take her back to his native village. But the play also reflects Hansberry's own activism in its push towards the future, its sense of racial pride, and the family's daring foray into white territory. Reflecting the contemporary struggles of African Americans to find social acceptance, the play conveys a sense of endurance, survival, and hope. (*See also* African American Drama)

Further Reading

Carter, Steven R. *Hansberry's Drama: Commitment Amid Complexity.* Urbana: U of Illinois P, 1991.

Cheney, Anne. *Lorraine Hansberry.* Boston: Twayne, 1984.

Domina, Lynn. *Understanding "A Raisin in the Sun": A Student Casebook to Issues, Sources, and Historical Documents.* Westport, CT: Greenwood Press, 1998.

Effiong, Philip U. *In Search of a Model for African-American Drama: A Study of Selected Plays by Lorraine Hansberry, Amiri Baraka, and Ntozake Shange.* Lanham, MD: UP of America, 2000.

Kappel, Lawrence, ed. *Readings on "A Raisin in the Sun."* San Diego: Greenhaven Press, 2001.

Karen C. Blansfield

RAKOSI, CARL (1903–2004) Jewish American poet and psychiatric social worker. Rakosi was born in Berlin, Germany, on November 6, 1903, and died a century later in San Francisco. His parents separated while he was still an infant, and he spent his early childhood with his mother's family in Hungary. His father, meanwhile, had immigrated to the United States and remarried. In 1909 Rakosi joined his father's new family in Chicago. It was while studying at the University of Wisconsin in the early 1920s that he began to write poetry and publish it in various magazines. His work drew the attention of some of the major poets at the time—including T. S. Eliot and Ezra Pound—and through his correspondence with them he was introduced to poets who would greatly influence the course of his artistic career: **George Oppen**, **Charles Reznikoff**, and **Louis Zukofsky**.

Rakosi's early poetry reflects his modernist temper as well as his fascination with the English language and its imaginative and symbolic possibilities. His *Two Poems*, published in 1931, reveals his poetic kinship with Eliot and Pound, whose works he greatly admired. By the late 1930s, however, Rakosi—largely because of Zukofsky's encouragement—increasingly began to write poetry in the Objectivist mode. Like his fellow Objectivists, Rakosi suggested that art should reflect objective reality rather than subjective consciousness and that every poem should function as a self-contained linguistic and formal unit. His new poetic credo, however, inevitably led to a major crisis: his incremental politicization during the 1930s, his eventual membership in the Communist Party, and his strident advocacy of Marxism proved fundamentally incompatible with his alignment with the Objectivist movement. The crisis led to his self-imposed silence, and for nearly three decades—from 1941 to 1967—Rakosi abandoned poetry, which, he felt, was an inadequate vehicle to effect radical social change. He resumed poetry writing in the mid-1960s and published six more volumes of poetry. *The Collected Poems of Carl Rakosi*, published in 1986, offers an excellent introduction to work that spans early modern to postmodern eras.

Only recently have critics begun to assess the significance of Rakosi's work in the context of the Jewish tradition in American poetry. In his revealing interview with Burton Hatlen in 1986, Rakosi confesses that he had little awareness of his Jewishness while growing up in Chicago. Only when he was an undergraduate student at the University of Wisconsin, surrounded by Anglo-Saxon students and faculty, did he become increasingly conscious of his Jewish otherness. And his political radicalization during the 1930s was at least partly a response to the genocidal **anti-Semitism** in central Europe. When asked to comment on the impact of his diasporic Jewish consciousness on his poetry, Rakosi identified four elements: "very great moral seriousness," "a sense of moral purpose," an "existential intensity," and a sharply developed sense of "humor and irony" (Hatlen 108).

Further Reading

Hatlen, Barton. "Interview with Carl Rakosi." *Sagetrieb* 5.2 (1986): 95–123.
Heller, Michael, ed. *Carl Rakosi: Man and Poet.* Orono, ME: National Poetry
    Foundation, 1993.

Emmanuel S. Nelson

RAMA RAU, SANTHA (1923–)   Indian American travel writer, novelist, and dramatist. Santha Rama Rau was born in Madras, the child of Sir Benegal Rau, a diplomat who was a leader the movement for Indian independence, and Dhanvanthi Handoo, a Kashmiri Brahmin and a social activist who became an advocate of Indian family planning program. Although, for the most part, Rama Rau has lived and been educated abroad, graduating from Wellesley in 1945, remembrances of life in India and "the strong universe of family" influenced all of her major works.

Home to India is an autobiographical account of both her culture shock on her return to India after college and her growing awareness of herself as an Indian. The book received the Harper Book Find award in 1945. Her grandmothers, strong matriarchs, represent traditional cultural values. In the coming-of-age novel *Remember this House* (1956), the heroine is at first infatuated by the ideal of romantic love embodied in the relationship of an American couple she befriends, but she comes to accept her grandmother's view that love will follow marriage, and chooses a man her family approves. The travel books *East of Home* (1950) and *A View to the Southwest* (1957) explore, in part, negative aspects of **colonialism**, as does her autobiography *Gifts of Passage* (1961). Rama Rau's ability to capture human interest with her entertaining attention to conversation, manners, and customs is evident in this personal narrative, which links together some of her best magazine pieces. Much of her work appeared in popular magazines, such as *Holiday, The New Yorker,* and the *Saturday Review.* Perhaps her most influential writing is her dramatization of E. M. Forster's *Passage to India*, critically applauded in London and New York, and the basis for a motion picture. Judging this version "excellent and sensitive," Forster praised Rama Rau as "an Indian writer of celebrity and distinction"(Rama Rau 63–64).

Further Reading

Gebhard, Ann O. "Santha Rama Rau." *Writers of the Indian Diaspora.* Ed.
    Emmanuel S. Nelson. Westport, CT: Greenwood Press, 1993. 357–62.
Rama Rau, Santha. "Recollections of E. M. Forster." *E. M. Forster: A Tribute.* Ed. K.
    Natwar-Singh. New York: Harcourt, Brace, & World. 1964. 50–64.

Ann O. Gebhard

RAMOS, LUIS ARTURO (1947–)   Ramos has been an associate professor in the Bilingual Spanish/English Graduate Creative Writing Program at the University of Texas, El Paso, which is the only bilingual creative writing masters program in the U.S. since 1992. He has won several national and regional literary prizes in Mexico. Among them, he is the winner of the 1980 Colima Narrative Award for his first novel, *Violeta Peru*, and the 1998 Colima Latin American Narrative Award for his third novel, *Este era un gato*.

Ramos is renowned in the American and Latin American academia for his creative literary work. He is known as one of the most important and talented writers of the Mexican borders. Ramos has published four novels in Spanish, and one of them has been translated into English. He has also published several collections of short stories and critical essays as well as five books of children's literature. In addition, he has written a book of chronicles titled *Crónicas desde el país vecino*. This book is a reflection on the cultural border conflicts between Mexicans and Anglos.

He has published the novels *Violeta Perú, Within These Walls, La mujer que quiso ser Dios*, and *La casa del ahorcado*. Among them, *Within These Walls*, originally titled in Spanish *Entremuros* and retitled in Spain as *La ciudad de arenas*, is one of the most important novels written by the author. In this novel Ramos fictionalizes the history of the Spanish exile in Mexico. Another novel of importance is *Violeta Perú*. In this novel the author plays with the postmodern condition in the life of the main character, whose life fluctuates between cultural borders. Ramos's creative work has transcended the boundaries of his native Mexico. His short stories have been published in almost twenty anthologies in Spanish, English, and German. Luis Arturo Ramos' work reflects the cultural impact of the Mexican American community in the United States and Mexican borders. That is why he has been considered one of the foremost Mexican writers on border literature. In his creative work the struggles of the Mexican community in the border are key elements of the narration and plot.

Ramos's ample knowledge on Chicano and Mexican literature has also placed him among the most outstanding literary critics of Mexican and Mexican American literature in the United States and Mexico. He has served on the editorial board of several literary journals in the United States and Mexico and is a reviewer of *Azatlán*, an important refereed journal dealing with Chicano studies in the United States. He has also been the director of publication and executive editor of the Veracruzana University Press in Mexico. (*See also* Border Narratives)

Further Reading

Contreras, Francisca. "Exilio, Historia y Discurso en Intarmuros de Luis Arturo Ramos." Thesis, Universidad Veracruzana. 1993.

Williams, Raymond, and Blanca Rodriguez. *La narrative postmoderna en Mexico*. Mexico: Universidad Veracruzana, 2002.

Amarilis Hidalgo de Jesús

RAMOS, MANUEL (1948–) Chicano novelist, lawyer, and scholar. Ramos is best known for his crime fiction novels, which draw on his legal training in order to explore the problematic treatment of Chicanos by corrupt legal and political systems.

Ramos was born in Florence, Colorado, into a Mexican American family with links to the Mexican Revolution: One of his grandfathers served in Pancho Villa's army. After gaining a degree in law from the University of Colorado, Ramos subsequently worked as an attorney in the Denver legal aid program, a job that involved giving legal aid to those in dire economic and social need. His promotion to the position of the director of advocacy for Colorado legal services has entailed the overseeing of an extensive legal aid program across the state. This first-hand experience of the law has provided Ramos with an awareness of the criminal underworld and the injustices experienced by the Chicano community. It is this insight that forms the inspiration for his fiction.

Ramos has written a number of detective novels that feature the Chicano lawyer-detective Luis Móntez, who investigates the murky underbelly of the Denver crime scene. This central character is drawn from the hard-drinking, fast-living mould of detectives who inhabit the U.S. hard-boiled genre of crime fiction popularized by writers such as Dashiell Hammett and Raymond Chandler in the 1940s and 1950s. Similarly, Ramos evokes a nightmarish world in which the police are corrupt, the detective is fallible, and violence on the street prevails. However, Ramos introduces a new twist into his fiction by exploring a range of contemporary political issues related to the realities of being Latino in a white-dominated society. Ramos has won several prizes, including the Colorado Book Award and the Chicano/Latino Literary Award, the latter presented to him by the University of California at Irvine.

Ramos' first novel, *The Ballad of Rocky Ruiz* (1993), is set within the context of the Chicano Civil Rights Movement, as it deals with the investigation by the detective Móntez into the deaths of various Chicano political protestors. His second novel, *The Ballad of Gato Guerrero* (1994), continues a political agenda by revealing the problems of domestic abuse, gang violence, and police cruelty. In *The Last Client of Luis Móntez* (1996), Ramos explores the detective's interaction with the criminal drug underworld. Similar themes of racism and urban violence are also explored in his subsequent novels, including *Blues for the Buffalo* (1997) and *Mooney's Road to Hell* (2002). The latter exposes the problems caused by the trafficking of undocumented immigrants. In his most recent work, *Brown on Brown* (2003), Ramos delves into Chicano-Anglo conflicts concerning control over water rights in the Anglo San Luis Valley.

Manuel Ramos continues to publish fiction, practice law, and teach classes in Chicano literature at the Metropolitan State College of Denver.

Further Reading

Ramos, Manuel. "The Postman and the Mex: From Hard-Boiled to *Huevos Rancheros* in Detective Fiction." *Hopscotch: A Cultural Review* 2.4 (2001): 160–67.

Helen Oakley

RANDALL, DUDLEY (1914–2000)   African American poet, founder of the **Broadside Press**, publisher, editor, librarian, and teacher. Born in Washington, DC, he moved to Detroit with his family in the early 1920s. His father, a politically oriented preacher and sometime laborer at Ford, took him to hear African American intellectuals such as **W. E. B. Du Bois**, **James Weldon Johnson**, and **Walter White**; Randall's poetry reflects their political and intellectual legacies as well as the impact of the Great Depression, World War II, and the Black Nationalist and Civil Rights eras. Randall worked as a laborer in the foundry at Ford in Dearborn, Michigan, from 1932 to 1937 and then became a clerk at the post office. He served overseas in the U.S. Army Air Corps from 1943 to 1946. Upon his return home, he earned a BA in English at Wayne State and an MA in Library Science at the University of Michigan in 1951 and began his professional life as a librarian; at the end of his career, he was employed at the University of Detroit, where he was also the poet in residence.

Randall began Broadside Press with twelve dollars of his own funds in 1965; its first publication was his own broadside, "The Ballad of Birmingham," written to commemorate the murder of four girls in a church bombing in that city. Broadside became one of the major institutions of the **Black Arts Movement** of the 1960s and 1970s. It promoted and demonstrated the link between the liberation struggles of black people and the preservation and development of the historical and literary traditions of African Americans. For these reasons, Broadside has been described as the most important black press in America. Broadside provided an alternative to mainstream presses and a venue for both emerging and established black writers who, in turn, supported Randall's efforts; for example, in the late 1960s and early 1970s, **Gwendolyn Brooks** selected Broadside to publish her poems and chose it, over Harper and Row, to publish her autobiography, *Report from Part One* (1972). Broadside also published the work of earlier writers such as **Sterling A. Brown** and brought it to younger generations of readers. Between 1965 and 1985, when Randall sold the press for a second time and retired (from 1977 to 1982, the press was owned by the Alexander Crummell Memorial Church, although Randall remained a consultant), Broadside also published **Nikki Giovanni**, **Etheridge Knight**, **Sonia Sanchez**, Don L. Lee (**Haki R. Madhubuti**), **Margaret Walker**, **Audre Lorde**, **Robert Hayden**, LeRoi Jones (**Amiri Baraka**), **Larry Neal**, and James Emanuel. As this list demonstrates, Broadside published a wide range of poetry and supported and promoted the work of black women writers. Randall also made the publications of the press available to a cross-section of African American readers: The broadside and pamphlet formats were an inexpensive way to disseminate poetry. Broadside also established a Critical Series—publishing the critics Addison Gayle, **Houston Baker Jr.**, and Bernard Bell—sponsored regular poetry readings, and produced recordings.

Randall's own poetry has been described as work that bridges the gap between the **Harlem Renaissance** poets—among them, those who influenced him, **Jean Toomer, Countee Cullen**, and **Paul Laurence Dunbar**— and those of the Black Arts Movement. Ranging from highly formal to free verse, his work incorporates both autobiographical elements and urgent political commentary. Randall's work was published in magazines and several important anthologies, including books edited by **Arna Bontemps** and **Langston Hughes**, in the 1960s. Broadside's first book of poetry, *Poem Counterpoem* (1966), was a collaborative project between Randall and another Detroit poet, **Margaret Danner**. Randall published subsequent books and pamphlets with Broadside, as well as with Madhubuti's Third World Press and another Detroit publisher, Lotus Press. Although an important poet, Randall's legacy is primarily that of Broadside Press and its recognition and support of several generations of African American writers. (*See also* African American Poetry)

Further Reading

Ampadu, Lena. "The Message in the Melody: An Interview with Dudley Randall." *Callaloo* 22.2 (1999): 438–45.

Boyd, Melba Joyce. *Wrestling with the Muse: Dudley Randall and the Broadside Press.* New York: Columbia UP, 2004.

House, Gloria, Albert M. Ward, and Rosemary Weatherston, eds. *A Different Image. The Legacy of Broadside Press: An Anthology.* Detroit: Broadside P and U of Detroit Mercy P, 2004.

Melhem, D. H. "Dudley Randall: A Humanist View." *Black American Literature Forum* 17.4 (1983): 157–67.

Thompson, Julius E. *Dudley Randall, Broadside Press, and the Black Arts Movement in Detroit, 1960–1995.* Jefferson: McFarland, 1999.

Robin Lucy

RANDALL, MARGARET (1936–)   Jewish American essayist, poet, political commentator, and activist. Margaret Randall was born in New York City in 1936. Originally her last name was Reinthal, but her parents, because of their anti-Semitic self-loathing, changed their family name to Randall. Although Randall was not raised as a Jew, she has tried to make her four children aware of their Jewish heritage and has tried to keep the history alive for them.

At the age of eleven she and her family moved from New York City to Albuquerque, New Mexico, where she attended public schools. She spent one year at the University of Mexico before leaving the United States for Spain. After her year abroad she moved to her birthplace of New York City, where she pursued her writing career. In 1961 she moved to Mexico with her ten-month-old son. Subsequently, in 1966, Randall became a Mexican citizen. For twenty-three years she lived outside of the United States, in Mexico, Cuba, and Nicaragua.

Randall moved to Mexico with the hope that she would find an environment where she would be able to concentrate on her writing and her son simultaneously. While in Mexico she coedited the bilingual journal, *El*

Corno Emplumado. Published quarterly, the journal included works from writers all over Latin America in three sections: the prose, the letters, and the poetry. All three segments explored the political and personal realms of the contributors. She also gave birth to three daughters and published several volumes of poetry and prose while there.

In 1969 Randall left Mexico with her four children and relocated in Cuba. While there, she worked for the Cuban Book Institute. She also started to focus on women and their oral history in her writing and photography. She began to document the lives and struggles of Cuban women and, in 1972, published *La Mujer Cubana Ahora.*

The year 1980 took Margaret Randall from Cuba to Nicaragua, where she continued to concentrate on the lives of the women around her. She recorded the first-hand stories of Nicaraguan women while living there in her book *Sandino's Daughters: Testimonies of Nicaraguan Women in Struggle* (1981).

In January of 1984 Randall decided to return to the United States and began to teach Women's Studies and American Studies at the University of New Mexico. A few months after her arrival in her native country, she made up her mind that she would like to stay there. However, when she took out Mexican nationality in 1966, she unknowingly lost her United States citizenship. She was forced to apply for permanent resident status.

The United States **Immigration** and Naturalization Service, after forcing Randall to wait seventeen months, denied her petition for permanent residency. The reason for their decision was based on the McCarran-Walter Immigration, Naturalization, and Nationality Act of 1952. This act empowered the Department of Justice to deport immigrants or naturalized citizens engaging in subversive activities. Because Randall had exercised her First Amendment right to freedom of speech and criticized the U.S. policies in Vietnam and Central America as well as publishing writings that disagreed with the ideologies of the government, she was given twenty-eight days to leave her country.

She did not leave, however. She stayed on to fight; numerous writers defended her right to live in the United States. During this time she published a collection of poetry, *The Coming Home Poems* (1986). The proceeds from the sale of the book were donated to a legal defense fund in Margaret Randall's name. This collection includes poems before and after she returned to the United States. Several of them are autobiographical meditations on her changing relationship with her country and poignant explorations of complex shifts in her own personal and political consciousness.

Her following collection of poetry, *Memory Says Yes* (1988), touches on these subjects but delves deeper into Randall's political beliefs. Poems such as "Letter from Managua: one and two," show her political outrage as to the United States government's interventions in Nicaragua. As well, *Memory Says Yes* has poems that address her grandfather who sexually abused her.

The abuse she went through is further discussed in Randall's 1987 autobiographical nonfiction work, *This Is About Incest.* The book starts with prose sections that describe different stages of how she came to terms with her abuse. "This is about language," she titles one of the sections, and another as "This is about art." Here she recalls memories of abuse, silence, and shame and the incremental healing process. The next section of the book includes poems such as "The Second Photograph," in which she works through her anger toward her grandfather, a Christian Science practitioner who used his power to take advantage of her. Photographs of her grandfather are integrated with the poetry. Some are the originals and others have been modified by Randall to express her pain and anger. A number of them include images of mushrooms, which she had always been frightened of, she believes, because of their phallic resemblance.

Part of the Solution/Portrait of a Revolutionary (1973) is also an autobiographical book by Randall. The introduction is written by Robert Cohen, another North American expatriate living in Latin America and father of her youngest daughter, Anna. The book has excerpts from her diary from when she was living in Cuba. It reveals the effects that the revolution and the socialist society had on her life and her ways of thinking about her own and the government's place in the public. It also includes more of her poetry and essays that she wrote during this period in her life. She also includes a section of translations of Latin American revolutionary writers, such as León Felipe, Leonel Rugana, and Carlos Maria Gutiérrez. And, significantly, some of the essays are intensely personal: They focus on her lesbianism that she had concealed from the public for many years.

Further Reading

Byrd, Carole. "The Voices and Lives of Latin American Women Writers." *Feminist Collections* 18 (Fall 1996): 8–12.

Byrne, Judith. "Getting Our Money's Worth." *Lesbian Review of Books* 3 (Spring 1997): 18.

Molyneux, Maxine. "Not So Dutiful Daughters." *Women's Review of Books* 11 (September 1994): 18.

Katherine M. Miller-Corcoran

RAPHAEL, LEV (1954–)   Jewish American novelist and essayist. Although Lev Raphael is the author of several popular academic mysteries featuring Nick Hoffman, it is his short story collection *Dancing on Tisha B'Av* (1990) and the novels *Winter Eyes* (1992) and *The German Money* (2003) that have earned him a distinctive place in the contemporary Jewish literary **canon**. As a child of **Holocaust** survivors and as a gay man, he writes about the destruction wrought by cultures of shame and secrecy as well as the joys and challenges of coming out and coming home to Jewish communities.

In his autobiographical collection of essays, *Journeys and Arrivals: On Being Gay and Jewish* (1996), Raphael chronicles growing up in a home haunted by the Holocaust and his estrangement from an affirmative Jewish life until he reached adulthood. Significantly, the challenges of his early life shaped his literary mission: Like many second-generation writers, he views his fiction as Jewish memory work; he also sees his writing as a bridge between Jewish and queer communities. Both the title story of *Dancing on Tisha B'Av* as well as "Abominations," the final story of the collection, focus on Nat, his new lover Marc, and Brenda, Nat's sister. In the title story, Nat and Marc are exiled from their Orthodox community when it is discovered that they are gay. Nat's response to this expulsion is to go dancing on Tisha B'Av, the solemn fast day that commemorates the destruction of the Second Temple. Significantly, Brenda finds her brother's sexuality more discomforting than the homophobia that disallows him from embracing all parts of his self. However, in "Abominations," Brenda's consciousness is raised by a continuum of hate crimes; when Nat's dorm room is destroyed as a result of arson, Brenda links the violence of homophobia to that of **anti-Semitism** and becomes an ally. Thus Raphael counters the abominations of hate with a developing narrative of solidarity.

Like most second-generation writers, Lev Raphael is haunted not only by the past but also by the dangers of literary witnessing from the historical and geographical distance of contemporary America. The narrator of "The Tanteh" is a high school senior who uses his Great Aunt Rose's Holocaust memories as material for an English assignment that is subsequently published in the school's yearbook. After reading this story, the Tanteh is plagued by nightmares and flees the only family home she knows in order to return to Europe. She dies in Prague. Shortly after her death, the narrator receives a postcard that she had written before her death; in that short missive, she excoriates him for stealing her story. Here Raphael explores the boundary between memorialization and appropriation.

In *The German Money,* a novel that took twenty years to write (and had its earliest incarnation in the short story "Inheritance"), Raphael returns to the question of appropriating the Holocaust. Paul, the narrator of the novel, is forced to confront his past when his mother, Rose, unexpectedly dies and leaves him the money that was paid to her by the German government. Given his estrangement from his cold, silent mother, Paul strives to understand her motivation for leaving him this legacy. Through Mrs. Gordon, his mother's elderly neighbor, Paul discovers that the silence with which he was raised was not that of suffering but rather that of fear: His mother had assumed the identity of a woman who had died in a camp. For stealing the life story of Mrs. Gordon's best friend in the Vilna ghetto, Rose is sentenced to death: Mrs. Gordon confesses to Paul that she murdered his mother. Ultimately, Raphael mobilizes conventions of the mystery genre to indict those who desecrate Holocaust memory.

Dancing on Tisha B'Av was the winner of the 1991 Lambda Literary Award; that short story collection as well as his novels *Winter Eyes* and *The German Money* has received critical attention from scholars working on Holocaust literature. Thus Raphael's work has become one of the bridges linking Jewish and queer literary studies. (*See also* Jewish American Gay Literature)

Further Reading

Berger, Alan L. *Children of Job: American Second-Generation Witnesses to the Holocaust.* Albany: State U of New York P, 1997.

Buchbinder, David. Gaiety on Tisha B'Av: Sexuality, Subjectivity and Narrative Closure in the Work of Lev Raphael. *Canadian Review of American Studies* 28.2 (1998): 163–76.

Helene Meyers

RAY A. YOUNG BEAR (1950–) Native American poet and novelist. For more than three decades, the poetry of Ray A. Young Bear, one of the most prominent voices of the Native American Renaissance, has appeared in prestigious American literary journals and Native literature anthologies. A member of the Meskwaki Nation of central Iowa, Young Bear grew up in the Tribal Settlement in Tama County, where he and his wife Stella live today. The settlement, which is not a federal Indian reservation, is unique. The purchase of land along the Iowa River in 1856 by Young Bear's great-great-grandfather, a Sacred Chieftain, enabled the People of the Red Earth to return to the eastern woodlands after their forced federal relocation to the Kansas prairies. The tribal community remains tightly knit. In 1993 Young Bear, who attended Pomona College and several Iowa universities, was awarded an honorary doctorate in letters by Luther College. He has taught as a visiting faculty member at The Institute of American Indian Arts, Eastern Washington University, the University of Iowa, and Iowa State University, as well as the Meskwaki Indian Elementary School.

Young Bear's first language was Meskwaki, and he composed his early poems in Meskwaki, afterwards translating them into English. Tribal language and culture remain profoundly important to him. In 1983 he and his wife cofounded the drum and dance group now called Black Eagle Child, and Young Bear frequently opens his readings with traditional Meskwaki songs of his own composition. Several of these have been published in bilingual versions. Young Bear also incorporates bilingual dialogue into his fiction. His publications include four books of poetry—*Waiting to Be Fed* (1975), *Winter of the Salamander: The Keeper of Importance* (1980), *The Invisible Musician* (1990), and *The Rock Island Hiking Club* (2001)—a fictional autobiography in poetry and prose, *Black Eagle Child: The Facepaint Narratives* (1992), and a closely related novel, *Remnants of the First Earth* (1996), which received the 1997 Ruth Suckow Award.

In his work Young Bear strives to maintain a balance between a need to incorporate the tribal worldview and a need to protect Native spirituality. This balancing act is the essence of "The Significance of the Water Animal." Young Bear invokes the elements of life on earth as physical reality growing seamlessly out of an old story. The faith that grounds this story, ultimately, is a faith in constant change. Young Bear's early poems offer glimpses into an elusive reality grounded in the logic of dream, where images shift suddenly. They are almost inexplicable lyric narratives weighted by deep sorrow. His later poems tell stories from his life.

Perhaps the most accessible key to Young Bear's work is the multi-genre **trickster** narrative, *Black Eagle Child: The Facepaint Narratives.* Laced with pop culture references and psychedelic rock lyrics, it reads like a roisterous science fiction comedy, complete with supernatural strobe light. Time spins forward and backward as Edgar Bearchild finds his place in, and ultimately disappears into, the stories of the Black Eagle Child community. Like many small communities with horny teenagers, sexual secrets, petty jealousies, and rigid pecking order, Black Eagle Child is also the kind of place where a car can outwit the police in a hot pursuit. If Junior Pipestar flees the settlement, Edgar Bearchild keeps returning. He is returning for the first time when this irreverently reverent chronicle of the supernatural begins. Edgar's exploration of tribal spirituality begins on Thanksgiving 1965. He is fourteen when he is guided through his first hallucinogenic experience by the elders of the local Well-Off Man Church, a thinly disguised version of the Native American Church. Edgar is a full-time working writer when, ten years later, Young Bear's story shifts from poetry to prose, sketching details of tribal and personal history and fast-forwarding to 1987 and Edgar's chance sighting of a long-lost buddy at a tribal celebration in Washington State. Time circles back, quickly, however, when Edgar notes that his friend died in a car wreck in 1976. When this story finally shifts back to poetry, Edgar himself is invisible, subsumed in stories of community healers and witches, the bewitched and the healed. *Remnants of the First Earth* continues Edgar's saga in prose fiction. (*See also* Native American Mythology)

Further Reading

Bruchac, Joseph. "Connected to the Past: An Interview with Ray A. Young Bear." *Survival This Way: Interviews with American Indian Poets.* Tucson: U of Arizona P, 1987. 337–48.

Ellefson, Elias. "An Interview with Ray Young Bear." *Speaking of the Short Story.* Ed. Farhat Iftekharuddin, Mary Rohrberger, and Maurice Lee. Jackson: UP of Mississippi, 1997. 35–44.

Linda Lizut Helstern

RECHY, JOHN (1931–) Mexican American novelist. John Rechy, who was born Juan Francisco Rechy in El Paso, Texas, on March 10, 1931, first came to prominence in the 1960s as the author of sexually explicit depictions of homosexual subculture. Most early critics concentrated on the shocking and strongly autobiographical subject matter of his novels—Rechy used his extensive experiences as a male hustler as the basis for his fiction—and soon the author was labeled a gay writer. Rechy has stated that he does not like labels of any sort and hopes that eventually he will just be considered a writer who is gay. Recently, Rechy's substantial contributions to Chicano literature have been recognized, as has his role as a regional writer with the focus on Los Angeles, the "City of Lost Angels." Although Rechy has been gratified that he has finally been accepted as a Chicano writer, he has always seen himself as an outsider, an outlaw. In some of his interviews he has conceded that he has never seen himself totally fitting in the gay or the Chicano world.

Early in his career Rechy was not only labeled a gay writer but also an accidental one because the documentary style of his first novels gave critics the false impression that Rechy was lacking craftsmanship and artistry. Rechy has therefore felt the need to defend himself, and he has stressed on numerous occasions that he considers himself a literary writer and that all of his books are consciously structured and have undergone numerous revisions. Without false modesty he has stated that he is an excellent writer, a writer who is as good as any other writing today, and much better than most. The fact that he recently received several lifetime achievement awards is a sign that the importance of his oeuvre is finally being recognized. In 1997 he was honored by the PEN Center USA-West; in 1999 he received the Publishing Triangle's William Whitehead Lifetime Achievement Award; and in 2001 he received an award from the University of Southern California.

A close look at Rechy's novels reveals that they are indeed carefully structured and that they are a part of a long literary tradition. Essentially, all of Rechy's works are quest narratives using elements of the picaresque novel and the bildungsroman as well as Gothic literature. The author told Ramon Renteria of the *El Paso Times* that he enjoys the challenge of taking a very old form and making it seem modern. Rechy's protagonists are in a never-ending search for (sexual) **identity**, salvation, redemption, and grace. *City of Night* (1963), Rechy's groundbreaking first novel, established the pattern. The unnamed narrator traverses the United States, exploring the homosexual subculture in New York, Los Angeles, and New Orleans in search of self-affirmation and sexual identity, and meeting various colorful characters along the way, the most memorable of whom is Miss Destiny, a drag queen. The book's protagonist is a hustler who sells his body to other men and who refuses to show any affection to his clients. Being a Chicano man, he is confined to a world of machismo, which only permits a sexually active role. Patrick O'Connor has shown that this stereotype of Latin masculinity, personified by the nameless narrator, together with the stereotype of Latin femininity, the Latin drag queen, connect Rechy's book to Latino literature. The novel, which had its origin in a letter that described Rechy's experiences during carnival season in New Orleans and which he reworked into the short story "Mardi Gras" (published in the progressive *Evergreen Review*), was a commercial success but took an initial drubbing by the critics. Rechy was especially incensed by Alfred Chester's vitriolic review for the *New York Review of Books,* which was titled "Fruit Salad" and which questioned the existence of the author. Another critic who savaged Rechy's novel was Peter Buitenhuis, who wrote in the June 30, 1963, edition of the *New York Times Book*

Review, "Mr. Rechy can hardly be called a novelist. He lacks the art to shape experience into developing narrative; he has little of the craftsmanship, nothing of the detached lucidity which makes the true novelist" (3).

Rechy was not deterred by such criticism and, in 1967, published *Numbers,* which can be considered a sequel to *City of Night* and which, according to Rechy's biographer Charles Casillo, is based on the author's experiences while traveling to Los Angeles with his beloved mother Guadalupe. While his mother was staying with his sister in Torrance, Rechy went on a ten-day sexual binge in order to prove to himself that he was still a sexual magnet. Like his creator, Johnny Rio, the protagonist of *Numbers,* sets himself a goal of thirty sexual conquests—hence the title of the novel—in an attempt to reaffirm his desirability and to keep the damaging effects of time at bay. Casillo has pointed out that the death Rechy describes in *Numbers* is the "death of youth" (181). *This Day's Death* (1969), which Rechy considers the worst book he ever wrote, is based on the author's close relationship with his strong-willed but ailing mother and his arrest in Griffith Park in Los Angeles for public indecency. Jim Girard, the novel's protagonist, divides his time between caring for his ill mother in El Paso and defending himself in Los Angeles against the unfounded charges. According to Casillo, Girard thus faces two kinds of prison: the metaphorical one of his suffocating relationship with his mother and the real one he might have to enter as a result of the trial (197).

Having explored the homosexual subculture in detail in his first three novels, Rechy expanded his themes in his next novels. *The Vampires* (1971), one of the author's personal favorites, shows the influence of Edgar Allen Poe, comic strips, and Hollywood films and is based on Rechy's visit to the secluded Chicago mansion of a wealthy heterosexual admirer. In the operatic novel dozens of colorful characters play dangerous, sadomasochistic mental games initiated by Richard, the mansion's eccentric owner, and Malissa, a mysterious, witchlike woman. *The Fourth Angel* (1972) refers to Jerry, a sixteen-year-old, who, like the novel's author, is mourning the recent death of his mother and who joins a group of hardened teenagers. These "lost angels" are led by a girl, Shell, who invents cruel mind games with strangers in order to keep boredom at bay and who takes drugs in order to cope with emotional pain. *Bodies and Souls* (1983), which David William Foster has called one of the very best contemporary novels about Los Angeles, "a sort of urban Pilgrim's Progress" (*Studies in 20th Century Literature* 25 [Winter 2001]: 196), also features several disillusioned teenagers who have traveled to the City of Angels in search for a modern paradise promising salvation only to be obliterated in a bloody shootout on a freeway overpass. Rechy stated in the introduction to the 2001 reprint of the novel that Los Angeles is a main character in many of his novels, and in this one a central character throughout. It was his intention "to explore beneath the clichés too often expressed about Los Angeles: its spurious obsession with artifice, not substance, its lack of defining center, its courtship of extremity, its mindless narcissism—that is, its want of profundity, of soul." As an homage to Hollywood, Rechy reproduced scenes from classic movies with the intention to "strip away romance and sentimentality from the old films in order to expose camouflaged violence." He conceived *Bodies and Souls* as an alternating series of Technicolor and black-and-white scenes.

The Sexual Outlaw (1977), subtitled *A Non-Fiction Account, with Commentary of Three Days and Nights in the Sexual Underground,* also employs cinematic elements. Rechy described the book as "the literary equivalent of a film documentary influenced by Robbe-Grillet's theories on the new novel. Plotless and black-and-white, it is a minute-by-minute accounting of three days and three nights of anonymous sex as Jim roams the sexual underground of Los Angeles" (Casillo 252). The book was conceived as a powerful statement of gay rage against heterosexual fascism and as a provocative defense of promiscuity. Because Rechy characterized *The Sexual Outlaw* as "a documentary," this book has sometimes been ignored in studies of the author's fiction. For Rechy, however, the line of fiction and nonfiction is blurred, and he does not see any rigid separation, as he told Richard Canning. One of his works-in-progress is tellingly titled *Autobiography: A Novel.* The title of Rechy's 1979 novel, *Rushes*, directly alludes to its connection with the cinema: Rushes is not only the name of the gay bar that serves as the book's setting, it also refers to film footage shot during a given day without editing or soundtrack. Rechy combines cinematic elements with allusions to the Catholic mass and the Stations of the Cross in *Rushes.* It was intended as an allegory on the destructiveness of Christian rituals as well as an examination the self-hatred of gay men caused by heterosexual oppression. Considering Rechy's strong political engagement, it is surprising that he has not explicitly dealt with the devastating AIDS pandemic. He comes close to dealing with the subject in *The Coming of the Night* (1999), which describes the sexual odyssey of a large cast of characters during a single day in the summer of 1981 in Los Angeles. While alluding to the approaching crisis in the title and mentioning "a strange illness . . . Something mysterious, something new, something terrible," Rechy seems to give the reader the impression that time has stopped in the early 1980s. Consequently, O'Connor has called the book "not only a disappointment but a significant one" (416). Rechy has indicated that *Autobiography*, his work-in-progress, will directly deal with AIDS.

In the late 1980s and early 1990s, Rechy created a cycle of novels featuring memorable female characters. *Marilyn's Daughter* (1988) describes the quest of Normalyn Morgan, a young woman from Gibson, Texas, for her true identity. Normalyn is raised by Enid Morgan, one of Marilyn Monroe's closest friends, and when Enid commits suicide she leaves a note for Normalyn that states Marilyn Monroe is her real mother. Normalyn's quest leads her to Los Angeles, where she encounters an array of colorful characters, among them a gang of teenagers called the Dead Movie Stars, reminiscent of the groups of alienated youths in previous novels. *The*

Miraculous Day of Amalia Gomez (1991), which is Rechy's most overtly Latino book, revolves around a twice-divorced Mexican American woman in Los Angeles who searches for meaning in her life after she witnesses the apparition of a cross in the sky. Rechy describes the book's origin in the introduction to the 2001 edition as follows: "On a spring day in Los Angeles, I looked up into a clear sky and saw two wisps of clouds intersect to form a very discernible cross. I watched until a breeze smeared the impression. What would one of the Mexican American women I grew up among think if she had seen that cross? What if such a woman's life was in crisis? Would she see that cross as a desperate sign of hope?" Religious elements also abound in *Our Lady of Babylon* (1996), which is based on the book of Revelation and which deals with the fate of fallen women throughout the ages. Rechy's most recent novel, *The Life and Adventures of Lyle Clemens* (2003), a picaresque bildungsroman inspired by Henry Fielding's *The History of Tom Jones* (1749), describes the hilarious trials and tribulations handsome, naive, and—for a change—heterosexual Lyle has to endure in artificial and seductive Las Vegas and Los Angeles before he can discover his real self. The novel proves yet again Rechy's ability to recast old literary conventions into something original and new. (*See also* Mexican American Gay Literature)

Further Reading

Bredbeck, Gregory W. "John Rechy." *Contemporary Gay American Novelists.* Ed. Emmanuel S. Nelson. Westport, CT: Greenwood Press, 1993. 340–51.

Casillo, Charles. *Outlaw: The Lives and Careers of John Rechy.* Los Angeles: Advocate Books, 2002.

O'Connor, Patrick. "John Rechy." *Latino & Latina Writers.* Ed. Alan West-Duran. New York: Charles Scribner's Sons, 2004. Vol. 1, 405–23.

Karl L. Stenger

REDDING, J. SAUNDERS (1906–1988)   African American literary critic, social historian, novelist, and anthologist. He published eight books, among them one novel; along with Arthur P. Davis he edited a highly influential anthology, *Cavalcade: Negro American Writing from 1760 to the Present* (1971).

His parents both graduated from Howard University, and Redding attended Lincoln University for one year before joining his brother Louis (later a lawyer) at Brown University in 1924. Fired after teaching three years at Morehead College in Atlanta, he returned to Brown and received his MA in 1932. In 1933 he had a graduate fellowship to Columbia University, and in 1936 became chairman of the English department at Southern University in Baton Rouge, Louisiana. In 1944 he received North Carolina's Mayflower Cup Award for the best book of the year. He received a Guggenheim Fellowship in 1944, and in 1949 Brown University invited him to be a visiting professor. Ultimately, he became the Ernest I. White Professor of American Studies and Humane Letters at Cornell University.

His first book, *To Make a Poet Black* (1939), traces the development of black literature from 1970 to the 1930s. He shows, period by period, how the "purpose or necessity" of historical circumstances shaped a practical rather than a speculative literature. Chronologically, he analyzes the evolution of African American literature from the forerunners, including **Phyllis Wheatley**, to the **New Negro** and ending with such folk artists as **Sterling Brown** and **Zora Neale Hurston**.

To Make a Poet Black, the title of which is taken from a poem by **Countee Cullen**, foreshadows later themes in Redding's work. A pervasive concern is the conflict between the conservative philosophy of **Booker T. Washington** and the progressive philosophy of **W. E. B. Du Bois**. In the national debate between these two **race** leaders, Redding was committed to integration, but, like Washington, he believed African Americans are "earth-proud" people who must reestablish a spiritual connection with their agrarian roots. Consequently, toward the end of *To Make a Poet Black*, he rejects the sensationalism and escapism of the **Harlem Renaissance** and lauds the folk writers who are returning to the Southern scene and the more representative vernacular of the people.

No Day of Triumph (1942) was written after Redding received a Rockefeller Fellowship in 1940 that allowed him to make an investigative tour of the South. It contains a beautifully written forty-two page autobiographical introduction in which we learn the legacy of his two grandmothers, one sternly and bitterly black, the other conscious of her light pigmentation. His parents were hard-working middle-class people, the first to buy a home on an all-white street in Wilmington, Delaware. His father was a teacher then a postal worker who, to afford a large family, worked cutting corn during summer vacation. The family had striven so hard to improve themselves that it took some adjustment—especially on the part of his mother—to accept the change of the rest of the street to black ownership a few years later.

The rest of *No Day of Triumph* is devoted to Redding's odyssey—both physical and spiritual—throughout the South to recover the "lusty stream of culture which had nourished us." In the course of his travels, he encounters white bigots, self-absorbed black doctors, snobbish Negro collegians, friendly farmers, and many others in the complex fabric of American life. Ultimately, he decides we do not have a black problem or even a white problem but a profoundly complicated human situation; and he rediscovers that his **race**'s core values reflect the highest common denominator shared by all people: "integrity of spirit, love of freedom, courage, patience, hope."

His only novel, *Stranger and Alone* (1950), allows Redding to return to some of the major concerns of his earlier work. Sheldon Howden, the main character, is alone because he remains a stranger to fellow blacks and their collective best interests. The book, which appeared two years before **Ralph Ellison**'s *Invisible Man*, portrays Sheldon as a Dr. Bledsoe–like figure in the late 1930s and early 1940s. In a time of economic and social flux—the

Depression and World War II—Sheldon clings to the notion that he can attain individual power at the expense of other blacks if he can subtly manipulate whites into thinking he is doing their bidding. But in the process, he *does* do their bidding.

His relationships with his wife, Nan, and his mistress, Gerry, demonstrate his ethical emptiness. On racial issues he is morally bankrupt as well. He is too busy protecting his position as state superintendent of Negro schools to protest grossly inequitable social conditions in the South. One of the central images of the novel—the county courthouse clock that has not run for years—symbolizes Sheldon's inability (or unwillingness) to change. He aspires to be white because he does not "know what time it is on the clock of the world." *Stranger and Alone* ends with the betrayal of his fellow blacks who have organized a mass registration of voters. In the racial war, Sheldon is a Black Quisling.

They Came in Chains: Americans from Africa (1950) brims with historical facts and sociological analysis tracing the advent of **slavery** on pre-U.S. territory in 1619 up to the post–World War II era. The book ends with a chapter on "The Larger Hope," paying tribute to President Truman and "courageous and outspoken Eleanor Roosevelt," who along with other forward-thinking Americans betokened the promise of social equality.

Redding began *On Being Negro in America* (1951) by saying: "This is personal." It is, in fact, an intensely personal argument for integration three years before the U.S. Supreme Court decision in *Linda Brown vs. the Board of Education of Topeka, Kansas*. He tells of being frozen between two contending impulses—to help and to avoid—as he watched a white woman die in the snow. He goes on to analyze the psychological impact of historical events on racial reality. But he does not want the human crisis solved by the slow process of historical inevitability; he wants to solve the disease of segregation immediately. At the time, his position—although he was self-avowedly Christian and patriotic—was considered audaciously radical.

In 1952 the U.S. State Department sent Redding on what it called a temporary foreign assignment. In 1954 he published *An American in India*, a personal reaction to the newly independent nation, officially nonaligned but flirting with Communism. He predicted ongoing dilemmas for India.

The Lonesome Road (1958) devotes chapters to **Sojourner Truth**, **Frederick Douglass**, Daniel Hale Williams, W. E. B. Du Bois, **Marcus Garvey**, Paul Robeson, and Joe Louis, among others. The following year Redding received his second Guggenheim Fellowship and engaged in a much publicized symposium—the First Conference of Negro Writers—at which he delivered "The American Negro Writer and His Roots." His last book *The Negro* (1967), billed as a concise survey, deals forthrightly with the dehumanizing agency of slavery but ends with the hope that the Lyndon Johnson administration will usher in a new era of social justice.

Toward the end of his career, Redding directed the National Endowment for the Humanities' division of research and publications. He also received numerous academic honors and recognition for his personal and scholarly investigations of race in America. (*See also* African American Autobiography)

Further Reading

Berry, Faith. "Saunders Redding as Literary Critic of Langston Hughes." *Langston Hughes Review* 5.2 (1988): 24–28

Gates, Henry Louis, Jr. "Introduction." *To Make a Poet Black*. Ithaca: Cornell UP, 1988. vii–xxviii.

Savery, Pancho. "'Git a Stool. Let Me Tell You Something': Call and Response in *No Day of Triumph*." *Black American Literature Forum* 24 (Summer 1990).

Leonard J. Deutsch

REED, ISHMAEL (1938–) African American novelist, poet, songwriter, satirist, essayist, playwright, and editor. Winner of the MacArthur Genius Award, Ishmael Reed is a man of many talents. His most significant achievements are his innovative, multidimensional novels, especially *Mumbo Jumbo* (1972), which was nominated for the National Book Award, and *The Last Days of Louisiana Red* (1974), which earned Reed the 1975 Rosenthal Award from the National Institute of Arts and Letters. However, he has also produced several remarkable volumes of poetry, one of which, *Conjure* (1972), was nominated for the National Book Award. Some of his poetry and songs have been set to music by Kip Hanrahan and recorded. Reed also took these poems and songs on a European tour with the Ishmael Reed Band. In addition, he has written and staged plays and operas as well as edited numerous anthologies, many of which are multiethnic. Along with several other writers of color, Reed cofounded the Before Columbus Foundation, which issues the American Book Awards.

Reed's novels were experimental and satirical from the outset. His first novel, *The Free-Lance Pallbearers* (1967), depicted a dictator named Harry Sam who ruled a country bearing his name, indicating how much he controlled it. Harry Sam spoke with a Texas accent, held barbecues, and kept disappearing into an outhouse from which his excrement flowed over the country. Although Harry Sam was recognizably Lyndon Johnson, and the novel offered a commentary on the Vietnam War, his actions and their consequences updated the Greek and Shakespearean concept that the character of the ruler determined the spiritual welfare of the country and that corruption at the top could lead to spiritual illness throughout.

Reed's second novel, *Yellow Back Radio Broke-Down* (1969), was a broadside in his cultural war with the historical establishment. His protagonist, a black Hoodoo cowboy named the Loop Garoo Kid, took on not only rancher businessman Drag Gibson and the Pope but also various established views about the "winning" and "civilizing" of the West by whites. The anachronistic use of a helicopter by the Kid's Indian ally Chief Showcase implied the inseparability of past and present in American society. Reed made this point in a similar way in his novel *Flight to Canada* (1976), in which his slave/writer Raven Quickskill fled to Canada in a commercial airplane. Reed implied that the greed and lust for power that underlay **slavery** continue today in corporate America. He challenged both historical "truths" and contemporary business morality by depicting Quickskill's master Arthur Swille behaving like a modern lobbyist by loaning money to both confederate leaders and Abraham Lincoln so that he would continue to profit no matter who won.

Reed's greatest challenge to historians was in *Mumbo Jumbo*, in which he assaulted the Eurocentric slant on Western Civilization from Ancient Egypt to the present. In his view, the central conflict was between two churches: the Western church, presided over by a glum Christ, and the African church, inspired but not controlled by a dancing Osiris. The militant arm of the Western church was the Wallflower Order, composed of those who cannot dance and use force to keep others from doing so. The Order's enemy was the Jes Grew Movement, a benevolent virus that infected people with the desire to express themselves in creative and often jubilant ways. Reed opposed any monolithic social structure, preferring pluralism and multiculturalism.

In writing *Mumbo Jumbo*, Reed used and lovingly parodied the conventions of detective fiction, in the same way that he employed the conventions of the western in *Yellow Back Radio Broke-down* and of the **slave narrative** in *Flight to Canada*. He has regarded all of these as forms of popular expression sneered at by the standard bearers of a repressive culture. He was also drawn to slang for the same reason. Detective fiction is the popular form that seems to have attracted him the most, because he also used it in several other novels: *The Last Days of Louisiana Red* (1974), *The Terrible Twos* (1982), *Reckless Eyeballing* (1986), and *The Terrible Threes* (1989). However, he has usually blended it with satire and sometimes with science fiction.

In *The Last Days of Louisiana Red*, Reed employed one of the same spiritual detectives that he used in *Mumbo Jumbo*—Papa Labas—but the spiritual illness of Western Civilization that he tracked down this time was somewhat different. Louisiana Red and its subsidiary disease, Moocherism, involved the many ways oppressed workers and self-proclaimed revolutionaries fought and tormented each other while their true enemies, capitalist billionaires, went about their business untouched. For example, feminist rebel Minnie Yellings (the pun is intentional) was shown to be a descendent of both Cab Calloway's Minnie the Moocher and Sophocles' Antigone, and her protest activities were exposed as parasitical because she invariably shouted down the voice of people she claimed to represent.

Reed continued to applaud humanity's multiplicity of talents and cultures and to stress the importance of seeking durable values in pre-Western and non-Western sources such as Ancient Egyptian religion and Voodoo in *The Last Days of Louisiana Red*. However, he added Confucianism to his non-Western values this time, and this altered his perspective a bit. Instead of focusing on boisterous outbursts of joy as with Jes Grew, he depicted the quieter pleasures of listening to soft **jazz** piano music and playing chess and asked that people show consideration to each other.

Reed's satire on feminist Minnie Yellings provoked the first wave of feminist protests against his writing. *Reckless Eyeballing,* which portrayed Eva Braun as having survived World War II and become an arbiter of feminist literary expression, raised these protests to the level of tidal waves and he was frequently denounced as a misogynist. Reed has argued in a number of essays that he was only attacking certain excesses of **feminism**, particularly white feminism, and pointed out that his works have been supported by a number of black feminists. His more recent play *The Preacher and the Rapper* (2000) even skewered the anti-woman attitudes of both rap music and the Judeo-Christian-Islamic religious traditions. At the end of the play, the preacher Reverend Jack Legge, while remaining a Christian, was converted to a prochoice, anti-male chauvinist position. The rapper too abandoned his sexism and insensitivity toward women.

Like *The Preacher and the Rapper,* Reed's most recent novel was very even-handed in its satire. Just as his play attacked both rappers and those who would censor rap, *Japanese by Spring* (1993)—probably provoked by Reed's teaching experiences at the University of California at Berkeley and elsewhere—tore into all sides of an academic power struggle. It showed the Eurocentric, Japanese-fearing, all-white, all-male administration being replaced by one dominated by Asia-centered, American despising, fanatical Japanese with numerous shifts in alliances among scholars of widely differing backgrounds and disciplines. As before, Reed plugged for pluralism over power plays.

Reed's play *Hubba City* (2000) was also prompted by personal experience. As with *Japanese by Spring,* however, experience merely suggested a direction, and Reed's imagination took the idea and ran with it. In 1979 Reed moved to a neighborhood in Oakland, California, where he observed drugs being sold openly and other criminal activities flourishing without police interference. From this situation, Reed constructed a play around the plight of two elderly retired couples living in a neighborhood with young kids selling drugs on the street and a crack house everyone knows about. The couples instituted a crime watch, but the police never used their information or came when they called. Reed's play not only depicted police corruption but also implied government complicity in the availability of crack to black neighborhoods.

The Reed Reader (2000) provides an overview of his work. It includes excerpts from all nine novels, eight essays, many poems and two plays. It is an excellent place to start with Reed, and most readers will come to the conclusion that the MacArthur Genius Award was justified. (*See also* African American Novel)

Further Reading

Bell, Bernard W. *The Afro-American Novel and Its Tradition.* Amherst: U of Massachusetts P, 1989.

Carter, Steven R. "Ishmael Reed's Neo-Hoodoo Detection." *Dimensions of Detective Fiction*. Ed. Larry N. Landrum, Pat Browne and Ray B. Browne. Bowling Green, OH: Popular Press, 1976.

Steven R. Carter

REICH, TOVA RACHEL (1942–)   Jewish American writer. Reich is the author of three published novels, shorter fiction, and reviews. She is known for her political and religious satire and engages in her fiction with Jewish Orthodoxy and fundamentalism, **feminism**, and questions of Jewish American **identity** and the Jewish "Other."

Born as Tova Rachel Weiss in Liberty, New York, into an Orthodox family in 1942, Reich grew up to speak and read English, Hebrew, and Yiddish. In addition to her high school education, she studied at *yeshivot* (religious schools) and remains committed to religious study. Both her parents descended from rabbinical families: Her father, an Orthodox rabbi, immigrated to Israel; her three brothers are also rabbis.

After her graduation with a BA from Brooklyn College of City University of New York (1964) and her MA from New York University (1965), Reich held various teaching posts at American universities and was a visiting writer at the University of Maryland from 1991 to 1992 and in 1994. She is married to psychiatrist Walter Reich, who was the director of the United States **Holocaust** Memorial Museum from 1995 to 1998, and lives in Maryland.

Reich's first novel, *Mara* (1978), also her first published work of fiction, recounts the story of an American rabbi sending off his nubile, yet naïve, daughter named Mara to Israel, there to be educated and to find a Jewish spouse. Although darkly comical, Reich's novel sounds a bitter note, as is indicated by its title, *Mara,* the Hebrew word for bitter and also the protagonist's name. Already, in this novel, Israel and its meaning for American Jews emerge as central concerns of Reich's. For her second novel, *Master of the Return* (1988), she received the prestigious Edward Lewis Wallant Award, established to honor outstanding works of fiction that have significance for Jewish Americans. Yet *Master of the Return* is set entirely in Israel, among the followers of a Hasidic sect whose objective is the restitution of the Temple Mount and the erection of the Third Temple. In this novel, Reich explores satirically both the phenomenon of the return to the land of Israel and to the Jewish faith, the *teshuva,* (particularly of American Jews) and the nature of religious fanaticism and ecstasy. Her third and, to date, last novel, *The Jewish War* (1995), has been described in reviews as "lively, intelligent, disturbing" (Brown); as "outrageously funny, wickedly irreverent" (Steinberg); and as "alternately chilling and hysterical" (Graham). That in referring to *The Jewish War* most critics feel the need to resort to the use of opposites is indicative of the novel's ambivalent potential: "Readers will be either delighted or scandalized, depending on the particulars of their piety and their political perspective" (Kirschenbaum 311f). *The Jewish War* chronicles the rise and fall of a fictitious group of secessionist Jewish settlers who, at the end of the twentieth century, create the Kingdom of Judea and Samaria with a view to promoting redemption. Weaving together in her narrative the opposing doctrines of radical Zionist religious settlers, ultra-Orthodox anti-Zionists, liberal Zionists, and evangelical fundamentalists, Reich in *The Jewish War* once again probes the dimensions of religious fanaticism and the meaning of the land of Israel, both religious and political. A fourth novel of Reich's, *Birth Wish*, remains unpublished.

Unfortunately, as yet uncollected is Reich's shorter fiction, which has appeared in *Atlantic Monthly, Harper's, Commentary,* and elsewhere since 1979. Among the most disturbing of her stories is probably "Mengele in Jerusalem" (1986), in which a Holocaust survivor, come to Israel on a spiritual quest, meets with Reb Mengele, the sadistic concentration camp doctor Josef Mengele turned Hasid. For her "The Lost Girl" (1995) Reich was presented with the National Magazine Award for Fiction in 1996. With "The Third Generation" (2000), in which the granddaughter of Holocaust survivors decides to become a Catholic nun in a convent built on the outskirts of Auschwitz, Reich proves that she remains sensitive in her work to questions of morality, redemption, and Jewish identity. (*See also* Jewish American Novel)

Further Reading

Furman, Andrew. *Israel through the Jewish-American Imagination. A Survey of Jewish-American Literature on Israel, 1928–1995.* Albany: State U of New York P, 1997. 175–95.

Glazer, Miriyam. "Orphans of Culture and History: Gender and Spirituality in Contemporary Jewish-American Women's Novels." *Tulsa Studies in Women's Literature* 13 (1994): 127–41.

Kirschenbaum, Blossom S. "Tova Reich (1942–)" *Contemporary Jewish-American Novelists. A Biocritical Sourcebook.* Ed. Joel Shatzky and Michael Taub. Westport, CT: Greenwood Press, 1997. 305–13.

Pinsker, Sanford. "New Voices and the Contemporary Jewish-American Novel," *Jewish Book Annual.* Ed. Jacob Kabakoff. New York: Jewish Book Council, 1991. 6–20.

Axel Stähler

REVARD, CARTER (1931–) Native American poet and essayist. Named a Rhodes Scholar in 1952 and given the tribal name Nompeh-wahthe, relative of thunder, by his Osage grandmother, mixed-blood Carter Revard has given voice to Native experience in a manner that bridges divides, not only between rural Oklahoma and urban America but between centuries, continents, and academic disciplines. His poetry collection *An Eagle Nation* (1993) was honored with the Oklahoma Book Award, and in 2000 Revard was named Writer of the Year in Autobiography by the Wordcraft Circle of Native Writers for his essay collection *Family Matters, Tribal Affairs* (1998). His publications also include the poetry collections *Ponca War Dancers* (1980) and *Cowboys and Indians Christmas Shopping* (1992) and the mixed-genre memoir *Winning the Dust Bowl* (2001). Revard's work has been included in such important anthologies as *Returning the Gift, Earth Power Coming, I Tell You Now,* and *The Norton Anthology of Poetry.*

Carter Revard was born in the Osage Agency town of Pawhuska, Oklahoma, and grew up on a farm in the Buck Creek Valley, where he, his twin Maxine, and their siblings all graduated from the one-room school. Winning a radio quiz scholarship to the University of Tulsa enabled Revard to keep his promise to his dying grandfather to attend college. After studying at Oxford, Revard was awarded his PhD by Yale University in 1959. A scholar of medieval English literature, linguistics, and Native literature, he taught at Amherst College and, from 1961 until his retirement in 1997, at Washington University in St. Louis. He has been an active member of the American Indian Center of St. Louis and the St. Louis Gourd Dancers.

Revard's personal essays, laced with humor and irony, are often as intimate and colloquial as if he were telling the stories in person. In "Walking Among the Stars" Revard brings to life a family whose members are ultimately connected with a much greater world. If he shares the story of Aunt Jewell and the courage song that inspired his own writing career, he also remembers "Uncle Frank" Phillips, whose Bartlesville-based petroleum company profited so richly from Osage oil. Revard introduces himself ceremonially as a member of a family universe that is not only far-flung but almost infinitely expandable. The uncles, aunts, grandparents, great-grandparents, cousins, siblings, nieces, and nephews—inlaws and outlaws, Osage, Ponca, and Irish—he recalls with deep affection in his essays and poems are almost as numerous as the stars.

Revard insists that the best poems, lyric as well as narrative, are grounded in story. Often, as in "An Eagle Nation," he centers all of the lines on the page, his way of flashing each one in front of the reader like a small revelation. In this poem, Revard tells the story of a visit with Aunt Jewell and her innumerable grandchildren to the Oklahoma City Zoo and the Red Earth powwow. As this elder in her wheelchair greets a bald eagle who has been wounded and will never fly again, the conception of family expands yet again. When Aunt Jewell addresses the bird very quietly in Ponca, respectfully calling him "brother," the eagle listens with rapt attention and responds shrilly to the astonishment of dazed onlookers. He had totally ignored a white man's well-intentioned clicking and whistling. Aunt Jewell is moved to tears. At the powwow, Revard links the history of migrations and meetings at Osage dances that had made his relatives family with eagle migrations. All of the circles come together to affirm the power of tribal life itself in the presence of so many individuals dancing to a single drum–heart beat.

Revard almost effortlessly turns personal story to political ends. In his gentle but pointed satire on the territorial claims of Columbus, "Report to the Nation: Repossessing Europe," Revard motors across Europe from England almost, but not quite, to the summit of Mount Olympos, claiming all this previously unclaimed territory in the name of the Osage elders. At the heart of the satire stand four poems. Published separately in other volumes, these poems offer a lesson from the oral tradition about shaping meaning through context. Here they serve as a quiet reminder that, despite Columbus, the real tribal issue at stake is not land ownership but respectful and reciprocal relationship among all the beings alive in a dynamic, ever-changing universe. Revard's poems evoke details of the natural and human worlds precisely. Often, as in "Rock Shelters," he moves deftly beyond the physical to configure a tribal universe akin to that understood by contemporary science. From a vista high above Buck Creek, the poem asks us to observe the flowing stream and to see life beyond the point where the flow turns from water to oil. As humans move on to claim other galaxies, our greed and violence will follow us, Revard observes, inserting himself into the scene once again, but we will always depend upon the land, spiritual now as much as physical, to sustain us. "To the Muses in Oklahoma" lauds the living seasons of the pond Revard's family built on their farm, altering the natural world, whereas "As Brer Coyote Said" celebrates the blackberry, both in its seasonal changes and, fierce with thorns, as a force of change, creating and sustaining wildness on land that has been disturbed. Through the glitter of crystals inside a rock, "Stone Age" moves us to a sense of wonder, as so many of Revard's poems do. The starry sky is, quite literally, the mystery of the infinitely expanding universe visible to the naked eye. (*See also* Native American Poetry)

Further Reading

Bruchac, Joseph. "Something That Stays Alive: An Interview with Carter Revard." *Survival This Way: Interviews with American Indian Poets.* Tucson: U of Arizona P, 1987. 231–48.

Scarberry-Garcia, Susan. "'I Have More Than One Song': Singing and Bird Songs in the Work of Carter Revard." *Studies in American Indian Literatures* 15.1 (Spring 2003): 53–59.

Wilson, Norma. "The Mythic Continuum: The Poetry of Carter Revard." *The Nature of Native American Poetry.* Albuquerque: U of New Mexico P, 2000. 15–30.

Linda Lizut Helstern

REYES, GUILLERMO (1962–) Chilean American playwright and professor. Many of Guillermo Reyes's plays push the boundaries of theatrical representations of gay Latinas and Latinos. Reyes skillfully intertwines discourses of gender, sexuality, **identity**, **immigration** status, and politics, frequently using comedy to combat cultural taboos in the panethnic Latino community. Although Reyes is not of Mexican descent, his work is often included in discussions of Chicano theater because he writes so many Chicana and Chicano characters.

Reyes was born in Chile and moved to the United States at the age of nine. His playwriting career began while he was an undergraduate at the University of California at Los Angeles (UCLA). In 1986 the South Coast

Repertory Theatre's Hispanic Playwrights Project held a reading of Reyes's unpublished play *Exile from L.A.* While earning a master of fine arts in playwriting from the University of California at San Diego (UCSD), Reyes wrote *The Seductions of Johnny Diego,* a comedy about an Irish/Chicano dysfunctional family, which includes a gay brother. The play was staged by the UCSD Theatre Department in 1990, directed by noted Chicano director Tony Curiel.

After graduating from UCSD in 1990, Reyes moved to L.A., where he wrote the script to his best-known play *Men on the Verge of a His-Panic Breakdown.* This one-man show consists of nine monologues that explore gay Latino identity in the United States from widely different perspectives. The characters embody diverse viewpoints in terms of their immigration/citizenship status, Latino heritage, age, professions, and attitudes toward their sexuality. In their own ways, each of the characters probes the ways in which ethnicity and sexuality intersect and inform one's identity.

The first production of *Men on the Verge* at the Celebration Theatre in West Hollywood received Theater L.A.'s Ovation Award for Best World Premiere Play and Best Production in 1994. The show has also been produced in San Francisco's Theater Rhinoceros, San Jose's City Lights, and Playwrights Preview Productions of New York City. The New York production earned Reyes the 1996 Emerging Playwright Award and an Off Broadway run at the 47th Street Playhouse.

In 1996 the Celebration Theatre also produced the world premier of another of Reyes's widely celebrated works: *Deporting the Divas,* directed by Jorge Huerta. The central character, Michael González, is a Chicano immigration officer who falls in love with Sedicio, an illegal Mexican immigrant who he meets in his Spanish class. Sedicio already speaks both English and Spanish fluently but takes Spanish classes to meet men. From the start, Sedicio has a clear grasp of his identity, his sexuality, and the ways in which he can comfortably navigate life on both sides of the border. Michael, on the other hand, struggles to learn Spanish, feels conflicted about his identity, and represses his sexuality. Rather than dealing with the reality of his attraction to Sedicio, Michael daydreams of the perfect woman: a tango-dancing drag queen named Sirena. The characters struggle with issues of **assimilation** and the crossing of sexual, political, linguistic, and geographic borders.

Divas has been produced at the Borderlands Theatre in Tucson and the Diversionary Theater in San Diego. The 1996 production of *Divas* at Theater Rhinoceros in San Francisco received a nomination for Best Original Script by the Bay Area Critics Circle and won the Bay Area Drama-Logue Award for Playwriting.

Reyes became a professor at Arizona State University in 1996 and now heads the playwriting program there. That same year the Actors Theatre of Louisville produced his romantic comedy *Chilean Holiday,* which was subsequently published in the anthology *Humana Festival '96: The Complete*

Plays. Reyes's play *A Southern Christmas* won the 1997 National Latino Playwrights Award, and in 2003 his comedy *Sunrise at Monticello* was the runner-up for the same award. Also in 2003, Reyes directed the world premier of *Places to Touch Him*, which won the AriZoni Theater Award for Best Original Play Production. His most recent play, *Men on the Verge 2*, premiered at the Borderlands Theater in Tucson in 2004. His other works include *Bush Is a Lesbian*, *Mother Lolita*, *Miss Consuelo*, *The West Hollywood Affair*, *Allende by Pinochet*, and *Sirena, Queen of the Tango*, which is a spin-off of *Deporting the Divas.*

Further Reading

Huerta, Jorge. *Chicano Drama: Performance, Society and Myth.* Cambridge: Cambridge UP, 2000.

Lockhart, Melissa Fitch. "Buenos Aires on the Border: Sirena: The Transvestite Tango Diva in the Theater of Guillermo Reyes." *Ollantay Theater Magazine* 9.18 (2001): 70–83.

Ashley Lucas

REZNIKOFF, CHARLES (1894–1976)   Jewish American poet and novelist. Reznikoff is one of the most important Jewish American poets of the twentieth century. Closely associated with the Objectivist movement, Reznikoff labored for most of his life in relative obscurity, only obtaining some degree of literary popularity in the 1960s. Nevertheless, he remains one of the most accomplished and influential figures in Jewish American letters.

Reznikoff was born the son of immigrant parents from Russia and grew up in the Jewish neighborhood of Brownsville, in Brooklyn, New York. After a brief flirtation with journalism at the University of Missouri, Reznikoff returned to New York, where he attended New York University's Law School, graduating second in his class. Although he was admitted to the New York Bar in 1916, Reznikoff never practiced law but instead earned his living through a series of editorial jobs, research positions, and translation work. Reznikoff's background in law would help to expose him to some of his subject matter, however, particularly in 1928 when he was engaged to work on an encyclopedia of law called Corpus Juris. Many of the trials he witnessed and read about during this period would make their way into Reznikoff's major work, *Testimony.*

A family story told that Reznikoff's grandfather, in Russia, was a poet as well as an itinerant merchant. When he died in another town, the man's belongings, including his collection of writings, were returned to his family. Reznikoff's mother, fearing that her father's writing (which she could not read) might contain something seditious and put the whole family in danger, burned the manuscripts. Reznikoff's desire to see his work published, therefore, remained constant, but unlike many of his contemporaries, Reznikoff was not much of a self-promoter, and was often content to publish his poems and short plays at his own expense. In fact most of his early collections, including his first, *Rhythms* (1918) were published in this way. By the 1930s, Reznikoff's association with the Objectivist Press would help him publish to a slightly wider audience, and later, in the 1960s and 1970s, Black Sparrow Press would help rescue Reznikoff's reputation from relative obscurity by reprinting his work.

Reznikoff's association with the Objectivist movement begins as early as 1929, when he met **Louis Zukovsky** and **George Oppen**. The Objectivist movement in American poetry has been garnering greater attention in recent years and is sometimes seen as a predecessor to postmodern ideas of poetics because of its disdain for sentimentality and its attention to language. Originally an offshoot of Ezra Pound's Imagism, the Objectivists similarly focused on the empirical rather than the symbolic image. The idea was to capture one's subject with as little adornment in excess verbiage and flowery description as possible. Objectivism was more socially engaged than Imagism, and its practitioners tended to be more politically left-wing than the modernists of the Pound school. Most of the poets associated with objectivism—Louis Zukovsky, George Oppen, and **Carl Rakosi**—were Jewish, although with widely varying degrees of knowledge and affiliation. Reznikoff, Zukovsky, and Rakosi were all the sons of immigrants and maintained deep emotional ties to a sense of Jewish **identity**, and Reznikoff in particular struggled to reconcile his poetics with his loyalty to his ethnic identity.

Reznikoff's poetry demonstrates a precise control of language and a willingness to allow images to speak for themselves with little extraneous adornment. This is not to say, however, that Reznikoff's poetry is without complexity or literary allusion. On the contrary, subtle references to the Bible, classical literature, and other works are prevalent, and probing intelligence often underlies his impartial descriptions. The portrait that emerges from Reznikoff's poetry is that of a speaker highly attuned to the urban landscape, to its characters and music. Once asked why he had not yet accepted an invitation to visit Israel, Reznikoff was said to have answered that he had not yet finished exploring Central Park.

Reznikoff's two long poetic works, *Testimony* and *Holocaust*, are the most dramatic uses of his reportage style, using the words of victims and perpetrators of crimes to stand on their own, without commentary. *Testimony* is a massive collection of witness statements and confessions drawn from trial materials in American courts from the nineteenth century. The material is grouped by region and subject, rather than literary theme, and the lack of authorial comment, especially as the material accumulates, increases the stark effect of the descriptions, creating a powerful montage of images, voices, and stories. Of course there's no question that Reznikoff selected, managed, and edited the pieces he included in these major works, but they nevertheless seem the closest to fulfilling the early modernist ideal of writing nothing that an average person might not say. *Holocaust* (1975) performs similar work in response to the European tragedy and likewise attempts to encompass the massive material by letting testimonies speak for themselves, one after the other.

In 1929 Reznikoff self-published a book of poems titled *By the Waters of Manhattan*, which included a short autobiographical prose piece. Playing off the biblical phrase, "By the waters of Babylon we sat down and wept," the title came to be a favorite of Reznikoff's, and he would later use it for his selected poems in 1962. The prose piece attracted the attention of the publisher Charles Boni, who would later print a book-length memoir-novel with the same title in 1930. *By the Waters of Manhattan* has become perhaps Reznikoff's best-known work, and traces the experiences of Reznikoff's mother Sarah Yetta, leading to her **immigration** to the United States. Reznikoff would later fill in the rest of his family's remarkable story with *Early History of a Sewing Machine Operator*, which was in fact written collaboratively with Reznikoff's parents.

With regard to his ethnic heritage, Reznikoff frequently wrote about his admitted lack of knowledge of the Hebrew language and Jewish rituals as well as the accompanying dissociation this caused him as a modern man. But he also wrote with increasing affection for the history and legacy of Judaism, and in some ways Reznikoff's poetic aesthetic could be linked to his understanding of Judaism's role in his understanding of the world. As Reznikoff's reputation grows, a deeper understanding of his poetic achievement and its connection to his ethnic identity seem to follow.

Further Reading

Bernstein, Charles. "Reznikoff's Nearness." *My Way: Speeches and Poems.* Chicago: U of Chicago P, 1999.

Fredman, Stephen. *Menorah for Athena: Charles Reznikoff and the Jewish Dilemmas of Objectivist Poetry.* Chicago: U of Chicago P, 2001.

Hindus, Milton, ed. *Charles Reznikoff: Man and Poet.* Orono, Maine: National Poetry Foundation/U of Maine P, 1984.

Adam Sol

RICE, ELMER (1892–1967) Jewish American playwright, director, novelist. Elmer Rice—originally named Elmer Leopold Reizenstein—is one of the most versatile and eclectic writers of the early twentieth century. Although he wrote well over fifty plays, as well as many novels, essays, and short stories, he is remembered primarily for two works: his innovative Expressionistic play *The Adding Machine* (1923) and his stringent social exposé *Street Scene* (1929), which won him the Pulitzer Prize. And although most of his other plays lack the power and bite of these stringent social dramas, he is often considered to be the first significant modern American playwright.

After earning a law degree at New York University and graduating cum laude in 1912, Rice abandoned the profession a year later to pursue writing full-time, although he drew upon his law experience for material. His first play, *On Trial* (1914), is a mechanically structured murder mystery that proved

Elmer Rice. *Courtesy of the Library of Congress.*

a huge success, bringing Rice money and fame. Despite its flaws, the play is credited for its creative use of cinematic flashback techniques. Still, recognizing its dramatic weaknesses and determined to improve his craft, Rice enrolled at Columbia University, where he studied drama, participated actively in theater activities—including directing—and continued writing plays, most of which focused on legal, political, and social topics.

The first play to display his mastery of the dramatic art was *The Adding Machine,* a remarkably prescient and contemporary play born of the Industrial Age but reflecting the devaluation of the individual and the regimentation of modern life that has become even more disturbingly relevant in the twenty-first century. Its central figure, aptly named Mr. Zero, anticipates a reward for his quarter century of loyal service as a bookkeeper with an unnamed firm, but, instead, his boss announces that he is to be fired and replaced by an adding machine. Deranged by an insensitivity he cannot comprehend, Mr. Zero murders his boss, is convicted by a puppetlike jury, and subsequently executed. Expressionistic techniques such as tilted platforms, intensified music, and mouths that move without speaking intensify the dramatic impact and social ideas of the play.

By contrast, *Street Scene*—considered by many to be Rice's best work—utilizes more naturalistic techniques in its bleary depiction of tenement life and adultery, incorporating an ethnically diverse cast of about fifty characters, including Irish, Jewish, Italian, German, and immigrants from other countries. The play highlights these ethnic differences as well as individual dissatisfactions. Rose Maurrant, a young Irish office worker, is engaged to a Jewish man, Sam Kaplan, an engagement much disapproved of by the gossipy neighbors. Sam's own sister even tells Rose to stick to her own kind. Mrs. Maurrant is having an affair with a married milk-company businessman, and when Maurrant—the building's janitor—unexpectedly catches them, he murders them and is later arrested. Rose decides to cut off her engagement, fearing the marriage would lead only to poverty and unhappiness, and prepares to move away from the city with her younger brother to start a new life. In 1947 Rice and Langston Hughes transformed the play into a musical, collaborating with composer Kurt Weill.

In 1935 Rice accepted a post as director of the New York wing of the Living Newspaper, which was part of the Federal Theatre Project, founded by Hallie Flanagan under the auspices of the New Deal's Works Progress Administration initiated by President Franklin D. Roosevelt. The Living Newspaper was a kind of cinematic documentary revue that dramatized contemporary events through song, dance, lighting, vignettes, and other devices, drawing its text from actual newspapers, speeches, and other texts of the day.

However, trouble immediately arose with the first planned New York production, *Ethiopia*, which was to include speeches from Haile Selassie and Mussolini, as well as the transcription of a broadcast by Roosevelt. But when the government barred the project, Rice angrily resigned in a very public news conference, noting that he had been fighting censorship for fifteen years and would not serve a government that placed politics over freedom and democracy.

Rice continued his own campaign against society's ills. In 1937 he helped found the Playwrights' Producing Company, which staged some of his later plays and which continued to express his deep concern with social, economic, moral, and political issues. He also served on the board of the American Civil Liberties Union (ACLU), as president of the American Authors League, and as the first president of the Dramatists' Guild, which he founded. (*See also* Jewish American Theater)

Further Reading

Durham, Frank. *Elmer Rice.* New York: Twayne, 1970.

Hogan, Robert. *The Independence of Elmer Rice.* Carbondale: Southern Illinois UP, 1965.

Lee, Joanna, et al., eds. *Street Scene: A Sourcebook.* New York: Kurt Weill Foundation for Music, 1996.

Rice, Elmer. *The Living Theatre.* New York: Harper, 1959.

———. *Minority Report: An Autobiography.* New York: Simon & Schuster, 1963.

Karen C. Blansfield

RICE, SARAH WEBB (1909–)   African American activist and memoirist. Prompted by family friend Louise Westling, an English professor at the University of Oregon, Sarah Rice shared the story of her active life in a single volume, *He Included Me* (1989). Taking its title from twin incidents in which she and her mother before her felt plenitude in God's plan in the midst of daunting poverty, *He Included Me* works in the tradition of oral narrative and is notable as a contribution to Southern black women's autobiography.

With Westling as editor and scribe, Rice provides a first-hand account of life first in Eufala, Alabama, and later in Jacksonville, Florida. She describes a vital, woman-centered community from which she gathered strength and to which she owed her allegiance. Rice's faith, commitment to service, and refusal to be victimized made her a respected leader and political organizer in her church (first African Methodist Episcopal, then Baptist, after her 1953 marriage to Andrew Rice) and in the rural Southern communities where she worked as a teacher and a domestic.

Rice was prompted to tell her story and, by extension, the story of her particular time and place, by family and friends who understood the value of her courage, self-determination, and unusually pragmatic resolve. Rice's elevated status within her community and her substatus in the dominant white world in which she worked make her story a compelling addition to the growing literature documenting the "peculiar sisterhood" between Southern black and white women.

Born only two generations removed from **slavery** time into a deeply segregated South, Rice was raised to have confidence in her abilities by her formidable, hard-working parents. Her mother, Lizzie Janet Lewis Webb, was a teacher, and her father, Willis James Webb, was a minister, as well as a sharecropper and storekeeper. The ambitious young Sarah was taught to achieve through "work and scuffle." At harvest time, Webb writes, if "you weren't at school, you were either chopping cotton, hoeing cotton, replanting corn, or hoeing around the corn."

This hardscrabble life did nothing to diminish Webb's spirit. Even as a young child she exhibited the self-assurance and quick-wittedness that would, in later years, make her a natural leader. Early in her book, she recalls an encounter she had as a girl with a school principal, who was ready to administer a "strap" to the frightened six-year-old offender. Instead of submitting to his grown-up version of punishment, she found her voice and saved herself "'with a lie on [her] daddy'." "'Professor Wilson,' she has the nerve to say, 'my daddy said you're too big to be picking on a little girl like me'." This strong sense of fair play and an indefatigable drive to challenge falsely held authority and the prevailing status quo characterize Rice's life and work.

Well into her nineties, Rice still lives in Jacksonville, where she is celebrated as a true "elder": a wise, compassionate, accomplished teacher, prodding later generations to continue organizing for social change.

Further Reading

Frost, David. *Witness to Injustice*. Jackson: University of Mississippi Press, 1995.

Rouse, Jacqueline A. Rev. of *He Included Me*. *Journal of American History* 78.1 (June 1991): 361.

Kate Falvey

RICH, ADRIENNE CECILE (1929–) Jewish American poet, essayist, and feminist theorist. In her eighteen volumes of poetry and four prose works, Adrienne Rich reveals her sensitivity to her own and to the world's pain. No other poet has so clearly articulated the ideals of the twentieth-century feminist movement. Her development as a writer enacts a vision and revision of her poetics in form and content, reflecting her developing sense of self in the world.

Born in Baltimore, Maryland, on May 16, 1929, Rich grew up in a privileged and cultivated household. Arnold Rice Rich, her father, was a professor of forensic medicine at Johns Hopkins; her mother, Helen Jones Rich, abandoned a promising career as a concert pianist to marry. To carry out the father's strict ideas about education, her mother educated Rich and her younger sister at home until the fourth grade, when they were sent to private school. Arnold Rich was Jewish, but his children were reared as Episcopalians. Commenting upon her paternal grandparents' choice of a military school for their son, Rich writes, "With whatever conscious

Adrienne Rich. *Courtesy of the Library of Congress.*

forethought, Samuel and Hattie sent their son into the dominant Southern WASP culture to become an 'exception,' to enter the professional class." In a poem eulogizing Hattie Rich, the poet observes that during World War II the word *Jewish* was barred from the household. Both her mother and father felt that such a silence was necessary *if* the family were to assimilate successfully into their traditionally closed Southern society. Later in life, Rich became acutely aware of how cultural silences protect privilege and determined that her writing would disrupt such silences.

Ambitious for success for his talented elder daughter, Arnold Rich participated actively in her education, sharing with her his large library of nineteenth-century poetry and setting her exercises in poetic form. But as she matured, Rich came to bitterly resent her father's patriarchal control and to take a strong stand against all patriarchy. In *Of Woman Born: Motherhood as Experience and Institution* (1976), she records her struggle with her father, "for my right to an emotional life and selfhood."

Nevertheless, early on Rich realized at least part of her father's ambition for her. At Radcliff College, she completed her first book of poetry *A Change of World* in 1951, and in that year graduated with honors as a Phi Beta Kappa. W. H. Auden selected the work for inclusion in the prestigious Yale Younger Poets series. In his introduction Auden noted Rich's debt to established poets

Frost and Yeats and praised her "craftsmanship, for its evidence of a capacity for detachment from the self and its emotions" (Gelpi and Gelpi 278). These poems are skillfully written, formal in use of meter and rhyme, traditional in theme, and exhibit Rich's characteristic vivid imagery and striking metaphor. The frequently anthologized "Aunt Jennifer's Tigers" presages Rich's life-long concern about constraints on woman's creativity.

Following upon this success, she received a Guggenheim Fellowship to travel in Europe, travel reflected in many of the poems in her second volume, *The Diamond Cutters* (1955). The title poem is a metaphor for the craft of poetry and her view at the time, also expressed in "Love in a Museum," of the necessity for the artist to maintain emotional distance from his/her subject. The gently ironic "Living in Sin" reflects its author's growing understanding of the limitations of the ideal of romantic love. The book is dedicated to A. H. C., Alfred H. Conrad, an economist teaching at Harvard and the poet's husband.

The fifties was a decade of intense domesticity. Although Rich recognized the split between, as she puts it, "the girl who defined herself in writing and the girl who defined herself in her relationships with men, at the time she believed that only through marriage and motherhood would she be entirely fulfilled as a woman. Despite his academic credentials, her parents did not approve of Conrad, who was Brooklyn-born with an East European background—"a Jew of the wrong kind," their daughter commented. Between 1955 and 1959 Rich gave birth to three sons. She found domesticity and motherhood isolating and very difficult. Reflecting on this period of her life from the vantage of the 1970s, she remembers with bitterness "'the solitary confinement of a life at home enclosed with young children."

Of Woman Born: Motherhood as Experience and Institution (1976) is a prose work in which Rich makes clear how radicalizing her experience with marriage and motherhood had been. In it she combines autobiography and research in a unique way. Many readers found her personal revelations shocking.

> Sometimes I seem to myself, in my feeling toward these tiny guiltless beings, a monster of selfishness and intolerance. Their voices wear at my nerves, their constant needs . . . fill me with despair at my own failures, despair too at my fate, which *is* to serve a function for which I was not fitted.

Here Rich forcefully breaks a traditional silence; she refutes the idea that for women motherhood *is* instinctual and always gratifying. She sees the culture's idealization of motherhood as a patriarchal stratagem of control. For the first time, the gifted white intellectual finds herself to be marginalized.

> My husband was a sensitive, affectionate man who wanted children and who—unusual in the professional, academic world of the fifties—was will-

ing to help. But it was clearly understood that this "help" was an act of generosity; that his work, his professional life was the real work in the family.

After the birth of her children, Rich did not publish again for eight years. When she did publish *Snapshots of a Daughter in Law* (1963), its tone, form, and content differed markedly from her earlier work. Bitter and allusive, fragmented in the manner of Eliot's *Wasteland*, the title poem demonstrates the extent to which she had come to feel woman's victimization. She describes how this poem came to be written.

> The poem was jotted in fragments during children's naps, brief hour in a library or at 3:00 A.M. after rising with a wakeful child. Over two years I wrote a ten-part poem called "Snapshots of a Daughter-Law" (1958–1960), in a longer looser mode than I'd ever trusted myself with before. It was an enormous relief to write that poem.

In this volume Rich writes in a new voice, reflecting her sense of victimization and a greater willingness to address directly her lived experience. Unlike her earlier works, *Snapshots* was either ignored by establishment critics or condemned for its negativity and emotion.

In 1966 Rich published *Necessities of Life*, continuing her effort to create a more woman-centered, politically conscious aesthetic. Poems depict her relationships with her father ("After Dark"), with her child ("Night Pieces to a Child"), and with her husband ("Like This Together" and "Marriage in the Sixties"). By that year the family had moved to New York City, where her husband had taken a teaching job at Columbia University. Rich became involved in the intense political ferment of the time—anti–Vietnam War demonstrations and the **Civil Rights Movement** as well as the feminist movement. Teaching writing to disadvantaged inner-city students in the SEEK program at City College heightened her sensitivity to class and race issues. In 1969 she published *Leaflets*, which included "Ghazals: Homage to Ghalib." In this series of poems, Rich experimented with a form developed by the Indian poet Ghalib (1797–1869), who lived in Delhi during the brutal imposition of British rule, a period that Rich identified as politically turbulent as her own. Although Rich is by no means a confessional poet, poems written in this decade reveal her increasing sense of isolation in her marriage. In 1970 she separated from her husband. Later that year, Alfred Conrad drove a rental car all night to the family's summer home in Vermont, where early in the morning he shot himself. Only much later in her life does the poet publicly explore that subject.

Increasingly, Rich envisions **feminism** as enabling the creation of a more beneficent society. In the foreword to her first published essay collection, she writes of "a world dominated by passive-aggressive men and by male institutions dispensing violence." The *Will to Change* (1971) reflects her strong resolve to use poetry as a means of presenting alternatives to patriarchy. In "The Burning of Paper Instead of Children" Rich invokes the story of Joan of

Arc and blends poetic images of her private pain with prose to depict her despair. In the poem's conclusion, she identifies the inadequacy of language as part of the human problem. She becomes determined "to find language and images for a consciousness we are just coming into."

The title poem of *Diving into the Wreck* (1973), winner of the National Book Award for Poetry, enacts a theme of empowerment through a process of discovery. Its central symbol is a woman's archetypal descent into a deep black sea where an aged wreck disgorges its cargo, and her ascent is fortified by a unique, perhaps androgynous, understanding. Although various critics have debated the nature of the persona and symbols in this suggestive narrative, the central figure seems to be another version of the redemptive woman Rich describes in the last stanza of "Snapshots of a Daughter-in-Law." In poems such as "Rape" condemnation of men is more forceful. On the dust jacket of this volume, she writes, "I feel this book continues the work I've been trying to do—breaking down the artificial barriers between private and public, between Vietnam and the lovers' bed." Increasingly, her commitment to sexual politics leads her to radical feminism.

In *Dream of a Common Language* (1978) Rich suggests a new social contract based on a lesbian sense of community that would replace the abusive institutions of patriarchy. At the center of this volume, "Twenty-One Love Poems" is an impassioned, erotic tribute to her lover. In the sequence, images of torture, urban decay, and environmental degradation contrast with the warmth and beauty of the lovers' relationship. Although the affair ends in estrangement, Rich feels that such a relationship could become the basis of a new kind of community. She considers heterosexuality to be a culturally imposed institution like class or race. In her influential critique of the injustice of this cultural imposition, "Compulsory Heterosexuality and Lesbian Existence," Rich posits that all women exist on a "lesbian continuum" that, for many, involves feminine connectedness, "woman-identified experience," and, for some, is a fully expressed "lesbian existence." Whatever degree of female bonding exists, all such bonding creates essential resistance to patriarchy, which she has come to believe is the source of all oppression. Thus female bonding would contribute to a cultural transformation to benefit all humanity. A tribute to such bonding is embodied in "Phantasia for Elvira Shatazev," the leader of a female climbing team, all of whom died in an assault on Lenin Peak in 1974.

Written about this time, "From an Old House in America," the Vermont house in which she lived with her husband, presents to the poet bitter images of an American history of exploitation of women: a girl giving birth chained in the hold of a slave ship, witch trials, the perilous isolation of the frontier woman. Later, in the transitional work *A Wild Patience Has Taken Me This Far* (1981), she writes about the same house in "Integrity," a poem that takes its first line from the volume's title. This later poem, again like much of Rich's poetry, an interior monologue, employs a quite different tone. Here the house is the destination of a carefully detailed boat passage.

Although the poet recognizes anger, still, in feelings generated by the house, she also admits to feelings of tenderness. Such sentiments are also expressed in her eloquent tribute "Grandmothers." "The Spirit of Place" is a long dialogue on the actual and psychological landscape of Western Massachusetts addressed to **Michelle Cliff**, an Afro-Caribbean writer who has been her partner since 1976. Later poems in the volume are prompted by their relationship and subsequent move to California. In the next decade Rich's poetry becomes less polemic and more philosophic.

Rich's essays frequently illuminate and extend the concepts expressed in her poetry. Published by W. W. Norton, the firm that has published almost all of her poetry, her four volumes of essays are *On Lies, Secrets, and Silence: Selected Prose 1966–1978* (1979); *Blood, Bread, and Poetry: Selected Prose 1979–1986* (1986); *What Is Found There: Notebooks on Poetry and Politics* (1993); and *Arts of the Possible: Essays and Conversations* (2000). Perhaps the best critical analysis of her work is in her own "When We Dead Awaken: Writing as Re-Vision" (from *On Lies*). Few essays are more important in understanding her poetry after the seventies than "Split at the Root: An Essay on Jewish Identity" (1982).

Throughout her adult life Rich considered herself Jewish. In this essay she explores a significant traumatic experience of her youth, her recognition of her father's **anti-Semitism**, reflected in his desire to assimilate to a conservative Southern culture and his rejection of her choice of husband. Part of her strong hatred of patriarchy is rooted in her negative feelings toward him. In a moving final paragraph she writes of the effect of her upbringing on her sense of self.

> Sometimes I feel I have seen too long from too many disconnected angles: white, Jewish, anti-semite, racist, anti-racist, once-married, lesbian, middle-class, feminist, expatriate southerner, *split at the root*—that I will never bring them whole.

In her later poetry she becomes reconciled to some of these discordant elements. In "Sources" in *Your Native Land, Your Life* (1986) she identifies with the Jews of the **Holocaust** but also reveals her understanding of the pain hidden by her father's arrogance and recognizes that her father and her husband had much in common. For the first time, in *Contradictions: Tracking Poems,* she writes of the pain of the rheumatoid arthritis she has suffered since her twenties.

In *An Atlas of a Difficult World: Poems* 1988–91 Rich continues her self-described role as "Philosopher of oppression." A remarkable series of poems, "Eastern War Time" concerns anti-Semitism and its ultimate expression in the Holocaust, vividly dramatized in poem number five of that series. "1948 Jews" is a personal reflection. Her next book *Dark Fields of the Republic: Poems 1991–1995* maintains her criticism of history's tragedies, like the Holocaust, as well as the contemporary culture's lies and cruelties, but also includes the playful "Sending Love."

During her long and prolific life, Rich has had appointments at ten universities, including Cornell, Brandeis, Harvard, and Stanford; been awarded numerous honorary doctorates; and received many awards for her poetry, such as the Robert Frost Silver Medal of the Poetry Society of America. In 1994 she received a MacArthur Fellowship, which supported her work for five years. During that time she completed *Midnight Salvage: Poems 1995–1998* and, so far, her final book *Fox: Poems 1995–1998*.

A gifted poet and committed intellectual, Adrienne Rich eloquently confronts historic and contemporary injustice. An ardent feminist, she is deeply engaged by the redemptive power of poetry. Although she envisions a better world, her writing is firmly grounded in the realities of this one, which she portrays in exact and striking images. (*See also* Jewish American Poetry, Jewish American Lesbian Literature)

Further Reading

Gelpi, Barbara Charlesworth, and Gelpi, Albert, eds. *Adrienne Rich's Poetry and Prose*. New York: W. W. Norton & Company, 1993.

Keyes, Claire. *The Aesthetics of Power: The Poetry of Adrienne Rich*. Athens: U of Georgia P, 1986: *Reading Adrienne Rich: Reviews and Re-Visions*. Ed. Jane Roberta Cooper. Ann Arbor: U of Michigan P, 1984.

York, Liz. *Adrienne Rich: Passion, Politics, and the Body*. London: Sage Publications, 1997.

Ann O. Gebhard

RICHARDSON, WILLIS (1889–1977)   African American playwright, essayist, editor, and director. Willis Richardson was a pioneering African American dramatist: the first to have a nonmusical play performed on Broadway, author of over forty plays, an early proponent on a theory of black theater, and an important anthologist of black plays for both adults and young people.

Much of Richardson's early upbringing, including his place of birth and parentage, remains shrouded in mystery. It is generally believed that he was born in Wilmington, North Carolina, on November 5, 1889. After the outbreak of **race** riots in Wilmington in 1898, the family moved to Washington, DC, where Richardson would attend the M Street School (later called Dunbar High School), the first all-black public high school in the United States. Among his teachers was playwright Mary Burrill, who encouraged the youth to develop his literary instincts. Because of financial reasons, Richardson was unable to pursue higher education, instead taking a position with the Bureau of Engraving and Printing in 1911, where he would remain until his retirement in 1954. In 1914 he married Mary Ellen Jones and the couple gave birth to three daughters.

Richardson actively began a career in playwriting after seeing a performance of **Angelina Grimké**'s *Rachel* in 1916. He decided to focus on ordinary black folk, "the soul of a people," of their struggles and triumphs, and told in their vernacular. The main thrust of Richardson's plays was always to educate people and to dispel stereotypes of blacks. This belief is clearly laid out in several essays he wrote on black drama in the 1920s. His plays seldom concern interracial conflicts but instead stress the need for better cooperation between members of the race.

His first published play for adults, *The Deacon's Awakening* (1920), advocating equal political rights for black women, demonstrates the need for intraracial harmony. This is also portrayed in *Mortgaged* (1924), in which two brothers quarrel over the best way to uplift the race, through business or education. The dangers of internal struggles within the community are set forth in such plays as *The Broken Banjo* (1925), where a man is betrayed by his brother-in-law, and *The Flight of the Natives* (1927), in which a slave's escape is thwarted by another slave.

Richardson's dramas were a staple of such black companies as the Krigwa Players, the Ethiopian Art Players, and the Gilpin Players. *Mortgaged*, for example, was the first play written by a black person, other than a student, to be produced by the Howard Players. *The Chip Woman's Fortune* (1923) was the first nonmusical black Broadway production. This play, about a simple woman who has secretly saved up a fortune, displays a model of how the black community can be supportive of one another.

About twenty of Richardson's plays have been published, some in such periodicals as the *Crisis* and in the important anthologies *The New Negro* (1925), edited by **Alain Locke**, and *Plays of Negro Life and History* (1927), edited by Locke and Montgomery Gregory. However, many are contained in Richardson's own anthologies, *Plays and Pageants from the Life of the Negro* (1930), the first all-black collection of drama in American literature; *Negro History in Thirteen Plays* (1930), coedited with May Miller; and *The King's Dilemma and Other Plays for Children* (1956).

Richardson was a groundbreaking figure in African American theater. Yet, despite his achievements, he found it increasingly difficult to have his plays produced and published. Over half of his plays remain unpublished. However, in recent years, with the renewed attention on the **Harlem Renaissance** and on the history of black theater, this seminal figure has begun to gain the attention he has long deserved. (*See also* African American Drama)

Further Reading

Gray, Christine Rauchfuss. *Willis Richardson, Forgotten Pioneer of African-American Drama.* Westport, CT: Greenwood Press, 1999.

Peterson, Bernard L. "Willis Richardson." *Black World* 26 (April 1975): 40–48, 87–88.

Sanders, Leslie Catherine. *The Development of Black Theater in America: From Shadows to Selves.* Baton Rouge: Louisiana State UP, 1988.

Louis J. Parascandola

RIDGE, JOHN ROLLIN [YELLOW BIRD] (1827–1867) On March 19, 1827, essayist, novelist, poet, and newspaperman John Rollin Ridge was born into a prominent Cherokee family at New Echota (near present-day Rome, Georgia). In 1835—believing that assimilating into white society was the Cherokees's only hope for survival—John Rollin's grandfather, Major Ridge, along with his father, John Ridge, and two uncles, Stand Watie and Elias Boudinot, joined a group of twenty men in signing the Treaty of New Echota. Under Cherokee law, the penalty for this act, which provided for the cession of all Cherokee lands east of the Mississippi River and which led to the forced removal of thousands of Cherokees from their Southern Appalachian homeland, was death. Consequently, on June 22, 1839, Rollin's grandfather, his father, and one of his uncles were assassinated by anti-Removal factions in Indian Territory (now Oklahoma).

Ridge, who was only twelve years old at the time, witnessed the murder of his father, an event that would greatly impact the rest of his life. Fearing for their safety, the young boy's mother, Sarah Northrup Ridge, moved her family from Indian Territory to Fayetteville, Arkansas, and in 1843, Ridge was sent to Massachusetts to attend the Great Barrington Academy.

In 1845 he returned to Fayetteville to study law; his dream, however, was to become a writer. After marrying Elizabeth Wilson (a white woman he had met in Massachusetts) in 1847, Ridge settled in Arkansas and began publishing poems and articles on Cherokee history and politics in local newspapers.

Another tragic event in 1849, however, changed the course of Ridge's life once again. In an altercation many believed to be a set-up that was designed to murder him, Ridge killed David Kell, a Cherokee man believed to be one of the assassins of John Ridge. Fearful of an unfair trial, he moved with his wife and daughter to California, where he quickly resumed his writing. In 1854, he published his popular novel, *The Life and Adventures of Joaquin Murieta, the Celebrated California Bandit*. Ironically, the book, whose protagonist commits murders in the name of justice, is a condemnation of **racism** against Mexican Americans, not Native Americans. Some critics, however, view *Joaquin Murieta* as Ridge's verbal attempt to avenge the death of his father; others believe that his prime motivation for writing the novel was money.

In 1857 Ridge became the first editor of the *Sacramento Daily Bee*, a newspaper with which he remained the last seventeen years of his life. Although most of his editorials were political in nature, Ridge also used the *Bee* as a forum for reviewing literary works, publishing his own poetry, publicizing Indian speeches, and defending female journalists.

Ridge considered himself primarily a poet, and the title of his best-known poem, "Mount Shasta" (1852), is inscribed on the author's grave marker. He also wrote love poems, patriotic poems, and philosophical poems, and a collection titled, simply, *Poems* was published posthumously in 1868.

John Rollin Ridge died on October 5, 1867, and is buried in the Greenwood Cemetery at Grass Valley, California.

Further Reading

Farmer, David, and Rennard Strickland. *A Trumpet of Our Own: Yellow Bird's Essays on the North American Indians.* San Francisco: Book Club of California, 1981.

Parins, James W. *John Rollin Ridge: His Life and Words.* Lincoln: U of Nebraska P, 1991.

Ginny Carney

RIGGS, LYNN (1899–1954) The only American Indian dramatist to achieve critical acclaim during the 1920s and 1930s, Lynn Riggs was born on August 31, 1899, in Indian Territory, near present-day Claremore, Oklahoma. His father, William Grant Riggs, was a rancher and a banker, and his Cherokee mother, Rosa Gillis Riggs, was a housewife. Lynn's mother died of typhoid fever when he was only two years old, but before Rosa died, she secured a Cherokee allotment for her son, which later helped to support him. Six months after the death of Rosa, Mr. Riggs married another Cherokee woman, Juliette Scrimsher Chambers. Juliette, however, was not "the motherly type"; she was especially cruel to Lynn, who was eventually sent to live with his Aunt Mary Brice.

As a young boy, Lynn Riggs was an avid reader who also had an aptitude for music and learned hundreds of old Cherokee chants. He was also an expert horseman and cowboy, but his real dream was to become an actor.

In 1912 Riggs entered Eastern University Preparatory School in Claremore. After graduating in 1917, he traveled to Chicago and New York, where he worked at a variety of jobs, ranging from janitor to proofreader for the *Wall Street Journal.* While in New York, he attended as many plays as possible, acted in cowboy movies, and continued to write drama and poetry.

In 1920 Riggs returned home and entered the University of Oklahoma, where he majored in speech. There he continued to write poetry, and in 1921 he produced his first play, *Cuckoo.* During his senior year at the university, the young playwright contracted tuberculosis and went to Santa Fe to recuperate. His second play, *Syrian Knives,* was produced there in 1925.

While in France on a 1928 Guggenheim Fellowship, Riggs wrote his most famous play, *Green Grow the Lilacs.* The play, a colorful tale of life in Indian Territory, premiered on Broadway January 26, 1931, ran for sixty-four performances, toured the Midwest, and was nominated for a Pulitzer Prize. In 1943 Riggs's play was adapted by the famous Broadway team of Richard Rodgers and Oscar Hammerstein into the internationally acclaimed musical *Oklahoma!*

Riggs's only play about Indian people, *The Cherokee Night,* explored the alienation and conflict often experienced between mixed-blood youth, born of Cherokee people and Caucasian settlers, and restrictive adults. Although it played at Hedgerow Theater in 1932 and Federal Theater, New York City, in 1936, this experimental, achronological play was not easily understood by audiences. Today, however, it is being studied with renewed interest by American scholars.

During his lifetime, Riggs wrote thirty plays, numerous short stories, two books of poetry (including a volume titled *The Iron Dish*), and an unfinished novel, as well as scripts for several movies. Lynn Riggs died of stomach cancer in New York City on June 30, 1954, and is buried in Oklahoma. (*See also* Native American Drama)

Further Reading

Braunlich, Phyllis. *Haunted by Home: The Life and Letters of Lynn Riggs*. Norman: U of Oklahoma P, 1988.

Erhard, Thomas A. *Lynn Riggs, Southwest Playwright*. Austin, TX: Steck-Vaughn Company, 1970.

Ginny Carney

RISHEL, MARY ANN MALINCHAK (1940–)   Slovak American short story writer and novelist, textbook author, and professor. "Staus" (1977) is a short story that affectingly depicts a twentieth-century Slovak American adjusting to life after the sudden death of his wife. "Uncle Perk's Leg" (1979) is a chatty, mock-serious narration by Staus's niece about an amputated leg. Rishel's novel-in-progress *The Devin Gate* concerns Slovak Americans and Slovaks living through recent political changes in Central Europe.

Resilience and perduring hope among members of the same Slovak American family distinguish both "Staus" and "Uncle Perk's Leg." In "Staus" the character Staus is always thinking but says little. From his musings the reader learns that he and Martha were older when they married after World War II but suited each other well. Then, she just peacefully died in his arms on that Friday, and his life changed forever. Adjusting to Martha's absence reveals her unique place in Staus's life. Helping his sisters in various tasks seems to ameliorate his sorrow. They think that Staus should get on with his life by marrying Sara Antonszik, an old family friend and sister of Staus's sister Irene's husband, but he will have none of this. Reserved Staus, however, is the one who helps soothe bad feelings and hurts in the family, lest these fester and menace family ties. In the end, Staus and his siblings become a community of support for one another living without their spouses.

The story time for "Uncle Perk's Leg" actually precedes that of "Staus." In this story Staus's wife Martha is still alive. Staus's young niece (no name given), daughter of his widowed sister Irene, is the first-person narrator. Because of his arteriosclerosis Uncle Perk, the husband of Staus's sister Kate, needs to have his right leg amputated. Since her father's death when she was a year old, Uncle Perk has been like a father to Staus's niece and her brother. Ironically, the amputation is quite a minor concern. It is the funeral for the amputated limb that causes the major crisis because precisely the size of the amputated body part is what necessitates such a ritual according to Fr. O'Donovan. The ensuing discussion of where to bury the amputated limb carefully anticipates that someday the rest of Perk should be readily united with it. The funeral occurs, but inexplicably without priest and proper ritual. Not long after this, Perk's actual death, his loss to the family, is now better appreciated through his niece's tale of his amputated leg.

The Devin Gate presents eighty-year-old Zuzanna Koval. After fighting in the Slovak National Uprising in World War II, she immigrates to the United States, where she spends the next fifty years quietly raising eight children. Because of an enigmatic invitation to a wedding in Slovakia, Zuzanna returns to her homeland with her granddaughter. There she encounters Marushka, her estranged Roma friend and fellow partisan, the real reason for Zuzanna's return. In the end, only through Marushka can Zuzanna satisfy her yearning for quest and self-discovery.

Gerald J. Sabo

RIVERA, EDWARD (1944–2001) Puerto Rican novelist and short story writer. Rivera was born in Orocovis, Puerto Rico. At the age of seven, his parents immigrated to New York City, where he lived most of his life. In the Spanish Harlem, he attended both parochial and public schools, the Art Students League in his senior year and the Pratt Institute for a semester. Following his graduation from high school, Rivera worked in offices, factories and did odd jobs in the city. He also worked at the central branch of the New York City Public Library. When he turned nineteen years old, Rivera enrolled in evening classes at the City College of New York. But his aspirations of a college career where postponed when he was drafted in the U.S. Army, where he became a typist stenographer.

After his discharge from the Army, Rivera worked for a year in a bank as a filling clerk and form-letter typist. During this time, he also resumed his college evening studies and obtained an associate degree in English. After the completion of his associate degree, Rivera continued with his studies in English. He earned a BA in 1967 from the City College of New York and received a master's degree in fine arts from Columbia University. Rivera died in New York City at the age of sixty-two as a consequence of a heart attack. By the time of his death, he was working as an assistant professor of English at City College in New York City.

Rivera's novel *Family Installments*, published in 1982, has been considered groundbreaking literature of Puerto Ricans in the United States. This autobiographical novel was first written in the form of short stories that were originally published in magazines and journals. In this novel, Rivera approaches from a third-person narration the history of the migration of a father and a son in New York City. In this novel, through the third-person narrator, a first-person narrator discourse emerges, bringing an adult perspective to the story—that of the narrator's father. The father's narration is antagonized by Santos, the youngest narrator in the novel. In this use of narration, the reader sees the experience of the Puerto Rican people's emigration from two different perspectives: the old and new generation of immigrants. In the novel the father is constantly searching for the American dream through the images of seduction that the immigrants have created, whereas his son, Santos, acquired the dream through education. In the novel the images of the naïve idealism of the false modernization discovered by the father are contrasted with the modernization process that his son is living through education. Rivera uses these two perspectives to portray the transition between the oral culture and the written culture in his novel.

Several stories written by Rivera have been published in anthologies, journals, and newspapers. (*See also* Puerto Rican American Novel)

Further Reading

Natterman, Udo. "International Fiction vs. Ethnic Autobiography: Cultural Appropriation in Mark Twain and Edward Rivera." *International Fiction Review* 28.1–2 (2001): 13–22.

Sanchez, Marta. "Hispanic and Anglo-American Discourse in Edward Rivera's *Family Installments.*" *American Literary History* 1.4 (1989): 853–71.

Amarilis Hidalgo de Jesús

RIVERA, JOSÉ (1955–)   Puerto Rican American playwright and screenwriter. Author of the widely produced play *Marisol* (1992), Rivera explores themes of **identity** in his work: maintaining one's personal identity in a rapidly and frighteningly changing world and maintaining one's cultural identity in a strange land.

Rivera comes from a family of storytellers, which he cites as an intrinsic part of being Puerto Rican. His family's stories, he says, blur the lines between fantasy and reality, and this trait is evident in his own playwriting. He has remained closely connected with his heritage through family tradition, through visits to Puerto Rico and family still living there, and through serious exploration of that heritage in his work.

During the great migration of Puerto Ricans to the United States, especially to New York City in the 1940s and 1950s, Puerto Rican drama began to flourish in New York's theater scene, eventually supplanting Spanish theater as the dominant Hispanic theater in the United States. Perhaps the most successful Puerto Rican American playwright thus far is Rivera, author of the popular *Marisol*, *Cloud Tectonics* (1995), *References to Salvador Dalí Make Me Hot* (2000), and *Sueño* (1998), a freewheeling adaptation of Pedro Calderón de la Barca's Spanish Golden Age classic play *Life Is a Dream* (1636).

Rivera was born in Puerto Rico but raised on Long Island, where he saw his father work as many as three jobs at any one time to support his family. Rivera's work has been criticized by some for "not being Hispanic enough" and by others for being "too Hispanic." Full of excess and fantasy, Rivera's plays are often classified as "magic realism," and he counts Latin American magic realist novelist Gabriel García Márquez, under whom he studied at a Sundance Institute workshop in 1989, as an influence, though he prefers not to label himself a "magic realism writer," saying instead that magic realism is just another literary tool that can be put to service when appropriate. He refers to it as a particularly poetic method of getting at a character's inner psychology. His plays negotiate the space between the real and the fantastic, as in *Marisol*'s exploration of a postapocalyptic New York. Ruptured violently, society must begin anew as the old order falls. Populated with angels and idiots, the play explores issues of gender and religion against a backdrop of dreams and nightmares.

His play *The House of Ramon Iglesia* (1983) premiered at New York City's Ensemble Studio Theatre and subsequently aired on the Public Broadcasting Corporation series *American Playhouse. Each Day Dies at Sleep* (1990) premiered in a coproduction between Circle Repertory Company and Berkeley Repertory Theatre, certainly high-profile theaters at which to debut a work, but it was *Marisol* that would establish him as a nationally recognized, in-demand playwright. It has proven popular among regional theater groups since it premiered at the Actors Theatre of Louisville in Louisville, Kentucky, in 1992 and won the 1993 Obie Award for Outstanding Play after a run at the New York Shakespeare Festival. *Marisol* is set in the boroughs of New York City as the year 2000 fast approaches. Marisol, a young Latina, is saved by a combat-boots-clad angel as she is on the verge of being mugged at knife-point on the subway. The angel later shows up at Marisol's home to tell her that the apocalypse is nigh and that New York will soon undergo massive fires and abandonment by most of its populace. The angels have declared war on their ailing, senile God, and New York is the battleground. The denizens of Heaven take to the streets of Earth with tommy guns, and humans take sides in the war before eventually beginning a rebellion of their own. Many of the play's gruesome events, including the subway attack, are based on Rivera's experiences as a former New Yorker and derive from his anxiety about the disintegration of positive social relations in the complex modern world. Though dealing with grand themes and mysticism, *Marisol*'s characters always seem fully human and developed, or developing, as they struggle to maintain their senses of self in an explosive, shifting environment.

References to Salvador Dalí Make Me Hot, which starred Rosie Perez and frequent Rivera actor John Ortiz in its 2001 New York production at the

José Rivera. *AP/Wide World Photos.*

Joseph Papp Public Theater, again juxtaposes the fantastic with the real, this time to explore the Gulf War. The main character in *Sueño*, played by Ortiz at Hartford Stage in its original production, is never quite sure if he is living in reality or in a dream. *Adoration of the Old Woman* (2002) concerns a Puerto Rican family undergoing generational conflict while dealing with identity issues resulting from Puerto Rico's status as a United States territory and as a country with its own distinctiveness. Though the play tackles the issue of Puerto Rican independence versus United States statehood, it frames the theme within a plot concerning an old woman whose bed is haunted by her dead husband's lover's ghost, a story based on what is purportedly a true experience of Rivera's great aunt, whom he had visited in Las Arenas, Puerto Rico.

Rivera's plays have been produced all over the country at such prestigious theaters as the Public Theater/New York Shakespeare Festival, which sponsors the annual Festival Latino; Playwrights Horizons; and the Mark Taper Forum. He has received Fulbright, National Endowment for the Arts, Rockefeller, and Whiting Foundation grants. His first feature film screenplay, *Motorcycle Diaries* (2004), is a road story of personal transformation partly based on Che Guevara's diaries. He created the smart but short-lived cult television series *Eerie, Indiana* (1991–1992). Along with Gabriel García Márquez and his mother—a dazzling storyteller, according to Rivera—he counts novelists Thomas Mann and Günter Grass as influences. José Rivera currently makes his home in Los Angeles. (*See also* Puerto Rican American Drama)

Further Reading

Landau, Tina. Foreword. *Marisol and Other Plays*. José Rivera. New York: Theatre Communications Group, 1997. ix–xiii.

Rich, Frank. "The Angel of No Hope Visits New York." *New York Times* (May 21, 1993): C3.

Rivera, José. "*Marisol*: A Production History." *TheatreForum* (Fall 1992): 22.

Jeffrey Godsey

RIVERA, TOMÁS (1935–1984) A writer, scholar, and university administrator whose 1971 novel *. . . y no se lo trago la tierra (. . . and the earth did not devour him)* won the first *Premio Quinto Sol*. This novella was made into a feature film and is among the most studied works of Chicano literature. Rivera was born in Crystal City, Texas to Mexican immigrants. Because of their migrant work Tomás missed much school. Nevertheless, in 1969 he received a PhD in romance languages and literature, and in an astonishing ten years moved up the ranks to became Chancellor of the University of California, Riverside—the first minority so honored in the UC system. Along with his award-winning novel, he published poetry, short stories, and essays. Some work was posthumously published: *The Searchers: Collected Poetry* (1990), *The Harvest: Short Stories by Tomás Rivera* (1989), and *Tomás Rivera: The Complete Works* (1995).

. . . and the earth did not devour him was translated by Hermino Rios C., and later by Evangelina Vigil-Piñon. Rolando Hinojosa-Smith produced an English "rendition": *This Migrant Earth* (1987). *. . . and the earth did not devour him* powerfully depicts the miserable conditions endured by Mexican migrants between 1945 and 1955. A young, nameless protagonist is the primary narrator, but there are other voices that sometimes act as chorus. Structurally, the novel consists of twelve chapters that roughly correspond to a year because Rivera is interested in cycles of life and harvest. Before each chapter there is a one-paragraph vignette that usually relates to the following story or to the previous one. The prologue introduces a lost year, and then the narrator falls asleep and dreams of his past—the stories that follow. The epilogue "Under the House," employs flashbacks that tie together many of the stories and add further detail. The protagonist wants to recapture all of the people from his past and embrace them. Though initially a boy is under the house, ultimately a man emerges from where he had gone to "think in peace." This tranquil setting—representative of his subconscious—allows him to make a discovery and experience an epiphany. Through memory he recaptures a lost year, and then desires to recall all the past years and all the people from them.

The first story of the collection concerns a young Mexican boy being accidentally shot by the Anglo rancher who does not want workers wasting time drinking water. This sets the tone for Rivera's narrative, but what keeps the work from being overly didactic is his style and craft, his subtlety, as well as his sense of humor, and humanity.

In "The Night the Lights Went Out" Rivera characteristically renders a complexity of voices by alternately using Ramon, Juanita, Ramiro, and neighbors as contributing narrators. Ramon, a spurned and jealous ex-boyfriend still wants to control Juanita, who insists on going to a dance without him, so he attempts to cut off the building's power supply and ends up electrocuting himself. What Rivera renders so well are the different speakers who elevate this tragic couple to a Romeo-and-Juliet-like status by concluding that Ramon must have killed himself over unrequited love.

At the center is the title story in which the protagonist finds his voice and curses God for the sunstroke of his father and brother, and for the tuberculosis of relatives. His mother, meanwhile, merely lights candles and implores God for mercy—which the boy thinks is useless. The novel's title could be loosely translated as "and lightening did not strike him," which traditionally conveys what happens to those who blaspheme. The boy curses God, but the ground does not swallow him. His cursing becomes a powerful act of self-determination and empowerment, which is significant since in the first paragraph the narrator is "at a loss for words." Cursing God also serves as a rejection of his mother's Catholicism, which is associated with superstition and passivity. Rivera's depiction of religion is clear: priests and nuns are dirty-minded; a minister's wife runs off with a carpenter; a mother bargains with God—her palpitating heart in exchange for her son's safety; a priest blesses cars for five dollars each and then vacations in Spain. Rivera also makes oblique allusions to ideas of Aztec sun-worship and human-sacrifice.

The double entendre of "When We Arrive," a story of migrant workers traveling like cattle in a truck, suggests the idea of interminable travel; more significantly, the repetition of the title conveys the notion that these migrants will never arrive economically or socially. Despite dehumanizing hardships, one character—suffering from diarrhea—is able to maintain humanity and transcend difficulties through his concern for others and, even more dramatically, by gazing skyward and reveling in the beauty of stars punctuating a black sky. His unwillingness to succumb to his squalid circumstances gives him courage to endure and, ultimately, to overcome such conditions.

Rivera's other collection, *The Harvest*, has not received enough critical attention although the first five stories are masterpieces of Chicano literature and rise to mythic proportion: "The Salamanders" is a gripping allegory about those socially and economically disenfranchised; "On the Road to Texas: Pete Fonseca" is about a *pachuco* who seduces a single mom and fools a migrant community; "Eva and Daniel" is a poignant story of love lost; in "The Harvest" mild magical-realism depicts the migrant worker's connection to the earth's rhythms; and in "Zoo Island" José empowers a migrant camp by counting everyone and putting up a sign, "Zoo Island Pop 88 ½." All of these uncommon stories are among Rivera's best. One story is a fragment from Rivera's lost novel *La casa grande del pueblo*; another pays homage to Jorge Luis Borges.

Despite Rivera's early death, his literary reputation is assured. His stories, novel, and poetry chronicle the life and struggles of dispossessed migrants. Although Rivera drew from his own life, his exceptional literary talent renders works rich in interpretation, nuance, and compassion.

Further Reading

Lattin, Vernon E, ed. *Contemporary Chicano Fiction: A Critical Survey.* Binghamton: Bilingual Press, 1986.

Lattin, Vernon E., Rolando Hinojosa, and Gary Keller, eds. *Tomás Rivera, 1935–1984: The Man and His Work.* Tempe, AZ: Bilingual Press, 1988.

Olivares, Julian, ed. "International Studies in Honor of Tomás Rivera." *Revista Chicano-Riqueña* 13.3–4 (1985).

Sommers, Joseph, and Tomás Ybarra-Frausto, eds. *Modern Chicano Writers.* Englewood Cliffs, NJ: Prentice Hall, Inc., 1979.

Paul Guajardo

ROBBINS, DOREN GURSTEIN (1949–) Jewish American poet and activist. A rarity among American poets of his generation, Doren Robbins has been called by Pulitzer Prize winner Philip Levine "a new Adam" whose "first priority [is] naming the unnamed, noting the unnoted, filling in all the details of those lives that have waited for ages . . . at the frontiers of poetry for an invitation to come in" (147).

In his collection of autobiographical prose poems, *Parking-Lot Mood Swing*, Robbins recounts an incident indicative of his essential attitude. As he read Robert Desnos's "Last Poem" aloud to college students, he found himself weeping. He did so, he says, because he cares so much about passion. Such passion is a multifaceted insistence on absolute love, absolute justice, and the absolute dignity of the individual. Robbins, a self-taught writer who attended college and sought graduate degrees only after working many years as a cook and carpenter, exhibits this passion even in his earliest poems, which often explode with rage against specific injustices.

Such fulmination against injustice is not generic. Nor is it merely the passion of youth. As Philip Levine notes, Robbins is "consumed by what has driven him to fury" (148). Twenty-five years after the publication of his first book, Robbins continues such unflinching zeal in his 2001 poetry collection, *Driving Face Down*, which won the prestigious Blue Lynx Prize. Here, for example, he focuses on the gritty underbelly of Los Angeles, a city he knows well for having grown up there; and his portraits of people, including family, disclose fervor against injustices visited upon them, whether they be political victims from as far away as El Salvador, Croatia, or the Ukraine, or working-class comrades closer to home.

But Robbins's is not only an angry passion. Within his poetry collections are numerous ardent love poems and emotional elegies. He exhibits palpable compassion for urban inhabitants like an eighty-four-year-old woman, or a market worker who has deformed fingers from the Death Camps, or even for a broken-winged pigeon he manages to save from being tormented by two young hoodlums.

The poet Thomas McGrath has said that Robbins's work is unified by both anger and love. Other critics and reviewers have compared him with Francois Villon, Louis-Ferdinand Celine, Henry Miller, and **Gerald Stern**, writers whose work is equally intense. Indeed, Robbins is an ecstatic poet whose vision is uncompromised, whose poems are rich with extraordinary attention paid to the often undocumented, ordinary lives that deserve it. His is a deeply rooted devotion, as is evident from his first collection of poems.

Doren Robbins has given more than one hundred readings of his work and published more than eighty poems in American and international literary journals, among them *The American Poetry Review*, *Kayak*, and *International Poetry*. He has written eleven books and won such awards as the Anna Davidson Rosenberg Award from the Judah Magnes Museum (1996), an Oregon Literary Arts Fellowship (1996), and a Loft Foundation Fellowship (1985). He has an MFA from the University of Iowa and completed graduate coursework toward a PhD at Indiana University of Pennsylvania. Robbins teaches at Foothill College, Los Altos, California, where he is cochair of the creative writing department and director of the Foothill Writers' Conference.

Further Reading

Levine, Philip, "Forward to *Dignity in Naples and North Hollywood*." *Sextet One: Six Powerful American Voices.* Ed. Victor di Suvero and Jeanie C. Williams. Santa Fe, NM: Pennywhistle Press, 1996. 146–48.

Andrea Hollander Budy

RODGERS, CAROLYN (1945–) African American poet and activist. Carolyn Rodgers's place in the African American literary tradition was first established with her association with the Chicago Organization of Black American Culture in the 1960s. Rodgers was instrumental at that time for helping to promote poetry as a black art form. Much of her poetry from this time period comes from the perspective of a militant black woman; however, her sensitivity is revealed through her writing as she struggles with the many contradictions found in the African American cultural revolution.

Although Rodgers's early poems received criticism for their language, she is credited for using them to break down walls that were in place for black women writers. Incorporating obscenities and playing with black speech patterns were ways for Rodgers to come to grips with her personal struggles and to reconcile the inconsistencies of the world around her. Although other black artists at the time were utilizing these unconventional methods, it was considered particularly courageous for a woman poet to use them. *Paper Soul* (1968), Rodgers's first published collection of poetry, reveals poems that suggest, in their subjects as well as in their radical language, cultural revolution in act or in spirit. In this collection, Rodgers employs vivid, forceful language to address the contradictions she sees around her and to explore themes such as love (and a woman's need for it), religion, **identity**, male-female relationships, and, of course, revolution. Moreover, Rodgers expresses concern over the role of women in the **Black Arts Movement**, who she sees as being forced into contradictory roles of revolutionary harshness and soft femininity. In this way, while Rodgers' poetry serves as a voice for all black artists in the 1960s, her role as a strong advocate of black women also emerges even in her earliest writings.

Whereas revolution remains a major part of her second collection of poetry, *Songs of a Blackbird* (1969), Rodgers's increasing concern with the black woman poet also clearly becomes a more dominant theme. The real shift in Rodgers's writing, however, can be seen in her work *how I got ovah*, which was published in 1975. With the transition into a new decade, Rodgers's work also transitions away from the militant spirit and apparent struggles of her early poetry to softer, more introspective writing. While Rodgers continues to explore social concerns in her later poetry, her writing reflects her maturity and growth; in fact, most of her political poems in this collection end with a sense of peace and hope. By her later poems, Rodgers's language is more consistent and her works are centered more on love. These poems explore new themes such as the church, the family, and women. Rodgers's love for black people, and for black women in particular, comes through in all of these poems.

Since her movement away from the militant arts movement, Carolyn Rodgers's poems have continued to reflect a sort of evolving **feminism**, which focuses on her reflections on herself and the world around her. Like many black female writers, she has come to recognize the influence of the black women who have gone before her, particularly her mother. Many of Rodgers's poems reveal the impact that her mother has had on her, from her mother's religious beliefs to her views of relationships. At the same time, Rodgers's poetry reflects a quest for self-definition apart from outside forces. Her search for identity and for potential, both for herself and for black women in general, is evident in these writings.

Throughout her many years in the literary scene, Carolyn Rodgers has proven herself to be an important voice for African American women. From her involvement in revolutionary literary movements to her exploration of themes important to black women in particular, Rodgers has actively worked toward breaking down the walls that hold back black artists and women in society throughout her career. For this work, Rodgers has received numerous awards, from the first Conrad Kent Rivers Memorial Fund Award in 1968 to the **Gwendolyn Brooks** Fellowship. With her published works and numerous accomplishments, Carolyn Rodgers can certainly be recognized as one of the most notable new black poets. (*See also* African American Poetry)

Further Reading

Evans, Marie, ed. *Black Women Writers (1950–1980): A Critical Evaluation.* Garden City, NY: Anchor/ Doubleday, 1984.

Henderson, Stephen. *Understanding New Black Poetry.* New York: William Morrow, 1973.

Lee, Don L. *Dynamite Voices: Black Poets of the 1960's.* Detroit: Broadside Press, 1971.

Randall, Dudley. *The Black Poets.* New York: Bantam, 1971.

Jessie N. Marion

RODRÍGUEZ, JOE D. (1943–)   Mexican American novelist, critic and teacher. Rodríguez's fictional and critical work explores the themes of Mexican American cultural **identity** and the horrors of war. Rodríguez was born in Hawai'i into a racially hybrid family. The union of his Mexican grandfather with his Indian grandmother and the subsequent marriage of his Mexican American father to his Puerto Rican mother provided Rodríguez with a multilayered cultural identity. After a year of studying microbiology at the University of Texas at Austin Rodríguez dropped out and returned to Hawai'i. The **racism** he had encountered in Texas formed a marked contrast to the relative inclusiveness of the environment in Hawai'i. After abandoning a course at the University of Hawai'i Rodríguez moved with his family to San Diego, where he took on a variety of temporary jobs and experienced a period of homelessness.

From 1965 to 1966 Rodríguez served in Vietnam as a nurse, and it is this experience that provided him with the inspiration for his novel *Oddsplayer* (1989) which takes Joseph Conrad's *Heart of Darkness* as a point of departure, rather in the manner of Francis Ford Coppola's *Apocalypse Now* (1979). The three chapters of the novel correspond respectively to early morning, midday, and twilight, thus forming a metaphorical progression through the day. Rodríguez draws on pre-Columbian and Judeo-Christian motifs and imagery in order to dramatize the Vietnam conflict. However, in contrast to the by now familiar vision of the Vietnam soldier driven toward mental breakdown as a result of the carnage of the war, Rodríguez suggests that the conflicted state of mind of many of the book's characters derives from deeply disturbing personal experiences that had occurred prior to the war and remained unresolved. The diverse cast of characters provides scope for Rodríguez to explore the various problems experienced by Latinos, African Americans, and Anglo-Americans. The narrative style of the novel owes much to the fragmentary and ludic quality of Latin American writers such as Julio Cortázar, whose view of life as a game has had a profound influence on Rodríguez's work.

Rodríguez finally gained his BA in philosophy at the University of San Diego State University in 1967, and in 1977 he completed a PhD on Nathaniel Hawthorne at the University of California at San Diego. He now works as a professor in the department of Mexican American studies at San Diego State University. In critical articles such as "United States Hispanic Autobiography and Biography: Legend for the Future" Rodríguez explores the complex process of constructing a sense of cultural identity as a Hispanic citizen living in the United States.

Joe D. Rodríguez is currently working on a number of literary projects concerning **multiculturalism** in the United States, among them a novel focused on the life of anthropologist John Peabody Harrington, who strove to save Indian cultures.

Further Reading

Joe D. Rodríguez. "The Chicano Novel and the North American Narrative of Survival." *Denver Quarterly* 16 (1981): 64–70.

Helen Oakley

RODRÍGUEZ, LUIS J. (1954–) Mexican American writer. Luis J. Rodríguez has distinguished himself as a writer of poetry, short stories, children's literature, and memoir. He garnered substantial acclaim for his autobiography, *Always Running: La Vida Loca, Gang Days in East L.A.* (1993). The autobiography describes his descent as an adolescent into a life of street gangs, random violence, and heavy drugs.

As he grew up in southern California, Rodríguez was arrested numerous times for his criminal activities. By the time he was fifteen, he was already a homeless high school dropout. When he was eighteen, however, he decided to abandon his gang affiliation and rehabilitate his direction in life.

With help, he quit drugs, and after taking various odd, mostly manual-labor jobs, he began to work as a journalist. This experience with reporting marked the beginning of his new life as a writer. As he covered homelessness and labor issues during this period of his life, Rodríguez's commitment to social activism solidified.

Rodríguez's first published works were poetry collections. Both *Poems Across the Pavement* (1989) and *The Concrete River* (1991) portray urban life as a volatile mixture of despair, poverty, violence, hope, and hurt. Although *Always Running* also reflects Rodríguez's orientation toward unveiling the underside of American society, he has mentioned that he wrote it to save his firstborn son, Ramiro, from repeating the errors of his father. Some readers complain that *Always Running* glamorizes gang membership and portrays rape and other forms of violence with insensitivity, but others praise its honesty and the warning it provides about the perils and emptiness of life in a gang.

As part of his ambitious commitment to redirecting youth away from gangs and crime, Rodríguez has hosted numerous workshops in schools and juvenile detention facilities. In addition, he has written two books for children. The first, *América Is Her Name* (1998), tells the story of América, a young girl from Oaxaca who must contend with dislocation, **racism**, and gender oppression. Rodríguez uses this story to validate the experiences of immigrant children and to inspire both children and adults to lift the restrictions that have foreclosed Latinas' dreams and ambitions. *It Doesn't Have to Be This Way* (1999), Rodríguez's follow-up book for children, portrays a young boy's negotiation of an invitation to join a local gang. Through this story, Rodríguez emphasizes the dangers of gangs in order to encourage readers to re-examine any inclination to see gangs as a pathway to manhood.

Other works by Rodríguez include *Trochemoche* (1998), a poetry collection; *Hearts and Hands: Creating Community in Violent Times* (2001), a work that offers strategies for understanding and ending youth violence; *The Republic of East L.A.* (2002), a collection of short stories; and *Music of the Mill* (2004), Rodríguez's forthcoming first novel. (*See also* Mexican American Autobiography, Mexican American Children's Literature)

Further Reading

Rodríguez, Andres. "Contemporary Chicano Poetry: the Work of Michael Sierra, Juan Felipe Herrera, and Luis J. Rodríguez." *Bilingual Review* 21.3 (1996): 203–18.

Phillip Serrato

RODRIGUEZ, RICHARD (1944–)   Mexican American intellectual, television and radio commentator, journalist, and essayist, Rodriguez writes for Pacific News Service, periodicals such as *Harper's* and the *Los Angeles Times*, and the Public Broadcasting Service show *The NewsHour with Jim Lehrer*. Richard Rodriguez exploded on the literary scene with his controversial first book, *Hunger of Memory: The Education of Richard Rodriguez, An Autobiography*, published in 1982. Ten years later *Days of Obligation: An Argument with My Mexican Father* (1992) appeared. In 2002 Rodriguez, who spells his name the English way rather than with the original Spanish accent (*Rodríguez*), published *Brown: The Last Discovery of America*, which he says "completes a trilogy on American public life and [his] private life."

Hunger of Memory begins the trilogy. Though subtitled "An Autobiography," Rodriguez notes that the book is a collection of six "fugue-like" essays, "impersonating an autobiography." The six essays and prologue reveal the history of Rodriguez's education, beginning with his uncomfortable entry into the "public" English-language classroom of the local Catholic school from the "private" intimacy of a Spanish-language household, and moving to an epiphany of sorts as a Fulbright researcher in the British museum. There he rejects the secure academic career waiting for him as he rejects the benefits of affirmative action that, he believes, unjustly make that career possible for him and not for others. And thus begins his career as a freelance writer. As language is the tool of his trade, so it is one of the main subjects of *Hunger of Memory*. An oft-excerpted section anthologized under the title "Public and Private Language" lies at the heart of his argument. At its simplest, "private" language was the Spanish of his household and family, while "public" language is the English he learned at school, the English the nuns asked his parents to use instead of their native Spanish. But more than language, it is education itself that creates an unbridgeable distance between him and his parents.

Rodriguez has been harshly criticized, and deeply praised, for his stance on affirmative action and bilingual education in *Hunger of Memory*. Other Chicanos (or Mexican Americans) in particular have rejected his views as harmful to the progress of the Chicano movement, while conservatives have seen his views as sensible. He, on the other hand, considers himself to the left of center, but has resisted the group **identity** implied by a "movement." He complains of the lack of diversity present in an all-encompassing group identity that inherently limits the identity of the individual.

Days of Obligation: An Argument with My Mexican Father (1992), selected as a finalist for the Pulitzer Prize in 1993, was received less contentiously than *Hunger*. The "days of obligation" of the title come from the Catholicism ever-present in Rodriguez's writing. A practicing Catholic is obligated to attend mass on Sundays and certain holy days of obligation, which at their most pared down include the Ascension (Easter), the Immaculate Conception, and the birth of Christ (Christmas). Composed of ten chapters and an introduction, Rodriguez places himself, literally and figuratively, in Mexico and California in search of an ethnic and sexual identity. On location in Mexico with a British television camera crew, he searches for his "parents' village," just the right image for a European audience. But Rodriguez ranges through time as well as space. "India" contemplates the Indians of the Americas who later became Native Americans. He examines the story of La Malinche, who, as consort of the Spanish conquistador Hernán Cortés, gave birth to the first Mexican, a *mestizo* mix of Indian and Spanish. In his (revisionist) version she is the seductress of Spain rather than the victim of rape. She is the defiled Indian juxtaposed with Mexico's Virgin patron saint, Our Lady of Guadalupe, who appeared to a humble Indian boy in 1531. And like Mexico itself, Rodriguez cannot avoid his own heritage as a Mexican (American) with Aztec ancestors.

In "Late Victorians" Rodriguez examines sexual identity and reveals a sexual orientation only hinted at in *Hunger of Memory*. He sketches a history of gay life in San Francisco, noting that the "gay-male revolution had greater influence on San Francisco in the 1970s than did the feminist revolution. But then came the AIDS epidemic of the 1980s, and with it the phone calls reporting the diagnosis or death of one friend after another. One dying friend tells him that he, Rodriguez, will be the only one spared the AIDS plague, because he is "too circumspect."

"In Athens Once" he visits Tijuana, a bustling town across the border from San Diego, during Holy Week. In other chapters, Rodriguez visits "The Missions" founded by Father Junípero Serra, who founded twenty-one missions, all a day's walk apart. He tells the story of the legendary bandit Joaquín Murietta. He discusses Catholicism and visits a "Junky church" in "The Latin American Novel" and delves into the immigrant experience in "Asians." Visiting various locations in California and Mexico, Rodriguez takes the reader to physical spaces inhabited by history—the history of the past, recorded by its inhabitants, and the history of the future of America, the place and the idea that no one can resist. What is America? And who is American? are questions central to *Days of Obligation*, but no less central is Rodriguez's self-definition, his tracing of his own identity as Catholic, Mexican American, and gay, along with a kind of redefinition of the cultural contributions of those elements to America.

In *Brown: The Last Discovery of America* (2002), Rodriguez completes his trilogy. With a preface and nine chapters, *Brown* is a series of meditations not on the color brown, but brown as impurity, says Rodriguez. Even the cover of the book is brown, with its brown title word and a photo of the author designed to reveal his own brownness, his Hispanic-ness, and most especially his Aztec features.

According to Rodriguez, **race** in America has always been an issue of white and black, of what he calls "white freedom and Negro disadvantage." From Alexis de Toqueville's "triad" of white, Indian, and Africa, America moved to a dichotomy of white and black; race, not class, as the great American divide. Thanks to the administration of President Richard Nixon ("Poor Richard"), race became five categories: Black; White; Native American/Eskimo; Asian/Pacific Islander; and Hispanic, or black, white, red, yellow, and brown. The Hispanic was born, what Rodriguez calls "The Third Man." Unlike other racial categories, being Hispanic depends on culture, not blood: "there is no such thing as Hispanic blood." With the invention of the Hispanic (sometimes known as the Latino), the specificity of national identity—Peruvian, Mexican, Honduran—was erased, and affirmative action and bilingual education were born. Rodriguez remains firmly against affirmative action and the notion of "minority" as numerical rather than cultural because, once again, race, not class, is the issue. In his view, that is, the poor white kid has less chance of getting into college than the middle-class Hispanic.

Rodriguez remains equally unconvinced of the need for bilingual education, which he sees as a program that creates disadvantages for young children and prevents their **assimilation** into mainstream America. It is perhaps ironic that Rodriguez himself had to learn Spanish in college, though it was his first language.

In *Brown* Rodriguez is much more open about being Catholic and, perhaps paradoxically, about being gay. He compares himself with the church's fathers, her popes, because none of them create life. He contrasts as well the white Anglo-Saxon Protestant pronoun "I" with the brown Catholic pronoun "we" (*nosotros*). He alters the standard historical vision of America as East-West. With the trans-border agreement of NAFTA (the North America Free Trade Agreement) and the continuing influx of Hispanics, America is now North-South. Blond-haired, blue-eyed Anglos order *burritos* and say "*sí, gracias.*" In keeping with his stance on affirmative action, Rodriguez would do away with race altogether as a category. Not black versus white, but brown. Impurity, as he calls it, is the fusion of races, the fusion of cultures, and it is precisely this fusion, or confusion, that Rodriguez sees as America's best hope.

Though Rodriguez's works are often shelved in the Sociology section, he might better be categorized as a cultural critic, a kind of participant-observer who makes no pretense of objectivity. He ignores the notion of political correctness, emphasizes the individual over the collective, and envisions the history of the future, rather than the past. For Rodriguez, the optimistic history of the future is brown. (*See also* Bilingualism, Mexican American Autobiography, Mexican American Gay Literature)

Further Reading

Alarcon, Norma. "Tropology of Hunger: The 'Miseducation' of Richard Rodriguez.' *The Ethnic Canon: Histories, Institutions, and Interventions.* Ed. Liu D. Palumbo. Minneapolis: U of Minnesota P, 1995. 140–52.

Fine, Laura. "Claiming Personas and Rejecting Other-Imposed Identities: Self-Writing as Self-Righting in the Autobiographies of Richard Rodriguez." *Biography* 19 (Spring 1996): 119–36.

Schilt, Paige. "Anti-Pastoral and Guilty Vision in Richard Rodriguez's *Days of Obligation.*" *Texas Studies in Literature and Language* 40.4 (Winter 1998): 424–41.

Torres, Hector A. "'I Don't Think I Exist'" Interview with Richard Rodriguez." *MELUS* 28.2 (Summer 2003): 164–202.

Linda Ledford-Miller

RODRÍGUEZ MATOS, CARLOS A. (1949–) Puerto Rican poet and literary critic. Drawing on his identity as a gay Latino man, the poetry and criticism of Rodríguez Matos explores constructions of masculinity and Hispanic culture. Carlos Antonio Rodríguez Matos was born in Naranjito, Puerto Rico, where he lived until 1979, when he came to the United States to complete his PhD at the University of Wisconsin—Madison. He has lived in New Jersey since the 1970s, but he still considers himself a "Puerto Rican" rather than an American writer. Rodríguez Matos has helped to raise consciousness regarding gay rights: He and his partner have adopted a boy, and they are considering adopting a girl. His criticism on Puerto Rican poetry is groundbreaking, as it has been instrumental in ensuring that "gay" poetry was given its own distinct category. Rodríguez Matos has also put together the first Hispanic anthology of AIDS literature titled *Poesída: An Anthology of AIDS Poetry from the United States, Latin America and Spain* (1995). The word "poesída" combines the Spanish term for AIDS, SIDA, with the word for poetry, "poesía."

Rodríguez Matos's first book of poetry, *Matacan* (1982) was designated as one of the best five poetry books in Puerto Rico in 1982. Here the author aims to play with the concepts of philosophical and love poetry, drawing on cultural influences derived from religion, music, and film. The first two sections, "Para llegarte," and "Morisquetas," focus on humorous love poetry with a philosophical dimension. The third section, "Llama de amor vivita (jarchas)," deals with love but with an absence of humor, and the final section, "Baquine Punk de Peter Blade," is more cynical. Rodríguez Matos's second book of poetry, *Llama de amor vivita (jarchas)*, was published in the Dominican Republic in 1988 and illustrated by the Puerto Rican artist Victor Amador. This book constitutes a development of the third section of *Matacan*, as its four sections ("Zero," "One," "Two," and "Three") explore different stages of love, tracing a movement from a sense of loneliness to the collective.

In addition, Rodríguez Matos is the author of an influential critical book on the subject of the Spanish picaresque writer, Guzman de Alfarache, titled *Guzman de Alfarache, el narrador Picaro* (1985), which analyses the narrative function of the trickster figure, illustrating how the entire narrative is an attempt by the narrator at deceiving the implied reader. This was one of two critical works used by Professor Nina Davis in her book *Autobiography as Burla in the Guzman de Alfarache* (1991).

Rodríguez Matos currently works as a professor of Spanish at New Jersey's Seton Hall University, where he continues to write poetry and critical works. (*See also* Puerto Rican American Gay Literature)

Further Reading

Rodríguez Matos, Carlos A. "To Be Gay, Puerto Rican, and a Poet." *ANQ: A Quarterly Journal of Short Articles, Notes, and Reviews* 10.3 (1997): 25–37.

Helen Oakley

ROETHKE, THEODORE (1908–1963) German American poet, author of children's books, and essayist. Roethke's childhood impressions of nature that he formed in the commercial greenhouses in Saginaw, Michigan, that were owned by his father and uncle had a profound impact on the way he treated the subjects and imagery of his poetic creations. A love of the organic world and a development of the self during the journey called life are intertwined in his intense lyricism. His poems, ranging from being written in strict meter and regular stanzas to free verse poems filled with surrealistic and mystical elements, continue to be held in high regard by critics and readers alike. Some scholars, quoting Roethke's psychiatrists, have pointed out that the poet's most productive periods occurred immediately after his serious mental breakdowns. His most popular and frequently anthologized poem "My Papa's Waltz" (1942), which describes a paradoxical father-son relationship, might reflect the poet's own thoughts about his father, who died when Theodore was fifteen years old.

Theodore (Huebner) Roethke spent his childhood and early teenage years growing up in a German American family in Saginaw, Michigan. His father, Otto Theodore Roethke, the son of Wilhelm Roethke—who had moved to Saginaw from Germany with his three sons, Emil, Karl (aka Charles), and Otto in 1872—was a floriculturist and greenhouse owner; his mother, Helen Marie Huebner Roethke, also of German American origin, was a homemaker. She had a profound impact on Theodore's school choice, reading development, and study habits. First, young Roethke attended John Moore School, where he studied reading, writing, arithmetic, and, for an hour a day, German. In 1921 his mother sent Theodore away to Arthur Hill High School because she was opposed to his attending Saginaw High School. As a freshman, Theodore wrote a speech addressing the Saginaw chapter of the Red Cross, which reached an international audience by being translated into twenty-six languages. Trying to dispel the myth that smart boys are "sissies," Theodore joined a high school athletic fraternity, Beta Phi Sigma, at the end of his freshman year; he became involved in sports as a substitute on the basketball team and a member of the track team.

The year of 1923 became a turning point for young Theodore's family: In February, his uncle Charles committed suicide, and in April, his father died of cancer. Consequently, young Theodore had to mature quickly. He became the first one in his family to attend a university by enrolling in the University of Michigan at Ann Arbor; as one of his summer jobs, he worked at the Heinz Pickle factory. In 1929 Roethke graduated magna cum laude from the University of Michigan, after which he entered Michigan Law School. However, he dropped out of law school to pursue a master's degree in literature at the Harvard Graduate School. Since the Great Depression weighed heavily on his family's finances, he decided to withdraw from school and accept a teaching position as an instructor in English at Lafayette College in Easton, Pennsylvania. During his four years there, three of his poems were published in a small magazine called *The Harp*; this is officially seen by critics as the start of his career as a poet. To support himself, Roethke took another teaching position, again as an instructor in English, at Michigan State College (now University) in 1935; in this environment he wrote more poetry, befriended such individuals as William Carlos Williams, **Stanley Kunitz**, and Louise Bogan. In November of his first year at Michigan State Roethke, however, had a mental breakdown, which forced him to be hospitalized at Mercywood Sanitorium in Ann Arbor for three months. For the next academic year, Roethke was hired by Pennsylvania State University in University Park as an instructor; by then his poems had been appearing regularly in reputable magazines such as *Poetry* and *The Saturday Review*. In 1939 he was promoted to the rank of assistant professor of English.

Roethke's first collection poetry titled *Open House*, which consists of forty-seven poems, was published in 1941; W. H. Auden, Elizabeth Drew, and other critics reviewed this first book favorably. Since Roethke preferred less hierarchical teaching and less formal learning environments, he decided to leave Penn State and take a position as an assistant professor of English at Bennington College in Vermont in 1943. In 1945 various aspects of his academic and personal life contributed to another one of Roethke's bouts of depression, which lead again to another hospitalization, and he was treated with experimental shock therapy.

The same year, patient Roethke was awarded his first Guggenheim Fellowship, which allowed him to spend the majority of his time writing poetry instead of teaching. The result was Roethke's second collection of poems, *The Lost Son and Other Poems*, which was released in 1948 after Roethke had accepted a position as an associate professor at the University of Washington in Seattle following another semester-long stint at Penn State in 1947. This volume, often considered his best, represents Roethke's energizing visions reflected in the organic world, which accompany the self while loving and living during the journey called "life." In 1948 Roethke was promoted to professor of English, a position he held until 1962, when he was appointed poet-in-residence there.

Praise to the End! (1951), a third collection of poetry, was completed in Seattle during the academic year and in the summer in Saginaw after Roethke had received a second Guggenheim Fellowship; it was followed by *The Waking: Poems 1933–1953* in 1953 after he, a confirmed bachelor, had married Beatrice O'Connell, a former Bennington student, and they had gone on their European trip to Italy, where they stayed at W. H. Auden's villa at Ischia, and then on to Switzerland and France in 1952. *Words for the Wind* came out in 1958 after Roethke had experienced his mother's death in 1953, suffered several mental ailments between 1953 and 1957, and gone on another trip to Europe. Roethke's *I Am! Says the Lamb* (1961) was the first of his collections of children's poetry to be published while he was alive. His last collection of poetry, *The Far Field*, had been completed as a first draft in 1963 before he died while swimming at a friend's pool on August 1, 1963.

He was buried next to his parents in Oakwood Cemetery in Saginaw, his birthplace.

As mentors, W. H. Auden, Louise Bogan, Babette Deutsch, Stanley Kunitz, and William Carlos Williams provided the gifted Roethke with encouragement but were unable to prevent him from plunging into periods of deep depression. On the other hand, Richard Hugo, Carolyn Kizer, David Wagoner, and James Wright form the quite successful quartet of former Roethke students. As a poet, his influences include William Wordsworth, William Blake, Christopher Smart, John Donne, Sir John Davies, Walt Whitman, William Butler Yeats, T. S. Eliot, and Dante Alighieri.

For his poems published in *Poetry*, Roethke received the Levinson Prize in 1951; in 1954, the poet was awarded the Pulitzer Prize in poetry for *The Waking: Poems 1933–1953*. Roethke received the National Book Award for *Words for the Wind* in 1959 and again in 1965—this time posthumously—for *The Far Field*. In 1959 Roethke received three other awards: the Edna St. Vincent Millay Award, the Longview Award, and the Pacific Northwest Writers Award. In 1962 Roethke was presented with an honorary Doctorate of Letters from the University of Michigan. In the same year, he received the Shelley Memorial Award for Poetry and the Poetry Society of America Prize, and, in 1958, the Bollingen Prize in Poetry from Yale University Library.

A good deal of Roethke's essentially confessional work was published posthumously (*The Far Field* [1964], *Sequence, Sometimes Metaphysical* [1964], *On the Poet and His Craft* [1965], and *Collected Poems* [1966]), exerting a significant influence on fellow poets, such as Sylvia Plath, Ted Hughes, James Dickey, and Robert Bly. In his poetic creations, sadness and joy—similar to his medical condition in life, which was diagnosed as a "bipolar disorder"—dominated as recurring stages in the self's attempts to reach new levels of awareness.

Further Reading

Bowers, Neal. *Theodore Roethke: The Journey from I to Otherwise.* Columbia: U of Missouri P, 1982.

Brooks, Cleanth, and Robert Penn Warren, eds. *Conversations on the Craft of Poetry.* Fort Worth, TX: Holt, Rinehart & Winston, 1961. 48–62.

Deutsch, Babette. *Poetry in Our Time.* New York: Doubleday, 1963.

Harjo, Joy. "On Theodore Roethke." *Poetry Speaks: Hear Great Poets Read Their Work from Tennyson to Plath.* Ed. Elise Paschen and Rebekah Presson Mosby. Naperville: Sourcebooks: 2001. 180–184.

Malkoff, Karl. *Theodore Roethke: An Introduction to the Poetry.* New York: Columbia UP, 1966.

Mills, Ralph J., ed. *Theodore Roethke: Letters.* St. Paul: U of Minnesota P, 1968.

Parini, Jay. *Theodore Roethke: An American Romantic.* Amherst: U of Massachusetts P, 1979.

Seager, Allan. *The Glass House: The Life of Theodore Roethke.* Boston: McGraw Hill, 1968.

Stiffler, Randall. *Theodore Roethke: The Poet and His Critics.* Washington, DC: American Library Association, 1986.

"Theodore Roethke." *Poetry Speaks: Hear Great Poets Read Their Work from Tennyson to Plath.* Ed. Elise Paschen and Rebekah Presson Mosby. Naperville, IL: Sourcebooks, 2001. 179.

Waggoner, Hyatt H. *American Poets from the Puritans to the Present.* Boston: Houghton Mifflin, 1968.

Wagoner, David, ed. *Straw for the Fire: From the Notebooks of Theodore Roethke, 1943–1953.* New York: Doubleday, 1972.

Claudia A. Becker

ROGERS, WILL (1879–1935)   Native American author, actor, and humorist. The youngest child of mixed-blood Cherokees, Clem and Mary Rogers, William Penn Adair Rogers was born in Indian Territory (now the state of Oklahoma) in 1879.

In 1829—just one year before Congress passed the Indian Removal Act, calling for the removal of all Southeastern Indian tribes to Indian Territory—Will's Cherokee grandparents, Robert and Sallie Vann Rogers had voluntarily moved from the state of Georgia to the Going-Snake district near the present town of Westville, Oklahoma. Robert Rogers soon became a prosperous farmer and rancher; however, in the summer of 1842, he was murdered, leaving behind his widow, a six-year-old daughter, and a three-year-old son, Clem (who would later become the father of Will).

Clem, who is said to have hated school, was nevertheless an ambitious young man who, like his father, became a wealthy rancher and a well-known Cherokee politician. In 1858 Clem married Mary Schrimsher, whose family had walked the infamous Trail of Tears in 1839. Clem and Mary, only nineteen years old at the time of their marriage, became parents to eight children, three of whom died before Will was born. His seventeen-year-old brother, Robert, died of typhoid fever in 1883, leaving Will as the only boy in the family.

Like his father and grandfather, Will had a special love for horses. By the time he was four years old, he was already a good rider, and he later became such a skilled roper that he was listed in the *Guinness Book of World Records* for his feats with a lasso.

When Will was ten years old, however, his carefree life was shattered by the death of his beloved mother, the person most responsible for her son's love of books. During his late teens, Will, who had dropped out of school in tenth grade, left home due to conflicts with his father and traveled to South Africa with the Wild West Show. Billed as "The Cherokee Kid," he did roping tricks, which later took him to Australia and New Zealand with the Wirth Brothers Circus and, later, earned him appearances at the World's Fairs in St. Louis and New York City.

In 1908 Will Rogers married Betty Blake; he was fond of saying, "When I roped her, that was the star performance of my life." They had four children.

Will Rogers. *Courtesy of the Library of Congress.*

Following his marriage, Rogers's vaudeville acts evolved from the exhibition of his skills with the lariat to an act that included humorous observations about people, politics, and life. Soon, the "cowboy philosopher," as he came to be known, was the most popular man in America.

In 1918 Rogers began acting in silent films, including *Laughing Bill Hyde* (1918) and *The Ropin' Fool* (1921). Throughout his career, he starred in seventy-one movies and several Broadway productions. In 1934 he was voted the most popular male actor in Hollywood.

In addition to his career as an actor, Rogers became a prominent radio broadcaster and political commentator. His stage monologues were so well-liked that he began putting them into writing. In 1919 he published his first two books: *The Cowboy Philosopher on the Peace Conference*, and *The Cowboy Philosopher on Prohibition*. In 1923 he began writing a nationally syndicated newspaper column (some 4,000 of his columns were printed during his lifetime). That same year Rogers published his *Illiterate Digest.* In 1926 *The Saturday Evening Post* sent him to Europe as an unofficial ambassador for President Calvin Coolidge. The articles he wrote during that trip were later published in book form as *Letters of a Self-Made Diplomat to His President.* In 1927 *Not a Bathing Suit in Russia*, based on Rogers's travels in the Soviet Union, was published.

Unfortunately, the life of America's most beloved celebrity was cut short at the age of 55. In 1935, during a trip to Alaska with aviator Wiley Post, their small plane crashed, and both men were killed.

The wit and humor of Will Rogers live on today, however, for, as President Franklin Delano Roosevelt once observed, "[Will's] humor and his comments were always kind. His was no biting sarcasm that hurt the highest or the lowest of his fellow citizens. When he wanted people to laugh out loud, he used the methods of pure fun. And when he wanted to make a point for the good of mankind, he used the kind of gentle irony that left no scars behind it."

Further Reading

Carter, Joseph H. *Never Met a Man I Didn't Like: The Life and Writings of Will Rogers.* New York: HarperCollins, 1994.

Yagoda, Ben. *Will Rogers: A Biography.* Norman: U of Oklahoma P, 2000.

Ginny Carney

ROIPHE, ANNE RICHARDSON (1935–)   Jewish American feminist and writer. Roiphe addresses in her fiction and nonfiction the conflicts between roles traditionally ascribed to women and their desire for an independent identity and explores questions of (female) Jewish **identity** between the parameters of America, Israel, and Judaism.

Born in New York in 1935 as Anne Roth, Roiphe was raised in an upper-class, Upper East Side milieu of affluent assimilated Jews. In 1957 she graduated from Sarah Lawrence College. In the following year she married Jack Richardson and, after her divorce in 1963, the psychotherapist Herman Roiphe in 1967. She lives in New York.

Her first novel, *Digging Out* (1967), autobiographic and an example of the Jewish-American novel of experience, was published under Roiphe's first married name of Anne Richardson. Better known is her second novel, *Up the Sandbox!* (1970), considered to be a feminist "classic" and a "landmark" portrayal of women's motherhood and career conflicts. In this satirical novel, Roiphe tells the story of a college-educated young mother who suffocates in the domestic routine of her married life and desperately seeks to escape in fantasies of alternative selves. Most controversial among her novels is, perhaps, *Lovingkindness* (1987), an example of what has been referred to as a Jewish American literature of the theological imagination (Glazer 81). In this novel, Roiphe explores in much detail the transitional state of the "returnee," to Israel and to the Jewish faith. Through her story, the reader witnesses the metamorphosis of the narrator's daughter from an insecure American dropout girl into an Orthodox Jewish woman living in Israel. Confronted with the emerging "other" in her daughter, and against her innermost resistance, the narrator (who shares many characteristics with the author) finally comes not only to accept her daughter's decision but, having relearned "cultural relativism" and having been made aware of her own spiritual dearth by recurrent dreams of Rabbi Nachman of Bratslav, finds herself compelled to reconsider her own existence as a secular and feminist Jewish American intellectual. In view of the biography of its author, *Lovingkindness* is perhaps the most intimately personal of Roiphe's novels: Her eldest daughter, the writer Emily Carter, became an alcoholic and drug addict. Roiphe gave an account of her daughter's illness in *Fruitful. A Real Mother in the Modern World* (1996), a work of nonfiction, shortlisted for the National Book Award, in which Roiphe censures the women's movement for its failure to effectively address issues of child care and parenting. In *The Pursuit of Happiness* (1991), a five-generation novel about a Jewish immigrant family finding its way in, and out of, America, Roiphe explores once more the meaning of Israel for American Jews as they acquire fortunes, strive for and achieve **assimilation** and status, and finally turn toward the Jewish State.

Already in 1981 appeared Roiphe's first memoir, *Generation without Memory: A Jewish Journey in Christian America*, in which she describes her experiences in the United States and inquires into the place of the Jewish people in American society. This was followed in 1999 by her second memoir, *1185 Park Avenue.* A chilling portrait of the author's dysfunctional early family life, her narrative also captures the social and historical circumstances of prosperous Jewish life in New York from the thirties onward.

In addition to her novels, Roiphe published a great number of articles and reviews in *Vogue, Redbook, Glamour, Working Women, Family Circle,* and elsewhere, and wrote a bimonthly column for the *New York Observer.* In many of her magazine contributions she addressed the issues central also to her earlier fiction: **feminism**, family life, and child care. Roiphe's latest novel, *Secrets of the City* (2003), was serialized in *The Forward* before being published in book form. Foregoing her familiar terrain, yet a witness to her closeness to the throb of civilization, this novel, set in an unnamed city that is really New York, is in many ways an attempt to come to terms with the aftermath of the terrorist attacks on September 11, 2001.

Further Reading

Furman, Andrew. *Israel Through the Jewish-American Imagination: A Survey of Jewish-American Literature on Israel, 1928–1995.* Albany: State U of New York P, 1997. 153–173.

Glazer, Miriyam. "Male and Female, King and Queen: The Theological Imagination of Anne Roiphe's *Lovingkindness,*" *Studies in American Jewish Literature* 10 (1991): 81–92.

Halio, Jay L. "Anne Roiphe: Finding Her America," *Daughters of Valor: Contemporary Jewish American Women Writers.* Ed. Jay L. Halio and Ben Siegel. Newark: U of Delaware P, 1997. 97–111.

Axel Stähler

ROLFE, EDWIN (1909–1954)   Jewish American poet. Born as Eddie Fishman in Philadelphia, Rolfe was the son of working-class, Ukranian immigrant parents, both of whom were active in leftist social movements. Rolfe took up their politics at an early age, joining the Young Communist League in high school. He became a freelance writer for the Communist paper *The Daily Worker* in the late 1920s, and advanced to become its Features Editor in 1933. In 1937 he joined the International Brigades in the Spanish Civil War, an experience that was to animate his work for the rest of his life. After World War II, he was blacklisted by the House Un-American Activities Committee. The rest of his short life was spent with his wife, Mary, fighting Joseph McCarthy's witch hunts on the home front.

Rolfe is primarily remembered as a poet who produced three major books of poetry, *To My Contemporaries* (1936), *First Love, and Other Poems* (1951), and *Permit Me Refuge* (1955). In addition, his poems appeared in a variety of leftist publications of his era, such as the periodicals *The Daily Worker* and *Partisan Review,* in the collaborative poetry collection *We Gather Strength* (1933), as well as in the influential collection *Proletarian Literature in the United States* (1934). Rolfe also wrote prose works: *The Glass Room* (1945), a mystery novel that was turned into a lucrative, Warner Brothers film starring Humphrey Bogart and Lauren Bacall, and *The Lincoln Battalion* (1939), a history of the American volunteers in the Spanish Civil War.

Each of his three major collections dealt with a particular phase of the history through which Rolfe lived. In order, these were the Great Depression and its attendant social struggles in the United States, the Spanish Civil War, and the post–World War II persecution of suspected radicals. The scholar Cary Nelson has noted that what unites Rolfe's poetry is a sense of bearing witness to history, the sense that we must speak to the events unfolding around us. His poems do not come from the perspective of a detached or cloistered observer, but from someone whose day-to-day life is deeply and personally affected by that history. Rolfe thus intended his poems not just to "bear witness" to history, but to intervene in the dynamic social struggles of the day.

His first independent book, *To My Contemporaries*, narrates the traumas and struggles of the Great Depression, and its poems cover subjects such as lynching, revolutionary martyrs, marching on May Day, the nuances of Party work, and the slow death of the worker under capitalism. Perhaps the most important, underlying "intervention" the collection puts forward is the necessity of effacing the boundary between self and other. For the world to be redeemed of its suffering, Rolfe suggests, new affective bonds must arise under the banner of communist revolution that bridge the gap between region, nation, class, and sentiment. "Definitions," for example, offers a call to put aside personal animosities within the ranks of the movement in favor of a unifying ethos of love; "These Men Are Revolution" envisions a future map without lines or distinct territories; and perhaps "Credo" goes furthest in obliterating the very notion of "I."

Despite his shifting historical focus, this theme continues in Rolfe's subsequent books of poetry. His collection *First Love, and Other Poems*, represents Republican Spain of the Spanish Civil War (1936–39) as a space where the perfect unity between self and other was achieved for a brief moment. Since many of these poems were written after his return to the United States, the book also reflects a strong desire to keep the memory of this unity fresh. By resurrecting the war in poetic form, Rolfe not only instills the reader with a sense of its monumentality, but also uses its example as a didactic lesson for future generations. One of the means by which Rolfe communicates the intensity of his experiences in Spain is by recurrently figuring the country as a romantic lover; one such poem, "Eligia," was so powerful that it brought Ernest Hemingway to tears for one of the few times in his life.

Permit Me Refuge, Rolfe's book focusing on the McCarthy-era United States, continues Rolfe's pursuit of a language of solidarity. The poem "Catalogue of *I*" echoes old themes by metaphorically figuring the entire diversity of humanity—even those who profit by war—as an inseparable facet of himself. But the collection also reveals a more consistent sense of anguish and desperation than his previous books, as if Rolfe is narrating from within an occupied territory. The unity of self and other he had been trying to forge all his life through poetry was clearly difficult to maintain after World War II, when former comrades saved their own skins by turning against each other in the public trials of the House Un-American Activities Committee. Nonetheless, Rolfe even registers betrayal through his lifelong belief in human inseparability. In "Ballad of the Noble Intentions," for example, he shows that by destroying others, the ex-radical-turned-stool-pigeon has actually annihilated himself. Rolfe unfortunately died of a heart attack before the era of communist witch-hunts ended and before the new mass movements of the 1960s were to inspire new ballads of solidarity.

Further Reading

Kalaidjian, Walter. "'Deeds Were Their Last Words:' The Return of Edwin Rolfe." *College Literature* 24 (1997): 55–69.

Nelson, Cary. "Lyric Politics: The Poetry of Edwin Rolfe." *Edwin Rolfe: Collected Poems*. Ed. Cary Nelson and Jefferson Hendricks. Urbana: U of Illinois P, 1993.

Nelson, Cary and J. Hendricks. *Edwin Rolfe: A Biographical Essay and Guide to the Rolfe Archive at the University of Illinois at Urbana-Champaign*. Urbana: U of Illinois P, 1990.

Chris Vials

RØLVAAG, OLE EDVART (1876–1931) Norwegian American novelist and man of letters. O. E. Rølvaag is considered the preeminent figure in Norwegian American literature. His novel *Giants in the Earth*, a story of Norwegian Americans settling the Dakota prairie, transcended the usual constraints of ethnic literature and found a wide American audience in translation. He was also an important essayist, critic, and mentor within Norwegian American literary circles and a professor of Norwegian literature at St. Olaf's University, where he helped found the Norwegian American Historical Association.

Rølvaag's novels explore the steep psychological toll that emigration exacted on Norwegian Americans, including the loss of their deep-rooted traditions and culture without adequate replacements and frequent estrangements from their more acculturated children. As with other Norwegian American cultural leaders, Rølvaag hoped to alleviate these and related problems through the retention of a Norwegian ethnic culture among Norwegian Americans, and central to this project was the use of Norwegian as a literary language. Simultaneously, Rølvaag fundamentally considered his writings to be "American literature in Norwegian," and, while Norwegian authors such as Henrik Ibsen and Jonas Lie were among his strongest literary influences, he freely adapted the conventions of American fiction to his work. Also, the alienation, rootlessness, and generational conflict that Rølvaag explored through the prism of the emigrant were frequent themes of the Modernist American authors concurrent with Rølvaag.

Rølvaag was born on the island of Dønna, just south of the Arctic Circle, where his family had earned their living as fishermen for generations. Restless and seeing the United States as a place to try himself on a larger scale, Rølvaag emigrated in 1896. Much of his early experience found its way into his first published book, *Amerika Breve* (1912; *The Third Life of Per Smevik*, 1971). An epistolary novel, Per's letters to his family describe his gradual, painful assimilation. Like Rølvaag, Per first labors as a farmhand on the Great Plains, then works his way through college, eventually becoming a teacher. Offsetting his successes are struggles with English, disenchantment at the shallowness of the mores of many Americans, and a continual sense of loss at leaving his native country and family. Eventually, like Rølvaag, Per comes to realize that the United States has become his proper home, although he will never be entirely at home there.

Rølvaag's next novels examined the psychology of greed and materialism, qualities that Rølvaag dishearteningly observed in his fellow Norwegian Americans. In *Paa glemte veie* (*On Forgotten Paths*, 1914) Chris Larsen loses his health in attempting to tame the prairie and his soul through avarice and rejection of his Lutheran teachings; his daughter Mabel strives and succeeds in saving it. *To Tullinger* (1920; *Two Fools*, 1920; revised as *Pure Gold*, 1930) shows the degeneration that cultural rootlessness exacts on a second-generation couple. Greed becomes a force that Lars and Lizzie Houglum find themselves helpless to resist, and their obsession with money comes to replace other values and relationships and is made to satisfy all longings. When they die, their fortunes are inadvertently destroyed with them.

In *Længselens baat* (1921; *The Boat of Longing*, 1933), Rølvaag uses his childhood experiences to describe poetically the childhood of Nils Vaag in northern Norway. Nils immigrates to Minneapolis as a young man, but, as with many of the Norwegian American characters, finds acculturation difficult in the gritty urban environment. While his fellow traveler Per disappears with a slick businessman and Weismann, his poet roommate, cannot transcend his alcoholism, Nils strives to remain true to his native ideals and gains some respite through the sympathetic Kristine Dahl. Nils is last seen, however, as an itinerant worker no longer in contact with his parents, seemingly unable to adapt his sensitive nature to its best use in the United States. Nils's father eventually goes in search of his son, but is refused admission at **Ellis Island**.

Rølvaag's first novels reached primarily Norwegian Americans in the Midwest, but with *Giants in the Earth* (1927; published in two volumes as *I de dage*, 1924 and *Riket grundlægges*, 1925) he became a best-selling author. The work details the struggles of a settlement of Norwegian American pioneers and, in particular, the differing psychological responses to emigration of Per Hansa Holm and his wife Beret. Per Hansa, enterprising and optimistic, finds peace and purpose in owning and working the prairie, while Beret breaks down in spiritual alienation at its vast strangeness, becoming religiously obsessive and at times incapacitated. The novel concludes with the death of Per Hansa in a blizzard, an ending that has been interpreted both as showing Per Hansa's heroism and his hubris.

The saga continues in *Peder Seier* (1928; *Peder Victorious*, 1929) and *Den signede dag* (1931; *Their Father's God*, 1931), following Per Hansa and Beret's youngest child Peder as he struggles to Americanize himself. Peder comes to represent what Rølvaag saw as some of the most poignant tragedies of **immigration**; he rejects his rich ethnic heritage for a shallow rationalism incorporated from American culture, and, as one of the second generation, he inevitably moves into worlds that Beret cannot understand. Peder makes an ultimate break with his marriage to the Irish Catholic Susie Doheny, but the union proves incompatible and his attempt to fully join American life through a try at political office leaves him disillusioned. Beret remains a major figure in the two novels. While she fulfills the dream of Per Hansa by successfully developing their farm, Beret is never reconciled to her removal to the United States, and, throughout, embodies the tensions and complexities of the emigrant.

Rølvaag died on November 5, 1931, from chronic heart ailments, his death helping to hasten the end of the Norwegian American literary sub-culture that he had championed. Rølvaag's most consistent theme is the cost of immigration, but he also recognized his own literary achievements were inextricably tied to his often painful experience in multiple worlds. Rølvaag lived a version of what is called the American dream; to become university educated, a professor, and an author would have been unlikely, if not impossible, in Norway. That his works serve to show the price of that achievement demonstrates one of the ambivalences Rølvaag saw as inherent in the emigrant's experience. (*See also* Norwegian American Literature)

Further Reading

Eddy, Sara. "'Wheat and Potatoes': Reconstructing Whiteness in O. E. Rølvaag's Immigrant Trilogy." *MELUS* 26.1 (Winter 2001): 129–49.

Haugen, Einar. *Ole Edvart Rølvaag.* Boston: Twayne, 1983.

Reigstad, Paul. *Rølvaag: His Life and Art.* Lincoln: U of Nebraska P, 1972.

Thorson, Gerald Howard, ed. *Ole Rølvaag: Artist and Cultural Leader.* Northfield, MN: St. Olaf College P, 1975.

Sue Barker

ROSCA, NINOTCHKA (1946–) Filipino American novelist, journalist, and political activist. Rosca's lifelong commitment to social justice informs all of her writing. Her novels, *State of War* (1988) and *Twice Blessed* (1992), were the first political novels on the Philippines by a Filipino American woman to be published in the United States; *Twice Blessed* won the American Book Award in 1993.

Rosca started producing short stories as an undergraduate at the University of the Philippines; as a graduate student in comparative literature she joined the movement against dictator Ferdinand Marcos. In the late 1960s several of her short stories, among them "A Parable of Evil," appeared in magazines such as the *Philippines Free Press.* Her first book, *Bitter Country and Other Stories* (1970), is a collection of these early pieces, criticizing the

Filipino educated elite for lack of social and political concern. In 1968 she became managing editor for *Graphic* magazine, wrote columns denouncing government abuses, and helped focus media coverage on political issues: corruption, human rights violations, and militarization, including problems caused by U.S. military bases in the Philippines.

When Marcos imposed Martial Law in 1972, Rosca was among the dissidents arrested, spending six months in military detention at Camp Crame. This experience provided the backdrop for *The Monsoon Collection* (1978), the stories of which draw parallels between the experience of political prisoners and that of the nation as a whole, imprisoned in tyranny. This collection was published in Australia, not in the Philippines, for Rosca's safety; after her release, she had to submit all her writing to military censors.

In 1977, to avoid the possibility of further arrest, Rosca left the Philippines for the United States as a political self-exile, attending (aided by the U.S. embassy in Manila) a writers' program at the University of Iowa. She taught briefly at the University of Hawai'i in Manoa and then moved to New York City, where she worked at a publishing house. She completed a novel on the Philippines, *State of War*, in 1982, but could not interest American editors in it. Under the Marcos regime it could not be published in the Philippines; it circulated in mimeographed form. Discouraged, Rosca temporarily gave up fiction and devoted herself to human rights organizations such as Friends of the Philippines and the Gabriela Network. She visited the Philippines in 1986, after the People Power revolution and Marcos's flight to Hawai'i, and produced a journalistic reportage, *Endgame: The Fall of Marcos* (1987).

State of War found a publisher in 1988; a complex interweaving of past and present, its action centers on a radical plot to assassinate an unnamed dictator, "the Commander," during the riotous merrymaking of a traditional festival. Tracing the family histories of the young plotters, it portrays the country's idyllic distant past, followed by the oppressive Spanish and American colonial regimes. Rosca traces the roots of contemporary tyranny back to the colonizers; the Commander and the soldiers who torture the protagonists, Anna and Adrian, have learned from outsiders to brutalize their own people. When the plot against the Commander fails, Anna finds hope in living in solidarity with peasants and envisioning her unborn son as chronicler of their history and aspirations.

Twice Blessed can be read as a roman à clef; knowledgeable readers can identify many figures from Philippine political history in the novel's satiric recasting of Ferdinand and Imelda Marcos as the megalomaniac twins Hector and Katerina Basbas. However, the novel also works as a farcical parable on the arrogance of power everywhere, highlighting the dictators' almost casual use of violence, their cynical political machinations, and the lavish spectacles that create for them a pseudo-mythical image, hiding their corruption. The novel is not pure farce, ending with their ally, Teresa, realizing with dismay that in collaborating in the twins' political rise she has plunged the nation into nightmare.

Rosca continues to write, currently at work on a novel combining Philippine history with the lives of Filipino Americans in the United States. Strongly opposed to being classified as a third-world writer, she has made her mark by showcasing the political plight of her own country, as a microcosm of the whole world. (*See also* Filipino American Novel)

Further Reading

Casper, Leonard. "Minoring in History: Rosca as Ninotchka." *Amerasia Journal* 16.2 (1990): 201–10.

———. "Ninotchka Rosca." *American Ethnic Writers.* Ed. David Peck. Pasadena, CA: Salem Press, 2000.

Leonard, Shannon T. "Ninotchka Rosca." *Asian American Novelists: A Bio-Bibliographical Critical Sourcebook.* Ed. Emmanuel S. Nelson. Westport, CT: Greenwood Press, 2000. 308–12.

Manalo, Isabel. "Writer in Exile." *The Progressive* 61.1 (January 1997): 15–16.

Dolores de Manuel

ROSE, WENDY (1948–) Native American activist, anthropologist, essayist, poet, and professional artist. Wendy Rose's place in Native American literature stems from her illumination of historical injustices toward Native peoples, her application of her marginalized status to provide enlightening perspectives into the Native condition, and her journey as a mixed-blood writer struggling with issues of self-**identity**.

Central to Rose's writings is a personal struggle for place. Her father was full-blooded Hopi; her mother was of Irish and Miwok descent. Rejected by her mother's people and unable to enroll in the Hopi tribe since Hopi tribal membership is determined through the mother's bloodlines, Rose's mixed-blood status brings with it the sting of alienation from both white and Native cultures and places Rose in the company with other contemporary mixed-blood writers such as **Paula Gunn Allen**, Tiffany Midge, and **Linda Hogan**.

Her first book of poetry, *Hopi Roadrunner Dancing* (1973), includes themes of lost heritage, quests for both cultural identity and self-identity, and survival. The focus is on the poet's own struggles as a minority woman; however, the book includes some poetry reflective of the politically turbulent era of the 1960s and 1970s.

Rose's second book of poetry, *A Tribal History* (1976), manifests a maturity, as Rose's subject matter concentrates on more global concerns and offers social criticisms by highlighting losses sustained by Native people separated from their language and their culture. Influenced by her study of anthropology, Rose acquires a double-sighted perspective, seeing the world from the viewpoint of both the object under study and the scientist. In this work, Rose gives voice to the victims who have been silenced, objectified, and commoditized by the dominant culture.

Academic Squaw: Reports to the World from the Ivory Tower (1977) reveals the anger behind injustice. Continuing to provide victims with a voice, one of her most moving poems, "I Expected My Skin and My Blood to Ripen," allows readers to hear a young Lakota mother's chilling recount of her baby's violent death and the subsequent looting and mutilation of Indians by frenzied soldiers at Wounded Knee. Commoditization and exploitation arouse Rose's ire, and she strives to raise awareness of inequity.

In Rose's fourth book, *Builder Kachina: A Home-Going Cycle* (1979), Rose returns to emphasizing the quest for self-identity and tribal connections. Inspired after a visit with her father whereby Rose lamented her loss of tribal connections, her father reassured her that, although she felt "cut off" from her culture, she had the ability within to build her own new roots as a bridge to her cultural heritage and her native lands.

Lost Copper (1980) is a testament to a theme of survival. Like most mixed-blood writers, Rose is caught between two worlds but chooses to side with her Indian identity. This book highlights Rose's spiritual connection to the earth, praises figures that the poet admires, and continues to deliberate her mixed-blood ancestry.

Book six, *What Happened When the Hopi Hit New York* (1982), features poetry of travel, stopovers, and urban scenes viewed through both a scientific and a creative eye. Rose's successive book, *The Halfbreed Chronicles and Other Poems* (1985), is often hailed as her strongest work. Exploitation and injustice are pervasive themes as is the celebration of the female spirit that has the power to create new life in two ways—to actually give birth and to open the eyes of the world by becoming a global conscience that initiates change.

Rose's next publication, *Going to War with All My Relations* (1993), is a culmination of themes that permeate Rose's career: concern for the earth, for women, and for the turn academic anthropology has taken. Some critics have hailed this book as her most polemic, for it also attacks the cultural phenomenon of "white shamanism," or the appropriation of Native spirituality, customs, art forms, and identity by non-Indians. *Now Poof She Is Gone* (1994) follows a similar vein, and *Bone Dance: New and Selected Poems; 1965–1992* (1994) is a collection spanning nearly thirty years of writing. Her pan-Indian approach allows Rose's works to provide readers access to the struggles facing many urban Indians in today's society. (*See also* Native American Poetry)

Further Reading

Bruchac, Joseph. *Survival This Way: Interviews with American Indian Poets*. Tucson: Sun Tracks and U of Arizona P, 1987.

Coltelli, Laura. *Winged Words: American Indian Writers Speak*. Lincoln: U of Nebraska P, 1990.

Wilson, Norma C. *The Nature of Native American Poetry*. Albuquerque: U of New Mexico P, 2001.

Witalec, Janet, ed. *Smoke Rising: The Native North American Literary Companion*. Detroit: Visible Ink Press, 1995.

Patricia R. DiMond

ROSEN, NORMA (1925-)   Jewish American novelist, short story writer, and essayist. A writer who embraced Judaism only after years of ambivalence, Norma Rosen's work often focuses on Jewish individuals or Jewish issues, but her themes transcend ethnicity as she examines the intellectual and moral ambiguities of our time.

Her most critically acclaimed work, *Touching Evil* (1969), uses the **Holocaust** as an image of an evil so pervasive that it touches the lives of everyone, Jew and Gentile alike. The story is told from the point of view of two Christian women, Jean Lamb and her younger pregnant friend, Hattie Mews. Jean first experiences the terror of the Holocaust through photographs and Hattie becomes immersed in the tragedy when she and Jean watch the Eichmann trials on television. Meanwhile, the Holocaust becomes increasingly personal, images internalized as metaphors for the characters' own pain. Hattie identifies with the women who gave birth in the camps, and Jean imagines that she is like the woman who claws her way from the bottom of a pile of corpses. As each woman suffers her own losses, she is haunted by her experience as a witness through the imagination.

Because she believes that the Holocaust was the central event of the twentieth century, Rosen continued to mine its significance in her next novel, *At the Center* (1982). The novel's protagonist, Hannah Selig, the child of survivors, is struggling to understand good and evil. Her journey leads her to an unlikely place, the Bianky Family Planning Center, an abortion clinic, where Hannah finds a job for which she feels qualified because of her personal acquaintance with grief. Not only were her parents victims of the Holocaust, but when they came to this country to renew life, they were brutally murdered in their own home. In the face of this horror, Hannah questions the nature of God and the authenticity of her parents' Orthodox Jewish belief. She would like to talk to God, but, like her biblical namesake, she is silenced. She understands finally that she can embrace life only when she lets go of bitterness, and so she leaves the clinic and sets out on her own Jewish journey.

In her next novel, *John and Anzia: An American Romance* (1989), Rosen returned to the realism that characterized her first novel, *Joy to Levine* (1961), and much of her early short fiction. *John and Anzia* is a fictionalized account of the love affair between John Dewey, dean of Teachers College at Columbia, and Anzia Yezierska, a poor Russian Jewish immigrant, who became a successful novelist.

Rosen's most recent full-length work, *Biblical Women Unbound* (1996), is a somewhat playful reinterpretation of the lives of fourteen biblical women. Despite the surface humor, Rosen is serious in using the tradition of *midrashic* storytelling to give voice to women in the Bible. Rosen addresses the concerns of women that never occurred to the male rabbis as she revises the familiar biblical narratives from a feminist perspective.

Rosen's personal journey from secular Jew to biblical scholar is the subject of several of the essays in *Accidents of Influence: Writing as a Woman and a Jew in America* (1992). She describes being raised in a secular household, where ties to the family's Jewish heritage had been nearly severed. Her mother remained angry that women were exiled from the world of religious observance, while Norma, as a child, yearned to belong to the community of Jews rejected by her parents. She found her way into Judaism over a period of many years that began with her marriage to Robert Rosen, an observant Jew and Holocaust survivor, for whom Judaism held spiritual and intellectual meaning. In an autobiographical story, "What Must I Say to You" (1963), Rosen describes an altercation between a young couple over the hanging of a *mezzuzah*, the scroll containing the words of Deuteronomy that observant Jews hang on doorposts. Feeling betrayed by a God who allowed the Holocaust, the wife rejects the *mezzuzah*, only to be rebuked by the husband, who tells her that she does not know enough about the symbols of Judaism to discard or judge them. Eventually Rosen would study at Jewish Theological Seminary and increasingly return to the traditions enabling her to connect with her Jewish past.

In recent years Rosen has written short stories and essays and has been working on a novel, a fragment of which appeared as "How Much Room Does a Man Need" (1992). Although she continues to explore Jewish themes, she has also written about the art of literary creation as well as ongoing moral concerns.

Further Reading

Berger, Alan. *Crisis and Covenant: The Holocaust in American Jewish Fiction.* Albany: State U of New York P, 1985.

Klingenstein, Suzanne. "Norma Rosen." *Jewish American Women Writers: A Bio-Bibliographical and Critical Sourcebook.* Ed. Ann R. Shapiro. Westport, CT: Greenwood Press, 1994. 350–57.

Kremer, S. Lillian. "The Holocaust in Our Time: Norma Rosen's *Touching Evil.*" *Studies in American Jewish Literature* 3 (1983): 212–22.

Ann R. Shapiro

ROSENFELD, ISAAC (1918–1956) Jewish American novelist, poet, critic, and short story writer. After World War II, Rosenfeld became an important spokesman for the Jewish writer in America, whom he considered "an expert in alienation." Though a prolific writer, he published only one novel, *Passage from Home* (1946), during his short lifetime. His stories, essays, and literary criticism appeared in *Partisan Review, Commentary, New Leader, New Republic,* and *Nation.* After his death, some of his best writing was collected in a posthumous volume of essays, *An Age of Enormity: Life and Writing in the Forties and Fifties* (1962), and in a collection of short stories, *Alpha and Omega* (1966).

In nearly all of Rosenfeld's fiction, alienation is the dominant theme. One of his best stories, "The Hand That Fed Me," features an alienated American Jew, bogged down by his unemployment while the war rages in Europe, who vainly and rather pathetically tries to insinuate himself into a

Russian girl's life. The setting and the protagonist are clearly reminiscent of *Dangling Man*, published in the same year (1944) by **Saul Bellow**, who was Rosenfeld's friend and a major literary competitor at the time. The title story of Rosenfeld's volume, "Alpha and Omega," presents a series of vignettes of equally lonely, alienated characters—a postman, a janitor, a prostitute, a dancer, and a paralytic—whose lives are connected only because they happen to live in the same building.

Rosenfeld's only novel, the autobiographically inspired *Passage from Home*, tells the story of Bernard, a Jewish adolescent who is totally estranged from his father and stepmother. Confused between the two components that make up his **identity**, Bernard flees the traditional Jewish world represented by his father and his religiously observant grandparents, and moves in with his secular, Americanized aunt, Minna. He even hooks her up with a cousin by marriage, Willy Harpsmith. Although he initially sees Minna's bohemian lifestyle as an attractive alternative to the Jewish milieu of his home, he soon becomes disgusted with the physical filth (the cockroaches he discovers in the sink, the bedbugs that assault him every night) as well as the moral filth in Minna's life: She now shares her bed with Willy, but has kept it a secret from everyone that she has been married for the past six years to the sleazy owner of a derelict saloon. When their ménage à trois breaks up after only one month, Bernard returns to his father, hopeful of a reconciliation, only to discover an unbridgeable gap between them. The sensitive adolescent has indeed passed from home.

Rosenfeld's literary criticism features some excellent essays on authors, such as **Abraham Cahan**, Franz Kafka, Aldous Huxley, George Orwell, **James T. Farrell**, William Faulkner, Ernest Hemingway, **Richard Wright**, Andre Gide, Henry Miller, and Simone Weil. They are often passionate appeals for the creation of strong characters in a humanist literature of commitment.

An important theme in Rosenfeld's nonfiction writing is the moral and emotional consequences of the **Holocaust**. Soon after the war, when the subject was still a taboo, Rosenfeld was already accusing Americans of indifference in the face of Jewish suffering in Europe. He explicitly relates the creation of a generation of alienated underground men who populate all of his fiction to the rise of fascism and the Holocaust. Not these underground men, but the people who go about their lives as if nothing had happened, are the ones who are really insane, Rosenfeld argued. For, an awareness of the European disaster, its eradication of the normal categories of good and evil, should make our former lives impossible.

Although he was considered one of the most promising talents of Jewish American fiction in the early forties, Rosenfeld suffered from a severe writer's block, and his second and still unpublished novel, *The Enemy*, was rejected by several publishers. After his death from a heart attack, four more manuscripts were discovered in his apartment, but they too remain unpublished to this day. Some critics argue that Rosenfeld's later work—

most conspicuously his last story, "King Solomon"—suggests that he had finally rediscovered his source of inspiration. In his foreword to *An Age of Enormity*, Saul Bellow remembers his late friend as a brilliant, warm man who died alone, almost like a Rosenfeld character, in a shabby furnished room on Chicago's Walton Street.

Further Reading

Bellow, Saul. "Foreword." *An Age of Enormity*. Ed. Theodore Solotaroff. Cleveland: World Publishing Company, 1962. 11–14.

Shechner, Mark. "From Isaac Rosenfeld's Journals." *Partisan Review* 47.1 (1980): 9–28.

Philippe Codde

ROSSI, AGNES (1959–) Italian and Irish American fiction writer. Rossi writes within the conventions of realistic fiction and is regarded as part of the recent group of writers that includes **Carole Maso** and **Mary Caponegro**, who engage indirectly with their *italianità*, choosing instead to focus on gender, and, to a lesser degree, class, in her fiction. Rossi was born in Paterson, New Jersey, and raised in suburban Upper Saddle River, to a second-generation, middle-class Italian American father and Irish American mother who maintained strong ties to their immigrant parents' working class origins.

Rossi's first short story collection, *Artists and Athletes* (1987), won the 1986 New York University Creative Writers Competition. Its ten stories—brief, fragmentary, and spare—explore the boundaries of human connection and communication. Her second publication, *The Quick* (1992), comprises a novella (the eponymous piece of the collection) and six short stories. The narrator of "The Quick," Marie Russo, becomes a confidante to and emotional prop for Phyllis, a coworker who loses her thirty-eight-year-old husband to a heart attack. Marie's bond to Phyllis, a motif characteristic of much of Rossi's work, is one forged out of loss and of the experience of being female; we witness the foundering of Marie's own marriage and learn of her difficult relationship with her Italian American working class father. The remainder of the collection examines significant life passages: sexual awakening, reclamation of parent-child connections, the sale of a childhood home. Rossi's powerful first novel, *Split Skirt* (1996), is somewhat more experimental in narrative technique, alternating chapters of two women who find themselves cellmates for three hot days one July. Despite significant differences in age and social class, Mrs. Tyler and Rita, the novel's central characters, discover common ground in female experience as they tell one another their life stories. Her most recent novel, *The Houseguest* (2000), focuses on her maternal heritage, narrating the life of Edward Devlin, an Irishman who abandons his daughter and flees to America following his beloved wife's death. The novel shares with Rossi's other works the theme of loss, particularly loss through death, and its devastating results—especially the fracturing of fragile psyches and tenuous familial bonds.

Rossi's writing opens up significant critical questions of self-definition for the Italian American writer. Critical response to her work, particularly from scholars of Italian American literature and culture, emphasizes the way she disguises her ethnic **identity**. Rossi disavows any deliberate attempt to mute or avoid her ethnic heritage in her fiction, noting that although she was always highly conscious of her parents' ethnicities and took pride in identifying herself accordingly, she believes that truthful portrayals of women's lives is imperative in contemporary culture. She is currently writing a novel exploring the intersection of class and gender division within a small suburban community. (*See also* Italian American Novel)

Further Reading

Bona, Mary Jo. *Claiming a Tradition: Italian American Women Writers.* Carbondale: Southern Illinois UP, 1999.

Giunta, Edvige. "Speaking Through Silences, Writing Against Silence." *Writing with an Accent: Contemporary Italian American Women Authors.* New York: Palgrave, 2002. 71–91.

Mimi Pipino

ROSTEN, LEO (1908–1997) Jewish American novelist, humorist, lexicographer, and social scientist. A writer with a broad range of interests and abilities, Leo Rosten is most known for his humorous books about language, in particular *The Education of H*Y*M*A*N K*A*P*L*A*N* (1937) and *The Joys of Yiddish* (1968).

Rosten received a PhD in political science from the University of Chicago and taught and wrote about social science at several schools, including Yale University and Columbia University. Perhaps it is this interest in society and communication that led Rosten to write so frequently about language. His comic collection of stories about immigrants learning English, *The Education of H*Y*M*A*N K*A*P*L*A*N*, was based on his own experience teaching English to adults. Hyman Kaplan, a Jewish immigrant eager to learn English properly, has an unusual dialect and pronunciation and a habit of getting the language comically wrong. The scholar in Rosten tried to be accurate in depicting the life of Jewish immigrants in America, in particular through their language usage. This book was popular during its time, but some might consider the ethnic humor mocking or overdone today.

The Yiddish language is based on medieval German, written in Hebrew letters, and combined with and influenced by Hebrew itself, Aramaic, Slavic languages, and other European tongues. It was traditionally the secular, everyday language of the Eastern European Jews, while Hebrew was used for religious purposes, and, as a result, it was a folk language that didn't command much respect. Rosten helped change this with his work. Yiddish is a rare language now, and even when Rosten wrote, it was clear that, because of various twentieth-century events, namely the tragedy of World War II, it was no longer a commonly used language. Nevertheless, Yiddish was and is essential to Jews, in particular because it is the everyday tongue for religious Jews and also because it is a way for Jews, who were, until recently, a stateless group of people spread throughout various countries in the **diaspora**, to communicate and connect despite geographical boundaries. *The Joys of Yiddish* is a lexicography that liberally uses jokes to illustrate the words and their meanings. Through the words and the accompanying stories and jokes, Rosten also describes the attitudes and personalities of Eastern European Jews and Jewish Americans. Rosten, who moved with his parents from Poland to the United States at a young age, and grew up speaking Yiddish at home, describes the language in an enter-

Leo Rosten. *AP/Wide World Photos.*

taining and lively way, using humor to explain words that are often untranslatable. In *The Joys of Yiddish* and its sequel *Hooray for Yiddish* (1982), Rosten not only explores Yiddish and the Yiddishkeit culture, but also the fascinating influence of Yiddish on English.

Leo Rosten wrote screenplays, melodrama, detective novels, social science, economics, and many other genres, but it is as a champion for Yiddish that he is most renowned. (*See also* Yiddish Literature)

Further Reading

Golub, Ellen. "Leo Rosten." *Dictionary of Literary Biography: American Humorists 1800–1950 Part 2: M–Z.* Ed. Stanley Trachtenberg. Detroit, MI: Bruccoli Clark, 1982.

Brett Jocelyn Epstein

ROTH, HENRY (1906–1995) Jewish American fiction writer. After thirty years of neglect, Henry Roth's first novel, *Call It Sleep* (1934), was recognized as a classic of **immigration** fiction and a pioneering contribution to American Jewish literature. Roth himself abandoned a literary career but in a late burst of creativity published his second novel, *A Star Shines Over Mt. Morris Park* (1994), sixty years after his first. In his final years, the octogenarian author overcame the debilitating agony of rheumatoid arthritis to produce thousands of manuscript pages, most of which appeared in *Mercy of a Rude Stream* (1994–98), an autobiographical tetralogy whose last two volumes were published posthumously.

Drawing on Roth's own experiences as a young immigrant from Austro-Hungarian Galicia, *Call It Sleep* begins in 1907, when two-year-old David Schearl arrives, with mother Genya, at Ellis Island. The novel focuses on David's troubled childhood during the years 1911–1913, as a stranger in a strange land. Constructed out of four sections, each defined by a different image, "The Cellar," "The Picture," "The Coal," and "The Rail," *Call It Sleep* recounts the coming of age of a hypersensitive Jewish boy forced to cope alone with the mysteries of sex, religion, and love. He can count on nothing as reliably as the enmity and abuse of his father, Albert, a surly man embittered by disappointment.

Call It Sleep is attentive to details of life among the tenements of the Lower East Side, a tumult of conflicting sensations that make it easy for little David, who cannot make himself understood to a kindly Irish cop, to become lost a few blocks away from home. But the book is most memorable as a cacophonous record of culture clash, one that makes its English into a subtle instrument for rendering the collision of languages, including Yiddish, the first language of the Schearls, as it was of Roth, as well as English, German, Hebrew, Italian, and Polish. It makes effective use of stream of consciousness to render the perspective of a child assaulted by disparate impressions in an alien world he neither controls nor understands.

Though *Call It Sleep* received enthusiastic reviews, it was attacked in the Marxist *New Masses* for being too introspective and ignoring the plight of the proletariat. Roth had joined the Communist Party, and he took to heart the leftist critique. It was the midst of the Depression, and *Call It Sleep*, whose publisher went out of business, did not sell well before falling out of print. Roth determined to write something more consequential, and he set to work creating a novel about a feisty working-class hero from the Midwest. However, he filled barely a hundred pages before inspiration flagged and he abandoned the project. He also abandoned New York City and the literary life, moving with Muriel Parker, a musician whom he met in 1938 at the artists' colony Yaddo, and their two sons to rural Maine. For two decades, living under primitive conditions, Roth wrote little, eking out an income from slaughtering ducks and geese, as well as picking blueberries, chopping wood, fighting forest fires, and working in a mental hospital.

In 1964 when *Call It Sleep* was re-published as an Avon paperback, a fervent tribute by critic **Irving Howe** on the front page of the *New York Times Book Review* turned the book into an unexpected best seller. Roth, now famous, was asked repeatedly what he was working on and what he had written during the thirty years since the first appearance of *Call It Sleep*. He tried to resume writing, initially without much success. But, at the outset of the 1967 Six Day War, Roth, shocked by the prospect of Israel's annihilation, repudiated Marxist universalism and reaffirmed his Jewish **identity**. He later claimed that submission to the formulas of socialist realism and alienation from the wellspring of his art, the Jewish community, depleted his ability to write. In the final decade of his long life, Roth took up where he had left off in 1934.

Mercy of a Rude Stream begins in the summer of 1914, a few weeks after *Call It Sleep* concludes. Its protagonist, called Ira Stigman, might be David Schearl, or Henry Roth. Narrated by a retrospective, ailing author in his eighties who longs for death but also for a final act of literary redemption, the four volumes of the series—*A Star Shines Over Mt. Morris Park, A Diving Rock on the Hudson* (1995), *From Bondage* (1996), and *Requiem for Harlem* (1998)—trace a life from ages eight to twenty-two that closely resembles its author's. Like Roth himself, Ira clashes with his father, and he, too, is expelled from Stuyvesant High School for stealing classmates' pens. Even more shameful is the revelation that Ira maintained sexual relationships with both his sister and his first cousin. Roth's inability, until the end, to unburden himself of persistent, secret guilt over incest, accounted in part for his writer's block. By the end of *Requiem for Harlem*, Ira moves out of his dysfunctional family's meager flat in northern Manhattan down to Greenwich Village, to live with a poet and professor twelve years his senior. Named Edith Welles, she is a thinly disguised rendition of Eda Lou Walton, who served for ten years as Roth's mentor, lover, and Muse. Roth dedicated *Call It Sleep* to Walton and the final, agonizing decade of his life to summoning up remembrance of things past repair.

In 1987 Mario Materassi, Roth's friend and Italian translator, assembled a volume of his stories, essays, and interviews that he published under the title *Shifting Landscape*. Arranged in chronological sequence, the book functions as a kind of intellectual autobiography. However, Roth's literary impulses were almost always autobiographical. In *Call It Sleep* as well as the later novels, he offers up vivid versions of himself that are, despite the vagaries of literary reputation, both anguished and enduring. (*See also* Jewish American Novel)

Further Reading

Kellman, Steven G. *Redemption: The Life of Henry Roth.* New York: W. W. Norton, 2005.

Lyons, Bonnie. *Henry Roth: The Man and His Work.* New York: Cooper Square, 1976.

Studies in American Jewish Literature 5.1 (1979) [Henry Roth issue].

Wirth-Nesher, Hana, ed. *New Essays on Call It Sleep.* New York: Cambridge UP, 1996.

Steven G. Kellman

ROTH, PHILIP (1933–)   Jewish American novelist and short story writer. Philip Milton Roth, in a career that spans over four decades and nearly thirty books, explores the moral complexities of what it means to be a middle-class Jew in modern America. In a fictional world that moves from realistic, serious depiction to surreal, comic adventures, Roth's protagonists put up defenses in their struggle with self-**identity**, suffering, and sexuality. More

Philip Roth. *AP/Wide World Photos.*

than any other writer of contemporary fiction, Roth uses wit, irony, satire, and caustic humor both to celebrate and transcend "the Jewish question." As he continues to experiment with many different comic modes, Roth still manages to write about what causes people pain and to explore very serious, universal concerns.

Born March 19, 1933 in Newark, New Jersey, as the oldest child of first-generation Jewish American parents Herman and Bess Finkel, Roth grew up in the city's middle-class section of Weequahic. He attended Newark schools, and from 1950 to 1951, he enrolled at the Newark branch of Rutgers University. When his father's career as an insurance salesman improved, Roth was able to transfer to Bucknell University, where he received a BA in 1954. In 1955 he received an MA degree from the University of Chicago, where he also taught English.

Roth spent two years in the U.S. Army from 1955 to 1956, where he wrote press releases and, on off hours, wrote the short stories that later became his first published work. He returned to the University of Chicago to pursue a PhD, but he dropped out of the program in 1957 to work for the *New Republic.*

In 1959 Roth married Margaret Martinson Williams, a divorced mother of two. The couple separated three years later without having children of their own; she was killed in a car accident in 1968. Roth married the actress Claire Bloom in 1990; the couple had lived together since 1976. Following their separation three years later, Bloom wrote a memoir of their life together, *Leaving a Doll's House* (1996).

Roth has been writer-in-residence or visiting writer at the University of Iowa's Writer's Workshop, the University of Pennsylvania, Princeton University, the State University of New York, and Hunter College, from which he retired in 1992. Roth spends part of the year working in his two-story office near the 1790 colonial farmhouse on forty acres in Litchfield County, Connecticut, where he has lived since 1976.

Philip Roth's first published short story was in the *Chicago Review* in 1954, and his "Defender of the Faith," published to some criticism from Jewish readers in *The New Yorker*, followed in 1955. These two stories, along with three other stories and the title novella, *Goodbye, Columbus* (1959), earned Roth the National Book Award and established him as an innovative voice in American literature. This book is a satirical portrait of the suburban, self-possessed Patemkins, a Jewish family that strives to assimilate into the mainstream American culture. It received good reviews, but it also angered some Jewish readers. Roth was also accused of being anti-Semitic, a charge that has followed his career and one that he alternately ignores or refutes through interviews, essays, or through his mouthpiece protagonist and alter ego, Nathan Zuckerman. This attack on Roth reached a critical stage at a symposium at Yeshiva University in 1962. Roth was not only openly reviled and hated by the audience; he had to be protected as he left the venue.

His first full-length novel, *Letting Go* (1962), met with favorable reviews. Roth followed that black comedy with *When She Was Good* (1967), a novel in the realistic mode. Its protagonist, Lucy Nelson, is one of Roth's few independent women. In 1969, with the publication of his most famous work, the comic masterpiece *Portnoy's Complaint*, and the motion picture version of *Goodbye, Columbus*, Roth became internationally successful. *Portnoy's Complaint* is the story of Alexander Portnoy and his coming of age in a middle-class Jewish New York world. His puberty-driven obsessions and his overpossessive Jewish mother further aggravated those Jewish readers who thought Roth was making fun of Jews and stereotyping them. Some called the book offensive and pornographic, but it established Roth as a major writer.

The 1970s saw Roth expanding his satiric view to include such institutions as politics and baseball, and he also introduced recurring protagonists and narrators David Kapesh and Nathan Zuckerman, the latter variously called Roth's alter ego, id, impersonator, and surrogate voice. *Our Gang* (1971) is a parody and political satire that recalls Orwell and Swift. Its six short chapters chronicle the life of President Trick E. Dixon, an attack on President Nixon. *The Breast* (1972) is a Kafkaesque fantasy and black humor novella in which Kapesh turns into a giant breast. In *The Great American Novel* (1973) baseball becomes folklore, and Roth mythologies the American pastime.

Nathan Zuckerman is introduced in 1974's *My Life as a Man*, a work that deepened Roth's fiction, which was becoming more self-reflexive and postmodern. In two long stories, a failed writer tries to make sense of his life. Roth uses the novel partly to chronicle his failed marriage. In 1975 Roth published *Reading Myself and Others*, a collection of essays and interviews. One of its essays, "Looking at Kafka," is his most famous, and the ghost of Kafka, both his themes and style, illuminates much of Roth's work. *The Professor of Desire* (1977) continues the life of David Kapesh. *The Ghost Writer*

(1979) is a Jamesian parable in which Zuckerman revives Anne Frank at age fifty. Both farce and fantasy, it is a parable of artistic identity. In many of his works, Roth explores the question of what it means to be an artist, a Jewish writer in the modern world. Roth, as noted before, uses Nathan Zuckerman, a man much like Roth himself—of the Jewish faith, a writer, and born in Newark—to answer and befuddle his critics, and as a way to blur the bounds of fiction and real life. Roth has spent a lifetime portraying his characters, and he explores the relationship between fact and fiction, both in his narratives and in his autobiographical memoirs. His ultimate concerns, what it means to be a Jewish writer and what that writer's relationship is to his culture, have shaped his work throughout his career. By putting these concerns in the mouth of Zuckerman and other fictional selves he refers to as "Philip" or "Philip Roth," Roth both identifies with and distances himself from his protagonists.

In 1981 Roth published *Zuckerman Unbound*, in which his protagonist, much like himself, is beleaguered by celebrity and controversy. *The Anatomy Lesson* (1983) is the third in a trilogy about Jewish angst. Zuckerman, now forty, is a novelist full of self-pity and guilt. The novel deals with pain, anger, and remorse. Two years later Roth published *Zuckerman Bound*, bringing together the three previous Zuckerman novels and *The Prague Orgy*, a novella-length epilogue. Roth is clearly in the confessional, autobiographical school, using Zuckerman here and elsewhere not only to be his mouthpiece for Jewishness and all its attending cultural and intellectual problems, but also to confound himself by having Zuckerman interact with a fictional Roth. *Zuckerman Bound* illustrates how the life of a man and the life of a character are blurred in various genres of fiction.

The Counterlife (1986), Roth's tenth book, is an ingenious look at how we transform our lives. In this fifth installment of the character, Nathan Zuckerman has published the controversial *Carnovsky*, an obvious reference to the notoriety and condemnation Roth received from *Portnoy's Complaint*. The following year, Roth published *The Facts: A Novelist's Autobiography*. Its central narrative, an informal reader's guide to Philip Roth, is preceded by a letter from Zuckerman. The 1990 novella *Deception* is the first of a trilogy of works that explores the nature of storytelling itself. The protagonist is a novelist named Philip Roth, fifty and married. The book is a series of notebooks kept by "Roth," and so the book becomes a literary game that questions the genres of autobiography and fiction.

Patrimony: A True Story (1991) and *Operation Shylock* (1993), which Roth labeled "self-reverential fiction," complete the trilogy begun with *Deception*. The first is a poignant memoir of Herman Roth, who, at age eighty-six, suffered an incurable brain tumor. Roth's account of how he took care of his father—Herman Roth died in 1988—and the indignities of old age, both compassionate and funny, began as a journal Roth kept in between writing his novels. *Operation Shylock: A Confession* is the story of Moishe Pipik, who impersonates the protagonist Roth. Again, the lines between fact and fiction are obscured. The book is also an analysis of Jews and Judaism, though Roth seldom uses his fiction to take a stand about who is or is not a Jew.

Sabbath's Theater (1995), Roth's twenty-first book, is the story of Morris "Mickey" Sabbath, an arthritic, suicidal puppeteer obsessed with sex and death. In his next novel, *American Pastoral* (1997), Roth returns to Nathan Zuckerman, now sixty-two, who, on going to a class reunion in 1968, meets Seymour "Swede" Levov. Roth weaves a tale of three generations and uses Levov to represent the All-American Boy, an ex-athlete from Weequahic High in Newark. The novel, divided into Paradise Remembered, The Fall, and Paradise Lost, explores American identity, idealism, and conventions. Roth's last novel of the 1990s, *I Married a Communist* (1998) again includes Zuckerman.

The Human Stain (2000) was the second of Roth's novels to be made into a feature film, in 2002. The narrator is a self-absorbed Nathan Zuckerman, who recalls the events of the summer of 1998 at Athena College. Roth uses Dr. Coleman Silk, a light-skinned African-American trying to pass for a Jewish intellectual, to explore the political correctness of modern America and present a gloomy vision of personal and political agendas. In 2001 Roth published two works, *The Dying Animal* and *Shop Talk*. The first, a funny, erotic novella that filters characters through the intellect of David Kapesh, explores the sexual era of the 1960s. The latter is a collection of interviews with Milan Kundera and Primo Levi, among others, and an essay on **Saul Bellow**'s fiction.

One of the hallmarks of Philip Roth's lasting impact is that he will be the third living American author to be published in the Library of America series, beginning in 2005. Such an endorsement testifies to the staying power and artistic success of Roth's work, including three National Book Awards (1959, 1995, and 1997) and the Pulitzer Prize in 1997 for *American Pastoral*. Many critics see no diminishing in the power of his fiction; his later works have received more critical attention and awards than did his early phenomenal successes more than thirty years ago. Roth continues to examine what it means to be a Jewish writer in the modern world, and he writes with a deft comic realism that sees the absurd in all life situations.

Further Reading

Baumgarten, Murray, and Barbara Gottfried. *Understanding Philip Roth.* Columbia: U of South Carolina P, 1990.

Cooper, Philip. *Philip Roth and the Jews.* Albany: State U of New York P, 1996.

Halio, Jay. *Philip Roth Revisited.* New York: Twayne, 1992.

Lee, Hermione. *Philip Roth.* New York: Methuen, 1982.

McDaniel, John. *The Fiction of Philip Roth.* Haddonfield, NJ: Haddonfield House, 1974.

Milbauer, Asher Z., and Donald G. Watson, eds. *Reading Philip Roth.* New York: St. Martin's Press, 1988.

Pinsker, Sanford, ed. *Critical Essays on Philip Roth.* Boston: G. K. Hall & Co., 1982.

Rogers, Bernard F. *Philip Roth.* Boston: Twayne Publishers, 1978.

Gary Kerley

ROTHENBERG, JEROME (1931–)   Jewish American poet and critic. Jerome Rothenberg has had a gigantic career, one that has spanned over forty years, and one that grows increasingly important and influential with each generation. Always an innovator of language, he has also been a leader in setting the political agenda for contemporary poets. He has been an anthologist, a **canon**-maker, a critic, and a cultural historian. All of these interests have made him a natural respondent to the study of the **Holocaust**. Rothenberg has written over twenty books of poetry and put together several major anthologies of postmodern poetry, including *Shaking the Pumpkin* (1972) and *A Big Jewish Book* (1978). In his subject matter, he has broadened and innovated contemporary American and international poetry. His wide influence, his eclectic interests, his dedication to cultural particularities, and his background as an historian—all brought him quite naturally to a study of Jewish **ethnicity** and to an important discussion of the Holocaust. Two of his collections, *Poland 1931* and *Khurbn*, have been important contributions to Holocaust literature

In the 1960s Rothenberg devoted his poetry to studying the sounds and rhythms of Native American discourse, paying close attention to the recognition of cultural particularities and origins. He labeled this poetry ethnopoetics, a type of poetry that could explore both the cultural myth and archetype of the Native American experience, but also could be quite readily imported to explore his own ethnicity and **identity**. Ethnopoetics was uniquely suited to the American seventies, a decade in which many ethnic minorities became interested in uncovering their own cultural identities. Yet, in a crucial way Rothenberg's devotion to ethnopoetics should not be confused with the more leisurely pursuit of one's roots that became popular at this time. For Rothenberg, ethnopoetics is a way of seeing and saving the world: "A poetics for me is as personal (as distinguished from an imposed) theology might be for a person with a serious belief in God or a metaphysics for another kind of searcher after what is real or true or both."

Two collections of his poetry have dealt quite specifically with his own ethnopoetics, In the 1960s, while Rothenberg devoted his poetry to studying the sounds and rhythms of Native American discourse, he was paying close attention to cultural particularities, origins and natural idioms of speech. Ethnopoetics brought together poetic and anthropological consciousness. The first goal of this linkage was to translate archaic poetries; the second was to show that many of the concerns of contemporary culture could find a link in much earlier civilizations. Another major anthology appeared on this topic: *Symposium of the Whole: A Range of Discourse Towards an Ethnopoetics* (1983), which he coedited with Diane Rothenberg. Clearly, ethnopoetics has been a major contribution to postwar American poetry, and is perhaps Rothenberg's single most-noted accomplishment.

Using ethnopoetics, Rothenberg could explore both the cultural myth and archetype of the Native American experience, but he could also easily connect contemporary Jewish American culture to Native American. In fact,

Rothenberg moves easily between these models, often interchanging the two identities. This could have been a politically dangerous technique, yet critics have extensively praised Rothenberg's ethnopoetics as a unique kind of borrowing that allows the dignity of the giver and taker to remain not only undisturbed, but celebrated, illuminated, and clear. Because Jerome Rothenberg understands his own origins, because he knows his fathers and how his being arises from theirs, he can accept and articulate his Seneca experience justly. It is possible to reverse this claim; that is, that Rothenberg's initial interest and success in describing Native American history and devastation led him to articulate the history and devastation of his own ancestors. Whatever the case, there can be no doubt that Rothenberg's descriptions of Jewish American culture are interwoven with his work on Native Americans.

Rothenberg's stature as a poet has grown with the importance of post-modern critique. As poets and literary critics have rejected many of the values of Modernism, rejecting ideas of universality in favor of cultural specificity, ethnopoetics has been even more fervently embraced. Moreover, many of today's most critically esteemed Language poets cite Rothenberg's experimentation with language as a major influence on their own work. With these changes in evaluation, Rothenberg's reputation has continued to advance. *Poland 1931* and *Khurbn* significantly contribute to the canon of Holocaust literature, and Rothenberg's influence in the national and international poetry canons will continue to be felt for many generations.

Further Reading

Cott, Jonathan. "Conversations with American Writers." *New York Times Book Review* (January 13, 1985): 18.

Gitenstein, Barbara. *Apocalyptic Messianism in Contemporary Jewish American Poetry.* Albany: State U of New York P, 1986.

Zalenski, John. "Rothenberg's Continuing Revolution of the Word." *North Dakota Quarterly* 55.4 (Fall 1987): 202–16.

Hilene Flanzbaum

RUDMAN, MARK (1948–) Jewish American poet, essayist, educator, and translator. Mark Rudman was born in New York City and grew up in various locations throughout the Midwest. He currently lives in New York City, where he is an Adjunct Professor at New York University. Rudman holds a bachelor's degree from the New School for Social Research (now New School University) and a MFA degree from Columbia University. He is a recipient of fellowships from the National Endowment of the Arts and the Guggenheim Foundation, and has taught poetry and creative writing courses at numerous colleges and universities, including New York University and Columbia University.

Rudman, a very prolific poet and essayist, has a unique poetic style in which he alternates between poetry, prose, and conversation. He is best known for his series of poetry books known as the "Rider Trilogy." Comprising three books, *Rider* (1994), for which he received the National Book

Critics Award for Poetry, *The Millennium Hotel* (1996), and *Provoked in Venice* (1999), the trilogy provides the reader with a semiautobiographical, diasporian journey in which the narrator examines his relationships with his family, Jewish heritage, and the world in which we all live. In *Rider*, Rudman establishes a unique conversational tone that is carried throughout the three books, where the narrator often speaks to a disembodied omnipotent voice (dubbed The Rider) who comments on, criticizes, and consoles the narrator. The Rider (the voice), which seems to be an amalgamation of Rudman's deceased stepfather, Rabbi Sidney, and a very familiar friend (perhaps the narrator's own inner voice), provides the narrator with an outlet to reflect upon his childhood, his relationships with his stepfather, his natural father, son, and mother. *Rider* offers a glimpse into the conflicts that the narrator experienced trying to reconcile his Judaism with his secularism, while growing up in various predominantly Gentile locations. Though the narrator has many typical conflicts with his stepfather, the rabbi, he ultimately realizes that his stepfather was much more of a true father to him than his own natural father. As such, *Rider* is a tribute and an elegy to Rudman's deceased stepfather.

Rudman continues his examination of relationships in *The Millennium Hotel*. In this collection, the narrator, once again accompanied by The Rider, examines his strained relationship with his natural father and their forced togetherness, as illustrated through past vacations together. The narrator also reflects on his current relationship with his own son, as well as his past romantic and erotic relationships with women. Though the narrator is a secular Jew, his conflicting emotions about his Jewish heritage are also examined in numerous poems throughout the book, such as "The Millennium Hotel—Prologue and Lament" and "The Millennium Hotel—Semaphore." These poems, among others, express sadness, reverence, joy, and ambivalence toward the narrator's Jewish traditions.

In the third book of the series, *Provoked in Venice*, the narrator from *Rider* and *The Millennium Hotel* uses a family vacation to Italy as a backdrop to examine contemporary society and its relationship to literature, film, art, and history—with a particular focus on Judaism in Italy and the unfortunate reality of **anti-Semitism**. In "A Winter Night in the City of God" the narrator is disgusted to find anti-Semitic graffiti on a wall in Rome, and in "Venice Less and Less" the narrator is saddened by the deserted synagogues in Venice and reflects on the impact that the **Holocaust** had on the Jews in that city. As in the other two books of the trilogy, the narrator is accompanied on his journey by The Rider, who offers insight and guidance at various stages throughout the book. Topics addressed in *Provoked in Venice* also include familiar subjects such as the underlying conflicts with his natural father and relationships with his son and wife.

Though much of Rudman's poetry is focused on the narrator's search for a healing sense of self, Rudman draws on traditions of other great poets, such as Quintus Horatius Flaccus (Horace) and Johann Wolfgang von

Goethe. In *Provoked in Venice*, three poems, "Against Odds Against," "The Desert of Empire," and "In Your Own Time," are, as Rudman calls them, Horatian palimpsests, where he updates themes in Horace's Roman world with those of a contemporary American world. The shift from contemporary culture to classic history and their interrelatedness is a thematic and stylistic nuance found throughout Rudman's works.

Rudman's most recent book of poetry, *The Couple* (2002), is a collection of four poem sequences that analyze and examine relationships between two people. For example, "Long-Stemmed Rose" examines the extremely erotic and somewhat volatile relationship between a younger man and an older woman who is herself a victim of sexual abuse. Other couples in the book range from the Greek mythological characters Perseus and Andromeda, to the Rat Pack with Dean Martin and Jerry Lewis. In typical Rudman style, he mixes poetry and prose to paint a vivid, subtle, and accessible picture of the complexities that exist in all human relationships.

Rudman's other poetry collections include *The Nowhere Steps* (1990), *By Contraries and Other Poems* (1987), as well as several limited editions and chapbooks, including *In the Neighboring Cell* (1982) and *The Killers* (2000), which was written in memoriam to the victims of the Columbine High School shootings in 1999. Rudman has also written several poetic prose books, including *Realm of Unknowing* (1995), and has edited and translated several other works.

Further Reading

Christophersen, Bill. Review of *The Millennium Hotel*. *Poetry* (March 1998): 339–46.

Ellis, Steven R. Review of *The Millennium Hotel*. *Library Journal* (November 15, 1996): 65.

Kaganoff, Penny. Review of *Memories of Love*." *Publishers Weekly* (March 10, 1989): 81.

Orr, Linda. "Form and the Father: On Mark Rudman's Poetry." *Agni Review* 35 (1992): 299.

Shires, Nancy. Review of *Diverse Voices: Essays on Poetry*. *Library Journal* (March 15, 1993): 78.

Smith, Dinitia. "Pure Poetry." *New York* (April 18, 1988): 63.

Marcel Trommel

RUIZ, RONALD (1936–) Mexican American novelist. Ronald Ruiz's first novel, *Happy Birthday Jesús* (1994), tells the story of Jesús Olivas, a Chicano farm worker who grows up in Fresno, California, in the 1950s. He is raised by his grandmother, a religious fanatic who abuses him physically and psychologically. She punishes him by forcing him to wear a diaper while lying in a make-shift crib sucking on a baby bottle. She continues this practice well into Jesús's teenage years. She also makes him kneel on a concrete floor with a brick in each of his outstretched hands for long periods of time or until he collapses while she watches him from behind a nearly closed door. The grandmother carries out her abuse with the tacit support of a Catholic priest.

In response to the physical and psychological repression to which he is subjected, Jesús grows up weak and timid, but also terribly angry—a time bomb waiting to explode. Society fails him at all levels: family, church, school, and eventually the criminal justice system in its most extreme form, the prison. When he turns eighteen he assaults the priest, almost killing him. Represented by an incompetent public defender before a racially insensitive court, Jesús is sent to San Quentin Prison where he suffers the physical and psychological devastation of gang rape. He spends sixteen years in prison, most of it in isolation. Upon his release, he returns to his hometown, where his grandmother and the priest are now deceased. Far from being rehabilitated, he commits a vicious murder and then seeks to make amends with the only person who had befriended him as a child.

Happy Birthday Jesús is a difficult novel to read because of its graphic depictions of violence, sexual aggression, and child abuse. It has been compared to **Richard Wright**'s *Native Son* because of its brutal realism. Notwithstanding the morbid conditions under which Jesús is forced to live and the absolute lack of any real possibility for him to lead a normal life, the novel does not generate a sense of hopelessness. The gripping and memorable conclusion of the novel firmly establishes a character who is at once in all his contradictory complexities both a ruthless murderer and a deeply hurt but compassionate human being. Ruiz, a criminal attorney for almost forty years, has written two other novels: *Giuseppe Rocco*, about an immigrant family coming to terms with the American Dream, and *Big Bear*, a mystery about a Chicano lawyer defending an Anglo physician accused of murdering his wife. Readers will find *Giuseppe Rocco* and *Big Bear* less disturbing than *Happy Birthday Jesús* but just as memorable.

Marcial Gonzalez

RUIZ DE BURTON, MARIA AMPARO (1832–1895)

Mexican American novelist. Ruiz de Burton was the first Mexican American to write novels in English. Her two novels, *Who Would Have Thought It?* (1872) and *The Squatter and the Don* (1885), are known for their unflattering depictions of "Yankee" culture from her distinctive vantage point as a Mexican by birth and an American by the consequences of history.

Her first novel, *Who Would Have Thought It?*, is a historical romance about Lola Medina, the child of aristocratic Mexican parents, born while natives in the Southwest hold her mother captive. Lola is rescued by the benevolent Dr. Norval and taken to live with his family in New England, where she falls in love with Dr. Norval's gallant son, Julian. Although this romance drives the plot, the real substance of the novel is the unrelenting critique of hypocrisy and greed among many Northerners involved in the Civil War. In their attempts to manipulate Lola and rob her of a fortune in gems and gold, the characters surrounding her serve as symbols of Anglo-Americans who poured into the Southwest at the close of the Mexican-American war, dispossessing many *Californios* of their land and treating them as second-class citizens. Although critical of the racism exhibited by Dr. Norval's wife and others toward Lola, Ruiz de Burton unfortunately reveals her own **racism** by demonizing the native peoples of the Southwest and insisting on Lola's essential **whiteness**.

Ruiz de Burton had much in common with Lola. Born into the Mexican aristocracy of Baja California, she fell in love with Henry Stanton Burton, a Captain in the American army that invaded Baja in 1846. Just before the signing of the treaty of Guadalupe-Hidalgo in 1848, Captain Burton sent his fiancée north to Monterey, where she would automatically become an American citizen under the provisions of the treaty. The couple was married in 1849 and moved to San Diego in 1852, where they homesteaded a large parcel of land known as Rancho Jamul until Captain Burton was called back to the East Coast in 1859.

Living in New York, parts of New England, and Washington, DC, Ruiz de Burton began moving in prestigious circles. In 1861 she attended the first inauguration of President Lincoln and claimed a personal friendship with the First Lady. Many of her observations from this time period are recorded in her correspondence to fellow *Californio*, General Mariano Guadalupe Vallejo. These observations, including frequent examples of profiteering, corruption, and a very unflattering portrait of President Lincoln, also fill the pages of *Who Would Have Thought It?* While serving in the Union Army, Ruiz de Burton's husband contracted malaria and died in 1869. Shortly thereafter, Ruiz de Burton returned to San Diego and became embroiled in the land disputes that would plague her for the rest of her life and serve as the foundation for her second novel.

The California Land Act of 1851 required *Californios* to legally defend their claims to lands granted to them by the Spanish or Mexican governments before 1848. This process was lengthy and costly. In *The Squatter and the Don*, Don Mariano finds the claim to his estate challenged by numerous Anglo-American squatters. Greedy railroad barons eventually displace these squatters. As in the earlier novel, a romance between Don Mariano's daughter, Mercedes Alamar, and Clarence Darrell, a squatter's son, drives the conventional plot, which holds the more substantive social and economic critiques together.

Her scathing critiques of the relationship between America's famous robber barons and their allies within state and federal legislatures place Ruiz de Burton within the best muckraking tradition of American literary realism. Unfortunately, her imagined antidote to the ruthlessness she associated with capitalism and representative democracy was a highly idealized version of noblesse oblige, the obligation of a privileged aristocracy to assume a paternal role toward the common majority. The refinement and civility of this hereditary Mexican aristocracy is everywhere contrasted with the crass materialism of Anglo-Americans. Disdain for "Yankees" is mediated, however, by the inclusion of "natural" aristocrats, such as Julian Norval and Clarence Darrell, with whom high-born Mexican heroines might marry, bringing the two cultures happily together.

Further Reading

McCullough, Kate. "Maria Amparo Ruiz de Burton's Geographies of Race, Regions of Religion." *Regions of Identity.* Stanford, CA: Stanford UP, 1999. 131–84.

Montes, Amelia Maria de la Luz. "Maria Amparo Ruiz de Burton Negotiates American Literary Politics and Culture." *Challenging Boundaries: Gender and Periodization.* Ed. Joyce Warren and Margaret Dickie. Athens: U Georgia P, 2000. 202–25.

Jennifer A. Gehrman

RUKEYSER, MURIEL (1913–1980)   Jewish American poet, political activist, literary theorist, teacher, and biographer. As a Jewish, bisexual, leftist, feminist woman, Muriel Rukeyser has often been defined by her political activism. Unfortunately, such a definition not only earned her a voluminous Federal Bureau of Investigation file but also caused many literary critics of her era to dismiss her writing as didactic and stilted. More recent literary critics have celebrated Rukeyser's use of modernist innovations to bridge the gap between the personal and the political and to unite disparate groups in battles against oppression.

Rukeyser was born into an affluent Jewish family living on the Upper West Side of Manhattan. She attended Vassar College before dropping out in 1932 to write poetry from her family's home. In 1933 Rukeyser traveled as a reporter for *Student Review,* a Communist youth magazine, to Scottsboro, Alabama, to cover the trial of nine young African American men accused of raping a white woman. While in Alabama, she was arrested for informing African Americans about a conference for African American students at Columbia University. Though she was quickly released, she contracted typhoid fever while in prison. Her experiences in Alabama made a deep impression on Rukeyser, as can be seen in the poem "The Lynching of Jesus," which is part of a cycle of poems in *Theory of Flight* (1935).

Theory of Flight, Rukeyser's first collection of poems, was published through the prestigious Yale Younger Poets Series. Her unique poetic voice can be heard even in this early volume. Writing mostly in free verse, Rukeyser juxtaposes a wide range of references, from Joan of Arc to Kodak cameras. These juxtapositions create unfamiliar associations between things in the mind of the reader, thus causing him/her to see the world from a new perspective. The poem that introduces this volume, "Poem out of Childhood," contains the aphorism that summarizes Rukeyser's sense of purpose as a poet: "Not Sappho, Sacco." Sappho refers to a figure in Greek mythology, and Sacco refers to Sacco and Vanzetti, two Italian Americans who were unfairly accused of conspiring to overthrow the United States government. In this short line, Rukeyser declares that poets of her generation should engage in contemporary political events instead of merely playing with allusions to old myths. She is not saying, however, that modern American poetry should be devoid of all such allusions. Rukeyser uses allusions to myth to convey the meaning behind the politics of her time.

Rukeyser's next poetry collection, *U.S. 1* (1938), contains the stunningly powerful sequence of poems titled "The Book of the Dead." Basing these poems on her trip to Gauley Bridge, West Virginia, in 1936, she examines the legal case of miners who were dying from silicosis (a disease in which silicate enters a miner's lungs and restricts his breathing). "The Book of the Dead" is a literary montage of lyrical verse, historical narrative, character sketches, interviews, and transcriptions, shaped into verse, of the trial against the mining company that neither informed its miners of the danger of silicate nor protected them from it. The narrative voice of the poetry sequence acts as a historical witness of the tragedy at Gauley Bridge. Furthermore, this voice delineates the exploitation of the miners and forces the reader to consider his/her complicity in this tragedy. Modernist innovations serve the ends of radical politics in her complex text. Largely regarded as Rukeyser's masterpiece, "The Book of the Dead" stands as a towering achievement in modernist literature.

Radical political themes are explored throughout *U.S. 1*. Indeed, Rukeyser's political commitments surface, in one form or another, throughout her literary work. Some of her detractors claim that the political nature of her work prevents it from attaining universal appeal, and others contend that she sacrificed her artistic integrity to a Leftist agenda. Neither assessment does justice to the power of her work. Although Rukeyser had ties to the Communist Party of America during periods of her life, she was always independent in her thinking and did not submit to calls for censorship by Party leaders. Furthermore, Rukeyser's poems celebrate humanity above political doctrine. Thus, a poem like "Mediterranean," which recounts the evacuation of Rukeyser and other international Leftists from Barcelona's Anti-Fascist Olympic Games at the outbreak of the Spanish Civil War in 1936, conveys the human heartbreak at the inception of war instead of advancing a particular political agenda.

Rukeyser also considers Jewish **identity** in many of her poems, but her most succinct and profound statement on this theme appears in a section of the long poem "Letters to the Front," first published in *Beast in View* (1944). This section, referred to by its first line as "To be a Jew in the twentieth century," says that declaring one's Jewish identity makes one a target for oppression (a point underscored by Hitler's Final Solution) but that refusing this identity burdens Jews with a guilty conscience. At the same time, the poem also presents Jewish identity as a blessing, for it connects Jews to a tradition entrenched in the fight for social justice. Judaism, for Rukeyser, had more to do with principles of justice than with the laws of the sacred texts.

Although Rukeyser was most accomplished as a poet, she also produced a number of nonfiction texts. A particularly odd text is her biography of nineteenth-century physicist Willard Gibbs, published in 1942. The biography opens with a description of the Amistad mutiny, a slave ship revolt that had no explicit connections to Gibbs. Here again, she injects unfamiliar associations into the mind of the reader. A more successful text is *The Life of Poetry* (1949), a treatise on the purpose and power of poetry. In it, Rukeyser describes poetry as a social force that not only delights the imagination but also has the power to change the material world. When Rukeyser taught poetry seminars at Sarah Lawrence College and Vassar College in the 1950s and 1960s, she conveyed this understanding of poetry to her students, asking them to examine poems both as vital artifacts of an earlier age and portals into possible futures. It is important to note that though such a perspective on poetry was unconventional, departing from standard notions of figurative language and meter, Rukeyser's method was no less rigorous than conventional literary analysis. Furthermore, *The Life of Poetry* anticipates more recent trends in literary criticism, such as New Historicism, that place literary works in their historical contexts.

In 1947 Rukeyser gave birth to her only son, William, whom she raised on her own. Becoming a career-oriented, single mother ten to fifteen years prior to the full blossoming of American feminism in the 1960s was a radical political statement in itself. Rukeyser, though, added to this statement by writing poems about pregnancy and motherhood, such as "Night Feeding" from *Selected Poems* (1951). Ignoring social taboos and pioneering the notion of personal as political, she spoke the unspeakable about women's bodies. She also explored her own bisexuality in verse, most famously in the exquisitely blunt "Orgy" from *The Speed of Darkness* (1968).

In the last years before her death in 1980, Rukeyser engaged in a flurry of radical political activity. She traveled to Vietnam in 1972 to protest the war, and in 1975 she stood vigil outside the South Korean prison that held poet Kim Chi Ha. The political poems in *Breaking Open* (1973) and *The Gates* (1976) are further evidence that Rukeyser's life experiences inspired her most engaging work. More specifically, "Despisals" reaffirms her faith that "we," the readers and writers of poetry, must take it upon ourselves to advance the case of humanity.

Muriel Rukeyser was a uniquely talented poet and writer who fearlessly articulated her convictions. Though her harshest critics condemned her as un-American, her modernist innovations and commitment to justice prove that she is an American original.

Further Reading

Gardinier, Suzanne. "'A World That Will Hold All the People': On Muriel Rukeyser." *Kenyon Review* 14.3 (1992): 88–105.

Herzog, Anne F., and Janet E. Kaufman, eds. *"How Shall We Tell Each Other of the Poet": The Life and Writing of Muriel Rukeyser*. New York: Palgrave, 2001.

Michael Yellin

RUSSIAN AMERICAN LITERATURE   The Russian presence in American letters dates back to the Romantic period. In the 1810s American readers learned of Paul Svenin (Pavel Svinin, 1787–1839), who, while stationed in Philadelphia from 1811 to 1812, contributed to *The Portfolio*, an early American periodical. (Standard Anglicized spelling or spellings of the writers' names are used wherever available; otherwise a simplified version of the Library of Congress transliteration will be used for both Russian names and titles). In 1813 Svenin's *Sketches of Moscow and St. Petersburg* appeared in Philadelphia in English. Another notable Russian on the American scene was Helena Blavatsky (1831–91), who, in 1875, founded the Theosophical Society in New York City, where her famous *Isis Unveiled* first appeared.

In the late nineteenth century and throughout the twentieth century many writers came to the United States from the Russian Empire and the Union of Soviet Socialist Republics (USSR) as immigrants and refugees, fleeing political repression, **anti-Semitism**, and censorship. Of the Russian immigrants who switched to English, the most successful was **Vladimir Nabokov** (1899–1977), who came to America in 1940. Already a famous Russian émigré author, Nabokov refashioned himself in the 1940s and early 1950s, becoming a great American writer. Nabokov spent his final decades writing American fiction in Switzerland, and insisting he was "as American as April in Arizona." The second most successful Russian in American letters was **Joseph Brodsky** (1940–96), who arrived in the United States in 1972 from Leningrad (now St. Petersburg) to win the Nobel Prize for Literature in 1987 and become a U.S. poet laureate, while mainly writing poetry in his native Russian. It would be difficult to eclipse or even match the literary stardom of these two writers.

What does it mean for an exiled Russian writer to become American? After decades of living in America, some Russian writers never become Americans—either in language or in the themes and spirit of their work. A case in point is Alexander Solzhenitsyn (1918–). Forced into exile from the USSR in 1974, Solzhenitsyn found refuge in Vermont in 1976. He continued writing exclusively in Russian, shunning vestiges of Americanization, voicing bellicose criticism of American society, and insisting he was in exile temporarily. Author of meditative works on the future and reconstruction of Russia, Solzhenitsyn returned to Russia in 1994, where he now lives.

In addition to a dearth of scholarship on the subject and the vastness of the Russian American literary landscape, one faces various difficulties of classification and methodology. "Russian" can define the writer's language, culture, ethnicity, country of origin, and so forth. For example, an émigré writer of Armenian parentage raised in Moscow and writing in Russian is likely to be seen as a Russian American writer, whereas an Jewish immigrant from Moscow writing in English on Jewish topics might be viewed as a Jewish American author.

Leaving theater, screenwriting, and journalism outside its scope, this brief article attempts a selective, chronological overview of Russian American literature from the 1920s until the present. Exploring some of the boundaries separating such categories as "Russian émigré literature in America," "Russian American literature," and "literature by Russian

Americans," it seeks to illustrate the variety of typologies and hyphenated entities that both frustrate and exhilarate a student of the Russian literary presence in America.

Russian émigré literature belongs mostly to the twentieth century and is conventionally divided into three "waves." The First Wave émigrés left Russia during and in the aftermath of the Russian Revolution of 1917 and the ensuing Civil War (1918–22). The Second Wave exiles left the USSR during and immediately following World War II; many of them were the so-called DPs (displaced persons). The majority of the Third Wave emigrants left the USSR in the 1970s and 1980s; they were Jewish or connected, by real or fictional family ties, to Soviet Jews. The last Third Wave writers came to the United States from 1987 to 1989 during the period of reforms in the USSR known as *perestroika* that led to the collapse of the USSR in 1991. The term Fourth Wave is sometimes used to refer to those who left in the last Soviet year and the first few post-Soviet years. During these years, leaving the USSR ceased to be a problem, whereas immigrating to the United States became increasingly difficult, as those trying to move to America were no longer treated as political refugees but rather as economic immigrants. Some of the differences between *late* Third Wave and Fourth Wave Russian American writers are better determined not chronologically but based on whether they perceive America as a new home or merely as a place of literary residence.

The shortcomings of chronological periodization become apparent when one considers the time when many First Wave émigré writers arrived in America. Whereas before 1940, the First Wave writers established major Russian literary centers in such European cities as Berlin, Paris, and Prague, the pre–World War II Russian literary life in America had been provincial. The scarcity of the Russian literary life in prewar America can be easily gleaned from the collective *Iz Ameriki: Stikhotvoreniia* (1925; From America: Poems). Very few important representatives of the First Wave reached the United States in the years before World War II; it was not until the early 1940s that writers such as Nabokov made the United States their home.

Mainly a writer of historical and philosophical novels, Mark Aldanov (1886–1957) had had several books published by Knopf even before he and his wife escaped from France to the United States in 1941. In the 1940s and early 1950s Aldanov was the most successful Russian writer in America. Translated into English and published by major New York City houses, his books included the novels *The Fifth Seal* (1943), *Before the Deluge* (1947), and *To Live as We Wish* (1952) and the short story collection *A Night at the Airport* (1949). America never became Aldanov's true home; he returned to Europe in 1947 and died in Nice.

Besides his original writing, Aldanov contributed to Russian American literature by cofounding with Mikhail Tsetlin (1882–1945, penname "Amari"), in 1942 in New York City, the émigré journal *Novyi zhurnal* (*The New Review*), still published today on a quarterly basis. *The New Review* replaced the Parisian *Sovremennye zapiski* (Contemporary Annals), the leading Russian periodical of the interwar period. In the 1940s and 1950s some of the best Russian prose and remarkable poetry appeared in *The New Review*, including works by Isaac Babel, Nina Berberova, Mikhail Bulgakov, Ivan Bunin, Georgii Ivanov, and Vladimir Nabokov. In the subsequent decades dissident literature smuggled from the USSR appeared in the journal, as did translations of such American writers as Saul Bellow and John Cheever. From 1946 to 1959 Michael Karpovich (1888–1959), an émigré historian, edited *The New Review*. Subsequent editors include Roman Goul (1896–1986), who moved to New York City in 1950 to continue writing and publishing historical novels (the sensationist *Azef*, 1962), and Yuri Kashkarov (1940–96), a writer who arrived in New York in 1977 and described his émigré travails in the unfinished novel *East-West*, serialized in *The New Review* in 1986. Edited by Third Wave poet Vadim Kreyd (1936–) since 1995, the journal continues to publish valuable archival and documentary materials.

Andrei Sedykh (1902–94), prose writer and journalist, arrived in New York City from France in 1942 and joined *Novoe russkoe slovo* (The New Russian Word), America's oldest Russian daily, founded in 1910; in 1973 he became its editor-in-chief and president. Sedykh presided over momentous changes as his paper's readership shifted in the 1970s, from the First Wave and Second Wave émigrés to ex-Soviet Third Wave readers. Sedykh's principal contribution to postwar émigré culture was his memoir, *Dalekie, blizkie: literaturnye portrety* (1962; Distant Ones, Close Ones: Literary Portraits).

No account of Russian American poetry of the First Wave is complete without Vladimir Korvin-Piotrovskii (1891–1966), Iurii (George) Ivask (1907–86), and Igor Chinnov (1909–96). Soon after the end of World War II, Korvin-Piotrovskii moved to California from Europe. *Pozdnii gost'* (A Late Guest), his two-volume collected works, appeared posthumously in Washington, DC in 1968–69. Iurii Ivask (1907–86), who had spent the interwar years in Estonia, received a PhD from Harvard in 1954 and divided his time between university teaching and writing. He edited *Na Zapade* (1953; In the West), a landmark anthology of Russian émigré poetry. Igor Chinnov, who was born in Riga, Latvia, and died in Daytona Beach, Florida, wrote his best poetry in America, where he moved to become a university professor in 1962. Marked by lyrical grotesqueness and subtle homoeroticism, Chinnov's books published in America include *Metafory* (1968; Metaphors), *Avtograf* (1984; Autograph), and others.

Few writers did more for the preservation of Russian émigré publishing than Sofiia Pregel' (1894–1972), poet, memoirist, and philanthropist, who founded the journal *Novosel'e* (Housewarming) in New York City in 1942. A U.S. citizen, Pregel' returned to Paris in 1948, publishing and editing *Housewarming* there until 1950. The émigré critic Marc Slonim (1894–1976), who taught Russian literature in postwar America, edited Pregel's posthumous

Poskdnie stikhi (1973; Last Poems). Finally, a brief mention should be made of Sofia (Sophie) Dubnova-Erlich (1885–1986), poet, essayist, translator, and memoirist, daughter of the great Jewish historian Simon Dubnov (1860–1941). In America, where she arrived in 1942, Dubnova-Erlich contributed to Russian and Yiddish publications. Dubnova-Erlich's memoir, *Bread and Matzos*, was partially serialized in the 1980s in the Third Wave émigré quarterly *Vremia i my* (Time and We); the complete text appeared in St. Petersburg in 1994.

In the foreword to the English translation of *The Gift* (1963), Nabokov wrote, "The tremendous outflow of intellectuals that formed such a prominent part of the general exodus from Soviet Russia in the first years of the Bolshevist Revolution seems today [written in Montreux in 1962] like the wonderings of some mythical tribe whose bird-signs and moon-signs I now retrieve from the desert dust. We remained unknown to American intellectuals (who, bewitched by Communist propaganda, saw us merely as villainous generals, oil magnates, and gaunt ladies with lorgnettes. That world is now gone. . . . The old intellectuals are now dying out and have not found successors in the so-called Displaced Persons of the last two decades who have carried abroad the provincialism and Philistinism of their Soviet homeland." Nabokov's remarks augment two key aspects of the postwar Russian literary life in America: the relative obscurity of Russian literary exiles in the American imagination and the ideological and aesthetic divides separating the writers of the First Wave and Second Wave.

The works of the Second Wave writers reflected the difficulties of their lives in Stalinist Russia, the experiences during World War II, during Nazi occupation, and in the DP camps in postwar Europe. Memoir and poetry were represented more prominently than fiction in the writing of these émigrés. Nikolay Narokov (1881–1969), who emigrated from Germany in 1950, was the most visible Russian prose writer of the Second Wave living in America. His best-known novel *Mnimye velichiny* (1952; *The Chains of Fear*, 1958), as well as his other fiction, depict post-revolutionary Russia.

Narokov's son, the poet Nikolai Morshen (1917–2001), became a well-known Russian American poet. He lived in California, and his books include *Tiulen'* (1959; Seal) and *Sobranie stikhov* (1996; Collected Verses). Perhaps the most celebrated poet of the Second Wave was Ivan Elagin (1918–87), who relocated to the United States in 1950. Elagin's American collections, such as *Kosoi polet* (1967; The Slanted Flight), spoke of his cultural fragmentation. The latter poems in Elagin's *Pod sozvezdiem topora: izbrannoe* (1976; Under the Constellation of an Ax: Selected Poems) were especially American in their themes. Elagin translated into Russian *John Brown's Body* by Stephen Vincent Benét (1979; Telo Dzhona Brauna). Among other Russian American Second Wave poets are Ivan Burkin (1919–); Boris Filippov (1905–91), poet and scholar who operated Inter-Language Associates, a major outlet of émigré publishing; and Valentina Sinkevich (1926–), author of the bilingual volume *Coming of Day* (1978) and founder of *Encounters*, an annual of émigré poetry.

The Third Wave gave America the largest constellation of its Russian literary artists, some of whom pursued publishing and writing in English. A number of them had been dissidents and left the USSR for reasons of political and ideological persecution. A key factor shaping the destinies of Third Wave writers was Jewish emigration from the USSR, which crested from 1977 to 1979, restarting in 1987. A number of Third Wave writers had been "refuseniks" (those whom Soviet authorities denied—"refused"—permission to emigrate) before being allowed to leave.

Some Third Wave writers came to America as mature, published authors and capitalized on their Soviet professional experiences, whereas others only began to publish abroad. For example, the New York-based poet Lev Khalif (1930–), who emigrated in 1977, recorded his literary past in the acerbic memoir-novel *TsDL* (1979; Central House of Writers) while remaining loyal to his poetic youth during Khrushchev's Thaw. In America, Russian writers of the Third Wave enjoyed vastly new publishing opportunities that were free of censorship and also encouraged self-publishing. Most Third Wave literary publications paid no honoraria, and some asked for a subvention fee. Few Russian immigrants could make a living as writers, and some resorted to other careers. Only several Third Wave Russian writers reached wider American audiences in translation. Few new literary careers flourished in America, and some Russian writers vanished after coming to the New World. Lev Mak (1937–), a poet from Odessa, emigrated in the 1970s, contributed for a few years to Russian Third Wave periodicals (*Time and We*), published two books, including the English-language *From the Night and Other Poems* (1978), and "disappeared" in the middle 1980s.

Although the Third Wave introduced dailies and weeklies (for example, the Los Angeles-based *Panorama*), Russian American communities formed in the 1970s and 1980s were much less concerned with the preservation of Russian culture abroad, as compared to their First Wave and Second Wave predecessors. Many readers looked to their writers for journalistic professionalism, occasional and measured doses of nostalgia, and Russian-language accounts of life in America, couched in traditional versification or simple representational prose. Only the elite few among Russian American readers were interested in formal experimentation.

Over the years, as the English skills of the Russian Americans improved; some of them stopped reading in Russian and grew increasingly skeptical of Russian American writing. The reform years and the collapse of the USSR brought about a publishing boom in Russia and the former Soviet republics that nearly paralyzed émigré literary publishing in America. For example, Ardis Publishers, founded in the 1971 by Carl Proffer (1938–84), published many works by Third Wave Russian American authors in the 1970s and 1980s, in Russian and in translation; by the late 1990s Ardis Publishers had ceased publishing new Russian titles.

At the same time, a number of Russian American writers, who had been unable to publish in the USSR, made their literary returns in the late 1980s and early 1990s. Questions such as "One or Two Literatures?", previously the realm of academic punditry, acquired practical significance in the 1990s as Third Wave Russian American writers began to compete with writers living in Russia in the literary marketplace of the former USSR. Although, with a few exceptions, repatriation of Russian writers living in America has not been common, Third Wave writers can visit the former USSR and meet with their audiences.

Third Wave writers displayed a wide span of ages and generations. Some Russian Americans arrived as teenagers and became bilingual authors, such as Nina Kosman (1959–), who immigrated in 1972 to Israel and later to America. Writing poetry in both Russian and English (e.g., *Po pravuiu ruku sna/To the Right of A Dream*, 1996), Kosman has distinguished herself as an English translator of Marina Tsvetaeva's poetry while also becoming a writer of English prose for adolescents (her novel *Behind the Border*, 1994). Yet many of the Russian American writers, especially those who came in the middle of their careers, have remained monolingual literary practitioners. Naum Korzhavin (1925–), poet and essayist, and victim of Stalinism, immigrated to Boston in 1973, remaining an anti-Soviet *Soviet* poet. His Russian poetry volumes published in the West include *Weavings* (1981). In *Ne tol'ko Brodskii* (1988; Not Just Brodsky), a collection of photographs and accompanying cultural anecdotes, Sergey Dovlatov reported Korzhavin's statement: "I don't write for Slavists, I write for normal people."

Third Wave Russian American writers have also brought with them a great diversity of pasts (ethnic, linguistic, religious, ideological) and a broad representation of formal trends (from stanch avant-gardists to sworn traditionalists). The commonality of Russian as the lingua franca of the educated Third Wave immigrants from the USSR has resulted in an interplay between Russian American writers and émigré writers from ethnic Soviet republics (for example, Ukraine and Lithuania). Several Russian poets, including Joseph Brodsky, Vladimir Gandelsman, and Marina Temkina have rendered into Russian the verses of the Lithuanian poet Tomas Venclova (1937–), who immigrated to America in 1977 and contributed to Third Wave publications. Also intriguing is the career of Igor Mikhalevich-Kaplan (1943–), who originally wrote in Ukrainian. Having emigrated in 1979, Mikhalevich-Kaplan settled in Philadelphia and eventually switched to Russian; in 1992 he founded the literary annual *Poberezh'e* (The Coast) and a publishing house of the same name, which has since issued over one hundred books by Russian American authors.

A famous Soviet writer since the 1960s, Vassily Aksyonov (1932–) arrived in America in 1980, the year his novel *Ozhog* (*The Burn*, written during 1969–75), appeared in America in Russian (the English translation was published in 1984). Although Aksyonov remained prolific and enjoyed success in translation, his American works, including *Skazhi izium* (1985; *Say Cheese!*, 1989), never eclipsed either *The Burn* or his other major novel, *Ostrov Krym* (1981; *The Island of Crimea*, 1983).

The extremes of Soviet history and ideology inform the literary imagination of Yuz Aleshkovsky (1929–), who emigrated in 1978. His novels *Ruka (povestvovanie palacha)* (1980; *The hand*, or, *The confession of an executioner*, 1990), *Kenguru* (1981; *Kangaroo*, 1986), and others allegorize the brutality and absurdity of the Soviet regime. Aleshkovsky's manner is distinguished by a manipulation of non-normative slang and criminal jargon.

Philip Isaac Berman (1936–) emigrated from Moscow in 1981 and settled in Philadelphia. In the USSR only a few of Berman's works had appeared, whereas in America he became well known after the publication of his metaphysical short novel *Registrator* (1984; Registry Clerk). Problems of a dual, Jewish-Russian **identity**, permeate Berman's literary imagination, as evidenced by his frequently anthologized, Yiddish-infused short story "Sara i Petushok" (1988; "Sarah and Rooster").

A self-disarming intonation, combined with bitterly satirical, often biographically based, first-person fictions of life in the USSR, typifies the works of Sergei Dovlatov (1941–90). A journalist and a prolific writer, Dovlatov was marginalized in the USSR. Only after his **immigration** in 1978 did a number of his books appear, including *Kompromiss* (1981; The Compromise) and *Zona: zapiski nadziratelia* (1982; *The Zone: A Prison Camp Guard's Story*, 1985). Dovlatov's latter fiction, including *Inostranka* (1986; *A Foreign Woman*, 1991), satirized the daily lives of Russian immigrants.

An autobiographical imperative, sexual openness, radical critique of bourgeois values, and provocativeness, have become the trademarks of the novelist, memoirist, and poet Eduard Limonov (1943–). After emigrating, Limonov wrote *Eto ia, Edichka* (1982; *It's Me, Eddie: A Fictional Memoir*, 1983); the novel's disparagement of American culture and lives of the Russian émigrés in New York City initially made publication difficult (it first came out in French translation). Limonov later moved to France, where he enjoyed a successful literary career and became a citizen in 1987. Returning to Russia in 1991, Limonov devoted himself to extremist political activities.

The writings of Sasha Sokolov (1943–) make ingenious use of a Beckettian stream of consciousness in order to depict a Soviet childhood and youth. Sokolov's major novel, *Shkola dlia durakov* (1976; *A School for Fools*, 1977) came out soon after his emigration in 1975. His other works, including *Palisandria* (1985; *Astrophobia*, 1989), conflate fantasy and history but do not match the power of the narrative voice in *A School for Fools*. Having lived in Vermont, Sokolov later settled in Canada.

The Odessan writer Arkady Lvov (1927–) emigrated in 1976, settling in the New York City area. Set during the Stalinist years, Lvov novel, *Dvor* (1982; *The Courtyard*, 1989), takes its architectonics from an Odessan courtyard, a narrative amphitheater where the protagonists' families are both the gladiators and the spectators. Jewish themes are central in much of his writing, including his short stories.

Jewish themes and protagonists also inhabit the fiction of Felix Roziner (1936–97), who came to Boston in 1985 after having first emigrated from the

USSR to Israel in 1978. His major novel *Nekto Finkelmaier* (1981; *A Certain Finkelmayer*, 1991), won the 1980 Dahl Prize (Paris). Roziner's protagonist is a genius Russian poet whose fate mirrors and mimics Joseph Brodsky's. Roziner's post-**Holocaust** novella *Lilovyi dym* (1987; "Purple Smoke" in *Commentary*, 1989) is told by a Jewish Lithuanian protagonist living in Israel in the 1980s.

David Shrayer-Petrov (1936–), fiction writer, poet, and memoirist, was unable to publish in the USSR throughout his nine years as a refusenik. Emigrating in 1987, Shrayer-Petrov settled in Providence, Rhode Island. Part dirge, part confession of a Jew's expired love for Russia, his second American collection *Villa Borghese* (1992) bridged Russian and émigré years. Gently ironic fiction about Russian Jewish émigrés in America appears on both sides of the Atlantic. In 2003 his *Jonah and Sarah: Jewish Stories of Russia and America*, came out in English in the Library of Modern Jewish Literature Series.

Third Wave prose writers also include Vasilii Agafonov (1942–), who emigrated in 1979 and published *Kniga Svin'i. Poema* (1995; Book of Swine. An Epic Poem); Mikhail Morgulis (1942–), who emigrated in 1977, published the magazine *Literaturnyi kur'er* (Literary Courier, 1981–87) in Chicago, and described his first trip back to Russia in *Return to the Red Planet: 22 Days in Gorbachev's Back Yard* (1989); Irina Muravyova (1952–), who moved to Boston in 1978 to publish poetry and fiction (three of her tales were collected in English as *The Nomadic Soul*, 1999); and Ludmila Shtern (1937–), who emigrated in 1975 and wrote a memoir about Joseph Brodsky (2001).

Among the Third Wave poets, Dmitri Bobyshev (1936–), has received much critical attention. Bobyshev emigrated from Leningrad in 1979. His most original book, *Zveri sviatogo Antoniia: Bestiarii* (1989; The Beasts of St. Anthony: A Bestiary), was marked by verbal artistry. A shift away from formal complexity and an emphasis on Christian metaphysics mark Bobyshev's collection *Angely i sily* (1997; Angels and Powers).

The *enfant terrible* of Russian American poetry, Konstantin K. Kuzminsky (1940–), emigrated from Leningrad in 1975. An avant-garde poet, Kuzminsky was the principal editor of the landmark compendium, *The Blue Lagoon Anthology of Modern Russian Poetry* (1980–1986). In recent years Kuzminsky has been mentoring a group of younger Russian American authors who publish the journal *Magazinnik*.

Mikhail Kreps (1940–94), poet and scholar, emigrated from Leningrad in 1974. Kreps wrote the first monograph about Joseph Brodsky, *O poezii Brodskogo* (1984; On Brodsky's Poetry). Author of several collections, including *Buton golovy* (1987; Bud of the Head), Kreps is best remembered for his collection of Russian palindromes, *Mukhi i ikh um* (1993; Flies and Their Intelligence). In 1997 the Michael B. Kreps Memorial Readings were inaugurated at Boston College, where he taught from 1981 until 1994.

Poet and literary scholar Lev Loseff (1937–), formerly of Leningrad, emigrated in 1976. Loseff's poetry is distinguished by distancing authorial irony and sophisticated versification. Having written criticism in English, Loseff also collaborates in translating his poetry. His émigré poetry collections include *Chudesnyi desant* (1985; Miraculous Sortie) and *Tainyi sovetnik* (1987; translated as both Privy Councilor and Secret Adviser).

Marina Temkina (1948–), a New Yorker since 1978, has published several collections of poetry, of which the most original is *Kalancha: Gendernaia lirika* (1995; Fire Station: Gendered Lyric). Temkina is the cofounder and president of the Archive for Jewish Immigrant Culture. Other Third Wave Russian American poets include Pavel Babich (1933–), who emigrated in 1980; Ina Bliznetsova (1958–), who emigrated in 1970; Mikhail Iupp (1938–), who arrived in America in 1981; Aleksandr Ocheretyansky (1946–), who emigrated in 1979 and founded the avant-garde annual *Chernovik* (*Draft*) in 1989; Sergei Petrunis (1944–), who emigrated in 1978; and Viktor Urin (1924–), who emigrated in 1977.

A separate case could be made for Third Wave Russian American writers who emigrated in their twenties and early thirties and have since transitioned to writing in English. Before emigrating in 1986, Mikhail Iossel (1955–) had contributed to Leningrad's *samizdat* (underground) literary publications. *Every Hunter Wants to Know . . . A Leningrad Life*, his debut collection of English-language stories about living in the stagnating USSR, appeared in 1991. Iossel coedited, with Jeff Parker, the collection *Amerika: Russian Writers View the United States* (2004) and continues to write in his native Russian and adopted English. Maxim D. Shrayer (1967–), son of David Shrayer-Petrov, emigrated in 1987. Poems written prior to emigration formed the bulk of his first collection, *Tabun nad lugom* (1990; Herd Above the Meadow). Shrayer's second and third collections, *Amerikanskii romans* (1994; American Romance) and *N'iukheivenskie sonety* (1998; The New Haven Sonnets) captured the experience of Americanization. In 1995 Shrayer made a transition to writing creative prose in English, which he occasionally translates or cotranslates for publication in Russian.

The disintegration of the USSR in 1991 changed the face of Russian American literature. The émigré writers in the United States were transformed from exiles to expatriates; the political system some of them had criticized ceased to exist. The late Soviet reform and the post-Soviet era have brought about the Fourth Wave of Russian writers in America, resulting in new types of cultural transplantations.

Vladimir Gandelsman (1948–) arrived in New York City from Leningrad in 1990. Joseph Brodsky's introduction to Gandelsman's first collection *Shum zemli* (1991; Hum of the Earth) launched the poet's career, ricocheting to Russia, where Gandelsman became a popular poet. He went on to found Ars-Interpres, a New York-based press that publishes bilingual, English-Russian editions of works by American poets.

Ilya Kutik (1960–) left Russia in 1990 already a published poet, spent almost five years in Sweden, and arrived in America in 1995 to become a university professor. A translation of Kutik's *Ode: On Visiting the Belosaraisk*

Spit on the Sea of Azov (1997) was printed in a bilingual edition. Although bilingual, Kutik continues to write poetry in Russian. His essays have been gathered in *Hieroglyphs of Another World* (2000).

Katia Kapovich (1960–) grew up in Moldova and in 1990 moved to Israel, where her first poetry collection appeared. Kapovich later moved to United States, published other books of Russian poetry, and gradually embraced writing in English. Kapovich's first English-language collection is titled *Gogol in Rome* (2004); she coedits *Fulcrum: An Annual of Poetry and Aesthetics* with the poet Philip Nikolaev (1966–), a former Muscovite who writes poetry in English.

Originally from Moscow, Irina Mashinskaya (1958–) emigrated in 1991. Her first collection, the bilingual chapbook *Potomu chto my zdes'* (1995; Because We Are Here), was followed by other collections of Mashinskaya's Russian poetry, including *Posle Epigrafa* (1997; After the Epigraph), where the best poems record the contortions of a Russian psyche in American suburbia, and translations of contemporary American poetry.

With all the changes of the 1990s the term "Russian American literature" has become even more problematic. Yet one cannot disregard the emergence, in the 1990s, of another group: Russian-born young authors, who were raised in the United States or came here as young men and women and began to compose or publish in English, cultivating in their works the theme of immigrant culture and the sense of duality it precipitates. Gary Shteyngart (1972–), who came from Leningrad as a child, recently published *The Russian Debutante's Handbook* (2002). Emigrating in 1994, Lara Vapnyar (1971–) began writing fiction in English. *There Are Jews in My House* (2003), Vapnyar's debut collection, features formally unassuming accounts of Russian life. Russian Americans who write in English include poet and translator of Russian avant-garde Matvei Yankelevich (1973–), who emigrated in 1977 and founded Ugly Duckling Presse in 1993, poet Eugene Ostashevsky (1968–), who has lived in the United States since 1979 and has published chapbooks of English poetry and translations; and others.

The transition of Russian American writers to English entails not only the linguistic and epistemological wherewithal, but also psychological, cultural, and social barriers, and also what for some émigrés remains a principled stance. The majority of Russian writers living in America, even those who came young enough to have transitioned, continue to write in Russian, and the works of only a few of them are available in English translation. Can they be considered *American* writers? Whatever the definition, Russian American literature is a conglomeration of individual voices, whose historical past and bicultural experiences form a unique body of literary works.

Further Reading

Bobyshev, Dmitrii, Vadim Kreid,, and Valentina Sinkevich. *Slovar' poetov russkogo zarubezh'ia.* Ed. Vadim Kreid. St. Petersburg: Izdatel'stvo Russkogo Khristianskogo gumanitarnogo universiteta, 1999.

Glad, John. *Conversations in Exile: Russian Writers Abroad.* Ed. John Glad; trans. Richard and Joanna Robin [from 1991 Russian ed.]. Durham, NC: Duke UP, 1993.

———. *Russia Abroad: Writers, History, Politics.* Intro. Victor Terras. Tenafly, NJ: Hermitage Publishers, Birchbark Press, 1999.

Morrison, R. H., ed. and trans. *America' s Russian Poets.* Ann Arbor, MI: Ardis, 1975.

Shrayer, Maxim D., ed. *Anthology of Jewish-Russian Literature: Two Centuries of Dual Identity in Prose and Poetry.* 2 vols. Armonk, NY: M. E. Sharpe, 2006.

Struve, Gleb. *Russkaia literatura v izgnanii* [incl. *Kratkii biograficheskii slovar' russkogo zarubezh'ia,* by R. I. Vil'danova, et al.]. 3rd ed. Paris: YMCA-Press; Moscow: Russkii put', 1996.

Margarit Tadevosyan and Maxim D. Shrayer

S

SÁENZ, BENJAMIN ALIRE (1955–)   Chicano novelist, poet, essayist, and teacher. Since the early 1990s Benjamin Alire Sáenz has emerged as a significant chronicler of the border-straddling metropolis formed by El Paso, Texas, and its Mexican neighbor, Ciudad Juárez. This border setting provides the physical and symbolic focus of Alire Sáenz's novels *Carry Me Like Water* (1995) and *The House of Forgetting* (1997), his short story collection *Flowers for the Broken* (1992), and the poetry collections *Calendar and Dust* (1991), *Dark and Perfect Angels* (1995), and *Elegies in Blue* (2002). Alire Sáenz has written bilingual children's picture books and the novel for young adults, *Sammy and Juliana In Hollywood* (2004). He is also an insightful essayist, his pet themes being the sociopolitical structures and dominant cultural protocols against which Chicana/o writers like himself have had to struggle in order to attain visibility and acceptance in a country that has historically devalued its Chicana/o communities.

Born in a working-class family near Las Cruces, New Mexico, Alire Sáenz's late high school and early adult years were marked by a growing politicization and interest in Catholic liberation theology. In the 1970s he began studying for the priesthood, first in Denver, Colorado, and then for four years at the University of Louvain, Belgium. However, by the early 1980s, Alire Sáenz had shifted his attention to creative writing and went on to complete degrees at the University of Texas at El Paso, Iowa, and Stanford. He currently teaches English literature at the University of Texas at El Paso.

Alire Sáenz's novel *Carry Me Like Water* encapsulates the author's concerns with place and **identity**. The novel is structured as an epic quest narrative in which various Chicana/o and Anglo characters attempt to imagine and construct a new "American" home in El Paso. The quest requires them to disclose repressed personal histories and to reassess the oppressive conditions of everyday life that impact Chicana/o, Anglo, and Mexican relations. Alire Sáenz's second novel, *The House of Forgetting*, also explores fraught Chicana/o and Anglo relations as seen from the perspective of Gloria Santos. Kidnapped from her home in El Paso by Thomas Blacker, an Anglo academic from Chicago, seven-year-old Gloria becomes the focus of Blacker's experiment to transform her into an ideal "American," educated in line with the Western literary and philosophical canon. Her "exile" ends in adulthood when she stabs her captor and leaves his house, only to realize that her Chicana identity and connection to El Paso have been destroyed. A similar concern with Chicana/o "exile" in the United States characterizes Alire Sáenz's poetry and short stories.

Despite Alire Sáenz's impressive publishing output, which amounts to a nuanced exploration of Chicana/o identity formation and borderlands resilience, Alire Sáenz remains a surprisingly underrated and neglected writer in Chicana/o studies.

Further Reading

Allatson, Paul. *Latino Dreams: Transcultural Traffic and the U.S. National Imaginary.* [Portada Hispánica Series no. 14.] Amsterdam and New York: Rodopi, 2002.

López-Pulido, Alberto. "To Arrive Is to Begin: Benjamín Sáenz's *Carry Me Like Water* and the Pilgrimage of Origin in the Borderlands." *Studies in Twentieth Century Literature* 25.1 (2001): 306–15.

Paul Allatson

SAID, EDWARD W. (1935–2003) Palestinian American critic, theorist, and autobiographer. Said was without question the foremost spokesman in English for the Palestinian people. He was also the leader of a school of thought, cultural studies, which examined writing in the context of historical culture; his fellow thinkers included Stuart Hall, Gayatri Chakravorthy Spivak, and Aijaz Ahmad. Said thus served in his lifetime as the meeting place of two distinct discourses: cultural studies and Palestinian nationalism. In his writing the two came closer together, cultural studies benefiting from the case of Palestinian (and postcolonial) writing and the Palestinian cause from the insights of cultural studies.

Said was born in Jerusalem, British Mandate Palestine, in November 1935. His father and mother, Wadie and Hilda Musa Said, were affluent Christians. The family moved a great deal, and in his childhood Edward was educated in Egypt. They returned to Palestine in 1947, before Israel's declaration of independence, and after a year joined many other Palestinians in leaving the country, eventually settling in the United States. After secondary education at Mount Hermon School in New England, young Edward Said entered Princeton University in New York where he earned his BA in 1958. He earned his PhD from Harvard in 1963 and was promptly

Edward W. Said gives the introductory lecture at the first European Art Forum. *Associated Press.*

hired as an instructor at Columbia University, where he remained a part of the comparative literature faculty until his death in September 2003.

Said's books span a thirty-five-year period, beginning in 1966 with a version of his doctoral thesis, *Joseph Conrad and the Fiction of Autobiography.* In 1968, in a collection of essays edited by Ibrahim Abu-Lughod in the wake of the Six-Day War, he contributed "The Arab Imaged," which became the basis for one of his major themes: the effect of cultural representation on people's lives. In 1973 he published *Beginnings,* an analysis of narrative indebted to French literary theory and to the Italian communist writer Antonio Gramsci's notion of self-exploration as key to ideology. A sabbatical year at Stanford University in 1975–76 resulted in his best-known work, *Orientalism* (1977). *The Question of Palestine* followed in 1979 and *Covering Islam* in 1981. In the 1980s, Said notably published *The World, The Text, and The Critic* (1983), a collection of essays, and *After the Last Sky: Palestinian Lives* (1986), a collaboration with photographer Jean Mohr. The 1990s saw *Musical Elaborations* (1991), an application of Said's ideas to the concert world and, more significantly, *Culture and Imperialism* (1993), Said's most comprehensive work on Western writing and its relation to the "Other" of the once-colonized world. A collection of essays and interviews on Palestinian struggle, *The Politics of Dispossession,* came out in 1994, followed five years later by a memoir, *Out of Place.* Said was working on yet another book at his death in 2003.

In the trilogy that established his critical reputation, *Orientalism, The Question of Palestine,* and *Covering Islam,* Said embarked on the task of changing the Western view of the Arab and Muslim world. In *Orientalism* he began by defining that field as it emerged in the nineteenth century, a scholarly discourse linked to European imperialism. Orientalist writers portrayed their subjects, the people of the "East," including Arabs and Indians, using a never-changing vocabulary of ideas and images: whereas Westerners were said to be dynamic, progressive, and developing, Easterners were regarded as lazy, irrational, and unchanging. *The Question of Palestine* applies this idea to Palestine, where a Western ideology, Zionism, used Orientalist vocabulary to forever alter the political landscape for millions of indigenous Arab people. *Covering Islam,* written in the wake of the Iran crisis of 1979–81, explores the way in which updated Orientalism has been fueled by American and Israeli national interests to radically shape Western images of the Muslim peoples.

Edward Said's role as professor of literature overlapped with his separate role as advocate for the Palestinian people. As America's best-known Palestinian intellectual, Said defended Palestinians against the blanket charge of terrorism and himself against the false charge of **anti-Semitism**. He accomplished these tasks eloquently, in the face of death threats; he thereby demonstrated how it is possible to blend literary criticism with progressive political activism. (*See also* Arab American Autobiography)

Further Reading

Aruri, Naseer H. "Professor Edward W. Said, Scholar Activist." *Holy Land Studies: A Multidisciplinary Journal* 2.2 (March 2004): 140–43.

Bove, Paul A., ed. *Edward Said and the Work of the Critic: Speaking Truth to Power.* Durham, NC: Duke UP, 2000.

Sprinker, Michael, ed. *Edward Said: A Critical Reader.* New York: Blackwell, 1992.

Barry Fruchter

SAIKI, PATSY SUMIE (1915–)   Japanese American fiction and prose writer. As a writer of fiction and nonfiction, Patsy Sumie Saiki is integral to the tradition of Hawaiian "local" writing. *Patsy Sumie Saiki: A Daughter of Hawaii* (2003), a video produced by Arnie Saiki, provides the only biography of Patsy Saiki to date. Made in response to the Japanese tradition of venerating those who reach the age of 88, the video provides an excellent biographical resource for scholars and the general public alike.

Patsy Saiki began writing at a mature age, publishing her first novel, *Sachie: A Daughter of Hawaii* (1977), at age sixty-seven and a collection of short stories, *Early Japanese Immigrants in Hawaii* (1993), at age eighty-three.

The first of her three books of nonfiction, *Ganbare, An Example of Japanese Spirit* (1982), depicts the experiences of 1500 Hawaiians of Japanese descent who were interned during World War II in disparate parts of the United States from Missoula, Montana, to Camp Forrest, Tennessee. *Japanese Women in Hawaii: The First One Hundred Years* (1985) celebrates the accomplishments of second-generation Japanese American women in Hawai'i, and Saiki's most recent nonfiction book, *Traveling Is Not Just for Sightseeing: INSIGHTseeing* (2000), documents her travels around the world. In addition, Saiki has written three plays: *The Return* and *The Second Choice* published in *University of Hawaii Plays* (1959) and *The Return of Sam Patch* in *Theatre Group Plays, 1966–67* (1967). All of Saiki's work relates the experiences of Japanese immigrants in Hawai'i, even as her work becomes more autobiographical, as in her most recent book of nonfiction. Stephen Sumida distinguishes Patsy Saiki as central to the tradition of "local Hawai'i writers" who, in the 1920s, began to publish fiction, poetry, and nonfiction that describe personal, family, and community experiences.

Sachie: A Daughter of Hawaii is central to this tradition. A first-person narrative of a thirteen-year-old girl, Sachie, the novel is divided into twelve chapters, each enfolding the events in each month of the year. This structure, Sumida argues, is unique in Hawaiian contemporary literature; the calendar device allows Saiki to enfold a number of "talk stories" while sustaining a continuing story line of Sachie's life. Sumida calls the sense of time in this novel "distinctly local and Hawaiian"; in other words, Sumida argues, "Saiki, in effect, tells time 'by event or person'" (93). The novel is not in any way sentimental as it portrays the conflicts between the Japanese values held by Sachie's parents and her efforts to own and hone her own American **identity**. Nonetheless, the depiction of Sachie's parents affirms their desire to hold onto Japanese values while making a place in this new world of Hawai'i.

A similar concern is addressed by Saiki in *Ganbare, An Example of Japanese Spirit*. As Saiki notes in her introduction to the book, the narratives reveal how "the Japanese spirit of *ganbare*—hold on! keep going! persevere!" helped detainees survive miserable conditions and great loss. All of the narratives are based on interviews and diaries of internees who fought against bitterness and despair in the internment camps. Her account includes documents (e.g., questionnaires used to determine loyalty to the U.S. government, lists of internees, etc.), photos, and maps, making this ethnography a valuable historical reference.

Saiki's short stories, again, reveal a particular history; this collection depicts the lives of the immigrants who came to Hawai'i in 1885 to work on the sugar plantations and the lives of their children. Some of the selections are purely fiction; others are not. "Two Artists," for example, portrays the lives of two second-generation Japanese American artists: weaver Alice Kagawa Parrott and potter Toshiko Takaezu. In each account, Saiki not only provides biographical information but graphic descriptions of each artist's work. In Takaezu's narrative, Saiki quotes Takaezu on her aesthetics: pots, she says, should not only have distinct visual and tactile attributes, but they should be made so that they can "sound." This is just one example of the nonfiction entries in what, overall, is a collection of short stories. "A Letter to a Daughter," for example, is a poignant story of an immigrant woman's life. It begins with a three-line letter written in the Japanese writing system called katakana. Saiki uses this letter as a device to reveal an intimate autobiography of a mother's life; each phrase of the letter unfolds into poignant reflections of this mother's fears, aspirations, and feelings of love and loneliness—and in the end, the letter becomes a gift that her daughter treasures far beyond its few words. (*See also* Hawai'i Literature, Japanese American Novel)

Further Reading

Luangphinith, Seri. "Patsy Sumie Saiki." *Asian American Novelists: A Bio-Bibliographical Critical Sourcebook.* Ed. Emmanuel Nelson. Westport, CT: Greenwood Press, 2000. 311–16.

Sumida, Stephen H. "Sense of Place, History, and the Concept of 'Local' in Hawaii's Asian/Pacific American Literature." *Reading the Literatures of Asian America.* Ed. Shirley Geok-lin Lim and Amy Ling. Philadelphia: Temple UP, 1992. 215–37.

———. *And the View from the Shore: Literary Traditions of Hawai'i.* Seattle: U of Washington P, 1991. 91–97.

Barbara Cantalupo

SAINT, ASSOTTO [YVES FRANÇOIS LUBIN] (1957–1994)   Haitian American poet, playwright, musician, and editor whose works articulated new identities and negotiated an increased visibility for black gay males. Writing in the time of devastation caused by AIDS, Saint conceived literature as a social force, contributing to the implementation of public changes and the inclusion of gay male voices into America. His poetry bears witness to the AIDS crisis and celebrates the solidarity and love of black gay men in the face of the disease. The seminal anthologies of gay black writing that he edited were published by the Galiens Press, the publishing house that Saint founded in 1989. Based in New York City, Saint was also the cofounder with his life partner, Jan Urban Holmgren, of Metamorphosis Theatre and the art-rock band, Xotika.

Saint's edited anthologies of gay black writing, *The Road Before Us* (1991), *Here to Dare* (1992), and *Milking Black Bull* (1995), participated in the vast reassessment of the position of black gay males within American society that took place during the 1980s and the 1990s. Douglas Steward has placed the three anthologies in the context of the social and literary revolution that began with the publication of Joseph Beam's collection *In the Life* (1986), to which Saint contributed with a piece from his multimedia theater piece, *Risin' to the Love We Need.* Beam called for a moratorium on the writing of white gay men and invited black gays to produce texts that would give visibility to homosexuals within the black community: "The bottom line is this: We are Black men who are proudly gay. What we offer is our lives, our love, our visions. We are risin' to the love we *all* need. We are coming home with our heads held up." Black gay men should become conscious that "Black men loving Black men is the revolutionary act of the eighties" (vii).

Saint's editorship is informed by the same desire to represent the variety of the black homosexual experience in America. Tellingly, in his essay "Why I write," Saint argues that his aim is to make black voices full participants of American life. His anthological projects avoid individualism to stress instead the power of a collective to engineer social and cultural transformations. Douglas Steward explains that "the editorial selection inherent in the production of anthologies 'frames' a certain voice for the work as a whole, unifying the collection. And yet, that voice nevertheless remains polyphonic and irreducible to a unitary discourse"(33). Saint's anthologies include some of the most celebrated American gay black voices such as **Essex Hemphill** and Joseph Beam and subvert the racial stereotypes to which black homosexuals are subjected.

Saint's own work shares with the anthological collections the awareness that **W. E. B. Du Bois**'s classical formulation of "double consciousness" can be queered and read as representing the status of being black and gay. The struggle for black rights goes hand in hand with the struggle for queer rights. In *Risin' To the Love We Need,* Francine, a drag queen, celebrates Josephine Baker's achievements as showing the way to black people to overcome the obstacles of the racist South. The character feels that events of racial and sexual pride—**Rosa Parks**'s refusal to move to the back of a bus in 1955 and the third world gay conference with its march in 1979—are an equally important part of her heritage.

The poems collected in *Stations* (1989) and *Wishing for Wings* (1994) are predominantly testimonial in nature and commemorate the heroism of black gay men in the face of AIDS, mourning the loss of friends and lovers. The opening poem of *Wishing for Wings,* explicitly titled "Writing About Aids," summarizes the sense of urgency and emergency that poetry should embody. Poetic texts are charged with the social function of chronicling the predicament brought about by the illness and the indifference of those in power. Both collections focus on poetic composition as an act of survival, breaking the silence that stands for death. Yet, as the poem "Shuffle Along" states, these survival rituals are often disturbing and not encouraging as they record the stages of physical and psychological disintegration through the agency of the virus. In the time of AIDS, poetry can be affirming only to a certain degree. The three-part prose, "No More Metaphors," interspersed through the poems of *Wishing for Wings* directly confronts the death of Saint's lover, a death that leaves the poet speechless, leading him to conclude that no word can effectively represent his despair. "No More Metaphors" also stands as the collection's political slogan, inviting gay black men to confront the illness frankly and in all its aspects, including the most disturbing ones such as the obstinate refusal of some to engage in "safe" sex. (*See also* African American Gay Literature, African American Stereotypes)

Further Reading

Beam, Joseph, ed. *In the Life: A Black Gay Anthology.* Boston: Alyson, 1986.

Steward, Douglas. "Saint's Progeny: Assotto Saint, Gay Black Poets, and Poetic Agency in the Field of the Queer Symbolic." *African American Review* 33.3 (Fall 1999): 507–18.

Luca Prono

SAKAMOTO, EDWARD (1940–) Japanese American playwright. Edward Sakamoto was born and raised in Honolulu, Hawai'i, and graduated from the University of Hawai'i in 1962. In 1966 Sakamoto moved to Los Angeles to work for the *Los Angeles Times.* Many of his plays are set in Hawai'i and question what "home" means. He received grants from the National Endowment for Arts and the Rockefeller Foundation, two Hollywood Dramalogue Critic's awards for *Chikamatsu's Forest* and *Stew Rice,* and the Hawaii Award for Literature.

Sakamoto first became interested in writing when he rewrote Robert Stevenson's *Treasure Island* for extra credit as a ninth grader, and he tried acting while he was a college student. The damaging stereotypes and the lack of substantial roles Asian American actors could play, however, discouraged him from continuing acting. As a student, he wrote *In the Alley* (1961), and the play was later published in an anthology of plays by the Kumu Kahua Theatre, *Kumu Kahua Plays* (1983). Moving to Los Angeles in 1966 aided Sakamoto's career as a playwright. Mako and other post–World War II generation Asian American actors were fighting against demeaning roles and advocating accurate Asian American representations in the media. In 1972 the East West Players (founded in 1965) and its director Mako produced Sakamoto's second play, *Yellow Is My Favorite Color* (1972), and in 1980–81, the Pan Asian Repertory Theatre produced it in New York City. The East West Players continue to stage many of Sakamoto's plays.

Sakamoto published *Hawai'i No Ka Oi: the Kamiya Family Trilogy* (1995), which includes *The Taste of Kona Coffee, Manoa Valley,* and *The Life of the Land.* Though Sakamoto's relocation to the mainland was a good career move, he questions his decision through his characters in the plays. In *The Taste of Kona Coffee* and *The Life of the Land,* for example, characters who relocate to the mainland, such as Jiro and Spencer, face alienation, isolation, and resentment from family members and friends upon their return home to Hawai'i. Another recurring issue that Sakamoto's ethnic Hawaiian characters face is the **assimilation** into the mainland, predominantly white culture when they move away from their island home. In *Stew Rice,* a play included in *Aloha Las Vegas and Other Plays* (2000) along with *A'ala Park* and *Aloha Las Vegas,* Russell becomes keenly aware of the differences between *haoles* and himself.

Theater reviewers and the public praise Sakamoto's plays, especially his effective use of Hawaiian pidgin English in the dialogue. Though many of Sakamoto's plays were produced by the East West Players in Los Angeles, the Pan Asian Repertory Theatre in New York City, the University of Hawaii, and Kumu Kahua Theatre in Honolulu, many of Sakamoto's manuscripts remain unpublished. (*See also* Hawai'i Literature)

Further Reading

Huot, Nikolas. "Edward Sakamoto (1940–)." *Asian American Playwrights: A Bio-Bibliographical Critical Sourcebook.* Ed. Miles Xian Liu. Westport, CT: Greenwood Press, 2002. 303–9.

Kyoko Amano

SALAAM, KALAMU YA (1947–)   African American poet, playwright, activist, and critic. Born Vallery Ferdinand III in New Orleans, he eventually adopted the Swahili name Kalamu ya Salaam, meaning "pen of peace." In the early 1960s he was active in the **Civil Rights Movement** in Louisiana, working with the National Association for the Advancement of Colored People (NAACP) and the Congress of Racial Equality (CORE). He attended Carleton College, Minnesota, for a year, then went into the army. Returning to New Orleans in 1968, he pursued further study and spent several years during the fervent period of the **Black Arts Movement** working with the Free Southern Theatre. Out of that organization came BLKARTSOUTH, an important locus of cultural nationalist production and theorizing in which Kalamu was a central figure. He later founded a number of other activist arts groups, WordBand (an ensemble combining poetry and music) and the Runagate Press. He is moderator of CyberDrum, an Internet listserv for black authors and other interested individuals. Kalamu ya Salaam still makes his home in New Orleans.

In his poem "Food for Thought," Kalamu insists that **blues** singers were the first significant black poets. Indeed, just as the blues has been seen as an essential ingredient in **jazz**, there is a very real sense in which Kalamu, along with many artists who came to the fore during the Black Arts Movement, see the blues as being at the heart of the literature of African Americans. Accordingly, he bases his work primarily on a blues aesthetic that is also informed by the rhythms and the dynamics of the black church. Both emphasize deep feeling that can put the expressive powers of language under intense pressure, yielding spontaneous, heightened forms of eloquence (see part two of "The Blues," one of his more important poems from the Black Arts period).

Kalamu ya Salaam is the author of *Hofu Ni Kwenu (My Fear Is For You)* (1973), *Ibura* (1976), *A Nation of Poets* (1989), *What Is Life?: Reclaiming the Black Blues Self* (1994), and numerous other volumes. Books he has edited include *Word Up: Black Poetry of the 80s from the Deep South* (1990), *From a Bend in the River: 100 New Orleans Poets* (1998), and *360°: A Revolution of Black Poets* (2001). His *The Magic of Juju: An Appreciation of the Black Arts Movement* (2004), along with his historical overview of the movement in

The Oxford Companion to African American Literature (1997), are essential reading for anyone interested in this extremely important and still insufficiently studied period of black expressive culture. Kalamu also has issued a spoken word CD, *My Story, My Song* (1996), on which his work can be heard performed to great effect.

Further Reading

Ellison, Mary. "Kalamu ya Salaam and the Black Blues Subversive Self." *Race & Class* 45.1 (2003): 79–97.

Thomas, Lorenzo. *Extraordinary Measures: Afrocentric Modernism and Twentieth-Century American Poetry.* Tuscaloosa: U of Alabama, 2000.

Robert Elliot Fox

SALINAS, LUIS OMAR (1937–)   Chicano poet. Considered by some as one of the most important Chicano poets writing today, Luis Omar Salinas's work, characterized by use of the surreal, is extensively anthologized. Although best known for his earlier work, Salinas continues to publish poetry and give public readings.

Born in Robstown, Texas, to Mexican parents, Salinas lived both in Mexico and later in California where he attended Bakersfield City College and California State University, Fresno. His first book, *Crazy Gypsy* (1970), received more critical attention than much of his later work. Influenced by Spanish surrealist poets, Salinas uses disjointed images of both the whimsical and the concrete, juxtaposing in "Aztec Angel" personified clouds and stark descriptions of malnourished children. Although not overtly political, this collection explores the breakdown of an oppressed people, describing gritty bar scenes, deaths, and loss, combining these with unlikely images of the natural world. Yet, through the sadness, anger, and chaos, one catches glimpses of pride; "Aztec Angel" ends with the proclamation that the speaker's mother was beautiful.

His later works are more direct and rely less on the surreal. For example, in the introduction to his next collection, *Afternoon of the Unreal* (1980), Salinas claims that he is an "existential hero" facing the loss and pain of life. The collection delineates these losses, specifically a childhood in Mexico ("Ode to the Mexican Experiences"), and loss through death ("Drunk Cemeteries," "Many Things of Death"). This collection, like *Prelude to Darkness* (1981) and *Darkness Under the Trees* (1982), continues to draw from images of everyday life—particularly sad but beautiful women and children—and to work toward self-definition.

Walking Behind the Spanish (1982) distinguishes itself from Salinas's other collections thematically. In this collection, Salinas focuses on defining his poetic and cultural influences, writing poems to César Vallejo, Miquel de Cervantes, Miquel Hernández, and Emiliano Zapata. This work also includes the much anthologized poem "My Father Is a Simple Man," in which the poet calls the father with a sixth grade education "a scholar," suggesting the poet's influences go beyond the literary.

Although his poetry does often reflect and comment on the social and political realities surrounding the poet, it is universality, stunning imagery, and deep emotions that make Salinas's poetry so memorable and so deserving of further study. (*See also* Mexican American Poetry)

Further Reading

Buckley, Christopher. "Any Good Fortune: An Interview with Luis Omar Salinas." *Quarterly West* 55 (2002): 149–57.

Rios, Alberto. "Chicano/Borderlands Literature and Poetry." *Contemporary Latin American Culture: Unity and Diversity.* Ed. C. Gail Guntermann. Tempe: Arizona State UP, 1984. 79–93.

Risco-Lozada, Eliezar, and Guillermo Martínez. Introduction to *Crazy Gypsy.* Luis Omar Salinas. Fresno, CA: La Raza Studies, 1970. 7–11.

Soto, Gary. "Luis Omar Salinas: Chicano Poet." *MELUS* 9.2 (Spring 1982): 47–82.

Veach, Cindy. "Interview with Luis Omar Salinas." *Northwest Review* 20.2–3 (1982): 238–41.

Angela M. Williamson

SALINGER, J. D. (1919–)   Part-Jewish, part-Irish American novelist and short story writer. Salinger is best known for the celebrated novel *The Catcher in the Rye* (1951) and for a critically acclaimed collection of short fiction, *Nine Stories* (1953). His later work, the Glass Family series (1955–65) received chiefly negative reviews because of its pervasive religious themes. However, some critics have credited the Glass series for its sharp portrayal of the assimilated Jewish bourgeoisie. After producing four books and twenty uncollected stories, Salinger stopped publishing in 1965, probably because of the negative criticism he had been receiving.

Jerome David Salinger was born in New York City on January 1, 1919. His father, Solomon, was Jewish and his mother, Mary, was Irish Catholic. The Salinger family was well-to-do and lived on Park Avenue. They did not practice the Jewish religion but celebrated Christmas with gift giving and a Christmas tree. Salinger attended public and private schools in Manhattan and graduated from Valley Forge Military Academy in Pennsylvania. He also took courses at Ursinus College in Pennsylvania, New York University, and Columbia University, but he did not take a college degree.

Salinger's first short story appeared in 1941. He continued to publish stories while serving in an Army intelligence unit in Europe during World War II, and he expanded two of his early stories into *The Catcher in the Rye*. After the immense success of *The Catcher in the Rye*, Salinger retreated to a farmhouse in the woods of New Hampshire to avoid scrutiny of his private life by intrusive fans and reporters. But his withdrawal only increased media interest. In one of the few interviews that Salinger ever gave, he explained that he continued to write, but that he did not plan to publish anymore during his lifetime.

The Catcher in the Rye is considered to be one of the best coming-of-age novels written in the twentieth century. It continues to be on the reading lists of many high schools and colleges all over the world. The novel is told by the seventeen-year-old Holden Caulfield who has flunked out of yet another prep school and wanders around in New York for two days before going home and confronting his parents. Holden's problem is that he can't stand the status consciousness and conformity of his "phony" peers and the prospect of dedicating his life to the pursuit of wealth and power.

When Holden's little sister, Phoebe, accuses him of not having any idea of what he wants to be when he grows up, Holden tells her that the only thing he wants to be is "the catcher in the rye." He imagines a big rye field at the edge of a steep cliff where a lot of children are playing, and he says that if the children are running and not looking where they are going, he has "to catch everybody if they start to go over the cliff." Unrealistic though this idea is, it not only reveals Holden's kindness, it also reveals his notion that children need to be saved from their own mistakes.

By the end of the novel, Holden's attitude has changed as a result of his experiences while roaming around in New York. These experiences include ordering a prostitute to his hotel room and being beaten up by her pimp, befriending a trio of nuns and talking about Shakespeare with them, and getting a lecture on growing up from a former English teacher who then proceeds to make "a flitty pass" at him. Holden's change becomes apparent in the novel's last scene when he sits on a park bench in the pouring rain and watches his sister Phoebe ride a carrousel. Holden is worried that Phoebe might fall off while trying to lunge upward and grab a gold ring, but he realizes, "The thing with kids is, if they want to grab for the gold ring, you have to let them do it, and not say anything. If they fall off, they fall off, but it's bad if you say anything to them." This comment shows that Holden has abandoned the idea of wanting to be the catcher in the rye and that he now has a more realistic and adult view of life.

Whereas *The Catcher in the Rye* is set entirely in a gentile milieu, some of the pieces in *Nine Stories* include characters from the Jewish bourgeoisie. Salinger lampoons that segment of American society in his portrayals of the protagonist's materialistic and superficial wife and mother-in-law in "A Perfect Day for Bananafish." However, he also draws an utterly positive image of an upper-middle-class Jewish woman in Boo Boo Tannenbaum, née Beatrice Glass, the central character in "Down at the Dinghy" (1949). The most celebrated piece in *Nine Stories* is the autobiographical "For Esmé—With Love and Squalor" (1950). It deals with the aftermath of the nervous breakdown of a Jewish Army Intelligence sergeant shortly after the end of World War II.

Salinger's narrative series about the Jewish-Irish Glass family develops the story of the life of Seymour Glass and his spiritual influence on his siblings. The Glass Family Series consists of "A Perfect Day for Bananafish" (1948), *Franny and Zooey* (1961), *Raise High the Roof Beam, Carpenters and Seymour—An Introduction* (1963), and "Hapworth 16, 1924" (*The New Yorker*, June 1965). In that series, we find that Seymour, Buddy, Zooey, and Franny

Glass are all deeply religious but that none of their ideas are Jewish ones. Instead, they quote texts from the New Testament, Zen Buddhism, classical Taoism, and especially from Vedanta Hinduism, the most ecumenical of the Eastern religions. The Glass series begins with Seymour Glass killing himself in "A Perfect Day for Bananafish," but then it gradually redefines Seymour's character. It winds up showing that Seymour did not kill himself because he was in despair but because he wanted to be reincarnated in a different life, one that would allow him to make better progress toward spiritual perfection and union with God than he could in materialistic America. (*See also* Jewish American Novel)

Further Reading

Alsen, Eberhard. *A Reader's Guide to J. D. Salinger.* Westport, CT: Greenwood Press, 2002.

French, Warren. *J. D. Salinger, Revisited.* Boston: G. K. Hall, 1988.

Grunwald, Henry. A. *Salinger: A Critical and Personal Portrait.* New York: Harper, 1962.

Lundquist, James. *J. D. Salinger.* New York: Ungar, 1979.

Eberhard Alsen

SANCHEZ, SONIA (1934–)   African American poet. Born in Birmingham, Alabama, and educated at Hunter College in New York City, Sonia Sanchez's strong female poetic voice was forged in the **Black Arts Movement** of the 1960s. Her collection *Homecoming* (1969) won the PEN writing award and established her as a politically active poet and teacher. A mother of two and a professor at Temple University since the mid-1970s, Sanchez has taken her role as a teacher quite seriously, seeing herself as an instrument in the education of children as well as undergraduates. To this end, she has published plays, poems, and short stories aimed at children including *It's a New Day: Poems for Young Brothas and Sistuhs* (1971) and *The Adventures of Fathead, Smallhead, and Squarehead* (1973).

Sanchez's own childhood was marked by an education in language and culture. Spending her first nine years in the Jim Crow South, she moved to Harlem to live with her father after the deaths of her mother when she was six and her grandmother three years later. In New York, she listened to the language of the street while she learned about Northern **racism**—both of which are crucial to her work as a poet. Despite having a stutter as a child, which first caused her to write poetry as a form of therapy and communication, Sanchez has performed and recorded her poems for years, including solo albums and collaborations with the likes of the a capella group Sweet Honey in the Rock. The music of her language is highly adaptable to musical and other recordings.

As a graduate student at New York University in the 1960s, Sanchez first heard **Malcolm X** deliver a speech on a Harlem street corner. The event proved crucial in solidifying Sanchez's racial politics, transforming her from an integrationist to a nationalist. She produced poetry associated with other Black Arts Movement members **Nikki Giovanni** and **Haki Madhubuti** (Don

Sonia Sanchez. *Photo by Leander Jackson. Courtesy of Sonia Sanchez.*

L. Lee) as part of the Broadside Quarter. She moved to San Francisco and became a teacher, agitating for the establishment of a black studies program at San Francisco College (now University). It was there that she published *Homecoming* and the follow-up, *We a BaddDDD People* (1970), both steeped in black vernacular and musical aesthetics.

In the early 1970s, Sanchez joined the Nation of Islam (NOI)—the organization Malcolm X had helped establish before being ousted in the year before his death. She was a staunch advocate of the group's nationalist agenda. But Sanchez never quite fit in the NOI because she was an outspoken woman. She wrote articles for the NOI newspaper, *Muhammad Speaks,* that argued for the equality of women in Islam by drawing on historical research; she was critiqued within the Nation for these pieces. So although she shared a sense of racial politics, she never could tolerate the misogyny of the Nation's practices. She believed that women had a strong, compelling voice to add to the struggle for racial equality and refused to adhere to the Nation's sexist notions that women should be relegated to silent supporting roles. Sanchez's voice was not one to be silenced and she left the Nation in late 1975.

Building on the work of **Langston Hughes** and **Gwendolyn Brooks**, Sanchez's vernacular poetry is explicitly political. Her poems can be confrontational even as they are formally innovative and based in black speech. In addition, Sanchez's words represent the spoken, collapsing spaces, using slang, and taking advantage of enjambment to propel her reader. The effect is an immediacy, a compelling sense of voice and poetic performance. As a result, her poems speak for and about a range of people within the African American community. They are vibrant, colorful, and well-crafted bits of speech, often trying to represent the spoken in language; for instance, she uses the spelling "blk" for "black." Throughout her poetry, Sanchez exhibits the same genealogical impulse that she showed in her *Muhammad Speaks* articles; she links contemporary racial and gender struggles to those found in history. At the same time, her work celebrates Afrocentric history and rituals as a corrective to the white supremacist culture of the United States.

Sanchez won the American Book Award from the Before Columbus Foundation for her volume, *homegirls and handgrenades* (1984). It includes poems that are lyrical and musical in addressing issues of **race**, the nation, and the legacies of the 1960s. Not simply seeking blame, Sanchez's poems are affirmative if defiant. She is highly critical of those who engage in self-destructive behaviors—be it abuse, drug use, or lechery. But she insists on affirming the possibility of redemption in part by showing how the self-destructive behaviors are linked to the degradation suffered under white patriarchy.

Sanchez's poems defiantly articulate the conundrum of black women, refusing both racial stereotypes and sexual degradation. Along with fellow African American feminist writers Giovanni and June Jordan, Sanchez produces an ultimately affirmative sense of community through her poetry. She celebrates the strength of black women, today and in the past. An influence on Ntzoke Shange, Tupac Shakur (whose biggest hit "Dear Mama" takes its title from a Sanchez poem), and countless others, Sanchez has maintained her political activism while achieving success in academia. An advocate for issues of class as well as race and gender, she is presently the Laura Carnell Professor of English and Women's Studies at Temple University.

In 1998, Sanchez published *Shake Loose My Skin: New and Selected Poems.* The collection spans thirty years of her poetry, revealing not only the strength of her voice but also the consistency of her commitments. Although there have been some significant changes since she began, Sanchez's voice still finds the lyricism in the vernacular and still is able to seek out the seams of inequality. (*See also* African American Poetry, African American Stereotypes)

Further Reading

Frost, Elizabeth. *The Feminist Avant-Garde in American Poetry.* Iowa City: U of Iowa P, 2003.

Gibson, Donald. *Modern Black Poets: A Collection of Critical Essays.* Englewood Cliffs, NJ: Prentice Hall, 1973.

Jones, Meta DuEwa. "Jazz Prosodies: Orality and Textuality." *Callaloo* 25.1 (Winter 2002): 66–91.

Tate, Claudia. *Black Women Writers at Work.* New York: Continuum, 1983.

Thomas H. Kane

SANDBURG, CARL (1878–1967)   American poet, political activist, folksinger, author of American fairytales, biographer, autobiographer, lecturer, and newspaper columnist of Swedish American origin. In his literary and nonliterary writings, Sandburg was a passionate advocate of the everyday working person and neglected children, those who may neither have the power nor the words to speak for themselves. He offers in his works valuable insights into the circumstances, spirit, and the worth of the American people. Some researchers have argued that Sandburg's unconventional metrics and rhythms in his poetry could be attributed to the fact that Swedish, not English, was his first language.

Carl Sandburg. *Courtesy of the Library of Congress.*

Carl August Sandburg, called "Charlie" by the family, spent his childhood and early teenage years growing up as the second of seven children in a typical working-class family of Swedish origin in Galesburg, Illinois. His father, August Sandburg, a Swedish immigrant, was a blacksmith's helper for the nearby Chicago, Burlington, and Quincy Railroad; his mother, Clara Anderson Sandburg, a Swedish immigrant as well, was a homemaker. From the time he was a young boy, Carl helped by delivering milk, harvesting ice, laying bricks, and shining shoes in Galesburg's Union Hotel; he quit school in eighth grade to become a day laborer to help support the family. During that time, he briefly traveled west to Kansas at age nineteen "with [his] hands free, no bag or bundle, wearing a black sateen shirt, coat vest, and pants, a slouch hat" (*Always the Young Strangers*). Conse-

quently, his firsthand experience meeting strangers mostly from working-class backgrounds, doing a variety of odd jobs, and traveling in an unorthodox fashion through the United States had a deep impact on his own views and his unique blend of styles, which one detects when analyzing his writings and listening to his recordings. Especially the stark contrast between rich and poor made him question the capitalist ideology. After becoming a volunteer in the Spanish-American War in Puerto Rico in 1898 he decided to return to his hometown of Galesburg to continue his education at Lombard College. To support himself, he became a call fireman. At Lombard College, he joined the "Poor Writers' Club," an informal literary organization founded by professor Phillip Green Wright, a talented scholar and political liberal. Its members met regularly to listen to and critique each other's poems. Beginning in 1903, Sandburg spent his time traveling around the country a second time, performing his poetry, playing the guitar, and talking about his dreams for America to high school and college audiences and to the American public at large. Because he showed a genuine interest in what the ordinary American in small towns, cities, and farms had to say, he began to collect sayings, slang terms, bits and pieces of folklore, stories, and songs he heard while on the road. Sandburg's first, second, and third collections of poetry titled *In Reckless Ecstasy*

(1904), *Incidentals* (1907), and *The Plaint of a Rose* (1908) were all printed in Wright's basement press—even after Sandburg had decided not to earn his academic degree. As a mentor, Wright provided the gifted Sandburg with encouragement but was unable to prevent him from dropping out in his senior year. The three chapbooks generated under Wright's guidance, however, were entirely overlooked by the critics and the general public.

Not only did Sandburg love the ordinary American's language, he was also deeply concerned with American workers' issues, in particular. He moved to Milwaukee in 1907 to become actively involved with the Wisconsin Social Democratic Party, whose headquarters were in Milwaukee. There he wrote and distributed political pamphlets and other materials, which reflected his leftist political views and Socialist sympathies; from 1910 to 1912 he worked as the secretary for Milwaukee's Socialist mayor. Before he and his wife, Lillian Steichen, the sister of the famous photographer Edward Steichen, whom he met at party headquarters in Milwaukee and married in 1908, moved to Chicago to take up a career in journalism, Sandburg started to submit some of his poems and some of his articles to various magazines. He worked as an editorial writer for the *Chicago Daily News* for several years, covering mostly labor issues. For his poem "Chicago" he received the "Levinson Prize"; this meant that he became recognized as a member of the Chicago Literary Renaissance, which included, for example, **Theodore Dreiser** and Edgar Lee Masters. In 1914, a group of his poems appeared in *Poetry* magazine, which brought him national recognition. With the publication of his book *Chicago Poems* (1916), Sandburg's poetic career took off; *Cornhuskers* (1918) and *Smoke and Steal* (1920), two collections of poetry about urban as well as agrarian America, further enhanced Sandburg's reputation as a poet.

Sandburg did not want to be only known for his poetry, although he kept on writing poetry all his life; in 1919, he published a book called *The Chicago Race Riots*, which focused on the social unrest in the city. In 1922 a collection of children's tales for his three daughters, *The Rootabaga Stories*, followed. His publisher, Alfred Harcourt, was so impressed by this book that he wanted him to create a biography of Abraham Lincoln for children. The project, however, turned after two years of intensive research on Sandburg's part into a biography for adults titled *Abraham Lincoln: The Prairie Years* (1926), which constituted Sandburg's first financial success. In a new house in the Michigan dunes, Sandburg completed four additional volumes: *Abraham Lincoln: The War Years* (1939), for which he was awarded the Pulitzer Prize in 1940. His novel, *Remembrance Rock* (1948), a second volume of folk songs titled *The American Songbag*—which included 280 folk songs, many of them printed for the first time—and an autobiography titled *Always the Young Strangers* (1953) followed after, in 1945, the Midwesterner Sandburg and his family had moved to Connemara, North Carolina, where their farm and the surrounding pastureland offered the solitude and peace of mind required for his writing; more than one-third of his oeuvre was produced there. His later collections of poetry, *Complete Poems* (1950), for which he was awarded a second Pulitzer in 1951, and *Honey and Salt* (1963), continued Sandburg's earlier attempts to celebrate the spirit and worth of the American people. In 1962 Sandburg became Illinois' first poet laureate; in 1964 he received the Medal of Freedom from President Lyndon Johnson. Although Sandburg died in North Carolina, where he was living at the time, his ashes were deposited, as he had requested, beneath a "remembrance rock," a red granite boulder in the garden behind the family's first home in Galesburg, Illinois. (*See also* Swedish American Literature)

Further Reading

Brown, Rosellen. "On Carl Sandburg." *Poetry Speaks: Hear Great Poets Read Their Work from Tennyson to Plath.* Ed. Elise Paschen and Rebekah Presson Mosby. Naperville, IL: Sourcebooks, 2001.

Paschen, Elise, and Rebekah Presson Mosby, eds. "Carl Sandburg." *Poetry Speaks: Hear Great Poets Read Their Work from Tennyson to Plath.* Naperville, IL: Sourcebooks, 2001.

Claudia A. Becker

SANDERS, DORI (1935–) African American novelist, cookbook author, and farmer. Raised on a family peach farm in upstate South Carolina, where she continued to work as an adult, Dori Sanders didn't become a published writer until late in life. The author of two novels, *Clover* (1990) and *Her Own Place* (1993), and a cookbook, *Dori Sanders' Country Cooking: Recipes and Stories from the Family Farm Stand* (1995), Sanders is known for her gentle, humorous, and loving portraits of rural South Carolinians who struggle with shifting racial and family relationships in the twentieth-century South.

Sanders was born in York County, South Carolina, the eighth of ten children. Her father was a farmer and local school principal who instilled a love of language in his children. In interviews, Sanders recalls growing up in a family of storytellers; she and her brothers and sisters had a favorite "storytelling rock" where they would spin their tales. She also grew up working on the Sanders farm, helping to sell the family-raised produce in a roadside vegetable stand. As an adult, Sanders frequently took odd jobs in the farming off-season, often writing bits and scraps of dialogue and observation when she had a chance. While working for a Best Western Inn in Maryland during the 1980s, Sanders was urged by one of her bosses to send her work out for publication. Although her first manuscript, a novel about Southern sharecroppers, was rejected by Algonquin Press as "melodramatic," the editor recognized Sanders's talent and encouraged her to try again.

The second manuscript Sanders sent Algonquin evolved into *Clover,* her first published novel. The book's narrator is ten-year-old Clover Hill, the daughter of a widowed school principal in a tight-knit African American farming community in upstate South Carolina. When Clover's father, Gaten Hill, decides to marry Sara Kate, a white woman he'd gone to college with, the community is suspicious and unwelcoming. An outsider not only by **race**, Sara Kate is also set apart by regional, educational, and class differences. Following Gaten's death in a tragic car accident just hours after their wedding, Sara Kate unexpectedly insists on raising Clover herself, against the wishes of the large, extended Hill family. The novel examines both the friction of interracial relationships as well as the gradual warming of both Clover and the larger community to the initially unwelcome intrusion of the white woman. *Clover* was praised by critics for the authentic, humorous, and refreshing voice of its ten-year-old narrator and for its loving and optimistic depiction of Southern rural life. The novel won the prestigious Lillian Smith award and was made into a television movie that aired on the USA Network in 1997.

Sanders's second novel, *Her Own Place,* tells the story of Mae Lee Barnes, the only daughter of South Carolina tenant farmers. Having married her husband as a teenager the day before he leaves to serve in World War II, Mae Lee works hard in a munitions factory while he is gone, saving up enough money to buy a small piece of land. Her husband returns home safely but eventually abandons Mae Lee, leaving her to raise their five children on her own. She develops into a tenacious and successful farmer, all the while dealing with various tribulations in her family and the larger community. Critically appreciated for its realistic depiction of ordinary, rural Southerners, the novel was also criticized by some reviewers who complained that it skipped across the surface of events without probing deeply enough into them.

Descriptions of food and cooking abound in both of Sanders's novels. It's not surprising, then, that this author, who considers herself a farmer first and a writer second, would pen a third book devoted to the topic of food. *Dori Sanders' Country Cooking: Recipes and Stories from the Family Farm Stand* was published by Algonquin in 1995. The book includes numerous downhome Southern recipes, featuring ingredients such as grits, country ham, sweet potatoes, collard greens, and of course the peaches that her family grew and sold. Mingled with the recipes are Sanders's reminiscences of growing up on a family farm: stories about gathering fresh eggs and about hog-killing time, about eccentric relatives, and about preparing the yearly feast called "The Big Eat." Like her novels, *Country Cooking* provides readers with a slice of African American life in the rural South.

Further Reading

Hubbard, Kim. "A Farmer's Tales: After Years of Growing Peaches, Dori Sanders Tried Writing—and Her Mind Proved Fertile Ground." *People Weekly* (July 19, 1993): 45–46.

Norris, K. Anthony. "Dori Sanders' Simple Eloquence." *American Visions* 8.2 (April–May 1993): 28–29.

Susan Farrell

SANFORD, JOHN (1904–2003) Jewish American novelist and historian. John Sanford belongs to the postimmigrant tradition of Jewish

American writers chiefly born in the United States who sought the freedom and equality promised by American society and whose disappointment led to their membership in the Communist Party in the 1930s and subsequent persecution during the McCarthyism of the 1950s.

Born into a middle-class Jewish family as Julian Shapiro in 1904, Sanford's writing career spanned more than seventy years and comprises a total of twenty-four published works. These works can be divided in three categories: novels and stories, the most significant being *The People from Heaven* (1943) and *A Man without Shoes* (1951); interpretations of American history, or personal histories, with the first, *A More Goodly Country*, appearing in 1975 and the most recent, *Intruders in Paradise*, published in 1997; and life writing, including a five-part autobiography, *Scenes from the Life of an American Jew* (1985–94), and a series celebrating his wife, screenwriter Marguerite Roberts, and their life together. After studying briefly at a number of colleges he received a degree from Fordham University Law School, was admitted to the New York State Bar in 1927, and later made a number of trips to Europe. At about this time, through his friendship with **Nathanael West**, he began writing fiction. Coupled with his call to Hollywood as a screenwriter in 1936 this (not unhappily) put an end to practicing law. Based on the first two volumes of the autobiography, through his departure for Hollywood, Sanford appeared to lack an interest in the traditional American pursuits of education and career and was considered more of a prodigal son. More importantly, as he himself notes, he was a man without even the slightest political consciousness: he believed his gradual radicalization by the late 1930s was a result of the execution of Sacco and Vanzetti.

Sanford's earliest novels are set in the Adirondack Mountains of New York State and depict the violence and bloodshed pervading the supposedly idyllic American countryside that he and West visited in 1931. He returns to this area in *The People from Heaven* and adds **racism** and **anti-Semitism** to the violence of his earlier works. In fact, Sanford's works convey the idea that institutionalized racism, various forms of discrimination, and fear of the Other are the foundation of the society. *A Man without Shoes* fictionalizes Sanford's own political growth through the travels of his Irish American alter ego, Danny Johnson, across the country as he witnesses the calculated oppression of the working class and minority groups. Both novels employ the reinterpretations of American history—counter-histories of the excluded—that comprise the series of personal histories Sanford embarked upon in the 1970s. His heroes include individuals who challenged the establishment, its racism, and oppression: **John Brown**, Lincoln, Sacco and Vanzetti, Emma Goldman, and numerous others whose names are unknown to his readers.

Sanford openly states in his autobiography and biographies of his wife that unlike other novelists-turned-screenwriters (he worked briefly in the studios) who had to put their literary efforts aside, he was able to continue writing since Marguerite Roberts, one of the highest-paid and respected screenwriters in Hollywood, supported not only Sanford but his father as well. Through the end of his life he was guilt-ridden for not preventing Roberts from joining the Party—the blacklist stole nine years of her creative life and, as an undeclared expression of solidarity, silenced Sanford for an eleven-year period between novels. He wrote his last novel in 1967 and spent the remainder of his career with personal histories and life writing. His works have not received any significant academic attention, but they still command a small but loyal and enthusiastic audience.

Further Reading

Mearns, Jack. "The Complex Legacy of John Stanford." *Firsts* 14.1 (2004): 40–51.

Roy Goldblatt

SANTIAGO, DANNY [DANIEL JAMES] (1911–1988) White American novelist who successfully, though only briefly, passed for a Mexican American writer and by doing so raised intriguing questions about authenticity and ethnic authorship. When *Famous All Over Town,* a novel about a Chicano working-class family from East Los Angeles, was published in 1983 most readers assumed the author, Danny Santiago, was a young Chicano fiction writer. Santiago won a prestigious award and $5000 from the American Academy and Institute of Arts and Letters for writing *Famous,* but he failed to show at the award ceremony to receive the prize, fueling suspicion about his **identity**. Sixteen months after the novel's release, John Gregory Dunne published an article in the *New York Review of Books,* revealing that Santiago was not a Chicano writer from East Los Angeles. His real name was Daniel James. Moreover, he was white, seventy-three years old, and a former member of the Communist Party. Subsequently, several Chicano critics and teachers called Santiago a fraud and excluded his novel from Chicano literature courses and research projects. In so doing, however, they raised an important question: Is it possible for a non-Chicano to write an authentic representation of Chicano experiences?

Daniel Lewis James was born in Kansas City, Missouri, in 1911, the only child of wealthy parents. He received a Bachelor's degree in Greek Classics from Yale in 1933. That same year he became involved with the John Reed Club, a literary group organized by the Communist Party. He joined the Party in 1938 and remained active for ten years while working as a screenwriter in Hollywood. James and his wife, Lilith, were subpoenaed to appear before the House Un-American Activities Committee on September 19, 1951, to answer questions about communist sympathizers. Lilith James later remarked, "They thought we would snitch" (Dunne 37), but the Jameses refused to cooperate. After the HUAC hearing, James was blacklisted and could no longer find work in Hollywood. It was during this time that he first began to use a pseudonym and write stories about Mexican American life in East Los Angeles. The Jameses worked as volunteer social workers in the Lincoln Heights community of East Los Angeles for twenty-five years. They started several youth clubs and promoted education as an alternative to gang violence (Dunne 41). They established close friendships and kinship ties with families in the neighborhood and became intimately familiar with the culture of the barrio.

Famous All Over Town details the collapse of a Chicano family and the destruction of their neighborhood. Chato, the novel's narrator and protagonist, is an eighth grade student, a poor achiever in school but a brilliant storyteller. Despite his intelligence, he is oblivious to what makes his world tick. Chato's father, Rudy, represents the values of machismo and imposes his views on other family members, either through persuasion or with his fists. Chato's rebellious seventeen-year-old sister, Lena, challenges her father's authority at the risk of physical abuse, but at times her loyalty to her father outweighs her rebelliousness. At one point, to console the man, she humbly tells him, "You could hit me, Papa . . . if it would make you feel better." Eleanora, Chato's mother, at first appears to be the stereotypical Mexican housewife, taking her licks and her husband's infidelity passively. But her strength lies in her ability to operate clandestinely within the confines of her patriarchal environment. Despite her reticence, Eleanora knows more than do the other characters in the novel, including how to control men when necessary. She stands as the glue that keeps the family together. She is also the only character to change and to display a sense of agency by deliberately acting to take control of her life. She knows what to keep to herself, what not to reveal—much like the control that Santiago/James attempts to wield over his own life through his use of a Latino pseudonym. Whatever judgment a reader may pass on these characters, and despite their obvious ideological defects, they are nonetheless complexly developed.

When Santiago's identity was revealed in 1984, Chicana/o critics had reason to be angry, given the many decades of institutionalized racist neglect of U.S. Latina/o writers by the mainstream publishing industry. But the antagonism expressed toward Santiago was for the most part misdirected; it needed to have been aimed at the systemic causes of **racism**, rather than at the author or the novel itself.

Further Reading

Dunne, John Gregory. "An American Education." *Crooning: A Collection.* New York: Simon and Schuster, 1990. 21–56.

Marcial Gonzalez

SANTOS, BIENVENIDO N. (1911–1996) Filipino American short story writer and novelist. One of the first writers to record the experiences of Filipinos in America, Bienvenido Santos is best known in the United States for his short stories; his work also includes several novels on social conditions in the Philippines. His prolific writing career spans five decades of the lives of Filipinos. In America, his characters keenly feel their distance from their homeland, struggling as early migrant workers in the 1940s, recognized as "lovely people" for their heroic stand against the Japanese during World War II, isolated in the 1950s and 1960s, and coping with **immigration** restrictions in the 1970s and 1980s. In the Philippines they struggle against repressive conditions: social, economic, and political. Santos is a central figure in what has been termed the Filipino American literature of exile; in simple terms, through straightforward and apparently artless prose he creates moving portraits of the lives of Filipinos, reflecting both a deep sympathy for their various plights and a commitment to social justice.

Santos grew up in Tondo, a Manila slum that appears in his works as "Sulucan," for him and for his characters the starting point for many journeys. The son of peasants who moved to Manila looking for opportunity, he found lasting artistic inspiration in his slum origins and in his rural roots. Ambitious, eager to make his way out of poverty, he started writing short stories in high school; they were first published when he was nineteen, in Manila's flourishing English-language press. He entered the country's foremost university, the University of the Philippines, and on graduating in 1932 became a teacher. In 1941 he went on to graduate study at the University of Illinois and Columbia University as a *pensionado*, a scholar of the Philippine Commonwealth government. Stranded by the Japanese occupation of the Philippines, one in a small community of students in exile, he was sent by the Philippine Embassy to lecture around the United States; he thus came to know the lonely lives of working Filipinos in cities and small towns around America, which were to form a central subject in his oeuvre. On his return to the Philippines in 1946 he became a university professor and administrator and continued to work on the short stories that were published in the Philippines as *You Lovely People* and reprinted in the United States in *Scent of Apples*, some of which have become widely anthologized. These stories of "hurt men," Filipinos in America during the 1940s and 1950s, are loosely connected by Ambo and Ben, recurring narrators and characters.

One of Santos's best-known stories is the title story, "Scent of Apples," where the narrator, an educated Filipino lecturing on the Philippines, encounters Celestino Fabia, one of the men often called *manongs*, or "old-timers," the first generation of Filipinos, or *Pinoys*, in America. Fabia, a farmer in the Midwest, is defeated by his American wife's assertion that "there's no such thing as a first-class Filipino" and his feeling that in spite of his homesickness, nobody in the Philippines remembers him. Another story that has received critical attention is "Quicker with Arrows." Its protagonist, Val, a rich Filipino student stranded by the war, is in a conflicted relationship with a working-class American woman, Faye. Less known but also of interest are "The Contender," featuring a lonely Pinoy ex-boxer who is going blind, and "Woman Afraid," showing a young American wife and her Filipino husband; their marriage is shattered by her fears of having mixed-**race** children who will be seen as "monkeys." Another story of "old-timers," alienated from their surroundings while simultaneously cut adrift from their own people, is told touchingly in "The Day the Dancers Came." Set in Chicago in the 1950s, its protagonist, Fil, is homesick and eager to welcome and entertain a group of young Filipino dancers but, finding that they avoid him, realizes that they must have been warned against old-timers like him.

After receiving several awards and writing fellowships, and traveling to the University of Iowa as participant and lecturer in the writers' workshop, Santos published two novels in 1965, both set in the 1940s: *Villa Magdalena* reflects social inequalities in the Philippines in the sagas of a wealthy clan and of its poorer neighbors, whereas *The Volcano* is the story of the Hunters, missionaries coming to the rural Philippines and experiencing anti-American sentiment. His next novel, *The Praying Man* (1982), appeared during the martial law years, first serialized in *Solidarity* magazine. When military censors banned it for political overtones in the portrait of Chris Magat, who is torn between prayerful impulses and predatory corruption, deeming it offensive to the Marcos regime in its exposure of graft, Santos went into exile in the United States as writer-in-residence at Wichita State University and became an American citizen. His next two novels are set there, returning to his familiar protagonists, lonely Pinoys far from home. *The Man Who (Thought He) Looked Like Robert Taylor* (1983) features the stories of many Pinoys, as witnessed by Sol, who, like them, in trying to be American loses his self-respect and his Filipino identity. "Immigration Blues," which is sometimes published as a separate short story, is part of this novel; its protagonist, Alipio Palma, another old-timer, enters an arranged marriage, helping a friend to circumvent immigration restrictions. Critics have called *What the Hell for You Left Your Heart in San Francisco* (1987), Santos's final novel, a quintessential Filipino American novel; it focuses on Filipinos in the Bay Area and their absorption of American culture. The protagonist, David Tolosa, like Santos an exile under martial law, is a teacher and editor of a magazine backed by successful Filipino immigrants; instead of allying himself with them, he is repelled by the shallowness of students and businessmen. He wanders the city streets and meets the underclass, feeling sympathy for these "little brown men and women" in their confusion and displacement.

Santos's work, although in part widely known to readers in the United States, has yet to be appreciated fully; his novels have been published only in the Philippines. Growth in the appreciation of the lost history of early Filipino Americans should bring with it a fuller awareness of the achievements of this seminal author. (*See also* Filipino American Novel)

Further Reading

Gonzalez, N. V. M., and Oscar Campomanes. "Filipino American Literature." *An Interethnic Companion to Asian American Literature*. Ed. King-Kok Cheung. Cambridge and New York: Cambridge UP, 1997. 62–124.

Mannur, Anita. "Bienvenido N. Santos." *Asian American Novelists: A Bio-Bibliographical Critical Sourcebook*. Ed. Emmanuel S. Nelson. Westport, CT: Greenwood Press, 2000. 317–22.

Dolores de Manuel

SAPIA, YVONNE V. (1946–)   Puerto Rican American poet, novelist, and community college instructor. Sapia's poetry has been published in many periodicals and anthologies, but it is her novel that places her in the literary tradition of East Coast writers such as **Nicholasa Mohr** and **Judith Ortiz Cofer**. She has published two collections of poems, *The Fertile Crescent* (1983) and *Valentino's Hair* (1987), and the novel *Valentino's Hair* (1991).

In discussing her poetry Sapia states that her work "explores relationships through the reconstruction of memories, dreams, and reflections of each poem's persona." She feels that she can best convey "the intense emotion of illuminating experience with sparse and carefully chosen language" (*Contemporary Authors* 192). The same sentiment can be applied to her fiction writing. The first publication, titled *Valentino's Hair*, was a personalized poem about Sapia's relationship with her father, but when she wrote the novel it became the story of a father and son.

Reading *Valentino's Hair* is an enriching experience as the plot contains thrilling ingredients of magic, *Santeria*, witchcraft, unexplained deaths, and an unsolved mystery. Set in a fascinating historical context, the 1920s, the novel raises important contemporary issues such as racism and forbidden love relationships. Facundo Nieves is confessing the story to his son Lupe as Facundo lies on his deathbed. As a young man in 1926 Facundo was called from his barbershop in an exclusive Manhattan hotel to cut the hair of Rudolph Valentino, who was staying in the hotel. Soon after, Valentino is taken seriously ill and dies within a few weeks. Facundo sees Valentino one more time when he is called to shave him in the hospital where he hears Valentino's last words to him, *"cuida el pelo"* (take care of the hair). Facundo has kept clippings from Valentino's haircut, and he takes them to a local *bruja* who tells him that hair is a powerful aphrodisiac. She also initiates him to the uses of enchanting elixirs.

During the first haircut that Valentino receives from Facundo he narrates a secret from his past to him. Facundo lives with this secret, plus his own secret that he experiences after he recklessly uses the power of Valentino's hair for his own pleasure. These are the secrets he must dispense with before he dies, and he chooses his son as the recipient. Facundo's narrative is interrupted and interspersed with the story of Lupe's coming-of-age in the South Bronx. By narrating the story of Lupe the author is introducing the reader to the Puerto Rican community of the 1960s and to the urban social issues that face a young non-white man. The closing chapter, and the final scene, is riveting as Facundo reveals his secrets to his son. *Valentino's Hair* is a memorable novel that sets Yvonne Sapia as a gifted storyteller and skillful writer.

Sapia has received several awards for her poetry. In 1989 the Arts Council of Tampa-Hillsborough County selected her as a winner in its first literary competition, and she received the Samuel French Morse Poetry Prize from Northeastern University Press in 1987 for *Valentino's Hair*, the poetry collection. *Valentino's Hair* was chosen by Publisher's Weekly as one of the best books of 1991.

Sapia's work appears in several anthologies, including *To Read Literature* (1992), *The Woman That I Am: The Literature and Culture of Contemporary Women of Color* (1993), and *Unsettling America: Race and Ethnicity in Contemporary American Poetry* (1994). Sapia has written a theatrical adaptation of *Valentino's Hair* and is planning to write a screenplay of the novel. (*See also* Puerto Rican American Poetry)

Further Reading

Alarcon, Daniel Cooper. "Shear Destiny: Yvonne Sapia's 'Valentino's Hair'." *MELUS* 23.1 (Spring 1998): 133–45.

Metzger, Linda, Hal May, Deborah A. Straub, and Susan M. Trosky, eds. *Contemporary Authors.* Vol. 126. Detroit: Gale Research, 1989. 392–93.

Rafaela G. Castro

SAPPHIRE The term "Sapphire" is a negative reference to an African American woman. African American women have been saddled with labels designating unattractive behavior since the days of **slavery**. The first and best-known example of the Sapphire stereotype appeared in the *Amos 'n' Andy* radio show, which premiered in March 1928 in Chicago and began national broadcasting in August 1929. Set in Harlem, the show started out as *Sam 'n' Henry* in 1926. The television version of *Amos 'n' Andy* premiered in 1951 and ran for two years. Of the various stereotypes into which the black woman has been cast, Sapphire is the only one that requires the presence of a black man. Originally the joke of plays and minstrel shows, she was set up to make her husband look inferior. Sapphire Stevens appeared in the *Amos 'n' Andy* radio show as the wife of Kingfish Stevens. Because the radio and the television series were insulting to African American women and men and cast the African American family in a negative light, they were cancelled after criticism by civil rights groups.

Ernestine Wade is the actress who popularized the Sapphire image as Kingfish's shrewish wife. She was confrontational; her intent was to belittle Kingfish and to make him appear incompetent. They engaged in an ongoing verbal duel. Based on this portrayal, any woman who belittled her husband, put him down, and made him look inferior was labeled a Sapphire. Other characteristics of Sapphire make African American women appear evil, stubborn, bitchy, hateful, and wisecracking.

Although the character first appeared in the early part of the twentieth century, the stereotype exists today; African American women are still given this label. The stereotype grows out of what at first appears to be positive qualities: independence, wit, loyalty, and strong opinions. However, in the media, these qualities are exaggerated to the point where they become negatives. A black woman who speaks her mind to men, is loud and annoying, and belittles her man is likely to be called Sapphire. She is seen with hands on hips, a finger pointing at him, and rudely making negative comments about him. She is in charge, stubborn, hateful, emasculating through verbal putdowns, and spiteful.

Women with these characteristics continue to be portrayed in the media. In old movies and in television reruns, newer versions of their old selves appear. Sapphire is seen in such characters as Florence on *The Jeffersons*, Dee on *What's Happening*, Harriet Winslow on *Family Matters*, Aunt Esther on *Sanford and Son*, and Nell Carter on *Gimme a Break*. Urban black women who are loud and rude can also be seen on *Law and Order* and *NYPD Blue*. The existence of the Sapphire image is supported by the media and continues to influence the manner in which African American women are depicted. (*See also* African American Stereotypes)

Further Reading

Guy-Sheftall, Beverly. "Sapphire." *The Oxford Companion to African American Literature*. Ed. William L. Andrews, Frances Smith Foster, and Trudier Harris. New York: Oxford UP, 1997. 644.

Gwendolyn S. Jones

SARACINO, MARY (1954–)   Italian American fiction and creative nonfiction writer. The daughter of a Tuscan American mother and an Apulian American father, Mary Saracino was born and raised in Seneca Falls, New York. She is the author of *Voices of the Soft-bellied Warrior: A Memoir* (2001), *Finding Grace* (1999), which was awarded the Colorado Authors' League 1999 Adult Fiction Mainstream/Literary Award, and *No Matter What* (1993), which was a 1994 Minnesota Book Award Fiction Finalist. Saracino's work has also appeared in *The Milk of Almonds: Italian American Women Writers on Food and Culture*, *Don't Tell Mama!: The Penguin Book of Italian American Writing*, *Hey Paesan!: Writing by Lesbians and Gay Men of Italian Descent*, *Writers Who Cook*, and in literary journals such as *Voices in Italian Americana* and *Italian Americana*. An excerpt from her novel *No Matter What* has been translated into Italian for the literary journal *TutteStorie*.

Both in her fictional and in her autobiographical work, Saracino questions the centrality and the sacredness of family and religion in the Italian American culture. In Saracino's novels, *No Matter What* and its sequel *Finding Grace*, the story is told by a ten-year-old girl, Regina, torn between the unconditional love for her mother, who is having an affair with a Catholic priest, and her desire to keep her family together. Rather than being a place of safety where everybody finds salvation and support, the domestic space of the family in these novels is the place where violence is perpetrated. Religion does not offer salvation, either: The Catholic priest is the cause of the family's disintegration, because Regina's mother elopes with him taking her daughters with her, and the church is merely the place where Regina's father takes refuge when the environment at home becomes too conflictive. In this context, the word "grace" acquires a secular meaning: In *Finding Grace*, Grace is the name of the old lady who comes to Regina and Rosa's help when they run away from their second home. For them finding Grace also means finding the grace, the peace, the support that both their family and religion have been unable to offer.

Central themes in her autobiographical writings are her relationship with her Italian American heritage and with Catholicism and her desire to articulate her own voice. In "Sunday Rounds" Saracino examines her position as an outsider in the Italian American community as a woman, an intellectual, and a lesbian. In *Voices of the Soft-bellied Warrior,* Saracino's attempt to regain her voice, which she had progressively lost, becomes a metaphor for the necessity for all women to break the silence that confines them to the definitions that patriarchal societies have created for them. (*See also* Italian American Lesbian Literature, Italian American Novel)

Further Reading

Giunta, Edvige. *Writing with an Accent: Contemporary Italian American Women Authors.* New York: Palgrave/St. Martin's Press, 2002.

Romeo, Caterina. *Donne che migrano, donne che ricordano: Memoria, migrazione, identità nei memoir delle scrittrici italo americane.* Rome: Carocci, 2004.

Caterina Romeo

SAROYAN, WILLIAM [SIRAK GORYAN] (1908–1981)   Armenian American playwright, fiction writer, screenwriter, and essayist. Saroyan was born in the immigrant Armenian community of Fresno, California, to Armenak and Takoohi Saroyan, refugees from the first wave of massacres that became a full-fledged genocide of Armenians in Turkey between 1896 and 1915. His father's death and the family's subsequent poverty forced Takoohi to place her four children in an orphanage for several years. Many biographers see this experience as the source of ongoing themes of exile and alienation in Saroyan's writing. Paired with these themes, however, is the author's trademark optimism and the consequent upbeat tone in many of his works. He acknowledged the tragedy that marked his people's history and identity but also refused to lose faith in what he saw as a universal "brotherhood." He refused to engage the politics and ideologies that influenced the work of many of his contemporaries in the 1930s, purposely maintaining a humanist attitude toward art and sometimes idealizing its power to unite people.

A prolific writer, Saroyan published over fifty plays, novels, short fiction collections, works for children, and memoirs. The most well-known portion of his career spans roughly twenty years between the 1930s and 1950s. He entered the literary scene in 1934 with his collection of stories titled *The Daring Young Man on the Flying Trapeze,* for which he quickly won the coveted O. Henry Award for short fiction. The stories in the collection helped to establish Saroyan's reputation as an absurdist humorist, leading one recent critic to compare him to Kurt Vonnegut. His later short fiction collection *My Name Is Aram* (1940) evidenced a much more nostalgic and semiautobiographical preoccupation with heritage and the complications of bicultural **identity** and **assimilation**. The stories capture the landscape of his childhood in the San Joaquin Valley and the lives of the immigrants working in California. In stories such as "The Pomegranate Trees" and "Seventy Thousand Assyrians," for example, he foregrounds cultural icons of the homeland and the motif of displacement.

Having established his name as a writer, Saroyan found even greater success in theater. Because his plays were sometimes divisive, he became a well-known and at times controversial artist in the 1940s. Some theatergoers found him brilliant and avant-garde, while others found his work to be self-indulgent and difficult to understand. Often described as the American counterpart of playwrights Samuel Beckett and George Bernard Shaw, Saroyan created theatrical works using a blend of absurdist humor, intellectual musing, and symbolic experimentation. Because of his nontraditional style and influences (including **Gertrude Stein**), Saroyan's works can most easily be described as "modernist" in approach; however, his works did not fit easily with the agenda of the influential New Critics, and at one

William Saroyan. *Courtesy of the Library of Congress.*

point he even engaged in a back-and-forth written battle with Ernest Hemingway. Clearly, Saroyan's work does not belong to one particular literary movement. Despite the confusion with which some of his plays were met, he was awarded the Drama Critics Circle Award and the Pulitzer Prize for drama in 1940 for the Broadway success *The Time of Your Life.* The non–plot-driven play assembles a group of American stereotypes (one of which was played by a young Gene Kelly) in a San Francisco bar to illustrate the contradictions inherent in American society. Even though he gained fame for winning the Pulitzer Prize, Saroyan became even more notorious for turning it down, refusing to accept the prize on the principle that the business world should not judge and attempt to influence the arts. Other plays include *Love's Old Sweet Song* (1941), *My Heart's in the Highlands* (1937), and *The Armenian Trilogy* (1986).

Disenchanted with Broadway after the failure of his play *The Beautiful People,* Saroyan was lured to Hollywood by Metro-Goldwyn-Mayer in 1941. Returning to the West Coast, he became interested in returning artistically to California settings and subjects such as those in *My Name Is Aram.* However, he knew the characters in his first film had to have broad national appeal to succeed in an America preparing to enter World War II. Apparently unbothered by the confluence of commerce and art that motivated his rejection of the Pulitzer, he set out to make his first screenplay a commercial success. After studying the formulas of Hollywood by watching popular films, he worked with famous child actor Mickey Rooney to customize a story of small-town American life during the war. The result, *The Human Comedy* (1943), won the Academy Award for Best Screenplay, and the novel he adapted from the screenplay quickly became a national best seller. The story follows a boy working as a bicycle messenger for a telegraph company, whose grim task of delivering news of war casualties to families in the community forces his coming-of-age.

In addition to a boost in his career, the Hollywood period provided Saroyan with other significant life changes, including a brief stint in the Army and his marriage to New York society debutante and aspiring actress Carol Marcus. The years spent in the military, in Hollywood, and within a turbulent marriage provided materials for Saroyan's semi-auto-biographical, somewhat disenchanted novels, *The Adventures of Wesley Jackson* (1946), *Rock Wagram* (1951), and *One Day in the Afternoon of the World* (1964). Like many American novels of the postwar era, these stories focus more often on a first-person narrator's interior conflicts, in contrast to Saroyan's earlier works that concentrated on communities of people in order to provide more generalized studies of human nature. *Rock Wagram* remains one of his most intriguing, but underappreciated, works. It explores and theorizes the sources of personal identity through the title character, an Armenian American actor going through a divorce from his Anglo American wife and struggling to stay connected to his children, maintain his sophisticated, independent lifestyle, and, simultaneously, reconnect with the Armenian community of his past. Other novels include the California Literature Gold Medal–winning fantasy novel *Tracy's Tiger* (1951), *The Laughing Matter* (1953), *Mama I Love You* (1956), and *Boys and Girls Together* (1963).

Saroyan moved away from Hollywood and continued to produce new manuscripts and rewrite earlier works of all genres in the latter half of his career. The 1970s found him turning frequently to memoir. He published personal essays for magazines and newspapers, as well as book-length autobiographical works, such as *Places Where I've Done Time* (1972), *Sons Come and Go, Mothers Hang in Forever* (1976), *Chance Meetings* (1978), and *Obituaries* (1979). These works amble through personal philosophical reflections, influential episodes in his life and career, famous acquaintances and collaborators, and places in which he traveled and lived.

Critics often note how prominent a writer Saroyan was at mid-century yet how quickly he has become seen as a "minor" figure in recent decades. His work remains important to the body of work by a generation of writers coming out of immigrant enclaves to contribute new voices to the American literary scene. In his honor, the William Saroyan International Prize for Writing was established by Stanford University Libraries and the William Saroyan Foundation in 2002. (*See also* Armenian American Literature)

Further Reading

Balakian, Nona. *The World of William Saroyan.* Cranbury, NJ: Associated UP, 1998.

Bedrosian, Margaret. "William Saroyan and the Family Matter." *MELUS* 9.4 (Fall 1982): 13–24.

Calonne, David Stephen. *William Saroyan: My Real Work Is Being.* Chapel Hill: U of North Carolina P, 1983.

Keyishian, Henry, ed. *Critical Essays on William Saroyan.* New York: G. K. Hall, 1995.

Lee, Lawrence, and Barry Gifford. *Saroyan: A Biography.* New York: Harper & Row, 1984.

Shinn, Thelma J. "William Saroyan: Romantic Existentialist." *Modern Drama* 15.2 (1972): 185–94.

Tracy Floreani

SCHAEFFER, SUSAN FROMBERG (1941–)   Jewish American writer. Born in Brooklyn, educated in New York City public schools, Susan Fromberg Schaeffer graduated from Brooklyn College, wrote the first dissertation on **Vladimir Nabokov** at the University of Chicago, and returned to Brooklyn College in 1966 and founded the MFA program in writing. She married Neil Jerome Schaeffer in 1970, raising two children with him in Brooklyn and Vermont. She found her voice as a poet in the first of six collections, *The Witch and the Weather Report* (1972). The realism of her earliest novels (*Falling*, 1973; *Anya*, 1974; *Time in Its Flight*, 1978) and more experimental work (*The Queen of Egypt*, 1980) gave rise to the hyperrealism and psychological acuity of her atypical historical novels. Retiring from Brooklyn, she was named Alexander White Professor of English at the University of Chicago (2002–2005). In a four-decade teaching and writing career, she published poetry, scholarly articles and book reviews, short stories, two works of fiction for young adults, and twelve novels, many translated into multiple languages. "Imagination is finally victorious over human justice," says Schaeffer in her introduction to Charlotte Brontë's *Villette* (Bantam, 1986; xxxiii), in a statement emblematic of her own work, less well known than it deserves, despite prizes and translation into several languages.

Reviewing *Falling* (*New York Times* May 20, 1973), critic and theorist Wayne Booth called Schaeffer the finest new talent "except maybe for **Cynthia Ozick**." More clearly than some subsequent reviewers, Booth recognized that the realism of Schaeffer's fiction did not overshadow its engagement with its true subject, the relations of mortality, imagination, and reality. Similarly attuned to the serious accomplishment of what some saw as simply another **Holocaust** novel, Cynthia Ozick commented that Schaeffer's second novel, *Anya*, "makes experience—no, *gives* it, as if uninvented, or as if, turning around in your room, you see, for the first time, what has happened, who you are, and what is there, and why." From *Granite Lady* (nominated for a National Book Award) to her most recent work in *Prairie Schooner*, the deceptively simple surface of Schaeffer's poetry similarly opens to profound vision.

As Schaeffer commented in a letter to the editor in the *New York Times* (July 18, 1993), "Fiction is a record of that conflagration that occurs when reality collides with imagination." Each of her works uniquely stretched the boundaries of the realistic novel. Reviewing *Time in Its Flight* (1978) in the Book of the Month Club newsletter, Clifton Fadiman compared it to works as dissimilar, in all but theme and distinction, as *War and Peace* and Thornton Wilder's *Our Town. Love* (1981), stereotyped by some critics as Jewish multigenerational family saga, transcends those limits by virtue of its hyperrealism and profound insight into character and motivation. It elicited enthusiastic praise from her fellow novelists Margaret Atwood and Rosellen Brown. Schaeffer, although she sometimes uses conventional romantic plots, subverts and transforms them. For example, both *Mainland* (1985) and *The Injured Party* (1986)—though mis-marketed as popular romances—interrogate the conventions of middle-aged womanhood that they represent.

Feminist overtones pervade all of Schaeffer's works, though not in any programmatic way. Working in a vein often ceded to male writers, Schaeffer transformed the genre of war novel in *Buffalo Afternoon* (1990), a brilliant fictional representation of Pete Bravado, Brooklyn-born American soldier, battered but not broken by Vietnam and the haunting presence of a young Vietnamese girl, the first in her village to encounter American forces. Hailed by veterans and Vietnam journalists, this novel was followed by a more experimental novella, *First Nights* (1993); a mysterious novel about **identity** focused on twins, *The Golden Rope* (1996); the playful *Autobiography of Foudini M. Cat* (1997); and *The Snow Fox,* (2004), an ambitious novel set in Japan, whose theme, again, is time and identity.

Susan Fromberg Schaeffer observed in relation to Nabokov's fiction that "Every serious book is an autobiography not of the author's observable, recordable life but of the author's imagination at the time of writing" (Schaeffer, Unreality of Realism 736). Her observation can be applied to her own work as well: Schaeffer's imagination opens diverse American worlds to her readers. (*See also* Jewish American Stereotypes)

Further Reading

O'Conner, Patricia T. "Surveying the Inner Landscape." *New York Times* (July 7, 1985): A18.

Schaeffer, Susan Fromberg. "'Bend Sinister' and the Novelist as an Anthropomorphic Deity." *Centennial Review* 17.2 (Spring 1973): 115–51.

———. "The Unreality of Realism." *Critical Inquiry* 6.4 (Summer 1980): 727–37.

Gail Berkeley Sherman

SCHOOLCRAFT, JANE JOHNSTON (1800–1841) Native American poet and storyteller. She was the first Native American woman to publish her work, which appeared in *The Literary Voyager* or *Muzzeniegun*, a literary magazine that she published with her husband. Her poems and essays represent the best of both Ojibwe and non–Native American worlds.

Schoolcraft was born Bame-Wa-Wa-Ge-Zhik-A-Quay, Woman of the Stars Rushing Through the Skies, in Sault Ste. Marie, on the Canadian border between Michigan and Ontario. She was the daughter of John Johnston, a Scots Irish fur trader, and Susan Johnston (Chippewa), formerly Ozha-gus-coday-way-quay, Green Meadow Woman. Jane learned to speak Ojibwe as a child and remained fluent in her tongue her entire life. She completed her formal education in Ireland, where she lived briefly with her father in 1909.

In 1823, Jane Johnston married Henry Schoolcraft, who lived with the Johnstons while working as a Native American agent for the Upper Great Lakes. She assisted him in collecting Native American tales and compiling his Chippewa vocabulary. Together, they published *The Literary Voyager or Muzzeniegun,* which included poems and essays on Indian culture.

Schoolcraft wrote under the pseudonyms "Leelinau" and "Rose." Under these pen names and the influence of her mother's teaching of Ojibwe lore, Jane wrote essays that trace the traditions of her Ojibwe tribe and retell many of its myths. She published her first tale, "The Origin of the Robin," in 1827. In this oral allegory, Schoolcraft relates the story of an old man who directs his only son to undertake the traditional practice of fasting to secure a guardian spirit, on whom his future depends.

Schoolcraft developed an interest in poetry from her father, who was pious, an avid reader, and an amateur poet. He tutored Jane and her seven siblings in history, religion, the classics, and English literature. Consequently, most of Jane's poems reflect a love of nature, gentle piety, and fondness of English pre-Romantic poetry. Her most poignant work expresses her grief over the loss of her first-born son, William. "Woman's Tears," "Lines Written Under Affliction," and "To My Ever Beloved and Lamented Son" detail her pain.

At Henry's encouraging of Jane to abandon her Ojibwe heritage and adopt Christian beliefs, she moved to New York with him and their three children. As a result, she wrote more traditional stories, demonstrating a clear, direct, engaging voice, and combining a forthright narrative style with poetic diction. Despite living the remainder of her life in isolation, Schoolcraft influenced contemporary English authors, such as Anna B. Jameson, Harriet Martineau, and Thomas McKenney. She died in New York in 1841. (*See also* Native American Poetry)

Further Reading

Ruoff, LaVonne Brown. "Early Native American Women Authors: Jane Johnston Schoolcraft, Sarah Winnemucca, S. Alice Callahan, E. Pauline Johnson and Zitkala-Sa." *Nineteenth Century American Women Writers: A Critical Reader.* Ed. Karen L. Kilcup. Malden, MA: Blackwell Publishers, 1998.

Ondra K. Thomas-Krouse

SCHULBERG, BUDD (1914–)   Jewish American novelist and screenwriter. Budd Schulberg is part of the postimmigrant tradition of Jewish American writers seeking the freedom and equality promised by American society and whose life was greatly affected by the McCarthyism of the 1950s. Having joined the Communist Party in the 1930s, he later broke with it and testified before the House Un-American Activities Committee (HUAC) during the 1950s. Author of five novels, numerous screenplays, and nonfiction, his major literary effort, *What Makes Sammy Run?*, explores the effect of the American success ethic on the immigrant.

Budd Schulberg was a "Jewish Prince." Son of an influential Hollywood production executive, he was groomed to take his place in one of the studio dynasties. Schulberg made a trip to the Soviet Union in 1934 and came back singing the praises of the "workers' paradise." This trip, his years at Dartmouth, and his later rejection of the production end for the creative aspects of screenwriting led him to adopt a political position that was anathema to the studio bosses. Moreover, the struggle of the Screen Writers Guild for union recognition fueled his attitudes. The guild struggle provides the backdrop for events in *What Makes Sammy Run?*

Published in 1941, the book describes the corrupt and exploitative practices employed by the studio system. Its criticism comes through the characterization of Sammy Glick, an uncultured, calculating upstart who achieved his rise to power across the backs of friends and acquaintances. Glick may be understood in terms of the Jewish tradition as **Abraham Cahan**'s David Levinsky or **Samuel Ornitz**'s Meyer Hirsch going West, denying his heritage, and pulling out all the stops. His struggle for success in Hollywood precludes even a cursory glance on his part at his earlier Lower East Side life. Unlike Cahan's or Ornitz's "American hero," the only sentimentality in Sammy is limited to his mother. By rejecting his **ethnicity**, his Jewish self, the figure of Glick, departs from the notion of the self-made man and the Jewish tradition of success and the pain the earlier characters suffer from their divided selves. For Sammy there is no time to rue the loss of what might have been, no pausing to think. There is only a single self desperately trying to maintain the achieved level of success, to say nothing of surpassing it. Using the metaphor of running, Sammy's constant state of movement, the author creates the ghetto escapist par excellence. The novel reinscribes the Jewish American narrative of success.

Sammy was attacked on two fronts: the Jewish moguls feared that Sammy Glick might be perceived as their younger mirror image; the Communist Party voiced ideological disapproval of Schulberg's independence for publishing the book without first gaining the Party's blessing. Ironically, this condemnation followed a glowing review in its own paper, *Daily Worker*. Excommunication by his "native" community and censure by his adopted one led to Schulberg leaving Hollywood and vowing never to return.

Schulberg did, however, return, and triumphantly. In 1954 he won the Oscar for best screenplay for *On the Waterfront*. The movie revolves around the struggle of Terry Malloy to choose between the code of silence of the docks—accepting the rules imposed by a corrupt union boss and upholding his power, his dictatorial right to decide who works, lives, and survives economically, and who is blacklisted—and opposing the existing system by testifying before the Waterfront Crime Commission, and bringing change to his environment. Moreover, *On the Waterfront* emphasizes the bravery of the informer, "the guts" essential to his actions.

The film has also been interpreted as a validation of Schulberg's own appearance before the House Un-American Activities Committee in 1951 after having been labeled a Communist. Coupled with his feelings toward the Communist Party regarding his novel and his avowed reason of "acting in obedience to a higher authority," Schulberg informed on friends and associates from his Party days. Such nobility may, however, be questioned: In the political climate of the times, refusing to testify would have resulted in blacklisting, the loss of a lucrative book contract, and precluded *On the Waterfront* (or *A Face in the Crowd*, 1958) from ever coming to the screen and winning an Oscar. Because of the controversy surrounding his two major works, Schulberg remains a conflicted figure in Jewish American literature and film.

Further Reading

Scholnick, Sylvia Huberman. "Money Versus *Mitzvot:* The Figure of the Businessman in Novels by American Jewish Writers." *Yiddish* 6.4 (1987): 48–55.

Schwartz, Nancy Lynn. *The Hollywood Writers' Wars.* New York: Alfred A. Knopf, 1982.

Roy Goldblatt

SCHUYLER, GEORGE SAMUEL (1895–1977) African American novelist and journalist. Schuyler's views proved to be quite controversial and unpopular among his contemporaries. He is reputed to have written the first African American satire. Born in Providence, Rhode Island, his family moved to Syracuse, New York, when he was very young. Because of his patriotic ideals, he dropped out from public school at age seventeen to join the U.S. Army, where he spent the next seven years. He participated in World War I and left the army as first lieutenant. After the war, he held different jobs until Philip Randolph hired him for *The Messenger,* a socialist-oriented newspaper. He worked there from 1923 to 1928, becoming its managing editor. Due to the controversies the paper raised under Schuyler's leadership, it was even investigated by the U.S. House of Representatives.

In the 1930s, he turned to novel writing with the publication of his full-length satire, *Black No More* (1931). Also drawing from other genres such as science fiction, the novel can be described as an antiutopia because it presents a society obsessed with color. The starting point is the invention of a procedure that "whitens" blacks, which almost the entire Harlem community takes advantage from. The result is that they become three shades lighter than whites themselves who begin suntanning in order to differentiate themselves from the whitened ones. So the color mania starts all over again. The book is an open denunciation of both the white and the black communities in America, which

George S. Schuyler. *Courtesy of the Library of Congress.*

finally sustain the system of racial prejudice. The critical reception of the novel represents the way in which Schuyler himself was unjustly criticized during his lifetime. Mistaking his intentions, most contemporary critics affirmed that the novel revealed Schuyler's betrayal to his own **race** due to his open allegiance to white ideology, specifically to its racial hierarchy. Therefore, the novel was rejected as **assimilation**ist propaganda and practically ignored until the 1980s when attention was finally paid to the satiric component unacknowledged by previous reviews.

He also published two other novels: *Slaves Today: A Story of Liberia* (1931), which examined the difficult conditions of workers in Liberia considered as "new slaves," and *Black Empire*, which was the collection of a series that he published in the *Pittsburgh Courier* from 1936 to 1937 under the pen name of Samuel I. Brooks and was not published until 1991. As far as nonfiction is concerned, he wrote *Racial Intermarriage in the United States* (1929)— where he defended interracial children as genetically superior thanks to their hybridity, basing it on his own experience of being married to a white woman artist named Josephine Cogdell and of raising their daughter Phillippa who became a talented pianist—and his autobiography, *Black and Conservative: The Autobiography of George S. Schuyler* (1966), which remains an invaluable source of information about his committed stance.

But probably his most influential work took the form of the numerous columns and articles he contributed to different papers and magazines throughout his life. His longest association was with the *Pittsburgh Courier* and lasted for almost forty years, both as a columnist and foreign correspondent in West Africa, Latin America, and the West Indies. He also wrote for noteworthy journals such as *The Nation* and *Reader's Digest*, among others. In addition, he was invited by **H. L. Mencken** to publish essays in *The American Mercury*. His most famous article, titled "The Negro Art-Hokum," appeared in 1926 in *The Nation* (and elicited another well-known essay, **Langston Hughes**'s "The Negro Artist and the Racial Problem"). Schuyler proclaims in it one of his most oft-quoted statements: "the Aframerican is a merely lampblacked Anglo-Saxon," basically referring to his belief in the equality of both races and thus in the impossibility to discriminate between their cultural legacies.

Apart from this polemical view, he has always been qualified as ultraconservative when, in fact, he was an ardent communist in the twenties. Schuyler's individualistic evolution—from communism to conservatism in the forties—branded him as a traitor, but he only anticipated the reaction of his own generation. Moreover, he was also interested in constantly delving into controversial issues, especially concerning the black political and intellectual elite of his day. Nevertheless, his contributions can be acknowledged as crucial to understanding the social and racial panorama of America in the first half of the twentieth century as current reassessments of his work have confirmed.

Further Reading

Nelson, Emmanuel. "George Samuel Schuyler." *African American Autobiographers: A Sourcebook*. Ed. Emmanuel S. Nelson. Westport, CT: Greenwood Press, 2002. 323–27.

Peplow, Michael. *George Schuyler*. Boston: Twayne, 1980.

Mar Gallego

SCHWARTZ, DELMORE (1913–1967) Jewish American poet and short story writer. Born in Brooklyn in 1913 to Jewish immigrants from Romania, Delmore Schwartz became a well-known poet, short story writer, and literary critic. Although he energetically professed himself to be the representative Jew, he traveled in the literary circles of his day, befriending the likes of Robert Lowell, **Saul Bellow**, and **Alfred Kazin**, and teaching Lou Reed in a poetry seminar at Syracuse University.

He received a BA in philosophy from New York University in 1935, attended Harvard for two years, and then dropped out of the graduate philosophy program to be a lecturer in the English department there for twelve years. He went on to be an instructor and then Visiting Professor at Kenyon College, Princeton University, the University of Chicago, and Syracuse University. But Schwartz is not remembered for his teaching. He is remembered for his breakthrough collection, *In Dreams Begin Responsibility* (1938), published by the independent, avant-garde publisher New Directions. The book consists of poetry, short fiction, a play, and lyrics. Most notable is the title story, which recounts the anxiety of the immigrant son, detailing the pressures of **assimilation** and the desire to repress ethnicity or use it to construct an identity.

In Dreams Begin Responsibility tells the highly autobiographical tale of familial dysfunction and the special insight of the immigrant son-artist to have access to articulate that dysfunction because he is neither of the old world and its faulty rituals nor fully assimilated into the new world. In it one can see Schwartz revealing the tension that would animate him and his works for the remainder of his career; his own sense of his Jewishness precludes him from easy assimilation, even while he can be critical of his parents' old world Jewishness. Schwartz's other short story collections include *The World Is a Wedding* (1948) and *Successful Love and Other Stories* (1962).

His poetry is recognizably confessional and, paradoxically perhaps, high modernist, filled with literary allusion while articulating feelings of alienation in an advanced industrial culture. Schwartz produced the verse play *Shenandoah* (1941) and the autobiographical book-length poem *Genesis* (1943) to critical acclaim. His collection *Summer Knowledge: New and Selected Poems, 1938–1958* (1959) won the prestigious Bollingen Prize for Poetry, making Schwartz the youngest recipient in the prize's history.

As an accomplished literary critic, Schwartz produced essays and reviews that articulated his position as one who came after T. S. Eliot and Ezra Pound. He won the Bowdoin Prize in the Humanities for his essay "Poetry as Imitation" in 1936. In another piece, "The Isolation of Modern Poetry," he critiques the shortcomings of New Criticism by showing how it relies on a false sense of objectivity and writes what might be considered the manifesto for confessional poetry; after modernism, confessional poetry is the next major movement in poetry that includes the likes of Schwartz, Robert Lowell, **Theodore Roethke**, Sylvia Plath, Anne Sexton, and several others.

Schwartz suffered from mental illness, living in sanatoriums and hotel rooms for twenty years. The causes of his illness are not known, but it manifests itself in his work and his life. He felt deeply the divided obligations of his artistic aspirations and his cultural inheritances; indeed, he may have internalized the covert **anti-Semitism** of certain high modernists even as he insisted himself to be the quintessential Jew. A belated modernist, he revered the achievements of Joyce and Eliot. And yet, he yearned for something fresh to say—"to make it new" in Pound's famous dictum—and to do so, he turned his ethnic and personal anxiety into poetry. He not only represented Jewish guilt; he lived it. Though he expressed skepticism about his own place in the pantheon of modernist artists, he openly aspired to be included in it. As a result of this tension, Schwartz was a volatile figure.

When he died in 1967 in the Columbia Hotel in New York City, he had been living as a recluse for more than a year without contact with any friends. Schwartz's voice is an important one in the context of Jewish American fiction, paving the way for the likes of John Berryman, **Bernard Malamud**, **Philip Roth**, and more recently, Nathan Englander. Not only is Schwartz to be found in allusions by Lowell and as a major character in Bellow's *Humboldt's Gift*, he is something of an influence for literary-rockers, having songs dedicated to him by Lou Reed and U2.

Further Reading

Aarons, Victoria. *A Measure of Memory: Storytelling and Identity in Jewish American Fiction.* Athens: U of Georgia P, 1996.

Atlas, James. *Delmore Schwartz: The Life of an American Poet.* New York: Farrar, Straus and Giroux, 1977.

Dike, Donald A. "A Case for Judgment: The Literary Criticism of Delmore Schwartz." *Twentieth Century Literature* 24.4 (Winter 1978): 492–509.

McDougall, Richard. *Delmore Schwartz.* New York: Twayne, 1974.

Rosenberg, Ruth. "Three Narrative Jewish Strategies in *Humboldt's Gift*." *MELUS* 6.4 (Winter 1979): 59–66.

Thomas H. Kane

SCHWERNER, ARMAND (1926–1999)   Jewish American poet, scholar, teacher, and translator. It would prove difficult to definitively locate Armand Schwerner within a particular school or circle of postwar American poets, but this is only one of multifarious difficulties that Schwerner's work presents to the reader. A short list of the groups that Schwerner is most often associated with includes ethnopoetics, the deep image school L=A=N=G=U=A=G=E, and possibly even the Beats due to his abiding interest in Buddhist thought and practice. If Schwerner is not immediately identifiable in any one school it is due to the sheer breadth and variety of his poetry; quite simply the work does not allow itself to be categorized easily. Schwerner presents a commitment not so much to a singular movement of group but instead commits his work to the experimental aspects of language over and above any doctrinaire affiliations.

Schwerner published over thirteen volumes of poetry and several translations during his lifetime. It is fortuitous that Schwerner's first published book of poetry, *The Lightfall*, coincided with the publication of his co-translation work with Donald M. Kaplan in *The Domesday Dictionary* (both in 1963). The interrelation between the archaic and the contemporary, the primitive and the new, would come to occupy all of Schwerner's work to a greater or lesser degree. Beginning with his early volumes, one can see Schwerner searching for the poetic means of catching glimpses of language presenting itself at the height of its potential for meaning. In a sense, Schwerner's concerns with the archaic/primitive elements of language are his guiding star through all his works. In the earlier work, these concerns manifest themselves in the "child voice" of poems such as "daddy can you staple these two stars together . . .," which emphasizes how language becomes so charged with meaning that it seeks to bridge the distance between like and unlike materials, between sameness and difference. In Schwerner's poetry, the sacred and profane mingle not so much in harmonies or symmetries but in clusters or complex constellations of image and sound. Take for example "Zoology 1" from *Seaweed*, which creates a strange list of animals and animal body parts that are not given in any recognizable "traditional" poetic structure. Instead, the poem develops a taxonomy of sounds where strange anatomies and associations are allowed to proliferate beyond the confines of any adherence to natural harmony that a less open and dynamic poem might unwittingly obliterate. Consequently, Schwerner's early and middle periods often emphasize openness, indeterminacy, spontaneity, and humor over and above the polished lyric gem. Nonetheless, the power of lyric courses through all of Schwerner's poetry in trace amounts, like precious ores in a dark cave.

If in "the violence around us" the poet asks "who is speaking?" it is because in the language of his early and middle works, one often finds that the single speaker, the ego of the poem, is missing or possibly diffusing through a field of different voices. Often it is the case that the voice is so dispersed that the poem emerges without an identifiable speaker. Schwerner's later works present a deepening interest in the tensions inherent in the recovery of the lyric voice. These tight lyrics are especially evident in the "bacchae sonnets 1–7" in *Sounds from the River Naranjana & the Tablets I-XXIV* (1990).

In order to perceive the full development of Schwerner's poetic voices one must turn to the epic long poem, *The Tablets.* Here, the poet's most recurrent concerns are joined in a "symposium of the whole" (to use Robert Duncan's phrase) that began in 1968 and continued until Schwerner's death. The early "Tablets" present a dynamic open and projective verse, with the farcical and profane humor (like many of his earlier works). The latter "Tablets" present Schwerner at the height of his concentration on lyric and beyond (including several notebooks on poetics and the process of composition). *The Tablets* presents the fullest expression of the poet, translator, scholar, teacher, and, lest we forget, trickster and is sure to be considered Schwerner's most powerful achievement as well as a major event in the history of American poetry. *The Tablets*, like all of Schwerner's works, explores the poem as a site of archaic mixtures of the self and other that are monstrous and beautiful, comic and tragic. (*See also* Jewish American Poetry)

Further Reading

McHale, Brian. "Archeologies of Knowledge: Hills' Middens, Heaney's Bogs, Schwerner's Tablets." *New Literary History* 30.1 (1999): 239–62.

Paul, Sherman. *In Love with the Gratuitous: Rereading Armand Schwerner.* Grand Forks, ND: North Dakota Quarterly Press, 1986.

Mikel Parent

SCOTT-HERON, GIL (1949–)   African American poet, novelist, singer, and musician. He is regarded as a progenitor of rap music as well as slam poetry. Born on April Fool's Day in 1949 in Chicago, Scott-Heron spent his early years living with his grandmother near Jackson, Tennessee, where he was one of three black children chosen to integrate the local elementary school during his eighth-grade year. The young Scott-Heron was unable to cope with the pressure of harassment by white students, however, and was soon sent to live with his mother in New York. There he was exposed to the work of influential black writers, including the artists of the **Harlem Renaissance** and especially **Langston Hughes**. He also encountered the work of radical poet and playwright Leroi Jones (who later became **Amiri Baraka**) while in New York, before leaving briefly to attend Lincoln University in Pennsylvania in 1967, where he won the Langston Hughes Creative Writing Award. He dropped out at the beginning of his second year in order to finish his novel *The Vulture.* This accomplished apprentice piece, published in 1970 to modest critical acclaim, is a thriller that pieces together the events leading up to a young man's murder through the testimony of various acquaintances. In the process it also depicts the gritty social conditions of a Harlem plagued by drugs, crime, and gambling.

As a writer Scott-Heron seems to have peaked early: He is probably best known today for his poem "The Revolution Will Not Be Televised" (1970) first published in the volume *Small Talk at Lenox and 125th Street* and recorded on his debut spoken-word album of the same name with a simple but compelling percussion accompaniment. This seemingly prescient poem is a stinging and witty indictment of the complacency cultivated by an image-driven consumer culture and a call for revolution to overthrow this lethargy and narcissism. A similar call to arms forms the subtext of Scott-Heron's second novel, *The Nigger Factory* (1972), about a student strike at a fictional university reminiscent of Lincoln University that boils over into an incipient revolution.

Despite his early success as a novelist and poet, as the 1970s progressed, Scott-Heron's career as a musician and singer began to overshadow his literary endeavors. With his long-time musical collaborator Brian Jackson, Scott-Heron broke into the R&B top-thirty charts with "Johannesburg" in 1975 and "The Bottle" in 1978. He continued to record prolifically into the early 1980s. But then, in a dark irony for someone who had always loudly denounced drug and alcohol use, Scott-Heron developed a well-publicized drug problem, and his recording and publication output has subsequently been sporadic. The importance and relevance of his early work, however, continues to grow.

Further Reading

Massa, Suzanne Hotte. "Gil Scott-Heron." *Contemporary African American Novelists: A Bio-Bibliographical Critical Sourcebook.* Ed. Emmanuel S. Nelson. Westport, CT: Greenwood Press, 1999. 416–20.

Shane Graham

SEACOLE, MARY (1805–1881)   Jamaican nurse and autobiographer. Mary Seacole's remarkable autobiography, *The Wonderful Adventures of Mary Seacole in Many Lands* (1857), is a combination of life writing and travel narrative. The book chronicles the life of an independent black woman who traveled the world, crossing racial, national, and gender boundaries to earn fame as a battlefield nurse at a time when sexism and **racism** were still very much obstacles to her achievements. At the time of its publication, Seacole was well known and celebrated for her heroism serving British soldiers during the Crimean War (1853–56), and her autobiography, only the second book by a black woman ever published in Great Britain, was a best seller in England.

Seacole was born Mary Jane Grant in 1805 in Kingston, Jamaica. Her father was a Scottish army officer and her mother was a free black Jamaican woman who ran a boarding house for local military officers, frequently using her expertise in herbal medicines to treat her clients' ailments. Fascinated by medicine from an early age, Seacole followed in her mother's footsteps to become a successful hotelier and a skilled nurse adept at treating tropical diseases and capable of performing minor surgery. After a brief marriage that ended with the death of her husband, she traveled with her brother, Edward, to the Spanish colony of New Granada, in Central America, to manage a hotel and practice medicine. After briefly returning to Jamaica, and assisting during the 1853 yellow fever outbreak, Seacole moved to London in 1854, eager to support Britain's military effort in the Crimean War. When she arrived, however, she was denied a position in Florence Nightingale's nursing corps on the grounds of her race. Undaunted, Seacole traveled to the front on her own and established and ran her own institution for British soldiers, a combination of store, mess hall, medical dispensary, and hospital. Known as "Mother Seacole" by the men she treated, she became widely heralded for her bravery, compassion, and skill, receiving numerous commendations and medals of valor from the British government.

Although Seacole describes her battlefield experiences in detail, her autobiography is remarkable not only for its depictions of the graphic human terrors of war but for its author's style and wit. Seacole was a cosmopolitan and educated woman, as capable of using sarcasm to ridicule slaveholders and racists as she was of writing moving depictions of death and destruction on the battlefield. Throughout her autobiography, Seacole's intellect, humor, and determination are apparent, as is her persistent optimism in the face of numerous difficulties.

After the war, Seacole spent the remainder of her life traveling back and forth between England and Jamaica before dying in London in 1881. All but forgotten for more than a century after her death, Seacole's autobiography has recently emerged as an important text for scholars of both travel writing and black women's autobiography. (*See also* African American Autobiography, African American Travel Narrative)

Further Reading

Fish, Cheryl J. *Black and White Women's Travel Narratives: Antebellum Explorations.* Gainesville: U of Florida P, 2004.

Woodard, Loretta G. "Mary Seacole." *African American Autobiographers: A Sourcebook.* Ed. Emmanuel S. Nelson. Westport, CT: Greenwood Press, 2002. 328–32.

Todd Dapremont

SEATTLE. *See* Chief Seattle

SEGAL, LORE [GROSZMANN] (1928–) Novelist, translator, and writer of children's books that illuminate Anglo Jewish and Jewish American experiences during and after World War II and that focus on the growing child as wise, imaginative, innovative, and resourceful. In *Other People's Houses* (1963), an autobiographical novel (or novel written as memoir), Segal recounts the life of Lore Groszmann, and her family, beginning in

1938 when ten-year-old Lore is sent on a child transport train from Austria to England where she is taken into several foster homes and ending with the family's resettlement in America in 1951, her father having died earlier in England and her grandfather in the Dominican Republic. Family burial places in different parts of the world during this **diaspora** is only one of the poignant facts in Segal's story of continuous and enforced transplantations for European Jews under Nazi rule. But she delivers horrifying facts and truths with blunt honesty and often self-deprecating humor. Lore, the child—and later the adult—is presented with all her faults. She is "critical, anxious, and overeager" as the author describes her child-self. She watches others and tries to imagine herself as she appeared to them, but what Segal presents is never an idealized portrait of herself or other family members. She (and they) can be selfish, overbearing, and thoughtless but also brave, caring, and sensitive.

From the moment she leaves on the kinder transport, Lore shoulders the entire burden of getting her parents out of Vienna, and she accomplishes the task by writing admittedly florid but moving letters to relatives already resettled in England. And always she has a mind of her own, as Segal depicts, with boisterous humor in a later picture book, *The Story of Mrs. Lovewright and Purrless Her Cat* (1985). Just as Lore, the child of *Other People's Houses*, could never show open affection or curry the favor of matrons, Jewish or Christian, who opened their English houses to her, Purrless will not "cozy" up to the controlling do-gooder, Mrs. Lovewright when she decides she must have a cat.

In *Other People's Houses*, Segal's subject, the displacement and transplantation of **Holocaust** survivors, intersects with several themes: the genesis of the child writer, storytelling as survival strategy, and imaginative creation as survival strategy. (Lore already knows she is a writer and that others depend on her writing for their lives even as she lands in England at the Dovercourt refugee camp.) This rendering of a child or adult self, encircled with calamities and learning to adapt, permeates all of Segal's work, whether she is picturing a family buffeted by but resisting cruelties of war in *Other People's Houses*, a European immigrant sorting out idioms, relationships, and **racism** in *Her First American* (1985), a cat with a mind of its own, or a child artist who cannot part with the present (a set of paints) he brings to the party, finally opening it himself and beginning, with comic exuberance, to produce a self-portrait (*Morris the Artist*, 2003).

Segal's warm and humorous ability to produce a child's eye view of the world and her focus on the plight of vulnerable children who face a puzzling and illogical world and who triumph through imaginative creation bring to mind the children's books of Jewish American artist Maurice Sendak. Both have created books about children suffering in the Holocaust, Segal in *Other People's Houses*, Sendak in *Dear Mili* (1988), based on a Grimm tale. In fact the Grimm tales have provided inspiration for both creators. Both selected then produced (she translated, he illustrated) the renowned collection, *The Juniper Tree and Other Tales from Grimm* (1973). Both have published picture book versions based on Grimm's fairy tales (*Dear Mili* and Segal's *The Bear and the Kingbird*, 1979). Both have produced stories of well-loved, mischievous children wreaking havoc on the family routine and then resolving their anger, boredom, or sibling jealousies through imaginative efforts: Sendak's *Where the Wild Things Are* (1963) and Segal's *Tell Me a Mitzi* (1970). Both Segal, in *Why Mole Shouted* (2004), and Sendak, in the Little Bear series (1957–68) written by Else Minarik, have created curious, stubborn, but endearing child animals in close knit families, exploring the world and learning from parents and grandparents.

Further Reading

Endelman, Todd M. *The Jews of Britain, 1625 to 2000.* Berkeley: U of California P, 2002.

Kaplan, Marion A. *Between Dignity and Despair: Jewish Life in Nazi Germany.* New York: Oxford UP, 1999.

Lanes, Selma. *The Art of Maurice Sendak.* New York: Harry Abrams, 1984.

Nina Mikkelsen

SEGUÍN, JUAN N. (1806–1890) Mexican American/Tejano memoirist and member of Texas's military. The *Personal Memoirs* (1858) of Juan Seguín represents one of the first documents of Mexican American border **identity**. It provides insight into one man's devastating experience with the installation of a white-dominated socioracial order in the southwest United States, which occurred when Mexico's northern territory became part of the United States.

Born in 1806 in what is now San Antonio, Texas, Seguín grew up to be a prominent man in Texas. Aside from holding a number of political positions, he was a renowned member of Texas's military. He enjoyed the praise that Sam Houston, Stephen F. Austin, and other distinguished Texans bestowed on him for his bravery and for his devotion to the independence of Texas from Mexico. In spite of his esteemed standing in political and military circles, however, by 1842 Seguín found himself resigning his posts and fleeing to Mexico to escape the pursuit of his military brothers. Rumors had begun circulating that Seguín was really sympathetic toward Mexico. It appears that the rash persecution of Seguín was nothing less than the result of Anglo Texans' eagerness to act on their racist resentment of the Tejanos in their midst.

Seguín organizes his *Personal Memoirs* around his traumatic fall from respectability. He begins this work with a description of his accomplishments and the various ways he has distinguished himself. By beginning in this fashion, Seguín strategically establishes himself as a worthy and loyal Texas citizen. As soon as he starts to retell the trauma and ruin that befell him, he figures himself as a man who has been wronged. Since Seguín wrote the *Memoirs* after returning to Texas from Mexico, they can be seen as motivated by a desire to clear his reputation and recuperate the esteemed standing he formerly enjoyed in Texas society.

Seguín's contemplation of his liminal standing in Texas society antici-pates more recent figurations of border identity by Chicano and Chicana critics and theorists, such as **Gloria Anzaldúa**, **Guillermo Gómez-Peña**, and José David Saldívar. As Seguín is not quite an "American" or a "Mexi-can," his life story dramatizes the betwixt and between nature of Chicano identity. In addition, Seguín's *Memoirs* offers insight into the decimating effect that the transformation of the racial order in the southwest United States had on Mexican men's sense of their masculine identities. As Seguín bemoans the loss of his masculinized status in Texas society, the emasculat-ing implications of the new racial order for Mexican men become apparent. (*See also* Liminality, Mexican American Autobiography)

Further Reading

Padilla, Genaro M. *My History, Not Yours: The Formation of Mexican American Autobiography.* Madison: U of Wisconsin P, 1993.

Serrato, Phillip. "Tragic Inflexibility: Outdated Ideals of Masculinity in Juan Seguín's *Personal Memoirs.*" *Journal of the American Studies Association of Texas* 34 (October 2003): 14–34.

Teja, Jesús F. de la. "The Making of a Tejano." *A Revolution Remembered: The Memoirs and Selected Correspondence of Juan N. Seguín.* Ed. Jesús de la Teja. Austin, TX: State House, 1991. 1–70.

Phillip Serrato

SÉJOUR, VICTOR (1817–1874)   African American playwright, nov-elist, and short fiction writer. Author of "Le Mulâtre" (The **Mulatto**)—argu-ably the first piece of fiction written by an African American—Séjour's work anticipates the literature of later African American writers who recast "main-stream" literary movements within an African American context.

Born in New Orleans, Louisiana, to free and prosperous parents, Juan Victor Séjour Marcouet Ferrand attended Sainte-Barbe Academy where he worked under the tutelage of black journalist Michel Séligny. When he turned nineteen, Séjour, like other free blacks in New Orleans, traveled to Paris. Here, he developed friendships with other writers of color, namely Alexandre Dumas, author of *The Count of Monte Cristo* (1844), and Cyrille Bisette, editor of the French periodical *La Revue des Colonies*. Séjour pub-lished both the short story "Le Mulâtre" (1837) and the Napoleonic ode "Le Retour de Napoléon" (1841) in *La Revue des Colonies*. While in Paris, Séjour developed a career as a playwright, staging more than twenty plays during the course of twenty-five years.

Notwithstanding his prolific career as a dramatist, Séjour's "Le Mulâtre" stands as his most renowned piece because it marks the beginning of Afri-can American fiction and boldly explores themes that were, at the time of its publication, taboo. This dark tale of miscegenation, rape, and murder tells the tragic story of Georges, a mulatto slave who, as the tale opens, is unable to identify his father. Divided into five sections, Séjour's frame tale begins when the narrator, a tourist, happens upon an "old negro" who tells him about Georges. As the narrator recounts the old man's story, readers learn the circumstances surrounding Georges's birth and his mother's death; observe Georges's heroism and dedication as he saves his master, Alfred, from a slave uprising; feel Georges's anguish when his master betrays him; and suffer Georges's shock as he discovers with murderous finality his father's **identity**.

Unlike nineteenth-century African American autobiographers **Frederick Douglass** and **Harriet Jacobs**, who could only mask the true hideousness of **slavery** behind a veil of **abolition**ist-inspired prose, Séjour offers a direct and explicit treatment of slavery's horrors and an outspoken critique of rape as a perverse element of the slave system. Like Edgar Alan Poe, Séjour details terror, violent death, sexual obsession, and the human psyche under extreme emotional strain; but Séjour departs from the American literary gothic tradition by grounding his tale in social reality, not in a world governed by the supernatural or scientific. As an African American who lived in Paris, and as a black writer who published on the periphery of the American literary scene, Séjour's life and work represent one component of the diverse collective that is black literature. (*See also* African American Drama)

Further Reading

O'Neill, Charles Edwards. *Séjour: Parisian Playwright from Louisiana.* Lafayette: U of Louisiana P, 1996.

Shanna Greene Benjamin

SENNA, DANZY (1970–) African American novelist and journalist. Senna received glowing reviews and numerous awards for her first novel, *Caucasia* (1998), published when she was not yet thirty. In addition to her fiction, Senna has published essays on racial politics and her experiences as the daughter of an African American father and white mother. Her second novel, *Symptomatic,* was published in 2004.

Born to a novelist/poet mother and a journalist father in Boston, Massachusetts, Senna received her BA from Stanford in American Studies in 1992. After working as a journalist in New York for *Newsweek,* Senna obtained her MFA from the University of California at Irvine in 1996.

Winner of the Stephen Crane First Fiction Award (1998) and the Whiting Writer's Award (2002), *Caucasia* has been widely praised as an absorbing, original, and highly skilled meditation on contemporary American racial politics. The novel is told from the point of view of Birdie, one of two daughters born in 1970s Boston to Sandy, a blue-blooded White Anglo-Saxon Protestant, and Deck, an African American professor. Birdie's sister, Cole, preferred by both parents, appears Black, whereas Birdie is light-skinned enough to be frequently identified as white. When their parents split up, Cole, Deck, and his African American girlfriend search for racial utopia in Brazil, while Sandy, convinced she is wanted by the Federal Bureau of Investigation, takes Birdie underground and tells her she must now pass as white. Chronicling Birdie's adventures in "caucasia," the novel portrays her sense of intense dislocation as she assumes a white **identity** and thus becomes an unwilling witness to white **racism**. Because it raises profound questions regarding the physical, social, and familial aspects of racial identity, the novel has provided fertile ground for contemporary critical arguments regarding the tangibility of **race** and the importance of "hybridity." Although Birdie's experiences seem designed to point toward the absurdity of essential definitions of race, Brenda Boudreau argues that the novel also disputes the idea that race is an insignificant "costume," because society renders the effects of that costume deep, abiding, and frequently painful.

Initial reviews indicate that Senna's second novel, *Symptomatic,* addresses similar themes. The novel describes the adventures of a biracial young woman who travels to New York to take up a prestigious fellowship. The heroine gradually becomes embroiled with an older woman who is also biracial and whose investment in the heroine turns obsessive and ultimately terrifying. Preliminary reviews have been mixed, with some critics diagnosing a "sophomore slump" and others praising the novel for its dark and gripping presentation.

Further Reading

Arias, Claudia M. Milian. "An Interview with Danzy Senna." *Callaloo* 25.2 (Spring 2002): 447–52.

Bourdreau, Brenda. "Letting the Body Speak: Becoming White in *Caucasia.*" *Modern Language Studies* 32 (Spring 2002): 59–70.

Gomez, Jewelle. "Review of *Caucasia.*" *Callaloo* 24.1 (Winter 2001): 363–73.

Hunter, Michele. "Revisiting the Third Space: Reading Danzy Senna's *Caucasia.*" *Literature and Racial Ambiguity.* Ed. Teresa Hubel. Amsterdam: Rodopi, 297–316.

Schmidt, Elizabeth. "Soul Mates." *New York Times Book Review* (March 15, 1998): 22.

Jane Elliott

SEPHARDIC LITERATURE   For the long path Sephardic literature has walked throughout centuries and continents, it has kept but one distinct feature: its oral quality. Eleventh- and twelfth-century Spain produced remarkable poets, namely Selomoh Ibn Gabirol, Yehudá Ha-Leví, and Mosef Ibn Ezra, whose compositions on love, friendship, religion, and cosmology were also commonly influenced by Arabian poetic techniques predominant in the eight-hundred-year period of Al-Andalus. In America, Sephardic literature originated from the oral legacy brought over by immigrants and developed through the genre of memoirs and lyrical compositions. They had a musical element that passed from generation to generation in the form of oral ballads and folktales. In the last part of the twentieth century, a literary corpus mainly integrated by female writers has emerged in America. Their texts mostly consist of short fiction that addresses the issues of historical heritage, memory, and **identity**.

The adjective "Sephardic" is applied to the Jewish people who originated from the Iberian Peninsula (taken from the book of Obadiah, Sephardim stands for Spain in Modern Hebrew) or to those who, without specifically coming from Spain and Portugal but willfully tracing their roots back to the Golden Age of Spanish Jewry, follow their cultural or religious practices. After the Spanish Reconquest and the creation of the Inquisition, Jews were expelled from Spain (those who forcedly converted in order to stay were called *conversos*, *marranos*, and *anusim*; some of them carried out Sephardic practices secretly and were called Crypto Jews).

Many communities in and out of Spain preserved the living tradition of oral poetry and the particularities of the Ladino or Judeo Spanish languages when they settled down in other territories. In 1654, a group of twenty-three Jews—mostly of Amsterdam Portuguese Sephardim origin—are believed to have formed the first Jewish American Community in the Dutch colony of New Amsterdam. New York's Shearith Israel (1654) and Philadelphia's Mikve Israel (1782) constituted landmarks for the perpetuation of Sephardic culture through prayers, readings (i.e., the Book of Lamentations), and chants that were brought over from Europe by trained Dutch cantors. It would be a mistake, therefore, to dissociate music from the formation of a Sephardic literary corpus. Among the most popular genres cultivated by this rich culture are ballads, folktales, lyric poetry, proverbs, and riddles. Sephardim had developed a culture of adaptation by which Old Spanish and European compositions in general were translated and modified in the Ladino language as to recreate a wide range of stories whose characters and content had well-known predecessors. Certain adaptations have proved to be very close to the originals both in quality and faithfulness to the subject matter. Such is the case of *Lady Alda's Dream,* one of the most traditional sixteenth-century ballads from Southern France. Because of the multi**ethnicity** of Sephardic settlements, texts have also adapted and enriched traditional epics with innumerable versions depending on the countries in which they developed. These variants have been rarely analyzed by literature studies, and they significantly vary from community to community. Renowned Spanish scholar Ramón Menéndez Pidal (1869–1968) documented more than a hundred versions of a folk song titled "Gerineldo." The theme of the difference of social rank as both an impossibility and a temptation for amorous relationships is represented in this case by Gerineldo, the King's servant, who is surprised by his master while in bed with the princess. In some variations his life is saved thanks to the princess's implorations to his father, whereas in others he is condemned to beheading. Many of them, Menéndez Pidal acknowledged, came from Sephardic settlements in Greece, Turkey, and North Africa; he also found a fifteen-year-old Catholic boy in Cuba who knew this song.

From their expulsion from Spain on July 31, 1492, and from Portugal in 1497, the **diaspora** would widely expand into different lands: from the Balkan and the North African areas of the Ottoman Empire to America. A significant number of descendants of the first generations who left Spain and Portugal to set off to America and settle down in the Caribbean, Central America, and South America made their way back to the main capitals of the United States. After the fall of the Ottoman Empire came a second wave of immigrants. Finally, a minor representation of European and African Sephardic Jews arrived after World War II. However, Sephardic literature has had to turn its pages with undeserved slowness: The cultural tradition of orality combined with an historical fear of **anti-Semitism** and the lack of resources present in immigrant life were core to the inconsistency of its written production.

During periods of adaptation to new lands, Sephardic Jews did not isolate themselves as much as Ashkenazis. Segregation was not a common feature among Sephardic Jews, and their integration within Muslim communities was considered customary. The outcome was a convivial atmosphere in which cultural exchanges were recurrent; however, their culture started dissolving within the neighboring influences. It was not until the twentieth century when the literary panorama witnessed the emergence of authors of Sephardic origin or who wrote about Sephardim in an array of themes coming from different walks of life. Yitzhak Navon's role as a politician and his service to the Argentinean and Uruguayan embassies did not hold him back from writing two musical plays based on Sephardic folklore: *Sephardic Romancero* (1968) and *Bustan Sephardi* ("Spanish Garden," 1970). He instead served as a model for many writers to come who, realizing the possibilities of literature embedded in the Sephardic culture, began to write in the middle or at the end of their careers that normally had nothing to do with literature. Matilda Coen Sarano was a foreign minister before publishing various collections of Sephardic stories; Sara Benveniste Benrey began writing poetry and comedy scripts in the 1980s; Rita Gabbai Simantov, a Cultural Officer in the Israeli Embassy, published her first poetic anthology in 1994. This late literature blossoming corresponds to an especially difficult period for Judeo Spanish literature during the postwar years, when almost no prose, drama, or poetry was produced.

In America, publications addressing the immigrant population made the development of certain journalistic and literary form possible. The first Ladino newspaper in New York and in the country, *La Amérika* (1910–25), was followed by a dozen of other attempts, most famously *La Vara* and *El Progresso*. There were opinion columns that soon gained a reputation among a considerable number of readers. Unfortunately, this diverse circulation came to an end with the closedown of the New York Ladino Press in 1948. Among the groups that have remained culturally active in the United States, Los Angeles, San Francisco, Seattle, and New York are the most successful in having kept the community's heritage alive.

In the 1970s Sephardic literary production was not especially flourishing, but Moshe Shaul and some collaborators launched the world's only cultural magazine written entirely in Judeo Spanish, *Aki Yerushalayim: Revista Kultur-*

ala Djudeo-espanyola. Currently, they release three issues every year. Another initiative is the association Ivri-NASAWI, headquartered in Los Angeles and with a chapter in New York that opened two years later, in 1998. Ivri stands for "Hebrew" or "border-crosser" and NASAWI is the acronym of the National Association of Sephardic Artists, Writers and Intellectuals. It was founded by Ammiel Alcalay Ruth Behar, Jordan Elgrably, and Victor Perera to unify the groups within the Sephardic and Mizrahi Jewry, and they organize the National Sephardi Literary Contest (NSLC). Other contributions to the preservation of the cultural heritage have been Al Passy's *Sephardic Folk Dictionary: English to Ladino, Ladino to English* in 1991 and *Ladino-English/English-Ladino Concise Encyclopedic Dictionary* by Elli Kohen and Dahlia Kohen-Gordon in 2000. One revealing fact that accounts for this lack of cohesion and strength in disseminating the Sephardic culture and literature has to do inevitably with the separation provoked by the two languages spoken by Jewish communities in America: Yiddish and Ladino. Although Yiddish became commonplace in American culture and an influence for English, Ladino rarely gained access to printed form.

There have been tensions between both groups and languages. Renowned anthropologist Ruth Behar illustrated them in her story "A Sephardi Air." Here, a girl analyzes the stereotypes that mark and distinguish Ashkenazi and Sephardi Jews, both of which she embodies because of her parents' different Jewish descent. Fortuna Calvo-Roth's "What! No Yiddish? Growing up Sephardi in Peru" accounts for the predominance of Ashkenazi culture in Peru, as it happens in most Latin American countries; she narrates how she was raised respecting Sephardic rites that her father, an immigrant coming from Turkey at the beginning of the twentieth century, had established in their home in Lima. In "My Cuban Story," Ester Levis Levine tells how being Jewish, Sephardic of Turkish origin, and Cuban makes her a "Juban" with many questions to face about issues of identity and belonging. Among the most well-known authors, Angelina Muñiz de Huberman occupies a distinguished place: She was the first writer to introduce Sephardic mysticism and the neo-historical novel in Mexico. She is a scholar, a poet, and a novelist whose work has been translated into several languages and is extensively published in many collections (e.g., *The Oxford Book of Jewish Stories*). Her narrative includes *La lengua florida* (*The Flowery Language*), the name that Muñiz de Huberman has given to Ladino and Judeo Spanish because of their incredible richness that the Sephardic peoples have kept blooming to the present day.

In *The Sun at Midday: Tales of a Mediterranean Family* (1997), Gini Alhadeff writes about her experience of being raised as a Catholic and discovering in New York her Sephardic Jewish roots when she was in her twenties. She elaborates a family map with exhilarating and witty prose that goes from Alexandria where she was born to her uncle Nissim, a **Holocaust** survivor and now a gynecologist in Queens. After this memoir, in 2003 she published the novel *Diary of a Djinn*. Also set in New York, Gloria DeVidas

Kirchheimer compiled eleven stories under the title *Goodbye, Evil Eye: Stories* (2000), in which she showcased the tensions around a Sephardic family and contemporary life in the United States.

In the last two decades there has been a revaluation of Sephardic identity, especially in relation to female writers. Academics have lately invested much research in recovering testimonies through pieces of short fiction. Such is the case of Marjorie Agosín, who has edited compilations of memoirs and short stories: *The house of memory: stories by Jewish women writers of Latin America* (1999) and *Taking Root: Narratives of Jewish Women in Latin America* (2002). She has also written fiction: *Las palabras de Miriam* (1999). In the film industry, there are movies such as "Every Time We Say Goodbye" (1986), a story by Moshe Mizrahi that depicts the relationship between a gentile American soldier and a Sephardic Ladino woman who lives in Israel after World War II.

Further Reading

Agosín, Marjorie, ed. *Taking Root: Narratives of Jewish Women in Latin America.* Columbus, OH: Center for International Studies, 2002.

Armistead, S. G., and J. H. Silverman. *The Judeo-Spanish Ballad Chapbooks of Yacob Abraham Yona.* Berkeley, U of California P, 1971.

Gerber, Jane S. *The Jews of Spain: A History of the Sephardic Experience.* New York: Free Press, 1992.

Lévy, Isaac Jack. *And the World Stood Silent: Sephardic Poetry of the Holocaust.* Urbana and Chicago: U of Illinois P, 1989.

Mann, Vivian B., et al. *Convivencia: Jews, Muslims, and Christians in Medieval Spain.* New York: George Braziller in Association with The Jewish Museum, 1992.

Matza, Diane ed., *Sephardic-American Voices: Two Hundred Years of a Literary Legacy.* Waltham, MA: Brandeis UP, 1997.

Menéndez Pidal, Ramón. "El Romancero sefardí; su extraordinario carácter conservador." *The Sephardi Heritage* I (1971): 552–59.

Yolanda Morató

SHAKIR, EVELYN (1938–)   Fiction writer, teacher, and scholar in the field of Arab American literature and women's studies. Daughter of Lebanese immigrants, Shakir grew up in Boston and received her BA from Wellesley College, MA from Harvard, and her PhD from Boston University. She is the author of *Bint Arab: Arab and Arab American Women in the United States* (1997), which comprises the testimonials of a number of Arab and Arab American women interviewed by Shakir. *Bint Arab* depicts a wide range of experiences narrated by women with mainly Lebanese or Palestinian heritage but with different social and religious backgrounds. The stories depicting these experiences start with what Shakir calls the First Wave of **immigration** extending between 1875 and 1925, then move to depict the shift between later generations of immigrants, and finally focus on the Second Wave of Arab immigration that dates from 1945 to the present. Shakir's biggest achievement in this book is giving a narrative voice to an often silenced community of women whose stories are frequently missing from the annals of Arab immigrant history.

The figure of the mother is a recurring thematic reference in Shakir's critical work on Arab American literature. In two articles published by *MELUS*, the first in 1988 and the second in 1991–1992 (volumes 15.4 and 17.3 respectively), Shakir focuses on the mother-son relationship in autobiographies by first-generation Arab Americans writing in the first half of the twentieth century such as Abraham Rihbany and Salom Rizhk. Shakir, in the second article, extends her analysis of the maternal figure by looking at autobiographies by second-generation Arab American male writers such as **Vance Bourjaily**, **William Peter Blatty**, and Eugene Paul Nassar. Highlighting the constant negotiation that they had to undergo between their ethnic background and mainstream American culture, Shakir shows the social constraints and personal dilemmas experienced by this group writing in the second half of the twentieth century.

Other essays by Shakir on Arab American literature and Arab American women have appeared in magazines and journals such as *Al-Jadid, American Transcendental Quarterly,* and *Frontiers.* Books featuring chapters by Shakir include *Crossing the Water: Arabic-Speaking Immigrants to the United States before 1940* (1987) and *New Immigrant Literatures in the United States: A Sourcebook to Our Multicultural Literary Heritage* (1996).

Shakir's short fiction has been published in *Post Gibran: Anthology of New Arab American Writing* (1999). The featured story "Remember Vaughn Monroe?" reveals the generational gap between first-generation Lebanese immigrants and their children, who grow up straddling the world of their parents on the one hand, with its conservative values and arduously preserved customs, and the more liberal American society on the other hand. The manner in which Shakir develops the story through the first-person point of view of the seemingly innocent narrator belies the author's discerning wit in depicting the full scope of an Arab immigrant mentality.

In 1999 Shakir taught at the Lebanese University in Beirut as a Fulbright scholar, and she is currently Associate Professor of English at Bentley College in Massachusetts.

Carol Fadda-Conrey

SHAMSIE, KAMILA (1973–)   Pakistani American novelist, teacher, and journalist. Having recently finished her soon-to-be-published fourth novel, *Broken Verses* (2005), Shamsie, at the age of thirty-one, is widely regarded as one of Pakistan's most accomplished young writers writing in English. In the company of such writers as Nicola Barker, Zadie Smith, and Sarah Waters, Shamsie was hailed in 2000 as one of "21 writers for the 21st century," by Orange Prize Futures, signifying her arrival on the world's literary stage as a powerful new voice. Shamsie is the latest in a line of remarkable literary women in her family beginning with her great-aunt Attia Hosain whose journalism, short stories, and seminal novel, *Sunlight* *on a Broken Column* (1961), paved the way for subsequent generations of South Asian women writing in English. Shamsie's grandmother, Jahanara Habibullah, has published a memoir of her life in Rampur titled *Remembrance of Days Past: Glimpses of a Princely State During the Raj* (2001), and her mother, Muneeza Shamsie, is a writer and editor whose anthology *A Dragonfly in the Sun* (1997) has been regarded as the definitive collection of post-Partition poetry and fiction written in English by Pakistani writers.

Surrounded by books and talk of books Shamsie has launched her literary endeavors in her place of birth, Karachi, a city whose culture, politics, and people form the foundations of all her writing. At the age of nine, an already devoted reader, she decided upon a career in writing and coauthored her first work, a forty-page exposition of dog heaven, at the age of eleven. In the manner of several of her characters, Shamsie left Karachi as a teenager to complete her higher education in America. She received her BA from Hamilton College in New York where she found creative inspiration from her mentor, poet **Agha Shahid Ali**. She went on to complete her MFA at the University of Massachusetts, Amherst. Her first novel, *In the City by the Sea* (1998), which began as a short story written during her undergraduate years at Hamilton College, became the subject of her master's thesis in creative writing. The novel was accepted for publication while she was still at the University of Massachusetts, and it proved to be both a popular and critical success, particularly in the UK and Pakistan.

In the City by the Sea, set in an unnamed Asian city, is narrated by eleven-year-old Hasan who, along with his close-knit and privileged family (his mother is an artist and gallery owner, his father a lawyer, and his uncle is in politics), is living, as Shamsie herself did, under an oppressive military dictatorship. Hasan has the usual concerns of any eleven-year-old boy: He loves cricket and the stars, has a fantastical imagination, and a crush on Zehra, the girl next door. His young life, however, takes unexpected turns when he witnesses another child falling to his death, and his Uncle Salman is arrested and accused of treason. The novel depicts a city, which the reader may assume is a fictionalized Karachi, under house arrest, divided by political upheaval, and it garnered Shamsie a shortlist nomination in 1998 for the Mail on Sunday/John Llewellyn Rhys Award in Britain. In 1999 she received the Prime Minister's Award for Literature in Pakistan for the same work.

Her second novel, *Salt and Saffron* (2000), evolved out of a short story called "Unspeakable Hunger." Although Shamsie roots the complex multigenerational story of the imaged House of Dard-e-Dil in Karachi, she develops a more cosmopolitan feel in *Salt and Saffron* by including references to and episodes in London and America. Aliya, the central character, returns from her American university for her summer holiday to Karachi and finds herself enamored with her traveling companion, Khaleel, a Pakistani American who it seems is from "the wrong side of the city": Liaquatabad, a poor Karachi neighborhood. As in all of her novels, Shamsie depicts the privilege of Karachi's elite and its perpetuation of social divisions based on class distinctions. Aliya's attraction to Khaleel is frowned upon by her upper-class family, and her budding romance with the unsuitable suitor parallels another unlikely match—a shameful family secret involving Aliya's "not-quite twin" Mariam Apa and the family cook, Masood. Aliya resolves to discover the truth amid the fiction of her aunt's doomed love story and her decision to run away with Masood. At the heart of the novel is an examination of family history, its intricacies, fears, legends, and secrets. Aliya, who can trace her ancestry back centuries to the Dard-e-Dil royal family, is the inheritor of a legacy of family stories with a host of colorful characters including the Starched Aunts, the Hairless Nawab, and the cursed "not-quite twins" Akbar, Sulaiman, and Taimur. Above all Aliya is a consummate storyteller and the novel speaks to the importance of the storytelling tradition and the difficulties it encounters when **colonialism**, war, separation, and displacement interrupt the flow of genealogical narrative.

Shamsie's third and most recent novel, *Kartography* (2002), earned her another shortlist nomination for the Mail on Sunday/John Llewellyn Rhys Award. A more ambitious novel than her previous two, *Kartography* is set again in the author's beloved Karachi in the 1980s and 1990s, with flashbacks to the early 1970s, all during times of war, ethnic violence, and betrayal. The main story revolves around soul mates Raheen and Karim, now both in their early twenties, children of privileged Pakistani upbringings by parents who share a close friendship and a past secret. Growing up in a time and place of great political instability, Raheen and Karim, along with their contemporaries, the dashing Zia and the demure Sonia, form an unbreakable bond of friendship that lasts through their school days and into their adult lives as they move around the globe. Raheen, the novel's narrator, touchingly notes that "Karachiites come together in times of crises with attitudes which suggest that no matter what else we are in our lives . . . our real vocation is friendship." The strength of the novel lies in its exploration of the very different ideas and expectations of two generations of Pakistanis. Shamsie has commented that her novels are told from the perspective of the children of the young men and women of the optimistic 1950s and 1960s. *Kartography* depicts the experiences of both Raheen's parents' generation prior to and during the Bangladesh War of 1971 and Raheen's generation, living in a Karachi much different from the one envisioned by the previous generation. During the Bangladesh War, and before either child was born, Raheen's father was engaged to be married to Karim's mother and Karim's father to Raheen's mother. Surprisingly and mysteriously the couples swap partners but remain close. As children Raheen and Karim know little about their parents' pasts or about the secret that binds them. Eventually, an adult Raheen realizes that everyone, including Karim, knows the truth and that it has something to do with her father's past behavior and a devastating choice he once made. Knowledge of this choice drives Karim away from Raheen to London where he indulges in his love of mapmaking and draws maps of Karachi. Raheen knows she must confront her father about his history if there is to be any hope of reconciliation with Karim.

In addition to her fictional writings, Shamsie has authored several journalistic pieces that have appeared in the *Guardian, Prospect,* and *New Statesman.* She writes largely of political, social, cultural, and **identity** issues pertaining to Pakistan and its relationship with India and the world. She is also a visiting assistant professor at Hamilton College where she lives for part of the year and teaches courses in creative writing. Since 1998 she has been involved in a multination writing project called "I Belong," sponsored by the British Council. Shamsie was awarded, in October of 2004, with the British Council 70th Anniversary Cultural Relations Award for her substantial contribution as a mentor and workshop facilitator for the project. Although Shamsie's efforts have been applauded in her homeland of Pakistan, she is now unquestionably recognized internationally as a substantial literary talent and representative voice for a new generation of Pakistanis.

Further Reading

Curtis, Sarah. Review of *In the City by the Sea* by Kamila Shamsie. *Times Literary Supplement* (December 18, 1998): 19.

King, Bruce. Review of *Salt and Saffron* by Kamila Shamsie. *World Literature Today* 74.3 (Summer 2000): 588–89.

Dana Hansen

SHANGE, NTOZAKE (1948–)   African American feminist, poet, playwright, actor, dancer, director, and teacher. Shange's works offer a forthright glimpse into the psychological and social realities of life as a black woman in the latter part of the twentieth century. She has revolutionized American theater with her unique style, known as a choreopoem, a combination of dance, music, mime, and poetry. Shange's most famous choreopoem is her first Broadway hit, *for colored girls who have considered suicide/ when the rainbow is enuf.*

for colored girls started as a coffee shop novelty act and grew into a Broadway success; *for colored girls* opened in the Booth Theater and played a total of 867 performances, 747 of which were on Broadway. When the play was first introduced to New York audiences, it was like nothing they had previously experienced, and they embraced this avant-garde piece that at the time was unique in terms of both form and subject matter. After its long Broadway run, *for colored girls* toured throughout the United States and internationally.

In this genre-defying work, Shange translates the intense personal pain of growing up black and female into art; the series of vignettes combine to form a celebration of blackness and femaleness. The mood of the piece peaks at exhilaration and plummets into despair as the focus shifts from the coming-of-age story of a black girl, to teenage uncertainties, to motherhood, and to adulthood. The music of the 1960s—primarily **blues** and

Motown—provides the soundtrack to the character's experiences and the rhythms for the choreography and dance segments.

In the first vignette, the Lady in Yellow reminisces about her decision to lose her virginity on the day of her high school graduation. She embraces this rite of passage and brags that with her first sexual encounter, she has joined the ranks of the grown-up, adult world.

In the next series of vignettes, the tone shifts. The Lady in Blue shares how she came to love being black through embracing traditionally black art forms, such as music and dance. The cast explodes into the meringue and the bomba to the Afro-Latin music of Willie Colon. In the next vignette, an interruption by the Lady in Red, the mood becomes dark. She speaks about breaking up with her boyfriend by inventorying his inconsiderate behavior and his shortcomings in a letter to him. The mood continues to darken as this segment ends by addressing the topic of acquaintance rape. The women share their common experiences, which are so alike that they blend into a single statement that could represent the experiences of "every woman."

Ntozake Shange. *AP/Wide World Photos.*

In the next section, the taboo topics of abortion and exotic dancing are addressed. The Lady in Blue shares the story of her abortion while the Lady in Purple, calling herself Sechita, describes the degrading and yet empowering work of exotic dancing. Sechita becomes a metaphor for the various roles ascribed to women throughout history; through exotic dancing, Sechita becomes all things to all people as she shifts from naïve, to sage, to slut, to deity. In this well-crafted piece, the burlesque and the divine collide in the most unexpected circumstances.

The next series of vignettes blurs the line between reality and metaphor. In one example of this, a young girl in St. Louis transforms a boy named Toussaint Jones into the man of her dreams—**Toussaint L'Ouverture**. In another piece, a woman chooses the freedom and power acquired through promiscuity to overcome the largest threat in the urban jungle—intimacy.

The women pour over stories of loss; The Lady in Green combines humor and anguish in the story of a breakup gone awry. With bluesy language and a catchy refrain, she inventories the "stuff" of her life that she lost at the end of the relationship. Some of the items are more innocuous, such as clothes and records, while other items, such as her pride and sexual prowess, are vital. The other ladies respond to her story by confabulating a list of common excuses for bad behavior in relationships. The Lady in Blue proclaims that she does not need more apologies; consequently, she will become more like the unapologetic men in her life. She proclaims that both she and her future partners will take responsibility in the relationship rather than perpetually apologize for repeated mistakes.

At this point, *for colored girls* segues into the climax, the saga of Crystal and Beau Willie Brown. Beau Willie is the most developed male character in this piece. Through developing Beau Willie, Shange gives the audience a glimpse into his victimization by a racist society and his poor life choices. Beau Willie is separated from his family and is forbidden by a restraining order to see his children. Despite this fact, Beau Willie obsessively schemes about how he can win back his family and regain his status as the man of the house. In a deranged attempt to reunite his family, Beau Willy defies the restraining order, breaks into the apartment, and dangles the children out of the fifth-story window while demanding that Crystal take him back. Crystal is so distressed that she cannot respond to Beau Willie's threat loudly or quickly enough; Beau Willie drops the children to their deaths.

Crystal's lack of voice and assertion are key to interpreting this piece. At the moment of Willie's assault, she loses her voice; however, with the help and support of the other characters, Crystal regains her ability to speak as she conveys the largest tragedy of her life. As Crystal finds her voice and gives meaning to her experiences, she moves past dysfunction and self-hatred to finding God within herself. The other women mimic this mantra, which becomes a celebration and act of protest against societal oppression.

Many of Shange's other works are thematically similar to *for colored girls*. In 1977, *A Photograph: A Study of Cruelty,* a more conventional work best described as a poem-play, opened to mixed reviews. In 1978, Shange returned to the choreopoem with *Spell #7,* a work about the struggles of black artists. Shange's adaptation of Bertolt Brecht's *Mother Courage and Her Children* premiered in 1980; Shange's version takes place in post–Civil War America, and Mother Courage is an emancipated slave. Later that year, *Boogie Woogie Landscapes,* a dream-motif piece, premiered at the Kennedy Center in Washington, DC. Shange's next major production, *From Okra to Greens/A Different Kinda Love Story: A Play/With Music & Dance,* is adapted from her book of poems, *A Daughter's Geography.*

In 1982 Shange's *Three for a Full Moon and Bocas* and her adaptation of *Educating Rita* were produced in Los Angeles and Atlanta. Also, Shange's autobiographical novel, *Betsy Brown,* was adapted to the stage and was performed at the New York Shakespeare Festival in 1983. In 1987, the unpublished play, *Three Views of Mt. Fuji/A Poem with Music,* premiered at the Lorraine Hansberry Theatre in San Francisco, and in 1989 the play *Daddy Says* was published. Shange's volume of poetry, *The Love Space Demands,* was adapted for the stage in 1998 and was performed at the Painted Bride Art Center in Philadelphia and the Crossroads Theater in New Jersey.

Shange was commissioned to adapt Harriet Beecher Stowe's *Uncle Tom's Cabin* for the stage in 2000, and in 2002 Shange was a Visiting Professor at the theater school at DePaul University and a Visiting Artist at Brown University. During this time, Shange collaborated with South African Ladysmith Black Mambazo on a musical, *Nomathebu,* which played at the Kennedy Center in Washington, DC, and Chicago's Steppenwolf Theater. In 2003, while a Visiting Professor at the University of Florida, Shange completed a new choreopoem, *Lavender Lizards & Lilac Landmines.*

Critics of Shange's work raise concerns about her unconventional approach to theater. Harsh critics contend that Shange has yet to write a real play and claim that her works are ill-structured and unpolished. However, most critics praise Shange for her commitment to experimentation. Shange's unique use of language, for example, has dazzled literary and theater critics alike.

Shange has taught at various institutions across the country including Sonoma State College, Mills College, Rice University, City College of New York, Douglass College, and the University of Houston. She was the Mellon Distinguished Professor of Literature at Rice University, the Artist in Residence at Villanova University, and the Writer in Residence at Maryland College of Art. Her many awards include Obie awards for her adaptation of *Mother Courage and Her Children* and *for colored girls,* the *Los Angeles Times* Book Review Award for Poetry for her collection of plays, *Three Pieces,* and Outer Critics Circle, Audelo, and *Mademoiselle* awards for *for colored girls.* Shange also has been the recipient of Tony, Grammy, and Emmy nominations.

Throughout the span of her nearly thirty-year career, Shange has produced poems, children's books, short stories, cookbooks, novels, dramas, essays, and other pieces; her works present a vision in which blacks struggle together to overcome a racist society. As a significant voice in American Theater, Shange remains on the cutting edge of traditional performance conventions. Her major contribution, the choreopoem, will continue to astonish future audiences. (*See also* African American Drama)

Further Reading

Brown-Gillory, Elizabeth. *Their Place on the Stage: Black Women Playwrights in America.* Westport, CT: Greenwood Press, 1988.

Lester, Neal. *Ntozake Shange: A Critical Study of the Plays.* New York: Garland Publishing, 1995.

"Ntozake Shange." *The Playwright's Art: Conversations with Contemporary American Dramatists.* Ed. Jackson R. Bryer. New Brunswick, NJ: Rutgers UP, 1995. 205–20.

Carrie J. Boden

SHANKAR, S. (1962–)   Indian American novelist, poet, and scholar. S. Shankar's work stands beside other Indian American literature by chronicling both south Indian life and the condition of the migrant. Born in India, Shankar lived in several countries before attending college in Madras. His earliest writing was primarily poems. In 1987 Shankar gained a larger audience with the production of his one-act play *After the Party* and publication of *I as Man*, a collection of poetry. The same year he also moved to America to begin a PhD at the University of Texas at Austin.

Critically, most attention has been focused on his debut novel, *A Map of Where I Live* (1997). Set in Madras and the fictional Lilliput from Jonathan Swift's *Gulliver's Travels*, the novel follows two separate first-person narratives. One narrative is the journal of RK, a Madras native recently returned from the United States who is waiting to enter law school. RK eventually becomes involved with a local political election between a grassroots labor candidate, Shanthamma, and a corrupt politician from the powerful party machine. The election process becomes progressively violent until Shanthamma is murdered. RK becomes increasingly conscious of the economic and political disparity between classes and is forced to examine the nature of "home" and **identity**. The second narrative is told through the voice of Valur Vishweswaran, who is living again in Madras after a journey to Lilliput. Despite his exploitation and mistreatment by leaders of the fascist state, Valur becomes so assimilated that he is willing to undergo a medical experiment that will reduce his body to a miniature statue. Eventually forced to return to Madras, he carries with him the biases of the Lilliputians against his own people. Through political allegory and the juxtaposition of fantasy and reality, *A Map of Where I Live* both indicts society's ills while bringing focus to the various struggles associated with migration and return.

Shankar's more recent work includes a translation of the Tamil play *Water!* (2001); he has coedited the anthology *Crossing into America: The New Literature of Immigration* (2002). His critical book *Textual Traffic: Colonialism, Modernity, and the Economy of the Text* examines works by Joseph Conrad, **Zora Neale Hurston**, V. S. Naipaul, and **Richard Wright**. Shankar currently teaches at the University of Hawaii.

Further Reading

Iyer, Nalini. Review of *A Map of Where I Live*. ARIEL: A Review of International English Literature 29.1 (1998): 271–73.

John, Joseph. Review of *A Map of Where I Live*. World Literature Today 72 (1998): 209–10.

David R. Deborde

SHAPIRO, ALAN (1952–)   Jewish American poet, essayist, book reviewer, writer of memoirs, translator, editor, and professor of English and creative writing at the University of North Carolina, Chapel Hill, who has held prior academic posts at noteworthy institutions such as

Northwestern University and Stanford University. He has received numerous awards, including the Lila Wallace/*Reader's Digest* Award, nominations for National Book Critic awards, a writing fellowship from the Open Society Institute of New York, a Guggenheim Fellowship, and two National Endowment for the Arts Fellowships. His poetry, essays, and reviews have appeared in numerous journals and newspapers, such as *The Paris Review, Chicago Review, Critical Inquiry, TriQuarterly*, and the *Christian Science Monitor.*

An eloquent critic and explicator of his works, Shapiro has often spoken of the role his ethnicity has played in his creative process, as in a 2002 interview with the *Atlantic Unbound*:

> The **identity** of the Jewish-American poet, say, or of an American poet of any racial or ethnic stripe, it seems to me, adheres in the hyphen. My identity is essentially American because of its impurity, its mongrel status— the fact that it's pieced together from a wide variety of histories. . . . I want to be able to devise a way of writing that can make a place for all those influences. (McHenry, "Aesthetics of Inadequacy")

Shapiro cites among his diverse formative experiences reading the Torah, hearing Yiddish as a child, being raised in a conservative Jewish house-hold, attending Hebrew school, living through the Cuban Missile Crisis and Vietnam, and being schooled in the "Classical and Christian literary traditions—traditions that are themselves amalgams of different languages, different conquered and conquering cultures, city-states, empires."

Although many of Shapiro's poetic works, autobiographical in nature, deal with his Jewish cultural influences, *The Last Happy Occasion* (1996), nominated for a National Book Critics Circle Award, specifically considers his Jewish cultural heritage and how it has influenced his work. *The Last Happy Occasion* "moves continually back and forth between poetry and per-sonal experience, examining as concretely as possible how certain poems taught [him] over time to read [his] own and other people's lives, and how those lives, in turn, have shaped [his] understanding of certain poems." Here Shapiro describes his "awkward reverence" of Judaism's "ritual observances, renunciations and restrictions" that, as a child, were "dead forms invented by dead people to be mechanically, superficially, and hypo-critically followed by the living." He relays how he came to "respect" the impulse for communal worship and yearn for the consolations . . . ritual observances have brought to others." As he brings the book to a close, Shaprio tells about his son's *bris*, his family's tradition of telling stories, and his own homecoming—Shapiro's return to America, to his family, and to Jewish culture.

Two of Shapiro's recent works deal with the tragic loss of siblings. *Vigil* (1997), a memoir, chronicles his sister's death of breast cancer at forty-nine. His poetry collection *Song and Dance* (2002) memorializes his brother's death of brain cancer. Shapiro's early works consist of *After the Digging*

(1981), containing two historical narratives—one of the nineteenth-century Irish potato famine and the other of seventeenth-century American Puritans—and *The Courtesy* (1983), a collection of autobiographical lyric poems. His other poetry collections include *Happy Hour* (1987), which was awarded the William Carlos Williams Award by the Poetry Society of America, *Covenant* (1991), *Mixed Company* (1996), and *The Dead Alive and Busy* (2002), for which he received the Kingsley Tufts Poetry Award.

Shapiro has also written many essays and reviews and authored a collection of literary criticism, *In Praise of the Impure: Poetry and the Ethnical Imaginations: Essays 1980–1991* (1993). There he calls the imagination the "life-redeeming agent of impurity," at odds with "the human impulse for the pure, the unambiguous, the perfectly controlled." Shapiro argues that poetry enacts "ethical play," turning what is "most difficult to know" into "an ethical problem which we then attempt to solve." According to Shapiro, poems, narrative forms, are both "connected with implicit social, psychological, and linguistic actions" and are "the elegiac gifts of human consciousness."

His current projects include translations of Greek tragedy for an ongoing series published by Oxford University Press.

Further Reading

McHenry, Eric. "An Aesthetics of Inadequacy: Interview with Alan Shapiro."
Atlantic Unbound: The Atlantic Monthly Online (May 30, 2002), http://
www.theatlantic.com/unbound/interviews/int2002-05–30.htm.

Blake G. Hobby

SHAPIRO, DAVID (1947–) Jewish American poet, art critic, and violinist. David Shapiro was born January 2, 1947, in Newark, New Jersey, to Irving and Fraida Shapiro. His father was a physician and his mother a singer and teacher. Growing up, Shapiro was surrounded by poetry and music, which influenced his career tremendously. In 1970 Shapiro married Lindsay Stamm, who is a professor of architecture. They have one son, Daniel. Shapiro attended Clare College, Cambridge University, and Columbia University, where he received his PhD with distinction in 1973. He currently resides in New York City.

Shapiro has had a long and distinguished career. He has taught at Columbia University, William Paterson College, and Cooper Union. Shapiro is also a professional violinist, and he has played with the New Jersey Symphony. He has also worked as an Editorial Associate for *The New Yorker* and for *Art News,* and he has collaborated on architectural projects with architect John Hejduk. Shapiro has worked as a curator of poetry shows and is a specialist in teaching poetry to children for the New Jersey and the New York Council of Arts. He has authored several works of literary criticism, such as *John Ashbery: An Introduction to the Poetry* (1979), and works of art criticism, such as *Jim Dine: Painting What One Is* (1981). Shapiro is also a distinguished poet and the recipient of several awards including the

Gotham Book Mart Avant Garde Poetry Award in 1962, the Merrill Foundation Fellowship in 1967, and the Creative Artists in Public Service Award for Poetry in 1974.

One of Shapiro's earlier volumes of poetry, *January: A Book of Poems* (1965), contains poems that were written during his teens. Many of these poems contain imagery of natural elements, such as the wind, ocean, birds, and changing seasons. Shapiro's musical influence is also apparent in several of these poems, such as "Dying to Music," and "Five Songs." There are also many poems that discuss concerns and issues of family, such as "Poem for Berele Chagy," which is an emotional two-stanza poem about the death of Shapiro's grandfather in 1954. There are also four poems in this volume titled "Canticle," which is defined as a song whose words are taken from a biblical text. The first poem appearing in the volume is "Canticle" and is written in three parts, each concerned with some element of nature: clouds, crickets, and red birds. The second canticle poem dealing with lost love is "Canticle as Grieving," and this poem is written in two parts. The third "Canticle" is written in four parts and is an intense poem composed of several natural elements: rocks, shores, fire, grasshoppers, birds, and whirlwinds. The most complicated of the canticle poems is the fourth, which is written in thirty-one two-lined stanzas and includes various ideas about religion and love.

Some of Shapiro's later volumes of poetry include *Lateness: A Book of Poems* (1977), *To An Idea: A Book of Poems* (1984), and *House (Blown Apart): A Book of Poems* (1988). One of his more recent volumes, *After a Lost Original: A Book of Poems* (1994), utilizes dream-like imagery, personification, and metaphor in a manner that adds flare and complexity to language. Shapiro includes his own version of the Lord's Prayer that exemplifies his linguistic sensitivity and examines the use of liturgical language. Shapiro's ongoing engagement with nature is apparent in his poem "The Seasons," which was written about Jasper John's five-painting series titled "The Seasons." Shapiro's most recent volume, *A Burning Interior: New Poems* (2002), contains poems concerned with religious material, such as "A Cross for Joseph," which takes a quizzical, yet reverent approach to Christian tradition and the differing interpretations of Jesus' teachings. Shapiro also includes an elegy for his friend, architect John Hejduk, as the opening sequence. Other poems offer insightful psychological explorations, such as "Winter Work," which discusses the loyalty of a dog compared to that of his master, and "A Family Council," which are actual minutes from Shapiro's family meetings when he was seven years old. Two other poems, collaborated with his son, "God's Shadow" and "Black Silk," evaluate the child's sense of nature, society, and religion as he grows and changes.

A prolific writer, Shapiro continues to write poetry, produce scholarly works, and contribute essays to various periodicals.

Further Reading

Fink, Thomas. *The Poetry of David Shapiro*. Rutherford, NJ: Fairleigh Dickinson UP, 1993.

———. "Tracing David Shapiro's 'The Seasons'." *Contemporary Literature* 37.3
  (1996): 416.

Sarah Delarco

SHAPIRO, KARL (1913–2000) Jewish American poet, critic, and
editor. From the outset of his long career, Karl Shapiro received critical
acclaim for his poetry, which frequently adopts as its theme the tensions
between the poet's Jewish heritage and his home in the American South.
  V-Letter and Other Poems (1944) won Shapiro the Pulitzer Prize, which in
turn led to his being offered the position of Poetry Consultant at the
Library of Congress and an associate professorship at Johns Hopkins University in his native Baltimore. His prior efforts were less auspicious but
still brought Shapiro success. A first, privately printed collection of poetry,
Poems (1935), earned him a scholarship to Johns Hopkins, though it was
otherwise unremarkable; he enrolled in 1937 but left without a degree in
1939. Shapiro's first major book, *Person, Place, and Thing* (1942), won *Poetry*
magazine's Levinson Prize and the praise of such leading critics as Allen
Tate and Louise Bogan.
  But *V-Letter* truly established Shapiro's critical reputation, marking him
especially as a talented writer of war poetry. Drafted into the Army in 1941,
Shapiro served in New Guinea. The experience of wartime service provided the basis of the collection, as the title suggests; servicemen writing
home used the V-Mail system of the United States Armed Forces. "The
Leg," for example, ponders the relation between an amputated leg and the
rest of the body; "Full Moon: New Guinea" captures the ordeal of waiting
out bombing raids; and the speaker in "The Gun" addresses his weapon
and assumes moral responsibility for the violence it enacts. (**Howard Nemerov**, another Jewish American poet writing about the Second World War,
offers an interesting point of comparison.)
  Shapiro's military service was a productive creative period. In addition
to *Person, Place, and Thing* and *V-Letter*, he published *The Place of Love* (his
second book, printed privately in 1942) and *Essay on Rime* (1945), a collection of literary criticism in verse (the title of which makes reference to Alexander Pope's *An Essay on Criticism*). In the latter volume, Shapiro attacks
the state of contemporary poetry and criticism, as he would also do in *In
Defense of Ignorance* (1960), a volume of prose essays. In these works, Shapiro places himself in opposition to the high modernist tradition of T. S.
Eliot and Ezra Pound and defends the importance of the personal voice in
poetry. Shapiro's own poems, so often deeply interested in the details of the
lives of ordinary individuals, embody the values he promoted in his critical
writing.
  In addition to poetry about war, *V-Letter* also includes poems such as
"Shylock," which takes its epigraph from Shakespeare's *The Merchant of
Venice*, and "Jew," a sonnet that laments the fate of Jews everywhere.
Although he was not particularly religious, Shapiro's middle-class Jewish

upbringing informed much of his poetry. "University," for instance, from *Person, Place, and Thing,* describes the de facto segregation of American colleges.

These concerns become most explicit in two later collections, *Trial of a Poet* (1947) and *Poems of a Jew* (1958). *Trial of a Poet* takes as one of its subjects the trial for treason of Ezra Pound, whose **anti-Semitism** and engagement with fascist politics Shapiro publicly denounced when he served as a judge for the Bollingen Prize in 1948. Shapiro voted against awarding the prize to Pound; the committee, which included among others T. S. Eliot and W. H. Auden, nonetheless selected Pound as the winner. Shapiro later won the Bollingen Prize himself, sharing it in 1969 with **John Berryman**.

Poems of a Jew makes reference to a wide range of aspects of Jewish culture, from the Hebrew alphabet to biblical characters to the **Holocaust** and the creation of Israel. In poems such as "Teasing the Nuns" and "The Crucifix in the Filing Cabinet," moreover, Shapiro focuses on the experience of being Jewish in a predominantly Christian culture. "The First Time" recounts a young man's first sexual experience and reveals the intrusion of casual anti-Semitism into even the most intimate of encounters. At once personal and public, these poems employ the details of lived experience to record the difficulty and anxiety associated with contact between Jewish and non-Jewish Americans. This theme places Shapiro at the heart of a tradition of Jewish American poetry. He also deserves to be read in comparison to the noted Jewish Canadian poet A. M. Klein.

Shapiro's other works include *The Bourgeois Poet* (1964), *White-Haired Lover* (1968), *Adult Bookstore* (1976), *Love and War, Art and God* (1984), *Adam and Eve* (1986), and *The Old Horsefly* (1992), as well as two volumes of selected poems and one volume of collected poems. Much of this poetry pursues and develops the themes of the earlier works.

Among his other achievements, Shapiro edited *Poetry* magazine from 1950 to 1956 and *Prairie Schooner* from 1956 to 1966, while he was teaching at the University of Nebraska. He also taught at other universities, including the University of Illinois at Chicago and the University of California, Davis. Shapiro also wrote his autobiography and was well regarded as a public critic. (*See also* Jewish American Poetry)

Further Reading

Reino, Joseph. *Karl Shapiro.* Boston: Twayne, 1981.

Nicholas Bradley

SHAW, IRWIN (1913-1984)   Jewish American novelist, short story writer, dramatist, and screenwriter. Over the course of his long and consistently productive career, Irwin Shaw was praised for the seriousness of intention, the complexity of conception, and the technical proficiency that he brought to his work. Yet, his critical reputation has suffered because, at the height of his career, the popularity of his work—and especially of the film and television adaptations of his work—created the impression that he had sold out. Moreover, in an era marked by wild formal experimentation, his more subtle but nonetheless meaningful manipulations of narrative elements were hardly noticed.

Born in 1913 in New York City, Shaw received a public-school education and then enrolled in Brooklyn College during the depths of the Great Depression. At a time when political radicalism was widespread, especially among artists and intellectuals, and when literary work was judged by its social and political relevancy, Shaw began his career as a writer of dramas in the "proletarian" mode, most notably *Bury the Dead* (1936). In this same period, he began establishing himself as a writer of short stories, contributing to many leading periodicals, including the *New Yorker* with which he had a long relationship. Indeed, almost to the end of his life, Shaw would continue to write stories of considerable merit, and even those critics who have been inclined to denigrate his novels have generally found much to praise in his short fiction. His *Short Stories: Five Decades* (1978) remains a landmark in the history of the genre, and his story "The Girls in Their Summer Dresses" is still one of the most frequently anthologized American short stories.

Likewise, Shaw's first novel, *The Young Lions* (1948), remains one of the major novels about World War II. Treating the stories of three soldiers—two Americans (one a liberal White Anglo-Saxon Protestant and the other Jewish) and one German—the novel explores the social and political complexities just under the surfaces of the public attitudes toward the war on each side. The climax of the novel may be its major flaw, for there is too much disproportion in the way that the three soldiers coincidentally encounter each other in moments that are nonetheless charged with great thematic significance. Still, although Shaw's novel does not quite achieve the sustained intensity and the philosophical breadth of **Norman Mailer**'s *The Naked and the Dead*, it is clearly a much more serious attempt to understand the war than, say, **Herman Wouk**'s *The Winds of War*.

Shaw's second novel, *The Troubled Air* (1950), is concerned with communist witch hunts in the radio industry. Interestingly, the mixed reception of this novel led Shaw to emigrate to France, where he lived for most of the rest of his life. *Lucy Crown* (1956) treats a woman's adultery. *Two Weeks in Another Town* (1960) and *Evening in Byzantium* (1973) provide an insider's view of the movie industry by way of a film location in Italy and the Cannes Film Festival. *Voices of a Summer Day* (1965) presents a character study of an emotionally isolated middle-aged man, and it can be viewed as a corollary to *Lucy Crown*. Through the saga of a representative family, *Rich Man, Poor Man* (1970) and its sequel *Beggerman, Thief* (1977) chronicle the immigrants' gradual **assimilation** into the mainstream of American life. *Nightwork* (1975) and *The Top of the Hill* (1979) depict the lives of the affluent and of the rogues who are drawn to the exclusive resorts of Europe. Finally, in *Bread upon the Waters* (1981) and *Acceptable Losses* (1982), contemporary versions of the morality tale and the meditation on mortality emerge from engagingly told but wholly compelling stories. Indeed, several critics have suggested that these last two novels are so remarkable in their execution that they may provide the basis for a broader reevaluation of Shaw's achievement as a novelist.

Further Reading

Giles, James R. *Irwin Shaw.* Boston: Twayne, 1983.

———. *Irwin Shaw: A Study of the Short Fiction.* Boston: Twayne, 1991.

———. "Irwin Shaw's Original Prologue to *The Young Lions. Resources for American Literary Study* 11 (Spring 1981): 115–19.

Milic, Louis T. "Naming in Shaw's *The Young Lions.*" *Style* 23 (Spring 1989): 113–23.

Moorhead, Michael. "Hemingway's 'The Short Life of Francis Macomber' and Shaw's 'The Deputy Sheriff'." *Explicator* 44 (Winter 1986): 42–43.

Reynolds, Fred. "Irwin Shaw's 'The Eighty-Year Run'." *Explicator* 49 (Winter 1991): 121–23.

Martin Kich

SHEA, SUZANNE STREMPEK (1958–) Polish American novelist, memoirist, and journalist. Suzanne Strempek Shea is concerned with women's self-discovery within small, Polish American, Massachusetts communities and writes in her detail-oriented style how these women find their own paths apart from the traditional, and apart from the American mainstream. Her works include the novels *Selling the Lite of Heaven* (1994), *Hoopi Shoopi Donna* (1996), *Lily of the Valley* (1999), and *Around Again* (2001) and the memoir *Songs from a Lead-lined Room: Notes—High and Low—from My Journey through Breast Cancer and Radiation* (2002). Before turning to novel writing, she was a reporter for the *Springfield Union-News* of Massachusetts and the *Providence Journal* of Road Island.

Shea's first novel, *Selling the Lite of Heaven,* is about a thirty-two-year-old unnamed narrator living at home with her parents in a Polish Catholic neighborhood, whose husband-to-be leaves her to become a priest. Because of this bizarre situation, the narrator, who considers herself plain, is shy, and often unquestioning, goes through a process of self-discovery as she tries to sell her engagement ring, meeting all types of prospective buyers, some humorous and some loathsome. In the novel, we see two generations of Polish Americans: the immigrants and those born in the United States. For the narrator, following her mother's old traditions makes her a social oddity. Although late in coming, the narrator is finding her place in this world over the course of the novel. At points, *Selling the Lite of Heaven* has a chance to become cliché, but the twists and turns of the plot allow the novel, like its narrator, to keep dignity.

The 2002 memoir, *Songs from a Lead-lined Room: Notes—High and Low—from My Journey through Breast Cancer and Radiation,* is Shea's vivid account of her ordeal with a cancer diagnosis and the ensuing treatment. Shea is able to find humor in the worst of places, and her memoir offers encouragement for those who go through similar ordeals. While documenting every detail, from the material to the emotional, Shea knows that she was one of the lucky ones, and that her original diagnosis could have been much worse. Shea feels fortunate, showing the powerful help of family and friends. At the end of her memoir, she lists books she found helpful in getting her through her ordeal. In addition, Shea found journal writing very helpful, the entries of which evolved into this memoir. Shea also uses her book to bring about awareness of Molly Bish, a sixteen-year-old lifeguard who was abducted at about the same time of Shea's struggle. The memoir is powerful work of encouragement in getting through a horrible situation. (*See also* Polish American Novel)

Further Reading

Tempska, Urszula. "From (Ethnic) Mama's Girl to Her Own (New Ethnic) Woman: Gender and Ethnicity in Suzanne Strempek Shea's *Selling the Lite of Heaven.*" *Something of My Very Own to Say: American Women Writers of Polish Descent.* Ed. Thomas S. Gladsky and Rita Holmes Gladsky. Boulder, CO: East European Monographs, 1998. 287–304.

Stephen Oravec

SHEPHERD, REGINALD (1963–)   African American poet. Reginald Shepherd was born in New York City and grew up in poverty in the Bronx. At fifteen, after the death of his mother, he moved to Macon, Georgia. He earned a BA at Bennington College and MFA degrees from Brown University and the University of Iowa. Shepherd has published four books of poetry—*Some Are Drowning* (1994), which won the 1993 Associated Writing Programs' Award Series in Poetry, *Angel, Interrupted* (1996), *Wrong* (1999), and *Otherhood* (2003)—and has edited *The Iowa Anthology of New American Poetries* (2004). He has also published essays on literary and cultural topics in journals and anthologies. Among many honors, Shepherd has received an NEA fellowship and a "Discovery"/*The Nation* award.

With four books in less than ten years, Reginald Shepherd is one of the more prolific poets of his generation. The books display a remarkable consistency in quality, representing one of contemporary poetry's most intense and distinctive voices. His is a richly musical, rhythmically complex verse that occasionally ventures into experimentalism. His poems, which rely on thought as much as feeling, strive, perhaps more than any other contemporary poet's, to achieve the beautiful in the face of the world's ugliness.

Given how many lists appear in his poetry, one could call Shepherd's poems collections of treasures, though some of these treasures are sources of pain as well as pleasure. There are numerous references to high culture and popular culture, with the poems traveling with ease, for example, between opera and nightclubs. They consider the physical world of geology and flowers and the human world of myth and history, pitting the demands and fleeting joys of reality against the consoling but often reproachful shadows of imagination. "World," from *Wrong,* interweaves the vagaries of dream and the depredations of the world the speaker (like all of us) won't survive. Shepherd's inclusiveness finds its most important figure in that of the city, particularly Chicago, where he lived for most of the 1990s. The city in these poems serves as a great theater of the human drama, where both historical and personal struggles play out.

A major theme in Shepherd's work is the intersection of homosexuality and **race** relations, where questions of desire and questions of **identity** blend into and wrestle with one another, and the desired other is also an antagonist. Shepherd's poems also frequently juxtapose the contemporary world and the world of classical antiquity, exposing both their continuities and their ruptures. Another important problem his poems take up is that of poetry itself. Shepherd displays, in poems such as "Semantics at 4 P.M.," from *Otherhood*, a keen awareness of both the sublime potential of poetry and its utter ineffectiveness against the ravages of death and destruction. Such considerations find a formal expression in Shepherd's persistent use of parenthesis. Through the interruptions of parenthesis, thought in Shepherd's poetry constantly turns back upon itself and questions itself.

Reginald Shepherd is a serious poet, one who refuses the pervasive irony with which many contemporary poets excuse themselves, but his poetry is never sanctimonious or smug. His poetry seeks to face and respond to the problems and contradictions of our day, while remaining painfully aware of poetry's limits. The pathos of this tension is well expressed in "A Plague for Kit Marlowe," from *Angel, Interrupted*, which takes the occasion of the AIDS epidemic to meditate on the relationship between art and death and in which the speaker expresses both his distrust of the beautiful and his continuing devotion to it. Against these terrible limits, Shepherd offers his formidable poetry.

Further Reading

Boxwell, David. "Reginald Shepherd." *Contemporary Gay American Poets and Playwrights: An A-to-Z Guide.* Ed. Emmanuel S. Nelson. Westport, CT: Greenwood Press, 2003: 398–405.

Bruhm, Steven. *Reflecting: A Queer Aesthetic.* Minneapolis: U of Minnesota P, 2001. 176–78.

Martin, Robert K. *The Homosexual Tradition in American Poetry: An Expanded Edition.* Iowa City: U of Iowa P, 1998: 270–73.

Rowell, Charles H. "An Interview with Reginald Shepherd." *Callaloo* 21.2 (Spring 1998): 290–307.

Lawrence L. White

SHERMAN, MARTIN (1938–)   Jewish American gay dramatist. Martin Sherman has spent much of his adult life residing abroad, and he has become known for exploring the inner life of the outsider. His plays have been produced in over forty-five countries and have garnered numerous awards. Sherman was born in Philadelphia, attended Boston University, and moved to New York City to establish himself as a playwright.

Sherman fell in love with England early on and relocated to London shortly after his **Holocaust** drama, *Bent* (1979), became a sensation.

Set in Berlin and Dachau during 1934–36, *Bent* was the first Holocaust drama to foreground the persecution of homosexuals by the Third Reich. Unapologetic in its realistic portrayal of love between men at a time when gay stereotypes were the norm, the play's opening scene in Max and Rudy's apartment after a night of excessive partying could be a slice of life from late-1970s New York. Only this is the Night of the Long Knives, when Adolf Hitler and his supporters have killed openly gay Nazi Party chief commander Ernst Röhm and are hunting down his associates. Max has unknowingly picked up Röhm's boyfriend, the strapping young, blond military man Wolfgang Granz. Tipped off by the married drag queen Greta, who performs at a local bar, the Gestapo arrives at the apartment to kill Wolf. Max and Rudy flee the scene and attempt to cross the border on foot, but they are caught and placed on a train to Dachau. In transit, Max encounters a younger man, Horst, who wears a pink triangle and explains that queers are the lowest class in the concentration camp. In order to save himself, Max denies his **identity** and is forced to kill Rudy, whom the guards have severely beaten.

The second act takes place in a rock quarry at Dachau. Although he is not Jewish, Max has bargained for a yellow star instead of a pink triangle by having sex with a dead girl in front of the guards. He gets Horst assigned to the same rock-moving duty so they can keep each other company. In a provocative yet tender scene, Max and Horst "make love" while moving rocks—bringing each other to climax verbally without touching or looking at one another directly. When they discover that Max has provided him with medicine, the guards kill Horst. After placing Horst's body in a ditch, Max finally accepts his identity and his ability to love; he dons Horst's pink triangle and walks into an electrified fence. With this play, Sherman thrilled audiences on both sides of the Atlantic and earned the Drama Critics Circle Award, the Dramatist Guild's Hull-Warriner Award and a Tony nomination. In 1997, *Bent* became a feature film, for which Sherman wrote the screenplay.

Sherman also found success with other well-researched period dramas. *When She Danced* (1985) portrays the strained marriage between the famous dancer Isadora Duncan and a much younger Russian poet. Mourning the loss of her drowned children and suffering from poverty and prejudice against her socialist views, Isadora struggles to open a European dancing school. *A Madhouse in Goa* (1989, pub. 1996) compares two periods in gay American history—the 1960s and 1990—which are separated by the Stonewall Riot and AIDS. *Rose* (1999) recounts a life that was lived from the inside but remembered from the outside, mostly through confusing lived reality with images from movies. Based on Sherman's Jewish grandmother—Rose was born in a Russian village during the Bolshevik Revolution, survived a Warsaw ghetto, immigrated to Atlantic City, and settled in warmer climates—the play examines several aspects of her life, including her coming to terms with her grandson's homosexuality. The play, which originally starred Olympia Dukakis, was nominated for a Laurence Olivier Theatre Award for Best New Play.

Sherman's recent work includes a stage adaptation of E. M. Forster's *A Passage to India* and a new version of a Luigi Pirandello play, *Absolutely! {perhaps}*, which was directed by Franco Zeffirelli in London and nominated for the 2004 Olivier Award for Best Revival. Sherman received a 2004 Tony nomination for Best Book of a Musical for *The Boy from Oz*, which was based on the life of Australian songwriter and cabaret performer Peter Allen and starred Hugh Jackman. (*See also* Jewish American Theater)

Further Reading

Clum, John M. *Still Acting Gay: Male Homosexuality in Modern Drama.* New York: St. Martin's Griffin, 2000 [orig. pub. 1992].

Shackelford, Dean. "Martin Sherman." *Contemporary Gay American Poets and Playwrights: An A-to-Z Guide.* Ed. Emmanuel S. Nelson. Westport, CT: Greenwood Press, 2003. 406–11.

Kenneth J. Cerniglia

SHOCKLEY, ANN ALLEN (1927–)   African American compiler, novelist, and short story writer. Ann Allen Shockley's place in African American literature rests on a series of firsts: She compiled and published the first directory of African American authors and the first handbook for black librarians; she published the first African American novel about an interracial lesbian relationship, the first short story collection on black and white lesbian relationships, and the first literary anthology of African American women writers from 1746 to 1933. These firsts come in the later stages of her writing career that began decades earlier, in 1945, with short stories published in the *Louisville Defender* in Louisville, Kentucky, her birthplace, and in *Fisk University Herald*, the student newspaper of her alma mater, Fisk University.

Shockley's pioneering reference books, *Living Black American Authors: A Biographical Directory* (1973) and *Handbook of Black Librarianship* (1977), met the needs of an expanding body of black writers and literary scholars in the 1970s who sought information on black American authors. *Living Black American Authors* includes biographical information omitted from standard reference books and alphabetically arranges its entries from Russell Adams to Andrew Sturgeon Nash Young. Most entries include facts about the authors' birth, education, family, professional experience, memberships, awards, publications, and mailing addresses. *Handbook of Black Librarianship*, coauthored with E. J. Josey, identifies for librarians those materials essential to establishing special collections of African American writings and offers pointers on how to maintain those collections. These two books, more than any others, were indispensable references for black scholars and for the preservation of African American library holdings.

Shockley filled another gap in black literature with her explicit depiction of the black lesbian in *Loving Her* (1978). A pioneer novel, *Loving Her* illuminates the identity struggles of Renay Davis, a black lesbian, forced into a traditional marriage after her schoolmate rapes and impregnates her at senior prom. She leaves her abusive, alcoholic husband, and she and her daughter flee to the home of Terry Bluvard, a white lesbian writer and Renay's lover. Shockley's detractors castigated her for writing this novel on a subject that the black community considered taboo. Her supporters praised the novel as a political statement validating the existence of black lesbians and as an affirmation of the black lesbian's triple vulnerability as a black, a woman, and a lesbian. Despite mixed reviews, the novel has been reprinted with Naiad Press (1987) and Northeastern University Press (1997).

The Black and White of It (1980) continues the theme of lesbian self-identity. Considered the first collection of short stories about lesbians written by a black woman, the collection reiterates the difficulties black women encounter in same-sex relationships and in defining themselves in a heterosexual environment. The stories address themes of denial, family rejection, infidelity, and jealousy.

Say Jesus and Come to Me (1982), Shockley's second novel, is the author's boldest statement against homophobia in the black Christian church. Reverend Myrtle Black, the lesbian minister-protagonist, parodies the self-serving, fornicating black male preacher and exposes the moral laxity and hypocrisy of black leaders dissembling goodness. Shockley's three works on lesbianism paved the way for younger writers such as **Barbara Smith**, **Cheryl Clarke**, and Raymina Y. Mayes to come out of the closet with their lesbian fiction, poetry, and essays.

Afro-American Women Writers 1746–1933: An Anthology and Critical Guide (1988) chronologically documents African American women writers from Lucy Terry to **Nella Larsen**. A very useful sourcebook on early black women writers, it includes a biography and bibliography for each writer and introduces important sociohistorical information to each period discussed.

Driven by social consciousness, a moral imperative, and a need to plug the gaps in black literature, Shockley wrote on weekends and worked during the week as assistant librarian at Delaware State College (1959–60), as curator of Negro Collection at University of Maryland, Eastern Shore (1960–69), and as librarian and head of Special Collections at Fisk University (1969–98). Her writing also came in spurts as she reared two children, now grown. Among her many awards, she has received Outlook Award for Outstanding Pioneering Contributions to Lesbian and Gay Writers (1990) and the American Library Association Black Caucus Achievement Award for Extraordinary Achievement in Professional Activities (2000). Shockley retired from Fisk University in 1998, and she still types her short stories with a manual typewriter. (*See also* African American Lesbian Literature)

Further Reading

Bogus, Sdiane Adams. "Theme and Portraiture in the Fiction of Ann Allen Shockley." Diss., Miami University, 1988.

Dandridge, Rita B. *Ann Allen Shockley: An Annotated Primary and Secondary Bibliography.* Westport, CT: Greenwood, 1987.

Rita B. Dandridge

SHOLEVAR, BAHMAN (1941–)   Iranian American novelist, poet, and psychiatrist. Sholevar began publishing his writing as an adolescent and distinguished himself as an adult in Iran as a literary translator. His translations into Persian include William Faulkner's *The Sound and the Fury* (1959) and T. S. Eliot's *The Waste Land* (1964). He published his first volume of poetry, *Epic of Life, Epic of Death,* in 1960 in Iran. Sholevar finished writing *The Night's Journey* in 1961 (English translation by the author was published in the United States in 1973), but was not granted a permit to publish it by the Iranian government until 1967 when the author was on a diplomatic mission in Europe. After political difficulties resulted from the publication of *The Night's Journey,* Sholevar fled Europe and came to the United States where he attended medical school.

The dominant themes in Sholevar's writing—whether poetry or prose—are displacement, cultural wanderlust, and a kind of uprootedness. Like many of his contemporaries, Sholevar's writing expresses a kind of bifurcation between his Iranian heritage and upbringing and a Western sensibility that is the result of his education and his many years of residence in the United States. Because of Sholevar's experience in translation, he writes in both English and Persian and has even adopted an American idiomatic language in his work. His writing also reflects his interest in experimenting with form and style. In his short story "The Coming of the Messiah" (published with *The Night's Journey* in 1973), for example, Sholevar uses very little punctuation. Although he capitalizes letters, he does not use periods to indicate sentence endings. More than other Iranian immigrant writers of his generation, Sholevar has not made Iran the singular focus of his work. He has adapted to the literary and cultural landscape of American society, while also portraying his alienation and exile as not solely the function of his own personal **immigration** experience, but as a condition of the postmodern period. He does, however, like other Iranian immigrant writers of his generation, include his own biography in his work. Although his fictional works are not autobiographical, it is clear that some of his characters are based on the lives and experiences of people like him who came to this country during the reign of Mohammad Reza Shah and who were at odds with that government and its policies and also feel a cynicism about the Islamic Republic. The rootlessness expressed in his writing is also a reflection of the large number of professional activities he has engaged in since his arrival in the United States. In addition to his literary activities as a translator and literary critic, he has also worked as a physician, psychiatrist, political activist, television commentator, and a professor of literature. He is a practicing psychiatrist and professor of psychiatry at Thomas Jefferson University in Philadelphia and authored *The Creative Process: A Psychoanalytic Discussion* with William G. Niederland (1982).

Sholevar is among the few early Iranian immigrant writers who have published both poetry and prose in English. His poetry collections include: *Making Connections: Poems of Exile* (1979); *The Angel with Bush-Baby Eyes and the Love Song of Achilles* (1982); *Odysseus' Homecoming and the New Adam: Poems of Renewal* (1982); and *Rooted in Volcanic Ashes* (1987). Sholevar's most recent publication is *Dead Reckoning* (1992), which again deals with the Iranian immigrant experience but this time from the perspective of the post-1979 revolutionary period. Sholevar uses narrative techniques and stylistic devices to present the personality of a "permanent alien" exiled from his nation and his culture. Torn between the legacy of his dead relatives and the decadence of his fellow immigrant relatives, Farhang Shadzad, an Iranian in Iowa, spends a weekend debating whether to return to Iran for his mother's funeral. His mother, like his father fourteen years earlier, has died on the birthday of their middle son, a leftist revolutionary who was tortured and executed by the Savak, the secret police trained by the U.S. CIA. The protagonist's Uncle J., a wealthy man and former cabinet minister in the Shah's government, and his Americanized older brother Cyrus urge him not to return to Iran. He nevertheless decides to go back and take whatever risks await him because the gesture will be what he considers the first authentic existential experience of his life. Once back in Iran, Farhang discovers tyranny has simply exchanged Western clothing for fundamentalist garb, and that now, as in the Shah's regime, money pushes buttons. (*See also* Iranian American Literature)

Further Reading

Naficy, Hamid. "The Poetics and Practice of Iranian Nostalgia in Exile." *Diaspora* 1.3 (1991): 285–302.

Rahimieh, Nasrin. "The Quince-Orange Tree, or Iranian Writers in Exile." *World Literature Today* 66.1 (Winter 1992): 39–42.

Persis Karim

SHULMAN, ALIX KATES (1932–) American Jewish novelist, memoirist, and feminist activist. Prominent after 1969 as a founder of the second wave of American **feminism** (the social movement dubbed "women's liberation" by the media), Shulman wrote a first novel that has endured as a classic account of coming to feminist consciousness. Equally well known for a "Marriage Agreement"(published in the inaugural issue of *Ms.* magazine) that named principles and allocated responsibilities for an egalitarian marriage, Shulman also contributed to the feminist rediscovery of Emma Goldman and wrote two moving memoirs, one breaking new ground in detailing the relationship between a daughter and her parents in the closing days of their lives, the other limning a brilliant account of a midlife urban woman's redefinition of herself in solitude on a Maine island. Active into the twenty-first century, Shulman edited, with Susan Koppelman, anthologies on feminist issues. In her most recent writing, Shulman reflects on what she sees as the comparatively limited achievements of the second wave of American feminism, reminding her readers of how easily those actions, laws, and ideas, like the accomplishments and actors of the first wave of feminism at the beginning of the twentieth century, could be forgotten or undone.

Born in Cleveland, Ohio, Shulman at age twenty deserted suburbia for Greenwich Village, where she participated in Beat life of the 1950s. She began graduate study in philosophy at Columbia University, married and divorced, remarried and had two children, began publishing (starting with short stories and children's books), and joined two early feminist groups: Redstocking and WITCH (Women's International Terrorist Conspiracy from Hell).

Shulman's controversial "Marriage Agreement," often reprinted, and often erroneously called a "Contract," was first published in 1970 in the second issue of the new feminist journal *Up From Under,* and was reprinted in various magazines as well as both legal textbooks and feminist anthologies. Although Shulman argues that her consciousness was slowly transformed into a feminist one from 1968 to 1972, she was attacked by **Norman Mailer** as well as by Joan Didion as a radical on the basis of the "Agreement," reprinted in magazines from *Redbook* to *New York Magazine* to *Life.* As Shulman said in 1990 about the article's core foundation, the equal value of all work within marriage, "it is no longer controversial but neither is it much practiced."

Memoirs of an Ex-Prom Queen (1972) analyzes the trap in which mid-twentieth-century women of the middle and upper-middle classes found themselves: that of trading on beauty to achieve stability in a successful marriage, the only "career" open to even the brainiest (of which the heroine, like Shulman, certainly was). Tracing the apparent dissolution of the marriage of a Fulbright scholar and his "Halfbright" wife who discovers sexual freedom in Europe, the novel is at its best in demonstrating in compelling, often witty and funny prose, how the sexual mores of the mid-century, white middle-class, suburban American pitted boy versus girl in what Shulman later called "The War in the Backseat," the stakes being sex or a future on the marriage market.

Burning Questions (1978), Shulman's second novel, successfully evokes the quandaries and concerns of the beginnings of Second Wave New York feminism, as it recounts the transformation of its heroine Zane IndiAnna. In her 1990 preface, Shulman accepted labeling it a "historical" novel, yet its rhetorical aims are clearly conversionary, and it comes complete with a selected bibliography of revolutionary writers from Angelica Balabanoff to Trotsky and the 1970's U.S. government records of hearings of intelligence collected on the radicals of the 1960s. *On the Stroll* and *In Every Woman's Life* similarly evoke the flux in women's lives in the 1970s. Incidental writing from the next several decades suggests Shulman's continuing involvement in feminist issues: domestic violence; the politics of aging, sexuality, and obesity; and the revisioning of relationships between daughters and mother. Her articles and work on Emma Goldman presented the legacy of earlier feminist theories for a new generation.

Although settings and characters are often recognizably Jewish, overtly Jewish themes are absent from Shulman's work, except for occasional references (e.g., to the father's "ghetto school" in *Ex-Prom Queen*). Her Jewish allegiance is apparent most explicitly in the two memoirs, where they emerge in discussion of cross-generational concerns (for example, Shulman's belated recognition of her mother's fundraising for Jewish and non-Jewish organizations as valuable civic work). In her writing and her life, Shulman is an ardent feminist. Her works made the emergence of that feminism from the middle-class Midwest of the mid-twentieth century more understandable. (*See also* Feminism)

Further Reading

Baker, Christina Looper, and Christina Baker Kline. "Mothers & Daughters: Honest Talk about Feminism and Real Life." *Ms. Magazine* (May 1996): 43–63.

Baumgardner, Jennifer. "Rerun 2: After the Prom." Review of *Memoirs of an Ex-Prom Queen*. *The Nation* (October 20, 1997): 40–42.

Bender, Marylin. Review of *Memoirs of an Ex-Prom Queen*. *New York Times Book Review* (April 23, 1972): 34.

Broyard, Anatole. "Books of the Times." Review of *On the Stroll*. *New York Times* (September 16, 1981): C25.

Broyard, Anatole. "Her Finite Variety." Review of *Burning Questions*. *New York Times* (March 18, 1978): C21.

Gologorsky, Beverly. "Ex-prom Queen Goes Home." Review of *A Good Enough Daughter*. *The Nation* (August 9, 1999): 40–42.

Tanenbaum, Leora. "The Liberation of an Ex-prom Queen." *Ms. Magazine* (November 1997): 82–84.

Whitman, Alden. "Feminist Writer Steps to the Fore." *New York Times* (April 25, 1972): 37.

Gail Berkeley Sherman

SIGNIFYING   Signifying relates to a specific form of communication found in traditional African American literature that combines elements of joking and lying with the use of traditional black dialect to form a genre of its own. The joking aspect can take on the form of insult or mockery, parody, or a playful exchange used as a test of linguistic wits. The lying aspect can be merely another layer of the inherent humor, or it can be used as a sign of power in a dialectic struggle between two characters. Signifying is also popularly known as "playing the doubles." There are elements of both literary humor and struggle for social power inherent in the art of signifying.

Signifying has its roots in the oral tradition of African American folk tales, examples of creativity used by those unable to read and write, often as a means of laying claim to the native language of power by utilizing the folk tales of one's country of origin. One of these tales is that of the signifying monkey himself, who is the epitome of the **trickster** figure often seen in oral folk tales. In written form, signifying can easily be seen in works such as the Uncle Remus stories penned by Chandler Harris in the late nineteenth century. The protagonist of Uncle Remus's tales, **Brer Rabbit**, is another classic trickster figure. Harris's tales remained popular into the middle of the twentieth century for the same reason that signifying continues to live in both oral and written forms: The trickster, through signifying, brings a sense of justice and the hope of overcoming oppression to those seeking empowerment and equality. This was especially important, of course, as the African American community struggled through the era of Reconstruction and the turbulent years that led up to the **Civil Rights Movement**.

Signifying often involves a reversal of meaning and an element of competition. Such can be seen in later examples of African American literature, as well as can the traditional model of signifying. The idea of signifying has laid the basis for a form of African American literary criticism formally formulated by **Henry Louis Gates Jr.** in which the traditional dialogue of signifying becomes a more sophisticated dialogue of sorts between different writers, critics, and social philosophers who build upon—or against—each other's work, most often with deep racial implications involved. Signifying also plays a part in popular culture, as it has since its inception in this country, with the oral practice of signifying continuing its usage within the African American community of our own day, for many of the same reasons that the phenomenon has always been popular. (*See also* African American Folklore)

Further Reading

Gates, Henry Louis, Jr. *The Signifying Monkey: A Theory of Afro-American Literary Criticism.* New York: Oxford UP, 1988.

Marrouche, Mustapha. *Signifying with a Vengeance: Theories, Literatures, Storytellers.* Albany: State U of New York P, 2002.

Watkins, Mel. *On the Real Side: Laughing, Lying and Signifying: The Underground Tradition of African-American Humor that Transformed American Culture, from Slavery to Richard Pryor.* New York: Simon and Schuster, 1994.

Terry D. Novak

ŠILBAJORIS, RIMVYDAS (1926–) Lithuanian American literary critic. Šilbajoris is the major Lithuanian literary critic in America who actively published both in Lithuanian and English and shaped the understanding of **Lithuanian American literature**. Born in Kretinga, Lithuania, Šilbajoris was forced into exile in 1944, when the outcome of World War II became obvious and the Soviet occupation of Lithuania unavoidable. He studied literature in Mainz (1947–49) and worked as a professor of Slavic and East European languages and literatures at the University of Ohio (1967–92). As a professor of Slavic and East European languages and literatures, he is well known for his studies of Russian literature. He published three books on Russian literature in English, *Russian Versification: The Theories of Trediakovskij, Lomonosov and Kantemir* (1968), *Tolstoy's Aesthetics and His Art* (1991), *War and Peace: Tolstoy's Mirror of the World* (1995), and edited such collections of articles as *The Architecture of Reading: Essays on Russian Literary Theory and Practice* (1976), *Encounters in Reading* (1979). In addition, Šilbajoris is the author of numerous articles on both Lithuanian literature and the literature of Lithuanian Americans. His English work consists of several books. *The Perfection of Exile: Fourteen Contemporary Lithuanian Writers* (1970) gives an interpretation of fourteen major Lithuanian American authors, *Mind Against the Wall* (1983) is an analysis of the literature of occupied Lithuania, and *A Short History of Lithuanian Literature* (2002) is an attempt to integrate both traditions into a coherent view of Lithuanian literature. Besides that, he is the author of more than a hundred articles (both in Lithuanian and in English) on Lithuanian and Russian literatures, as well as several books in Lithuanian, including *Words and Meaning: Literature Today in Lithuania* (1982) and a collection of articles, *Signs of Dispossession* (1992). Šilbajoris is the only critic consistently presenting Lithuanian and American Lithuanian literature in the American press.

Šilbajoris's main works on Lithuanian American literature had a profound impact on the understanding of Lithuanian American literature and its **diaspora**. Šilbajoris's literary criticism, originating as a combination of influences from the Russian formalist school, New Criticism and structuralism, aimed at evaluating literature as an aesthetic form of existential thought, but his analysis of the language of poetic works and its aesthetics was often contextualized within larger contexts of cultural meanings present in the texts. Šilbajoris reads Lithuanian American literature as both artistic and existential expression of individualities that were forced to run away from the totalitarian communist state and live as a group of displaced persons in exile. He understands this literature both as aesthetic expressions of individualities and as an attempt to rewrite and reshape certain cultural symbols and meanings and make them productive in the literature of exiles, and therefore in the American culture that these writers live in. However, these symbols and cultural allusions to Lithuanian culture are not always accessible without an extensive knowledge of Lithuanian culture, and Šilbajoris's work opened Lithuanian American literature for the general reader. (*See also* Lithuanian American Literature)

Further Reading

Skrupskelis, Alina et al., eds. *Lithuanian Writers in the West: An Anthology.* Chicago: Loyola UP, 1979.

Rimas Zilinskas

SILKO, LESLIE MARMON (1948–) Native American poet, novelist, short story writer, essayist, and photographer. Known previously for her short stories and poetry, Leslie Marmon Silko's place in Native American writing is permanently assured by her innovative first novel, *Ceremony*. Silko is one of the earliest Native American authors to celebrate the mixed blood Indian as a source of power and a symbol of the future of the Native peoples. Her works have met with a varied critical response for their inventive and often controversial addressing of issues pertaining to Laguna culture and the dilemma of **race** in America.

Major Works

Ceremony (1977) was published in the same year that Silko won the Pushcart Prize for poetry. Written during her sojourn in Alaska where she was greatly influenced by the landscape as well as the sense of exile from Laguna that she carried with her, *Ceremony* is Silko's attempt to recreate Laguna and its surroundings. Silko's male protagonist is a scorned, alienated half-white, half-Indian war veteran who is regarded as a failure when judged by white terms of heroism. Shell shock and survivor's guilt cause Tayo to spiral into an abyss of self-condemnation and despair. It emerges that part of the strategy to combat such despair and achieve wholeness is to recover, through ceremonial rites of healing, the tribal stories and women-centered traditions that have been too readily dismissed, abused, or discarded. In a modern world where Indians still live under the ignominy and injustice of a colonizing government's policies, where violence dominates and nuclear sites desecrate the natural landscape, *Ceremony* is a cautionary tale directed not only at the whites who work against Native integration, but also at the Indians who unthinkingly embrace the values of the white world to the detriment of their own people's welfare.

Storyteller (1981) is a multigenre collection of photographs, poems, tribal tales, short stories, personal recollections, and family lore. Together, the collection exemplifies how the act of storytelling is important to the process of linking the historical and mythical past spiritually to the happenings of the present. In the title story, "Storyteller," the Alaskan landscape has as much a role as the human characters: the powerful wintry weather denying any human attempt to shape the environment permanently for their own uses.

Almanac of the Dead (1991) is Silko's magnum opus. Ten years in creation, it caricatures a country united by the soulless binding of materialism, a nation that is spiritually doomed. Dealing with sovereignty, past and present oppression of the indigenous peoples, political unrest, the drug dealing scene, mixed-blood **identity** conflicts, corruption, bestiality as well as psychological and technological mayhem, *Almanac* is a narration of the self-destruction evident in an individualistic culture. In a dramatic restructuring of the American mythic mindscape, Silko, in an era ruled by immediate efficacy and militarism, nonetheless advocates a graduated process of change. Only thus can new ideas be introduced at a pace that is readily integrated by the community so that the transformation is constructive rather than disruptive and destructive. Hope for the future is represented by the gathering of a motley crew of characters who for personal reasons join in a community resistance to combat that force of despair. Highlighting the social and political specter of a national uprising, Silko depicts a multiracial army made up of Mexican migrants, disgruntled war veterans, the poor and the homeless, and the North American tribal peoples ready to fight for their rights to a place and land from which they had been earlier dispossessed. Here, identity is depicted as a fluid entity so much so that "enemy" whites can escape their prophesized disappearance through Silko's apparent solution of the sincere embracing of Indian values. In *Almanac*, the "Indian problem" is a universal problem, and the reader is drawn into the pattern of the plot and forced to partake in the judging of the characters' actions in the light of the author's terms for ultimate victory. Throughout, Silko is no mere propagandist for her beliefs. Rather she understands that despite her personal politics, alternatives need to be looked at objectively for a convincing evaluation of what to do next. The aesthetic underpinnings present in the complexity of the plot's design ensure that a simplistic, absolute reading of the novel's message is close to impossible.

Gardens in the Dunes (1999) is an historical novel harking back to the humanitarian and industrial contradictions of the Gilded Age at the turn of the nineteenth century. Here we have a white woman, Hattie, born to wealth but oppressed by her husband and the gendered values of the rigid society she lives within. Her state of physical and psychological captivity is mirrored in the Sand Lizard girl she saves and befriends, both being hemmed in by prejudices that persecute them less for what they have done but for who they are. Published twenty-two years after *Ceremony*, *Gardens* reflects Silko's increased engagement with the politics of religion, beliefs, and superstitions as a matter that extends across generations and countries. There is no simplistic civilized/savage dichotomy in the presentation of the Indians in *Gardens* for while highlighting the vulnerability of tribal survival in the modern world, the work challenges the privileging race as the great distinguisher of the "other." Silko walks a fine line in exposing the problematic dynamics of attempting to site difference without ultimately lapsing into oversimplification. She very deliberately introduces the issue of gender politics, with the anti-Indian elements also proving to be antifeminist. Unlike *Ceremony* and *Almanac* where the key characters whose spiritual lives we follow are often male, the onus of change and revival in *Gardens* lies with women. The Indians' struggle to survive the corruptions of the "new" world is clearly linked to a recovered spirituality grounded in the Ghost Dance, which opposes the closed reading of the Jesus story that the patriarchal, dominant-culture church propagates. In communicating her alternative reality, Silko manipulates the conventional tropes of the organized church, thus destabilizing the politically correct white religious message. Throughout, there is an irrevocable sense of the linkage between femaleness and fertility, of a sexualized women-centered society and the hope of fecundity in a truly new Eden. Providing a complex study of the relationship between tribal and European myths, the socio-cultural use of gardens, imperialism, collecting fauna and the issue of interracial as well as intercultural exchanges, *Gardens* highlights the complex overlapping of identity influences.

Silko's repertoire of work also includes a book of poetry titled *Laguna Woman* (1974); the self-published *Sacred Water: Narratives and Pictures* (1993); *The Delicacy and Strength of Lace* (1986), chronicling her correspondence with poet James Wright and exploring the process of creating a work; and *Yellow Woman and a Beauty of the Spirit* (1997), a collection of essays covering largely political issues such as **racism**, **immigration**, and tribal disenfranchisement.

Themes

Silko writes mainly from the identity of an American Indian even though she has a mix of Laguna Pueblo, Mexican, and white ancestry. At the core of her writing is a desire to identify what it is like to grow up on the fringes of identities, neither fully fledged Laguna nor white. This lack of belonging allows her to look at Native identity both from the insider and outsider perspectives. It also pushes her to forge a path whereby her Laguna heritage may coexist with prevalent twentieth-century Euro-American sensibilities. Historically, Laguna culture itself is heavily influenced by Hopi, Zuni, Jemez, and Navajo as well as miscellaneous European cultures. Thus the practice of incorporating other traditions into Laguna society has always been in evidence. Her early short story, "The Man to Send Rain Clouds," highlights the basic themes of tolerable assimilation in a humorous depiction of a burial ritual encompassing Laguna as well as Roman Catholic rites and beliefs. Similarly, the mythic role of Yellow Woman, mirrored in many of her heroines, reveals how the traditional and contemporary can coexist in that one easily misunderstood figure who transgresses boundaries for the greater purpose of spiritual service to the tribe.

Educated variously at Board of Indian Affairs schools and a Catholic school before attending the University of New Mexico, Silko locates much of her work in the Pueblo of Laguna where she grew up. Central to much of her writing is the issue of the interrelatedness of community, which she defines as comprising both the land and its people. American Indian communal and individual identities have been consistently compromised in the past five hundred years by the multiple atrocities inflicted upon the land and its peoples. Hence sovereignty, community, the vitality of an evolving tradition, and the need for continuity and change are recurring themes in her works. The function of humor in her texts lends perspective to the author's view of the world and balances her rigorous addressing of issues including the role of violence in resistance. As a holder of community stories to be passed on, Silko also takes on the responsibility of an historian, combating ignorance of Native history with knowledge, a key weapon to disarm the whites who typically have the monopoly on making meaning.

Style

The role of orature and the power of storytelling to heal are very real to Silko's vision. As a child Silko learned the folklore of the Laguna and Keres people through stories told by her grandmother and aunt. As a writer, she seeks to bring the dramatic oral experience of listening to a story into the reading of a printed story. The spider's web is an important structural metaphor for her writing, with the circularity of the work and its complex weaving of different strands of the narrative suggesting connections that are difficult to untangle or assail. Incorporating verse and prose with eloquently loaded spacing, the interrelatedness of all things is demonstrated in the nonlinear narrative of *Ceremony*. Similarly, in *Almanac*, the work loops back on itself, runs into prolonged digressions, and fills its 800 or so pages with a series of narratives within narratives. Here Silko is essentially telling several stories at once, stories interlinked to touch each other at certain symbolic points. In line with Silko's borrowings from Native oral tradition is her perspective of time. Chronological time, like linear narratives, only serves to limit one's view of the history and the world. In the organic cosmology that Silko adheres to, prophecies begun five centuries ago are still in the process of being fulfilled. Constantly experimenting with and subverting Western literary forms, Silko produces a seditious style that is in itself a critique of white conventionality.

Critical Reception

Lauded with critical acclaim for her stylistic achievement and multi-genre works, Silko, like many of her fellow writers, has also been criticized for exoticizing the Indian world she portrays. Despite her aim to stay true to her Laguna heritage, she has also been criticized by fellow Laguna writer, **Paula Gunn Allen**, for revealing tribal secrets in *Ceremony*, a situation that points to the complexity involved in forming an Indian aesthetic and critical methodology. Having left law school in favor of the activism of writing, it is unsurprising that Silko's more recent work has also been met with disapproval by mainstream critics who earlier found *Almanac* uncomfortably political. Yet new studies have begun to analyze the subversive nature of Silko's earlier works, which tie in with her political agenda, which has become more overtly evident in her later works. Storytelling as a weapon of war is a means made available both to the author as well as to her characters. As a creative artist and activist, Silko's works unceasingly undercut the supposed fixity of a situation, be the issue a geographical limitation or a gender, racial, or sexual stereotype. (*See also* Native American Novel)

Further Reading

Arnold, Ellen L., ed. *Conversations with Leslie Marmon Silko.* Jackson: UP of
  Mississippi, 2000.

Graulich, Melody, ed. *"Yellow Woman": Leslie Marmon Silko.* New Brunswick, NJ:
  Rutgers UP, 1993.

Salyer, Gregory. *Leslie Marmon Silko.* New York: Twayne, 1997.

Poh Cheng Khoo

SIMON, KATE (1912–1990)   Jewish American travel writer and
memoirist. As the author of a landmark in travel writing and the ultimate
New York guidebook *New York City, New York Places and Pleasures: An
Uncommon Guidebook* (1971), Simon is also remembered for the first of three
memoirs, *Bronx Primitive: Portraits in a Childhood* (1982), which was a finalist
for the National Book Critics Circle Award that year and also named by the
New York Times Book Review as one of the twelve best books of 1982.

Simon's family emigrated from Warsaw, Poland, in 1917 when she was
five. Moving between several neighborhoods before finally settling in the
Bronx, Kaila Grobsmith adopted the name Kate. While at Hunter College of
the City University of New York, Simon was immersed in the bohemian lifestyle and graduated with a bachelor's degree in English in 1935. Patterning herself after Edna St. Vincent Millay, Simon swore to avoid the
shriveled, fading fate of immigrant women in America.

Working in the publishing industry as a freelance editor for Alfred A.
Knopf from 1952 to 1959, Simon wrote book reviews of contemporary nov-
els for the *New Republic* and the *Nation.* She held various editorial jobs with
Book-of-the-Month Club and *Publisher's Weekly* and contributed articles to
the *New York Times, Vogue, Harper's, Harper's Bazaar, National Geographic,
Holiday,* the *Saturday Review,* and *Travel and Leisure.*

Simon recalled keeping a notebook with ideas for *New York City, New York
Places and Pleasures: An Uncommon Guidebook* (1959) as early as age fourteen
when she wandered the city and recorded all that she saw and experienced.
Crafting a warm depiction of the city, Simon's guidebook sold 100,000 copies
in its first three years and went through four revisions. Simon's taste, wit,
and distinctive voice departed from the plodding and dry guidebooks of that
era. Simon was lauded by reviewers for giving new life to the musty and bor-
ing genre of travel writing. Her curiosity about people, architecture, and sce-
nic beauty was unconventional, and this approach granted Simon a clear
advantage over other travel writers. She attributed her style and clarity to
constant condensing and revision of her work.

Simon's attention to uncommon details, straightforward manner, and
adventurous spirit was evident in subsequent guidebooks that she wrote
about Mexico, Paris, Rome, Italy, and England. Simon's passion for new
experiences coupled with her facility for getting to the heart of other places
transformed the paper on which her words were written and endowed her
destinations with energy.

Bronx Primitive: Portraits in Childhood (1982) was remarkable on several accounts. Simon's colorful expressions and lack of sentimentalism captured the harsh realities that she faced coming-of-age in New York City in 1916. Frank in her accounting of abortions, childhood sexual abuse, and gender inequality, Simon's depiction of the immigrant experience during the Great Depression is used as a college text in sociology courses.

Further Reading

Neuman, Shirley. "'An Appearance Walking in a Forest the Sexes Burn': Autobiography and the Construction of the Feminine Body." *Signature: A Journal of Theory and Canadian Literature* 2 (1989): 1–26.

Rebecca Tolley-Stokes

SIMON, NEIL (1927–)   Jewish American playwright and screenwriter. Neil Simon is a prolific, popular, award-winning playwright, known mostly for his romantic comedies and plays about urban American family life in the twentieth century, many of which are loosely autobiographical in nature. His plays have been very successful on Broadway and on film but have not garnered much attention from academics until recently. He was awarded the Pulitzer Prize for drama in 1991 for *Lost in Yonkers,* which seems to have enhanced his reputation as a serious playwright.

Simon was born in the Bronx, New York City, on July 4, 1927, and was reared there and in the Washington Heights section of Manhattan. His childhood was difficult but would later prove to be a great source of material for many of his best-known works. His mother sometimes had to take in boarders or send the children to stay with relatives because his garment salesman father often abandoned the family for extended periods. Simon and his older brother Daniel took refuge in comedy and in escapist trips to the movies.

After attending New York University, beginning his career as an Air Force journalist, and writing for television comedy shows with his brother for a few years, Simon went on to win Emmy awards in 1957 and 1959, followed in 1961 by the premiere of his first Broadway play, *Come Blow Your Horn.* The play focuses on two young bachelors, based in part on the Simon brothers, in their first apartment trying to break away from their domineering father. Simon then wrote the book for the 1962 musical *Little Me,* followed by two back-to-back hit Broadway plays: *Barefoot in the Park* in 1963 and *The Odd Couple* in 1965.

Barefoot in the Park deals with the problems of a young married couple living in a small, walk-up New York apartment. Simon drew upon his marriage to his first wife, Joan, in creating the relationship between buttoned-up Paul Bratter and his free-spirited bride Corie. Simon adapted the play for the screen in 1967, and the film starred Robert Redford and Jane Fonda. *The Odd Couple* centers on another mismatched pair: compulsively fussy Felix Ungar and relaxed, slovenly Oscar Madison. The two men are forced to share an apartment when their marriages fall apart, and find that living together as room-

Neil Simon. *Photo by Al Ravenna. Courtesy of the Library of Congress.*

mates can be just as stressful. Simon's 1968 screen adaptation, starring Jack Lemmon and Walter Matthau, was a great success, which led to a subsequent hit television series starring Tony Randall and Jack Klugman. In 1985 Neil Simon wrote a new version of the play so that it could be cast starring two female roommates instead of men.

In 1966 Simon wrote the book for another musical, *Sweet Charity,* and his play *The Star-Spangled Girl* also debuted. He wrote the book for the 1968 musical *Promises, Promises,* and his play *Plaza Suite* premiered that same year. *Plaza Suite* is made up of three thematically linked one-act plays all set in the same New York hotel suite. Simon adapted it for the screen in 1971, and it was remade for television in 1987. His 1969 comedy, *Last of the Red Hot Lovers,* deals with unsuccessful attempts at adultery by a man undergoing a midlife crisis in the midst of the sexual revolution. Simon also wrote the 1972 film adaptation, which starred Alan Arkin.

Simon's next two plays were darker than his earlier work. 1970's *The Gingerbread Lady* tells the story of an alcoholic former cabaret star, and 1971's *The Prisoner of Second Avenue* focuses on the dehumanizing plight of contemporary urban life. Simon's second wife, Marsha Mason, starred in the 1981 film version of the former, titled *Only When I Laugh,* and Jack Lemmon and Anne Bancroft starred in the 1975 film version of the latter; both screenplays were written by Simon.

The Sunshine Boys, a bittersweet comedy about the reunion of an aging vaudeville team, premiered in 1972; Simon also wrote the screenplay for the 1975 Walter Matthau and George Burns film version. His next two projects would be adaptations of existing works, which did not meet with the same success. 1973's *The Good Doctor* is based on the short stories of Anton Chekhov and 1974's *God's Favorite* is based on the biblical book of Job.

Simon rebounded with *California Suite* in 1976, a play that applies the same organizational concept of *Plaza Suite* to a suite in the Beverly Hills Hotel. Again, Simon adapted the play to be filmed with an all-star cast in 1978. His next play, *Chapter Two,* which debuted in 1977, is a highly autobiographical look at a widower remarrying; Simon's wife Joan had died of cancer in 1973 and he had struggled with guilt about marrying Marsha

Mason soon after. Mason starred opposite James Caan in the 1979 film adaptation by Simon.

In 1979 Simon wrote the book for the musical *They're Playing Our Song* and followed that in 1980 with the play *I Ought to be in Pictures*, which Simon adapted for the screen in 1982, about a screenwriter whose now-grown daughter seeks him out after a sixteen-year separation. His 1981 comedy "Fools," about a schoolteacher in Russia, was not well received, but he would return in 1983 with the first in a now widely beloved trilogy of plays.

Brighton Beach Memoirs is the first of three plays that depict the life of Eugene Morris Jerome as he grows from an adolescent to a man. This first play in the Brighton Beach Trilogy is a nostalgic look back at a Jewish, Depression-era Brooklyn childhood not unlike Simon's own. Teenage Eugene, a budding writer, breaks the fourth wall by directly addressing the audience in journal entries that narrate his coming-of-age experience as it plays out on stage. Two years later, in 1985, came the second play in the trilogy, *Biloxi Blues*. It is six years later and Eugene is leaving home for the first time to serve in the Army. Out of his element in 1943 Mississippi, Eugene deals with the adult realities of sex, love, and prejudice on top of the duties and dangers of military service. He also takes another step down the path to becoming a writer as he is spared from combat duty to serve, as Simon did, as a military journalist. Simon later adapted the first two plays in the trilogy for the screen, starring Jonathan Silverman in 1986 and Matthew Broderick in 1988, respectively.

Just one year later in 1986, Simon finished his trilogy with *Broadway Bound*, which he adapted for television in 1992. The play, although still a comedy, has a more serious tone, as it deals with the breakup of the Jerome family unit and Eugene's full emergence into adult life. Eugene and his brother have just begun work as sketch writers for a late 1940s radio show, but as their careers take off and they prepare to move into the city to pursue them, they have to witness the painful dissolution of their parents' marriage, which leaves their mother struggling for the courage to go on with her own life. As Eugene tries to be a supportive son, he is forced to come to terms with the writer's dilemma he had already discovered in *Biloxi Blues*: the ethical question of how much one may use one's intimates as material for one's work.

In 1988 Simon's door-slamming dinner party farce, *Rumors*, a clear departure from the Brighton Beach plays, premiered on Broadway, but in 1991 Simon returned to the subject of the Jewish family in his Pulitzer Prize–winning *Lost in Yonkers*, in which two boys are sent by their widowed father to live with their grandmother and eccentric, dysfunctional extended family in 1942 Yonkers, New York. Simon also wrote the screenplay for the 1993 film starring Richard Dreyfus, Mercedes Ruehl, and Irene Worth.

In 1992 he broke with his usual largely realistic form to write an expressionistic piece called *Jake's Women*, in which a middle-aged man contemplates the myriad women in his life; it was adapted for television in 1996.

1993's *Laughter on the 23rd Floor* is about a team of television comedy writers in 1953; it was adapted for television in 2001. *London Suite,* another collection of thematically linked one acts, appeared in 1995 and was adapted for television in 1996. *Proposals* premiered in 1997, *The Dinner Party* in 2000, *45 Seconds from Broadway* in 2001, and *Rose's Dilemma* in 2003.

Broadway's Alvin Theatre was renamed the Neil Simon Theatre in his honor in 1983. (*See also* Jewish American Theater)

Further Reading

Bloom, Harold. *Neil Simon.* Bloomall, PA: Chelsea House Publishers, 2002.

Johnson, Robert K. *Neil Simon.* Boston: Twayne, 1983.

Konas, Gary, ed. *Neil Simon: A Casebook.* New York: Garland, 1997.

Koprince, Susan. *Understanding Neil Simon.* Columbia: U of South Carolina P, 2002.

McGovern, Edythe M. *Neil Simon: A Critical Study.* New York: Frederick Ungar, 1979.

Laura Grace Pattillo

SIMPSON, LOUIS (1923–)   Jewish American poet, critic, essayist, novelist, and teacher. Louis Simpson's place in the Jewish American tradition of writing rests on the elegance of his verse, mastery of traditional and free verse, and wide-ranging themes. To date, Simpson has published eighteen volumes of poetry, a novel, an autobiography, memoirs, and several volumes of literary criticism. Although Simpson's reputation is based on his entire body of work, he is most celebrated for his book of poetry *At the End of the Open Road,* which received the Pulitzer Prize in 1964.

Much of Simpson's most celebrated verse describes his combat experiences in World War II. Indeed, critics rank his poetry about combat as among the best produced in the second half of the twentieth century. Born in Jamaica to a Scottish father and Polish Jewish mother, Simpson moved to New York City in 1940 to attend Columbia University. The war intervened, however, and Simpson fought in the European campaign and in the Normandy D-Day invasion. All told, he served from 1943 to 1946. His bravery earned him two Purple Hearts and a Bronze Star. From this firsthand battle experience, Simpson drew inspiration for his first book of poetry, *The Arrivistes,* which he self-published in 1949. Many of the poems in this volume capture the fear and desolation of battle. For instance, the highly praised ballad "Carentan O Carentan" describes American troops ambushed by German troops. This ballad, often republished in anthologies, is one of the classic poems to come out of World War II. The powerful war poems are juxtaposed by love poems such as "Song: 'Rough Winds Do Shake the Darling Buds of May'."

Simpson's verse also traces the collapse of the American dream and the alienation of middle-class Americans. This is apparent early in his career in his second published book of poetry, *Good News or Death and Other Poems* (1955). "American Culture," for example, compares the optimism of America's beginnings with the despair of our present consumer-driven culture. This theme is amplified in later poems such as the brief "In the Suburbs" and the poems collected in *The Best Hour of the Night* (1983) and *In the Room We Share* (1990). These poems tell stories of ordinary people living lives of quiet desperation. As with his war poems, Simpson's poems on middle-class disaffection are ranked as among the best poems written on the subject.

There's a subtle but unmistakable irony to Simpson's criticism of mass culture, because in 1967 he accepted a position as an English professor at the State University of New York at Stony Brook, where he remained until his retirement in the 1990s. When Simpson first settled in Stony Brook, the region was largely vast expanses of potato and duck farms, but very quickly modest homes, McMansions, malls, and the other hallmarks of middle-class suburban life pushed the farmers ever eastward

From his first poems, Simpson's mastery of traditional forms is evident. Speaking of the poems in that collection, critic Ronald Moran notes that Simpson "often sounds like an Elizabethan song-maker or like a Cavalier poet" (Moran, *Contemporary Authors Online* 5). The regular metrics and traditional meter often serve to underscore the stress and turmoil of contemporary life.

In the second half of the 1950s, however, Simpson turned to more experimental poetic forms, most notably free verse and conversational diction to inhabit the American character and vernacular. *A Dream of Governors* (1959) marked the beginning of Simpson's use of free verse. Adapting Walt Whitman's use of the catalog technique to contemporary concerns, Simpson lists archetypal contemporary American images: automobiles, television, highways, and malls. Simpson's debt to Whitman is nowhere more clear than in "Walt Whitman at Bear Mountain" (1963), in which he attacks Whitman's cheery hopefulness about America's culture.

However, it wasn't until 1963 with the publication of *At the End of the Open Road* that Simpson plunged headlong into poetic experimentation, using not only free verse but also colloquial language and surreal vivid imagery. Despite the change in forms—or perhaps because of it—Simpson has never deviated from his stance as a detached observer. In this, he stands in sharp contrast to his contemporary "Confessional Poets," most notably Robert Lowell, Sylvia Plath, and Anne Sexton.

In addition to his poetry, Simpson has also published two volumes of letters, brief memoirs, essays, and speeches: *Selected Prose* (1988) and *Ships Going Into the Blue* (1995). He also wrote the novel *Riverside Drive* (1962) and full-length memoirs *North of Jamaica* (1972) and *The King My Father's Wreck* (1995). His literary criticism includes *Three on the Tower* (1975), *A Revolution in Taste* (1978), *A Company of Poets* (1981), and *The Character of the Poet* (1986).

Despite this varied and prodigious output of prose, Simpson's reputation at this point largely rests on his poetry. Together, *At the End of the Open Road*, *The Arrivistes* (1949) and *The Best Hour of the Night* (1983) are ranked with the seminal American poems of the late twentieth century. For his ability to enable us to notice things that are all around us that normally escape our notice, Simpson adds a new dimension to our awareness of ourselves and our world.

Further Reading

Lensing, George S., and Ronald Moran. *Four Poets and the Emotive Imagination.* Baton Rouge: Louisiana State University, 1976.

Laurie Rozakis

SINCLAIR, JO (RUTH SEID) (1913–1995)   Jewish American novelist. Jo Sinclair was born on July 1, 1913, in Brooklyn, New York. In 1907, her Yiddish-speaking family arrived in the United States from Russia via Argentina. Although better employment lured her carpenter father to Cleveland in 1916, they would remain poor. Thus, the valedictorian of 1930 started earning immediately after high school although she knew at fourteen that she wanted to write. Authorship, she was convinced, would free her from the "ghetto" and her family's "illiter[acy] in the soul." Escape, however, would not be easy. The clash between Jewish immigrant culture and the world of American letters would resonate throughout her oeuvre.

"Erscht schwartz is weiss und weiss is schwartz. A gantze welt tantzed und freyd sach!" (Once black is white, and white, black, the world will rejoice). This Yiddish saying, from Sinclair's third novel, prefigures major themes: against ethnocentricity, for tolerance, against religious dogmas, and for flexible gender identities.

Civil rights, a consistent theme, also enters her first published story, "Noon Lynching" (1936). By 1938, while she worked on the WPA, several more tales saw print. Yet Sinclair lacked the confidence she would gain through Helen Buchman. A Southerner "who had grown up in wealth," Buchman introduced "the waif" to "high cultural" sophistication that both fed and appeased her "constant . . . fear and insecurity as a writer." A lay psychoanalyst, Buchman was midwife to Sinclair's first novel, *Wasteland*, which won the $10,000 Harper prize.

"Like a cry tearing its way out of the throat," *Wasteland* evokes "the emotional frustrations of Jewish life in America," Richard Wright wrote, for Sinclair has "said about the Jewish family what [he had been] trying to say about the Negro." **Anti-Semitism** instills self-hatred in Jake Braunowitz, a photographer who "passes" as John Brown. In therapy, Jake is helped by his sister, Debby, one of the earliest lesbian characters in twentieth-century American fiction. She diagnoses "social wounds" that Jake works through toward acceptance of Jewishness as a universal ethics.

Sinclair's second novel, *Sing at My Wake* (1951), scrutinizes a Catholic family for its vulnerability in Protestant America. She continues to explore **identity** and **assimilation** in *The Changelings* (1955), referring to children who, despite parental prejudice, sense that human similarities outweigh differences. Specifically, thirteen-year-olds Judy Vincent, Jewish, and Clara

Johnson, Catholic and African American, approach friendship although each had been taught that the other was the enemy. Former gang leaders, they meet in a working-class neighborhood with empty flats that are sought by blacks. The Jewish homeowners, seeing in dark faces plummeting prices, slam their doors. Yet beneath the economic rationale is generalized fear of life. Many are refugees from Hitler; some have seen their families murdered. Although American anti-Semitism reached its apogee in the 1940s, the immigrants exhibit **racism** and teach hate as a displaced reaction to centuries of hostility. For most, Yiddish remains a tongue of the heart. The changeling generation, native English speakers, literally cannot talk to the old.

Intergenerational misunderstanding also pervades *Anna Teller* (1960). A feisty **Holocaust** survivor, seventy-five-year-old Anna, nicknamed "the General," flees the failed 1956 Hungarian uprising and enters the home of her only living son. Emil, who had emigrated in his twenties, confronts her with his early trauma, having been the less-loved child. He feels enormous guilt for not having rescued his brother Paul from the crematorium. At first, Anna's own "refugee trauma" prevents communication, her pride dictating behavior appropriate in Europe but not in the United States. Only when her grandsons contract typhoid from her run-down apartment does she accept new meanings.

The same linguistic inadequacy, or "creative death," haunts Sinclair's last work. A memoir and obituary dedicated to Helen Buchman, *The Seasons: Death and Transfiguration* (1993) features gardening and writing, including diary entries as Buchman lay dying. "Write me a book, Ruthie," Helen had repeatedly said. The result is a chronicle of patient friendship throughout the seasons of two women's lives.

Further Reading

Halley, Anne. "Afterword: The Family in Anna Teller." *Anna Teller*. New York: Feminist Press, 1992 [orig. pub. 1960]. 597–612.

McKay, Nellie. "Afterword." *The Changelings*. New York: Feminist Press, 1983 [orig. pub. 1955]. 323–37.

Uffen, Ellen Serlen. "America, 1945: Jo Sinclair's 'The Changelings.' *Exploring the Midwestern Literary Imagination*. Ed. Marcia Noe. Troy, NY: Whitston, 1993. 167–79.

Tobe Levin

SINGER, ISAAC BASHEVIS (1904–1991)

Jewish American writer. Isaac Bashevis Singer was the foremost writer in Yiddish, and his descriptions of the destroyed Eastern European Jewish world won him a large audience as well as the Nobel Prize. He also wrote frequently about Jewish immigrants to and **Holocaust** survivors in America, but his *shtetl* tales, which often described Hasidic people in Poland, nostalgically evoke Jewish life before the Nazis ended it with World War II and are the most popular of his works.

Isaac Bashevis Singer. *Courtesy of the Library of Congress.*

Singer was born in Warsaw into a poor and pious Jewish family. He had a religious upbringing, partially in Warsaw and partially in the small Polish village where his grandfather was the rabbi, and he attended a rabbinical seminary, but when he moved to Warsaw in 1923, he gradually became a secular Jew, though he maintained a belief in God. His older brother, the novelist Israel Joshua Singer, was a strong influence, and it was in part because of him that Singer became a secular rather than religious Jew. In Warsaw, Singer worked as a translator, an editor at the Yiddish journal *Globus*, and a writer of essays, reviews, and stories. In 1935, encouraged by his brother who was already in America, he immigrated to New York. He worked there at the Yiddish *Daily Forward* newspaper. Many of his fictional works were serialized in the newspaper before being translated and published in English in book form.

Singer started writing fiction in the late 1920s, and *Satan in Goray* was his first novel (published in Yiddish in 1935 and then in English in 1955). It is still widely considered his best novel. The story takes place in the seventeenth century and revolves around a town's belief in a false messiah. This belief brings people happiness and harmony, and they look forward to the arrival of the messiah and to the salvation he will bring. The town's residents fall into a hysteria verging on insanity as they await their messiah. However, it turns out to actually be Satan who has taken over the town, rather than a messiah. The novel can also be read as a symbolic depiction of the political situation in Europe, where various parties and leaders made false promises that enticed and seduced, but ultimately disappointed.

Gimpel the Fool (published in 1953 in the *Partisan Review* and in 1957 in a collection of short stories) is the short story that first introduced Singer to non-Jewish-speaking readers. It is about a gullible man who is mocked and taken advantage of. However, he cannot imagine why anyone would lie to him or treat him like a fool. Gimpel simply accepts life as it comes and always retains his faith in God. A truly good person, Gimpel is not the fool others try to make him out to be.

The Family Moskat (1950), which recreates the lost world of Polish Jewry, is a saga about a large Jewish family and about the old way of Jewish life clashing with modernity. The main character, Asa Heshel Banet, is based loosely on Singer himself. Asa Heshel, a young man from a religious family, moves from a small village to Warsaw, where he discards his background and becomes assimilated. Torn between women and between desires for what he wants to do with his life, and caught in the difficulties of current events, such as the approaching world war, Asa Heshel is also representative of the problems Jews faced at the time, and perhaps continue to face. Fitting into society, **assimilation**, and self-determination are essential issues in this novel and *The Family Moskat*, which can be seen as a sort of Jewish epic, remains ultimately ambiguous. Even the powerful and wealthy Moskat family cannot avoid extinction.

Singer's works depicting the destroyed Jewish life in Poland are more successful than those about life in America. It was understandably difficult for him to accept the destruction of the life he knew best, and thus the Old World and its issues and problems—the struggle for existence, the conflict between secular and religious Jewish life, the suffering of Jews throughout time, evil, and the constant threat of extinction—were his focus. His fiction about this world is secular and yet also spiritual and realistic, but also the stories are like fairytales, and often written in the language of liturgy, with biblical allusions and symbols. The stories about American life, in contrast, have less of a magical and otherworldly feel, but they have a similar theme: the assimilation of Jews into the larger society or, in other words, the loss of Jewishness because of both internal and external conflicts. A sense of hopeless fatalism characterizes many of his works.

Though famous and respected primarily for his stories about traditional Jewish life in Poland in a variety of times periods, Isaac Bashevis Singer's skill as a storyteller is obvious in his fiction of various styles, lengths, and topics. He won the Nobel Prize in 1978, the only Yiddish author ever to do so. (*See also* Yiddish Literature)

Further Reading

Burgin, Richard. "Isaac Bashevis Singer Talks . . . About Everything." *New York Times Magazine* (November 26, 1978): 24 and (December 3, 1978): 38.

Hadda, Janet. *Isaac Bashevis Singer: A Life.* New York: Oxford UP, 1997.

Brett Jocelyn Epstein

SKLAREW, MYRA (1934–) Jewish American poet, essayist, short fiction writer. Much of Sklarew's published writing explores Jewishness: her maternal grandmother's family's experiences in small villages in Lithuania, the **Holocaust**—particularly in Lithuania, Jewish writers, Israel, Talmudic and other rabbinical writings, and, currently, the relationship between the neuroscience of memory and Holocaust testimony. The recipient of the Anna Davidson Rosenberg Poetry Award, the National Jewish Book Council Award in Poetry, the Di Castagnola Award, and the PEN Syndicated Fiction Award, Sklarew was the president of the artist community Yaddo. Her work has been recorded for the Library of Congress's Contemporary Poets' Archive. Born and raised in Baltimore and, since 1961, living in Bethesda, Maryland, Sklarew is a professor of literature at American University, where she has also been codirector of its MFA program in creative writing.

Sklarew's work often reflects her undergraduate training at Tufts University as a biologist as well as her work years at Cold Spring Harbor Laboratory and Yale University School of Medicine, where she studied bacterial genetics and worked in neurophysiology on frontal lobe function and memory, respectively. A poetry course from John Holmes at Tufts and Writing Seminars at Johns Hopkins with Elliot Coleman influenced and inspired her to continue writing, an activity she began as a small child who wrote stories and poems to cheer a teacher who was saddened by her brothers' military service in World War II. In 1941, Sklarew felt the impact of the Nazis more directly: she became aware of the murder of her family members who remained in Lithuania and that knowledge has infused her life as well as her work. Since 1993, she has journeyed to Lithuania nine times to interview bystanders, witnesses, and survivors (rescuers, collaborators). She has tried to heal the loss of her family through walking their streets and fields. The poems in *Lithuania* (1995) speak to the history of both people and place; it is a narrative of experiences—Sklarew's and the Lithuanians' who tell their stories of 1941 and 1942 as well as the stories of the victims of townspeople and the Einsatzgruppen. The poem "Lithuania" unfolds the terrible histories of Kovno, Stutthof, Ponar, Vilnius, and Keidan. The book includes poems about Warsaw, Israel, birth and death, and some of the biblical figures whose stories invite retelling. In both Yiddish and English, *The Witness Trees* (2000) takes her readers to the ironic pastoral beauty of Keidan, Lithuania, and the massacres that the countryside masks.

The scope of Sklarew's work is dazzling: The eight books of poetry and one of short fiction are *In the Basket of the Blind* (1975), *From the Backyard of Diaspora* (1976), *Blessed Art Thou, No-One* (1982), *The Science of Goodbyes* (1982), *The Travels of the Itinerant Freda Aharon* (1985), *Altamira* (1987), *Like a Field Riddled by Ants* (1988), and *Eating the White Earth* (1994). *Lithuania: New & Selected Poems,* (1997), *The Witness Trees* (2000), and *Over the Rooftops of Time* (2003), a collection of poems, essays, and stories, demonstrate the range of her observations and the depth of her insights, as do the journals in which she has published, from *Poetry* to the *Journal of the American Medical Association* to the *Journal of Pastoral Counseling.*

Further Reading

Anon. "A Poet's Parable in Prose." *Washington Jewish Week* (July 21, 1988): 14.

Guber, Susan. *Poetry After Auschwitz.* Bloomington: Indiana UP, 2003.

Myrna Goldenberg

SLAVE NARRATIVE.   *See* African American Slave Narrative

SLAVERY   Various forms of chattel slavery, in which masters owned their slaves as property, were legal and widely practiced throughout England's colonies in North America and the Caribbean, and throughout the Southern United States for the first nine decades of the country's history. It is difficult to overstate how central slavery was to the American economy and political life, and especially to Southern life and culture. Slavery was enshrined in the Constitution; the White House and Capitol building were partly built with slave labor; the railroads that made possible the country's continual westward expansion and development were built in part by slaves; the majority of U.S. presidents from the Revolutionary War to the Civil War were slave owners; and one of the bloodiest and most divisive wars in U.S. history was fought largely over the right of southern states to keep slavery legal. Slavery was a brutal institution in which the (almost always white) masters kept the (usually black) slaves under control through any means at hand, including violence, but in which the slaves were never entirely defeated or controlled by the masters.

In the Americas, modern slavery began with Christopher Columbus's first encounter with the New World in 1492, when he wrote to his patron, Queen Isabella of Spain, about what good slaves the inhabitants of the Caribbean islands would make, and he ordered his crew to capture several Arawak Indians to bring back to Europe as specimens. In the subsequent century, Spanish Conquistadors regularly enslaved the indigenous Americans to search for gold and other precious metals, but by the end of the sixteenth century the American Indian populace of the New World had been decimated through disease, war, and abuse and overwork in the mines. A global trade in African slaves arose to meet the insatiable demand for labor in the mines and plantations of those parts of Brazil, the Caribbean islands, and North America that were controlled by Spain, Portugal, England, France, Holland, and other European powers. Although the large majority of slaves who survived the horrific **Middle Passage** from Africa to the New World were destined for the huge sugar plantations in the West Indies and Brazil, a total of at least 600,000 Africans were brought to North America before the transatlantic slave trade was abolished in 1808. From this initial 600,000 sprang an American population of black slaves numbering 1.1 million by 1810, and almost 4 million in 1860. Although slaves played many roles in the United States, they were most commonly put to work on the cotton, tobacco, rice, and sugar plantations of the South.

Defenders of slavery devised numerous and sometimes contradictory arguments to justify the institution to themselves and to the outside world, typically using some combination of religion, biological theories of **race**, and paternalism. Some arguments offered scriptural evidence that God approved of blacks being kept as slaves; others suggested that Africans occupied an earlier stage of human evolution, were incapable of governing themselves, and were better off under the watchful eye of a white master. Much paternalistic proslavery rhetoric before and after **abolition** described the black slaves as simple children, contented and happy in the only life they knew or were fit for.

The reality from the slaves' perspective was much different. Of course, it is difficult to generalize about the experience of slaves, when chattel bondage was in fact a heterogeneous institution changing over time and differing widely from state to state—the experience of slaves in the deep South was different from that of slaves in the upper South, and different still from those in the northern colonies before the institution was gradually phased out; slaves on large plantations with dozens of other slaves lived differently than those belonging to small farmers with only a few slaves; men had a different experience than women. Nevertheless, most historians agree on certain generalizations about the experience and situation of American slaves: in every state they had the legal attributes either of personal property or "chattel," or of real estate; they were legally unable to own property or to be party to a contract, including a marriage contract; they were slaves for life, unless the master chose to free them, and the children of a slave woman always became slaves in turn; slaves were usually kept in a subsistence condition, with minimal clothing, housing, and food; masters had almost total control over the lives of their slaves, and could dispense almost any punishment short of deliberate murder or maiming without fear of consequences. Everywhere throughout the South, and especially in the Deep South, owners and overseers used the whip liberally to keep slaves in control and drive them to produce more and faster.

If slavery was a brutal and dehumanizing institution, the slaves never allowed themselves to be entirely controlled or dehumanized. In recent decades, much historical scholarship has focused on the slaves not as passive victims of a white system, but as subjects capable of rationality and action even within the heavily policed confines of the antebellum Southern plantation. In a few cases, slaves asserted their subjectivity through violent resistance, most famously and dramatically in the case of **Nat Turner**'s Rebellion of 1831, which was brutally put down by whites. But slave resistance took countless more subtle forms as well, from running away, to a collective refusal to work faster, and to subversive folk tales and work songs that secretly mock the overseer in code. The enslaved individuals struggled against all odds to maintain their family structures and kinship ties; they developed distinctive forms of religious practice and expression; and they engaged in unique modes of song and dance derived partly from their African heritage, partly from the culture of their European-descended captors, and partly from their own original genius.

By the middle of the nineteenth century, slavery was thoroughly entrenched and central to the economies of the South, but was also the source of bitter dispute between northern and southern states. The Dred Scott case of 1857, in which the Supreme Court denied citizenship and thus access to the courts for all blacks, further polarized the political situation and set the stage for the Civil War. In January of 1863, in the midst of that conflict, President Lincoln issued the Emancipation Proclamation, freeing all slaves in the rebel states. In 1865 Congress passed and the states ratified the Thirteenth

Amendment to the Constitution outlawing slavery. But the aftermath of the "peculiar institution" continues to affect race relations and questions of justice and power in the United States today, fourteen decades after its abolition.

Further Reading

Berlin, Ira. "American Slavery in History and Memory and the Search for Social Justice." *The Journal of American History* 90.4 (2004).

Kolchin, Peter. *American Slavery* 1619–1877. New York: Hill and Wang, 1993.

Stampp, Kenneth. *The Peculiar Institution: Slavery in the Ante-Bellum South.* New York: Vintage Books, 1956.

Shane Graham

SLESINGER, TESS (1905–1945) Jewish fiction and screenplay writer. Slesinger was a defining figure in the New York intellectual community of the 1930s whose works both chronicled and questioned her time. Slesinger's early family life influenced the direction of her writing. Reared in an assimilated third-generation Jewish household in New York, she grew up uninterested in Judaism, but with an open curiosity about literacy, self-expression, autonomy, sexuality, the dynamics of personal relationships, and the relationship between individuals and social structures. These themes would later become central to her work.

In the 1930s, Slesinger emerged as a new voice along with **Muriel Rukeyser** and other women writers who questioned the gendered limitations of leftist ideology and the intellectual community that supported it. Recognizing that the left supported gender equality in theory but subordinated it in practice, Slesinger and her contemporaries wrote texts that explored the often-silenced female voice in the intellectual community.

Slesinger got her start by publishing book reviews and short stories in *Menorah Journal, American Mercury, Forum, Modern Quarterly, The New Yorker, Pagany, Scribner's, Story Magazine, This Quarter,* and *Vanity Fair* in the early 1930s. Her only novel, *The Unpossessed,* was published in 1934. Growing out of Slesinger's experiences with *Menorah Journal* and her marriage to its assistant editor, Herbert Solow, the novel probes the relationship between radical and sexual politics. Slesinger satirizes several would-be leftist revolutionaries as they endlessly debate starting a magazine and wrestle with the role of the Jewish intellectual in American society. Basing her characters on Solow, **Lionel Trilling**, Clifton Fadiman, Elliot Cohen, and **Philip Ravh**, the driving forces behind *Menorah Journal,* Slesinger questions the purpose of intellectuals in a time of crisis and critiques them for their inability to connect with others in personal relationships. *The Unpossessed* was an unusual text because Slesinger dared to satirize the left from within and challenge leftists to know themselves and act on their principles. The novel was very successful, widely praised for its style and wit and declared the best novel of contemporary New York by reviewers. Not surprisingly, though, it also drew some criticism from the community it targeted for failing to fulfill political objectives sufficiently.

In 1935 Slesinger published *Time: The Present,* a collection of her short stories set in the 1930s. Many of the stories had previously appeared in magazines, but they found new life in connection with each other. Taken together, the stories comment on the process of human growth through depictions of everyday people who experience moments of revelation. Slesinger's dominant themes are emotional survival, sexuality, love, self-worth, and the search for **identity**. Reviewers were divided in their assessment of the collection. Although some found the stories overly sentimental, others praised Slesinger's ability to capture emotion and offer insight into ordinary lives without relying on stereotypes. The collection was enlarged and republished as *On Being Told That Her Second Husband Has Taken His First Lover, and Other Stories* in 1971.

Shortly after the publication of *Time: The Present,* Slesinger divorced her husband and separated from the circle of New York intelligentsia, moving to Hollywood where she pursued a career in screenwriting. Over the next ten years she wrote many popular screenplays, including *His Brother's Wife* (1936), *The Good Earth* (1937), *The Bride Wore Red* (1937), *Girls' School* (1938), *Remember the Day* (1941), and *Are Husbands Necessary?* (1942). Slesinger cowrote the screenplays for *Dance, Girl, Dance* (1940) and *A Tree Grows in Brooklyn* (1945) with Frank Davis, her second husband. At the time of her death from cancer, she had begun work on a novel about Hollywood.

Slesinger's small but important body of work moved the Jewish American narrative away from its established consideration of cultural clash toward explorations of the effect of personal and political events on the individual psyche. Rather than examining the position of the Jew within the binaries of Jew or gentile and immigrant or American, her texts looked at psychologically damaged characters navigating their own realms of family, friends, and society. Her insights into the struggles of women, in particular, make her voice an important one from the 1930s and 1940s. The recent reissue of *The Unpossessed* by Feminist Press is a tribute to Slesinger's lasting literary contributions.

Further Reading

Sharistanian, Janet. Afterword. *The Unpossessed: A Novel of the Thirties.* Tess
    Slesinger. New York: Feminist Press at the City U of New York, 1984. 359–86.

Amanda M. Lawrence

SLOVAK AMERICAN LITERATURE   Although Slovak Americans are among the largest Slavic ethnic groups in the United States, Slovak American literature has received little critical attention. Before World War I, millions of peasants left poverty-stricken villages in Slovakia, which was part of Hungary until Czechoslovakia was established in 1918. The majority immigrated to industrial centers such as Pittsburgh and Cleveland (where they were commonly referred to by the derogatory term "hunky"). The earliest generation of Slovak writers in the United States, at the beginning of the twentieth century, was represented by at least two significant figures: Gustáv Maršall-

Petrovský and Anton Bielik. Maršall-Petrovský was best known for his 1894 novel about the Slovak national hero Jánošík, but his works also included short stories about American immigrant life. Bielik was a prose writer and editor of the newspaper *Slovak in America* (*Slovák v Amerike*).

Almost none of the literature from this period has been translated into English, but Esther Jerabek's bibliography *Czechs and Slovaks in North America* does provide a thorough overview of Slovak American publications for those readers familiar with the Slovak language. An interesting counterpoint can be found in the short story "That Alluring Land" (1907) by Timrava, Slovakia's earliest woman writer. Timrava herself did not immigrate, but her story satirizes the image of America held by those left behind in Slovak villages: "That land glittered magically before their eyes. It was covered by luxuriant ears of grain strewn with the dollars that rained down abundantly upon the working man and jingled together like music" (117). The Slovak American experience of the early twentieth century can also be seen in the 1919 novel *Sanctus Spiritus and Company* by Edward A. Steiner.

Immigration to the United States dropped in the 1920s, partly due to restrictive immigration controls and partly to increased prosperity in Slovakia under the first Czechoslovak Republic (1918–38). The "Slovak State" (1939–45) was a highly ambiguous time in Slovak history, when an independent Slovak state was established for the first time, at the cost of close political cooperation with Nazi Germany. Czechoslovakia was reunified after the war, but soon became part of the Communist Eastern Bloc (from 1948 to 1989). Both the fall of the "Slovak State" and the rise of Communism led to significant new waves of immigration to the United States.

Although the Czechs and Slovaks are closely related ethnically and linguistically, neither group of Slovak Americans identified strongly with the unified Czechoslovak republic, especially after it became Communist. Religion (particularly the Catholic Church) has always been a stronger force among the Slovaks than among the Czechs, further separating the two groups; several of the most significant Slovak American writers were Catholic priests, which was not the case in **Czech American literature**. Nonetheless, a number of ethnic organizations, particularly those of a more academic nature, such as the Czechoslovak Society of Arts and Sciences, did seek to create bonds between Czechs and Slovaks in exile.

The leading Slovak American writer of the following generation was the poet and prose writer Miloš K. Mlynarovič. Among Mlynarovič's prose works are the short story collections *Novellas from American-Slovak Life* (*Novely z americko-slovenského života*, 1926) and *In the Shadow of Skyscrapers* (*V tieni mrakodrapov*, 1949). Mlynarovič attempted to relate the Slovak American struggle to that of other ethnic groups, particularly in his only novel, *Birds in a Maelstrom* (*Vtáčence vo víchrici*, 1956).

Slovak American literature of the postwar years was dominated by religious poetry, at a time when both religion and literature were under attack by the Communist regime in Slovakia. The literary journal *Most* ("bridge"), founded in Cleveland in 1954, was a center of Slovak American literary activity. In addition to Mlynarovič, its cofounders included the younger Catholic poets and translators Mikuláš Šprinc and Karol Strmeň. Both of them had begun their writing careers in Slovakia as part of the interwar Catholic Modernism movement, which brought the surrealism and symbolism of modern poetry together with Christian spirituality. The prolific Šprinc and Strmeň collaborated on the poetry collection *Pilgrims' Songs* (*Pútovné piesne,* 1950), which included Šprinc's *Vineyard* (*Vinohrad*) and Strmeň's *The Silver Legend* (*Strieborná legenda*). Šprinc's later poetry collections include *Travels and Destinies* (*Cesty a osudy,* 1957) and *Sonnets about Beauty* (*Sonety o kráse,* 1976), whereas Strmeň's most significant works include the collection *The Sign of the Fish* (*Znamenie Ryby,* 1969), partly inspired by the Soviet occupation of Czechoslovakia in 1968. Another Catholic Modernism writer who continued his literary career in America was the poet Rudolf Dilong, whose work includes *Toward the Light* (*Za svetlom,* 1954). A limited selection from the work of Šprinc, Strmeň, and Dilong can be found in the bilingual anthology *The Taste of a Lost Homeland* (2002).

The experience of second- and third-generation Slovak Americans (like that of many groups) was one of gradual improvement of social conditions, accompanied by **assimilation** and loss of cultural heritage. Few works by American writers of Slovak origin achieved critical or popular success, with one major exception: **Thomas Bell**'s 1941 novel *Out of This Furnace,* widely acclaimed as a masterpiece of American ethnic literature. *Out of This Furnace* begins on board a ship bound for New York in 1881, and follows the Slovak American Dobrejcak family through three generations to the labor movements of the 1930s. Bell's semi-autobiographical protagonist Dobie shows a keen social awareness that brings him to a greater appreciation of his own ethnicity, and he does not hesitate to confront the prejudices of the older generation of Slovak Americans. When one elderly woman complains about the decline of their neighborhood with the influx of "dirty niggers" who "live together like so many animals," Dobie responds mildly: "The very things the Irish used to say about the Hunkies the Hunkies now say about the niggers. And for no better reason" (330). At the conclusion of the novel, Dobie has overcome his old feelings of shame and bitterness about his Slovak background: "In their place were pride of achievement, a growing self-assurance, a certain degree of understanding that 'Hunky' was only one word in a whole disgraceful dictionary of epithets whose use would continue to spread humiliation and discord until society made that use as unprofitable as it was dangerous" (410). It is such humanist insights that carry Bell's novel beyond ethnic boundaries and ensure its place in American immigrant literature.

Several other Slovak American writers produced notable works in the subsequent decades, although none attained the lasting impact of *Out of This Furnace.* Alvena Seckar, the daughter of Slovak immigrants, portrayed the difficult life in West Virginia coal mining towns in her three books for children: *Zuska of the Burning Hills* (cited by the *New York Times* as an outstanding children's book in 1952), *Trapped in the Old Mine* (1953), and *Misko* (1956). The Slovak American writer **Michael Novak** was a leading figure in the ethnic studies movement of the 1970s, and his novel *Naked I Leave* (1970) fictionalizes his own spiritual and emotional journey. Fiction in English about the Slovak American experience also includes Jozef Pauo's novels about life in exile from Communist Czechoslovakia: *Unconquerables* (1958) and *Flight to Wonderland* (1963), and Michal Simko's novel *Mila Nadaya* (1968), which portrays Slovaks in New England.

As interest in America's multicultural heritage has grown, Slovak American literature has remained in obscurity, cut off from Slovak Americans and other potentially interested readers by a lack of translations. The predominance of poetry (a more difficult genre to translate, and one that is less widely read than fiction) among the work of the leading exile writers compounds the problem. Just as Slovakia itself has been traditionally overshadowed by other European nations, Slovak American literature has almost disappeared from the map of ethnic American literatures. Whereas most of it may have limited appeal to a wider readership today, the work of Slovak American writers is worthy of detailed study by bilingual literary scholars and historians as a largely forgotten piece in the mosaic of modern American **identity**.

Further Reading

Borkovec, Vera, ed. *The Taste of a Lost Homeland: A Bilingual Anthology of Czech and Slovak Exile Poetry Written in America*. Washington, DC: Czechoslovak Society of Arts and Sciences, 2002.

Cincura, Andrew, ed. *An Anthology of Slovak Literature*. Riverside, CA: University Hardcovers, 1976.

Jerabek, Esther. *Czechs and Slovaks in North America: A Bibliography*. New York: Czechoslovak Society of Arts and Sciences in America, 1976.

Laurence, Patricia Ondek. "The Garden in the Mill: The Slovak Immigrant's View of Work." *MELUS* 10.2 (1983): 57–68.

Petro, Peter. *A History of Slovak Literature*. Montreal: McGill-Queens UP, 1996.

Timrava. *That Alluring Land*. Translated by Norma L. Rudinsky. Pittsburgh: Pittsburgh UP, 1992.

Charles Sabatos

SLOVENE AMERICAN LITERATURE Slovenia—a territory split among Austria-Hungary, Italy, and Yugoslavia at separate times in history; an independent state since 1991 and a member of the European Union since 2004—has been a land from which persons have immigrated to the United States ever since the second half of seventeenth century. The earliest Slovenes in North America were Catholic missionaries Marko Anton (Marcus Antonius) Kappus (1657–1717), Friderik (Friedrich) Baraga (1797–1868), and Franc (Franz) Pirc (Pierz, 1785–1880). These and other late-nineteeth-century missionaries produced an enormous quantity of writings, such as letters, diaries, histories, Indian grammars and dictionaries, as well as religious books in Indian dialects. Some wrote poetry: for example, Kappus in Latin and Pirc in Slovene.

The biggest wave of migration of Slovene people followed at the turn of the century beginning in 1880s and stretching over the next decades until the implementation of U.S. quota laws of 1921 and 1924. Poor, uneducated immigrants established colonies in the West and Midwest at first; after 1900, they were drawn to Cleveland, Chicago, Pittsburgh, Detroit, Milwaukee, and New York, as well as the Minnesota Iron range, Kansas, and Colorado.

The third wave of Slovenes followed during and after World War II, consisting of political refugees who were well educated and more flexible than their predecessors. They did not settle in colonies, nor did they merge with earlier Slovene immigrants.

Most of the literature pertaining to the turn-of-the-century group was written in a simple, unpretentious style. Frequently nostalgic and sentimental, these works reflect upon life prior to emigration or they focus on immigrant experience, the tone ranging from hopelessness and despair to optimism and euphoria, from resigned acceptance to overt criticism of capitalist exploitation. Parallel to an equal division in their homeland, Slovene Americans were divided along ideological lines into Catholic and "progressive" authors. The first included poets Andrej Smrekar, Evstahij Brlec, and Ivan Zupan as well as short story writers John Jerich, Bernard Ambrožič, and John Plaznik and playwright Kazimir Zakrajšek. Zupan's collection of predominantly religious verses *Iz življenja za življenje* (1915) contains some formally and thematically simple, nostalgic, reflexive, and humorous poems; Father Zakrajšek's tragedy *Za srečo v nesrečo* (1932) is a moral play trying to dissuade prospective Slovene emigrants from even thinking of immigrating to the morally corrupt United States. The "progressive" group includes Jože Zavertnik, author of numerous proletarian short stories as well as a well-documented monograph on Slovene Americans, *Ameriški Slovenci* (1925), Frank S. Tauchar, Jože Ambrožič, Joško Oven, Anton Slabe, Louis Beniger, Frank Zaitz, Milan Medvešek, Anton Zaitz, Frank Česen, Mirko G. Kuhel, Frank Kerže, France Magajna, and Anton J. Terbovec. Many of the above were either editors of Slovene language newspapers or their regular contributors. Some wrote poetry but the majority were short story writers whose major characteristics include a realistic and naturalistic mode of narration, sharp criticism of capitalist exploitation, moralizing and occasional sentimentality.

Memoirs and autobiographies as well as mixed-genre memoir literature were published by first- and second-generation Slovene Americans. The oldest is anonymous (written by L.G. or L.C.), *V močvirju velemesta*, published in early 1920s in Cleveland: the life story of a Slovene immigrant woman packed with adventure, coincidences, and an obligatory happy ending. Jože Grdina published a memoir of his captivity in Russia during World War I, *Štiri leta v ruskem ujetništvu*, in 1925, followed by four books of travelogue between 1938 and 1963. While the doctor Frank Javh Kern reminisces about his beginnings in America in *Spomini ob tridesetletnici prihoda v Ameriko* (1937), the priest, Jurij M. Trunk, reflects upon the difficult time of plebiscite in Slovene Carinthia in Austria just after World War I in his book *Spomini* (1950). Trunk's major work, a 600-page history *Amerika in Amerikanci* appeared already in 1912. Gizella Hozian's reminiscences of her youth, *Spomini mladosti,* appeared in 1961, whereas Slovene American journalist Vatroslav Grill died before publication of his memoir of Slovene community in Cleveland *Med dvema svetovoma* (1979). Fred Bahovec combined autobiography with hunting stories in *Ljubljančan na Aljaski: spomini in lovske zgodbe* (1987). Franc Dornik (real name Pavlič) published his only book titled *Stickluft (Black Damp)* in 1969, recording in it his youth in native Trbovlje as well as his career as marine officer in Austrian navy up to the point of emigration just after World War I. Marie Prisland's *From Slovenia to America* (1968) falls short of its title's promise, being part history, part biography, memoir, and ethnography. In 1974 Sister Lavoslava Turk published *Pesem šolske sestre* that recreates, from the perspective of a nun, her interesting and meaningful life, focusing on her teaching career in Sheboygan, Wisconsin. Second-generation Slovene American Irene Planinsek Odorizzi's 1978 book *Footsteps Through Time* collects twenty-one autobiographies as told by Slovene immigrants and recorded, translated into English, and edited by Planinsek Odorizzi. Josephine Janežič's autobiography *Pepca's Struggle* (1989) records her and her family's ordeal during World War II as well as postwar departure for America. In some of the above cases, autobiography merges with biography. Many biographies were serialized, but those that appeared in book format include Frank J. Turk's *Slovenski pionir,* the biography of first Slovene immigrant in Cleveland in 1881; Giles E. Gobetz's *From Carniola to Carnegie Hall: A Biographical Study of Anton Schubel, Slovenian Immigrant Singer and Musical Pedagogue* (1968); *Love Moves Mountains: A Short Biography of Father Anthony Merkun, a Slovenian Refugee Priest* (1960), and *Slovenski ameriški slavček Ivan Zorman* (1991), Gobetz's biography of one of the foremost Slovene American poets. In 1977, *The Polka King: The Life of Frankie Yankovich, as Told to Robert Dolgan* was published. In 1985 G. E. Gobetz published the festschrift *Ohio's Lincoln Frank J. Lausche,* whereas William C. Bitter's *Frank J. Lausche: A Political Biography* appeared in 1975. Nancy Svet Burnett's *Slovenes in Rural Appalachia: An Oral History* (1992) is partly biography—relating of the author's parents' destiny after arrival in the United States—and partly a general history of Slovene immigration to the United States. Biographical writing peaked with **Louis Adamic**'s *The Cradle of Life* (1936), a fictionalized life story of Croatian painter Maximilian Vanka. Mary Molek's *Immigrant Woman* (1976) combines biography with autobiography.

Etbin Kristan's (1867–1953) reputation as a poet, prose writer, and dramatist had been well established in his homeland before immigration to the Untied States in 1922. He was an active socialist who became an important public figure within Slovene American community. He published little while in America—a collection of predominantly wartime short stories as well as a couple of immigrant tales *Povesti in črtice* (1945) and a story that looks back on his homeland during and after World War I, *Brata: povest iz še ne pozabljenih dni* (1948). He also wrote twelve plays that were repeatedly staged by Slovene American theaters. Influenced by Ibsen, he particularly loved to juxtapose the powerful and the ruling with the poor and exploited masses, where immigrants also belonged.

Ivan Molek's (1882–1962) career as a socialist author peaked in the 1920s and 1930s: he wrote poems, short stories, essays, and plays that were scattered, like Kristan's, among the pages of Slovene American left-wing press. He was a realist whose plastic narration and a capacity to join tragic and humorous elements made him one of the most popular Slovene American authors. His first naturalistic novel *Zajedalci* (1920), influenced by the Muckrakers, exposes the inhumanity of capitalism and the elusiveness of the American dream but focuses on the immorality of self-proclaimed doctors—"specialists in venereal diseases." This was followed by a trilogy— *Dva svetova* (1932), *Veliko mravljišče* (1934), and *Sesuti stolp* (1935). Its protagonist reveals some autobiographical features of the author, although Molek's purpose was clearly to write a model proletarian novel. *Čez hribe in doline*, Molek's fifth book, was published posthumously—in English translation—by his wife Mary. Although a prolific playwright, Molek published just one drama in book format; *Hrbtenica* (1926), a realistic three-act play with an allegorical prologue and epilogue, dealing with the theme of social criticism enhanced by a love story.

Zvonko A. Novak's (1882–1953) realistic-naturalistic long story *Iz Zapeške globeli* (1922) depicts Slovene immigrant life in America based on a stock theme and characters. Novak also published two pamphlets in book format.

Ivan Zorman (1889–1957) published six collections of poetry: *Poezije* (1919), *Pesmi* (1922), *Lirični spevi* (1925), an anthology *Slovene (Yugoslav) Poetry* (1928), *Pota ljubezni* (1931) and *Iz Novega sveta* (1938). They include patriotic and immigrant themes, reflexive and love lyrics, and humorous and occasional poems. Whereas patriotic poems yearn for an idyllic past but gradually give way to images of new American reality, Zorman's love poems range from spiritual to erotic, occasionally introducing an interesting mix of liturgical and sensual language. Nature looms large in his reflexive poems along with images of passing away and death, the latter taking over in his dark, desperate war poems.

Katka Zupančič (1889–1967) was a teacher who wrote mainly for the young. Her collection of seven short stories and five poems *Slike iz vsakdanjega življenja* appeared in 1946. A social critic, she wrote from the perspective of a child thus poignantly underscoring the aimlessness of human suffering. Her adult texts were less successful in their inability to disguise a far-too-obvious idea, such as her long story *S tujega na tuje* (1943).

Journalist, poet, and prose writer Janko N. Rogelj's (1895–1974) big literary idol was Slovene Ivan Cankar. His poems *Skrivnostni klic* (1967) contain immigrant themes and motives, such as nostalgic memories, elusive America, and resistance to Americanization. The short stories *Kruh in srce* (1962) and *Svoji k svojim* (1973) are stylistically polished, written in a highly lyrical language that reminds one of Cankar. Frequent humorous touches aim at social ills within the Slovene American community. Rogelj's four-volume memoir *Spomini* remains unpublished.

Jack Tomšič's (1897–1994) simple, descriptive verses, the themes of nostalgia and patriotism, nature and love, the use of conventional symbols and popular parables as well as his sonorous rhymes made him *the* poet of Slovene American community. He published two collections of poems, *Pognale so na tujih tleh* (1968) and *Človeku pojem* (1989).

Prose writer and dramatist Andrej (Andrew) Kobal (1899–1988) was, among other things, a journalist, university teacher, and employee of the Office of Strategic Services and Pentagon. First he published two plays, *Tolminec* (1931) and *Sakuntala* (1934), to be followed by a two-volume travelogue with elements of autobiography, memoir, and political history, *Svetovni popotnik pripoveduje* (1975, 1976). *Slovenec v službi F.B.I. in druge zgodbe ameriških Slovencev* (1981) is a biography of a Slovene American secret agent. Slovene American theaters often staged his other plays though none was published in book format.

Ivan Jontez (1902–79) was a lyrical poet, short story writer, and author of three novels. *Senca preko pota* (1940) is a naturalistic account of a Slovene American journalist's personal growth that leads him from unhappy marriage to a labor strike and a new beginning. *Jutro brez sonca* (1949) deals with the shooting down of an American plane in Slovenia after World War II. *Trouble on East Green Street* (1956) is an immigrant novel further complicated by the theme of racism but lacking in psychological insight.

Second-generation Slovene Americans authors are less numerous. Some published in newspapers and magazines and some of their work was anthologized, such as the short stories written by second-generation Slovene Americans John Modic, Jim Debevec, Stanley Zupan, and John Nielsen.

Frank Mlakar (1913–67) worked for the most prominent Slovene American author Louis Adamic for twelve years while both men lived in New York in 1930s. His novel *He, the Father* (1950) speaks about a young Slovene immigrant who ends up caught in a web of forces that appear to be beyond his control. This multilayered narrative focuses on the juxtaposition between natural and ethical laws—looking back on Dostoyevsky and Rølvaag—in its motives of crime and punishment and the divided heart of the immigrant. Although much praised by the critics, this nightmarish, pessimistic novel never became popular reading.

Mary Jugg Molek (1909–82) was a second-generation Slovene American whose poems in elaborate English were thematically removed from the daily concerns of immigrants, whereas her short stories and a biographical novel about her mother, *Immigrant Woman* (1976), focus on immigrant themes, such as survival, immigrant lifestyle, ancient ethical norms based on hard work, denial of pleasure, and strict morality. Molek translated into English and published her husband's novel *Two Worlds* (1978) as well as his memoir, *Slovene Immigrant History 1900–1950: Autobiographical Sketches* (1979).

Indifferent to her Slovene roots as a young girl, poet and short story writer Rose Mary Prosen (1931–) later tried hard to retrieve her memories. She published five booklets of poems, but only her 1980 collection, *Apples*, casts an eye upon her heritage, as symbolized by the apple, its synonyms and metaphorical substitutes. The apple represents the poet's source of experience, her tree of knowledge. Prosen's poetic expression is based on multiple connotations; she toys with punctuation and polarities; and she shuns no fantastic combination of seemingly incompatible words.

The number of post–World War II immigrant authors was relatively small. Mirko Javornik (1909–86), author of several books before emigration, published his second volume of essays, travelogue, criticism, and short stories, *Pero in čas* (1980), while living in the United States. Zdravko Novak (1909–71) "authored over two hundred short stories and articles, three dramatizations, and two major books, *Pota božja* (1957) and *Utrinki* (1959)" (Gobetz and Donchenko 225). Milena Šoukal's (1922–) 1969 collection *Pesmi* contains deeply intimate lyrical poems whose natural imagery orchestrates with her emotional life and ontological status. Marjan Jakopič (1923–78) published two collections of poems, *Vrbova piščal* (1955) and *Romanje pod sončnim lokom* (1979), his verses characterized by "powerful sentiment and nostalgia" (Glušič 300). Frank Bűkvič's (1923–95) collections of short stories, *Ljudje iz Olšnice* (1973) and *Zgodbe iz zdomstva in še kaj* (1979), thematically focus on life in native Prekmurje and immigrant life, respectively. His long war chronicle, *Vojna in revolucija* (1983), presents members of a Slovene family over a period of time beginning with the day Hitler occupied Prekmurje and ending after the war. Mara Cerar Hull's (1934) only published novel *Poletje molka* (1995) is partly autobiographical; it tells about a handicapped girl's ordeal during and after World War II.

Karel Mauser (1918–77), the most prolific writer of the group, had also published before emigration; his American publications include a long story *Mrtvi rod* (1963), his masterpiece, the trilogy *Ljudje pod bičem* (1963, 1964, 1966), as well as the novel *Kaplan Klemen* (1965). The trilogy focuses on man's inhumanity resulting from his adherence to political idea(l)s. Its characters, presented with deep psychological insight, fight for personal and religious freedom. *Kaplan Klemen* is a psychological study of a young priest's life, whereas Mauser's "American" short stories—*Vasovanje* (1982) and *Mačice v vazi* (1953)—relate social as well as psychological aspects of Slovene American life; so do his novels *Slum* (a fragment, 1952), *Vračanje* (1963), and *Večna vez* (published as *Srce nikoli ne laže*, 1991). His only collection of poetry, *Zemlja sem in večnost* (1978), appeared posthumously; its poems, described as being "reflexive and impressionistic in form" (Glušič 294), combine thought and emotion—their central idea the preciousness of life and beauty of the world.

Further Reading

Glušič, Helga. "Književnost novih slovenskih priseljencev v ZDA po letu 1945." *Slovenska izseljenska književnost 2. Severna Amerika.* Ed. Janja Žitnik and Helga Glušič. Ljubljana: Rokus and ZRC SAZU, 1999. 289–306.

Gobetz, Giles Edward, and Adele Donchenko. *Anthology of Slovenian American Literature.* Willoughby Hills, Ohio: Slovenski ameriški inštitut/Slovenian Research Center of America, 1977. 185–228.

Jurak, Mirko, and Jerneja Petrič, eds. *Ameriška proza od realizma do postmodernizma.* Ljubljana: Znanstveni inštitut Filozofske fakultete: 2001. 169–207.

Kuzmič Mihael. "Literarna dejavnost prekmurskih Slovencev v ZDA." *Slovenska izseljenska književnost 2. Severna Amerika.* Eds. Janja Žitnik and Helga Glušič. Ljubljana: Rokus and ZRC SAZU, 1999. 265–88.

Jerneja Petrič

SMITH, ANNA DEAVERE (1950–) African American playwright and performer. Anna Deavere Smith has created a body of theatrical work called *On the Road: Search for American Character.* Smith creates the pieces by interviewing people in select locales and later performing them using their own words. She developed the method that would lead to *On the Road* as exercises to teach students, but rather than asking a troupe of players to create each character, she assembled one-woman shows in which she plays all the parts herself.

Fires in the Mirror: Crown Heights, Brooklyn and Other Identities (1993) was Smith's first large-scale attempt to extend *On the Road* to address a specific event. The play explores the 1991 clash between Jews and blacks in that New York community. *Twilight: Los Angeles, 1992* (1994) examined the civil unrest following the Rodney King verdict. *House Arrest: A Search for American Character in and Around the White House, Past and Present* (2003) explores the mythic role that the presidency has played throughout American history.

Smith cites as influences the Free Southern Theatre, Ntozake Shange, and Allen Ginsberg. Others have connected her work to Brechtian theater, Cubist visual art, West African rituals, Faith Ringgold's story-quilts, talk shows, and Studs Terkel's oral histories. Smith's method also aligns with several African American aesthetic traditions, including found art, quilting, and **jazz**.

For *Fires in the Mirror*, Smith interviewed six hundred people in just eight days, two months after the violence abated. From the gathered recollections, she crafted her performance. Blacks and Jews had clashed following a car accident in which a Jewish van driver ran a red light and swerved onto the sidewalk killing a young black child and seriously injuring his cousin. That evening, a group of black men fatally stabbed a Hasidic scholar from Australia. The three days of riots that followed were a culmination of years of resentment between the Orthodox Jewish sect and Crown Heights's black majority. The conflict also reflected the pain, oppression, and discrimination these groups have historically experienced outside their own communities.

In accordance with her notion of adapting concepts of American character, Smith structures her text in such a way that issues related to character and **identity** formation are investigated in a circular fashion, from the general to the particular. The first two sections, "Identity" and "Mirrors," offer broad and speculative reflections on not just identity but how one sees or discerns the reality in which identities are constructed. From there, Smith locates specific issues of "Hair," "**Race**," "Rhythm," and "Seven Verses" to structure the dialogue pertaining to how the African Americans and Jews of the community come to describe and define themselves and each other. The drama concludes with the unambiguous "Crown Heights, Brooklyn, August 1991" section, which offers different perspectives on the actual events and their meanings. As the drama moves from general reflection to the specific issues that led to the incident documented, the audience confronts more difficult discussions of specific racist attitudes. Only the continuity of Smith's presence undercuts the authority of one group over another or of one individual over another.

The title of *Twilight: Los Angeles, 1992* was derived from the chosen name of one of Smith's characters, Twilight Bey, who hoped to organize a truce between the gangs of Los Angeles. The concept of twilight is both the introduction to and the coda for the limbo that Smith explores in this drama, and the character Twilight Bey himself functions like a surrogate for Smith's voice—one who speaks or communicates across seemingly insurmountable lines of hierarchy and difference. The metaphoric potential of twilight paradoxically recalls a time of danger and obscured vision, but also one of liminality and creativity. In *Twilight,* the bright light of fires reflected in a mirror becomes the dim light of a day ending, revealing new truths about identity but also new ambiguities.

In the spring of 1991, Rodney King, a black man, was severely beaten by four Los Angeles police officers after he led them on a high-speed chase. A nearby resident videotaped the beating. When the tape was broadcast on national television, there was an immediate outcry. The next year, when the police officers who beat King were tried and found not guilty, the city exploded with fury over the verdict. Three days of burning, looting, and killing followed the announcement. A declining economy, a growing hostility between the police and people of color, and the increasing assertiveness of marginalized ethnic communities all contributed to the preexisting tension. *Twilight* presented a multidimensioned challenge to Smith. The dispersed geography, the layered economic classes, and the multiple ethnic associations complicated her search for identity.

Sections of the play include "The Territory," which offers general assessments of the conditions that led to the uprising. "Here's a Nobody" traces different reactions to the beating of Rodney King and the resulting trial of the police officers involved. "War Zone" gives graphic renditions of the uprising itself, and "Twilight" and "Justice" deal with the aftermath and attempts to rebuild the community. The play concludes by circling back to the same issues raised in the prologue, in which a character traces a familial history of minority victimization.

House Arrest premiered not with Smith playing all the roles as she did before but with a group of twelve actors of different genders and races playing across lines of race, age, and gender to become Bill Clinton, Thomas Jefferson, Sally Hemings, celebrities, journalists, prison inmates, and academicians, among a vast array of historical and contemporary figures. The play was an ambitious attempt to renarrate U.S. history and interrogate presidential power and the role of the press. The play unfolds in multiple registers, juxtaposing historical material, interview excerpts, music, dance, and video.

Thematically, *House Arrest*'s point of view is revisionist history, highlighting the legacy of **slavery** and the complex intertwining of race, sexuality, and power that have been part of American democracy since the founding of the Republic. *House Arrest* was a significant development in Smith's work because she chose in this play to extend the earlier work in several ways. She makes use of several sources of textual material, including historical documents, a conventional fictive play that framed the action, first-person narrative/direct audience address, and the interview-based text that she used before. Video and television also were central characters, echoing the play's themes of media surveillance and saturation. The scope of the play expanded far beyond the analysis of a single contemporary urban crisis to encompass centuries of U.S. history presented in nonlinear juxtaposition. In all her works, Smith demonstrates the transformative nature of theater when it is applied to social justice. (*See also* African American Drama)

Further Reading

Connor, Kimberly Rae. "Negotiating the Differences: Anna Deavere Smith." *Imagining Grace: Liberating Theologies in the Slave Narrative Tradition.* Urbana: U of Illinois P, 2000. 194–238.

Lahr, John. "Under the Skin." *New Yorker* (June 28, 1993): 90–93.

Lewis, Barbara. "The Circle of Confusion: A Conversation with Anna Deavere Smith." *Kenyon Review* 15.4 (1993): 54–64.

Martin, Carol. "Anna Deavere Smith: The Word Becomes You." *Drama Review* 37.4 (1993): 45–62.

Kimberly Rae Connor

SMITH, BARBARA (1946–)   African American editor and essayist. Activist and scholar Barbara Smith has been a driving force behind the development of black feminist studies. In numerous anthologies and essays, Smith has explored the intersections between issues concerning **race**, gender, sexuality, and class while validating the unique and complex experiences of black women.

Smith received her BA from Mount Holyoke in 1969 and an MA from the University of Pittsburgh in 1971. She has taught at several universities, including the University of Massachusetts, Barnard College, and most recently New York University. Smith has also held several artist residencies, and until 1995 she was the publisher of Kitchen Table: Women of Color Press, the first American publisher for women of color. She cofounded Kitchen Press with **Audre Lorde** in the early 1980s.

Smith published her first book, *Toward a Black Feminist Criticism, Out and Out*, in 1977, the same year that the Combahee River Collective Statement was issued. This widely anthologized declaration, which Smith cowrote with Beverly Smith and Demita Frazier, describes the purposes of the Combahee River Collective, a feminist group founded in response to a growing sense of alienation among black women. The statement addresses sexism in the black community, and **racism** among women's groups, while also tracing the development of contemporary black **feminism**.

An understanding of the simultaneity of oppression has been a central theme of Smith's critical work. As she addresses specific concerns of black women, including reproductive freedom, lesbian and gay rights, expanded educational opportunities, housing, and environmental conservation, Smith offers an integrated approach to social reform and activism. In anthologies such as *All the Women Are White, All the Blacks Are Men, but Some of Us Are Brave: Black Women's Studies* (1982), *Home Girls: A Black Feminist Anthology* (1983), and *Yours in Struggle: Three Feminist Perspectives on Anti-Semitism and Racism* (1984), Smith has assembled a wide array of essays on the challenges and issues confronting black women. *All the Women are White,* for example, ranges from studies of historical representations of black women to discussions of the role of black women in the church and institutions of higher education. Smith has consistently articulated a liberatory politics that recognizes interlocking systems of oppression and seeks broad social reform at both a global and national level.

Smith has also made significant contributions to the study of African American literature. She was one of the first critics to approach classic black novels from both a feminist and lesbian perspective. By identifying lesbian themes and relationships in works not explicitly identified as homosexual, Smith explores such topics as the politics of heterosexuality and the destructive nature of gender roles.

Most recently, Smith published *The Truth That Never Hurts: Writings on Race, Gender, and Freedom* (1998), a collection of essays. She continues to lecture widely and to speak out on issues relevant to black women.

Further Reading

Culley, Margo, ed. *A Day at a Time: The Diary Literature of American Women.* New York: Feminist Press, 1985.

Stephanie Li

SONE, MONICA (née ITOI) (1919–) Japanese American autobiographer. Monica Sone's *Nisei Daughter* (1953) has been recognized as the first published autobiography of a Nisei (second generation) woman. This book is the only book that the author has written. *Nisei Daughter* was received approvingly in 1953; it was lauded for its candor, humor, and steering clear of bitterness and self-pity. Since reprinted in 1979, when the redress movement of the Japanese American community was initiated, Sone's book has been deemed as an important Asian American text that addresses the issues of **race**, **ethnicity**, and citizenship.

Sone's autobiography chronicles a young Nisei woman character's (Kazuko) life before, during, and after the **internment**. While the internment experience hinges together the pre- and post-internment life, a large portion of the narrative is contributed to the prewar childhood, described as a blissful and innocent period, but also overshadowed by some incidents of cultural conflict and racial tension. Like the majority of Japanese Americans during the war, Kazuko and her family went through repeated relocation and were forced to stay in prison cells euphemistically called "apartments." In mid-1943, as the War Relocation Authority opened channels for some Nisei women and men to leave the camps, Kazuko found her own "ticket"—employment and a white family sponsorship—to leave for Chicago. Later, she went to study in a liberal arts college in southern Indiana. In the Midwest, she still found it difficult to integrate into "mainstream" society, even as she tried to remain "invisible," that is, "nonoffensive" to the white majority. At the end of the book, the narrator sounded positive about her "double" **identity** and **assimilation** into "American" society, notwithstanding her experience of **racism** and incarceration. However, as some critics (e.g., Traise Yamamoto) point out, this optimist veneer is really a carefully engineered performance, which allows the Nisei woman narrator to educate non-Asian readers about the internment without offending them.

Sone's *Nisei Daughter* is often compared with **Jade Snow Wong**'s *Fifth Chinese Daughter* (1950) because both were published in the same period of time and share some characteristics, such as the dichotomization of Asianness and Americanness, the ethnic female subject, a coming-of-age plot, and, above all, a favorable outlook on assimilation. Yet the assimilational attitudes of these books should not be taken at their face value. Careful readers detect incongruent elements embedded in these narratives that really suggest ambivalence and ambiguity of "success stories" of the model minority. (*See also* Japanese American Autobiography)

Further Reading

Kapai, Leela. "Monica Sone." *Asian American Autobiographers: A Bio-Bibliographical Critical Sourcebook.* Ed. Guiyou Huang. Westport, CT: Greenwood Press, 2001. 321–27.

Kim, Elaine H. *Asian American Literature: An Introduction to the Writings and Their Social Context.* Philadelphia: Temple UP, 1982. 74–81.

Yamamoto, Traise. "*Nisei Daughter*, by Monica Sone." *A Resource Guide to Asian American Literature.* Ed. Sau-ling Cynthia Wong and Stephen H. Sumida. New York: MLA, 2001. 151–58.

———. *Masking Selves, Making Subjects: Japanese American Women, Identity, and the Body.* Berkeley: U of California P, 1999. 102–40.

Shuchen Susan Huang

SONG, CATHY (1955–) Korean/Chinese Hawaiian poet. Cathy Song is a well-acknowledged member of a younger generation of Asian American writers who represent the multicultural voice of Hawai'i. Many of her poems contain themes of Hawaiian immigrant history. She has published several collections of poems: *Picture Bride* (1983), *Frameless Windows, Squares of Light* (1988), *School Figures* (1994), and *The Land of Bliss* (2001). Her poems are widely published in journals and anthologies, including the *Hawai'i Review, Asian-Pacific Literature, Bamboo Ridge, The Greenfield Review, Hapa, New England Poetry Engagement Book, Seaweeds and Constructions, Tendril,* and *West Branch.*

Song was born in 1955 in Honolulu, Hawai'i. Her father is a Korean descendent, and her mother is a Chinese descendent. After attending the University of Hawai'i for a while, she transferred to Wellesley College, in Boston, where she earned her BA in 1977. She earned a master's degree in creative writing from Boston University in 1981. She published *Picture Bride,* her first collection of poems, in 1983, and it brought her acknowledgement as a prospective young poet. Richard Hugo chose *Picture Bride* for the Yale Series of Younger Poets. In addition to the 1982 Yale Series of Younger Poets Award, Song won many awards, including the Shelley Memorial Award from the Poetry Society of America, Hawai'i Award for Literature, and National Endowment for the Arts Fellowship. She returned to Hawai'i in 1987. She is currently a lecturer at the University of Hawai'i at Manoa and lives with her husband and children in Honolulu.

The major themes of Song's poems come from her observation of life as an Asian Hawaiian woman from a historical perspective. Many of her poems describe the Asian Hawaiian immigrant history and culture, such as plantation life, the history of the picture bride, the search for freedom, loneliness, and family connectedness. Song's works explore some of the popular themes of Asian American literature: many of her poems are about the experience of her family and community, and her parents and grandparents are popular subjects of her poems. Just as the narrator of **Maxine Hong Kingston**'s "No Name Woman," in the first chapter in ***The Woman Warrior***, speculates on the story of her aunt, Song's *Picture Bride* searches for the story of her grandmother as a picture bride. Through identification and imagination, Song constructs herself and the communal self of Asian American women. She often uses visual images and everyday language, which portray ordinary life with clarity and compassion.

Visual images are a major resource in Song's poems. In plain language, she describes the ordinary activities of people, such as cooking and putting on makeup. These visual images of actions also correspond to the poet's activity of interpreting the life of people and history. Through the presentation of simple actions, Song examines the culture and history, especially of Asian American women. Images of houses, such as kitchens, windows, rooms, curtains, and doors, appear as background; they are not only the part of the setting, but also are artifacts designed to reveal the hidden story of life. Domestic space or household goods uncover the lives of women and their sociocultural condition. For example, her poem "Humble Jar" in *Frameless Windows, Squares of Light*, uses buttons her mother collects in a jar as the central image to reveal her mother's life, which is marginalized and undervalued from the outside world.

One of the unique elements of Song's poetry collection is the use of visual art pieces to highlight the style and themes of her poems. *Picture Bride* contains paintings by Georgia O'Keeffe and eighteenth-century Japanese artist Kitagawa Utamaro's works. O'Keeffe's flower paintings project the sense of the balance and reconciliation between traditional and nontraditional womanhood in her poems. These art pieces in her poems also depict the relationships between the creative process of art, literature, language, and the cultural and social phenomena that Asian Americans experience.

Song's poems intertwine reality, language, and art. Using her imagination, she bridges her immigrant ancestors, parents, and other Asian Americans with herself in her poems, successfully showing the connection between communal history and personal issues. In terms of style, Song's presentation of ordinary life with vivid imagery and clear language provides a fresh perspective on language and culture. (*See also* Hawai'i Literature)

Further Reading

Fujita-Sato, Gayle. "'Third World' as Place and Paradigm in Cathy Song's *Picture Bride*." *MELUS* 15.1 (Spring 1988): 49–72.

Wallace, Patricia. "Divided Loyalties: Literal and Literary in the Poetry of Lorna Dee Cervantes, Cathy Song and Rita Dove." *MELUS* 18.3 (Fall 1993): 3–19.

Youngsook Jeong

SONG OF SOLOMON   **Toni Morrison**'s third novel, *Song of Solomon* (1977), is now a **canon**ical African American novel that explores the theme of quest for **identity** and for preserving a sense of community in its rich references to **African American folklore** tradition and history.

Morrison chooses a male protagonist, Milkman Dead, for her National Book Critics' Circle Award–winning novel, and this choice counters her foregrounding of female characters in her previous two novels—*The Bluest Eye* (1970) and *Sula* (1973). Milkman, caught between his father's black middle-class materialism and his aunt, Pilate's, traditional values, is alienated from his community and his cultural roots. Increasingly preoccupied with his family's past and troubled with his alienation, he embarks upon a physical and spiritual journey into the South. The original reason for this journey is to recover the gold that caused the rift between Milkman's father and his sister, Pilate. Milkman's father believes that Pilate stole a bag of gold when he and Pilate escaped from the South. What he does find, however, is liberating knowledge instead of the gold: when he overhears the name *Solomon* from a song that some children sing as they play a game in a little Virginia town, Milkman realizes that the song is part of his family history and that the "Solomon" in the song is his great-grandfather, a slave who escaped his bondage by flying back to Africa.

In *Song of Solomon*, Morrison also places her narrative in a larger political context of the **Civil Rights Movement** of the 1960s by incorporating historical events, such as the murder of Emmett Till, and through the characterization of Milkman's best friend Guitar Bains, who represents a radical political position. Guitar is a member of a secret revolutionary group called the *Seven Days*. Rejecting all racial uplift strategies, the Seven Days members are dedicated to avenging racial violence: when a black person is murdered by whites, the member responsible for that day of the week avenges the death by the same manner. At the end of the novel, Milkman and Guitar find themselves locked in physical struggle, and, then, Milkman leaps off a cliff, surrendering to the wind and riding it.

In *Song of Solomon*, a text that is infused with biblical allusions, mythologies, African American folklore and the history of **slavery**, the Great Migration, urbanization, and the Civil Rights Movement. Morrison illustrates how ancestral and cultural roots are vital to the preservation of the African American communities through her protagonist, who ultimately embraces the richness of his ancestry and heritage.

Further Reading

Kubitschek, Missy Dehn. *Toni Morrison: A Critical Companion.* Westport, CT: Greenwood Press, 1988.

Wagner-Martin, Linda. "'Close to the Edge': Toni Morrison's *Song of Solomon.*" *Teaching American Ethnic Literatures.* Ed. John R. Maitino and David R. Peck. Albuquerque: U of New Mexico P, 1996. 147–57.

Willis, Susan. "Eruption of Funk: Historicizing Toni Morrison." *Black Literature and Literary Theory.* Ed. Henry Louis Gates Jr. New York: Routledge, Chapman, and Hall, 1990. 263–83.

Seongho Yoon

SONTAG, SUSAN (1933–2004)   Jewish American writer and activist. Susan Sontag was a leading voice in cultural, artistic, and political thought around the globe. Her brilliant career in writing includes essays, novels, films, and plays. During her lifetime, she was an indefatigable activist in culture, art, and politics. Her fiction and nonfiction have appeared widely in periodicals, including the *New Yorker*, the *Nation*, the *New York Review of Books*, the *Times Literary Supplement*, *Antaeus*, *Parnassus*, and the *Threepenny Review*. As an essayist, she has garnered an attentive and admiring audience through her probing insight into a diverse and rich catalog of subjects: photography, pornographic literature, fashion, aesthetics, surrealism, illness, war, and terrorism.

Sontag was born in 1933 in New York City but grew up in Tucson, Arizona. Her father had a fur-trading business in China, where he died of pulmonary tuberculosis when she was five years old. Her mother, Mildred, married Nathan Sontag seven years later. Susan was a precocious young woman, entering the University of California at Berkeley at the age of fifteen in 1948 and graduating with a BA from the University of Chicago in 1951. She completed graduate studies at Harvard University (MA in English, 1954; MA in philosophy, 1955).

Adulthood responsibilities came early in her life. At the age of seventeen, she married Phillip Rieff, a sociology lecturer, and two years later gave birth to her son, David. She divorced in the late 1950s.

Susan Sontag. *Courtesy of the Library of Congress.*

It was during the 1950s and 1960s in New York City that Sontag formed her attitudes on how marginalized ideas can move to the center of the social and cultural text to transform the individual and world. She joined the intellectual crowd of the *Partisan Review* while teaching at City College of New York, Sarah Lawrence College, and Columbia University. She also held a one-year post as writer-in-residence at Rutgers University. In those two decades, she gained confidence as a young writer by contributing to the *Atlantic Monthly, Harper's, Nation,* and the *New York Review of Books.* Writing became her passion as well as her immediate tool for self-transformation. Her voice has been described as highly intellectual but articulate, independent but social, and critical but optimistic.

Sontag first gained prominence in the early 1960s as an essayist whose intellectual and emotional zeal challenged prevalent attitudes on art, culture, and society. *Notes on Camp* (1964)—thoughts on people divided into social and cultural groups—was her first entry into the difficult genre of essay writing. Her 1968 description of a sojourn to Hanoi during the Vietnam War gives evidence of Sontag's politically charged consciousness. As a social critic and human rights activist, her statements have been both combustible and conciliatory: "America is founded on genocide" and "Is it true that war never solved anything?" referring to Kosovo. Early on she discovered Edith Hamilton's mantra on the written word: "A word is no light matter."

An early essay that quickly brought her recognition in the study of art is "Against Interpretation," the principal essay collected in *Against Interpretation and Other Essays* (1968). This durable work is a postmodernist look at the problem of interpreting art forms. Her polemic argues that a reliance on deciphering art based on conventional codes or interpretation supplants the actual work with the hegemony of the interpreter. To interpret art transforms it and is a "revenge of the intellect upon the world. To interpret is to impoverish, to deplete the world—in order to set up a shadow world of meanings." Essentially, the actual work is lost in the translation.

In addition to the recurrent theme of transformation, Sontag's writing explores closing the gap between human illness and artistic expression, the body and consciousness. This subject of illness as a metaphor for society first emerged with her 1976 introduction to *Antonin Artaud: Selected Writings*. Artaud, the French surrealist dramatist and writer was, as Sontag referred to him, "one of the last great exemplars of the heroic period of literary modernism." Despite being a tormented genius and spending nine years in an asylum for the insane, Artaud amassed an eclectic body of work in aesthetics and theater. Theater, for Artaud, was to be devoted to myth, magic, and gesture, and not the power of the intellect through words. His modernist denunciation of the traditional artistic **canon** erupted with his declaration: "No more masterpieces!" a statement Sontag, a radical individualist in her own right, often reverberated through her essays and nonfiction works that question cultural norms and fossilized ideas.

While Artaud compares a theater experience to the unseen and assaulting effects of a plague, Sontag likens the theater to a visit to the surgeon or dentist. The theater offers "a kind of emotional and moral surgery upon consciousness" and "the audience should not leave the theatre 'intact' morally or emotionally."

On Photography (1976) is a collection of essays published originally in the *New York Review of Books*. Rather than prolonging the debate as to photography's role as a true art form, Sontag's work surfaces as one of the initial challenges to the use and effect of the barrage of photographs and images on society in a media-based and image-conscious culture. *On Photography* is also a return to Sontag's theme of deconstructing long-held social metaphors that constrict individual transcendence. Her concepts, which seek to free the photographic image from mimetic interpretation, have influenced photographers like Annie Leibovitz.

Sontag later returned to this link between corporeal and mental malady and society in *Illness as Metaphor* (1978) and *Aids and Its Metaphors* (1988), two complementary texts. While her work with Artaud was purely intellectual, her subsequent ideas in *Illness and Metaphor* and *Aids and Its Metaphors* are deeply personal and emotive. She breaks from traditional acceptances that human illness is a metaphor for an ailing society.

Illness as Metaphor became Sontag's personal response to her battle with what had been diagnosed as terminal metastatic breast cancer. Through unconventional therapy, she recovered from her first bout with cancer. Her response to the illness has been described as both "intellectual and emotional." *Illness as Metaphor* contends that the notion of illness in individuals and groups like women with breast cancer has erroneously become transformed, through metaphor, to a comment on the moral and cultural decay of a society. Such misguided transference creates the guilt-encrusted scenario that one's illness is somehow deserved. *Aids and Its Metaphors* is an expansion of the earlier work, criticizing the rampant social ridicule and punishment associated with AIDS. Sontag was diagnosed with uterine cancer in 1998.

Although Sontag had always had a passion for writing novels, it was not until *The Volcano Lover, a Romance* (1992) that she was able to transform herself artistically from social essayist to mature novelist. Her earlier attempts at the novel genre (*The Benefactor*, 1963; *The Death Kit*, 1967) did not bring the acclaim she enjoyed in nonfiction. She wrote *The Benefactor* at the age of thirty. This symbolic and experimental work concerns how the protagonist strives to incorporate his outlandish dreams into his daily life. *The Death Kit*, encountering mixed reviews, also explores the incongruity between dream and reality.

The Volcano Lover reveals the well-honed craft of the writer. Lurking behind the historical love story, set at the end of the eighteenth century, is the author's intellectual and feminist examination of the changing shape of Western civilization since the Age of Enlightenment. Original in its layered texture and provocative in its ideas, the novel has been praised as a historical romance. Her novel *In America* (1999), based on a real story of a woman's search for self-transformation, received the National Book Award in 2000.

In drama, Sontag wrote and directed plays in the United States and Europe. In 1993 she directed Beckett's absurdist drama *Waiting for Godot* in the besieged Sarajevo. Amid the backdrop of bombing and rifle fire from the war raging outside the theater, Sontag's unflagging determination in theater brought to the city a rallying point of resistance to tyranny.

In the medium of film, Sontag wrote and directed four feature-length films, including *Duet for Cannibals* (1969), *Brother Carl* (1971), *Promised Lands* (1974), and *Unguided Tour* (1983).

Her nonfiction work *Regarding the Pain of Others* (2003) is a probing and haunting work that explores the impact that the unrelenting barrage of savage images from the news media and movies of war, disasters, and social violence have on society. This much acclaimed work represents the peak of Sontag's many talents and interests, incorporating the essay, nonfiction, photography, film, media, and other disciplines. The work offers a haunting look at historical images, such as famine; bloodshed; and mass death as seen in the Civil War and World Wars I and II; as well as contemporary horrific images from Rwanda, Bosnia, and New York City on September 11, 2001. In this exploration, Sontag challenges a reader's attitudes regarding sympathy and obligation toward others.

Over her career, Sontag received many awards, including the American Academy Ingram Merrill Foundation Award (1976), National Book Critics

Circle Award for *On Photography* (1977), Academy of Sciences and Literature Award (Germany, 1979), National Book Award for *In America* (2000), Malaparte Prize (Italy, 1992), Commandeur de l'Ordre des Arts et des Lettres (France, 1999), Jerusalem Prize (2001), Prince of Asturias Prize (Spain, 2003), and Peace Prize of the German Book Trade (2003). She also received a five-year fellowship from the MacArthur Foundation. As a human rights activist, she served in the late 1980s as president of the American Center of PEN, the international writers' organization dedicated to freedom of expression and the advancement of literature.

Throughout her impressive career as an essayist, novelist, dramatist, and literary and social critic, Sontag confronted audiences with challenging images and ideas. Her role has remained to transform society into a more open and accepting world body. In a new edition of *Against Interpretation*, published thirty years after it initial appearance, Sontag looks back on her career as a woman of letters: "I saw myself as a newly minted warrior in a very old battle: against philistinism, against ethical and aesthetic shallowness and indifference." As an outspoken, leading woman of letters, her ideas have had considerable influence on topics that are the province of all peoples, such as war, terrorism, human rights, and illnesses. Sontag died of cancer on December 27, 2004, in New York City.

Further Reading

Kennedy, Liam. *Susan Sontag. Mind as Passion.* Manchester, UK: Manchester UP, 1995.

Poague, Leland. *Susan Sontag: An Annotated Bibliography, 1948–1992.* New York: Garland Publishers, 2000.

Rollyson, Carl. *Reading Susan Sontag: A Critical Interpretation to Her Work.* Chicago: Ivan R. Dee, 2001.

Rollyson, Carl, and Lisa Paddock. *Susan Sontag: The Making of an Icon.* New York: W. W. Norton, 2000.

Sayres, Sohnya. *Susan Sontag: The Elegaic Modernist.* New York: Routledge, 1990.

Michael D. Sollars

SOPRANOS, THE   Setting new benchmarks for social realism, narrative complexity, and psychological penetration, this weekly hour-long Home Box Office (HBO) Television series about the New Jersey Mafia first ran in January 1999 and in short order established itself as both the most popular show on cable television and the most highly praised in the history of the medium. Its creator is David Chase, formerly with *The Rockford Files* and other shows, and he took this project to HBO because, as a subscriber-only network, they could allow him artistic control, especially regarding sex and violence. The writer-director proved himself a video auteur; he developed each season about Tony Soprano and his struggles to keep his family together while retaining Mafia control so that its thirteen episodes presented a dramatically escalating and thematically coherent vision of dog-eat-dog America that was at once hilarious and harrowing. Vincent Canby, of the *New York Times*, praised the format as well as the content, declaring each season of *The Sopranos* a "megamovie"—worthy company to longer works by Fassbinder and Von Stroheim.

More common comparisons are to Scorsese and Coppola, and the series has spawned a number of booklength examinations, the best of which is the collection of essays *A Sitdown with the Sopranos*. Yet the show has also renewed the controversy over the representation of Italian Americans in popular media. Each season triggers a public outcry from organizations such as the National Italian-American Foundation, an irony given not just the critical agreement regarding the show's quality, but also the fact that Chase himself claims Italian descent; his grandparents' name was *DeCesare*.

The Sopranos makes use of rarified techniques like dream sequences and sharply placed cultural references, but it depends most on an old-fashioned and unstinting realism about its personalities and the damage they do each other. Chase and his colleagues maintain a searing fidelity to money-driven and family-saddened American dynamics. The best episodes have the intensity and intimacy of great kitchen-sink drama. It demands such emotional subtlety of its two principals, James Gandolfino as Tony and Edie Falco as his wife Carmela, that their performances have made them celebrities; both they and the show have earned a number of Emmy awards.

Despite its popularity and esteem, and despite the many laughs each episode delivers, *The Sopranos* remains television *noir*. It dwells in an often-terrifying social circle, severely stunted and based on a threadbare outlaw code. Carmela and the other women in the show have moments of steely power, but they remain largely helpless, creatures of pure skin. Conversely, Tony may invite sympathy—his counseling sessions are a continuing feature, illuminating not only about his character but also about the changing world around the therapist's office—yet this is one media mobster who remains a thug, always a predator on the disenfranchised and the poor, and never a figure to be envied like the lordly Don Corleone. Rarely have honesty and entertainment been so closely combined. (*See also* Italian American Film)

Further Reading

Barecca, Regina, ed. *A Sitdown With the Sopranos: Watching Italian-American Culture on TV's Most Talked-About Series*. New York: Palgrave MacMillan, 2002.

Canby, Vincent. "From the Humble Mini-Series Comes the Magnificent MegaMovie." *New York Times* (October 31, 1999): Arts & Leisure, 1.

Domini, John. "Dinosaur in the Train Station: Four Years of the *Sopranos* Phenomenon." *North American Review* 288.2 (2003): 38–42.

Lavery, David, ed. *This Thing of Ours: Investigating the Sopranos*. New York: Columbia UP, 2002.

John Domini

SORRENTINO, GILBERT (1929–)   Italian American novelist, poet, essayist, and short story writer, long based in New York City and later a professor at Stanford, best known for a series of experimental novels of the 1970s and 1980s. Sorrentino's books are acute in their observations on society and psychology, yet unconcerned with conventions of character or narrative; they foreground instead a play with forms, adapting everything from antique devices like rhyming quatrains to contemporary models like celebrity interviews. A lifelong devotee of William Carlos Williams, like him Sorrentino has proven prolific yet stubbornly outside the norm, so that he has earned only intermittent esteem, and publication has come generally in small presses. Nonetheless, the fiction has been praised by **Philip Roth** and **Don DeLillo**, and a *Selected Poems* appeared in 1981. That same year *The Review of Contemporary Literature* devoted an entire issue to his work, and in 2001 Sorrentino was one of three others to which another issue was devoted.

Brooklyn-born, his mother Irish and father Italian, his first book was a collection of poetry, *The Darkness Surrounds Us,* in 1960. His first novel, *The Sky Changes,* came six years later, and shortly after that Sorrentino entered a remarkably productive ten- or twelve-year period that saw a variety of novels at the top of his idiosyncratic form.

This began with *Steelwork* (1970), a scrapbook narrative that combines several voices and perspectives to portray the immigrant Brooklyn of mid-century as a stunted mockery of the American dream. With *Imaginative Qualities of Actual Things* (1971; the title is from William Carlos Williams) Sorrentino brought off another scabrous collage, often hilarious, portraying the lower levels of the New York arts scene. The slender *Splendide-Hotel* (1973) uses the alphabet as its organizing principle and has little truck with story. *Mulligan Stew* (1979) runs far longer and was widely reviewed, but nearly buries its plot of a novelist going mad beneath parodic games and metafictional trickery. A return to more ordinary subjects came with *Aberration of Starlight* (1980), a multivocal enactment of family dysfunction and deceitful love in 1930s New York, and then *Crystal Vision* (1981) took roughly the same concerns and milieu and turned them magical and uproarious. No clear critical consensus on these novels has emerged; each has been nominated as Sorrentino's greatest accomplishment. One can see, though, that in general the author moved further from realism in subject matter while, at a technical level, stepping up his experimentation.

The same period also saw the well-received poetry of *Corrosive Sublimate* (1971) and the *Selected Poems.* On top of that, Sorrentino was writing book reviews and essays, collected eventually in *Something Said* (1984), and short stories, including "The Moon in Its Flight" (1971), which appears in a few anthologies.

Later the play with fictional devices dominated his work above other elements, as seen in the trilogy *Odd Number* (1985), and *Rose Theater* (1987), and *Misterioso* (1989), collected as *Pack of Lies* in 1997. His latest, *Little Casino* (2002) returns to more recognizable human territory, but its unhappy postwar Brooklynites too are presented in fragments of diverse types of prose, including dream language. Overall, Sorrentino may be seen as helping define the farther parameters of contemporary American literature, combining intense awareness of ethnic and social realities with a rare freedom of imagination and form. Dalkey Archive Press has reissued most of his earlier work, and he has won many major fellowships, including the Guggenheim and the Lannan. (*See also* Italian American Novel)

Further Reading

Andrews, David. "Gilbert Sorrentino." *Review of Contemporary Fiction* 21.3 (2001). 7–57.

———. "The Art is the Act of Smashing the Mirror: A Conversation with Gilbert Sorrentino." *Review of Contemporary Fiction* 21.3 (2001): 60–68.

Domini, John. "Blue Without Blues: Gilbert Sorrentino and the Subversion of the Novel." *Boston Phoenix* (July 5, 1983): section 3, 7+.

O'Brien, John, ed. *Gilbert Sorrentino* [Special Issue]. *Review of Contemporary Fiction* 1.1 (1981): 4–189.

———, ed. "Casebook Study of Gilbert Sorrentino's *Imaginative Qualities of Actual Things*." *Review of Contemporary Fiction* 23.1 (2003): 5–181.

John Domini

SOTO, GARY (1952–)   Latino poet. Perhaps the most widely known contemporary Mexican American poet, Gary Soto has produced a great deal of work in other genres as well: novels, young-adult novels, short stories, essays, plays, memoirs, nonfiction, and children's books. He has even written a libretto for the Los Angeles Opera. Unlike other prolific authors who have been criticized for publishing their work indiscriminately, Soto has received much recognition for his work in a number of genres, and the great appeal of his other work has ultimately enlarged the readership for his poetry, in which he has made his most lasting contribution to American letters.

Soto was born in Fresno, California, and throughout his life he has continued to live within a relatively short distance of his home ground. The agricultural region of central California has provided him with both the impetus to write and the material about which to write. A poet of the laboring poor, Soto lost his own father to a work-related accident when only five years old. His father ironically became a haunting presence in the Soto home because his mother staved off being overwhelmed by grief by discouraging any references to him. Many of Soto's poems attempt to resurrect the father whom he hardly got to know by reconstructing him from the memories and memorabilia of family and friends—and, more broadly, from the cultural memory and artifacts of the time and place that produced him. In Soto's poetry, time is always referential as well as linear, and personal and communal truths are almost always complementary, even when they seem initially to be at odds.

In 1975 Soto married Carolyn Sadako Oda, the child of Japanese Americans who had been interned during World War II. Their marriage and the birth of their daughter, Mariko Heidi, infused Soto's poetry with a more broadly multicultural sensibility and has given a greater universality even to his poetic

Gary Soto. *Courtesy of Gary Soto.*

portraits of Mexican Americans. In addition, Soto's intense interest in his daughter's development not only led to his writing for younger readers but also added fresh layers of meaning to his poetic attempts to reconcile the past and present, to his attempt to recapture formative experiences and not only to understand them as an adult but also to consider how he may have perceived and understood them as a child.

As an undergraduate student at California State University in Fresno, Soto had the fortuitous opportunity to enroll in creative-writing courses presented by the poet **Philip Levine**. These courses caused Soto for the first time in his life to become an avid reader of poetry—and especially of contemporary poetry. His reading, as well as the work he produced for Levine and the feedback that he received, convinced him both that he could become a capable poet and that he should use his own experiences and his own community and heritage as the primary subjects of his poetry. Indeed, although Soto has developed a very distinctive poetic style, the degree to which he has been influenced by Levine's own work can be seen in the following aspects of his work: first, in his recurring interest in the meaning and consequences of labor and his refusal to indulge in populist idealizations of the laborer; second, in his creation of a poetic idiom that is colloquial, rather than inflated or arcane, but that, rather than merely reproducing or replicating speech, transforms familiar expression into something more pointedly poetic; third, in his subtle manipulation of poetic forms and of the poetic line to create an organic connection between how the poem looks and reads and what it says; and, finally, in his reliance on close attention to detail and in his sparing—and therefore all the more emphatic—use of figures of speech.

The best poems from Soto's first seven collections are available in his *New and Selected Poems* (1995), for which he received the National Book Award and well as several other awards. His subsequent collections have included *Junior College* (1997), *A Natural Man* (1999), and *Shadow of the Plum* (2002). (*See also* Mexican American Poetry)

Further Reading

Bus, Heiner. "Sophisticated Spontaneity: The Art of Life in Gary Soto's *Living Up the Street.*" *Americas Review* 16 (Fall–Winter 1988): 188–97.

de la Fuente, Patricia. "Entropy in the Poetry of Gary Soto: The Dialectics of Violence." *Discurso Literario* 5 (Autumn 1987): 111–20.

———. "Mutability and Stasis: Images of Time in Gary Soto's *Black Hair*." *Americas Review* 17 (Spring 1989): 100–107.

Erben, Rudolf, and Ute Erben. "Popular Culture, Mass Media, and Chicano Identity in Gary Soto's *Living Up the Street* and *Small Faces*." *MELUS* 17 (Fall 1991–1992): 43–52.

Ganz, Robin. "Gary Soto." *Updating the Literary West*. Fort Worth, TX: Western Literature Association/Texas Christian UP, 1997. 426–33.

Lee, Don. "About Gary Soto." *Ploughshares* 21 (Spring 1995): 188–92.

Manson, Michael Tomasek. "Poetry and Masculinity on the Anglo/Chicano Border: Gary Soto, Robert Frost, and Robert Hass." *The Calvinist Roots of the Modern Era*. Ed. Aliki Barnstone, Michael Tomasek Manson, and Carol J. Singley. Hanover, NH: UP of New England, 1997. 263–80.

Olivares, Julian. "The Streets of Gary Soto." *Latin American Literary Review* 18 (January–June 1990): 32–49.

Torres, Hector A. "Genre-Shifting, Political Discourse, and the Dialectics of Narrative Syntax in Gary Soto's *Living Up the Street*." *Critica* 2 (Spring 1988): 39–57.

Martin Kich

SOULS OF BLACK FOLK, THE

Published in 1903, *The Souls of Black Folk* is **W. E. B. Du Bois**'s collection of fourteen prose pieces that blend literary forms such as the essay, short story, and memoir to articulate one of the most stirring accounts of the black experience in the post-Reconstruction United States. Though nine key pieces were circulated in periodicals as early as 1897, their inclusion in this volume forms the crux of Du Bois's rethinking African Americans' history as well as their future.

"The Forethought" and the opening chapters introduce the text's central metaphors. The preface boldly declares that "the problem of the Twentieth Century is the problem of the color line," by which Du Bois means not simply the political and socioeconomic barriers to citizenship and property that legalized segregation levels against African Americans but also the divide within the black psyche that renders its "Negro" consciousness irreducible to its "American" one. The latter concept Du Bois refers to as "double-consciousness" in "Of Our Spiritual Strivings." But he is careful not to stigmatize this condition, for such "second-sight," "this sense of always looking at one's self through the eyes of others," locates the possibility for genuine and lasting democratic change in the United States in the hands of those who possess a dialectical vision borne out of oppression. The aesthetic upshot of double-consciousness is perhaps most strikingly reflected in the epigraphs for each chapter (save the last), which set a selection of verse from the Western literary **canon** alongside a bar of music from a folk **spiritual**.

Du Bois's vision is partial to the extent that it counters the project of racial uplift advocated by the leading African American spokesman of the time,

Booker T. Washington. In his chapter on Washington and "Of the Training of Black Men," Du Bois claims that the vocational approach to uplift accommodates itself to the political, social, and, perhaps most damaging, psychic logics of segregation in exchange for "larger chances of economic development." What he calls for instead is the "higher training" of African Americans in the liberal arts, which would ground black struggle for equality in discourses of universal reason and shared cultural knowledge. Though Du Bois has often been critiqued for this paradigm's sexist and elitist traits, his defense of the life of the mind could also be said to assert the fundamental humanity of African Americans as thinking and feeling subjects and thus to validate the black experience across the color line. The volume's most affectively charged contributions, "Of the Passing of the First-Born" and "Of the Coming of John," are testaments to this impression.

Du Bois put his writing to varied political ends as his long and prolific career unfolded, but the spirit behind his critical and poetic sensibilities, evoked most profoundly in this book, remained a constant. Likewise, Du Bois's turn-of-the-century valuation of African American humanity has encouraged generations of readers to understand the fate of the souls of black folk as part and parcel of their own.

Further Reading

Hubbard, Dolan, ed. "*The Souls of Black Folk: One Hundred Years Later.* Columbia: U of Missouri P, 2003.

Rampersad, Arnold. *The Art and Imagination of W. E. B. Du Bois.* Cambridge, MA: Harvard UP, 1976.

Stepto, Robert B. "The Quest of the Weary Traveler: W. E. B. Du Bois's *The Souls of Black Folk.*" *From Behind the Veil: A Study of Afro-American Narrative.* Urbana: U of Illinois P, 1979. 52–91.

Sundquist, Eric J. *Swing Low: "The Souls of Black Folk."* To Wake the Nations: Race in the Making of American Literature. Cambridge, MA: Harvard UP, 1993. 457–539.

Kinohi Nishikawa

SOUTH ASIAN AMERICAN FILM   South Asian American film attempts to register the specificity of the experiences of Indian immigrants to the United States even though as a genre, it concentrates almost exclusively on the post-1965, second wave of Indian **immigration**. The distinction between the two phases of Indian immigration is notable because whereas the first wave of Indian immigrants in the early twentieth century was composed almost exclusively of male migrant laborers on farms, the second wave included men and women who went on to pursue a diverse range of professions upon arrival. The genre's attention to the second wave of largely professional Indian Americans features two notable subcategories: films that centrally engage the relationship between Indian Americans and India; and films that address the relationship between different Indian Americans.

Indian American films that focus on the relationship between Indian America and India typically feature the story of an Indian American returning to India. Mira Nair's *Monsoon Wedding* (2001), for example, tells the story of Hemant, a young man—born and raised in India—who, having lived in the United States for a few years, decides to return to India for a marriage arranged by his parents. Hemant meets the prospective bride only to hear her confess to him that she has been having an affair with her former lover. *Hyderabad Blues* (1998) by Nagesh Kukunoor similarly features the story of a young Indian American man in his late twenties returning to India, this time after an absence of twelve years. Though initially uninterested in his parents' exhortations that he get married, Varun soon falls for Ashwini, the best friend of his friend's wife. From the beginning, however, their relationship encounters problems specific to cultural misunderstandings between the two about topics such as expressions of affection in public, familial approval, and the expectation that Ashwini give up her job as a doctor in India to join Varun in Atlanta.

Both *Monsoon Wedding* and *Hyderabad Blues* recount stories of young Indian American men who find themselves forced to reappraise themselves, their life, and thoughts about relationships after returning to India, even if only for a short period: Hemant has to quickly dispel preconceptions about arranged marriage ensuring a devoted Indian wife, while Varun has to confront and dispel his girlfriend's negative preconceptions about Indian American men. In narrating stories of Indian American men changed by Indian women, the films suggest that India—represented as a woman—has something valuable to teach (male) America qua Indian Americans. Both films can thus be read as feminist narratives about women of the "Third World" teaching arrogant men from the "First World" lessons about life and living. *Leela* (2001) offers an interesting variation on this theme. In this provocative movie, a strikingly beautiful middle-aged female visiting professor from India falls in love with her nineteen-year-old Indian American male student. Their relationship transforms them both substantially: the woman discovers new freedoms that allow her to leave an unhappy marriage to a philandering poet in India; the young student, who is thoroughly assimilated into American culture, reclaims his Indianness.

The second category of Indian American films—namely, those that dramatize relationships between different Indian Americans—includes films such as *American Desi* (2001), *American Chai* (2001), *ABCD* (1999), *Mississippi Masala* (1991), *Chutney Popcorn* (1999), and *My Own Country* (1998). The films focus on generational tensions between Indian Americans, or on issues involving gender, sexuality, and romantic relationships between Indian Americans. *American Desi*, *American Chai*, *ABCD*, and *Mississippi Masala* all centrally feature the clash between twenty-something Indian Americans and their parents.

In *American Desi* and *American Chai*, for example, the main characters—in both cases a young, male Indian American college student—confront their habit of avoiding all things Indian in order to escape the memory of their claustrophobic family experience. In *American Desi*, Krishna Reddy starts dating Nina Shah, an Indian American girl, and consequently becomes interested in Indian dance. Likewise in *American Chai,* Sureel—a college senior who has hidden his interest in music from his parents for years—overcomes his distaste for things Indian when he falls in love with Maya, another Indian American woman, and starts a band which plays a fusion of Western and Indian music. This trope of young Indian Americans reconciling conflicts with their family and Indian heritage is reversed in the films *ABCD* and *Mississippi Masala,* both of which represent Indian Americans who are so suffocated by the constraints and expectations of their family that they ultimately decide to minimize their interactions with other Indians and Indian Americans. In *ABCD,* Raj and Nina, the two children, defy their mother's expectations: Nina marries her white American boyfriend despite her mother's efforts to arrange her marriage to the son of an Indian family friend, while Raj backs out of his arranged marriage and quits his job. In *Mississippi Masala,* the girl resolves to elope with her boyfriend—who happens to be African-American—and leave town in order to escape the stifling atmosphere of her job working as a cleaner of rooms in her family's local motel.

Notable about all of these films is that they represent Indian Americans in the process of deciding to what extent they wish to be associated with India and Indians. The films represent the parents of Indian Americans as India and Indians: rejecting parental expectations affirms the specificity of first-generation Indian American desires and aspirations while conversely, acting in accord with parental desire—by marrying another Indian American, for example—suggests that Indian Americans, although "American," are nevertheless at heart, "Indian." Interestingly, all four films—*American Desi, American Chai, ABCD,* and *Mississippi Masala*—depict the degree of Indian American interest in knowing about India through the question of whether or not they form romantic attachments to other Indian Americans.

Chutney Popcorn and *My Own Country* depart from questions about Indian American **identity** and its relation to Indianness by focusing on issues of sexuality within the Indian American community. *Chutney Popcorn* features a young, gay Indian woman's decision to act as a surrogate mother for her infertile older sister, and the consequences of that decision after her sister confesses she is no longer interested in raising the child. *My Own Country,* meanwhile, dramatizes the experiences of an Indian American doctor in a small town in Tennessee diagnosing patients with HIV.

Both categories of Indian American film—those that focus on the relationship between Indian America and India, and those that feature relationships among Indian Americans—variously attempt to portray the specificity of being an Indian American in contradistinction to other immigrants to the United States. As a whole, the genre focuses on the challenges Indian Americans face because of cultural gaps between themselves and India/Indians, generation gaps between parents and children, and otherwise on the heterogeneity of the Indian American community. Importantly, however, the almost singular attention paid by Indian American films to issues involving family and personal identity eclipses commentary on other aspects of Indian American life, such as interethnic **racism** and political activism. This lack of attention to overtly political questions sharply differentiates the genre of Indian American film from other ethnic American film. (*See also* South Asian American Literature)

Further Reading

Avakian, Monique. *Atlas of Asian-American History.* New York: Media Projects Inc., 2002.

Bose, Purnima, and Varghese, Linta. "Mississippi Masala, South Asian Activism, and Agency." *Haunting Violations: Feminist Criticism and the Crisis of the "Real."* Ed. Wendy Hesford and Wendy Kozol. Chicago: U of Illinois P, 2001. 137–69.

Chute, David. "Monsoon Wedding (Film Review)." *Film Comment* 38.1 (2002 January/February): 72–73.

Mehta, Binita. "Emigrants Twice Displaced: Race, Color, and Identity in Mira Nair's *Mississippi Masala.*" *Between the Lines: South Asians and Postcoloniality.* Ed. Deepika Bahri and Mary Vasudeva. Philadelphia: Temple UP, 1996. 185–204.

Singh, Jaspal. "Globalization, Transnationalism, and Identity Politics in South Asian Women's Texts." *Michigan Academician* 35.2 (2003 Summer): 171–88.

Arnal Dayaratna

SOUTH ASIAN AMERICAN LITERATURE   The first significant American writer of South Asian descent was Dhan Gopal Mukerji (1890–1936). Often referred to as "that Hindu writer" by his contemporaries, Mukerji enjoyed considerable popularity during the 1920s. He was a graduate of Stanford University and his interpretations of Hindu folklore, philosophy, and scriptures are said to have influenced such diverse American authors as Van Wyck Brooks, T. S. Eliot, Lewis Mumford, and Eugene O'Neill. Born near Calcutta (India) in 1890, he came to the States in 1910, via Tokyo University, earned a graduate degree at Stanford University, where he taught as Lecturer in Comparative Literature until 1916; in 1918, he married Ethel Ray Dugan, an American school teacher, became a prolific writer, and died in New York in 1936 (at his own hands). In nearly fifteen years, he had published seven books about Indian fables, philosophy, and civilization; three plays, two books of poems, eleven children's books, and an autobiography. His beguiling animal stories became widely popular; one of them, *Gay Neck: The Story of a Pigeon* (1928), won the year's John Newbery Medal for "distinguished contribution to children's literature." This story of an army pigeon's death-defying friendship with his trainer would be produced as a filmstrip by Miller-Brody in 1973.

If Rudyard Kipling had written jungle stories solely for children's entertainment, Dhan Gopal Mukerji used them to embody the folk wisdom and the spiritual truths of the Hindu life—mainly its principles of tolerance, nonviolence, and truth. By using animals as protagonists of his tales, the animals that worked in unison with humans, he sought to dramatize the psychological benefits of living in harmony with nature. His work, sensitive and eloquent, seems to have been written with a fullness of love for all forms of life. As a literary pathfinder, he blazed the trails that other South Asian talents would follow for a while. However, those who followed him, albeit invariably better artists, would find Mukerji's grand humanistic vision unsuitable to their purpose. His autobiography, *Caste and Outcast* (1923), recently reissued by Stanford University Press (2002), has grabbed the attention of modern, especially postcolonial, scholars by its historical accuracy about the sorry status, and the questionable reception, of immigrants from minority communities.

The following essay, sectioned according to genres, deals chronologically with the South Asian Americans' achievements in various literary categories, beginning with the memoirs, then to poetry, and ending with fiction. A word about the criteria of inclusion: an open country like the United States has welcomed writers and professionals even if they came merely to work, and not to settle here; the nature of this publication, however, permits the inclusion of only those who can be rightly called American. Also, it may be said, the essay draws upon but a selection of the American writers of Indian and Pakistani descent, especially upon those who have either already made a name for themselves or are beginning to draw public attention.

Memoirists

In his recent book, *Modern South Asian Literature in English* (2003), Paul Brians speaks of "a profound and ever-growing international appetite for fiction by South Asian authors" (3), confirming the popular belief that South Asian Americans have excelled only in fiction. However, contrary to the general notion, South Asian American writers' contributions to nonfiction genres—especially to autobiography and poetry—have surprised well-informed readers not only by the freshness, elegance, and wit of their stance and narratives but also by the unusual content of their works. It is fitting that the essay should begin with a survey of the domains the least suspected to have been cultivated by South Asian American writers.

Ved (Prakash) Mehta (1934–), arguably, towers over contemporary autobiographers writing in America. The fifteen-year-old boy who came from India to the Arkansas School for the Blind, in Little Rock, and went on to earn a BA from Pomona College and a BA Honors from Balliol College of Oxford University, an MA, also from Oxford, and another MA from Harvard, ended up working as a staff writer for *New Yorker*. He has had a full share of exclusions from the five cultures he had known: the Indian, British, and American; the *New Yorker*'s; and of the blind. So, to share his stories and his insights, he embarked on autobiography on an epic scale, one that would keep him returning for thirty-two years to different segments of his life. Unleashing the series "Continents of Exile" in 1972, a metaphor for a life of exclusions, Mehta has just completed the eleventh, and perhaps the final, installment of his memoirs, the first being *Daddyji* (1972) and the last, *The Red Letters* (2004), both dealing with the long and the powerful shadow his father's life cast upon him. Each memoir, organized around a central metaphor, seeks to capture the shifting seasons of the soul at various stages of the author's life. Together, the eleven parts of the autobiography encompass the grand architecture of an eventful memory of seventy years.

Now, Mehta's memory, in the grand autobiographical tradition, is by no means made up of family relatives or personal events alone. Like Nirad C. Chaudhuri (1897–1999) and V. S. Naipaul (1932–), the two other famous political analysts of Indian **diaspora**, Ved Mehta has freely commented upon India's social and political conditions. *Portrait of India* (1970) inaugurates his life-long engagement with the political scene of the country he had left behind. He returns to the subject in *Mahatama Gandhi and His Apostles* (1977), if only to note the decline of Gandhian idealism among his disciples and political successors, a loss that spelled the national betrayal of a great promise. *The New India* (1978), *A Family Affair: India Under Three Prime Ministers* (1982), and *Rajiv Gandhi and Rama's Kingdom* (1994) round off his cold, detached analyses of the home conditions. Mehta has, thus, been a pilgrim of two worlds: of the rich internal world of his personal memory and psyche—its reports contained in his memoirs; and of the human world of material forces—its accounts recorded in his histories of India's contemporary politics.

Not all South Asian memoirists, however, display an equal interest in, or awareness of, the wider forces of history. **Meena Alexander** (1951–), poet, novelist, and critic, concentrates, in *Fault Lines* (1992), on her personal past as an allegory of an exiled woman's situation, of the dislocation of a person moving across cultures and borders, searching for her self and assessing the nature of the influences that shaped her poetic persona. Commenting upon the changes in the revised issue of *Fault Lines* (2003), Michael W. Cox, in the celebrated autobiography's review, published in *South Asian Review* 25.1 (2004), rightly observes that Alexander goes "to unearth something much closer to the truth and essence of who she is and how she came to be the present self" (351). Meena Alexander, thus, becomes the story of Meena Alexander's crafted memoir. Within that province, she searches with the alacrity—nay, the tenacity—of an Isis for the fragments of a global woman's **identity** scattered across continents, poring over them to piece together a human form. The result, one must say, is well worth the effort, for the reader is at once pulled into, and drawn along, the intriguing paths of a personal memory.

Sara Suleri (1953–), a memoirist, public intellectual, and literary critic, born in Pakistan, educated in Lahore and at Indiana University, has emerged as an intriguing and humorous autobiographer. A born stylist, wielding an exquisite language, she can nail down a sharp detail in a phrase, or light up an entire life in a sentence. Her first work, *Meatless Days:*

A Memoir (1989), deals not only with the loves and tensions of a growing family but also with the conflicted existence of Pakistan torn asunder by the 1971 war with India. Nobody escapes the gloom and oppression of those times—neither a thriving family, nor an individual's psyche. Suleri's second memoir, *Boys Will Be Boys* (2003), celebrates her father's passion for politics as well as his lust for life. In "an elegy" for her Pip, the "patriotic and preposterous," an intense inner monologue is directed here at the dead father, in a manner not unlike Sylvia Plath's. In both the works, the lives of the young keep getting mangled by the history of the country. Suleri's narrative, by turns gentle, bitter, or funny, veers away from making bold historical judgments. Her voice, cool when it could be screaming, can as well be read as a measure of personal desperation as of artistic discipline.

Poetry

The body of South Asian American poetry is indeed slim but is not insignificant. Several factors can satisfactorily account for its slimness: only a few of the South Asian creative writers have devoted themselves exclusively to poetry; most of them come from a younger generation, which has not rendered its full account yet; and two very gifted poets have been lost in the very prime of their lives—**Agha Shahid Ali**, to cancer, and **Reetika Vazirani**, to suicide.

A. K. Ramanujan (1929–93), poet, translator and folklorist, linguist, scholar and academician, is widely acknowledged as the doyen of the American poets of Indian descent. Educated at the University of Mysore, then earning a PhD in linguistics at Indiana University (1963), he arrived at the University of Chicago in 1962 to join its departments of South Asian Languages and Civilizations, where he would stay, until his death, to shape the course of South Asian Studies. A transnational and transcultural genius, elected to the American Academy of Arts and Sciences (1990), Ramanujan was honored with *Padma Sri*—one of India's highest civilian awards—by the president of India and awarded the MacArthur Fellowship by the prestigious Chicago-based foundation. His poetry, laced with mischief and mysticism, written in modernist—almost laconic—English, manages alternately to carry hints of the Himalayan breeze, the metropolitan pollution, and the monsoons of the South. The narrator's voice there, sensitive yet unsentimental, cuts like a scalpel through life's daily illusions. Philosophic or ironic, playful, naughty, or just whimsical, Ramanujan's poems, much like Eliot's, or Robert Frost's, begin in surprise and end in joy. So creative was his life that the publication of four volumes of poetry, six works of translations—four of them of classical Tamil and Kannada poems—and the coauthorship of four works did not exhaust his energy. Since his death, another five volumes of poems, essays, and oral tales have joined the body of his work, and more are in the offing.

Agha Shahid Ali (1949–2001), poet, critic, and translator, has had a phenomenal success in poetry, were success measured by the boldness to modify an established tradition and to influence the very course of poetry. One of Chaucer's contributions to English poetry has been that he imported the Petrarchan sonnet from Italy; one of Ali's contributions has been that he brought Urdu ghazal from India and grafted it on to the body of American poetry. He accomplished this, first, by writing some intense and winsome ghazals in English himself; and then by translating some of the best ghazals of the legendary poet of Pakistan, Faiz Ahmed Faiz, under the title *The Rebel's Silhouette* (1995); and, finally, by persuading, as Ellen Bryant Voigt says in "In Memoriam, Agha Shahid Ali: 1949–2001," "innumerable and some unlikely American poets to commit the elaborate ghazal" (Norton Poets online). A poem of formal discipline, where the first couplet sets up the rhyme and the refrain for the entire poem, the second line of whose succeeding couplets repeats the refrain, ghazal was antithetical to the contemporary American poetry entranced by free verse. Ali, in compelling poetic attention to his work, won respect for the restricted form new to the American poetry, so that when he gave his first reading at the Academy of American Poets, James Merrill would come to listen to his work. Amitav Ghosh gives an astute assessment of Agha Shahid Ali's contribution in his article "'The Ghat of the Only World': Agha Shahid Ali in Brooklyn." He says "the formalization of the ghazal may well prove to be Shahid's most important scholarly contribution to the canon of English poetry" (*Nation* 274.5 [2002], 31). Still another influence emanates from Ali's poetry: a multicultural blend of mythologies—the Arabic, Hindu, Persian, and the Greek—one that imparts density to his own work and demonstrates to our mythless age the central importance of the poets' historic memory to their art. What is more, experimental and playful, Ali refused to be circumscribed by the traditional and the exotic alone. He mastered some elaborate and complex forms of European poetry—especially the sestina and canzone—claiming a special place in the American poetry for South Asian voices. In view of his multiple achievements, it will be some years before Ali's full significance as poet can be assessed.

Meena Alexander, poet, memoirist, novelist, and critic has, with her eight volumes of poetry, produced a remarkable body of verse. At once reflective, intense, and lyrical, a fresh voice enters contemporary American poetry with her. Especially, as one who has lived in four continents (Asia, Africa, Europe and North America) and who speaks five languages (Arabic, English, French, Hindi, and Malyalam), Alexander brings a genuine cosmopolitan awareness to bear upon issues of **feminism** that are invariably the subjects of her poems. So, as with Eliot's narrator in "The Love Song of J. Alfred Prufrock," the "I" of Alexander's narrator keeps splitting into an individual and a universal person, a particular sufferer transforming into a type, in this case a universal woman—especially a postcolonial woman with harsh penalties attached to her color. The lines of her latest poems, the ones written after 9/11, especially the ones appearing in *Raw Silk* (2004), carry in their solemn march the stoic echoes of HD's *The Walls Do Not Fall*, which dealt mainly with Londoners' endurance and courage during the 1940s' Battle for Britain.

Chitra Banerjee Divakaruni (1957–), poet, novelist, essayist, and social counselor, has published four volumes of poetry. In a way, her poetry reflects the spirit that she considers to be the lifeblood of good art: "Compassion and empathy." And Divakaruni's compassion is pretty wide—for a self-willed child ("Leroy at the Zoo"), the ruthless Irish nuns in India ("The Infirmary"), and the battered immigrant women in the States (*Black Candle*). Her poetry, consequently, deals with the multicultural world that Divakaruni lives and moves in. And, deriving from personal experiences, her poems blend immigrant sociology with autobiography, their lines often rolling out as declarations of a humanistic commitment. Surprisingly, they deal as easily with the Indigo past of India as with a modern Yuba City School, stitching South Asian memories onto the American landscape.

Reetika Vazirani (1962–2003), a poet and literary editor, published two volumes of poetry in her brief lifetime, and several pieces, besides, but which still remain to be collected. Intense exuberance presides over her poems, where a reckless playfulness often surprises the reader with freshly minted words or remorseless sentiments. The poems of her first collection, *White Elephants* (1996), fastening their attention upon what naturally catches a newcomer's eye—the differences between *the here* and *the there*, between *theirs* and *ours*—resolve themselves into emotional dialectics. Her second book of poems, *World Hotel* (2002), which won the 2003 Anisfield-Woolf Book Award meant "for books that explore the richness of human diversity," is the work of a knowledgeable, almost a disillusioned, person who not only understands but also accepts human infidelity and forgives opportunism, ignoring lovers' indifference or their sudden falling off. Written with gusto, but almost in haste, it is urban poetry without a trace of sentimental nostalgia. The second book is, indeed, postmodernist to the core, teasing us to speculate where Vazirani might have arrived had she lived beyond her youthful years.

Fiction

The field of fiction has, indeed, been the glorious playground where South Asian American writers have racked up an impressive record of enduring value. First, there is an abundance of talent here: every six months or so a new author, generally a woman writer, turns up with a bright and dazzling book, the title quickly noted and widely promoted. Then, together, they have created a critical mass of fresh and varied South Asian writing. Finally, the quality of their contribution to American fiction has entitled one (**Bharati Mukherjee**) to a National Book Critics Circle Award (1998), and another (**Jhumpa Lahiri**) to a Pulitzer Prize. Not only are the best of these authors distinguished by awards, they are also recognized by regular inclusion in school and college curricula and anthologies.

Roughly since the late 1950s, the South Asian English fiction had been known in the West generally, and in the States particularly, through the comic works of R. K. Narayan—*The Financial Expert* (1952), *The Guide* (1958), and *The Vendor of Sweets* (1967); the philosophic novels of Raja Rao—*Kanthapura* (1938), *The Serpent and the Rope* (1960), *The Cat and Shakespeare: A Tale of Modern India* (1965); and the intense tales of Kamala Markandaya—*Nectar in a Sieve* (1954), *A Handful of Rice* (1966), and *The Nowhere Man* (1972). However, as a tributary of the American fiction, the South Asian American novel truly begins with the arrival of Bharati Mukherjee on the scene. In our chronological scheme, however, Bapsi Sidhwa must take precedence, as Anita Desai's latest phase of work, the one of American orientation, must be recognized here as well.

Anita Desai (1937–), short story writer, novelist, and critic, is identified as an Indian, rather than as a South Asian American, writer both on account of her subject and her domicile. For more than a decade, though, she has lived in and written about America, and hence the last phase of her work demands an acknowledgment here. Beginning with *Journey to Ithaca* (1995), which sends a young American couple on a tedious journey through India—virtually on their painful trials through India's ashrams—Desai's attention shifts to the American scene. Progressively, the plot of the next novel, *Fasting, Feasting* (1999), unfolds from India to the States, following a young Indian student who gets lost among the mazes of his abnormal American host family. Her latest novel, *The Zigzag Way* (2004), the narrative of a historian's search for his family roots spreading out from States, through Mexico, to England, paints vivid scenes of contemporary Mexican life. The three novels, open-ended, tentative, and experimental, bespeak of immense resilience in the author who, after publishing eleven novels, can break an altogether fresh ground. Her virtue as artist now, as earlier, seems to lie in the sensitivity and assurance with which she handles the contemporary idiom of the global middle-class professionals. Now witty, then sardonic, her narrative becomes a source of pleasure in itself—yes, even when the story becomes a bit tedious. She remains a bright and intelligent observer of the world's social and political scene.

Bapsi Sidhwa (1938–), a Pakistani American novelist of Parsi descent, has added sociopolitical novels with a fine overlay of humor. Whether dealing with heartless wife abuse by Pakistani tribesmen, as in *The Bride* (1983), or the social manners of the Parsi community in Pakistan, as in *The Crow Eaters* (1992) she gives a comic treatment even to the issues poignant or painful, thus gathering a distance from her subjects. Because she selects her characters from minorities, servants, and vendors, her fiction proves her to be pushing the marginalized or the misrepresented to center stage. Because of this social commitment, even a fictionalized personal memoir in her hands begins to approximate to a cultural and political record, as *Crack-*

ing India (1991), a young Parsi girl's account of the upheaval in the wake of the Partition, amply demonstrates. It is remarkable that the novel, which describes the sexual maturing of Lenny, can be read not only as her passage from innocence to knowledge but also as a feminist allegory. For, after all, the novel scours the female world governed as much by patriarchy as by a colonial regime, portraying thus the helpless condition of the young woman maimed by polio and governed by forces beyond her control. By turns humorous and raucous, Sidhwa's fiction excels at the portrayal of characters with a patina of westernization, of which the finest example is *An American Brat* (1993).

Bharati Mukherjee (1940–), novelist, short story writer, essayist, and critic, is "the Grande Dame of the Indian diasporic fiction," as **Vijay Lakshmi** says in her essay "Bharati Mukherjee," in *The Routledge Encyclopedia of Postcolonial Literatures* (2005). With seven novels, two collections of short stories, and three books of nonfiction and several polemical essays to her credit, Mukherjee's claim to an eminent place in the contemporary fiction is not likely to be challenged seriously. On the contrary, her position has been strengthened by more than the volume of her work. The way she has turned the expatriate novel into a variation of American writing puts her at the head of the compatriot practitioners of the craft. By the example of her work as much as by her polemical essays, she has demonstrated how the writing of newcomers can, and ought to, move beyond the ghettoized community of expatriates, and escape the perpetual rehearsals of the nostalgia of a home left behind. She argued for, and has achieved, a veritable immigrant community's novel, whose characters fight not to preserve their identity but to transform it, affecting, while striving to be assimilated by, the larger body politic.

Above all, what gives Bharati Mukherjee's work an easy currency is her craft. It is not only her exquisite story lines, but also her tightly knit yarns and seamless narratives, all delivered in the limpid prose of modern Americana, that have won her a wide readership. Her protagonists, mostly upwardly mobile women who, constantly in the process of becoming, keep on launching out in search of a new identity, a new destiny, or an enriching fulfillment of their lives, have stuck a deep chord in the heart of contemporary generation. In keeping with the characters' ceaseless search, her plots, the hieroglyphs of internal and external motions, delineate a world in constant flux, where one who stops must stagnate. Her novels have thus opened up an avenue of new attitude for the characters in transit, one leading to hopeful and energetic assertiveness in the face of the general uncertainty and indifference they encounter in the host country. A remarkable feature of her superb stories of personal relations, whether located in Calcutta or Bombay, New York or Detroit, Montreal or San Francisco, is their circumambient universe. A family's tale is grounded in the Indian National Movement; a life is mangled by Canadian racism, or a family's future is twisted by American violence. Their various envelopes effectively displace the characters' isolating exoticism with global modernism. However, in as much as the fortuitous violence of her women's lives shapes her plots, Mukherjee's work seems to suffer from the limitations that brand the turbulent early fiction of Joyce Carol Oates.

Gita Mehta (1943–), novelist, journalist, social activist and cultural commentator, has achieved well-deserved recognition in academic circles as well as the public media. She first attained fame with *Karma Cola: Marketing the Mystic East* (1979), a tightly knit and fast-paced account of the credulous crowd that went to India for a pop salvation of the soul. The narrative, spiked with lightning puns and crackling with wit, at once won an audience across the English-speaking world that found its postmodernist turn of mind perfectly reflected by it. For the generation of the 1970s, it seemed to do what T. S. Eliot's "Love Song of J. Alfred Prufrock" had done for the Europe of the 1920s: It cleverly and faithfully reflected the contemporary skepticism with cool detachment. Gita Mehta's fiction, meager but precious, represents two Indias: the colonial, in *Raj: A Novel* (1989), and the mystical, in *A River Sutra* (1993). In *A River Sutra*, like a thread (*sutra*), as Pradyumna Chauhan notes in his article "Gita Mehta," in *The South Asian Novelists in English* (2003), "the holy river Narmada flows through the novel, just as the great brown god Mississippi does through *The Adventures of Huckleberry Finn*, linking diverse lives and stories, myths and memories, rituals and dreams" (151). One such novel is enough to ensure an author's place in the history of South Asian American fiction.

Vijay Lakshmi (1943–), short story writer, novelist, critic, and social commentator, has attracted global attention not only through her publications in *Paris Transcontinental, Orbis* and *Wassafiri* (United Kingdom), *Femina* (India), *Short Story* (United States), but also through translations of her work in Chinese, French, and Spanish. Fascinated by the phenomenon of global mobility, she writes of the emotional losses and psychological consequences of deracinated communities, whether Jewish, Russian, or South Asian. Although her protagonists are often women, and although women pay the heaviest price for their emotional and physical transplantation, her characters are hardly ever victims. Well-educated and cosmopolitan, her heroines take charge of their destinies by readjusting to the changed circumstances of their lives, by borrowing the humane and rational practices of the host culture, by dedicating themselves to the needs of new society, or simply by starting out as entrepreneurs in the new land of opportunities. Believing that each human being lives alone in the castle of their skin, she coasts by popular ideological pronouncements that presume all human beings to be standardized like parts of a Ford motor car. Her chief domain is, rather, the world of the interior atmosphere of the mind, forever fluid, amorphous, and evanescent. To find a match to her lyrical stories fraught with poetic images that stun the reader with their deadly accuracy and brightness, one has to go to Virginia Woolf's impressionistic passages. Anne D. Ulrich finely sums up this poetic quality in her article "Vijay Lakshmi," in *Writers of the Indian Diaspora* (1993). She says of Lakshmi's narratives: "When her characters' fears are greatest, 'horses thunder across the plains of the mind, against skies of liquid fire.' When the moments are tender, 'the fragrance of jasmine and bela,' which the narrator wants so much to pack in a box to carry to America, falls off hands 'in tufts of cotton' and disappears" (179). Lakshmi's magical powers in capturing existentialist moments decidedly remain unsurpassed in contemporary American fiction.

Amitav Ghosh (1956–), anthropologist, essayist, journalist, and novelist, has carved out a reputation for prolific fiction that takes the reader's breath away. Reinforced by sound research, Ghosh's fiction cuts broad swaths through history as well as geographies—especially as represented by his last three novels: *The Calcutta Chromosome* (1996), *The Glass Palace* (2000), and *The Hungry Tide* (2004). He recreates in his *In an Antique Land: History in the Guise of a Traveler's Tale* (1993) a twelfth-century Indian servant's relation to his Tunisian Jewish master, a prosperous merchant first settled in Egypt, then in Aden. In the process, the novel delivers the contrary worlds of the two parties: the mud-walled Cairo of the master and the lush Malabar Coast of the servant. Filtered through the vision of a modern, Oxford-trained, anthropologist, the bondsman's story of eight hundred years ago, although reconstructed from medieval letters and chronicles, acquires a powerful clarity about the relationships between two old civilizations and their economic and social practices. The pervasive irony of the slave-compatriot's reading, and judging, the slave-master's documents ensures the reader's unflagging interest. However, Ghosh's work is no more a pure novel than Joyce's *Ulysses* is a classical epic. Provided with biographical information, bibliographic footnotes, and a factual prologue, in addition to blending various genres, its narrative unambiguously redefines the boundaries of the modern novel.

The Glass Palace, chronicling the fortunes of three generations, sweeps through the history of Bengal, Burma (Myanmar), and Malaysia, unfolding a panorama of Southeast Asia through war and peace, a truly Tolstoyan canvas of an imperial history done, and delivered, by a "postcolonial" subject. With his historical works, Ghosh opens up a new territory for the contemporary American novel. His fictional achievement, though, refuses to be confined to only a single category. *The Calcutta Chromosome: A Novel of Fevers, Delirium and Discovery* is a brilliant piece of science fiction that reads like a fast-paced mystery thriller. No matter in which type of fiction it is embedded, Ghosh's cross-cultural narrative, urbane and elegant, always ripples with gentle humor, verging at times on witty sarcasm. At work, behind all his fiction, is a highly intelligent and deeply moral mind, one anchored in wholesome sanity.

Chitra Banerjee Divakaruni (1956–), starting out as a poet, has arrived at a respectable place in the South Asian American fiction. Her novels no less than her stories are well known in, and outside, academia. And she has produced a robust body in genres as varied as children's fiction, such as

Neela: Victory Song (2002); mythical writing, in *The Conch Bearer* (2003); the novel of magic realism, in *The Mistress of Spices* (1997), and realistic fiction, in *Sister of My Heart* (1999). Extremely popular—indeed, a best seller—she writes mostly about the plight and the travails of immigrant women as they seek to find their feet in the new country. Adventurous and creative as Divakaruni's characters are, one suspects that they are run through a formulaic trail to vindicate a feminist ideology. It is such commitment alone that can satisfactorily explain the repetitive patterns of stories in the hands of a richly imaginative writer. The abiding virtue of Divakaruni's fiction, at times sentimental and often melodramatic but always experimental, is that it boldly engages in the creation of alternate realities.

Vikram Chandra (1961–), filmographer, novelist, and short story writer, has collected handsome credits for his fiction as well as for his work with films. "Passionately interested in movies," as he confessed in his interview with Kevin Mahoney (1998), Chandra has been associated either as actor, director, scriptwriter, or co-producer, with four films: *The Disenchanted* (1990), *Left Luggage* (2000), *The Quarry* (2000), and *Mission Kashmir* (2000), working with John Lynch, Jonny Phillips, Sylvia Esau, Oscar Peterson, and Jody Abrahams. For his fiction—*Red Earth and Pouring Rain* (1995), and *Love and Longing in Bombay* (1997)—he has won the Commonwealth Writers Prize for Best First Book and the Commonwealth Writers Prize for the Eurasia region. Chandra's fiction is remarkable for a ceaseless experimentation in form, and for its postmodernist resistance to genre and the inclusion of kitsch and skepticism. The action of *Red Earth and Pouring Rain,* an extensive epic stretching across three continents (Asia, Europe, and America) over three centuries, is mediated by a ghost narrator. Subverting the orderly—indeed, the organic— conventions of classicism, Chandra's fiction resorts to multiple and fractured narratives, creating a feel of multiverse. For his next work, as Chandra told Kevin Mahoney in a summer 1998 interview, he deliberately decided "to do a story of drawing-room warfare . . . a ghost story . . . a detective story, a love story, and a story about work and money" all, together, granting the writer "a many-layered apprehension of the city of Bombay" (www.geocities.com/ SoHo/Nook/1082/vikram-chandra.html). Whether caressing, or interrogating, the traditional forms of stories, Chandra links the five stories by a framing tale, all of them ending as so many meditations upon fictional form. There is something Joycean in Chandra's conscious exploitation of literary forms.

Jhumpa Lahiri (1967–), short story writer and novelist, is a popular fiction writer whose stories have appeared in *Harvard Review, Story Quarterly,* and *The New Yorker.* The focus of her work is personal relations, yes, even when they extend across oceans. By threading her narrative through their entanglements, Lahiri seeks not to dazzle, even less to shock, but only to reveal, to take the reader into the hidden recesses of personal ties, where festering might have begun but of which the persons involved may not have any inkling. As Paul Brians says in *Modern South Asian Literature in*

English (2003), "the relationships in her stories are a series of missed connections" (196). Whether working on the smaller scale of stories, or the larger canvas of a novel, Lahiri explores the physical and psychological dislocation of her immigrant characters. And in her pursuit, she employs the Jamesian method of cross-lighting the diverse characters, by juxtaposing their respective cultures together, in this case the Indian and the American. Her observation and treatment of the habits and attitudes of the second-generation characters rings true, while her portraits of *desis* (of Americanized versions of the people of Indian descent) visiting or touring India are but superficial accounts of certain stereotypes. Robin E. Field accurately observes in "Writing the Second Generation: Negotiating Cultural Borderlands in Jhumpa Lahiri's *Interpreter of Dreams* and *The Namesake*": "Lahiri's most overt project in *The Namesake* [2003], and in several of her short stories as well, is the differentiation between generations in regard to the importance and understanding of cultural roots" (*South Asian Review*, XXV: 2 [2004], 165). This disparity has earned Lahiri's work the charge of being "inauthentic," especially from South Asian critics who regard themselves as the only qualified purveyors of genuine cultural artifacts. Howsoever the future settles the charge against her, one thing is clear: as an artistic interpreter of cultural maladies, Jhumpa Lahiri hardly needs any apologies.

Anjana Appachana (1972–), story writer and novelist, deals in her fiction with the daily lives of ordinary Indian women, which, seemingly uneventful, are haunted by physical assaults, hardships, and psychological violations. *Incantations and Other Stories* (1992) recounts in various frames how the oppression of women comes not from men alone; it comes too from other women as well as the victims' collaboration with the perpetrators and their own silence. In *Listening Now* (1998), a novel made up of the life stories of six women, no one particular group or gender is blamed for women's situation and suffering, but everyone and everything about the woman's life—the folk ways, the customs, the rituals, the expectations—are alike shown to be responsible for their plight. Appachana is too much taken up, in words of Eliot's "Preludes," with "this infinitely gentle and infinitely suffering thing" to be drawn into heated debates about the politics of gender. The center of her well-told fiction is, primarily, a woman's experience of being alive with all her buried desires and pains, fantasies, and passions.

In sum, the South Asian American literature has been varied, vibrant, and abiding. New voices are breaking onto the scene, from such novelists as Kiran Desai, Amina Ali, **Manil Suri**, and **Indu Sundaresan**, a historical novelist of discernible power; they are going to provide the staying power for the coming decades. And their predecessors' impatience with social wrongs, their passion for change, their engagement with literary forms, and their freshly minted language, are all likely to have far-reaching consequences for contemporary American fiction, and not just for South Asian American fiction. After all, the work of their peers—V. S. Naipaul, Salman

Rushdie, and Vikram Seth—has already altered the landscape of the modern English novel. The transformation taking place across the Atlantic holds a lesson—indeed, a promise—for the contemporary American literary scene. (*See also* Diaspora, South Asian American Film)

Further Reading

Bahri, Deepika, and Mary Vasudeva, eds. *Between the Lines: South Asians and Postcoloniality.* Philadelphia: Temple UP, 1996.

Brians, Paul. *Modern South Asian Literature in English.* Westport, CT: Greenwood Press, 2003.

Chauhan, Pradyumna S. "Anita Desai." *South Asian Novelists in English: An A-to-Z Guide.* Ed. Jaina C. Sanga. Westport, CT: Greenwood Press, 2003. 47–53.

———. "Gita Mehta" *South Asian Novelists in English: An A-to-Z Guide.* Ed. Jaina C. Sanga. Westport, CT: Greenwood Press, 2003. 149–52.

Mukherjee, Meenakshi. *The Perishable Empire: Essays on Indian Writing in English.* Delhi: Oxford UP, 2000.

Nelson, Emmanuel S., ed. *Reworlding: The Literature of the Indian Diaspora.* New York: Greenwood Press, 1992.

———, ed. *Writers of the Indian Diaspora: A Bio-Bibliographical Critical Sourcebook.* Westport, CT: Greenwood Press, 1993.

Ross, Robert, ed. *International Literature in English.* New York: Garland, 1991.

Sanga, Jaina C. *South Asian Novelists in English: An A-to-Z Guide.* Westport, CT: Greenwood Press, 2003.

Wong, S. C. *Reading Asian American Literature: From Necessity to Extravagance.* Princeton, NJ: Princeton UP, 1993.

Pradyumna S. Chauhan

SPENCE, EULALIE (1894–1981) African American playwright. Spence was one of the more experienced female playwrights of the **Harlem Renaissance** movement whose works are marked by strong female characters and whose career was geared toward staging her plays. Born in the British West Indies, Spence immigrated as a child to the United States with her family. Spence settled in New York, attended Wadleigh High School and New York Training School for Teachers. She earned her BS at New York University in 1937 and a MA in speech from Columbia in 1939. Spence was a student of the National Ethiopian Art Theatre School, for which her first production, *Being Forty*, was staged at the Lafayette Theatre in October 1924. She taught elocution and English at the Eastern District High School in Brooklyn, where she also directed plays.

Unlike many of her contemporaries who congregated in Washington, DC, Spence remained in New York, maintaining her ties to Harlem's community. Harlem figured prominently in Spence's work; she portrayed the city's poverty, its people, and struggles. Besides writing thirteen plays, Spence was a community activist in educational theater, directing her own plays and those of other playwrights, including Eugene O'Neill. In the late 1920s, Spence helped establish the Dunbar Garden Players and was an active member of **W. E. B. Du Bois**'s Krigwa Players, initially in residence at the Harlem Branch of the New York Public Library. The Krigwa Players mounted several of Spence's dramas from 1926 to 1927.

Spence contributed significantly to race drama. Her plays held popular appeal during their time, were recognized by leading African American journals, and were staged primarily for black audiences. Receiving five play competition awards sponsored by *Crisis* and *Opportunity*, Spence earned more recognition in these one-act play contests than any of her peers. Moreover, *Fool's Errand* garnered the Samuel French Prize at the national Little Theatre Tournament in New York City following its 1927 premiere by the Krigwa Players. Her published plays include *The Starter* (1927), *Foreign Mail* (1927), *The Hunch* (1927), *Episode* (1928), *Help Wanted* (1929), and *Undertow* (1929).

With the exception of *Her* (1927), *La Divina Pastora* (1929), and *Undertow*, Spence wrote comedies that initially appear free of racial concerns. Nevertheless, feminist and **race** politics underscore much of Spence's drama. Her characters are identifiably black and encounter racial and cultural issues, as demonstrated in *The Starter* and *Hot Stuff* (1927), which introduce difficulties facing African Americans, such as prostitution, materialism, immorality, and urban poverty.

In *Hot Stuff*, Fanny, an immoral, manipulative gambler, prostitutes her body and uses other people for her desires. Spence therefore projects a degenerative Harlem where blacks do whatever they can to survive. Spence also interweaves a sense that African Americans need to be doubly guarded and self-aware by portraying characters asserting their needs and desire for self-determination.

Likewise, the racial concerns stir just below the surface in *Her*, a mystery play in one act. Initially it portends to be a retribution drama in which the ghost of a Philippino woman haunts her husband, Mr. Kinney, for his mistreatment. Like Susan Glaspell's *Trifles*, the protagonist ("Her") is absent. Of note is that Mrs. Kinney is a foreigner who attempts to find her place and identity in a strange country. *Her* is also the story of the victimization of the African American wife, Martha, who works multiple jobs to support her husband.

The rich performance history of Spence's productions is all the more important given that Spence advocated for the performance of drama, which distinguishes Spence from many of her contemporaries who were primarily interested in writing plays to be read. Indeed, in "A Criticism of the Negro Drama," (*Opportunity*, June 1928) Spence argued against underutilizing the dramatic form. Further, Spence challenged prospective playwrights to sharpen their skill by avoiding propaganda drama and instead focusing on the common life of African Americans. She wanted audiences to be entertained rather than alienated or antagonized.

Always the practical playwright, Spence recognized the need to balance audience demand with appropriate subject matter. Therefore, although Spence worked with **W. E. B. Du Bois**, she disagreed with his ideals regarding protest race drama, and was influenced by Alain Locke and Montgomery T. Gregory's tenets of the folk play and art theater. (*See also* African American Drama)

Further Reading

Burton, Jennifer, ed. *Zora Neal Hurston, Eulalie Spence, Marita Bonner, and Others: The Prize Plays and Other One-Acts Published in Periodicals*. New York: G. K. Hall & Co., 1996.

Perkins, Kathy. *Black Female Playwrights: An Anthology of Plays before 1950*. Bloomington: Indiana UP, 1989.

Shafer, Yvonne. *American Women Playwrights, 1900–1950*. New York: Peter Lang, 1995.

Adrienne C. Macki

SPENCER, ANNE (1882–1975)   African American poet. Primarily an artist of the **Harlem Renaissance**, Mrs. Spencer's national career spanned the years 1920 to 1931 during which fewer than thirty poems appeared in print. She never published a volume of her work and given the difficulty and obscurity of her poetry, her influence declined during the **Black Arts Movement** of the 1960s and 1970s. Not even J. Lee Greene's excellent biography—containing forty-two poems and a solid analysis of their meaning—has served to revive general interest in Spencer's finely crafted work.

She was born on a plantation in Henry Country, Virginia. Her father, Joel Cephus Bannister, was of mixed ancestry: black and white but primarily Seminole Indian. Her mother, Sarah Louise Scales, descended from a former slave and a Virginia aristocrat. Annie was born when Sarah was only sixteen years old.

Her parents became permanently estranged after the father, a saloon-keeper, publicly humiliated her mother; when Sarah retrieved her young daughter, who was being used as a show piece to entertain the white bar patrons, her husband spanked Sarah. Her mother took Annie to the small town of her brother, Nathan, in Bramwell, West Virginia. For the next several years she lived a sheltered life in this wealthy town where nine of the 150 denizens were millionaires.

Entering Lynchburg Baptist Seminary in 1893, where she stayed for six years, she received a liberal education and met her future husband, Edward Spencer. At a school picnic she also met future friend **W. E. B. Du Bois** when she was fifteen years old. Her biographer records that even as a young woman, Anne Spencer never felt inferior to whites and found their **racism** stupid. Her valedictorian speech bravely addressed the plight of blacks in the United States.

In May of 1901 she married Edward and eventually gave birth to four children, one of whom—a boy—died after eleven hours. She did little housework, preferring to garden and write instead. But she was more socially involved and committed than indicated in her poetry, most of which gives little sense of her racial **identity**. When, for example, the

National Association for the Advancement of Colored People (NAACP) wanted to establish a chapter in Lynchburg, Virginia, in 1918, Anne and her husband invited the NAACP organizer, **James Weldon Johnson**, to be their houseguest when everyone else was too intimidated to do so. A little later—and about thirty years before Rosa Parks—a feisty Anne Spencer refused to move to the Jim Crow section of a Lynchburg trolley.

Her first published poem, "Before the Feast at Shushan," based on the Book of Esther, appeared in *Crisis* (1920). James Weldon Johnson included five of her poems in *The Book of Negro American Poetry* (1922); "At the Carnival" was published in Robert T. Kerlin's *Negro Poets and Their Poems* (1923); Louis Untermeyer included Spencer and **Claude McKay** in his anthology, *American Poetry Since 1900* (1923); "White Things" appeared in *Crisis* (March 1923); "Lady, Lady," appeared in *Survey Graphic* (March 1925); Alain Locke included Spencer in his groundbreaking the *New Negro* (1925); "Lines to a Nasturtium" appeared in *Palms* (October 1926); "Rime for the Christmas Baby" appeared in *Opportunity* (December 1927); and ten of her poems appeared in **Countee Cullen**'s *Caroling Dusk* (1927).

During this time, the Spencers traveled little but much of the black world visited them at 1313 Pierce Street in Lynchburg, including Paul Robeson, **Langston Hughes**, George Washington Carver, Adam Clayton Powell, Roland Hayes, W. E. B. Du Bois, **Sterling A. Brown,** and James Weldon Johnson. Brown wrote "To a Certain Lady, In Her Garden (For Anne Spencer)."

"White Things," one of her few poems explicitly in the protest tradition, decries the tyranny that whites exercise over blacks. She describes a lynching in which a black man's burned skull is a "glistening awful thing"; the skull's whiteness symbolizes America's effort to subvert God's law and to deracinate black America. A dozen years later, a similar poem, "Between the World and Me," was written by **Richard Wright**.

Most of her poems, however, teem with classical and historical allusions. "Sybil Speaks" and "Life-Long, Poor Browning" are typical titles. Commonly she creates a fictional persona, such as in "Letter to My Sister" (Anne did not have a biological sister) and in "The Wife-Woman," a first-person poem about a widow whose husband was buried in Flanders Field, France, after World War I (Mrs. Spencer was a widow only when Edward died in 1964 at the age of eighty-eight).

"At the Carnival" celebrates the spiritual and formal beauty of the Girl of the Diving Tank. She represents the ideal that stands above "malodorous" reality, which has its sordid odors of sausage and garlic permeating the "blind crowd." The diving girl has a purity that will be tainted by the "bacilli of the usual and the expedient." Consequently, the poet implores Neptune to "claim his child"; that is, to let her die so as to preserve her purity. Beauty can only survive on an ideal level—such as in a poem or in the garden or in literal immortality.

Spencer retreated from the literary world in the 1930s, especially after James Weldon Johnson was killed in an automobile accident in 1938. She worked as a librarian at Dunbar High School until 1945. In 1949, her elegy for Johnson, "For Jim, Easter Eve," appeared in *The Poetry of the Negro, 1746–1949*, an anthology by Langston Hughes and **Arna Bontemps**.

One needs a dictionary and an encyclopedia at hand to read her poetry. Her work tends to be as cryptic and demanding as Emily Dickinson's. Obscure as her poetry is, she was, nonetheless, a politically aware and committed human being. Her life and her aesthetics were alike in one essential way: They were both brilliantly individualistic and defiant of conventional norms.

Her garden house, which she called Edankrall (meaning Ed and Anne dwelling), was her Eden, her sanctuary. The garden and her home are Virginia Historic Landmarks listed in the National Register. The Friends of Anne Spencer Memorial Foundation perpetuates her name. (*See also* African American Poetry)

Further Reading

J. Lee Greene. *Time's Unfading Garden: Anne Spencer's Life and Poetry*. Baton Rouge: Louisiana State UP, 1977.

Leonard J. Deutsch

SPEWACK, BELLA COHEN (1899–1990)   Jewish American journalist, playwright, screenwriter, publicist, and autobiographer. Bella Spewack collaborated with her husband Sam to write over thirty Broadway plays and screenplays between 1930 and 1960. Among the well-known classics are *Boy Meets Girl* (1935), *Weekend at the Waldorf* (1945), *My Three Angels*, and *Kiss Me, Kate* (1948). Her literary legacy was more recently enhanced by the posthumous publication of her immigrant autobiography written when she was twenty-two years old. *Streets: A Memoir of the Lower East Side* is a vivid portrayal of poverty and ambivalent **assimilation** in New York immigrant neighborhoods in the early part of the twentieth century.

Bella Cohen emigrated as a child from Romania to the United States in 1902 or 1903. Her mother, Fanny, was divorced and Bella's childhood was spent in poverty. Fanny supported Bella's intellectual ambitions, which, at the time, involved the struggle to finish high school. Charitable organizations supporting the family pressured Bella to help the family by going to work after elementary school. Her tenacity in pursuit of education is documented in her memoir.

After high school, Bella found secretarial work, and rapidly started writing articles for the *New York Call*. Soon she was writing full-time for a variety of magazines. She married Sam Spewack in 1922 and they traveled to Europe as newspaper correspondents. While working in Berlin and Moscow, Bella wrote her autobiography, though apparently she never pursued publication of the memoir. She wrote influential articles, including a series that affected rent laws in New York, and successful stories, including "The Laugh," which is found in the *Best Short Stories of 1925*. In 1926 her newspaper story was the first to introduce the woman who claimed to be Anastasia Romanov.

Bella and Sam Spewack returned to the United States and started writing plays. The Spewacks first collaboratively produced play was *The Solitaire Man* in 1927. Their first Broadway success, in 1932, *Clear All Wires,* is a satire based on journalists abroad. The couple collaborated on other early Broadway successes, such as *Boy Meets Girl* (1935–36) and *Leave It to Me!* (1938). Their movie collaborations include *My Favorite Wife* (1940) and *Weekend at the Waldorf* (1945). In 1948, *Kiss Me, Kate* opened with Cole Porter's music, a modern version of Shakespeare's *Taming of the Shrew. Kiss Me Kate* won a variety of awards, was produced abroad, and made into a movie.

Bella Spewack was involved in the United Nations Relief and Rehabilitation Agency after World War II. She continued her work as a publicist for different organizations, including the Girl Scouts, for whom she invented what she later called the "heinous, heinous cookie." Sam Spewack died in 1971 and Bella Spewack died in 1990. In 1993 Columbia University produced an exhibition *From Russia to "Kiss Me Kate": The Careers of Sam and Bella Spewack.* In 1995, the Feminist Press published *Streets,* originally serialized in *The Tenement Times,* a museum publication edited by Ruth Limmer. Limmer's Introduction contextualizes Spewack's story and elaborates upon the importance of the realistic details.

Further Reading

Elias, Lois Raeder. Afterword. *Streets: A Memoir of the Lower East Side.* Bella Spewack. New York: Feminist Press at the City U of New York, 1995. 159–173.

Limmer, Ruth. Introduction. *Streets: A Memoir of the Lower East Side.* Bella Spewack. New York: Feminist Press at the City U of New York, 1995. ix–xxxviii.

Muir, Lisa. "Rose Cohen and Bella Spewack: The Ethnic Child Speaks to You Who Never Were There." *College Literature* 29.1 (Winter 2002): 123–143.

Kristine Peleg

SPIEGELMAN, ART (1948–) Jewish American graphic novelist. The recipient of a special award from the Nobel prize committee in 1992, Art Spiegelman is best known for *Maus I & II* (1986, 1991), a comic book rendition of the **Holocaust** that envisions the participants—Jews, Germans, Poles—represented as their derogatory Nazi stereotypes—rodents, cats, and pigs. As a comic taken seriously as literature, *Maus* bridges the gap between high and low culture. As an absorbing story, it hovers between fiction and nonfiction, listed in the *New York Times Book Review* as a "fiction" best seller until Spiegelman objected. And as an animal fable, it self-consciously blurs its own metaphors; the Jews drawn as mice are plagued by too-real rats in their hiding place. *Maus* is "Tom and Jerry" turned deadly serious.

Maus tells the story of Vladek Spiegelman, Art's father, during World War II. Vladek's recollections begin in the mid-1930s, in Czestochowa, Poland, where he meets and marries Anna Zylberberg, Art's mother. The gradual encroachment of the Nazis haunts their early married life, shadowing the happiness of their successful textile business and beloved firstborn son, Richieu. Volume I, "My Father Bleeds History," follows the Spiegelmans through various hiding places in the Jewish ghetto, carefully documenting the architecture of their bunkers, and ends in the winter of 1944, when Vladek and Anja accept an offer to be smuggled into Hungary. However, the smugglers betray them and the Spiegelmans are instead taken to Auschwitz. Volume II, "And Here My Troubles Began," depicts Vladek's survival in the concentration camps. At first he is aided by a Polish guard who trades food and clothes for lessons in English. In his later jobs as tinsmith and shoemaker he is able to see and assist Anja, who has been taken to nearby Birkenau. Vladek describes the beginning of his troubles as the closure of Auschwitz and his deportation to Dachau, where he contracts typhus and nears death. The story closes with the end of the war, Vladek and Anja's homecoming, and their journey to America.

Maus is ultimately as much Art's story as Vladek's, as suggested by a brief prologue set during Art's childhood in Rego Park, Queens. Deserted by his friends when his roller skate breaks, the ten-year-old Artie goes to his father for consolation and is told, "Friends? Your friends? . . . If you lock them together in a room with no food for a week . . . *then* you could see what it is, friends!" *Maus* represents Art's attempt to come to terms with the tragedy that he did not experience, but that haunts his life. The framing story that depicts the process of researching, writing, and drawing *Maus* shows him grappling with family members both absent and present. He admits to sibling rivalry with Richieu, who could do no wrong since he was killed in the war before Art's birth and lived on only as a memory and a photograph; he longs to recover his mother's recollections of the war, written down before she committed suicide in 1968. Art's father confesses to destroying the diaries in a fit of despair, prompting Art to call him a murderer. Vladek himself is a major concern; Art worries that depicting his father's bad habits, including neurotically counting pills, saving bits of telephone wire and other odds and ends, and insulting a black man picked up as a hitchhiker, will only reinforce Jewish American stereotypes. He also wrestles with the success of his own work, turning down offers for merchandising and film rights and feeling pressured to be a spokesman of the Holocaust.

The wide acclaim earned by *Maus* has made Spiegelman the cartoonist of choice when scholarly commentary is called for, and he has produced introductions for works and collections including Richard H. Minear's *Dr. Seuss Goes to War*, on Theodore Seuss Geisel's World War II political cartoons; *Barefoot Gen*, Keiji Nakazawa's semiautobiographical manga of the Hiroshima bombing; and *Tijuana Bibles*, underground comics from the 1930s, 1940s, and 1950s.

Inspired as a child by the subversive style of *Mad Magazine*, Spiegelman knew as a teenager that cartoons were his métier. A participant in the underground comics boom in San Francisco in the late 1960s and early 1970s, he worked on *Young Lust*, a parody of 1950s romance comics; *Arcade*, an anthology attempting to mainstream satirical underground comics; and Marvel's *Comix Book*. In these works, known as "comix" both for "comixing" words and art and to emphasize their often X-rated content, he was already working with themes that would come to fuller fruition in *Maus*. His comix often featured Jewish black humor, and "Prisoner on the Hell Planet," a piece on his mother's suicide later included in *Maus*, appeared in *Short Order Comix* in 1973. From 1980 to 1984, Spiegelman and his wife Francoise Mouly edited the influential comix anthology *Raw*. *Raw* showcased works by the old stars of comix and introduced its audience to both newer American artists and those already established in Europe but previously unavailable in the United States. *Maus* was first serialized in the anthology as well.

Although most of Spiegelman's work has been for an adult audience, recently he has created works for children, such as the Little Lit series, also edited with Mouly. Like *Maus*, Spiegelman's stories for children often involve transformation of people and animals. *I'm a Dog!* (1997), complete with leash, wagging tail, and fuzzy places to pat, tells the story of a dog turned into a book by a wizard's curse. "Prince Rooster: A Hasidic Parable," Spiegelman's contribution to *Folklore and Fairy Tale Funnies* (2000), tells of a human prince who is convinced he is really a rooster.

Returning to historical tragedy, his most recent project *In the Shadow of No Towers* (2004) addresses the terrorism of September 11, 2001.

Further Reading

Geis, Deborah R., ed. *Considering* Maus: *Approaches to Art Spiegelman's "Survivor's Tale" of the Holocaust*. Tuscaloosa: U of Alabama P, 2003.

Hirsch, Marianne. *Family Frames: Photography, Narrative, and Postmemory.* Cambridge, MA: Harvard UP, 1997.

Jaime Cleland

SPIRITUALS The musical counterpart to slave narratives, the spirituals have assumed a dominant presence in the canon of American folk song. They have transcended their particular context and symbolically represent a universal hope of liberation from oppression. The spirituals are principally associated with African American church congregations of the antebellum South and the earlier, more informal, and sometimes clandestine gatherings of enslaved people. Their creation, the result of a process of mutual influence and reciprocal borrowing, is credited to evangelical sermons and hymns, biblical stories, traditional African chants and praise songs, and the combined experiences of enslaved people in the South.

Most important for interpreting the meaning of the spirituals is an appreciation of the context—social and religious—in which they were performed and the insight they lend into the extraordinary power of music to shape the experience and conscious identity of a people. In the spirituals, enslaved people critically analyzed their conditions, fashioned a creative theological response, indicted their oppressors without overtly denigrating them, reasserted the influence of an African sensibility, and empowered themselves by exercising a form of resistance that would endure longer than the conditions to which they were subject.

The spirituals created by enslaved people became a unique means to "keep on keeping on" under the physical and psychological pressures of daily life, testifying to the belief that the supernatural interacted with the natural and humanity had a decisive role to play in accomplishing liberation. In creation as well as performance they exhibited the essential characteristics of spontaneity, variety, and communal interchange. The form of the spirituals was flexible and improvisational, thereby able to fit an individual slave's experience into the consciousness of group, creating at once an intensely personal and vividly communal experience.

The spirituals, as the cultural product of enslaved Africans, used rhythms and beats of various homelands. The distinguishing musical aesthetic of the spirituals derives from West African percussive forms, multiple meters, syncopation, extensive melodic ornamentation, a call and response structure, and an integration of song and movement, each involving improvisation. Call and response embodies the foundational principle behind the performance of the spirituals, denoting the ritual requirement of what is necessary for completion. Very much a ritual act, when spirituals were sung by enslaved people they amplified their desire for liberation and created conditions of sacred space and time wherein the biblical stories of which they sang were transformed and the history of the ancient past became the history of the present.

Designed to communicate on more than one level, the spirituals sometimes functioned as coded songs to communicate information between enslaved people. **Booker T. Washington** affirmed that the freedom in their songs meant freedom in this world and **Frederick Douglass** insisted that references to Caanan implied the North. But formally and thematically, spirituals were open to change and improvisation as a spiritual in one situation might mean something else in another. In nearly every instance, however, there is an intertwining of theological and social messages.

When the Civil War opened up the society in which enslaved Africans were confined and brought them in to large-scale contact with the world outside the plantation, Northerners came to appreciate their distinctive music. As with ex-slave narratives, the African American authorship of the spirituals was challenged at first. But in an 1867 article published in *The Atlantic Monthly,* Thomas Wentworth Higginson, a militant New England abolitionist who commanded the first freed slave regiment to fight against the Confederacy, was among the first to describe how he heard spirituals.

Synthesizing sacred and secular meaning, the spirituals drew images from the Bible to interpret their own experience, measuring it against a wider system of theological and historical meaning. Three themes dominate spirituals: the desire for freedom, the desire for justice, and strategies for survival. God is a liberator who is involved in history who will "trouble the waters" of oppression. Many spirituals like "Joshua Fit the Battle of Jericho" are drawn from biblical texts that stress God's involvement in the liberation of the oppressed. Although God's liberating work was not always concretely evident, enslaved people were confident that "You Got a Right" to "the tree of life."

The songs also stress a need for enslaved people's own participation in God's liberation, to be "Singing With a Sword in My Hand." They viewed their cry of "Let My People Go" as answered with the Emancipation Proclamation, when "Slavery Chain Done Broke at Last." God makes justice for the righteous and the unrighteous because "All God's Children Got Wings," but "everybody who's talking about heaven ain't going." Anyone who stands against liberation is called to account, "Were You There When They Crucified my Lord?" Jesus represents both an historical savior and whoever helps the oppressed. Jesus functions in a more personal way than God does, and is affirmed both in his divinity and humanity, especially his identification with the oppressed who believe that "A Little Talk With Jesus Makes It Right." Hence his birth is an occasion to "Go Tell It on the Mountain."

Songs like "Steal Away" may have served as a means to convene secret resistance meetings, whereas "Deep River and My Home is Over Jordan" may imply a wish to cross over to Africa or to the North. But getting to freedom is what occupies many of the lyrics that take as a theme a tired sojourner struggling through a hostile landscape while leaning and depending on God. Portraying a struggle against oppression in a variety of metaphors, many spirituals focus on the difficult movement through space and time, but with the confidence to cheer the "Weary Traveler." Spatial and temporal metaphors of movement employing a variety of methods—sailing, walking, riding, rowing, climbing—all appear for a people "Bound to Go."

The spirituals actually and symbolically moved a people toward liberation when they sang, "We Are Climbing Jacob's Ladder," even if they could only "Keep Inching Along." Noting the threat of adverse physical conditions, the creators appropriated symbols from their own situation and describe searching for God in the wilderness, rocks, darkness, storms, and valleys. Lyrics from songs such as "O Stand the Storm," gave inspiration to endure. Although an enslaved person often felt "Like a Motherless Child," faith is affirmed because "All My Troubles Will Soon Be Over." Sometimes a lonely sojourner is aided by heavenly transportation, as in "Swing Low, Sweet Chariot," or the activity of the **Underground Railroad** that invites "Get on Board, Little Children." But the destination is always freedom. Many writers of all ethnicities have invoked the spirituals, conscious that in doing so they were calling forth the spirit of a people struggling to be free, a people who asserted that "Before I'll be a slave/I'll be buried in my grave/And go home to my Lord and be free." (*See also* African American Slave Narrative)

Further Reading

Cone, James. *The Spirituals and the Blues*. New York: Seabury Press, 1972.
Lovell, John. *Black Song: The Forge and the Flame*. New York: Macmillan, 1972.

Kimberly Rae Connor

STEIN, GERTRUDE (1874–1946)   Jewish American writer. Stein lived and wrote unconventionally. She was the daughter of well-off German Jewish immigrants and, after a peripatetic youth—some early years in Vienna and Paris, later childhood in California, study at Radcliffe College (with William James), and the Johns Hopkins University—Stein spent most of her creative years as an expatriate in France, living first with her brother Leo and then with her companion Alice Toklas. Stein engaged ethnicity as a theme in many of her writings, especially her early novels, but in an indirect style. For Stein, representing **identity** involved processes of abstraction. She explored these processes in several ways, challenging conventions of narrative and drama and blending together poetry and prose, fiction and autobiography. Stein not only believed it was important to continuously find innovative modes of representation but to creatively represent the ways we represent. Stein claimed that living surrounded by foreign language allowed her the space to experiment with English, to free words from worn-out use by juxtaposing them in new ways. Although some critics ridiculed her most experimental writing when it first appeared and preferred the "lost generation" writers she mentored, Stein has since been recognized as one of the most important American modernists. Recent critics have begun to look more closely at how Stein's aesthetics relate to her feminist, racial, and ethnic politics. Like the imprecise pronouns she preferred, Stein has proven hard to pin down. Much of the meaning of her words she left to their beholders.

In the early years of the twentieth century, Stein moved to Paris, turned her apartment into a salon filled with collected artwork, and played hostess to modern artists and writers. Stein began to write her first published novel *Three Lives* (1909) while looking at a painting by Cézanne and she later claimed her flattened, decentered style was inspired by his. Two of Stein's protagonists are inarticulate working-class German American women who lead repressed and oppressed lives far removed from any idealized American dream. Their stories ring with understated irony; desire and death are depicted succinctly, in unadorned prose and with a detachment that paradoxically heightens their tragedy. Thus Stein levels the relationship between surface and depth, writing and feeling. The repeated use of ethnic tags and vague adjectives has the strange effect of simultaneously investing and emptying them of meaning, bringing the whole process of conventional characterization to the attention of readers. Stein tried to achieve complex, immediate characterization in "Melanctha," the most experimental section of *Three Lives*, through a constant recurring and beginning again and by the pairing of descriptive words with gerunds so that protagonists are captured in a kind of prolonged present. Stein

Gertrude Stein. *Courtesy of the Library of Congress.*

wrote this story while she was posing for Picasso's portrait of her with a masklike face. Refitting some of her old dialogue, Stein masked or translated *Q.E.D.*, her earlier autobiographically inspired fiction of failed lesbian liaison, as "Melanctha," the story of a failed African American romance. Form and content mirror each other as the narration meanders through the thought and talk of Melanctha and Jeff. The relationship between them founders because they have incompatible personalities, which are depicted in psychologically grounded and racially stereotypical terms.

Stein also explored the way generations and time shape identity. Her enormous second novel, *The Making of Americans* (completed 1911, published 1925), begins as a chronicle of how younger members of two immigrant families negotiate inheritance and independence in becoming American. Although it deals with departure from the Old World and education in the New, this is no standard ethnic saga. Its style is jarring; Stein believed that innovative artists similarly felt the drag of the past and struggled to innovate. The novel self-consciously describes the narrator's attempt to capture in an immediate way the inner lives of members of three generations as variations on the basic types that make up all of humanity. By the end of the novel, Stein's strives to portray how experience feels as it occurs and her prose is full of participles in long, paratactic sentences about "being living." She was aiming for a coincidence of experience with representation so that writing becomes dramatic.

In many of her portraits and in *Tender Buttons* (1914), Stein further tried to close the time and distance gaps involved in representation by abandoning plot, describing through suggestion, and foregrounding the processes of perception and description. In this way she composed verbal equivalents of persons and objects. In a parody written in the 1920s, the sexually charged "As a Wife Has a Cow: A Love Story," eroticism is palpable but Stein's abstract explicitness confounds convention. In *Four Saints and Three Acts* (1932), a take-off on baroque opera on religious subjects, Stein hoped her characters would not seem defined through relationships to others or in time but just as beings in the landscape. The opera is full of vague everyday language, counting and puns, nonsequiturs and snippets of familiar phrases and rhymes, missing punctuation and syntax. Stage directions were sung. Stein came to think of this kind of suggestive but playful abstract leveling as a distinctly twentieth-century American aesthetic. Recently critics have begun to explore the ways Stein's widely noted and traveled opera, which was set to music by Virgil Thompson and performed by an all-black cast, participated in the racialism, popularizing, and Americanization of modernism.

Stein was aware of the ways her voice and audience complicated her identity. The book that made her a household name was an act of domesticated ventriloquism. In the best-selling *Autobiography of Alice B. Toklas* (1933), Stein tells the story of her home and social life in Paris in the voice of Toklas, though Stein reveals herself as author at the end. In *Everybody's Autobiography* (1937), which tells of her visit to the United States in the mid-1930s, Stein shows how self-conception is affected by celebrity status. Stein believed representations that are retrospective and aware of the recognition of others translate the self. These two books are written in a conversational style that actually discloses little that is intimate; their modes blur the external and the subjective. In them Stein manages to portray herself as a famous genius without hiding the constructedness of this portrayal.

War in Europe impacted Stein's life and writing. Stein and Toklas spent part of World War I in Majorca and then went to back to France and volunteered as aid workers; Stein wrote about some of their experiences in the collection *Geography and Plays* (1922). During World War II, Stein stayed in occupied France, leaving her Jewish identity, both figuratively and frightfully, up for grabs. Critics are still deciphering Stein's relationships with collaborationists/protectors at this time of tremendous risk. Her wartime writings, the novel *Mrs. Reynolds* (written 1942, published 1952) and the autobiographical *Wars I Have Seen* (1945), capture how daily home and neighborhood life is heightened and deprived by war. Stein composes the war as a collection of perceptions and war stories, a chronicle of the way people interact, feel, think, and talk during war. Eerily missing is the wider destruction of the war. After the arrival of American troops, Stein and Toklas moved back to Paris, where Stein reunited with old friends and enjoyed spending time with American GIs. She died of cancer a few months later.

Further Reading

Bartlett Hass, Robert, ed. A *Primer for the Gradual Understanding of Gertrude Stein.* Los Angeles: Black Sparrow Press, 1971.

Burns, Edward, and Ulla Dydo. "Gertrude Stein: September 1942 to September 1944." *The Letters of Gertrude Stein and Thornton Wilder.* New Haven: Yale UP, 1996. 401–21.

Dearborn, Mary. "*The Making of Americans* as Ethnic Text." *Pocahontas' Daughters: Gender and Ethnicity in American Culture.* New York: Oxford UP, 1986. 169–88.

North, Michael. "Modernism's African Mask: The Stein-Picasso Collaboration." *The Dialect of Modernism: Race, Language, and Twentieth Century Literature.* New York: Oxford UP, 1994. 59–76.

Stimpson, Catharine. "The Mind, the Body, and Gertrude Stein." *Critical Inquiry* 3.3 (1977): 489–506.

Wagner-Martin, Linda. *"Favored Strangers": Gertrude Stein and Her Family.* New Brunswick: Rutgers UP, 1995.

Watson, Steven. *Prepare for Saints: Gertrude Stein, Virgil Thomson, and the Mainstreaming of American Modernism.* New York: Random House, 1998.

Yael Schacher

STERN, ELIZABETH GERTRUDE LEVIN (1889–1954)   Jewish American writer and social activist, known for writing immigrant biographies and a classic feminist autobiography. Elizabeth Gertrude Levin Stern was a writer who at various times used the following pseudonyms: Eleanor Morton, Leah Morton. E. G. Stern, Elisabeth Stern, and Elizabeth Gertrude Stern. She married Leon Stern, worked as a night school principal, supervised welfare work in Philadelphia, and directed two New York settlement houses. She wrote features in the *New York Times* and a regular column in the *Philadelphia Inquirer*.

Elizabeth Stern wrote two autobiographies: *My Mother and I* (1917), and *I Am a Woman—And a Jew* (1926), under the pen name of Leah Morton. With her husband, she coauthored *A Friend at Court* (1923), a "casebook" of an idealized female probation office. Stern also wrote *This Ecstasy* (1927), *When Love Comes a Woman* (1929), *A Marriage Was Made* (1928), *and Gambler's Wife* (1931), all about women and their various social roles. A collection of her newspaper columns, *Not All Laughter: A Mirror to our Times* (1937), shows her long interest in family relationships. Stern wrote well-researched biographies including *Memories: The Life of Margaret McAvoy Smith* (1943), *Josiah White, Prince of Pioneers* (1946), and *The Women in Gandhi's Life* (1953).

The autobiography, *I Am a Woman—And a Jew*, was a best seller in the 1920s and has become a classic of immigrant autobiography. This work has been both praised for great frankness and psychological insight and discredited as inauthentic, imposter ethnicity. Early reviews laud the book for being the actual experiences of a real woman and for illuminating the psychological aspects of the age-old cleavage between Jew and gentile. Leah Morton, the narrator, leaves her immigrant Jewish rabbinical family for public schools, a college degree, and a career in social work. She casts aside the rigidity of Jewish orthodoxy by marrying a gentile. Leah Morton becomes an example of the industrious immigrant who through training, education, and intelligence becomes a leader in the field of social work, a well-respected writer, and an example for women to use their talents to benefit their families and their communities.

While the topics of **feminism** and women's suffrage are implicit in this story, the explicit theme is the developing sense of the importance of the Jewish ethnic heritage to the narrator. This is a book of unusual spiritual odyssey. Leah Morton's break with her past and **assimilation** into a multicultural America lead her eventually to self-discovery, and she realizes her most authentic self in admitting and celebrating her nature as both a woman and a Jew.

The narrator shows a keen interest in the psychology and behavior of ethnic, racial, and religious groups, and their interrelationships. She experiences the various aspects of being Jewish in America, first as a constant handicap and finally as strength through ethnic identification. Her characters discuss religious intolerance and persecution, quotas against Jews, **anti-Semitism**, the Ku Klux Klan, and the pull of Zionism. She personalizes the various approaches of spiritual leaders, the place of the pastor, priest, or rabbi in church or synagogue, and the function of the laity as board members, directors, and club women.

Stern says in the voice of Leah Morton that the Jew faces handicaps in the world, but that every Jew has an ability to express personally the accumulated genius of his or her race so that the individual is not only self-acclaimed but is also the mirror of his or her people. The identification rests not in religious creed or ritual but in shared heritage.

However, the racial authenticity and **ethnicity** that the author extols in *I Am a Woman—And a Jew* appear to be a writer's construction. Elizabeth Stern's son has revealed that his mother was not the Orthodox East Prussia-born daughter of Rabbi Aaron Levin and his wife Sarah. Thomas Noel Stern in his memoir *Secret Family* (1988) recounts that when he reproached his mother about the misrepresentations in the autobiography, she answered, "It makes me what I want to be. It shows our family as I want people to see us." Thomas Stern says that his mother was neither an immigrant nor a Jew and that she was in fact the Pittsburgh-born illegitimate child of a Welsh Baptist mother, Lillian Morgan, and a German Lutheran father, Chris Limburg. She was placed with the Levins as a foster child and lived with them from the age of seven to seventeen. Her adoptive father, Aaron Levin, sexually abused her and forced her to have an abortion at the age of fourteen.

The character that speaks in the first person may not in reality be a Jewish immigrant, but she is clearly a woman alienated from her family and in search of a heritage and a culture. This story is something more complex than a popular version of the preexisting genre of female autobiography; it is fiction created out of real life, based on the experiences and beliefs of its author, and presented in the guise of autobiography. It represents the power of the intellect and the imagination to transform the inadequacy of the real into a superior fictional alternative. (*See also* Jewish American Autobiography)

Further Reading

Zierler, Wendy. "In(ter)dependent Selves: Mary Antin, Elizabeth Stern, and Jewish American Women's Autobiography." *The Immigrant Experience in North American Literature: Carving Out a Niche.* Eds. Katherine B. Payant and Toby Rose. Westport, CT: Greenwood Press, 1998. 1–16.

Arbolina L. Jennings

STERN, GERALD (1925–)   Jewish American poet who bridged the religious and secular through art. Gerald Stern is regarded as a major poet in American letters. His distinct and passionate poetic voice resonates with both his traditional Jewish heritage and his American roots. Typically, Stern's poetry lauds the individual and mundane subject. He combs the past and present and foreign and native worlds in search of the inconsequential and marginalized object that will act as a window to a new better understanding of the world around us. The poet's verse characteristically champions a homeless person, a scurrying rodent, or a meadow filled with trees. These are Stern's little mysteries of life for which the reader gains a fresh and sometimes dazzling perspective. Over the past three decades, Stern has amassed an impressive number of volumes of verse.

The son of Eastern European immigrants, Stern was born into a second-generation Jewish family in Pittsburgh, Pennsylvania. He studied at the University of Pittsburgh, where he began an interest in writing poetry. After graduating in 1947, Stern served in the Army Air Corps, specializing in counterintelligence (1946–47). He later entered Columbia University, where he earned a master's degree in literature (1949). His interests during his studies in the middle of the twentieth century gravitated toward modernists like Ezra Pound, T. S. Eliot, **Theodore Roethke**, and W. B. Yeats, as well as traditional poets like John Donne, John Keats, Samuel Taylor Coleridge, Robert Browning, and William Wordsworth. He pursued a doctoral degree at Columbia, studying under Lionel Trilling, but withdrew after a year. Stern's poetry exhibits the literary strength of the moderns along with the pastoral and imaginative wanderings of the romantics.

After leaving Columbia, Stern entered the teaching profession. His marriage to Patricia Miller in 1952 produced two children. The couple was divorced in the 1980s. After a number of posts in secondary education, Stern joined the English faculty at Temple University in 1956. Since then he has taught at various institutions, including the University of Pittsburgh, Sarah Lawrence College, Columbia University, and Somerset Community College. From 1982 Stern has held a tenured faculty post in poetry at the University of Iowa Writers' Workshop. He has also been a visiting professor at Princeton and New York University.

Stern's emotive verse exhibits a quintessential neoromantic perspective. Marked frequently with allusions to the bible and references to the classical world, his poems clearly draw from both American and British romantics. Stern has singled out one poem in particular, "The One Thing in Life," collected in *Lucky Life* (1977), as most accurately representing his aesthetic position. His attraction to the overlooked and neglected world is to "a place no one else wanted." Mining this new rich terrain, Stern has earned a coveted comparison to the American romantic poet Walt Whitman, who spoke on behalf of every individual. His atypical choice of personae and subjects reflects the dogma in Wordsworth's *Lyrical Ballads* published at the beginning of the nineteenth century. Keats's classical and romantic confluence is also present in Stern's poetry.

Stern's first major published work is the book-length poem, *Pineys* (1969). It is an ambitious and long work of epic proportions that chronicles the history of the Pine Barrens, a wilderness clan of southern New Jersey. This disappointing early book is fraught with formal considerations such as lines of strict iambic pentameter and algebraic formulas as logical extensions of metaphors. Clearly, this work shows the artificial influence of the high modernists Eliot and Pound. Compared with his later, more mature works, *Pineys* reveals an author in search of his true voice.

With *Rejoicings* (1973), the poet achieved a bittersweet sense of accomplishment. While the collection of poems failed to produce critical or commercial success, *Rejoicings* discloses Stern's continued hunt of his own unique poetic persona, the mask through which he would eventually speak over the next several decades. Rather than the stylized and forced voice in *Pineys*, *Rejoicings* reveals an unfettered personal voice, the nascent evidence of Stern's trademark persona: a emotively charged, sentimental, comic and ironic, idiosyncratic, and joyful view of the world. These upbeat characteristics largely conflicted with other poets of his time who were more inclined toward confessional revelations and angst.

It was not until Stern was fifty years old that he achieved national acclaim with the publication of *Lucky Life*. This volume is a quintessential work in which the poet, through an elegiac and romantic style, infuses the ordinary object or person with grand if not metaphysical qualities. Emotions seem bare and accessible. Stern's delicately etched work draws strongly upon his Jewish heritage, infusing the images with a biblical strength. Memory and imagination create vibrant and colorful images in a pronounced literate style. Stern's voice remains distinct and strong, but never effaced or detached. His concern remains with the unheralded object. *Lucky Life* brought Stern the Lamont Poetry Prize in 1977.

Paradise Poems (1984) demonstrates another major transformation that began in *Rejoicings* a decade earlier. This change is marked by Stern's more personal and mature voice, which eclipses the sometimes tedious and stilted masks in earlier poems. Although Stern continues to instill in his verse images sharply patterning the past and present, the author transcends the everyday treatments in favor of an emphasis on universal themes. The ordinary—always anchored to the earth—is subsumed under the magical spell of the ethereal and metaphysical. The temper of voice has achieved the resolute and resilient.

Stern's *This Time: New and Selected Poems* (1998) brought the poet the prestigious National Book Award. This tour de force represents the culmination of the poet's repertory. The uniqueness of this collection is its multicultural window into unseen and often subterranean social, religious, and emotional concerns. Expertly drawn are the sublime and the wretched, existing side by side like twin siblings. This collection continues an underlying theme that is prominent in Stern's early poem "The Goons are Leaving" (*Rejoicings*). The poet's persona struggles with the haunting paradox: "we live in grief and ecstasy." The fusion of two seemingly disparate images is characteristic of Stern's canon. These odd bedfellows include the religious and the prosaic, human and animal, classical and contemporary, and the past and the present.

Stern is widely identified through his unique persona. Often written in the first person, his poems call upon a wide spectrum of narrators through whom the author speaks: a folksy gardener and a rabbinical sage, trees and weeds, and birds and rodents. Stern's voice is often comic and ironic, playful and prophetic. He is sometimes regarded as a confessional poet like Sylvia Plath and Robert Lowell. Self-revelation comes through themes of suffering, waste, and ruin, although typically Stern uses irony and humor. His collection *Last Blue* (2000) follows many of his previous themes and treatments that deconstruct neatly separated traditional binary signifiers like good and evil.

Stern, a dedicated and prolific poet, has received numerous regional and national honors during his literary career, including the National Endowment for the Arts, Guggenheim fellowship, Lamont Poetry Prize for *Lucky Life,* and the National Book Award for *This Time: New and Selected Poems.* His poems have also been honored by such prestigious journals as the *Paris Review* and *American Poetry Review.*

Further Reading

Sommerville, Jane. *Gerald Stern: The Speaker as Meaning.* Detroit: Wayne State UP, 1988.

———. *Making the Light Come: The Poetry of Gerald Stern.* Detroit: Wayne State UP, 1990.

Stitt, Peter. *Uncertainty and Plenitude: Five Contemporary Poets.* Iowa City: U of Iowa P, 1997.

Michael D. Sollars

STEWART, MARIA W. (1803–1879)   Early African American journalist, feminist, and activist. Born during the period of **slavery** in American history, but never a slave, Maria Stewart was one of few African American writers of the nineteenth century who were willing to risk life and limb to rescue her people from physical and mental slavery.

Maria Stewart was born in Hartford, Connecticut. Orphaned by the age of five, she was sent to a clergyman's family where she served until she was fifteen years old. She then supported herself through domestic service and participated in Sabbath School and literacy training. She married James W. Stewart in 1826 and adopted his middle initial. The marriage was short, for James, a successful middle-class businessman died, three years into the marriage. After her husband's death, Stewart was cheated out of her inheritance by a group of unscrupulous white businessmen. Her loss was further compounded when **David Walker**, a family friend and in many ways a mentor, died under suspicious circumstances.

Stewart was influenced by the political activism of David Walker, author of the political manifesto *The Appeal in Four Articles*. Stewart, though constantly threatened, was undaunted in her responsibility to educate her people. Stewart used the Bible as her primary tool and demonstrated through it, as did the Negro **spirituals**, that God would punish slaveholders for their various offenses against Africa's children.

Stewart was the first person to argue convincingly that black women must leave domestic service and seek careers outside the home, reminding women that they must fulfill an obligation to educate themselves and their daughters.

Considered America's first black woman political writer, Stewart's writings are a combination of call to action and religious appeal. Although her work is often overshadowed by the work of her contemporaries, **Frances E. W. Harper** and **Sojourner Truth**, her work is still as powerful today as it was in the 1830s.

Stewart's most active period was from 1830 to 1834; her speeches and essays include "Religion and the Pure Principles of Morality" (1831); "Cause for Encouragement" (1832); "Lecture Delivered at the Franklin Hall" (1832); "An Address Delivered Before the Afric-American Female Intelligence Society of America" (1832); "An Address Delivered at the African Masonic Hall" (1833); "Mrs. Stewart's Farewell Address to Her Friends in the City of Boston" (1833).

Writing essays and exhortations, on women's rights rooted in religious principles, Stewart encouraged blacks to realize their equality to whites and to educate themselves to rise above their given circumstances. Stewart prophesied, for though she wrote in the nineteenth century, many might argue that her admonitions are needed in the twenty-first century.

Stewart's first essay and her most anthologized work, *Religion and the Pure Principles of Morality, the Sure Foundation on Which We Must Build*, was first published in the abolitionist paper, *The Liberator* in 1831. In this work, Stewart outlines the work African Americans must do to stake their claim in America. She argues that although equal in every way to white Americans, African Americans, who built the country with their toil and tears, need to work tirelessly toward building both a religious and educational foundation, making necessary sacrifices, to ensure the future of African America. She encourages women to leave domestic service and enter their own enterprises; she promotes entrepreneurship that leads to uplifting the entire **race**. She then turns to a fierce indictment of Americans, warning that they cannot expect to keep African Americans in darkness and that God has assured vengeance and repayment for those who long-deprived African Americans of advantages to improve the mind and the spirit. She closes with encouragement to her brothers and sisters to turn their attention to knowledge and improvement and put their trust in the living God. He will surely deliver, she assures, with a mighty hand and an outstretched arm.

Further Reading

Richardson, Marilyn, ed. *Maria W. Stewart, America's First Black Woman Political Writer: Essays and Speeches.* Bloomington: Indiana UP, 1987.

Romero, Lora. *Home Fronts: Domesticity and Its Critics in the Antebellum United States.* Durham, NC: Duke UP, 1997.

Chandra Tyler Mountain

STRAND, MARK (1934–)   Jewish American poet, short story writer, essayist, translator, and children's author. The United States Poet Laureate from 1990 to 1991, Mark Strand belongs to a tradition of American Romantic poets that includes Ralph Waldo Emerson, Emily Dickinson, and Wallace Stevens.

Mark Strand's lyric poetry is typically noted for its surrealistic qualities and for its spareness of diction. A prolific and widely honored poet, Strand has shaped his career around intense explorations of the self and the relation of the individual to the world. Strand does not typically write about Jewish experience or **identity** in the manner of, for example, Karl Shapiro; he is not usually considered in terms of his being a Jewish poet. Indeed, Strand's poetry, which places little emphasis on matters of autobiography or the politics of personal identity, stands apart from much writing of the late twentieth century that pays particular attention to issues of **race**, gender, class, and sexuality.

Strand is principally a poet of ideas and abstracted emotion. He does not document the material details of life in contemporary America, but instead participates in a tradition of philosophical and metaphysical writing. This is not to say that Strand ignores the world around him. In fact, he is a skilled and sensitive observer of the natural world. But Strand's career can be read as a sustained attempt to investigate the nature of the self.

His first volume of poems, *Sleeping with One Eye Open* (1964), attracted little attention. His subsequent collections, *Reasons for Moving* (1968) and *Darker* (1970) developed the themes of isolation and division that the first book introduced. *Selected Poems* (1980) followed the four collections of the 1970s, but Strand then published no poetry until *The Continuous Life* in 1990.

Although the later poetry can be seen as variations on Strand's major themes, it also displays an interest in renewal and luminosity. *The Continuous Life* (1990) also demonstrates the range of poetic forms Strand employs. The collection includes short lyrics, brief as well as extended prose poems, rhymed quatrains, and dramatic fragments. The book's trajectory leads from "The Idea," the first poem, to "The End," the last. "The Idea" expresses a human desire to know the unknowable, whereas "The End" claims that not all men know what waits for them upon death. As do many of Strand's works, these poems show a profound interest in the power and limits of human knowledge, as well as and an affinity for images of light and brilliance. ("The Coming of Light," the first poem in *The Late Hour*

[1978], appears to equate light with love, a pairing of particular importance to Strand.)

The book-length poem *Dark Harbour* (1993) won the Bollingen Prize. The work, composed of forty-five sections, begins as the speaker leaves a town's Main Street and embarks on a journey of discovery. The speaker describes the town and the natural landscape in terms that suggest the sublime. This reflective work ranges in tone from the melancholy to the exuberant. Section XXXIV considers the strained relations between humans and nature, and includes a quotation taken from William Wordsworth's preface to *Lyrical Ballads.* This direct reference to Wordsworth suggests the importance of the Romantic tradition to Strand. Indeed, one of Strand's most notable critics, Harold Bloom, argues that he belongs to a tradition of Romanticism in American poetry that includes, among others, Ralph Waldo Emerson, Walt Whitman, Wallace Stevens, and A. R. Ammons.

In seeming contrast, poems such as "Elegy for My Father (Robert Strand, 1908–68)," from *The Story of Our Lives* (1973), or "For Jessica, My Daughter," from *The Late Hour,* show a more obviously personal side. Even in these poems, however, Strand continues to explore the relation of the self to others.

Despite his recurring attention to the natural world, Strand is not strongly affiliated with any particular region. Born in Summerside, Prince Edward Island, Canada, Strand moved to the United States in 1938. Like so many other contemporary poets, Strand has long been affiliated with universities. He took a BA at Antioch College in 1957 and a BFA from Yale in 1959, and he was a Fulbright fellow at the University of Florence in 1960–1961. He then took an MA from the University of Iowa in 1962. Since then, Strand has taught at many American universities, notably the University of Utah (1981–93), the Johns Hopkins University (1993–98), and the University of Chicago.

Further Reading
Bloom, Harold. *Figures of Capable Imagination.* New York: Seabury, 1976.
Kirby, David. *Mark Strand and the Poet's Place in Contemporary Culture.* Columbia: U of Missouri P, 1990.

Nicholas Bradley

STREET, THE   Written with the assistance of the Houghton Mifflin Literary Fellowship Award and published in 1946, **Ann Petry**'s novel became the first by an African American woman to sell over 1 million copies. *The Street* builds on the examples of **Paul Laurence Dunbar**'s *The Sport of the Gods* (1902) and **Richard Wright**'s *Native Son* (1940) in the cultivation of black literary naturalism. At the same time, it marks the historical crossover of black women's writing into mainstream American reading publics.

Recently divorced from her husband and estranged from her father, the independent and self-reliant Lutie Johnson is nevertheless filled with hope that she will be able to start a profitable new life for herself in New York City.

Lutie and her son, Bub, move into a run-down apartment in a tenement on Harlem's 116th Street, and, despite her immediate surroundings, the iconic image of Benjamin Franklin as the quintessential self-made individual looms large in Lutie's thoughts. But the reality of her situation as a single black mother living in a world where economic opportunity and social advancement are foreclosed to her lot is highlighted by the characters who prey on her optimism: Superintendent Jones targets Lutie as the object of his perverse sexual fantasies and persuades Bub to steal letters from mailboxes; tenant and madam Mrs. Hedges wants to enlist her as a prostitute; bandleader Boots Smith uses her to secure his own job and advance his own career; and white slumlord Junto, Petry's narrative counterpoint to Franklin, orchestrates the entire web of exploitation through his ownership of the tenement, its first-floor brothel, and the bar in which Boots's band plays.

The one glimpse of a silver lining comes when Lutie is given the opportunity to sing for Boots's band. But her sense of relief is cut short by a series of depressing events: Jones's attempted rape of Lutie; Junto's demand that Boots find a way to make Lutie his personal concubine or risk losing his job; Boots's subsequent extortion of her; and Bub's arrest by the post office authorities. Alone, destitute, and desperate, Lutie finally appeals to Boots for funds to retain a lawyer for Bub. Before she allows him to determine her fate with Junto, however, Lutie, in a fit of pent-up rage, takes matters into her own hands and clubs Boots to death with a candlestick. She instantly recognizes the weight of her crime and flees the city, leaving her incarcerated son behind.

As with most naturalist writers, Petry has received criticism for investing in an irrevocably bleak portrait of contending human interests and desires. But her narrative, cannily situated as it is at the nexus of **race**, class, and gender exploitation, compels the genre to examine the intersecting dynamics of social inequality, particularly as they bear on black women. In that light, the novel presents a singular (anti)heroine whose capitulation to extreme conditions of socioeconomic, sexual, and psychic oppression articulates one of the most damning literary critiques of the so-called American Dream. (*See also* African American Novel)

Further Reading

Barrett, Lindon. "(Further) Figures of Violence: *The Street* in the U.S. Landscape." *Blackness and Value: Seeing Double.* Cambridge: Cambridge UP, 1999. 94–128.

Hicks, Heather. "'This Strange Communion': Surveillance and Spectatorship in Ann Petry's *The Street.*" *African American Review* 37.1 (2003): 21–37.

McBride, Kecia Driver. "Fear, Consumption, and Desire: Naturalism and Ann Petry's *The Street.*" *Twisted from the Ordinary: Essays on American Literary Naturalism.* Ed. Mary E. Papke. Knoxville: U of Tennessee P, 2003. 304–22.

Pryse, Marjorie. "'Pattern against the Sky': Deism and Motherhood in Ann Petry's *The Street.*" *Conjuring: Black Women, Fiction, and Literary Tradition.* Ed. Marjorie Pryse and Hortense J. Spillers. Bloomington: Indiana UP, 1985. 116–31.

Kinohi Nishikawa

SUÁREZ, MARIO (1925–1998) Mexican American short story writer, and teacher of Chicano literature, Mexican and Southwest history, and Southwest folklore. Mario Suárez, an important writer in the evolution of Chicano literature, is credited with being among the first Chicano writers to create authentic Chicano characters living in a realistic, albeit poor and humble, multicultural community in Tucson, Arizona.

Born, raised, and educated in Tucson, Arizona, Suárez enlisted in the U.S. Navy upon graduating from high school. He returned to Tucson at the end of World War II in 1945 and enrolled at the University of Arizona, where he studied literature and creative writing. Almost immediately, Suárez found he had a talent for colorfully depicting a Tucson barrio and giving voice to its Chicano residents. Encouraged by a professor to submit his work to the *Arizona Quarterly*, he had five narratives published in the summer 1947 issue. "El Hoyo," "Señor Garza," "Cuco goes to a party," "Loco-Chu," and "Kid Zopilote," have since been republished many times in periodicals and anthologies. In 1948 and 1950, the *Arizona Quarterly* also published "Southside Run," "Maestría," and "Mexican Heaven."

Suárez's El Hoyo barrio is portrayed from the inside out, only as a local dweller could see it. With precise details, Suárez reveals the narrow streets of El Hoyo, the weeds, the garbage. The local inhabitants—Señor Garza, the regional philosopher and owner of Garza's Barber Shop; Cuco, a Mexican immigrant who doesn't quite fit in with his in-laws; and Kid Zpoilote, a young Chicano who returns from Los Angeles with *pachuco* tendencies—are portrayed with compassion and understanding as both insiders and outsiders of El Hoyo. A melancholic sense of nostalgia permeates Suárez's narratives as he presents a tight knit urban community that is struggling to preserve its changing historical, cultural, and linguistic values.

It is said that Suárez greatly appreciated and was influenced by the writings of John Steinbeck, particularly his novel *Tortilla Flat* (1935), which depicts a multicultural community in Monterey, California. Suárez's writing also brings to mind the work of another Chicano writer, **Rolando Hinojosa** (1929–) and his fictional community of Klail City of Belken County, Texas.

Throughout his life, Suárez wrote stories and several novels that were never published. In the past fifty years, his stories have appeared in countless publications and now the University of Arizona Press in 2004 is publishing a collection of his work titled, *Chicano Sketches, Short Stories by Mario Suárez*. The publication includes eight never before published stories, along with eleven of his well-known narratives.

Further Reading

Lilley, James D. "The Short Way of Saying Mexicano: Patrolling the Borders of Mario Suárez's Fiction." *MELUS* 26.3 (Fall 2001): 100–118.

Rafaela G. Castro

SUÁREZ, VIRGIL (1962–) Cuban American novelist, short story writer, poet, and editor. Virgil Suarez has published five novels, a book of short stories, and several poetry collections, and has edited four anthologies of Cuban American poetry and prose. He received an MFA from Lousiana State University in 1987 and currently teaches creative writing at the University of Miami in Coral Gables, Florida. Suarez arrived in the United States from Cuba when he was twelve years old. Thus, he retains vivid childhood memories of his homeland, many of which are recounted in his works.

One of his most insightful works, *Spared Angola,* is a collection of essays, poems, and short stories tied together by a narrative thread. The book begins by presenting the mature character, who is reunited with a relative he barely remembers, but who reveals to him that by leaving Cuba before that country's involvement in the African country's Civil War, he was "spared Angola." The work seems to be divided into three distinct parts, all containing memoir, short story, and poetry. The first part recounts the life of the young narrator in Cuba who is essentially unaware of the drastic turn his life will eventually take. In one of the section's most profound passages, Suarez relies on symbol as well as magical realism when describing a neighborhood tree. When playing around the tree with his friends, the narrator finds evidence of Santeria, a mixture of Catholic religion and traditional African ritual. Not even this odd mixture of faiths can save the tree, however, as it is struck by lightning and dies. Suarez's suggestion that the death of this magnificent tree is akin to the death of his homeland is written in a prose that is almost poetic.

It seems no coincidence, then, that in the last several years Suarez seems to be focusing more on his poetry, and he has published four books of verse in the last several years. *You Come Singing* (1998) is similar to *Spared Angola* as it seems a tribute to the past. In this book of poetry, however, Suarez incorporates memories of Spain and Los Angeles, two places where he himself has lived, in addition to poems of Cuba. *In the Republic of Longing* (1999), as the title implies, again contains a nostalgic element, but the book is clearly divided between Cuba and America, giving equal praise to the latter.

In addition to his prolific creative output, Suarez deserves added recognition as an important editor of Cuban American literature. With Delia Poey he has coedited *Iguana Dreams: New Latino Fiction* (1992) and *Little Havana Blues: A Cuban-American Literature Anthology* (1996), and most recently he is the editor of *American Diaspora: Poetry of Displacement* (2001). (*See also* Cuban American Poetry)

Further Reading

Dick, Bruce Allen. *A Poet's Truth: Conversations with Latino/Latina Poets.* Tucson: U of Arizona P, 2003.

Manso, Leira Annette. "Going Under and Spared Angola: Memories from a Cuban-American Childhood: A Contrapunteo on Cultural Identity." *Bilingual Review/La Revista Bilingüe* 24.3 (1999): 295–98.

Eduardo R. del Rio

SULERI GOODYEAR, SARA (1953–)   Pakistani American scholar and memoirist. A professor of English at Yale University, a founding editor of *The Yale Journal of Criticism* and an editorial board member of *The Yale Review* and *Transition,* Suleri Goodyear received her BA at Kinnaird College in Lahore, Pakistan, in 1974. Two years later she received her MA from Punjab University and went on to graduate with a PhD from the University of Indiana in 1983. She is the author of *The Rhetoric of English India* (1992), a seminal work of postcolonial criticism that explores, through a variety of diverse literary texts generated by the British colonization of India, the hegemonic power of language and "cultural tale-telling" to define the subcontinent and sustain popular, and, in Suleri Goodyear's estimation, the unproductive, inaccurate, and even dangerous, Western notions of Eastern alterity and cultural incompatibility. At the core of much of Suleri Goodyear's dense and provocative prose is the desire to assert the dangers of representing and fetishizing "otherness" and the "East-West" divide.

Whereas the publication of *The Rhetoric of English India* confirmed her as an invaluable voice in literary criticism, Suleri Goodyear's highly respected position in the Pakistani American tradition, the South Asian English literary tradition, and in the field of postcolonial studies, results in large measure from the success of her now iconic 1989 memoir, *Meatless Days.* Her first major work, *Meatless Days* is an account of Suleri Goodyear's upbringing in postpartition Pakistan. The daughter of a Welsh mother and scholar and the prominent Pakistani political journalist Z. A. Suleri, author Suleri Goodyear depicts her childhood and adolescence as times of extremes— great joys and terrible tragedies. The turbulent history of a newly independent Pakistan is woven into Suleri familial history and the complex relationships of siblings, parents, and grandmother. The memoir is particularly concerned with the joyfully intimate coterie of Suleri women and the gnawing emptiness left by the tragic death of the eldest sister, Ifat, and later the death of Suleri Goodyear's mother. In reckoning with her past in Pakistan, and coming to terms with her emotional and intellectual development that would lead her away from her homeland and "the company of women" to pursue her studies in the United States, Suleri Goodyear articulates a tremendous loss of a sense of self and place. Yet, as Oliver Lovesey notes, she "embraces in America the responsibility and tragedy of postcolonial hybridity"(46) by examining and accepting her multifaceted **identity** and preserving her Pakistan in the memories of her sisters and mother.

Suleri Goodyear's most recent publication, *Boys Will Be Boys: A Daughter's Elegy* (2003), is in many ways a revisiting of her childhood Pakistan of *Meatless Days,* this time revealing the details of what might be her most complicated and impactful relationship: that with her father, Z. A. Suleri, known to her simply as "Pip." It is to Pip that Suleri Goodyear writes, in a sort of dialogue with the deceased, as she pays tribute to a man of great character and contradiction. An almost mythic portrayal of Pip emerges as Suleri Goodyear describes his enigmatic presence in a room and his singular ability to arouse both fear and awe in his children, and especially in Suleri Goodyear, with whom he seems to have shared a particularly strong intellectual bond. One aspect of this bond was a mutual love and appreciation of Urdu poetry; therefore, peppered throughout the text are lines of Urdu poetry and poems penned by Suleri Goodyear—an attempt, perhaps, to sustain the connection not only with her proudly Pakistani father but also with her homeland, which for her are essentially one and the same. While *Boys Will Be Boys* is, like *Meatless Days,* concerned with the past, although in a less nostalgic manner, it is also addresses the present and offers insight into Suleri Goodyear's life in the United States with her academic career and new husband. Whereas in *Meatless Days,* "Sara" appeared only as aspect of the collective identity of the Suleri family, in *Boys Will Be Boys,* one has a better sense of Suleri Goodyear as an individual who has, fourteen years after the publication of her first memoir, perhaps at last fashioned for herself a sense of self and place.

Suleri Goodyear's ability to intelligently, reverently, and at times comically, underscore themes of loss and cultural displacement makes her an indispensable voice in postcolonial criticism speaking to the experiences of **immigration** and adaptation. (*See also* Postcolonialism, South Asian American Literature)

Further Reading

Lovesey, Oliver. "'Postcolonial Self-Fashioning' in Sara Suleri's *Meatless Days."*
  Journal of Commonwealth Literature 32.2 (1997): 35–50.
Ray, Sangeeta. "Memory, Identity, Patriarchy: Projecting a Past in the Memoirs of
  Sara Suleri and Michael Ondaatje." *Modern Fiction Studies* 39.1 (1993): 37–58.

Dana Hansen

SUNDARESAN, INDU (1969–)   Indian American novelist. Continuing in the long tradition of the Indian epic, Indu Sundaresan's two novels of historical fiction introduce Western readers to one of the most powerful figures in Indian history. *The Twentieth Wife* (2002) and *The Feast of Roses* (2003) tell the story of Mehrunnisa, a penniless orphan who would later become known as the empress Nur Jahan, possibly the most powerful female in seventeenth-century Mughal India.

The Twentieth Wife begins in 1577. Abandoned by her family, Mehrunnisa is introduced to the emperor's court by fate. As an eight-year-old, she witnesses the first marriage of the Emperor Jahangir and decides that she will one day be his wife. First she will be married to another man, later assassinated on Jahangir's order, and will be forced to contend with rival courtesans and political courtiers, all of whom seek to prevent her marriage to the Emperor. With patience, cunning, and destiny, Mehrunnisa enters the royal harem as Jahangir's twentieth and most beloved wife. Tediously researched and grounded in historical fact, Sundaresan's first novel presents the *zenana* (harem culture) as a powerful influence in Mughal government, and through the depiction of Mehrunnisa illustrates how one woman could transcend the historical restrictions against her gender.

The sequel novel *The Feast of Roses* details Mehrunnisa's life as Nur Jahan, "the light of the world," and increasingly the power behind the throne. As her relationship with Jahangir grows, Nur Jahan all but assumes sovereignty in the empire. She incurs the wrath of Jahangir's other wives and his government ministers, who sense their control over him waning. Despite the political division, and despite the conflict between her own desires and her obligations as empress, Nur Jahan's courage and strength of character allow her to form a junta with her father, brother, and the prince Khurram and position her daughter to marry the next emperor. Drawing on seventeenth-century travel narratives and memoirs of the Mughal rulers, Sundaresan again succeeds in creating an entertaining and historically accurate picture of court life in Mughal India.

Indu Sundaresan currently resides in Washington. (*See also* South Asian American Literature)

Further Reading

Raghunathan, Jeanine K. Review of *The Feast of Roses. Library Journal* 128 (June 15, 2003): 102–3.

Reale, Michelle. Review of *The Twentieth Wife. Library Journal* 127 (January 1, 2002): 155.

Zaleski, Jeff. Review of *The Feast of Roses. Publishers Weekly* 250 (May 19, 2003): 53.

———. Review of *The Twentieth Wife. Publishers Weekly* 248 (December 10, 2001): 49.

David R. Deborde

SURI, MANIL (1959–)   Indian American mathematician and novelist. A relative newcomer to the literary scene, Suri wrote his debut novel, *The Death of Vishnu*, over a period of five years and published it to critical and popular acclaim in 2001. An excerpt of the novel appeared in *The New Yorker* in February 2000. His only other literary publication is a short story titled "The Tyranny of Vegetables," which appeared in a Bulgarian journal in 1995. Heralded as one of *Time* magazine's "People to Watch," Suri, a professor of applied mathematics at the University of Maryland, Baltimore County, came to the United States in 1979 to pursue his academic studies. In the midst of a highly successful scholarly career with more than fifty mathematical publications, Suri has turned his attention to writing fiction in part to explore his Indian childhood and current status as an immigrant in the United States, and to address questions of historical memory, religious faith, and national and personal **identity**.

The Death of Vishnu, inspired by the events surrounding the death of an actual man named Vishnu with whom Suri was acquainted as a child growing up in Bombay, is a glimpse into the day-to-day life of several modern Indian families living in a small apartment building in Mumbai (Bombay). The building, a microcosm of and metaphor for the Indian nation divided by social and religious difference, is home to the sparring Hindu families, the Asranis and the Pathaks; the Muslim family, the Jalals, whose son Salim has caused shame and embarrassment for the Asranis by eloping with their daughter Kavita; and Mr. Taneja, a recluse living on the top floor. Coming and going from the building is a host of eccentric minor characters, mostly servants, who closely observe the affairs of the families, eagerly spreading rumors and false information, which lead to conflict and tragedy, adding to the severe depiction of a society in which deprivation and degradation are the norm and the misery of others is an opportunity for exploitation and personal gain.

As time passes in the building, among the living, life is rapidly coming to an end for Vishnu, who has entered into a dreamlike state, drifting somewhere between life and death. As the title of the novel suggests, the core of the story is the death of Vishnu, a one-time servant of the Asranis and the Pathaks. Now more a beloved friend and guardian of the building's occupants, he inhabits the stairwell landings of the building, moving ever farther up the staircase as he symbolically ascends the steps to heaven, with each floor representing a stage on the journey through attachment to the next level of enlightenment. As he lies silent, approaching death, Vishnu relives memories from his childhood and the years before he came to the apartment building, recalls intimate details of his beloved, and contemplates the possibility that he might, remarkably, be the god Vishnu. The novel, however, remains inconclusive as to whether Vishnu's divinity is metaphoric or actual. *The Death of Vishnu* is an expert blend of ancient Hindu mythology, religious and ethnic rivalries, the pervasive Indian film culture, caste and class conflicts, and India's struggle with modernity, as it recounts the undeniably tragic life of a man named for a god, but who is hopelessly humanly flawed.

Suri plans to follow *The Death of Vishnu* with two more novels to form a trilogy: *The Birth of Shiva* and *The Life of Brahma.* In the next book he anticipates continuing the story of the fascinating Ahmed Jalal, a character who finds himself torn between the desire for the rapture of religious faith, and an overwhelming skepticism of anything that cannot be rationalized.

In 2004 Manil Suri was awarded the prestigious Guggenheim Fellowship, popularly known as the "genius award." (*See also* South Asian American Literature)

Further Reading

D'Erasmo, Stacey. "Interview: Solving for X." Review of *The Death of Vishnu* by Manil Suri. *New York Times Book Review* (January 28, 2001): late ed., sec. 7, 9.

Gorra, Michael. "The God on the Landing." Review of *The Death of Vishnu* by Manil Suri. *New York Times Book Review* (January 28, 2001): late ed., sec. 7, 8.

Dana Hansen

SWADOS, ELIZABETH (1951–)   Jewish American composer, lyricist, novelist, playwright, screenwriter, musician, and educator. Born in Buffalo, New York, Swados considers her first foray into musical composition a calypso song created at age four. By age five, she had begun playing piano;

by ten, guitar; and by the time she was a teenager, she was performing as a folk singer. She also began writing short stories in her youth. Her passion for world music was furthered at Bennington College, where she enrolled at age sixteen. Although Swados was not raised in a religiously observant household, she identifies strongly with her Jewish heritage and specifically, she has said, with 1930s Jewish activism. In the 1960s, she played folk music in coffeehouses and at political rallies. During two college summers, she played guitar and sang with Pete Seeger and engaged in public protest against black lung disease while living with an Appalachian family (Chansky 440). Swados is presently on the faculty of Marymount Manhattan College.

Success as a composer came early for Swados, who left Bennington to perform professionally and was quickly discovered by Ellen Stewart, founder of New York's famous avant-garde performance venue, La MaMa E.T.C. There she began working with theater director Andrei Serban, composing the music for his productions of *Medea, Agamemnon,* and *The Cherry Orchard. Medea* earned the then twenty-one-year-old her first Obie. In the early 1970s, Swados toured Africa with theater director Peter Brook and his company and composed music for *Conference of the Birds.*

A concern for the human condition infuses her work, especially with regard to youth. She demonstrates an acute sense of social justice and stresses the need for sensitivity both toward others and oneself.

Swados developed *Runaways,* a 1978 musical about disenfranchised urban youth, from the stories of participants in an extended workshop, and earned four Tony Award nominations for the effort. Other notable youth-focused workshop-based projects include *The Hating Pot,* which toured New York City schools in the early 1990s with its message about coming to terms with racism and anti-Semitism and was made into a Public Broadcasting Service documentary; *The Violence Project* (2001); and *Jewish Girls* (2002), which addresses the problems and joys of being a young Jewish female in the United States.

Swados seeks to expand the range of the human voice as instrument. To this end, she often works with voices that are natural—from Old World traditions or the streets of urban America—not trained. Her compositional language experiments render pronunciation as important as melody and rhythm. In works such as *The Haggadah,* she invented sound language to capture environmental sounds. Swados has expressed interest in exploring music more as ritual than as concert and in asking what, in music, is of human value.

In the mid-1980s, she began writing liturgical music regularly, and in 1995, she released *Bible Women,* the first CD of her own music, excluding cast albums. The songs on *Bible Women* reflect Swados's life-long fascination with Judaism's sacred texts, relating their stories in musical styles ranging from gospel to jazz to 1990s pop.

A prolific artist, in addition to those theater pieces already mentioned, Swados created *Nightclub Cantata* (1977), *Alice in Concert* (1981), *Rap Master*

Ronnie (1985), *Doonesbury* (1986), *Esther: A Vaudeville Megillah* (1989), *Groundhog* (1992), and many more. She has written six children's books, three novels, and two autobiographical books, *Listening out Loud: Becoming a Composer* (1989) and *The Four of Us: The Story of a Family* (1991). *The Animal Rescue Store*, a collection of animal poems is forthcoming in spring 2005.

Her most recent projects include a children's book, *Hey You! C'mere: A Poetry Slam* (2002), which celebrates neighborhood children in their day-to-day experiences; and a musical, *Ten Years of Hope* (2004), which looks at the immigrant women who fled countries like El Salvador in search of a better life in America.

Swados has been nominated for Tony, Drama Desk, Ace, and Emmy awards and has won three Obies, Outer Critics Circle Awards, a PEN Citation, and an Anne Frank National Foundation for Jewish Culture award. She has received Guggenheim, Ford, and Covenant fellowships and a Stephen Spielberg Righteous Person Grant. In 2002, she became the first non-Catholic to receive the Media Images and Religious Awareness Award for *Missionaries*, about the 1980 rape and murder of three American nuns and a lay woman at the beginning of the Salvadoran civil war.

Further Reading

Blaney, Retta. "Heroic, Operatic Story of Four Women." Review of *Missionaries*. *National Catholic Reporter* (November 2000): 17.

Chansky, Dorothy. "Elizabeth Swados (1951–)." *Jewish American Women Writers: A Bio-Bibliographical and Critical Sourcebook*. Ed. Ann R. Shapiro. Westport, CT: Greenwood Press, 1994. 440–47.

Jennifer Lynn Lavy

SWEDISH AMERICAN LITERATURE   Swedish mass **immigration** to the United States began in 1846 when 1326 registered emigrants left Sweden for the newly established Christian communal colony of Bishop Hill, Illinois. Whereas many of the early immigrants left Sweden on religious grounds, the majority of Swedish emigrants during the nineteenth century were tenant farmers and landless farm laborers resolved to leave their class-bound and impoverished homeland for a fresh start in the New World. Attracted by the promise of free land, the immigrants took up homesteads on the prairies, or worked as laborers in frontier and urban centers. Toward the end of the nineteenth century, more than half of Swedish emigrants were urban industrial workers and more often than not young and single.

Emigration symbolized a break with tradition, a struggle to overcome hardship and a dream of success that had been impossible in Sweden owing to social restrictions and stifling class mentality. Increased conscription also played an import role, especially in the wake of World War I. By the 1930s, over a million, one out of every five Swedes, had made the journey across the Atlantic.

Swedish American literature begins with the letters (*Amerikabrev*) that immigrants wrote to their loved ones back home. Although the majority of these letters have been lost, many are kept in archives throughout Sweden and the United States. Early letters often paint an overly positive image of the immigrant experience to justify the emigration and tell little of the hardship and dissolution immigrants faced. Often passed around and even published in local Swedish newspapers these letters encouraged many emigrants to leave a meager life behind to try their luck in America. Toward the end of the nineteenth century, however, the letters become more realistic and describe both the emigrants' amazement as they arrived in the new land and experienced a sense of freedom they never felt in Sweden, as well as the adversity they often encountered. The literary value of these letters may be up for discussion, but their sociological and historical value is irrefutable.

The letters attest to the high level of literacy among Swedes. It is safe to assume that the majority of them were literate. Sweden's School Law of 1842 called for obligatory instruction in both reading and writing by qualified teachers and for the establishment of libraries in each parish; however, even as early as 1723, a parliamentary resolution had required parents to teach their children to read. During yearly parish catechetical meetings (*husförhör*), the parish priest would ask the members of his congregations to demonstrate their reading abilities, which would then be recorded in the meeting protocols.

Many newly arrived Swedish immigrants would develop the habit of reading newspapers on a regular basis. An estimated 650 newspapers and periodicals were published in Swedish, with a peak circulation of 600,000 in 1910, second only to the German-language publications of the non-English-language press. The newspapers served three important functions: to provide the immigrants with both Swedish and American news, to supply a forum for religious and political matters of interest, and to supply the often isolated immigrant with poetry, tales, and serialized novels to help alleviate the boredom of long winters at the homestead. The newspapers were often the only literature available and helped unite a diverse and dispersed community.

The first Swedish American newspaper was the short-lived *Skandinavien* (*The Scandinavian*), founded in New York in 1851. Among the more long-standing is the first independent newspaper *Svenska Amerikanaren* (*The Swedish American*, Chicago, 1866) and *Nordstjernan-Svea* (*The Northern Star-Svea*, New York, 1872). After having merged with other newspapers, these are still in print along with *California Veckoblad* (*California Weekly*, Los Angeles, 1909) and *Vestkusten–West Coast* (San Francisco, 1886).

The newspapers and journals published poetry and prose written by immigrants with various educational backgrounds but with one thing in common, a desire to express their feelings about the immigrant experience and what it meant to be Swedish in America. The prose often reflects their loyalty to their new land as well as their affection to the country they left behind. The poetry has three major themes: homesickness, childhood memories, and the Swedish landscape.

While the poems were usually written by the subscribers, the fiction was either European literature in translation or written by the newspaper staff. Among the more famous journalists/editors was Ernst Skarstedt (1857–1929), the son of a theology professor at the prestigious Lund University. Rather than following in his father's footsteps, he chose to emigrate at the age of twenty-one. In the United States, he worked as editor and contributor to several Swedish language newspapers.

Although many newspapers had literary supplements, there were also literary magazines such as *Valkyrian: Illustrerad månadsskrift* (*The Valkyrie: An Illustrated Monthly Magazine*, 1897), founded in New York by Charles Johanson, editor of *Nordstjärnan*. It looked to preserve Swedish values among the immigrants. The most well known of the literary magazines, *Prärieblomman kalender* (*The Prairie Flower Calendar*) was founded in 1900 in Rock Island, Illinois. Unlike most magazines that printed European work in translation, *Prärieblomman* promoted Swedish American writers. The first magazines, however, were church periodicals and contained no fiction and only a small amount of poetry on solely religious themes. Yet, the synod press soon began to publish magazines that contained moral and uplifting reading for the whole family and even journals targeting the young Swedish Americans, such as *Ungdomsvännen* (Friend of Youth, 1895), which gradually grew into an important illustrated cultural and literary journal. These magazines also reflected the Americanization of the younger generation by increasingly including texts written in English.

Many of the newspapers and periodicals occasionally published their serialized stories in book form. They would also print texts subsidized by the authors. The major Swedish American publishing house, the Augustana Book Concern, began printing in 1884, and laid the ground for what was to be a significant Swedish American literature. It was owned by the Lutheran Augustana Synod but did not limit itself to publishing religious work. By the turn of the century, it published the work of many major Swedish American authors. It was not, however, the only publishing house. Between 1891 and 1935, 343 Swedish-language publishing houses published 839 Swedish-language titles in almost 4 million copies.

The first Swedish American publication was a booklet of poetry published in 1872, titled *En svensk sång om den stora branden i Chicago af Anders Nilsson, arbetskarl* (*A Swedish Song about the Great Fire in Chicago by Anders Nilsson, a Laborer*). It was written by the journalist/poet Magnus Elmblad who emigrated in 1871 with a degree from the University of Uppsala. His first collection of poems, *Samlade dikter,* was published in Chicago in 1878. Among the Augustana Book Concern's publications were several books of significant value to the history of Swedish America that helped to establish a sense of shared identity among Swedish Americans: Vilhelm Berger's (1867–1938) *Svensk-amerikanska meditationer* (*Swedish-American Meditations*, 1902), Johan Person's (1868–1921) *Svensk-amerikanska studier* (*Studies on Swedish America*, 1912), and Ernst Skarstedt's *Svensk-amerikanska folket* (*The*

Swedish-American People, 1917). Skarstedt also wrote a significant study, *Våra pennfäktare* (*Our Ink-Slingers*, 1897), which included biographies of more than 300 Swedish American writers.

These journalists belonged to the first generation of Swedish American authors. They earned a living as journalists, editors, and ministers. Many, however, were distinctively different from the typical Swedish American immigrant in that they—like Elmblad and Skarstedt—belonged to the Swedish upper class. Leonard Strömberg (1871–1941) was a minister who came to the United States in 1895. Twenty-five years later, his books were among the most borrowed in Swedish libraries. Others, like Arthur Landfors (1888–1973) and **Joe Hill** [Joel Hägglund], emanated from the less fortunate in Swedish society, and became working class activists in the United States. Landfors was the son of an indebted farmer who came to Massachusetts in 1908. Although regarded as a working class writer, it was not until he settled in the United States that he became interested in Marxism. Although much of his poetry reflects his political stance, the poems that thematically address the immigrant's rootlessness and alienation made Landfors the most recognized Swedish American poet in Sweden. In fact, his two poetry collections, *Från smältungen* (*From the Melting Pot*, 1932) and *Träd som bara grönska* (*Trees That Turn but Green*, 1952) were published in Sweden and did not reach the Swedish American readers until years after their publication.

The poet and songwriter Joe Hill (1879–1915) was born Joel Hägglund, but, like so many other immigrants, he Americanized his name once in the United States, having arrived in 1902. Hill is the most globally known of all Swedish American writers, and a legend in his own time. A member of the Industrial Workers of the World (IWW), Hill spread the IWW's message to workers all around the country by putting new words to familiar tunes and hymns. Among his most famous songs are "The Preacher and the Slave" and "There Is Power in the Union." In November 1915 Hill was accused of murder on very shaky grounds and executed.

Joe Hill wrote his songs in English. His audience was not the Swedish American community but all North American workers. Most second-generation Swedish Americans wrote in English. Some were born in the old country but emigrated early enough to become native speakers of English. Among them were Gösta Larsson, Edita Morris, and Flora Sandström, who published numerous novels during the 1930s and 1940s. Because their work was in English, it was more likely to be published by American publishers than by Swedish American publishing houses. Most second-generation poets had little or no memory of Sweden. Their poetry celebrated the American landscape and did not reflect the concerns of the displaced immigrant. The writing also reflects the process of **assimilation** among the children of immigrants and blurs the distinction between Swedish American literature and American literature. One Midwestern writer who turned away from his Swedish background was **Carl Sandburg** (1878–1967), winner of two

Pulitzer Prizes. A dedicated socialist, Sandburg wrote about the working class in his poetry, such as in his *Chicago Poems* (1916).

Swedish American literature has as its central theme the culture shock of the immigrant experience. It is what makes this literature distinct from both Swedish and American literature but that creates a connection between it and other ethnic minority writing in North America. It represents a historical account for the psychosocial process of assimilation into American society.

Further Reading

Ander, O. Fritiof. *The Cultural Heritage of the Swedish Immigrant.* Rock Island, IL: Augustana College Library, 1956.

Ljungmark, Lars. *Swedish Exodus.* Carbondale: Southern Illinois UP, 1979. 108–15.

Skårdal, Dorothy Burton. *The Divided Heart: Scandinavian Immigrant Experience through Literary Sources.* Lincoln: Nebraska UP, 1974.

Joanna M. Daxell

SYRKIN, MARIE (1899–1989)   Jewish American author, journalist, educator, editor, poet, Zionist leader. Syrkin's Zionist essays; biographies of Jewish figures, including Golda Meir; and her reporting on the early stages of the **Holocaust**—along with her activism—all make her a singularly influential woman in the twentieth-century American Jewish community. Her work, polemic as it may now seem, provided intellectual and emotional foundations for American support for Israel.

Daughter of Labor Zionist organizer Nachman Syrkin and feminist Bassya Osnos Syrkin, Marie Syrkin was born in Switzerland, and moved to the United States when she was nine, after living in five countries. Syrkin's work reflects the tension between her individual aspirations as a poet and her community obligations of promoting Zionism among American Jews. Her personal life was unconventional; she married three times, first to Maurice Samuel (the marriage was annulled); to Aaron Bodansky, with whom she had two children; and finally to the poet **Charles Reznikoff**. Shared custody with Bodansky tied Syrkin geographically and financially to New York for a significant part of her life.

As she taught English at Textile High School, she also translated Yiddish poetry and edited the Labor Zionist journal, *Jewish Frontier*. On sabbatical, she wrote from Palestine about the disturbances of the 1930s. *Jewish Frontier* was responsible for the first reports in the United States of the Holocaust. During the war, she wrote articles and speeches promoting liberal **immigration** policies, including "Why a Jewish Commonwealth" in *The Nature of the Jewish Problem* (1943). She continued to teach, using the New York School system in *Your School, Your Children* (1944). Immediately after the war, she traveled in Europe to displaced-person camps in order to facilitate students' emigration.

Blessed Is the Match: The Story of the Jewish Resistance (1947) is one of the first books telling of the illegal immigration movements to Israel and the resistance against the Nazis. Set in Palestine, with Israel not yet a certainty, the book documents individual stories: the parachutists sent into Eastern Europe in the 1940s, the network of the underground in Europe, the battles in the ghettos, and resistance in Palestine. One of Syrkin's most powerful stories is about a teenage parachutist's mother. Hanna Senesch was sent to Hungary by the Jewish underground from Palestine to aid the partisans and was killed there by the Nazis. She is the author of the Hebrew poem "Blessed is the Match," and her heroism is remembered in Israel.

In 1950 Marie Syrkin joined the faculty at Brandeis University as an English professor, pioneering courses in Holocaust literature as well. She continued to write—*Golda Meir: Israel's Leader* (1963) and "Jewish Awareness in American Literature" in *The American Jew: A Reappraisal* (1967)—and to edit (*Hayim Greenberg Anthology* [1969]). Whereas *Gleanings: A Diary in Verse* (1979) was her long-deferred book of poetry, a collection of political essays, *The State of the Jews* (1980), appeared shortly thereafter. After retiring from Brandeis, she continued to write for *Foreign Affairs, New Republic, Commentary* and leading journals. Marie Syrkin's papers are located in the American Jewish Archives.

Further Reading

Kessner, Carole S. *The "Other" New York Jewish Intellectuals*. New York: New York UP, 1994.

Omer-Sherman, Ranen. *Diaspora and Zionism in Jewish American Literature: Lazarus, Syrkin, Reznikoff, and Roth*. Hanover, NH: Brandeis UP, 2002.

Kristine Peleg

SZE, ARTHUR (1950–)   Chinese American poet, translator, and professor of creative writing. Arthur Sze is acclaimed as one of America's best poets and translators. His work embodies a range of new possibilities for poetry, arising from his emulation and reinvention of poetic traditions that reach across cultural boundaries.

Sze's poetic career began with his translation of classical Chinese poems, which are an enduring source of inspiration for Sze, as well as a heritage that he seeks to reclaim and renew. Sze's early translations are published with his own poems in his first two collections, *Willow Wind* (1972) and *Two Ravens* (1976). Selections of these early translations are also included in Sze's sixth volume, *The Redshifting Web, Poems 1970–1998* (1998). His seventh volume, *The Silk Dragon: Translations from the Chinese* (2001), which is his first that is devoted entirely to translations, won the 2002 Western States Book Award for Translation. Sze's remarkable merits as a translator reside partly in his being a refined poet himself, partly in his knowledge of the Chinese language and the philosophies underlying the aesthetics of classical Chinese poetry, and partly in his understanding of translation as necessarily a transformational creative process that does not sacrifice accuracy or subtlety in the original texts.

Sze's relationship with classical Chinese poetry distinguishes his work from that of contemporary Chinese American poets. Unable to read the original, most contemporary Chinese American poets—with the exception of **Marilyn Chin, Ha Jin**, and Bei Dao, among others—encounter Chinese poetry only through secondary sources and seek to connect with the Chinese classical tradition usually through allusions to the best-known poets, or through imagist stylistic emulations. In comparison, Sze's evocation of the Chinese models are more extensive and innovative in terms of styles, aesthetics, and subject matter. At the same time, Sze achieves an openness to and inclusiveness of the world by integrating the ideogrammatic principle of juxtaposition in Chinese characters into his collage composition and sequence form. His fourth volume, *River River* (1987), marks the emergence of these major technical strategies that are capable of depicting both the diversity and interconnectedness of all things, which are two of the major themes of Sze's poems. Sze continues to explore those themes and technical possibilities in his later collections, *Archipelago* (1995) and *The Redshifting Web: Poems 1970–1998* (1998).

In addition to Chinese culture, Native American cultures also have a prominent presence in Sze's poems. Between 1978 and 1995, Sze was married to a Hopi weaver. He has been living in New Mexico since 1972, and has been teaching at the Institute of American Indian Arts in Santa Fe since 1984. The Native American view of the world as a delicately balanced web is embedded in the title of Sze's sixth volume, *The Redshifting Web: Poems 1970–1998* (1998), and in the themes and structure of the poems. To perceive the world as an expanding network is a central theme that Sze explores from various perspectives in his poems. This ecological view of the world underlies the ethics, aesthetics, and formal innovation of Sze's poetry. (*See also* Chinese American Poetry)

Further Reading

Tabios, Eileen. "Arthur Sze: Mixing Memory and Desire." Interview with a draft in progress of *Archipelago*. *Black Lightning: Poetry-In-Progress*. Ed. Eileen Tabios. New York: The Asian American Writers' Workshop, 1998. 3–21.

Zhou, Xiaojing. "'The Redshifting Web': Arthur's Sze's Ecopoetics." *Ecological Poetry: A Critical Introduction*. Ed. J. Scott Bryson. Salt Lake City: U of Utah P, 179–94.

Zhou Xiaojing

SZE, MAI-MAI (1905–1987)   Chinese American writer and artist. Seen as an important Chinese American writer during the Sino-Japanese War, Sze raises antiwar sentiment and immigrant experiences as important concerns of her writings. Crossing cultural boundaries, she, as the daughter of a Chinese ambassador, also attempts to deconstruct the binary opposition between East and West.

Writing in the 1940s, at a time when Western readers often expect exotic descriptions of the orient, Sze describes herself as a homeless cosmopolitan rather than as a tour guide of Eastern exoticism. In her autobiography, *Echo of a Cry: A Story Which Began in China* (1945), she records her life as a rootless Chinese American woman. Born in China, she was taken to England, cared for by an Irish nanny, sent to a private school in France, and then lived in New York. Revealing the difficulties of living in worlds that reject or marginalize her, she feels alienated in both her original and adopted societies. During a return visit to China for a birthday celebration, she expresses her feelings of disconnection from Chinese customs. In the western world, however, she discovers that her feelings of displacement and exile are even worse. For instance, in the United States she encounters the racial prejudice that confronts people of color when her skin color is subjected to racial slurs. On a painting trip to France, she is viewed as a curiosity. Throughout the book, she expresses feelings of displacement and exile wherever she is, and struggles to discover her sense of belonging. Sze's diasporic experiences show how difficult it is to determine one's identity after suffering so many relocations. She captures the profound loneliness and loss at the heart of immigrant experience.

Sze's antiwar sentiment is revealed in her novel, *Silent Children* (1948). Unlike early Chinese immigrant writers who write patriotic stories of the Sino-Japanese War in order to gain support for their mother nation, Sze does not show an urgent patriotism in this novel. Instead, in a surrealist setting, her narrative centers on a band of homeless children displaced from an unknown war who struggle to survive near the outskirts of a nameless city. With unknown nationality, the orphans work together for their future. As in her autobiography, which deals with the idea of homelessness, Sze uses the homeless and miserable condition of the orphans not only to criticize the dehumanization of war, but also to reflect the inner psychological condition of diasporic subjects.

In both works, Sze is also keen to the cultural stereotypes between East and West. In *Echo of a Cry*, she points out the fallacy of clear divisions between the two, and she tries to understand the difficulties of communication between the East and West in *Silent Children*. (*See also* Chinese American Autobiography, Chinese American Novel)

Further Reading

Ling, Amy. *Between Worlds: Women Writers of Chinese Ancestry.* New York: Pergamon P, 1990.

Su-lin Yu